THE MISHNAH ELUCIDATED

ששה סדרי משנה

SCHOTTENSTEIN EDITION

ששה
סדרי משנה

THE
MISHNAH
ELUCIDATED

זרעים

מועד

נשים

נזיקין

קדשים

טהרות

THE CZUKER EDITION OF SEDER ZERAIM

ArtScroll® Series

Rabbi Nosson Scherman / Rabbi Meir Zlotowitz
General Editors

A PROJECT OF THE

Mesorah Heritage Foundation

BOARD OF TRUSTEES

RABBI DAVID FEINSTEIN
Rosh HaYeshivah, Mesivtha Tifereth Jerusalem

JOEL L. FLEISHMAN
Chairman
Director, Sam & Ronnie Heyman Center on Ethics,
Public Policy, and the Professions, Duke University

HOWARD TZVI FRIEDMAN
Founding Partner,
Lanx Management, LLC

JUDAH I. SEPTIMUS
Pres., Atlantic Land Title & Abstract, Ltd.

RABBI MEIR ZLOTOWITZ ל"ז
Founder and President

RABBI GEDALIAH ZLOTOWITZ
President

RABBI NOSSON SCHERMAN
General Editor, ArtScroll Series

JOSEPH C. SHENKER
Chairman, Sullivan & Cromwell

JAMES S. TISCH
Chairman and CEO, Loews Corp.

AUDIT COMMITTEE

SAMUEL ASTROF
CFO/COO (Ret.) The Jewish
Federations of North America;
Partner (Ret.) Ernst & Young, LLP

JUDAH I. SEPTIMUS
Pres., Atlantic Land Title & Abstract, Ltd.

JOEL L. FLEISHMAN
Director, Sam & Ronnie Heyman Center on Ethics,
Public Policy, and the Professions, Duke University

JOSEPH C. SHENKER
Chairman, Sullivan & Cromwell

JAMES S. TISCH
Chairman and CEO, Loews Corp.

INTERNATIONAL BOARD OF GOVERNORS

JAY SCHOTTENSTEIN *(Columbus, OH)*
Chairman

STEVEN ADELSBERG
HOWARD BALTER
MOSHE BEINHORN
RABBI RAPHAEL B. BUTLER
EDWARD MENDEL CZUKER *(Los Angeles)*
REUVEN D. DESSLER *(Cleveland)*
BENJAMIN C. FISHOFF
YITZCHOK GANGER
JACOB M.M. GRAFF *(Los Angeles)*
HASHI HERZKA
JACOB HERZOG *(Toronto)*
AMIR JAFFA *(Cleveland)*
ELAN JAFFA
JACK JAFFA
LLOYD F. KEILSON
LESTER KLAUS
MOTTY KLEIN
ELLY KLEINMAN
EZRA MARCOS *(Tel Aviv)*
RABBI MEYER H. MAY *(Los Angeles)*
ASHER D. MILSTEIN

ANDREW J. NEFF
AARON J. ORLOFSKY *(Silver Spring)*
BARRY M. RAY *(Chicago)*
GEOFFREY ROCHWARGER *(Beit Shemesh / Teaneck)*
ZVI RYZMAN *(Los Angeles)*
A. GEORGE SAKS
JOSEPH A. SCHOTTENSTEIN
JONATHAN R. SCHOTTENSTEIN
JEFFREY A. SCHOTTENSTEIN
HERBERT E. SEIF *(Englewood, NJ)*
NATHAN B. SILBERMAN
A. JOSEPH STERN *(Edison, NJ)*
JACQUES STERN *(Sao Paulo)*
ELLIOT TANNENBAUM
SOL TEICHMAN ל"ז *(Encino, CA)*
THOMAS J. TISCH
GARY TORGOW *(Detroit)*
STANLEY WASSERMAN *(New Rochelle)*
JOSEPH H. WEISS
STEVEN WEISZ
SHLOMO WERDIGER

שִׁשָּׁה
סִדְרֵי מִשְׁנָה

ELUCIDATED

A PHRASE-BY-PHRASE
SIMPLIFIED TRANSLATION
WITH BASIC COMMENTARY

INCLUDES THE FULL HEBREW TEXT
OF THE COMMENTARY OF
RAV OVADIAH BERTINORO

SCHOTTENSTEIN EDITION

THE MISHNAH

THE CZUKER EDITION OF SEDER ZERAIM

Published by
ArtScroll®
Mesorah Publications, ltd

FIRST EDITION
First Impression ... November 2017
Second Impression ... January 2018
Third Impression ... February 2018
Fourth Impression ... November 2018

Published and Distributed by
MESORAH PUBLICATIONS, Ltd.
4401 Second Avenue
Brooklyn, New York 11232

Distributed in Europe by
LEHMANNS
Unit E, Viking Business Park
Rolling Mill Road
Jarrow, Tyne & Wear NE32 3DP
England

Distributed in Australia & New Zealand by
GOLDS WORLD OF JUDAICA
3-13 William Street
Balaclava, Melbourne 3183
Victoria Australia

Distributed in Israel by
SIFRIATI / A. GITLER — BOOKS
POB 2351
Bnei Brak 51122

Distributed in South Africa by
KOLLEL BOOKSHOP
Northfield Centre, 17 Northfield Avenue
Glenhazel 2192, Johannesburg, South Africa

ARTSCROLL® SERIES / THE SCHOTTENSTEIN EDITION
THE MISHNAH ELUCIDATED
CZUKER EDITION / SEDER ZERAIM VOL. 4
MAASER SHENI / CHALLAH / ORLAH / BIKKURIM

© *Copyright 2017, by MESORAH PUBLICATIONS, Ltd.*
4401 Second Avenue / Brooklyn, N.Y. 11232 / (718) 921-9000 / FAX (718) 680-1875

ALL RIGHTS RESERVED. *The Hebrew text of the Mishnah Elucidated has been edited,*
corrected, and newly set; the English translation and commentary —
including introductory material, notes, and insights –
as well as the typographic layout and cover artwork, have been written, designed,
edited and/or revised as to content, form and style.
Additionally, new fonts have been designed for the texts and commentaries.
All of the above are fully protected under this international copyright.

No part of this volume may be reproduced
IN ANY FORM — PHOTOCOPY, ELECTRONIC, DIGITAL MEDIA, OR OTHERWISE
— EVEN FOR PERSONAL, STUDY GROUP, OR CLASSROOM USE —
without WRITTEN permission from the copyright holder,
except by a reviewer who wishes to quote brief passages
in connection with a review written for inclusion in magazines or newspapers.

NOTICE IS HEREBY GIVEN THAT THE PUBLICATION OF THIS WORK
INVOLVED EXTENSIVE RESEARCH AND COSTS,
AND THE RIGHTS OF THE COPYRIGHT HOLDER WILL BE STRICTLY ENFORCED

ISBN 10: 1-4226-1912-5
ISBN 13: 978-1-4226-1912-4

Typography by CompuScribe at ArtScroll Studios, Ltd.
4401 Second Avenue / Brooklyn, N.Y. 11232 / (718) 921-9000
Bound by Sefercraft, Quality Bookbinders, Ltd. Brooklyn, N.Y.

SEDER ZERAIM VOL. IV

מסכת מעשר שני
TRACTATE MAASER SHENI

מסכת חלה
TRACTATE CHALLAH

מסכת ערלה
TRACTATE ORLAH

מסכת ביכורים
TRACTATE BIKKURIM

זרעים
מועד
נשים
נזיקין
קדשים
טהרות

Dedication of
This Volume

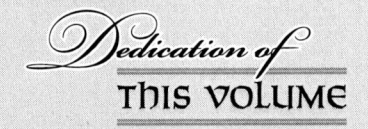

With both grieving hearts and profound gratitude, we dedicate this volume to the memory of

Rabbi Meir Zlotowitz ז"ל
הרב מאיר יעקב בן הגאון הרב אהרן ז"ל
ל' סיון תשע"ז

To others, he was the great visionary who changed and elevated the Jewish world. To us he was an intimate family friend, our adopted "uncle," guide, and mentor. The tragic news of his sudden loss stunned us all. A world without Meir Zlotowitz? Unthinkable!

But he taught us always to look ahead and never to despair. In this spirit, we dedicate this volume of Mishnah Elucidated to his glowing memory. The Gemara teaches that Seder Zeraim symbolizes *Emunah,* because no matter how hard a farmer works, he must have faith that his success depends on Hashem's blessing. Rav Meir planted seeds of Torah, and he did it with faith in Hashem. The crops of his imagination, initiative, and labor will continue to nourish the world for generations.

His life was a blessed gift to us and to Klal Yisrael.
His legacy will continue to teach us and his memory will always inspire us.

יהי זכרו ברוך

The Jaffa Family

Dedication of
CZUKER EDITION OF SEDER ZERAIM

This Seder is dedicated in loving memory of our beloved father,

Jan Czuker ז״ל
ר׳ יוסף ב״ר מנחם מענדל ז״ל
נפ׳ פסח שני תש״ע

Our father survived the Holocaust, but his faith and spirit remained intact. His determination to rebuild not only his own life and family but also those of others made him a generous supporter of many Jewish institutions and individuals in the community. His good cheer and charisma drew others to him. He was a loyal friend, always ready to help. He was a blessing to all who crossed his path.

Torah education, chessed, and ahavas Yisrael were all precious to him. A devoted father and grandfather, in words and deeds he instilled Jewish values in his children and grandchildren.

And in honor of our beloved mother,

Mrs. Susanne Czuker שתחי׳

She is the quintessential Eishes Chayil. Accomplished in her own right, her steady guidance and encouragement enabled our father to achieve all that he did. The love she has for her children and grandchildren lights up all of our lives. May Hashem bless her with many years of good health and the nachas of seeing that her offspring live up to her hopes and example.

Seder Zeraim deals with the laws of blessings, prayer, agriculture, and concern for the poor. Our parents' faith in Hashem and concern for the needy inspired all who knew them. When others despaired, they planted seeds in their new homeland that blossomed into thriving Torah communities.

Together they laid the foundations for us to carry on their Torah values and ideals, and fulfill their dreams. It is fitting, therefore, that this edition of Zeraim will honor our parents for generations to come.

Edward Mendel and Elissa Czuker
and Family

Dedication of
SCHOTTENSTEIN EDITION
THE MISHNAH ששה סדרי משנה
ELUCIDATED

The Mishnah Elucidated is lovingly dedicated in honor of
our parents and grandparents

Jerome ז״ל and Geraldine Schottenstein תחי׳
Leonard and Heddy Rabe שיחי׳

*T*hey were constant sources of strength
and role models of dignity,
integrity, loyalty to the past
and dedication to the future.

It is fitting that now,
as we dedicate The Mishnah Elucidated
we pay tribute to them,
for they symbolize to us
the values of our heritage,
their constant support day in day out,
and their encouragement
to go beyond our goals.

Jay and Jeanie Schottenstein

Joseph Aaron and Lindsay Brooke,
Jacob Meir   Jonah Philip   Emma Blake
Jonathan Richard and Nicole Lauren
Winnie Simone
Jeffrey Adam

PATRONS OF THE SEDARIM

The Mishnah is the basis of the Oral Law. In order to make this holy Torah legacy available to its heirs, these generous and visionary patrons have dedicated Sedarim/Orders of this edition of the Mishnah.

THE CZUKER EDITION OF SEDER ZERAIM

is lovingly dedicated by

Edward Mendel and Elissa Czuker and Family

(Los Angeles)

in loving memory of their beloved father

Jan Czuker ר' יוסף ב"ר מנחם מענדל ז"ל – ז"ל

נפ' פסח שני תש"ע

and יבל"ח in honor of their beloved mother

Mrs. Susanne Czuker שתחי'

THE GRYFE EDITION OF SEDER MOED

is lovingly dedicated by

Daniel and Dena Gryfe

in honor of their parents

Josh and Nadja Graff   Moishe and Michele Gryfe

and as an inspiration to their children

Koby, Rikki, Alexander, Benjy and Mia

and their siblings

**Elisha and Daniella   Zahava, Sabrina, Michal, and Tamara Graff,
Aviva and Gershon   Shoshana, Talia, and Esti Distenfeld,
Yehuda and Daniella   Yisroel, Aliza, Moshe, Ayelet, and Aryeh Graff**

ESTHER KLAUS EDITION OF SEDER NASHIM

is lovingly dedicated by

Lester Klaus

Ari and Fradie (Rapp) Goldsmith

Benjy and Raizy Chesner   Menachem and Avigayil Rapp Devorah, David and Esther
Shimmy, Bashi and Tzvi

Yankie and Sara Klaus   Bashie, Chedvah and Shimmy

Shmulie and Hindy Klaus   Dovie and Rachel Steier Esther   **Shana and Atara**

Moshe Klaus

in loving memory of our quintessential wife and mother

Esther Klaus ע"ה – אסתר בת צבי הירש ע"ה

נפ' ט"ו ניסן תשע"ז

PATRONS OF THE SEDARIM

THE BOOK FAMILY EDITION OF SEDER NEZIKIN

is dedicated by

Amy, Bob, and the Book Family

in memory of

Rabbi Meir Zlotowitz ז"ל

הרב מאיר יעקב בן הגאון הרב אהרן ז"ל

נפ' ל' סיון תשע"ז

DIAMOND FAMILY EDITION OF SEDER TOHOROS

is lovingly dedicated by

Dr. David and Tzipi Diamond
Dr. Tzvi and Yocheved Diamond
Yitzchok   Yoni   Rachel   Tali   Rose

in loving memory of our beloved parents and grandparents,

Dr. Isaac and Rose Diamond ז"ל

ר' יצחק ב"ר ברוך בענדיט ז"ל

נפטר ד' חשון תשמ"ו

חי' רויזא בת אברהם משה ע"ה

נפטרה ה' ניסן תשס"ט

PATRONS OF THE MISHNAH

With generosity, vision, and devotion to the perpetuation of Torah study,
the following patrons have dedicated individual volumes of
The Mishnah Elucidated.

SEDER ZERAIM

◆§ BERACHOS, PEAH, DEMAI

Aron and Aliza Hirtz
Eliezer, Binyomin, and Ariella

in memory of our grandparents
Leslie and Lillian Hirtz ז״ל
אליעזר בן ישעיה ז״ל
לאה בת יוסף הלוי ע״ה

Yossi and Adina Hollander
Eitan Yaakov, Yonatan Meir, and Eliana Devora

In memory of our father
Max Hollander ז״ל
מאיר בן אברהם משה ז״ל

We all join in paying tribute to the memory of
our beloved grandparents
Rev. Yonason Neiman ז״ל
יונתן בן יעקב יהודה ז״ל
Yuspah Devora Dear ע״ה
יוספא דבורה בת בילא ע״ה

◆§ KILAYIM, SHEVIIS

Anonymous

◆§ TERUMOS, MAASROS

In honor of
Ira A. and Barbara K. Lipman and Family

◆§ MAASER SHENI, CHALLAH, ORLAH, BIKKURIM

The Jaffa Families

in memory of
Rabbi Meir Zlotowitz ז״ל
הרב מאיר יעקב בן הגאון הרב אהרן ז״ל

PATRONS OF THE MISHNAH

SEDER MOED

◆§ SHABBOS, ERUVIN

Amir and Edna Jaffa
Eby and Shani Schabes, Eli, Yaakov, and Rikki
in revered memory of our grandparents ז"ל
ר' חיים ישראל ב"ר מאיר זאב ז"ל
ורעיתו אלטע ויטא (ויקי) בת ר' אשר זעליג ע"ה – פריד
ר' נפתלי הירצקא ב"ר מנחם משה ז"ל
ורעיתו רבקה בת ר' יונה ע"ה – קליין
הרב אליהו ב"ר שמעון ז"ל – קמנצקי
ר' משה ליב ב"ר שניאור זלמן ז"ל
ורעיתו בלימא בת ר' אברהם משה ע"ה – יפה
and יבל"ח in honor of our grandmother עמו"ש
Mrs. Anita Kaminetsky שתחי'

◆§ PESACHIM, SHEKALIM, YOMA, SUCCAH

Barry and Harriet Ray and Family
dedicated to the memory of our dear parents
Emanuel M. and Zira G. (Siegel) Ray ז"ל
ר' מרדכי ב"ר ברוך ז"ל
צירל בת שמואל ע"ה

◆§ BEITZAH, ROSH HASHANAH, TAANIS, MEGILLAH, MOED KATAN, CHAGIGAH

Norman and Cecily Davis
dedicated to the memory of our dear parents
Samuel and Sala Davis ז"ל
שלמה שמואל חיים בן דויד ז"ל
שינדל גיטל בת הרב צבי הירש הכהן ע"ה
Shaul and Yitta Cashdan ז"ל
שאול בן יוסף דוב הכהן ז"ל
חיה איטה בת חיים זליג ע"ה

SEDER NASHIM

◆§ YEVAMOS, KESUBOS

dedicated to the memory of
Rabbi Menachem Gottesman זצ"ל
הרב אהרן מנחם בן הרב אשר זעליג זצ"ל

PATRONS OF THE MISHNAH

ও§ NEDARIM, NAZIR
Andrew and Nancy Neff and Family
in honor of the ninetieth birthday of
our father, grandfather, and great-grandfather
Alan Martin Neff

ও§ SOTAH, GITTIN, KIDDUSHIN
Joseph and Sheila Bistritzky and Family
dedicated in loving memory of
our dear parents and grandparents
Leibel Bistritzky ז״ל
ר' יהודה לייב בן ר' מרדכי ז״ל
Edah Bistritzky ע״ה
איטא בת ר' שלמה ע״ה

SEDER NEZIKIN

ও§ BAVA KAMMA, BAVA METZIA
Robin and Warren Shimoff and Family
dedicated in honor of our very dear friends
Harry and Rachel Skydell

ও§ BAVA BASRA, SANHEDRIN, MAKKOS, SHEVUOS
Adam and Suri Sokol and Family
dedicated to the prodigious, awe-inspiring memory of
Rabbi Meir Zlotowitz ז״ל
הרב מאיר יעקב בן הגאון הרב אהרן ז״ל

ও§ EDUYOS, AVODAH ZARAH, AVOS, HORAYOS
Michael and Linda Elman
dedicated in loving memory of our dear parents
Julius Feigelman ז״ל
ר' יהודה ב״ר יחיאל מיכל ז״ל
Beatrice Feigelman ע״ה
בוניא בת ר' חיים אשר ע״ה
G. Leonard Rubin ז״ל
ר' גרשון ליפא ב״ר ליב עזריאל ז״ל
Bernice Rogoff Rubin ע״ה
באשא בת ר' בנימן ע״ה

PATRONS OF THE MISHNAH

SEDER KODASHIM

◆§ ZEVACHIM, MENACHOS
Shmuly and Batsheva Neuman and Family
dedicated in honor of our dear parents and grandparents
William and Gladys Neuman
Yanky and Perela Silber
Chaim and Suri Kassirer
Ruth Silber
and in memory of our dear grandparents

Avrohom Neuman — אברהם בן זאב יהודה ז"ל ז"ל
Magda Neuman — מלכה בת אברהם יצחק ע"ה ע"ה
Nechemia Rabenstein — נחמיה בן שמואל חיים הכהן ז"ל ז"ל
Freida Rabenstein — שרה פייגא בת שלמה אלעזר ע"ה ע"ה
Kalman Silber — קלונימוס קלמן בן יהודה לייב ז"ל ז"ל

◆§ CHULLIN, BECHOROS, ARACHIN
The Bak Families
dedicated in loving memory of our parents and grandparents

Bak — ר' שלום בן יהודה צבי ז"ל
Bak — ר' לייב בן ר' ניסן ז"ל
Zelmanovitz — הניא מלכה בת אברהם ישראל ע"ה
Scott — ר' ברוך בן חנוך ז"ל

and our uncles and aunts

Bak — ר' יצחק דוד בן יהודה צבי ז"ל
Bak — ר' גרשון בן יהודה צבי ז"ל
Zelmanowitz — מרים בת אברהם ישראל ע"ה
Zelmanowitz — חנה עקא בת אברהם ישראל ע"ה
Zelmanowitz — גיטל בת אברהם ישראל ע"ה

The Gastwirth Families
in memory of our beloved grandparents
Samuel and Beila Gastwirth ז"ל
ר' שמואל יעקב ב"ר צבי נחמן הלוי ז"ל
מרת בילה בת וואלף לייב הלוי ע"ה
Izzy and Ruthie Kalish ז"ל
ר' מרדכי יצחק ב"ר אהרן אבנר הלוי ז"ל
מרת רחל מרים בת מנחם צבי ע"ה

◆§ TEMURAH, KEREISOS, ME'ILAH, TAMID, MIDDOS, KINNIM
Sam and Laurie Friedland and family
dedicated in loving memory of our parents and grandparents

Friedland — ר' חיים מאיר בן שלמה זלמן ז"ל
Simon — ר' אליעזר בן משה יהודה ז"ל
Simon — שינא רחל בת דוד אליעזר ע"ה

PATRONS OF THE MISHNAH

SEDER TOHOROS

∞§ KEILIM (Vol. 1)
Woli and Chaja Stern
Jacques and Ariane Stern

לזכר ולעילוי נשמת
הורי ר׳ זאב
ר׳ צבי הלוי ב״ר חיים ומרים שטרן ז״ל
וזו׳ מרת דאכא ב״ר פרץ וברכה טאגר ע״ה
הורי חיה
ר׳ דוד אריה ב״ר יעקב ושינדל ברנר ז״ל
וזו׳ מרת איטלה (אירמה) ב״ר חיים ומדל שטרן ע״ה
אבי אריאן ר׳ יששכר טוביה ב״ר יוסף ופערל וייטמן ז״ל

∞§ KEILIM (Vol. 2)
Woli and Chaja Stern
Jacques and Ariane Stern

לכבוד ולזכות
אם אריאן רחל (רוז׳ה) ויטמן שתחי׳
ילדי ר׳ זאב וחיה
חיים אהרן ואריאלה ברכה סג״ל לנדא שיחיו
משה אפרים פישל ואילה (אנטי) קירשנבוים שיחיו
ילדי ר׳ יעקב ואריאן
יחזקאל וענת מינדל הרטמן שיחיו
מיכאל שלום ומרים אילנה פיינטוך שיחיו
צבי יונתן ומרים אביגיל שטרן שיחיו
יששכר טוביה ודבורה שטרן שיחיו
יחיאל משה ודאכא דינה מרזל שיחיו
ברוך משה ואיטלה טלי שטמברגר שיחיו

∞§ OHOLOS
The Gross, Strenger, Nadoff and Berger Families

in memory of our dear parents
Berish and Clara Berger ז״ל
יששכר בעריש בן יהושע ארי׳ ז״ל
שפרינצא בת אברהם ע״ה

∞§ NEGAIM, PARAH
Stephanie and George Saks

in memory of our dear friend
Rabbi Meir Zlotowitz ז״ל
הרב מאיר יעקב בן הגאון הרב אהרן ז״ל
and יבל״ח in honor of our dear friend
Rabbi Nosson Scherman שליט״א

PATRONS OF THE MISHNAH

◆§ TOHOROS, MIKVAOS

As people who cherish the opportunity to join together for the greater good of Klal Yisrael, we took upon ourselves to share in this beautiful opportunity to dedicate this volume of Mishnah so that Jews across the world can benefit from its wisdom.

PLATINUM **David and Chanee Deutsch** — Baruch Mappa — לז"נ ברוך בן אשר זעליג הלוי ז"ל
Benjamin (Binyamin) and Gabi Samuels In honor of our son Baruch

GOLD **Dovid and Tikvah Azman** In honor of our parents
Levi and Leeba Dessler לז"נ ר' צבי יעקב בן ר' חיים ז"ל
Ari and Ariella Deutsch לז"נ ר' משה יהודה בן יהודה ז"ל
Aryeh and Malky Feller לז"נ ישראל בן ישעיהו ז"ל   אהרן בן ישעיהו ז"ל
Chaim Sholom and Rivky Leibowitz לע"נ דבורה בת משה ע"ה — Debbie Leibowitz
Avi (Ryan) Melohn In honor of my parents and grandparents
Joseph (Yossi) and Malka Melohn In honor of Alexander, Don, and Kate
Shalom and Reena Vegh In honor of our parents
Michael and Katie Weisz לז"נ ר' משה דוד זצ"ל בן ר' נוריאל נ"י

SILVER **Families of Alfred and Maurice Friedman**
Laibel Gerson לז"נ עמנואל בן חיים יהודה ז"ל
Shari and Josh Goldberg In honor of our children, Evelyn and Phillip
Shmuel Umlas לרפואה שלמה אסתר בת מרים שתחי'

◆§ ZAVIM, TEVUL YOM, YADAYIM, UKTZIN

Aron and Rachel Solomon and Family
dedicated in memory of our dear father
ז"ל ישראל שלום ז"ל ב"ר יחזקאל ר' — Cheskel Solomon ז"ל
In honor of our dear Grandmother and Parents
Razi Solomon
Vera Solomon
Pinchus and Judy Solomon
Also in memory of our dear Grandparents
Lipa and Mindel Goldberger ז"ל
ר' חנניה יו"ט ליפא ב"ר שלום ז"ל   מינדל בת ר' דוד ע"ה
ז"ל ר' ישראל שלום ב"ר שמואל ז"ל — Yisroel Solomon ז"ל
Betzalel and Shaindel Solomon ז"ל
ר' בצלאל ב"ר דוב ז"ל   שיינדל בת ר' פינחס ע"ה
Yaakov Taivel and Rivkah Fixler ז"ל
ר' חיים אלטר יעקב טעבל ב"ר אליעזר ז"ל   רבקהביילא בת ר' צבי דוב ע"ה

══ **Mishnah Associates** ══

A fellowship of benefactors dedicated to
the dissemination of Mishnah Elucidated

❖

Phyllis and Chaim Shroot

══ **In Memoriam** — לזכר נשמת ══

Dedicated by the Mishnah Elucidated Associates
to those who forged eternal links

❖

אלכסנדר בן חיים צדוק ז"ל   צייריל בת ארי' ע"ה
יוסף בן אברהם יהושע ז"ל   פסאה חייענה בת ארי' לייב ע"ה

Patrons of the Sedarim ∻ Digital Edition

SEDER ZERAIM

is dedicated by
Yisroel (Ira) and Rochi Zlotowitz
In memory of the unparalleled marbitz Torah, our beloved father,
Rabbi Meir Zlotowitz ז״ל
הרב מאיר יעקב בן הגאון הרב אהרן ז״ל

SEDER MOED

is dedicated by
Uri and Devorah Dreifus
May the limud haTorah from the Digital Edition of Mishnah Seder Moed
be a zechus for our children:
Avigail and Menasche, Eli, Chani, Shevy, Shira and Penina

SEDER NASHIM

is dedicated by
Ezra Birnbaum
In honor of my Rebbeim and chavrusas, without whom my life would not be the same
**Rabbi Chaim Tzvi Yair Senter   Rabbi Mordechai Kamenetzky   Rabbi Casreal Bloom
Rabbi Yossi Weberman   Rabbi Binyamin Prince   Rabbi Chili Birnbaum**
Acharon Acharon Chaviv **R' Meir Zlotowitz ז״ל,**
whose vision and dreams allow me on a daily basis to fulfill mine.

SEDER NEZIKIN

is dedicated by
**Menachem and Binah Braunstein
Daniella, Talia and Aryeh**
In memory of our grandparents
Braunstein — הרב משה בן ישטכר בעריש ז״ל   מרת יענטא בת הרב ישראל חיים ע״ה
Reichner — הרב משה אברהם בן הרב אשי ז״ל   מרת מרים בת מנחם מענדל ע״ה
Tajerstein — הרב יעקב ארי׳ בן הרב שבתי ז״ל
Weisner — הרב בנימין צבי בן הרב אליעזר ז״ל

Pillars of the Mishnah

We wish to acknowledge in this volume the friendship of the following:

Sebastien Bensidoun

❧

Richard Berger

❧

Tirzo Cruz

❧

Lawrence and Judith Garshofsky

❧

William Hess

❧

Todd Pinchevsky

❧

Michael Scharf

❧

Herbert and Naomi Schechter

❧

Stuart Schnider

❧

Marsha Wolland

❧

In loving memory of **Rabbi Meir Zlotowitz** ז״ל
and in honor of his wonderful wife, **Mrs. Rachel Zlotowitz, and family.**
May you all continue his great legacy on behalf of Klal Yisrael.

Ezriel and Yaffa Munk

❧

The Written Word is Forever

We gratefully acknowledge the many Torah scholars who contributed to this volume.

General Editor:
Rabbi Chaim Malinowitz

Editorial Directors:
Rabbi Yosef Davis, Rabbi Yehezkel Danziger

Authors and Editors:
Rabbi Hillel Danziger, Rabbi Dovid Hollander, Rabbi Dovid Arye Kaufman,

Rabbi Zvi Goldberg, Rabbi Dovid Kaiser, Rabbi Yehudah Keilson, Rabbi Nechemya Klugman, Rabbi Henoch Morris, Rabbi Doniel Rose, Rabbi Mordechai Smilowitz, Rabbi Nahum Spirn

Scholars who reviewed and commented:
Rabbi Eliyahu Meir Klugman, Rabbi Moshe Rosenblum, Rabbi Yosaif Asher Weiss

We also wish to thank our technical staff who worked so diligently to produce this volume.

Proofreaders:
Mrs. Judi Dick, Mrs. Mindy Stern, Mrs. Faygie Weinbaum

Typesetters:
Mrs. Chumie Lipschitz
Mrs. Estie Dicker, Mrs. Esther Feierstein, Mrs. Toby Goldzweig

Illustrator: **Rabbi Yoav Elan**

Introduction

The Mishnah is the basis of the *Torah Shebe'al Peh*, the Oral Torah that was transmitted to Moses at Sinai. When conditions forced Rabbi Yehudah HaNasi and his compatriots to commit the Oral Torah to writing (completed in approximately 3950/190 CE), he composed the Mishnah in such a way that it could be understood only with the guidance of a teacher or with a broad knowledge of the subject matter. Therefore, the Mishnah cannot merely be read; it must be explained. One who has attained a basic knowledge of the entire Mishnah will find himself at home anywhere in the Talmud; he will have become familiar with the laws and concepts that were later discussed, broadened, and clarified by the Gemara and the countless commentaries. Traditionally, Mishnah has been studied not only by scholars, but also by students and laymen who had little knowledge of the Gemara. Obviously, therefore, Mishnah can be understood on many levels, from the most basic to the most scholarly. Additionally, because the Hebrew letters of the word משנה can be rearranged to spell נשמה, it is customarily studied as a source of merit for the departed, especially during the first year after their passing or on a *yahrzeit*.

✻§ The Schottenstein Edition

To a significant degree, this 22-volume **SCHOTTENSTEIN EDITION OF THE MISHNAH ELUCIDATED** will do for students of the Mishnah what the universally acclaimed Schottenstein Edition of the Talmud does for students of the Talmud, in the sense that it is at once succinct and clear. The new, elucidated **Translation** is based on the universally accepted interpretation of Rabbeinu Ovadiah of Bertenoro, commonly referred to as *the Rav* or *the Bartenura*. The translation adds words and phrases to make the Mishnah text read smoothly and clearly, without reference to the notes. Thus, one who reads the translation will gain a clear understanding of the basic text of the Mishnah. This is ideal for someone who wants to study the Mishnah for a *yahrzeit* or to review his learning. The **Notes** section clarifies and explains the Mishnah further by drawing, where necessary, on the Gemara or other classic Mishnah commentaries. In the rare instances when the consensus of the major commentators differs from the *Rav*, the translation and notes follow the consensus.

In the planning stages of this edition, many versions of the format were circulated for comment among our scholars and editors, as well as among lay readers. No suggestion was ignored. The approach was refined and refined again, until we arrived at this final version that, we feel, accomplishes the goal we to seek to achieve, with Hashem's help.

INTRODUCTION [xviii]

Many years ago, we were privileged to publish the widely acclaimed 44-volume Mishnah Series with the now-classic **YAD AVRAHAM** commentary, dedicated by **MR. AND MRS. LOUIS GLICK** in memory of their son AVRAHAM YOSEF ע״ה. The anthologized YAD AVRAHAM is an encyclopedic, in-depth commentary that presents many explanations and explores nuances and complexities, raises questions, and cites a wide variety of works on the Mishnah and Talmud. Its thoroughness has won the praise of even masters of the Talmud throughout the world, so that those who study and benefit from this new SCHOTTENSTEIN EDITION OF THE MISHNAH ELUCIDATED may turn to the Yad Avraham commentary when they wish to delve into the nuances of the Mishnah more deeply and explore a wider range of comments. Thus, in effect, the two editions complement each other.

The idea of producing an elucidated Mishnah patterned after the Schottenstein Edition of the Talmud was first put forward by our friend **TUVIA ROTBERG**. It was **RABBI ASHER DICKER** who suggested what eventually became the initial model for the format of this new series. We are grateful for their foresight.

This new MISHNAH ELUCIDATED represents yet another monumental undertaking by **JAY AND JEANIE SCHOTTENSTEIN**. Their previous historic projects — the Schottenstein Editions of Talmud Bavli and Talmud Yerushalmi, the Schottenstein Editions of the Interlinear Chumash, Prayerbooks, Megillah, and Haggadah; and the Schottenstein Edition of *Sefer HaChinuch/ Book of Mitzvos* — revolutionized the Torah study and Jewish lives of countless thousands, in homes, study halls, offices, commuter trains, and airplanes, wherever Jews have the desire and seek the opportunity to unite with their heritage. Thanks to Jay and Jeanie and their family, the Jewish world is a better place. Hundreds of thousands of Jews of all backgrounds have been touched by their vision and are now making Torah study and better prayer an integral part of their daily lives.

Now they have perceived a new need and, as always, they step forward to meet it. With their hallmark vision and generosity, they are enabling THE MISHNAH ELUCIDATED to bring the study of Mishnah within reach of all. This new series will add another jewel to the crown of their unprecedented service to the glory of Torah.

Gracious and generous, kind and caring, Jay and Jeanie open their hearts to countless people and causes. Quietly and considerately, they elevate the dignity and self-respect of those they help, they make their beneficiaries feel like their benefactors, and they imbue institutions with a stronger sense of mission. They not only give, they do.

In this dedication, Jay and Jeanie are joined by their children, **JOSEPH AND LINDSAY, JONATHAN AND NICOLE,** and **JEFFREY,** so the next generation of this regal family of Torah dissemination carries on the family tradition of responsibility for Klal Yisrael, present and future. Already in Columbus and beyond, they are adding luster to the legacy of their unforgettable grandfather JEROME ז״ל. As the years go by, this legacy will be joined by **JACOB, JONAH,**

[xix]   **INTRODUCTION**

and **EMMA**, as they take their places in the Schottenstein aristocracy of merit.

In the merit of their support of this and countless other Torah and *chessed* causes, may they all enjoy continued good health and success — and may the Jewish people continue to enjoy their leadership.

∞§ The Czuker Edition of Seder Zeraim

Seder Zeraim is dedicated by our dear friends, **EDWARD MENDEL AND ELISSA CZUKER**. We — and Klal Yisrael — are grateful for their generous support of major projects in Hebrew and English that are bringing Torah knowledge and love of learning to countless thousands of people around the globe. The Czukers feel a keen sense of responsibility to foster the growth and vitality of Torah life in their native Los Angeles and in Jewish communities everywhere. We are grateful and privileged for their personal friendship and their visionary support of our work.

ACKNOWLEDGMENTS

Over the years since the first ArtScroll book was published in 1976, we have been humbled to enjoy the guidance and encouragement of the great sages of the previous generation and our time. Their letters of approbation for various ArtScroll projects appear in volumes of those works. We are resolved בעזרת ה' to maintain the course set forth by them and their successors.

HAGAON HARAV DAVID FEINSTEIN שליט״א has been a guide, mentor, and friend since the first day of the ArtScroll Series, and we are honored that he regards our work as an important contribution to *harbatzas Torah*. Although complex halachic matters come to the Rosh Yeshivah from across the world, he always makes himself available to us whenever we consult him. He is also a founding Trustee of the Mesorah Heritage Foundation.

We are honored that this country's senior *roshei hayeshivah* have been so generous with their time and counsel. **HAGAON HARAV SHMUEL KAMENETSKY** שליט״א offers warm friendship and invaluable advice; **HAGAON HARAV AHARON SCHECHTER** שליט״א is unfailingly gracious and supportive; the Novominsker Rebbe, **HAGAON HARAV YAAKOV PERLOW** שליט״א, is a wise counselor, good friend, and staunch supporter of our efforts for *harbatzas Torah*. We are grateful beyond words to them all.

HAGAON HARAV DAVID COHEN שליט״א has been a dear friend for more than half a century; he places the treasury of his knowledge at our disposal whenever he is called upon, and has left his erudite mark on ArtScroll's projects from its inception. **HAGAON HARAV HILLEL DAVID** שליט״א is a warm and valued counselor and source of comment and advice. **HAGAON HARAV FEIVEL COHEN** שליט״א gladly interrupts his personal schedule whenever we call upon him.

A vast investment of time and resources will be required to make the twenty-two volumes of THE MISHNAH ELUCIDATED a reality. Only through the generous support of many people will it be possible not only to undertake and

INTRODUCTION [xx]

sustain such an important project, but to keep the price of the volumes within reach of the average family and student.

The Trustees of the MESORAH HERITAGE FOUNDATION saw the need to support the scholarship and production of this and other outstanding works of Torah literature. **HAGAON HARAV DAVID FEINSTEIN** שליט״א, as mentioned above, provides spiritual and halachic guidance. **PROF. JOEL L. FLEISHMAN** is the founding Trustee of the Foundation. It was he who recognized how much more could be accomplished with the aid of a Foundation. He conceived it and brought it into being. As chairman, he continues to guide us and lend his wisdom and prestige to our efforts. **SAM ASTROF** is nationally known in Jewish organizational life. His expertise and experience are invaluable. **HOWARD TZVI FRIEDMAN** is an old, dear friend and a fixture in the high echelons of public service. He unfailingly makes himself available. **JUDAH SEPTIMUS** is a *talmid chacham* and founding Trustee, who extends himself beyond belief in many ways, whenever he can be helpful. **JOSEPH SHENKER** is one of America's preeminent attorneys, a Torah scholar and good friend, who always makes time for our work. **JAMES S. TISCH**, one of the outstanding leaders of American industry and Jewish communal life, is a founding Trustee and a close friend. That such extraordinary people involve themselves closely with the work of the Foundation testifies to its importance. We are grateful to them and privileged to serve with them

We noted the Schottenstein family in the Introduction. **JAY SCHOTTENSTEIN** is chairman of the Board of Governors of Mesorah Heritage Foundation and has enlisted many others in support of its monumental projects. He and his wife **JEANIE**, and their children, **JOSEPH AND LINDSAY, JONATHAN,** and **JEFFREY,** have dedicated this SCHOTTENSTEIN EDITION OF THE MISHNAH ELUCIDATED.

ELLY KLEINMAN is a dear friend who is renowned for his warmth, integrity, judgment, and generosity. In addition to individual Talmud volumes, he is the Patron of several historic and popular projects: the 5-volume KLEINMAN EDITION OF KITZUR SHULCHAN ARUCH, an elucidation of a halachic classic, including the rulings of *Mishnah Berurah* and Rabbi Moshe Feinstein; the INTERACTIVE MISHKAN DVD; the English full-color MISHKAN volume, and its Hebrew counterpart; 43 volumes of the three series of the KLEINMAN EDITION OF DAILY DOSE OF TORAH; and the monumental 17-volume KLEINMAN EDITION OF MIDRASH RABBAH.

RABBI ZVI AND BETTY RYZMAN, loyal and devoted friends, are patrons of several Talmud volumes and the inaugural dedicators of a tractate of TALMUD YERUSHALMI. Rabbi Ryzman is an exceptional *talmid chacham,* an internationally renowned *maggid shiur,* author of many *sefarim,* and the epitome of the Jew who combines Torah study with business success — and gives priority to Torah. Most recently they have become the Patrons of this RYZMAN EDITION OF THE MISHNAH in Hebrew, which is already regarded as a classic, and which will be a major contribution to Torah study.

STANLEY AND ELLEN WASSERMAN are people of rare gentility, kindness, integrity, and dedication to worthy causes, both communal and private. They are patrons of several volumes of the SCHOTTENSTEIN EDITIONS OF THE

[xxi] **INTRODUCTION**

TALMUD — BAVLI AND YERUSHALMI, of volumes of RAMBAN, and of the KLEINMAN EDITION OF MIDRASH RABBAH. Their two current projects are already of historic proportions: The WASSERMAN EDITION OF THE ARTSCROLL SIDDUR is becoming the Siddur of choice throughout the world. The WASSERMAN DIGITAL INITIATIVE harnesses the era of technology in the service of Torah and tefillah. In their community and far beyond, the Wassermans are admired and respected not only for what they do, but for what they are.

ASHER AND MICHELLE MILSTEIN have dedicated three major projects: the MILSTEIN EDITION OF SEDER NASHIM in Talmud Yerushalmi, the MILSTEIN EDITION OF THE FIVE MEGILLOS in Midrash Rabbah, and the MILSTEIN EDITION OF THE LATER PROPHETS. Not content with *sponsoring* Torah works, he has become a major disseminator of Torah in a unique way, by arranging for the distribution of huge numbers of ArtScroll/Mesorah volumes to synagogues, organizations, and individuals throughout the world. We are gratified that they have chosen us as a vehicle to accomplish this goal, and that his brother **ELISHA SHLOMO MILSTEIN** has dedicated the MILSTEIN EDITION OF SEDER TOHOROS in Talmud Yerushalmi, and the MILSTEIN EDITION OF SEFER BAMIDBAR in Midrash Rabbah.

DANIEL AND DENA GRYFE have joined us as the first dedicators of Seder Moed in The Mishnah Elucidated. The Gryfes have earned admiration in Toronto as people who support a wide variety of Torah and *chessed* efforts, in Israel, Canada, and America. Although they are generous supporters of many mainstream yeshivas and kollels, they are especially devoted to Kiruv institutions and to organizations that help the needy and the childless. It is our privilege that they have chosen to add our work to their long list of important causes.

We are proud that **IRA AND INGEBORG RENNERT**, widely respected, generous supporters of a host of worthy causes, are the first dedicators of a Seder in Talmud Yerushalmi. By having dedicated the RENNERT EDITION OF SEDER ZERAIM in both the Hebrew and English editions, they were instrumental in bringing this work to fruition, and in making available the major source of the agricultural laws of the Land of Israel.

JACOB M.M. AND PNINA (RAND) GRAFF of Los Angeles are in the top rank of those who make the classics of our heritage accessible to today's Jews. They have dedicated SEDER MOED in the HEBREW EDITION OF TALMUD BAVLI, SEDER MOED in the ENGLISH EDITION OF TALMUD YERUSHALMI, and the GRAFF-RAND STUDENT EDITION OF RAMBAN. Thanks to them, countless people are able to navigate the Sea of the Talmud and understand Chumash through the eyes of Ramban.

EDWARD MENDEL AND ELISSA CZUKER of Los Angeles are modest people who resist honors, but their commitment to Torah dissemination speaks for itself. They have dedicated the ELUCIDATION OF THE TORAH'S COMMANDMENTS IN SEFER HACHINUCH/THE BOOK OF MITZVOS, BEREISHIS-NOACH IN MIDRASH RABBAH, and TRACTATE ROSH HASHANAH IN THE ENGLISH TALMUD YERUSHALMI and the classic CZUKER EDITION MIKRAOS GEDOLOS on Chumash, NEVIIM, and KESUVIM. Their generosity will be rewarded in the generations that will enter the world of enhanced Torah learning thanks to them.

INTRODUCTION [xxii]

YAAKOV AND BEATRICE HERZOG of Toronto have dedicated SEDER KODASHIM in the HEBREW TALMUD YERUSHALMI and SEFER DEVARIM OF RAMBAN. Their devotion to learning is inspiring. Reb Yaakov is a *talmid chacham* whose love of learning is infectious. Thanks to the generosity of Mr. and Mrs. Herzog, his zeal for learning will be extended to others through the volumes they make possible.

We are deeply grateful to **RABBI HESHIE BILLET**, a distinguished rav, teacher, and good friend; **JOSEPH AND SHEILA BISTRITZKY**, who, in their personal and business lives, epitomize unswerving loyalty to our Mesorah, and have always responded whenever called upon; **RABBI RAPHAEL B. BUTLER**, a constant friend and counselor, and the dynamic and imaginative founder of the Afikim Foundation; **NORMAN AND CECILY DAVIS**, of London and Jerusalem. The Davises are the parents of **RABBI YOSEF DAVIS**, the Editorial Director of this MISHNAH ELUCIDATED, and were the first dedicators of a volume in this new series; **RABBI YISRAEL H. EIDELMAN**, an effective, dedicated servant of Torah; **RABBI SHLOMO GERTZULIN**, whose competence and vision are invaluable assets to our people; **RABBI MOSHE M. GLUSTEIN**, an accomplished *marbitz Torah* and rosh yeshivah; **RABBI BURTON JAFFA**, the pioneer in giving hope to special children and their parents; **RABBI MICHOEL LEVI**, one of the community's most accomplished educators; **RABBI PINCHOS LIPSCHUTZ**, a leader in Torah journalism and a treasured friend; **RABBI SHIMSHON SHERER**, who inspires his congregation and honors us with his friendship; and **RABBI HOWARD ZACK**, a warm friend who is making an enormous impact for good in Columbus.

RABBI MEYER H. MAY of Los Angeles devotes his considerable acumen and prestige to the service of Torah. Thanks to him, many patrons have enlisted in support of the Foundation.

We are grateful also to many dear friends and loyal supporters. In alphabetical order, they are: **STEVE ADELSBERG**, a governor, and a dedicator in every edition of the Talmud; **REUVEN DESSLER**, a personal friend who adds luster to a distinguished family lineage; **YECHIEL BENZION FISHOFF**, the visionary, sensitive, and respected dedicator of several volumes; **ABRAHAM FRUCHTHANDLER**, who has placed support for Torah institutions on a new plateau; **LOUIS GLICK**, who sponsored the ArtScroll Mishnah Series with the Yad Avraham commentary; **HASHI HERZKA**, a pioneer dedicator and community activist; **MALCOLM HOENLEIN**, one of Jewry's truly great lay leaders, an eloquent and effective spokesman, who generously makes time to offer guidance and counsel; **SHIMMIE HORN**, patron of the HORN EDITION OF SEDER MOED of Talmud Bavli, a self-effacing person to whom support of Torah is a priority; **AMIR AND EDNA JAFFA, ELAN AND NOMI JAFFA**, and **JACK (YONA) AND CHANI JAFFA**, all members of the Board of Governors, who are glowing examples of the emergence of young leadership in their respective American Torah communities and around the world; **GEORGE KLEIN**, a major communal leader who has been in the forefront of Torah and community life for decades.

We are grateful to **MOTTY KLEIN**, dedicator of several Talmud volumes and of the OHEL SARAH WOMEN'S SIDDUR, a leader in his community and a force for Torah; **RABBI YEHUDAH LEVI**, whose service to Jewish children and worthy

[xxiii] **INTRODUCTION**

causes is extraordinary; **MOSHE MARX**, a respected and visionary supporter of Torah causes who prefers to remain in the background; **ANDREW NEFF**, dedicator of several volumes and a leader in his industry, who has made Mesorah his own cause; **DR. ALAN NOVETSKY**, the very first dedicator of an ArtScroll volume, who now resides in Jerusalem, and has continued his association and support over the years; **BARRY AND HARRIET RAY**, among the inaugural members of the Board of Governors, who have been warm personal friends for many years and were patrons of the earliest ArtScroll/Mesorah volumes before there was a Foundation; **DAVID RETTER**, scion of a distinguished family and a leader in his own right; **GEOFFREY ROCHWARGER** of Bet Shemesh, Patron of SEDER NASHIM in the Hebrew Talmud Bavli.

We are grateful to **HESHE SEIF**, who displays constant interest in our work. He is Patron of the SEIF EDITION TRANSLITERATED PRAYERBOOKS, who has added our work to his long list of important causes; **FRED SCHULMAN**, whose generous spirit invigorates his surroundings; **AUBREY SHARFMAN** is more than a Dedicator. He lends his verve and talent to many worthy causes and makes every effort to recruit others to join our work; **WARREN AND ROBIN SHIMOFF**, visionary people who discern a historic need and respond to it without being asked; **A. JOSEPH STERN**, Inaugural ArtScroll Patron of the SEFARD ARTSCROLL MACHZORIM and of Talmud tractates, whose warmth and concern for Torah causes are legendary; **NATHAN SILBERMAN**, a leader in his profession, who makes his skills and judgment available in too many ways to mention; **ADAM SOKOL**, a generous dedicator; **WOLI STERN** (São Paulo), a man of unusual warmth and sincerity who, with his son and partner **JACQUES**, honors us with his friendship.

We are grateful to **ELLIOT TANNENBAUM**, a warm and gracious inaugural Patron of every Talmud edition, as well as several other volumes, including the very popular *"Ner Naftali"* Eretz Yisrael Siddur, whose example has motivated many others; **GARY AND MALKE TORGOW**, precious and cherished friends. Gary is not only a visionary, but he turns his lofty vision into reality and enlists others to join him; **JOSEPH WEISS**, who has dedicated several volumes. He has made many astute comments as a contributing reader of Talmud Yerushalmi that were incorporated into the work, and he has influenced others to dedicate volumes; **STEVEN (CHANOCH) WEISZ**, a long-time personal friend and a true visionary whose infectious zeal for learning and service to good causes has brought many others under our banner; **SHLOMO WERDIGER**, an outstanding and selfless leader at the forefront of major causes, whose concern for the needs of Klal Yisrael is extraordinary, and who has been instrumental in our work since its inception; **YAAKOV WILLINGER**, an enthusiastic supporter; **MENDEL ZILBERBERG**, who carries on the family legacy of *askanus;* and להבחל״ח **HIRSCH WOLF** ז״ל, who was a valued friend and a fountain of encouragement from our very beginning, and an energetic, effective leader in many causes.

YERUCHAM LAX is more than an accountant. As a *talmid chacham* in his own right, he understands the importance of our work. His skill and expertise are indispensable in helping maintain our commitment to uncompromising accuracy.

INTRODUCTION [xxiv]

Enough cannot be said about our dear friend and colleague **RABBI SHEAH BRANDER**, whose graphics genius set the standard of excellence in Torah publishing. He is a *talmid chacham* of note who added more than one dimension to the quality of every volume. Reb Sheah is involved in every aspect of the project, from scholarship to production. He has earned the respect, trust, and affection of the entire staff, to the point where it is inconceivable to envision the past and future success and quality of the work without him.

MRS. CHUMIE LIPSCHITZ paginated the volume with her customary typographic expertise; **MRS. MINDY STERN** read the manuscript for accuracy with exceptional dedication and made many important suggestions; **MRS. JUDI DICK** contributed significantly with many valuable editorial comments; **MRS. ESTIE DICKER, MRS. ESTHER FEIERSTEIN,** and **MRS. TOBY GOLDZWEIG** provided typographic assistance.

The graphics skill and innovative work of **ELI KROEN** distinguish many of our works.

We express our appreciation to our esteemed colleague **SHMUEL BLITZ**, who continues to coordinate the activities of our authors and editors in Israel with dedication and distinction. On this side of the ocean, **AVROHOM BIDERMAN** and **MENDY HERZBERG** do the same, as they shepherd works from manuscript to computer to print.

MRS. LEA BRAFMAN, the comptroller of Mesorah Publications Ltd. virtually since our founding, is indispensable to the efficient functioning of our work. Her loyalty and competence are unexcelled. She is very ably assisted by **MRS. LEYA RABINOWITZ** and **MRS. ROBERTA FUCHS**.

MRS. SARA LEA HOBERMAN is the very loyal and effective comptroller of Mesorah Heritage Foundation. Both organizations are fortunate to have such a highly skilled and loyal staff.

We conclude with gratitude to Hashem Yisbarach for His infinite blessings and for the privilege of being the vehicle to disseminate His word. May this work continue so that all who thirst for His word may find what they seek in the refreshing words of the Torah.

Rabbi Nosson Scherman / Rabbi Gedaliah Zlotowitz

Cheshvan 5778/November 2017

מסכת מעשר שני
TRACTATE MAASER SHENI

זרעים
מועד
נשים
נזיקין
קדשים
טהרות

General Introduction

Tractate *Maaser Sheni* continues the topic of the last two tractates: the tithes that must be separated from produce grown in Eretz Yisrael. This tractate focuses on *maaser sheni,* the second tithe.

ಆೃ *Maaser Sheni*

The first portion separated from produce is *terumah*. A standard amount of *terumah* is 1/50 of the produce. *Terumah* is given to a Kohen and may be eaten only by a Kohen and the members of his household. After *terumah* is separated, the owner separates 1/10 of the produce that remains. This tenth is *maaser rishon* (*the first tithe*). It is given to a Levi, but may be eaten by anyone.[1] A second 1/10 is then separated from the produce that still remains. During the first, second, fourth, and fifth years of the seven-year *Shemittah* cycle, this second 1/10 is *maaser sheni*.[2] Unlike the other tithes, which are given to other people, *maaser sheni* is kept by the owner, but he must bring it to Jerusalem and eat it there.[3]

ಆೃ Produce subject to *Maaser Sheni*

Maaser sheni, like all tithes, is taken only from produce that grows in Eretz Yisrael (and, by Rabbinic law, from produce that grows in some surrounding areas). See General Introduction to Tractate *Terumos* and *Rambam, Hilchos Terumos* 1:1-9 for a description of the borders of Eretz Yisrael with regard to these laws.

The kinds of produce that are subject to *maaser sheni* are the same kinds that are subject to the other tithes (*Rambam, Hilchos Maaser Sheni* 1:12). In general, all edible produce that grows from the ground is obligated in these tithes, although some types of produce are obligated by Torah law and some only by Rabbinic law. See General Introduction to Tractate *Maasros*.

NOTES

1. The Levi, however, must first separate one tenth of the *maaser rishon* and give it to a Kohen; this tenth is known as *terumas maaser* and has the same laws as *terumah*.

2. During the third and sixth years of the cycle, a tithe known as *maasar ani* (*the tithe of the poor*) is separated instead of *maaser sheni;* it is distributed to the poor. The seventh year of the cycle is *Shemittah* (Sabbatical year), when certain agricultural activities, such as planting and plowing, are forbidden. If produce grows on its own during *Shemittah,* it must be left free for anyone to take. No tithes need to be separated from any produce that grows during *Shemittah*.

3. For a fuller discussion of the tithes, see General Introduction to Tractate *Terumos*.

◈§ Redemption of *Maaser Sheni*

A central focus of this tractate is the subject of פִּדְיוֹן מַעֲשֵׂר שֵׁנִי, *redemption of maaser sheni*.

A. Redemption and Deconsecration

If a person cannot or does not want to carry his *maaser sheni* to Jerusalem, he may transfer its sanctity to money. The produce becomes *chullin* (ordinary, non-sacred) and may be eaten anywhere. This process is known as פִּדְיוֹן, *redemption*. The money, which now has *maaser sheni* sanctity, must be brought to Jerusalem and used to buy food there. The sanctity then transfers to the purchased food, and it must be eaten in Jerusalem, in accordance with the laws of *maaser sheni*. The money (which now belongs to whoever sold the food) returns to *chullin* status and may be used for anything. This process is known as חִלּוּל, *deconsecration*, or *transfer of sanctity*.

B. Place of Redemption

Maaser sheni produce may be redeemed only outside Jerusalem. If it is brought into Jerusalem, it may no longer be redeemed. By Torah law, though, it may be taken out of the city and redeemed there. However, as a precaution against redeeming *maaser sheni* inside Jerusalem, the Rabbis decreed that a person may not even redeem *maaser sheni* outside Jerusalem if it has already entered the city. As a further precaution, they decreed that once *maaser sheni* produce enters the city, it may not be taken out at all (*Derech Emunah, Hilchos Maaser Sheni* 2:63). This concept is referred to as מְחִיצוֹת קוֹלְטוֹת, *the walls take hold*; that is, once *maaser sheni* produce enters the city, the walls of Jerusalem "take hold" of it and it may not be removed from the city or redeemed.[4]

If, however, it becomes *tamei* and thus unfit to be eaten (see below), it may be redeemed even inside Jerusalem. Whether it may then be removed from the city depends on how and where it became *tamei* (see Mishnah 3:9).

C. Methods of Redemption

Maaser sheni can be redeemed in either of two ways. Either a person sets aside some money and transfers the sanctity from the produce to the money, or he sells the produce to another person with the intention that the sanctity will transfer to the purchase money. In this second case, the sanctity transfers from the produce to the coins paid for it, and the produce, now owned by the buyer, becomes *chullin*.

It is not only the *maaser sheni's* owner who may redeem it. A person may redeem *maaser sheni* that belongs to someone else, by setting aside his own money to serve as its redemption.[5] The produce, now *chullin*, becomes his, and the money, which now has *maaser sheni* sanctity, is his as well, and he must eat it in Jerusalem.

There is one crucial difference between a person who redeems his own

---------------- NOTES ----------------

4. This law applies only to *maaser sheni* produce. Money with *maaser sheni* sanctity may be removed from Jerusalem (Mishnah 3:5).

5. The owner of the *maaser sheni* must give him permission to do so (see *Derech Emunah, Hilchos Maaser Sheni* 5:37).

[5] **MISHNAH MAASER SHENI** / General Introduction

maaser sheni and one who redeems *maaser sheni* that belongs to someone else. The Torah states (*Vayikra* 27:31) that when a person redeems his own *maaser sheni,* he must add a fee of one-fifth of the produce's value.[6] This extra fifth is added to the redemption money and also takes on *maaser sheni* sanctity.

This fifth is added only if a person redeems his own *maaser sheni* with his own money. If he redeems his *maaser sheni* with another person's money, or he redeems another person's *maaser sheni* with his money, he does not have to add a fifth.[7]

Maaser sheni is to be redeemed for its exact price (plus a fifth, when required), which must be determined based on the assessment of an expert merchant (see Mishnah 4:2). If, however, it is redeemed on any amount of money, it is valid after the fact — whether a large amount of *maaser sheni* is redeemed on a small coin or a small amount of *maaser sheni* is redeemed on a large coin (*Rambam, Hilchos Maaser Sheni* 4:18).

D. Further Exchanges

Once coins have been sanctified as *maaser sheni,* they may generally not be exchanged for other coins. There are exceptions, though: For example, if a person redeemed his *maaser sheni* on small coins, he may want to exchange them for larger coins so that he will have fewer coins to carry to Jerusalem (see Mishnah 2:8). And once he arrives in Jerusalem with large coins, he must exchange those for smaller coins, which he needs to make small purchases (see Mishnah 2:9).

Ideally, a person should spend his *maaser sheni* money in Jerusalem on animals that will be used for voluntary *shelamim* offerings. He may, however, use it for other food as well, as long as it meets certain criteria (see Mishnah 1:5; *Eruvin* 27b).

◆§ Using *Maaser Sheni*

Food with *maaser sheni* sanctity — whether produce separated as *maaser sheni* or food bought with money on which that produce was redeemed — must be eaten in Jerusalem. If a person eats it outside Jerusalem, he transgresses two of the Torah's commandments: a positive commandment to eat it in Jerusalem (*Devarim* 14:23),[8] and a prohibition on eating it outside Jerusalem (12:17 there).[9]

─────────── NOTES ───────────

6. This fifth is calculated as ⅕ of the value after the fifth is added. For example, if the produce is worth 4 *dinars,* he redeems it for 5 *dinars.* The extra *dinar* is ⅕ of the total after the fifth *dinar* is added — although it is ¼ of the *maaser sheni's* value (*Bava Metzia* 53b-54a).

7. If a person redeems his *maaser sheni* by selling it to another person, no fifth is added, because the produce is not redeemed with its owner's money but with the money paid by the buyer.

8. וְאָכַלְתָּ לִפְנֵי ה׳ אֱלֹהֶיךָ בַּמָּקוֹם אֲשֶׁר יִבְחַר, לְשַׁכֵּן שְׁמוֹ שָׁם מַעְשַׂר דְּגָנְךָ תִּירֹשְׁךָ וְיִצְהָרֶךָ, *And you shall eat before Hashem, your God, in the place that He will choose to rest His Name there — the tithe of your grain, your wine, and your oil.*

9. לֹא תוּכַל לֶאֱכֹל בִּשְׁעָרֶיךָ מַעְשַׂר דְּגָנְךָ וְתִירֹשְׁךָ וְיִצְהָרֶךָ, *You may not eat in your [outlying] cities the tithe of your grain, your wine, and your oil.*

This prohibition, however, does not take effect until the food is brought into

Maaser sheni may be used in any of three ways: it may be eaten, it may be drunk, and it may be rubbed on the skin (as with oil). Which use it may be put to depends on the type of food. Food that is typically eaten must be eaten; food that is typically drunk must be drunk, and items that are typically rubbed on the skin are rubbed on the skin.

Maaser sheni may not be eaten by a person who is *tamei*. Furthermore, one must safeguard *maaser sheni* from becoming *tamei;* if it does, no one may eat it. It is also forbidden to waste or destroy *maaser sheni,* and it may not be fed to animals.

◆§ Ownership of *Maaser Sheni*

Tannaim have a dispute whether a person actually owns his *maaser sheni*. R' Meir holds that *maaser sheni* is מָמוֹן גָּבוֹהַּ, *Divine property.* That is, *maaser sheni* does not actually belong to the person who holds it. It is God's property and the person who holds the *maaser* is permitted (obligated, in fact) to eat it in accordance with certain guidelines. R' Yehudah disagrees. He holds that *maaser sheni* is מָמוֹן הֶדְיוֹט, *property of the commoner.* That is, *maaser sheni* belongs to the person who holds it. He must follow certain guidelines in the way he uses it, but it is his property.

This dispute has a few ramifications, primarily whether a person can sell or give his *maaser sheni* to someone else. If he does not own it, he cannot sell it or give it away; he may use it only as the Torah allows him to; namely, to eat in Jerusalem.

◆§ *Maaser Sheni* Today

Maaser Sheni, like all tithes, must be separated even today from produce that grows in Eretz Yisrael.[10] However, when there is no Temple, *maaser sheni* may not be eaten (*Makkos* 19a). Therefore, the *maaser sheni* must either be left to rot, or, as is more commonly done, it is redeemed on a small coin and that coin is destroyed, for example, it is thrown into the sea (*Rambam, Hilchos Maaser Sheni* 2:2).[11]

NOTES

Jerusalem. If a person eats it outside Jerusalem before it was ever brought into the city, he does not transgress the prohibition on eating it outside Jerusalem (*Makkos* 19b; *Rambam, Hilchos Maaser Sheni* 2:6). He does, however, transgress the positive commandment to eat the *maaser sheni* in Jerusalem (*Derech Emunah* there 2:46).

10. There is a dispute among the Rishonim whether the obligation for tithes today is Biblical or Rabbinic in nature. The halachah follows those who rule that it is Rabbinic (*Shulchan Aruch* and *Rama, Yoreh Deah* 331:2).

11. As we have said, a redemption is valid even if a large amount of *maaser sheni* is redeemed on the smallest coin. Although this is generally valid only after the fact but not permitted in the first place, nowadays when the *maaser sheni* may not be eaten and must go to waste in any case, such a redemption is permitted (*Derech Emunah, Hilchos Maaser Sheni* 2:14).

Chapter One

- רע״ב -

מעשר שני — פרק ראשון (א) מעשר שני, אין מוכרין אותו. אפילו להוליכו לירושלים לפי שהוא קדש. וסתם מתניתין כרבי

[א] מַעֲשֵׂר שֵׁנִי, אֵין מוֹכְרִין אוֹתוֹ, וְאֵין מְמַשְׁכְּנִין אוֹתוֹ, וְאֵין מַחֲלִיפִין אוֹתוֹ, וְלֹא שׁוֹקְלִין כְּנֶגְדוֹ.

מאיר דאמר מעשר [שני] ממון גבוה הוא׃ ואין מחליפין אותו. לא יאמר לו הילך יין ותן לי שמן, שמן ותן לי יין׃ ואין שוקלין כנגדו. סלע של חולין כנגד סלע של מעשר שני, משום בזוי מצוה׃

---

[1] As explained in the General Introduction, *maaser sheni* is a tithe that must be separated from produce that grows in Eretz Yisrael during the first, second, fourth, and fifth years of the seven-year *Shemittah* cycle. The owner of the produce keeps the *maaser sheni,* but he must eat it in Jerusalem. If he does not wish to carry his *maaser sheni* to Jerusalem, he can transfer its sanctity to money, which he brings to Jerusalem and uses to buy food that he will eat there.

The Torah (*Vayikra* 27:30) labels *maaser sheni* קֹדֶשׁ לַה׳, *sanctified to Hashem*. This Mishnah lists a number of restrictions that apply to *maaser sheni* because of its sanctified status:[1]

מַעֲשֵׂר שֵׁנִי — *Maaser sheni* is subject to the following laws: אֵין מוֹכְרִין אוֹתוֹ — One may not sell it,[2] וְאֵין מְמַשְׁכְּנִין אוֹתוֹ — and one may not use it as security for a loan;[3] וְאֵין מַחֲלִיפִין אוֹתוֹ — and one may not trade it for another item. Although a person may eat his *maaser sheni,* it does not truly belong to him but rather is Divine property; thus, the person who holds it does not have the right to make transactions with it.[4] וְלֹא שׁוֹקְלִין כְּנֶגְדוֹ — In addition, **one**

NOTES

[1]

1. [Generally, when we refer to *maaser sheni,* we mean anything that has *maaser sheni* sanctity: either produce that was separated as *maaser sheni,* money to which that sanctity was transferred, or food bought with that money.]

2. The Mishnah forbids the type of sale where the produce remains *maaser sheni* and the buyer is responsible to eat it in Jerusalem. If, however, the sale is intended as a חִלּוּל, *transfer of sanctity* (sometimes known as פִּדְיוֹן, *redemption*), that is, the sale will *transfer* the sanctity from the produce to the purchase money, and the seller will then take that money to Jerusalem to buy food, the sale is permitted [and even encouraged when a person is unable to carry all his *maaser sheni* to Jerusalem] (*Rav* to Mishnah 4:6; see General Introduction).

3. [When a person lends money, he may take an item from the borrower to serve as security for the loan: if the borrower fails to repay the money, the lender keeps the security. *Maaser sheni* produce may not be used as security.]

4. The ownership of *maaser sheni* is actually a matter of dispute among Tannaim: R' Meir holds that *maaser sheni* is מָמוֹן גָּבוֹהַּ, *Divine property*. That is, *maaser sheni* does not actually belong to the person who holds it. It is God's property, and the person who holds the *maaser* is permitted (obligated, in fact) to eat it in accordance with certain guidelines. Our Mishnah follows this opinion. Therefore, our Mishnah rules that *maaser sheni* may not be sold, given as security, or traded, because a person cannot sell, give as security, or trade an item that does not belong to him (*Rav, Meleches Shlomo*).

R' Yehudah disagrees. He holds that *maaser sheni* is מָמוֹן הֶדְיוֹט, *property of the commoner.* That is, *maaser sheni* belongs to the person who holds it. He must follow certain guidelines in the way he uses it, but it is his property (*Meleches Shlomo*). [R' Yehudah agrees, though, that a person may not sell *maaser sheni,* give it as security, or trade it — but for a different reason: it is disrespectful to use a sacred item in such ways (*Yerushalmi,* with *Rash Sirilio*).]

[9] **MISHNAH MAASER SHENI** / Chapter 1: *Maaser Sheni*

וְלֹא יֹאמַר אָדָם לַחֲבֵרוֹ בִּירוּשָׁלַיִם, הֵילָךְ יַיִן וְתֶן לִי שֶׁמֶן. וְכֵן שְׁאָר כָּל הַפֵּרוֹת. אֲבָל נוֹתְנִין זֶה לָזֶה מַתְּנַת חִנָּם.

– רע"ב –

ולא יאמר אדם לחבירו בירושלים. לטיל אייר חון לירושלים, והכא קמשמע לן דאפילו בירושלים שקונין בדמיו מאכל ומשתה אינו רשאי להחליף: **וכן שאר כל הפירות.** אפילו אותן פירות דמעשר דידהו לא הוי אלא מדרבנן: **אבל נותנים זה לזה מתנת חנם.** כגון שמזמינו לאכול עמו על שולחנו. ודברי הכל היא, אבל לתת לו במתנה ממש לדברי האומר מתנה כמכר אסור:

---

may not weigh other items **against** [*maaser sheni*]; that is, a person may not use *maaser sheni* as a weight on a scale in order to determine the weight of something else,[5] because it is disrespectful to put a sacred object to such use. וְלֹא יֹאמַר אָדָם לַחֲבֵרוֹ בִּירוּשָׁלַיִם — **And** even **in Jerusalem a person may not say to his friend,** הֵילָךְ יַיִן וְתֶן לִי שֶׁמֶן — **"Take this** *maaser sheni* **wine and give me oil** in exchange." Although a person may spend *maaser sheni* money on food in Jerusalem, he may not exchange *maaser sheni* produce for different food.[6]

Until now, the Mishnah referred to standard *maaser sheni*, that is, produce obligated in *maaser sheni* by Torah law. The Mishnah adds:

וְכֵן שְׁאָר כָּל הַפֵּרוֹת — **And** all these activities are **likewise** forbidden for **all other** kinds of *maaser sheni* **produce,** even those that are only Rabbinically obligated in *maasros*.[7]

The Mishnah states a permitted use for *maaser sheni*:

אֲבָל נוֹתְנִין זֶה לָזֶה מַתְּנַת חִנָּם — **But** [people] **may give** each other *maaser sheni* as **a free gift;** that is, it is permitted to invite someone to a meal and serve him *maaser sheni* produce.[8]

--- NOTES ---

5. [A balance scale has two pans suspended from a bar. A weight (that is, an object of known weight; for example, a coin that weighs one ounce) is placed in one pan and an item, such as food, is placed in the other pan. When the pans balance, we know that the food weighs the same as the weight. *Maaser sheni* may not be used as a weight.]

6. When the Mishnah first said that a person may not trade *maaser sheni*, it referred to doing so outside Jerusalem — where it is forbidden to buy anything with *maaser sheni* (see Mishnah 5). The Mishnah now adds that even in Jerusalem, where it is permitted to buy food with *money* of *maaser sheni* (i.e., money to which he transferred *maaser sheni* sanctity), it is forbidden to exchange *produce* of *maaser sheni* for other food (*Rav*).

7. By Torah law, only grain, grapes, and olives are obligated in *maasros*. Most other forms of produce are obligated in *maasros* by Rabbinic law (see General Introduction).

8. It is only such a "gift" that is permitted. Since according to our Tanna *maaser sheni* is Divine property (see note 4), the person who holds it does not have the authority to give it to someone else as an outright gift. All he may do is grant a guest permission to eat it, since the right to eat it is a privilege that does belong to him (see *Rav;* see *Derech Emunah, Hilchos Maaser Sheni* 3:145).

[Since the Mishnah refers only to inviting someone for a meal, it uses the term "free gift" rather than "gift." A meal is something truly given for free, without expecting anything in return. An outright gift, on the other hand, is usually given in exchange for some favor received or hoped for (*Mishnah Rishonah*).]

משניות מעשר שני / פרק א: מעשר שני

[ב] **מַעֲשַׂר** בְּהֵמָה, אֵין מוֹכְרִין אוֹתוֹ תָּמִים חַי, וְלֹא בַעַל מוּם חַי וְשָׁחוּט, וְאֵין מְקַדְּשִׁין בּוֹ הָאִשָּׁה.

– רע"ב –

(ב) אין מוכרין אותו. דגמרינן גמולה גמולה מחרמים, נאמר במעשר (ויקרא כז) לא יגאל, ונאמר בחרמים (שם) לא ימכר ולא יגאל, מה להלן מכירתו עמו אף כאן מכירה עמו: תמים חי. והוא הדין נמי שחוט, שנאמר לא יגאל אינו נמכר לא חי ולא שחוט לא תמים ולא בעל מום. אלא תמים חי, חלבו ודמו קרבין על גבי המזבח והבשר אותו אוכלין הבעלים בירושלים. ובעל מום אוכלים אותו הבעלים בכל מקום. ואייתי דבטי למתני סיפא גבי בכור מוכרים אותו תמים חי, תני נמי רישא תמים חי: ואין מקדשין בו את האשה. דהוי כמכר.

---

[2] Having discussed whether it is permitted to sell *maaser sheni,* the Mishnah discusses whether it is permitted to sell two other types of sanctified items. The first is *maasar beheimah,* the animal tithe: Every year, a person must set aside one out of every ten cows, sheep, and goats that were born in his flock that year. The animals that he sets aside are sanctified: if they have no physical blemishes, they are brought as offerings; if they are blemished and thus unfit to be brought as offerings,[1] they may be eaten as ordinary meat. The Mishnah discusses whether animals that are *maasar beheimah* may be sold:

מַעְשַׂר בְּהֵמָה — An animal that is *maasar beheimah* is subject to the following laws: אֵין מוֹכְרִין אוֹתוֹ תָּמִים חַי — **One may not sell it** if it has **no blemishes and is alive** (in which case it is to be brought as an offering),[2] וְלֹא בַעַל מוּם חַי וְשָׁחוּט — **or if it has a blemish, whether it is alive or slaughtered** (in which case it is to be eaten by the owner).[3] וְאֵין מְקַדְּשִׁין בּוֹ הָאִשָּׁה — **And one may not betroth a woman with** any [*maasar beheimah* animal], because a betrothal has the same laws as a sale.[4]

The Mishnah discusses another type of sanctified animal: the *bechor.* A firstborn male cow, sheep, or goat is known as a *bechor* and must be given to a Kohen. If it is unblemished, the Kohen brings it as an offering. If it is blemished, the Kohen eats it as ordinary meat. The Mishnah discusses whether a Kohen may sell a *bechor* that he is given:

NOTES

[2]

1. [An animal that has any of certain physical blemishes (מום) is not valid to be brought as an offering. These blemishes are described in *Vayikra* 22:21-24 and *Bechoros* Chapter 6.]

2. The same applies even if the animal is no longer alive. The reason the Mishnah mentions only a live animal is because the first law taught in the next section of the Mishnah applies only to a live animal (see note 5). Therefore, the Mishnah mentioned a live animal here as well in order to contrast the two laws (*Rav*).

3. The prohibition of selling *maasar beheimah* is derived from verses in the Torah (*Rav*).

4. One way for a man to betroth a woman is to give her something of value (*Kiddushin* 1:1). It is forbidden to use *maasar beheimah* for this purpose, because a betrothal is similar to a sale: a person gets something (his wife) in exchange for a payment or gift. Thus, just as *maasar beheimah* may not be sold, it may not be used for betrothal (see *Rav*).

[11] **MISHNAH MAASER SHENI** / Chapter 1: *Maaser Sheni* 1/2

- רע"ב -

הַבְּכוֹר מוֹכְרִין אוֹתוֹ תָּמִים חַי, וּבַעַל מוּם חַי וְשָׁחוּט וּמְקַדְּשִׁין בּוֹ הָאִשָּׁה. אֵין מְחַלְּלִין מַעֲשֵׂר שֵׁנִי עַל אֲסִימוֹן וְלֹא עַל הַמַּטְבֵּעַ שֶׁאֵינוֹ יוֹצֵא, וְלֹא עַל הַמָּעוֹת שֶׁאֵינָן בִּרְשׁוּתוֹ.

הבכור מוכרין אותו תמים חי. משום דבבכור כתיב (במדבר יח) לא תפדה אבל נמכר הוא: ומקדשין בו את האשה. דממונו של כהן הוא ומותר למוכרו:
אסימון. מטבע שאין עליו צורה, ואין מחללין עליו מעשר שני דכתיב (דברים יד) וצרת הכסף בידך, כסף שיש עליו צורה: ולא על המטבע שאינו יוצא. דכתיב (שם) ונתת הכסף בכל אשר תאוה נפשך, פרט לכסף שאינו יוצא, שאינו יכול לקנות ממנו מה שהוא רוצה: ולא על המעות שאינן ברשותו. כגון שנפל כיסו לים הגדול אינו יכול לפדות מעשר שני על מעות שבתוכו, שהוא צריך לשכור מי שמט על פני המים להוציאו:

הַבְּכוֹר — A *bechor* is subject to the following laws: **מוֹכְרִין אוֹתוֹ תָּמִים חַי** — [The Kohen] who receives it **may sell it** if it is **unblemished** and **alive**.[5] **וּבַעַל מוּם חַי וְשָׁחוּט** — If it is **blemished**, the Kohen may sell it whether it is **alive** or **slaughtered**;[6] **וּמְקַדְּשִׁין בּוֹ הָאִשָּׁה** — and [a Kohen] **may betroth a woman with** [any of these *bechoros*].

The Mishnah returns to the laws of *maaser sheni*. As we have mentioned, a person may transfer the sanctity of *maaser sheni* onto coins, which he will spend on food in Jerusalem. The Mishnah lists a few types of coins that may not be used for this purpose:

אֵין מְחַלְּלִין מַעֲשֵׂר שֵׁנִי עַל אֲסִימוֹן — **One may not transfer sanctity from** *maaser sheni* **to a blank coin**, i.e., a coin-shaped piece of metal that has no official image imprinted on it; וְלֹא עַל הַמַּטְבֵּעַ שֶׁאֵינוֹ יוֹצֵא — **nor to a coin that cannot be spent**, such as a coin from another country that is not accepted in the place where he is; וְלֹא עַל הַמָּעוֹת שֶׁאֵינָן בִּרְשׁוּתוֹ — **nor to money that is not** currently **in his possession**, that is, coins that are not accessible, even though they belong to him.[7]

NOTES

5. This law applies only nowadays, when the Temple is not standing. Since the *bechor* cannot be brought as an offering, when it is given to the Kohen it simply becomes his personal property. [Unlike *maasar beheimah*, no verse forbids the sale of a *bechor*, and thus the Kohen may sell it.] While the Temple stands, though, a Kohen may not sell an unblemished *bechor*. Although it is given to him, he must bring it as an offering; it does not become his personal property and thus he may not sell it (*Tos. Yom Tov*, from *Temurah* 7b).

In addition, an unblemished *bechor* nowadays may not be slaughtered. The Kohen must keep it until it develops a blemish and only then may it be slaughtered and eaten. If it was slaughtered while unblemished, its meat is forbidden for benefit and must be buried. Therefore, the Mishnah states only that a *live* unblemished *bechor* may be sold. If it was slaughtered, it may not be sold because it is forbidden for benefit (*Tos. Yom Tov*).

6. A blemished *bechor* is always the Kohen's personal property, to eat as ordinary meat. Since no verse forbids its sale, the Kohen may sell it.

7. For example, if one's purse of money fell into the sea, he cannot transfer his *maaser sheni* onto the coins in the purse, even though technically they still belong to him (*Rav*).

These laws are all derived from verses in the Torah [*Devarim* 14:25-26] (*Rav, Bava Kamma* 98a).

משניות מעשר שני / פרק א: מעשר שני

[ג] **הַלּוֹקֵחַ** בְּהֵמָה לְזִבְחֵי שְׁלָמִים, אוֹ חַיָּה לִבְשַׂר תַּאֲוָה, יָצָא הָעוֹר לְחֻלִּין, אַף עַל פִּי שֶׁהָעוֹר מְרֻבֶּה עַל הַבָּשָׂר. כַּדֵּי יַיִן סְתוּמוֹת, מְקוֹם שֶׁדַּרְכָּן לִמְכֹּר סְתוּמוֹת,

– רע״ב –

(ג) **הלוקח בהמה לזבחי שלמים.** ממעות מעשר שני, שכך הוא עיקר מצות מעות מעשר שני לקנות מהם שלמים, דילפינן שם שם מגזרה שוה מהר טיבל: **ויצא** שאינה ראויה להקרבה, וקנאה ממעות מעשר שני לאכול אותה בשר תאוה, כלומר חולין: **יצא העור לחולין.** ואין צריך לאכול דמיו בירושלים: **יצא הקנקן לחולין.** ואין צריך למכרו ולאכול דמיו בקדושת מעשר בירושלים. והני מילי כשמוכר והקונה הדיוטים ואין נותנים עיניהם אלא בבשר לאכול וביין לשתות אבל אם אחד מהם אומן לעבד עורות, או יוצר חרס דעסקיו ודאי נותן עיניו בעורות או בקנקנין, נעשה כקונה זה בפני עצמו וזה בפני עצמו, ולא יצאו לחולין:

---

[3] When the sanctity of *maaser sheni* is transferred onto money, that money must be used to buy food, which takes on the *maaser sheni* sanctity. The next two Mishnahs discuss cases where a person spends *maaser sheni* money on food, and a non-food item is included in the sale:

הַלּוֹקֵחַ בְּהֵמָה לְזִבְחֵי שְׁלָמִים — **If someone buys a domestic animal** (a cow, sheep, or goat), with *maaser sheni* money, in order to bring it **as a shelamim offering,**[1] אוֹ חַיָּה לִבְשַׂר תַּאֲוָה — **or he buys a nondomestic animal** (for example, a deer), to eat **as ordinary meat,**[2] יָצָא הָעוֹר לְחֻלִּין — **the hide,** which is not food, **becomes *chullin*;** that is, it does not have any sanctity, even though the meat has *maaser sheni* sanctity.[3] אַף עַל פִּי שֶׁהָעוֹר מְרֻבֶּה עַל הַבָּשָׂר — **This is true even if the hide is worth more than the meat.** Since a person buys an animal for the meat and not the hide, the hide is not considered a significant part of the sale and does not take on *maaser sheni* sanctity.[4]

Similar cases:

כַּדֵּי יַיִן סְתוּמוֹת — **Someone buys closed jugs of wine** with *maaser sheni* money: מְקוֹם שֶׁדַּרְכָּן לִמְכֹּר סְתוּמוֹת — **if he is in a place where it is common** for wine **to be sold** in **closed [jugs],** that is, wine is always sold along with its

---
NOTES

[3]

1. Ideally, this is how *maaser sheni* money should be spent: on animals that will be brought as *shelamim* offerings (*Rav*). See Mishnah 4 note 2.

2. Literally, *meat of desire,* i.e., meat that is eaten as ordinary food rather than an offering (see *Rav*). [A nondomestic animal cannot be brought as an offering.]

3. Although the Mishnah uses the expression "it becomes *chullin*," in fact it simply *remains chullin,* because it never became sanctified at all (see *Rambam Commentary* and *Kesef Mishneh, Hilchos Maaser Sheni* 8:1).

4. When an animal is purchased, it can be assumed that both the buyer and seller intend to transact a sale of meat. Thus, the *maaser sheni* money went to purchase the meat, and that is what takes on sanctity. The hide just happens to come along with the sale because it is attached to the meat (*Rav; Rambam Commentary; Kesef Mishneh, Hilchos Maaser Sheni* 8:1).

If, however, the buyer or seller does consider the hide important in its own right (for example, he is a tanner, who uses hides for his trade), it can be assumed that the money was intended to pay for the hide as well and thus the hide takes on sanctity just as the meat does (*Rav*). Since *maaser sheni* money must be used for food, the buyer will be required to sell the hide and spend the money from its sale on food (*Tiferes Yisrael*).

[13] **MISHNAH MAASER SHENI** / Chapter 1: *Maaser Sheni* 1/4

יָצָא קַנְקַן לְחֻלִּין. הָאֱגוֹזִים וְהַשְּׁקֵדִים, יָצְאוּ קְלִפֵּיהֶם לְחֻלִּין. הַתֶּמֶד עַד שֶׁלֹּא הֶחֱמִיץ, אֵינוֹ נִלְקָח בְּכֶסֶף מַעֲשֵׂר. וּמִשֶּׁהֶחֱמִיץ, נִלְקָח בְּכֶסֶף מַעֲשֵׂר.

[ד] **הַלּוֹקֵחַ** חַיָּה לְזִבְחֵי שְׁלָמִים, בְּהֵמָה לִבְשַׂר תַּאֲוָה, לֹא יָצָא הָעוֹר

- רע״ב -

התמד. פסולת של ענבים שנתן עליהם מים: אינו נלקח בכסף מעשר. דכתיב כמו מים, ואזן בטעין פרי מפרי וגדולי קרקע: נלקח בכסף מעשר. דכיון שהחמיץ חשיב אוכל, והוא דרמא תלתא ואשכח ארבעתה: (ד) הלוקח חיה לזבחי שלמים. ואין קרבן

בא מן החיה, דכתיב (ויקרא א) מן הבקר ומן הצאן: ובהמה לבשר תאוה. חכמים גזרו שלא יקנו בהמה

---

jug, **יָצָא קַנְקַן לְחֻלִּין** — **the jug becomes** *chullin,* that is, it does not have *maaser sheni* sanctity. The transaction is considered a sale of wine; the jug simply comes along with it as per the local custom. Accordingly, only the wine takes on *maaser sheni* sanctity.[5]

הָאֱגוֹזִים וְהַשְּׁקֵדִים — Similarly, if someone buys **walnuts or almonds** that are in their shells, **יָצְאוּ קְלִפֵּיהֶם לְחֻלִּין** — **their shells become** *chullin;* that is, they do not take on sanctity, because they are not considered a significant part of the sale; they are simply included in the sale of nuts.

Not all food may be bought with *maaser sheni* money (this will be discussed further in Mishnah 5). One thing that may not be bought with this money is water. The Mishnah discusses whether *maaser sheni* money may be used for *temed,* a wine-flavored drink produced by soaking grape skins or seeds in water. When first made, it tastes like wine-flavored water; it later ferments and tastes like low-quality wine:

הַתֶּמֶד — The law for *temed* is as follows: **עַד שֶׁלֹּא הֶחֱמִיץ אֵינוֹ נִלְקָח בְּכֶסֶף מַעֲשֵׂר** — **If it has not yet fermented, it may not be bought with** *maaser sheni* **money** because it is considered [wine-flavored] water, and water may not be bought with *maaser sheni* money. **וּמִשֶּׁהֶחֱמִיץ נִלְקָח בְּכֶסֶף מַעֲשֵׂר** — **But once it has fermented, it may be bought with** *maaser sheni* **money** because it is considered food.

[4] The Mishnah discusses more cases where *maaser sheni* money is used to buy food, and a non-food item is included in the sale:

הַלּוֹקֵחַ חַיָּה לְזִבְחֵי שְׁלָמִים — **If someone buys** with *maaser sheni* money **a nondomestic animal** intending to bring it **as a** *shelamim* **offering,** which is impossible;[1] **בְּהֵמָה לִבְשַׂר תַּאֲוָה** — or a person uses *maaser sheni* money to buy **a domestic animal** to eat **as ordinary meat,** which is Rabbinically forbidden;[2] **לֹא יָצָא הָעוֹר לְחֻלִּין** — in these cases **the hide does not become**

NOTES

5. As in the previous case, if the buyer or seller considers the jug important (for example, he is a potter), the jug is considered a significant part of the sale and takes on sanctity (*Rav;* see note 4).

The next Mishnah will discuss the law where it is not customary to include a jug in a sale of wine.

[4]
1. A nondomestic animal may never be brought as an offering.
2. Although a person should ideally use

א/ד

משניות מעשר שני / פרק א: מעשר שני [14]

- רע"ב -

ממעות מעשר שני אלא שלמים, לפי שבראשונה היה מותר ליקח בהמה לבשר תאוה, כיון שראו שהיו הכל לוקחים בהמה לבשר תאוה ומבריחים אותה מעל גבי המזבח חזרו ואמרו לא

לְחֻלִּין. כַּדֵּי יַיִן פְּתוּחוֹת אוֹ סְתוּמוֹת, מָקוֹם שֶׁדַּרְכָּן לִמְכֹּר פְּתוּחוֹת, לֹא יָצְאוּ קַנְקַנָּן לְחֻלִּין. סַלֵּי זֵיתִים וְסַלֵּי עֲנָבִים עִם הַכְּלִי, לֹא יָצְאוּ דְמֵי הַכְּלִי לְחֻלִּין.

יקחו: **אין העור יוצא לחולין.** כלומר אינו בתורת זו שיצא העור לחולין, אלא לא קנה מעשר לא החיה ולא הבהמה, דנעשה כקונה שור לחרישה בדמי מעשר, דלא קנה מעשר: **לא יצא הקנקן לחולין.** כיון שנהגו למכור היין בלא הקנקן: **לא יצאו דמי הכלי לחולין:** לפי שדרך למכרן בלא הכלי:

---

chullin; that is, the status of the hide is irrelevant, because the sale is not valid. No sanctity is transferred: the money keeps its sanctity and not even the meat of the animal becomes sanctified.[3]

Another case:

כַּדֵּי יַיִן פְּתוּחוֹת אוֹ סְתוּמוֹת — If someone buys **jugs with wine,** whether the jugs are **open or closed,** מָקוֹם שֶׁדַּרְכָּן לִמְכֹּר פְּתוּחוֹת — in **a place where it is common** for wine **to be sold** out of **open [jugs],** that is, the wine is usually measured out and sold without the jug, לֹא יָצְאוּ קַנְקַנָּן לְחֻלִּין — **the jug does not become** *chullin,* that is, it takes on sanctity. Since a jug is not usually included in a sale of wine and this sale does include a jug, it is as though the jug is being purchased separately with part of the *maaser sheni* money; since it is bought with *maaser sheni* money, it takes on *maaser sheni* sanctity.[4]

A similar case:

סַלֵּי זֵיתִים וְסַלֵּי עֲנָבִים עִם הַכְּלִי — If someone buys **baskets of olives or baskets of grapes together with their container** (i.e., the basket), לֹא יָצְאוּ דְמֵי הַכְּלִי לְחֻלִּין — the amount of **money** that is the value **of the container does not become** *chullin.* That is, that money keeps its sanctity and does not transfer it

--- NOTES ---

maaser sheni funds to buy *shelamim* offerings (see Mishnah 3 note 1), the Torah allows him to use the money for any kind of meat. The Rabbis, however, decreed that a person may not use *maaser sheni* money to buy domestic animals unless they will be brought as offerings (*Rav*).

3. Since the sale is invalid, the hide is of course still *chullin.* Nevertheless, the Mishnah uses the phrase "the hide does not become *chullin*" to say that the sale is invalid in order to contrast this case with the cases in the previous Mishnah, where the question is whether the hide is *chullin* (*Meleches Shlomo*).

4. [Needless to say, the wine takes on sanctity, for wine is a valid *maaser sheni* purchase.]

Although a jug is not food and is therefore forbidden to be bought with *maaser sheni* funds, the transaction is valid and the jug takes on sanctity, unlike in the Mishnah's previous case, where the sale is simply void. This is because in the previous case the *entire* transaction was illegal. In this case, part of the transaction — the sale of the wine — was proper; thus, the transaction is valid even though it also includes a jug (*Hon Ashir, Rashash;* see the next note). [As a penalty for spending *maaser sheni* money on a jug, this person will now have to take some of his own money — the amount that the jug is worth — and use it for *maaser sheni*-appropriate food that he will eat in Jerusalem (*Tos. Yom Tov*). This is the penalty for misusing *maaser sheni* funds, as we will learn in Mishnah 7.]

[15] MISHNAH MAASER SHENI / Chapter 1: *Maaser Sheni* 1/5

– רע"ב –

[ה] **הַלּוֹקֵחַ** מַיִם, וּמֶלַח, וּפֵרוֹת הַמְחֻבָּרִים לַקַּרְקַע, אוֹ פֵרוֹת שֶׁאֵינָן יְכוֹלִין לְהַגִּיעַ לִירוּשָׁלַיִם, לֹא קָנָה מַעֲשֵׂר.

(ה) הלוקח מים ומלח וכו'. מים ומלח אין נקנים בכסף מעשר שני, דכתיב (דברים יד) ונתת הכסף בכל אשר תאוה נפשך, כלל, בבקר ובצאן וביין ובשכר, פרט, ובכל אשר תשאלך נפשך, חזר וכלל, כלל ופרט וכלל אי אתה דן אלא כעין הפרט, מה הפרט מפורש דבר שהוא אוכל וגדולי קרקע, דבקר וצאן וגדלים מן הצמחים שהם גדולי קרקע, ותלוש, ודבר המתקיים עד שמוליכין לירושלים, אף כל דבר שהוא אוכל וגדולי קרקע ותלוש ודבר המתקיים, יצאו מים ומלח שאף על פי שהן אוכל אינן גדולי קרקע, יצאו פירות המחוברים לקרקע, שאינן תלושים, יצאו פירות הנרקבים קודם שיגיעו לירושלים שאינן דבר המתקיים, שכל אלו אין נקנים בכסף מעשר: **לא קנה מעשר**. ולא חלה קדושת מעשר על הדבר הקנוי ולא יצאו המעות לחולין:

---

to the basket. Although the purchase of the fruit is valid and the fruit takes on sanctity, a basket is not food and thus may not be bought with *maaser sheni* funds. Therefore, the purchase of the basket is not valid; the money paid for the basket keeps its *maaser sheni* sanctity, and must be used to buy food.[5]

[5] The Torah (*Devarim* 14:26) gives four examples of what may be bought with *maaser sheni* money: *cattle, flocks [of sheep or goats], wine, and old wine*. The Sages teach that *maaser sheni* money may be used to buy only food that is similar to these examples. Our Mishnah discusses several items that do not meet this condition:

הַלּוֹקֵחַ מַיִם וּמֶלַח — **Someone buys** with *maaser sheni* funds **water or salt,** וּפֵרוֹת הַמְחֻבָּרִים לַקַּרְקַע — **or produce that is** still **attached to the ground,** אוֹ פֵרוֹת שֶׁאֵינָן יְכוֹלִין לְהַגִּיעַ לִירוּשָׁלַיִם — **or produce that cannot reach Jerusalem** without spoiling; in any of these cases, לֹא קָנָה מַעֲשֵׂר — **the** *maaser sheni* money **does not acquire** these items, that is, the purchase is not valid, because these items are not similar to the Torah's examples of what may be bought with *maaser sheni* money.[1] Thus, the money keeps its *maaser sheni* status and the items do not take on any sanctity.

--- NOTES ---

5. The basket does not simply come along with the fruit (as, for example, a hide comes with meat) because baskets are not generally included in the sale of fruit. Therefore, when a basket is included, it is considered a separate purchase. Since a basket is not food, that part of the sale does not take effect.

In the previous case — wine bought with a jug — the sale of the jug does take effect even though a jug is not food. Since wine cannot be held without a jug, the jug is considered part of the same transaction as the wine. Therefore, even where a jug is not automatically included in the sale of the wine, the jug and wine are considered part of the same transaction, and for that reason the sale of the jug takes effect (see the previous note).

Fruit, however, can be easily held without a basket, and thus the sale of the basket is viewed as its own transaction, completely unconnected to the sale of the fruit. Since a basket may not be bought with *maaser sheni* funds, this sale of a basket does not take effect at all (*Hon Ashir, Rashash*).

[5]

1. The Torah's examples — wine and animals — share four characteristics: (1) They are edible; (2) they are nourished from the ground (wine is made from grapes that grow in the ground, and animals are nourished by eating plants); (3) they are not attached to the ground; (4) they can easily reach Jerusalem without spoiling. Only items that share

א/ה

הַלּוֹקֵחַ פֵּרוֹת, שׁוֹגֵג, יַחְזְרוּ דָמִים לִמְקוֹמָן. מֵזִיד, יַעֲלוּ וְיֵאָכְלוּ בַּמָּקוֹם. וְאִם אֵין מִקְדָּשׁ, יְרָקְבוּ.

— רע״ב —

הלוקח פירות שוגג, שלא היה יודע שמכסף מעשר הוא קונה: יחזרו דמים למקומן. המוכר לוקח פירותיו ומחזיר הדמים, משום דהוי כמקח טעות, שאם היה יודע הלוקח שדמי מעשר הם לא היה לוקח בהם פירות הללו, משום טורח הדרך, וכיון דשוגג הוא בטל מקח: מזיד. שידע שבכסף מעשר הוא: יעלו ויאכלו במקום. אשר יבחר ה׳, כלומר בירושלים: ואם אין מקדש ירקבו. שהדבר הקנוי בכסף מעשר אינו נפדה טהור בריחוק מקום, כדתנן לקמן בפרק ג:

Maaser sheni money is supposed to be used to buy food *in* Jerusalem. The Mishnah discusses a person who buys food *outside* Jerusalem with this money:

הַלּוֹקֵחַ פֵּרוֹת — **Someone buys produce** outside Jerusalem with *maaser sheni* money: שׁוֹגֵג — **If he did so by mistake,** that is, he did not realize that the money had *maaser sheni* sanctity, יַחְזְרוּ דָמִים לִמְקוֹמָן — **the money is returned to its place,** that is, he returns the produce and receives his money back. It can be assumed that he never would have used the money if he knew it had sanctity; thus, the sale is considered a mistake and is void.[2] מֵזִיד — However, if he spent the *maaser sheni* money **purposely,** that is, he knew he was using *maaser sheni* money, the sale takes effect and the produce takes on *maaser sheni* sanctity.[3] Therefore, יַעֲלוּ וְיֵאָכְלוּ בַּמָּקוֹם — **it must be brought up and eaten in "the place,"** i.e., Jerusalem.[4] וְאִם אֵין מִקְדָּשׁ יְרָקְבוּ — **And if there is no Temple,** in which case *maaser sheni* produce may not be eaten at all — not even in Jerusalem — **it must be left to rot.**[5]

NOTES

all these characteristics may be brought with *maaser sheni* money. Water and salt, however, are not nourished from the ground, while attached produce and food that will spoil before reaching Jerusalem do not possess the last two qualities (*Rav*).

2. Any sale that is based on a mistaken premise is known as a מֶקַּח טָעוּת, *a mistaken sale,* and is void. Here, we can assume that this person would not have spent the money if he knew that it had sanctity, because he would not want the burden of carrying the purchased food to Jerusalem (*Rav*).

3. It is in fact forbidden to spend this money outside Jerusalem, but the transaction is valid after the fact if it was done deliberately (see *Meleches Shlomo*).

4. The Mishnah refers to Jerusalem as "the place," because that is how the Torah describes Jerusalem when discussing *maaser sheni*: The place that Hashem, your God, will choose (*Devarim* 14:25).

5. When there is no Temple, although *maaser sheni* must be separated from produce, it may not be eaten or used in any way; it must be simply left to rot (see *Makkos* 19a).

[Ordinary *maaser sheni* produce does not have to be left to rot in the absence of the Temple; the sanctity of the produce can be transferred onto a coin and the coin destroyed. In this case, though, where *maaser sheni* sanctity was already transferred onto money and from that money onto food, the sanctity cannot be transferred another time onto money. The only option is to allow the food to rot (*Rav*). If it becomes *tamei*, however, some Tannaim hold that its sanctity may be transferred onto a coin and the coin destroyed (see Mishnah 3:10).]

[17] **MISHNAH MAASER SHENI** / Chapter 1: *Maaser Sheni* 1/6-7

– רע״ב –

(ו) תקבר ע״י עורה. עם עורה, לפי שגם עורה אסור: (ז) אין לוקחין עבדים וקרקעות. לפי שאינן אוכל, ורחמנא אמר (דברים יד) בבקר ובצאן ואכלת שם:

[ו] **הַלּוֹקֵחַ** בְּהֵמָה, שׁוֹגֵג, יַחְזְרוּ דָמֶיהָ לִמְקוֹמָן. מֵזִיד, תַּעֲלֶה וְתֵאָכֵל בַּמָּקוֹם. וְאִם אֵין מִקְדָּשׁ, תִּקָּבֵר עַל יְדֵי עוֹרָהּ.

[ז] **אֵין** לוֹקְחִין עֲבָדִים וּשְׁפָחוֹת וְקַרְקָעוֹת וּבְהֵמָה טְמֵאָה מִדְּמֵי מַעֲשֵׂר שֵׁנִי.

---

[6] The Mishnah discusses how the above law — a purchase made outside Jerusalem with *maaser sheni* money — applies to live animals:

הַלּוֹקֵחַ בְּהֵמָה שׁוֹגֵג — **If someone** outside Jerusalem **buys an animal** with *maaser sheni* money **by mistake,** that is, he did not realize that the money had *maaser sheni* sanctity, יַחְזְרוּ דָמֶיהָ לִמְקוֹמָן — **the money** paid for [the animal] **is returned to its place,** that is, the sale is void; he returns the animal and gets back his money, which remains sanctified. Since he would never have bought the animal had he realized he was using *maaser sheni* funds, the sale does not take effect.[1] מֵזִיד — **However, if he spent the** *maaser sheni* **money purposely, the sale takes effect.**[2] Therefore, תַּעֲלֶה וְתֵאָכֵל בַּמָּקוֹם — **[the animal] must be brought up and eaten in "the place,"** i.e. Jerusalem. וְאִם אֵין מִקְדָּשׁ — **And if there is no Temple,** in which case it may not be eaten even in Jerusalem, it must be kept until it dies, and then תִּקָּבֵר עַל יְדֵי עוֹרָהּ — it **must be buried together with its hide,** since the animal and its hide have *maaser sheni* sanctity and may not be used in any way.[3]

[7] The Mishnah discusses additional items that may not be bought with *maaser sheni* money:

אֵין לוֹקְחִין עֲבָדִים וּשְׁפָחוֹת וְקַרְקָעוֹת וּבְהֵמָה טְמֵאָה מִדְּמֵי מַעֲשֵׂר שֵׁנִי — **We may not buy male or female slaves, land, or a nonkosher animal with** *maaser sheni* **money,** because *maaser sheni* money must be used to buy food.[1]

--- NOTES ---

[6]

1. See note 2 to the previous Mishnah.
[The animal referred to here is either a domestic animal that was intended as a *shelamim* offering, or a nondomestic animal that was intended as ordinary meat. If it was a domestic animal that was intended as ordinary meat, the sale is void in any case, as we learned in Mishnah 4 (*Rash,* from *Kiddushin* 56a).]

2. Although it is forbidden to make such a purchase, it is valid after the fact if it was done deliberately (see *Meleches Shlomo*).

3. Mishnah 3 taught that when someone buys an animal with *maaser sheni* money, the hide does not take on sanctity, because the buyer and seller are interested primarily in the meat; the hide simply comes along with it and thus remains *chullin* (see note 4 there). Here, though, since the meat cannot be used, we cannot say that the buyer and seller are primarily interested in the meat. Therefore, the hide is considered as much a part of the sale as the meat is, and both the hide and meat take on *maaser sheni* sanctity. Since, in the absence of the Temple, they may not be used in any way, both the hide and meat must be buried (see *Tos. Yom Tov*).

[7]

1. As we learned in Mishnah 5; see note 1 there. [Since a nonkosher animal may not be eaten, it is not considered food.]

משניות מעשר שני / פרק א: מעשר שני [18]

וְאִם לָקַח, יֹאכַל כְּנֶגְדָּן. אֵין מְבִיאִין קִנֵּי זָבִים,
וְקִנֵּי זָבוֹת, וְקִנֵּי יוֹלְדוֹת, חַטָּאוֹת, וַאֲשָׁמוֹת,
מִדְּמֵי מַעֲשֵׂר שֵׁנִי. וְאִם הֵבִיא, יֹאכַל כְּנֶגְדָּם.

– רע״ב –

יאכל כנגדן. כנגד מעות מעשר שני שהוליא בדברים הללו, יוליא משלו ויקנה דבר שהוא אוכל ויאכל בקדושת מעשר בירושלים.

והכא מיירי כשעברה המוכר ומשום הכי לא תנא לא יחזרו דמים למקומן. אי נמי מתניתין איירי במזיד, אבל שוגג יחזרו דמים למקומן: **קיני זבים וקיני זבות.** שתי תורים או שני בני יונה שחייבין הזבים והזבות להביא. וקיימא לן דכל דבר שהוא חובה אינו בא אלא מן החולין, שאין אדם פורע חובו במעות מעשר שני:

וְאִם לָקַח יֹאכַל כְּנֶגְדָּן — **And if someone did buy** any of these items with *maaser sheni* money, as a penalty **he must eat** with *maaser sheni* sanctity food that is **of equal value to [the money]** he spent illegally. For example, if he spent 10 *dinars* of *maaser sheni* money on a slave, he must take 10 *dinars* of *chullin* (i.e., non-*maaser sheni*) money and use it to buy food that he will eat in Jerusalem.[2]

As we have learned (in Mishnah 3), a person may (and should) use *maaser sheni* money to buy an animal for a *shelamim* offering, which is a voluntary offering. The Mishnah discusses whether a person may use *maaser sheni* money to buy certain offerings that he is *obligated* to bring:

אֵין מְבִיאִין קִנֵּי זָבִים — **We may not bring pairs of birds** as offerings **for** *zavim*,[3] **וְקִנֵּי זָבוֹת** — **or pairs of birds** as offerings **for** *zavos*,[4] **וְקִנֵּי יוֹלְדוֹת** — or **pairs of birds** as offerings **for women who have just given birth**,[5] **חַטָּאוֹת וַאֲשָׁמוֹת** — or ***chatas* or *asham* offerings**, **מִדְּמֵי מַעֲשֵׂר שֵׁנִי** — using ***maaser sheni* money**. Since these offerings are obligatory, they must be brought with one's personal money, not with *maaser sheni* money.[6] **וְאִם הֵבִיא יֹאכַל כְּנֶגְדָּם** — **And if someone did bring** them using *maaser sheni* money, as a penalty **he must eat food** that is **of equal value to [the *maaser sheni* money]** that he spent: he must take other money and spend it on food that he will eat in Jerusalem in accordance with the laws of *maaser sheni*.

--- NOTES ---

2. Mishnah 5 taught that if a person makes an improper purchase with *maaser sheni* money, the sale is not valid: the money still has *maaser sheni* sanctity and must be used to buy appropriate food. The buyer is not penalized because he has not actually spent the money. Here, though, the Mishnah refers to a case where the seller has left town with the money and cannot be found. The buyer is thus left with his purchase. Since he has spent *maaser sheni* funds improperly, he is given a penalty: he must take that amount from his own money and use it for *maaser sheni*-appropriate food (see *Tosafos, Kiddushin* 56a ד"ה מתקיף).

3. A *zav* (pl. *zavim*) is a man who is *tamei* because he experienced a certain type of bodily discharge (*Vayikra* 15:2-3).

4. A *zavah* (pl. *zavos*) is a woman who is *tamei* because she experienced a certain type of irregular menstrual bleeding (*Vayikra* 15:25).

To become fully *tahor*, a *zav* and *zavah* must bring two pigeons or two turtledoves as offerings (*Vayikra* 15:14-15; 29-30).

5. After a woman gives birth, she must bring certain offerings. A wealthy woman brings a bird and a lamb, while a poor woman brings two pigeons or two turtledoves (*Vayikra* 12:1-8). Our Mishnah refers to a poor woman.

6. Since a person is obligated to bring these offerings, if he uses *maaser sheni* to buy them he is essentially using *maaser sheni* money to pay a debt, and that is forbidden (*Rav*; see Mishnah 3:1).

[19] MISHNAH MAASER SHENI / Chapter 1: *Maaser Sheni*

זֶה הַכְּלָל, כָּל שֶׁהוּא חוּץ לַאֲכִילָה וְלִשְׁתִיָּה וּלְסִיכָה מִדְּמֵי מַעֲשֵׂר שֵׁנִי, יֹאכַל כְּנֶגְדּוֹ.

The Mishnah gives a general rule, and notes another permitted use of *maaser sheni* money:

זֶה הַכְּלָל — **This is the rule:** כָּל שֶׁהוּא חוּץ לַאֲכִילָה וְלִשְׁתִיָּה וּלְסִיכָה מִדְּמֵי מַעֲשֵׂר שֵׁנִי — **If any item other than** something used for **eating, drinking, or rubbing onto one's skin**[7] is bought **with** *maaser sheni* **money,** יֹאכַל כְּנֶגְדּוֹ — as a penalty [the buyer] must eat food that is **of equal value to [the** *maaser sheni* **money]** that he spent.

NOTES

7. In addition to food and drink, a person may spend *maaser sheni* money on oil to rub on his body. We will discuss this further in Mishnah 2:1.

Chapter Two

משניות מעשר שני / פרק ב: מעשר שני [22]

[א] **מַעֲשֵׂר** שֵׁנִי, נִתַּן לַאֲכִילָה וְלִשְׁתִיָּה וּלְסִיכָה, לֶאֱכֹל דָּבָר שֶׁדַּרְכּוֹ לֶאֱכֹל, לָסוּךְ דָּבָר שֶׁדַּרְכּוֹ לָסוּךְ. לֹא יָסוּךְ יַיִן וָחֹמֶץ, אֲבָל סָךְ הוּא אֶת הַשֶּׁמֶן. אֵין מְפַטְּמִין שֶׁמֶן שֶׁל מַעֲשֵׂר שֵׁנִי,

— רע״ב —

פרק שני — מעשר שני. (א) מעשר שני נתן לאכילה ולשתיה. דכתיב (דברים יד) בבקר ובצאן וביין ובשכר ואכלת שם, ושתיה בכלל אכילה. וסיכה כשתיה דכתיב (תהלים קט) ותבא כמים בקרבו וכשמן בעצמותיו: **לאכול דבר שדרכו לאכול.** שאם קנה בכסף מעשר פת ונתעפשה, יין והקריס, תבשיל ונבאש, אין מחייבין אותו לאכול דבר שאין דרכו לאכול כדי שלא יפסדו מעות של מעשר שני. אי נמי בקש לאכול תרדין לחין חיין או לכוס חטין חיות, אין שומעין לו, כיון שאין דרכן לאכלן כך: **אין מפטמין את השמן.** לשים לתוכו עיקרין וראשי בשמים, משום דבלעי דבלעי השמן ואזיל לאבוד, שהשרשים אינן נאכלין:

---

[1] The Mishnah discusses how *maaser sheni* may be used in Jerusalem:

מַעֲשֵׂר שֵׁנִי נִתַּן לַאֲכִילָה — *Maaser sheni* produce **is allowed** to be used in any of three ways:[1] **for eating,** וְלִשְׁתִיָּה — **for drinking,** וּלְסִיכָה — **and for rubbing** on one's skin.[2]

The Mishnah adds:

לֶאֱכֹל דָּבָר שֶׁדַּרְכּוֹ לֶאֱכֹל — We are **to eat** only **what is normal to eat.** Therefore, if *maaser sheni* produce spoils, it does not have to be eaten, because spoiled food is not normally eaten.[3] לָסוּךְ דָּבָר שֶׁדַּרְכּוֹ לָסוּךְ — **And we are to rub** only with **what is normal to rub.** לֹא יָסוּךְ יַיִן וָחֹמֶץ — **Thus, [a person] may not rub** his skin with **wine or vinegar** of *maaser sheni*, because these are typically used for eating and drinking, not rubbing; אֲבָל סָךְ הוּא אֶת הַשֶּׁמֶן — **but he may rub** his skin with **oil,** which is typically used for that purpose.[4]

The Mishnah considers more uses of *maaser sheni*:

אֵין מְפַטְּמִין שֶׁמֶן שֶׁל מַעֲשֵׂר שֵׁנִי — **One may not perfume oil of** *maaser sheni* by soaking spices in it. This is because the spices absorb some of the oil, and since the spices are eventually removed from the oil and thrown away, the

---

NOTES

[1]
1. When *maaser sheni* produce is brought to Jerusalem, it must be used in one of these ways, and if *maaser sheni* is redeemed for money, the money must be spent in Jerusalem on items that will be put to one of these uses (see *Rambam, Hilchos Maaser Sheni* 3:10).

2. For example, a person may rub *maaser sheni* oil into his skin.

These three permitted uses are learned from verses in the Torah: the Torah states explicitly that *maaser sheni* money should be used to buy food that will be eaten; drinking is always considered the same as eating; and it is derived from a Scriptural verse [*Psalms* 109:18] that rubbing one's skin with oil is considered

like drinking (*Rav*).

3. In general, it is forbidden to let *maaser sheni* food go to waste. If it spoils, though, one does not have to eat it.

The Mishnah's statement includes another law as well: that *maaser sheni* produce may be eaten only in the manner in which that type of produce is normally eaten: if it is a type of produce that is usually cooked, a person may not eat it raw, and if it is usually eaten raw, he may not cook it (*Rav*).

4. Similarly, a person may drink only liquids that people usually drink. For example, he may not drink plain oil, because that is not usually drunk (*Rambam, Hilchos Maaser Sheni* 3:11; *Derech Emunah* there 3:90).

[23] MISHNAH MAASER SHENI / Chapter 2: *Maaser Sheni*

– רע״ב –

וְאֵין לוֹקְחִין בִּדְמֵי מַעֲשֵׂר שֵׁנִי שֶׁמֶן מְפֻטָּם, אֲבָל מְפַטֵּם הוּא אֶת הַיַּיִן. נָפַל לְתוֹכוֹ דְּבַשׁ וְתַבְלִין וְהִשְׁבִּיחוֹ, הַשֶּׁבַח לְפִי חֶשְׁבּוֹן. דָּגִים שֶׁנִּתְבַּשְּׁלוּ עִם הַקַּפְלוֹטוֹת שֶׁל מַעֲשֵׂר שֵׁנִי וְהִשְׁבִּיחוּ,

ואין לוקחין בדמי מעשר שני שמן מפוטם. משום דבטעין דבר השוה לכל אדם, וזה אינו אלא למפונקים ולמעונגים: אבל מפטם הוא את היין. לעשותו ינומלין וכיוצא בהן: נפל. לתוך יין של מעשר שני כשהוא חוץ לירושלים דבש ותבלין, והשביח, חולקין את השבח לפי חשבון, כגון אם היין שוה ב׳ סלעים ודבש ותבלין שוין סלע והשביחו ועמדו על ד׳ סלעים, פודה את היין בב׳ סלעים ושני שלישי סלע: קפלוטות. כרתי פורו״ש בלע״ז:

וְאֵין לוֹקְחִין בִּדְמֵי מַעֲשֵׂר *maaser sheni* oil absorbed in them will go to waste. שְׁנֵי שֶׁמֶן מְפֻטָּם — In addition, **one may not buy spiced oil with** *maaser sheni* **money**, because spiced oil is used only by people with very refined tastes, and only types of food used by the average person may be bought with *maaser sheni* money.[5] אֲבָל מְפַטֵּם הוּא אֶת הַיַּיִן — **However, one may add spices to** *maaser sheni* **wine**, for although the spices absorb some wine, the spices are consumed together with the wine and thus no wine will go to waste.[6]

The Mishnah turns to another law related to spiced wine. If a person wants to redeem *maaser sheni* that is in a mixture with *chullin* ingredients, he needs to redeem only the value of the *maaser sheni* ingredients. However, when different ingredients are mixed to create a dish, the final product is often worth more than the sum of its individual ingredients. For example, if *maaser sheni* wine is mixed with *chullin* spices, the resulting beverage is worth more than the sum of the wine and the spices. The Mishnah explains how to calculate the value of the *maaser sheni* in such a beverage:

נָפַל לְתוֹכוֹ דְּבַשׁ וְתַבְלִין וְהִשְׁבִּיחוֹ — **If honey or spices fell into [***maaser sheni* **wine]**[7] **and as a result, [the mixture] went up in value**, that is, the spiced wine is worth more than the value of the ingredients on their own, הַשֶּׁבַח לְפִי חֶשְׁבּוֹן — **the added value is** calculated **by proportion**. To illustrate: Honey worth one *sela* fell into *maaser sheni* wine worth two *sela'im*, and the mixture is now worth four *sela'im*. If the owner wants to redeem the wine, he must redeem it for 2⅔ *sela'im*: Since the wine accounted for ⅔ of the mixture's original value, and the value of the mixture rose by one *sela*, he must add ⅔ of a *sela* to the wine's original value. דָּגִים שֶׁנִּתְבַּשְּׁלוּ עִם הַקַּפְלוֹטוֹת שֶׁל מַעֲשֵׂר שֵׁנִי וְהִשְׁבִּיחוּ — **Similarly, if (***chullin***) fish were cooked with** *maaser sheni* **leeks and [the resulting mixture] went up in value**, that is, the mixture is worth more

---

NOTES

5. Since items not used by the average person are usually very expensive, spending *maaser sheni* funds on them is considered a waste of the money (*Rash, Tosafos Chadashim*).

6. *Tiferes Yisrael*.

[However, a person may not *buy* spiced wine with *maaser sheni* funds, because spiced wine, like perfumed oil, is not something used by the average person (*Rashash*).]

7. Although the Mishnah's case is where honey and spices *fell* into wine, the same applies if a person deliberately added them to wine (*Pnei Moshe*).

[24] משניות מעשר שני / פרק ב: מעשר שני

הַשֶּׁבַח לְפִי חֶשְׁבּוֹן. עָשָׂה שֶׁל מַעֲשֵׂר שֵׁנִי שֶׁאֲפָאָהּ וְהִשְׁבִּיחָהּ, הַשֶּׁבַח לַשֵּׁנִי. זֶה הַכְּלָל, כָּל שֶׁשִּׁבְחוֹ נִכָּר, הַשֶּׁבַח לְפִי הַחֶשְׁבּוֹן. וְכֹל שֶׁאֵין שִׁבְחוֹ נִכָּר, הַשֶּׁבַח לַשֵּׁנִי.

[ב] **רַבִּי** שִׁמְעוֹן אוֹמֵר, אֵין סָכִין שֶׁמֶן שֶׁל מַעֲשֵׂר שֵׁנִי בִּירוּשָׁלַיִם.

– רע"ב –

הַשֶּׁבַח לַשֵּׁנִי. ופודה את הפת בשוויו, ואין חולקין השבח לטלים של חולין, אלא כל השבח למעשר שני, לפי שאין שבח טלים ניכר בפת: כל ששבחו ניכר. שֶׁבַח החולין ניכר במעשר שני, שהוסיפו החולין על המעשר במדה ובמשקל, אבל אם לא הוסיפו אלא בטעם אף על פי שנתעלה בדמים מחמת הטעם, אין זה שבחו ניכר: (ב) רבי שמעון אומר אין סכין וכו׳. קסבר לא ניתן שמן של מעשר שני לסיכה אלא לאכילה בלבד:

---

than the sum of the fish and leeks on their own, הַשֶּׁבַח לְפִי חֶשְׁבּוֹן — the added value is calculated by proportion.

In the next case, the law is different:

עָשָׂה שֶׁל מַעֲשֵׂר שֵׁנִי שֶׁאֲפָאָהּ וְהִשְׁבִּיחָהּ — If someone baked a dough of maaser sheni ingredients and its value went up, that is, the bread is worth more than the raw dough was worth, הַשֶּׁבַח לַשֵּׁנִי — the extra value is all added to the maaser sheni. Even though the reason it is worth more is because it was baked, which involves the use of (chullin) firewood, we do not say that some of the added value is attributed to the firewood. Rather, all the extra value is applied to the (maaser sheni) bread. If the owner wants to redeem it, he must redeem it for the full current value of the bread.

The Mishnah gives a general rule, which explains the difference between bread baked with chullin firewood and a food that contains both maaser sheni and chullin ingredients:

זֶה הַכְּלָל — This is the rule: כָּל שֶׁשִּׁבְחוֹ נִכָּר — In any case where the chullin item that causes the added value is recognizable, that is, we can measure the mixture and see that it contains chullin ingredients,[8] הַשֶּׁבַח לְפִי הַחֶשְׁבּוֹן — the added value is calculated by proportion. וְכֹל שֶׁאֵין שִׁבְחוֹ נִכָּר — But in any case where the chullin item that causes the added value is not recognizable, that is, we cannot tell by measuring the dish that it contains chullin, הַשֶּׁבַח לַשֵּׁנִי — the extra value is all added to the maaser sheni. Thus, where firewood causes dough to increase in value, the extra value is all added to the dough, because the firewood cannot be detected in the dough.[9]

[2] The previous Mishnah stated that maaser sheni oil may be rubbed on the skin. This Mishnah cites a view that forbids such a use:

אֵין סָכִין שֶׁמֶן שֶׁל מַעֲשֵׂר שֵׁנִי בִּירוּשָׁלַיִם רַבִּי שִׁמְעוֹן אוֹמֵר — R' Shimon says: — We may not rub with maaser sheni oil in Jerusalem; rather, maaser sheni

---
NOTES

8. For example, if honey is added to wine, the mixture increases in volume.

9. The chullin is considered "recognizable" only if it adds to the weight or volume of the dough. If the amount of chullin is too small to be measured by weight or volume, it is not taken into account, even if it can be tasted (Rav).

[25] MISHNAH MAASER SHENI / Chapter 2: *Maaser Sheni* 2/2

וַחֲכָמִים מַתִּירִין. אָמְרוּ לוֹ לְרַבִּי שִׁמְעוֹן, אִם הֵקֵל בִּתְרוּמָה חֲמוּרָה, לֹא נָקֵל בְּמַעֲשֵׂר שֵׁנִי הַקַּל. אָמַר לָהֶם, מַה, לֹא, אִם הֵקֵל בִּתְרוּמָה הַחֲמוּרָה מְקוֹם שֶׁהֵקֵל בְּכַרְשִׁינִין וּבְתִלְתָּן, נָקֵל בְּמַעֲשֵׂר שֵׁנִי הַקַּל מְקוֹם שֶׁלֹּא הֵקֵל בְּכַרְשִׁינִים וּבְתִלְתָּן.

— רע״ב —

אם הקל בתרומה. שאחה מודה דמותרת בסיכה, כדתנן בפרק שמיני דשביעית וכן בתרומה וכן במעשר שני, ולא קא מפלגת בתרומה: שהקל בכרשינין ובתלתן. של תרומה יותר מבמעשר שני, כדבעינן למימר לקמן, הלכך דין הוא שנקל בסיכה גבי תרומה. ואין הלכה כרבי שמעון:

וַחֲכָמִים מַתִּירִין — But the Sages permit rubbing with *maaser sheni* oil.[1]

The Sages support their ruling with a logical argument:

אם הקל בתרומה **[The Sages] said to R' Shimon:** אָמְרוּ לוֹ לְרַבִּי שִׁמְעוֹן — **If we are lenient concerning** *terumah,* that is, we allow a person to rub *terumah* oil on his skin,[2] even though *terumah* generally **has stricter** laws than those of *maaser sheni*,[3] לֹא נָקֵל בְּמַעֲשֵׂר שֵׁנִי הַקַּל — **should we not be lenient concerning** *maaser sheni* and allow it to be used for rubbing, since *maaser sheni* generally **has** more **lenient** laws?

R' Shimon responds:

אָמַר לָהֶם — **[R' Shimon] said to [the Sages]:** מַה לֹא — **What?** That is **not** a valid argument![4] אִם הֵקֵל בִּתְרוּמָה הַחֲמוּרָה — **While** here we are lenient when it comes to *terumah* although *terumah* generally has stricter laws, מְקוֹם שֶׁהֵקֵל בְּכַרְשִׁינִים וּבְתִלְתָּן — we are also **lenient with** *terumah* in other cases, such as **in the cases of vetch and fenugreek**;[5] נָקֵל בְּמַעֲשֵׂר שֵׁנִי הַקַּל — **should we be lenient about** *maaser sheni* just because it is usually more **lenient** than *terumah*, מְקוֹם שֶׁלֹּא הֵקֵל בְּכַרְשִׁינִים וּבְתִלְתָּן — **when there are cases where we are** *not* **lenient with** *maaser sheni*, **such as in the cases of vetch and fenugreek?** In other words, even though *terumah's* laws are stricter than those of *maaser sheni* in many ways, there are some laws — such as those regarding vetch and fenugreek — for which *terumah's* laws are more lenient. Thus, the fact that it is permitted to rub with *terumah* oil is no reason to say that it should be permitted to rub with *maaser sheni* oil.

───── NOTES ─────

1. The previous Mishnah, which states that *maaser sheni* oil may be rubbed on the skin, is the opinion of the Sages (see *Rav*).

2. *Sheviis* 8:2.

3. *Terumah* is generally considered stricter because it may be eaten only by Kohanim, while *maaser sheni* is permitted to everyone (*Tiferes Yisrael*).

4. Translation follows *Tos. Yom Tov.*

5. Vetch and fenugreek are bean-like plants usually used as animal feed. Regarding certain laws, vetch and fenugreek of *terumah* are treated more leniently than vetch and fenugreek of *maaser sheni*. These laws are taught in the next two Mishnahs.

משניות מעשר שני / פרק ב: מעשר שני

[ג] **תִּלְתָּן** שֶׁל מַעֲשֵׂר שֵׁנִי, תֵּאָכֵל צִמְחוֹנִים. וְשֶׁל תְּרוּמָה, בֵּית שַׁמַּאי אוֹמְרִים, כָּל מַעֲשֶׂיהָ בְּטָהֳרָה,

– רע״ב –

(ג) תאכל צמחונים. כשהן ירקות לחין, ולא יניחם עד שיגדלו ולא יהיו רחויות לאכילה. אבל בתרומה תאכל בין לחין בין יבשים: **בית שמאי אומרים כל מעשיה בטהרה.** אף על גב דתלתן לאו אוכל גמור הוא, ואין תרומה נוהגת בו אלא לפי שנאכל לקצת בני אדם, הלכך נחלק בטומאה, מכל מקום לבית שמאי צריך שיהיו כל מעשיה בטהרה ובנטילת ידים, כדין כל שאר אוכלים של תרומה שהנוגע בהם צריך נטילת ידים תחלה, וטעמא כדי שידעו שהם תרומה ולא יאכלו לזרים:

---

[3] In the previous Mishnah, R' Shimon said that vetch and fenugreek of *terumah* have more lenient laws than do vetch and fenugreek of *maaser sheni*. This Mishnah explains how this is true of fenugreek, a bean-like plant with edible stalks:[1]

תִּלְתָּן שֶׁל מַעֲשֵׂר שֵׁנִי תֵּאָכֵל צִמְחוֹנִים — **Fenugreek of *maaser sheni* must be eaten** when its stalks are **young** and moist. When fenugreek ripens further, its stalks turn hard and inedible. Since it is forbidden to cause *maaser sheni* to go to waste, a person must eat his fenugreek stalks before they become inedible. Fenugreek that is *terumah*, though, may be kept until it hardens.[2]

The Mishnah discusses another law about fenugreek that is *terumah*. *Terumah* may never be handled by a person who is *tamei*. In addition, the Sages decreed that even a person who is *tahor* must wash his hands before touching *terumah*; if someone touches *terumah* with unwashed hands, the *terumah* is considered *tamei*.[3] The Mishnah cites a dispute about whether this requirement applies to fenugreek, which has more lenient laws than ordinary *terumah*:[4]

וְשֶׁל תְּרוּמָה — With regard to **[fenugreek] of *terumah*:** בֵּית שַׁמַּאי אוֹמְרִים — **Beis Shammai say:** כָּל מַעֲשֶׂיהָ בְּטָהֳרָה — **Everything that is done to** prepare **it must be done in a state of purity;** that is, a person must wash his hands before touching it just as he must wash before touching other produce that is *terumah*. Although fenugreek is generally treated more leniently than ordinary *terumah*, the Rabbis decreed that it may not be touched with unwashed hands, so that people will remember that it is *terumah* and no non-Kohen will eat it.

NOTES

[3]

1. [In addition to the stalks, fenugreek contains seeds, which are used as spices. Our Mishnah discusses only the stalks, which are edible only when they are moist.]

2. Once fenugreek dries, it is fit only for animal feed. Since *maaser sheni* may not be fed to animals, fenugreek that is *maaser sheni* will have no use after it dries. Fenugreek that is *terumah*, though, may be fed to animals. Thus it may be kept until it dries, because it can then be fed to animals and will not go to waste. [Most *terumah* may not be fed to animals, but fenugreek is an exception; see *Derech Emunah, Hilchos Terumos* 6:10.] Thus, the law for fenugreek of *terumah* is more lenient than the law for fenugreek of *maaser sheni* (*Rav, Meleches Shlomo* citing *R' Yehosef*).

3. See *Bikkurim* 2:1.

4. As a rule, only produce that people eat is obligated in *terumah*. Fenugreek is used mainly as animal feed and is thus not obligated in *terumah* by Torah law. Since some people do eat the stalks when they are moist, though, it is obligated in *terumah* by Rabbinic law. However, it does not have the same stringencies as ordinary *terumah* (*Rav*).

[27] MISHNAH MAASER SHENI / Chapter 2: Maaser Sheni

חוּץ מֵחֲפִיפָתָהּ. וּבֵית הִלֵּל אוֹמְרִים, כָּל מַעֲשֶׂיהָ בְּטֻמְאָה, חוּץ מִשְּׁרִיָּתָהּ.

[ד] **כַּרְשִׁינֵי** מַעֲשֵׂר שֵׁנִי, יֵאָכְלוּ צִמְחוֹנִים,

- רע״ב -

חוץ מחפיפתה. שבלא נטילת ידים יכולים לחוף בהן ראשן. וכך היה דרכן לחוף ראשן בתלתן: כל מעשיה בטומאה חוץ משרייתה. במים, שצריך לנערותן בטהרה. שאם שורה אותן בלא נטילת ידים שריין מכשירתן לקבל טומאה, והוא מטמאן מיד בידיו. ואסרו זה בלבד משום היכר כדי שידעו שהיא תרומה: (ד) כרשיני. בלשון ערבי כרסנ״א, ואינם מאכל אדם אלא מדוחק בשנות רעבון:

חוּץ מֵחֲפִיפָתָהּ — **An exception** to this rule **is shampooing with [fenugreek** *terumah*]. A person may use *terumah* fenugreek to clean his hair[5] without washing his hands, because once it is used as shampoo it is no longer edible and there is no concern that a non-Kohen will eat it.[6]

The Mishnah cites Beis Hillel's opinion, which is based on a basic rule of *tumah*: that food can become *tamei* only if it has been "prepared" by becoming wet with one of seven liquids — one of which is water:[7]

וּבֵית הִלֵּל אוֹמְרִים — **But Beis Hillel say:** **כָּל מַעֲשֶׂיהָ בְּטֻמְאָה** — **Everything that is done to [***terumah* **fenugreek] may be done in a state of** *tumah*. The Sages did not require a person to wash his hands before touching fenugreek that is *terumah*, **חוּץ מִשְּׁרִיָּתָהּ** — **unless** he is **soaking it:** If a person soaks such fenugreek, he must wash his hands first, because soaking fenugreek with unwashed hands causes two things at once: it prepares the fenugreek to become *tamei* (by wetting it) and it makes it *tamei* (by bringing it into contact with unwashed hands). This action the Sages did forbid, as a reminder that it is *terumah*.[8]

[4] This Mishnah discusses how vetch that is *terumah* is treated more leniently than vetch that is *maaser sheni,* as mentioned in Mishnah 2:

כַּרְשִׁינֵי מַעֲשֵׂר שֵׁנִי יֵאָכְלוּ צִמְחוֹנִים — **Vetch that is** *maaser sheni* **must be eaten** when its stalks are **young** and moist. Vetch, like fenugreek, turns hard and inedible as it ripens. Since it is forbidden to cause *maaser sheni* to go to waste, a person must eat vetch before it becomes inedible. Vetch that is *terumah*, though, may be kept until it hardens.[1]

The Mishnah discusses two more laws that apply to vetch that is *maaser sheni;* these are matters for which vetch *maaser sheni* is different from other *maaser sheni* produce:

NOTES

5. Fenugreek was commonly used to make a form of shampoo.
6. See *Rambam Commentary*.
7. See *Vayikra* 11:38; *Machshirin* 6:4.
8. While Beis Shammai said that a person must (almost) always wash his hands for fenugreek, as a reminder that it is *terumah*, Beis Hillel hold that the Rabbis required less of a reminder. They ordered that a person wash his hands in only one case: where touching the fenugreek with unwashed hands would both prepare it for *tumah* and make it *tamei* at the same time. That requirement is enough of a reminder (*Rav*).

[4]

1. The reasoning behind this is the same as for fenugreek; see Mishnah 3 note 2.

משניות מעשר שני / פרק ב: מעשר שני [28]

- רע"ב -

וְנִכְנָסִין לִירוּשָׁלַיִם וְיוֹצְאִין. נִטְמְאוּ, רַבִּי טַרְפוֹן אוֹמֵר, יִתְחַלְּקוּ לְעִסּוֹת, וַחֲכָמִים אוֹמְרִים, יִפָּדוּ.

ונכנסים לירושלים ויוצאים. אף על גב דבשאר פירות קיימא לן דמעשר שני הנכנס לירושלים אין יכולין להוציאו משם, בכרשינין הקילו: יתחלקו לעיסות. ואינו כשאר מעשר שנטמא שפודין אותו ואפילו בירושלים, אבל כרשינים לפי שאינן מאכל אדם אין פודין אותן, דסבר רבי טרפון אין פודין את הקדשים להאכילן לכלבים, הלכך יתחלקו לעיסות טהורות של מעשר שני וישימו בכל עיסה ועיסה מן הכרשינים הללו שנטמאו פחות פחות מכביצה, דאוכל פחות מכביצה אינו לא מטמא מאחרים, ולא מטמא אחרים, וככה יאכלו אותן: וחכמים אומרים יפדו. כשאר מעשר שני. והלכה כחכמים:

וְנִכְנָסִין לִירוּשָׁלַיִם וְיוֹצְאִין — And [*maaser sheni* vetch] **may be brought into Jerusalem and** then **taken out** of the city. In contrast, other *maaser sheni* produce may never be taken out of Jerusalem once it is brought in.[2]

The next law involves *maaser sheni* that became *tamei*. Generally, if *maaser sheni* becomes *tamei*, it may be redeemed for money, which takes on its sanctity (see Mishnah 3:9). The law is different, though, for vetch that is *maaser sheni*:

רַבִּי טַרְפוֹן אוֹמֵר — R' Tarfon says that it may not be redeemed;[3] rather, **יִתְחַלְּקוּ לְעִסּוֹת** — it should be divided into small portions, which should be mixed together with larger, *tahor maaser sheni* doughs, so that in each dough, the small amount of vetch will be nullified by the larger amount of *tahor maaser sheni*.[4] **וַחֲכָמִים אוֹמְרִים** — But the Sages say: **יִפָּדוּ** — [The vetch] may be redeemed, just as with any *maaser sheni* that becomes *tamei*.[5]

---- NOTES ----

2. Like fenugreek, vetch is primarily used for animal feed and thus should not really be subject to *maaser sheni*. Since some people do eat the young stalks, though, it is obligated in *maaser sheni* by Rabbinic law. However, its laws are not as stringent as those of other forms of *maaser sheni*. Thus, while in general *maaser sheni* may not be taken out of Jerusalem once it is brought in (as we will learn in Mishnah 3:5), vetch may be removed from Jerusalem if it can be prepared more easily outside Jerusalem (*Rav*). [However, it must be brought back to Jerusalem to be eaten (*Meleches Shlomo*).]

3. R' Tarfon is concerned that if the vetch is redeemed, it will be fed to animals, since that is how vetch is usually used. Since we have a principle that sacred items may not be redeemed if they will then be fed to animals (*Temurah* 6:5; see Mishnah 3:11), R' Tarfon forbids redeeming this vetch (*Rav*).

4. This is an application of the principle of בִּטּוּל בְּרֹב, *nullification by the majority*, which states that when two substances are mixed, the majority substance nullifies the minority one. Based on this, the small amount of *tamei* vetch is nullified by the larger amount of *tahor* vetch and the mixture may be eaten (See *Tos. Anshei Shem*).

[The *tamei* vetch must be divided into portions smaller than the size of an egg; anything larger than that will transmit its *tumah* to the food that it touches and the whole mixture will become *tamei*. Food smaller than an egg, though, does not transmit *tumah* to other food (*Rav*).]

5. According to the Sages, the prohibition against redeeming sacred items to feed them to animals applies only to food usually eaten by people. Vetch, though, is generally fed to animals; therefore, although it may not be fed to animals while it has *maaser sheni* sanctity (see note 1), it may be redeemed and then fed to animals (*Yerushalmi*).

[29] **MISHNAH MAASER SHENI** / Chapter 2: *Maaser Sheni*

וְשֶׁל תְּרוּמָה, בֵּית שַׁמַּאי אוֹמְרִים, שׁוֹרִין וְשָׁפִין בְּטָהֳרָה, וּמַאֲכִילִין בְּטֻמְאָה. וּבֵית הִלֵּל אוֹמְרִים שׁוֹרִין בְּטָהֳרָה, וְשָׁפִין וּמַאֲכִילִין בְּטֻמְאָה. שַׁמַּאי אוֹמֵר, יֵאָכְלוּ צָרִיד.

– רע״ב –

שורין. במים ושפין על הבשר, בטהרה, בנטילת ידיס, שמתם ידיס שניות ופוסלות את התרומה: ומאכילין. לבהמה: יאכלו צריד. לשון יובש, כמו צריד של מנחות (פסחים כ, א) שהוא מקום של המנחה שלא הגיע שם שמן. כלומר יאכלו יבשים שלא יהא עליהס משקה בשעת אכילה, כדי שלא יהיה ניכר שהוכשרו לקבל טומאה:

The Mishnah now discusses vetch that is *terumah*. As mentioned in the previous Mishnah, a person is generally required to wash his hands before handling *terumah*. There is a dispute whether this requirement applies to vetch, which, like fenugreek, has more lenient laws than ordinary *terumah*:[6]

וְשֶׁל תְּרוּמָה — Regarding [vetch] that is *terumah*: בֵּית שַׁמַּאי אוֹמְרִים — Beis Shammai say: שׁוֹרִין וְשָׁפִין בְּטָהֳרָה — When **we soak** such vetch **or rub** it on the skin, we must do so **in a state of purity**; that is, a person must wash his hands before touching it, just as for ordinary *terumah*. וּמַאֲכִילִין בְּטֻמְאָה — But when **we feed** vetch to animals, we may do so **in a state of** *tumah;* that is, one does not have to wash his hands first. Although vetch does not have the same stringencies as ordinary *terumah*, the Rabbis decreed that when a person uses it for himself, he may not touch it with unwashed hands, so that people will remember that it is *terumah* and no non-Kohen will eat it.[7]

The Mishnah cites Beis Hillel's opinion, which is based on the principle that food cannot become *tamei* unless it is first "prepared" by becoming wet:

וּבֵית הִלֵּל אוֹמְרִים — But Beis Hillel say: שׁוֹרִין בְּטָהֳרָה — When we soak vetch, our hands must be *tahor*, וְשָׁפִין וּמַאֲכִילִין בְּטֻמְאָה — but we may rub vetch on the skin **or feed** it **to an animal in** a state of *tumah*. Only when a person soaks vetch must he wash his hands, because soaking vetch with unwashed hands causes two things as once: it prepares the vetch to become *tamei* (by wetting it) and it makes the vetch *tamei* (by bringing it into contact with unwashed hands). This the Sages forbade, as a reminder that this vetch is *terumah*. When used in other ways, though, the hands may be unwashed.[8]

Another opinion:

שַׁמַּאי אוֹמֵר — Shammai says: A person may handle vetch with unwashed hands, יֵאָכְלוּ צָרִיד — but [the vetch] should be fed to animals only when

---

NOTES

6. Since vetch is primarily used as animal feed, it is required in *terumah* only by Rabbinic law (see note 2 and Mishnah 3 note 4) and thus is treated more leniently than other forms of *terumah*.

7. In general, vetch is used in two ways: A person soaks it to soften it and then rubs it on his skin, or he feeds it to an animal. (Although the young stalks can be eaten by people, as the Mishnah said earlier, this is not commonly done.) The Sages decreed that before a person uses it for himself, namely, before he soaks it or rubs it, he must wash his hands. This is enough of a reminder that it is *terumah*. When feeding it to an animal, though, the hands do not need to be washed.

8. Beis Hillel hold that this one restriction is enough of a reminder (*Rash*).

ב/ה

- רע"ב -

כל מעשיהם בטומאה.
ואפילו הטריית. ואין
הלכה כרבי עקיבא:
(ה) מה שליקט ליקט
למעשר. כל מה שמלקט
הכל למעשר עד שישלים
דמי מעשר. ויתנה ויאמר.

רַבִּי עֲקִיבָא אוֹמֵר, כָּל מַעֲשֵׂיהֶן בְּטֻמְאָה.

[ה] **מָעוֹת** חֻלִּין וּמָעוֹת מַעֲשֵׂר שֵׁנִי שֶׁנִּתְפַּזְּרוּ,
מַה שֶּׁלָּקַט, לָקַט לְמַעֲשֵׂר שֵׁנִי
עַד שֶׁיַּשְׁלִים, וְהַשְּׁאָר חֻלִּין. אִם בָּלַל וְחָפַן.

אם כל מה שלקטתי הם מעות מעשר מוטב, ואם לאו אותם של מעשר שנשארו יהיו מחוללין על
אלו: **ואם בלל וחפן.** ואם לא ליקט אותן אחד אחד מכאן ומכאן, אלא שהיו בלולין ומעורבים ולקח
אותם מלא חפניו:

---

it is **dry.** According to Shammai, a person may not use vetch in a way that it is obvious that he is making it *tamei*. Since produce can become *tamei* once it is wet, if a person uses wet vetch with unwashed hands, it will be clear that he is making it *tamei*; this is forbidden. If the vetch is dry, though, it is not obvious that he is making it *tamei*, and the Rabbis did not require him to wash his hands.[9]

A final opinion:

רַבִּי עֲקִיבָא אוֹמֵר — **R' Akiva says:** כָּל מַעֲשֵׂיהֶן בְּטֻמְאָה — **Anything that is done with [vetch] may be done when a person is *tamei*.** The Rabbis made no decrees requiring a person to wash his hands before handling vetch.

[5] This Mishnah teaches what should be done if *maaser sheni* coins become mixed up with ordinary coins:

מָעוֹת חֻלִּין וּמָעוֹת מַעֲשֵׂר שֵׁנִי שֶׁנִּתְפַּזְּרוּ — ***Chullin*** **coins and** similar-looking ***maaser sheni*** **coins were scattered** and now we cannot tell which coins are which. If someone picks up the coins one by one, מַה שֶּׁלָּקַט לָקַט לְמַעֲשֵׂר שֵׁנִי — **whichever** coins he **picked** up first, **he picked** up for *maaser sheni*. That is, the first coins he collects are treated as *maaser sheni* coins, עַד שֶׁיַּשְׁלִים — **until he finishes** collecting the number of coins that belonged to *maaser sheni*. וְהַשְּׁאָר חֻלִּין — **The rest** of the coins are then treated as ***chullin***.[1] אִם בָּלַל וְחָפַן — **However, if the coins fell in a jumble and he scooped up a handful** at a time rather than one by one, the handfuls of coins are treated

---

NOTES

9. The vetch will still become *tamei* if it had once become wet. However, someone who sees a person using dry vetch does not know whether it has ever been wet. Since it is not obvious that he is making the vetch *tamei*, he does not have to wash his hands first.

[5]

1. For example, if there were 100 *maaser sheni* coins and 100 *chullin* coins, the first 100 coins he picks up are *maaser sheni* and the rest are *chullin*. This way, if a few coins will be lost at the end, the loss will be a loss of *chullin* and not of *maaser sheni* (Rambam Commentary).

Since he cannot be sure that the first 100 coins he collects are truly *maaser sheni*, he makes the following declaration after he collects 100 coins: "If all these coins are *maaser sheni*, all is well. If not, let the sanctity of all the *maaser sheni* coins still on the floor be transferred to any *chullin* coins that I have collected." Through this declaration, all the coins he picked up take on definite *maaser sheni* sanctity, and the rest of the coins are *chullin* (Rav).

[31] **MISHNAH MAASER SHENI** / Chapter 2: *Maaser Sheni*

- רע״ב -

לְפִי חֶשְׁבּוֹן. זֶה הַכְּלָל, הַמִּתְלַקְּטִים, לְמַעֲשֵׂר שֵׁנִי. וְהַנִּבְלָלִים, לְפִי חֶשְׁבּוֹן.

[ו] **סֶלַע** שֶׁל מַעֲשֵׂר שֵׁנִי וְשֶׁל חֻלִּין שֶׁנִּתְעָרְבוּ, מֵבִיא בְּסֶלַע מָעוֹת וְאוֹמֵר, סֶלַע שֶׁל מַעֲשֵׂר שֵׁנִי, בְּכָל מָקוֹם שֶׁהִיא, מְחֻלֶּלֶת עַל הַמָּעוֹת הָאֵלּוּ, וּבוֹרֵר אֶת הַיָּפָה שֶׁבָּהֶן:

לפי חשבון. שאם לזה מנה ולזה מאתים, נותן לזה של מנה שליש ולזה של מאתים שני שלישים:
(ו) שנתערבו. ורוצה להוציא של חולין חוץ לירושלים: מביא בסלע מעות. של נחשת שיש עליהם צורה, שהוין סלע של כסף: ובורר את היפה שבהן. שבשני הסלעים, ומחלל אלו המעות עליה, והסלע השני והמעות נשארים חולין:

לְפִי חֶשְׁבּוֹן — **by proportion.** For example, if two-thirds of the coins were *maaser sheni* and one-third were *chullin*, two-thirds of the coins in each handful are treated as *maaser sheni* and one-third as *chullin*.[2]

The Mishnah sums up:

זֶה הַכְּלָל — **This is the rule:** הַמִּתְלַקְּטִים לְמַעֲשֵׂר שֵׁנִי — **When [coins] are picked up** one by one, the first ones collected are all for *maaser sheni;* וְהַנִּבְלָלִים לְפִי חֶשְׁבּוֹן — **and** when [coins] are **jumbled together** and picked up by the handful, they are treated **by proportion.**

[6] Another case where *maaser sheni* and *chullin* became mixed together:

סֶלַע שֶׁל מַעֲשֵׂר שֵׁנִי וְשֶׁל חֻלִּין שֶׁנִּתְעָרְבוּ — **If** a silver ***sela* of *maaser sheni*** and a silver ***sela* of *chullin* became mixed up,** the owner can do the following:[1] מֵבִיא בְּסֶלַע מָעוֹת — **He brings a *sela*'s** worth of copper **coins,** וְאוֹמֵר, סֶלַע שֶׁל מַעֲשֵׂר שֵׁנִי בְּכָל מָקוֹם שֶׁהִיא — **and says, "The *sela* of *maaser sheni*, wherever it is** [i.e., whichever coin it is]**,** מְחֻלֶּלֶת עַל הַמָּעוֹת הָאֵלּוּ — **should have its sanctity transferred to these** copper **coins."** With this, the copper coins take on the *maaser sheni* sanctity and both *sela* coins become *chullin*. וּבוֹרֵר אֶת הַיָּפָה שֶׁבָּהֶן — **He then chooses the nicer of [the *sela* coins]**[2]

NOTES

2. In the Mishnah's previous case, where a person picked up one coin at a time, we consider each coin as it is picked up: each coin has an even chance of being one of the *maaser sheni* coins. It is therefore possible to say that the first coins picked up are all *maaser sheni*. Since this is possible, the Rabbis ruled that we should consider them as such, in order to save *maaser sheni* from possible loss (see note 1) — although the person must recite a declaration (see there) in order to make sure that they are *maaser sheni*.

In this case, though, where he picks up a handful of coins, it is unreasonable to say that the whole handful is *maaser sheni*. Accordingly, we assume that some are *maaser sheni* and some are *chullin*, based on the proportion of *maaser sheni* and *chullin* in the original mixture. In addition, since we cannot be certain that the coins he designates as *maaser sheni* are in fact those of *maaser sheni*, he must also make the declaration stated in note 1 in order to transfer the *maaser sheni* sanctity to those coins (*Tos. Yom Tov*).

[6]

1. [If he wants, he can simply treat both coins as *maaser sheni* and spend them both on food in Jerusalem.] The Mishnah assumes, though, that he wants to spend some of the money outside Jerusalem, and thus it gives a method by which he can resolve which coin is *maaser sheni* (*Rav*).

2. [As coins were used, they became rubbed out and lost some of their silver.]

— רע"ב —

מדוחק. כשהוא דחוק ואינו יכול לעשות בדרך אחרת: **ולא שיתקיים** כן. שישאר המעות של נחושת מעשר, אלא חוזר ומחללם על הכסף. ומי קשיא ולמה מביא בסלע מעות, יקח אחד משני סלעים שנתערבו ויאמר אם זו היא של מעשר מוטב ואם לאו הרי השני שהיא

של מעשר מחוללת עליה. אי שרייית ליה ליקח אחת מהן ולהתנות, חיישינן דלמא אתי למשקל חד מינייהו בלא תנאי: (ז) **לא יעשה אדם סלעיו דינרי זהב.** סלעים של כסף שיש לו ממעשר שני לא יעשה אותם דינרי זהב, שמא יהא מעלותיו עד שיחליף סלעיו ויתבטל מעלותו לרגל. ובית הלל סברי לא גזרינן:

וּמְחַלְּלָן עָלֶיהָ — **and transfers the sanctity from [the copper coins] to [the nicer** *sela***].** As a result, the nicer *sela* is *maaser sheni,* and the other *sela* and the copper coins are *chullin.*[3]

The Mishnah explains why he must transfer the sanctity back to a silver coin and does not simply leave it on the copper coins:

מִפְּנֵי שֶׁאָמְרוּ — He must transfer the sanctity back to a silver coin **because [the Sages] said** that **מְחַלְּלִין כֶּסֶף עַל נְחֹשֶׁת מִדֹּחַק** — **we may transfer sanctity from silver** coins **to copper** coins **only when we are forced** to do so (such as in this case, when there is no other way to separate the *maaser sheni* from the *chullin*), but not otherwise, because it is degrading to *maaser sheni* to transfer its sanctity from silver to the less-valuable copper.[4] **וְלֹא שֶׁיִּתְקַיֵּם כֵּן** — **But even when a person is forced to transfer the silver to copper, it should not stay that way;** **אֶלָּא חוֹזֵר וּמְחַלְּלָם עַל הַכֶּסֶף** — **rather, he must transfer the sanctity** from the copper coins **back onto silver.**

[7] The previous Mishnah discussed transferring *maaser sheni* sanctity from silver to copper. This Mishnah discusses a person who transferred his *maaser sheni* onto silver coins and now wishes to transfer the sanctity onto gold coins, so that he has less to carry when he goes to Jerusalem:

בֵּית שַׁמַּאי אוֹמְרִים — **Beis Shammai say:** **לֹא יַעֲשֶׂה אָדָם אֶת סְלָעָיו דִּינְרֵי זָהָב** —

NOTES

The "nicer" coin is the one that has more silver content (*Toras Chaim, Bava Metzia* 56a).

3. He could have accomplished the same thing by simply taking the nicer *sela* and saying, "If this *sela* is *maaser sheni,* all is well; if not, let the sanctity from the other *sela* be transferred to this one." However, the Sages did not allow a person to do this because they were concerned that he would forget to say the declaration and just pick one of the coins to treat as *maaser sheni,* when in fact the other coin is the *maaser sheni* one. Therefore, the Sages ruled that this person must first transfer the *maaser sheni* to copper coins and only then to the nicer silver coin. The fact that he is obligated to make a more complicated transfer will remind him to transfer the sanctity by means of a declaration (*Rav*).

4. *Rashi, Bava Metzia* 56a ד"ה מפני.

[The Mishnah refers to making such an exchange *outside* Jerusalem. Once a person brings his *maaser sheni* funds into Jerusalem, he may exchange the larger, silver coins for smaller ones in order to make small purchases. See Mishnahs 8-9.]

[33] **MISHNAH MAASER SHENI** / Chapter 2: *Maaser Sheni*   2/8

- רע"ב -

וּבֵית הִלֵּל מַתִּירִין. אָמַר רַבִּי עֲקִיבָא, אֲנִי עָשִׂיתִי לְרַבָּן גַּמְלִיאֵל וּלְרַבִּי יְהוֹשֻׁעַ אֶת כַּסְפָּן דִּינְרֵי זָהָב.

[ח] **הַפּוֹרֵט** סֶלַע מִמְּעוֹת מַעֲשֵׂר שֵׁנִי, בֵּית שַׁמַּאי אוֹמְרִים,

(ח) הפורט סלע ממעות מעשר שני. מי שיש לו מעות נחשת של מעשר שני, ובא לפורטן בסלע כסף להעלותו לירושלים מפני משאוי הדרך: בית שמאי אומרים בכל הסלע מעות. אם בא לפורטן יכול לפרוט כולן ולתת בשביל כל הסלע:

A person may not exchange his silver *sela* coins of *maaser sheni* for gold *dinars*; that is, if his *maaser sheni* was silver coins, he may not transfer its sanctity onto gold ones. If a person were allowed to do so, he might delay going to Jerusalem until he has enough *maaser sheni* to fill a gold coin.[1] וּבֵית הִלֵּל מַתִּירִין — But Beis Hillel permit transferring *maaser sheni* from silver to gold coins.[2] אָמַר רַבִּי עֲקִיבָא — R' Akiva said: אֲנִי עָשִׂיתִי לְרַבָּן גַּמְלִיאֵל וּלְרַבִּי יְהוֹשֻׁעַ אֶת כַּסְפָּן דִּינְרֵי זָהָב — I personally **changed the silver** *maaser sheni* coins **of Rabban Gamliel and R' Yehoshua for gold dinars,** as per Beis Hillel's ruling.

[8] The Mishnah now discusses whether a person may transfer *maaser sheni* sanctity from copper coins to a silver coin:[1]

הַפּוֹרֵט סֶלַע מִמְּעוֹת מַעֲשֵׂר שֵׁנִי — **Someone wants to exchange** many **copper coins of** *maaser sheni* **for a silver** *sela* **coin:**[2] בֵּית שַׁמַּאי אוֹמְרִים — **Beis**

---- NOTES ----

[7]

1. If a person has his *maaser sheni* in silver coins, he might wait until he has enough for a full gold coin before he brings it to Jerusalem. If a festival arrives before he has that amount, he might simply stay home, thereby failing in his obligation to visit Jerusalem for the festival. [Every Jewish adult male is obligated to travel to Jerusalem for each of the three festivals: Pesach, Shavuos, and Succos (*Devarim* 16:16).] To prevent this, Beis Shammai ruled that a person may never transfer his *maaser sheni* from silver to gold coins (*Rav*).

2. Beis Hillel hold that a person would not ignore his obligation to come to Jerusalem just because he does not yet

have enough *maaser sheni* for a gold coin (*Rav*; see *Bava Metzia* 45b).

[8]

1. [This Mishnah also appears in *Eduyos* 1:9.]

To understand the next two Mishnahs, it is useful to know certain denominations of money: The smallest coin is the copper *perutah*. 192 *perutos* equal one *dinar*. One *shekel* equals 2 *dinars*. One *sela* equals 2 *shekels*, or 4 *dinars*. See chart.

2. [As he accumulated *maaser sheni*, he transferred its sanctity to small copper coins, one at a time.] To make it easier to bring to Jerusalem, he wants to transfer the sanctity from the small coins to one large silver coin (*Rav*).

	Number of *perutos*	Number of *dinars*	Number of *shekels*	Number of *sela'im*
in a *perutah*	1	—	—	—
in a *dinar*	192	1	—	—
in a *shekel*	384	2	1	—
in a *sela*	768	4	2	1

בָּל הַסֶּלַע מָעוֹת. וּבֵית הִלֵּל אוֹמְרִים, שֶׁקֶל כֶּסֶף וְשֶׁקֶל מָעוֹת. רַבִּי מֵאִיר אוֹמֵר, אֵין מְחַלְּלִין כֶּסֶף וּפֵרוֹת עַל הַכֶּסֶף, וַחֲכָמִים מַתִּירִים.

- רע"ב -

וּבֵית הִלֵּל אוֹמְרִים. לֹא יפרוט אלא חציין, שהפרוטות יולאות בירושלים וכשיצא שם יהיה צריך לפרוטות מיד לקנות לצרכי סעודה, ואם ירוצו הכל אצל שולחני לפרוט יוקירו הפרוטות ונמצא מעשר שני נפסד. לפיכך ישאו פרוטות עמהן להוליא במקלת, ולכשיכלו יפרוט בכסף שבידו מעט מעט: שֶׁקֶל. הוא חלי סלע: אֵין מְחַלְּלִין כֶּסֶף וּפֵרוֹת עַל הַכֶּסֶף. מי שיש לו חלי דינר כסף של מעשר ופירות של מעשר שוה חלי דינר, לא יגרוס יחד לחללן על דינר: וַחֲכָמִים מַתִּירִין. בכי האי גוונא ט"י לירוף פירות, כיון שאין לו אלא חלי דינר כסף. אבל לחלל חלי דינר כסף ופירות שוה חלי דינר על סלע שהוא שני דינרין, מודים חכמים שאין מחללים. והלכה כחכמים:

Shammai say: בָּל הַסֶּלַע מָעוֹת — He may exchange all the copper **coins** — the value of an **entire sela** — for a silver sela. וּבֵית הִלֵּל אוֹמְרִים — **But Beis Hillel say:** שֶׁקֶל כֶּסֶף וְשֶׁקֶל מָעוֹת — He may exchange half of the copper coins, that is, the value of **a shekel** [a shekel is worth half a sela], for a **silver shekel,** but the other half of the copper coins, which are also worth **a shekel,** must be kept as copper **coins,** for the following reason. When a person arrives in Jerusalem with his maaser sheni money, he needs copper coins in order to make small purchases.[3] If everyone brought only silver coins to Jerusalem, they would have to exchange them there for copper, and there would be a large demand for copper coins, causing the price of copper coins to go up. To avoid this, Beis Hillel rule that a person should keep some of his maaser sheni in copper, so there will not be an overwhelming demand for copper in Jerusalem.[4]

Another dispute about exchanging maaser sheni money:

רַבִּי מֵאִיר אוֹמֵר — **R' Meir says:** אֵין מְחַלְּלִין כֶּסֶף וּפֵרוֹת עַל הַכֶּסֶף — **We may not transfer sanctity from** maaser sheni **money and** maaser sheni **produce together to the same silver coin.** For example, if someone has maaser sheni coins worth half a dinar and maaser sheni produce worth half a dinar, he may not transfer them both together to a single dinar coin. A transfer of maaser sheni is valid only if it is distinct and not mixed together with another transfer; money and produce may not be transferred together.[5] וַחֲכָמִים מַתִּירִים — **However, the Sages allow** such a transfer.[6]

NOTES

3. Silver coins had too much value to be used for ordinary day-to-day purchases. If a person comes to Jerusalem with a silver coin, he will need to exchange it for copper coins to buy food.

4. [Most people bring their maaser sheni money to Jerusalem at the same time — when they come for the festivals.] So many people trying to exchange silver for copper will cause the price of copper to go up and a person will receive fewer copper coins for his silver, which will be a loss of maaser sheni money. To avoid this, Beis Hillel want to make sure that the price of copper does not go up (Rav).

5. Rambam, Hilchos Maaser Sheni 5:15, as explained by Ri Korkos.

6. This ruling of the Sages does not apply in every case. They agree that if a person has enough small coins to transfer to a full coin, and enough produce to transfer to a full coin, he must transfer each — the money and the produce — to its own coin. They allow a "mixed" transfer only when a person does not have enough produce or enough small coins to fill its own coin.

[35] **MISHNAH MAASER SHENI** / Chapter 2: *Maaser Sheni*

- רע״ב -

[ט] **הַפּוֹרֵט** סֶלַע שֶׁל מַעֲשֵׂר שֵׁנִי בִּירוּשָׁלַיִם, בֵּית שַׁמַּאי אוֹמְרִים, כָּל הַסֶּלַע מָעוֹת. וּבֵית הִלֵּל אוֹמְרִים, שֶׁקֶל כֶּסֶף וְשֶׁקֶל מָעוֹת. הַדָּנִין לִפְנֵי חֲכָמִים אוֹמְרִים,

(ט) הפורט סלע של מעשר שני בירושלים. שהיה מחליף סלע שבידו ונוטל פרוטות להוציאן לצרכי סעודה מעשר: בית שמאי אומרים. אם בא להחליף כל הסלעים שבידו במעות, יחליף: ובית הלל אומרים. לא יחליף אלא חציין, שמא לא יהיה בעיר עד שיוציא את כולן, ויפקידם בעיר עד רגל אחר, והפרוטות מתעפשות, ואם יחזור ויחליפם בסלעים נמצא שולחני משתכר שני פעמים ומעשר שני נפסד. שמעון בן עזאי ושמעון בן זומא וחנן המצרי:

---

[9] This Mishnah discusses a person who arrives in Jerusalem with silver coins of *maaser sheni* and wants to exchange them for copper coins in order to buy food.[1]

הַפּוֹרֵט סֶלַע שֶׁל מַעֲשֵׂר שֵׁנִי בִּירוּשָׁלַיִם — **Someone who exchanges** a silver *sela* **coin of *maaser sheni* for copper coins in Jerusalem:** בֵּית שַׁמַּאי אוֹמְרִים — **Beis Shammai say:** כָּל הַסֶּלַע מָעוֹת — **He may exchange the whole** *sela* **for copper coins.** וּבֵית הִלֵּל אוֹמְרִים — **But Beis Hillel say:** שֶׁקֶל כֶּסֶף וְשֶׁקֶל מָעוֹת — **He must take change for one *shekel*'s** worth (half the *sela*) **in silver coins, and he may take change for the other *shekel*'s worth in copper coins.** He may not exchange the entire *sela* for copper coins, because we are concerned that he will not end up spending all the coins on food, but will save some for the next time he comes to Jerusalem. Since copper coins corrode over time and lose their value, they may be worth less by the next time he returns to Jerusalem, which will be a loss of *maaser sheni* money.[2]

Other Tannaim agree that a person may not take change for an entire silver coin at once, but disagree about how much change he may take:

הַדָּנִין לִפְנֵי חֲכָמִים אוֹמְרִים — **Those who debate before the Sages say:**[3]

---- NOTES ----

For example, he has half a *dinar's* worth of produce and half a *dinar's* worth of small coins. If he would transfer each to its own *dinar*, he would be left with two *dinars* that are each only half-sanctified with *maaser sheni*. In this case, the Sages allow him to transfer the money and the produce to the same coin (*Rav*).

[9]

1. [Although the previous Mishnah cited a dispute whether a person may transfer all his copper to silver, all agree that he may bring *some* silver to Jerusalem. This Mishnah discusses how he may transfer that silver.
Bear in mind that 1 *sela* is equal to 2 *shekels* or 4 *dinars*; see Mishnah 8 note 1.
This Mishnah also appears in *Eduyos* 1:10.]

2. He cannot simply exchange the copper coins back into silver coins (which do not corrode) before he leaves Jerusalem, because he will then have to pay an extra fee to the moneychanger: one fee when exchanging the silver for copper and another fee when exchanging the copper back for silver. This would be an unnecessary waste of *maaser sheni* money (*Rav*).

3. The students of the Sages would sit on the floor in front of their teachers and debate what they had been taught. Our Mishnah refers to a specific group of four scholars — Shimon ben Azzai, Shimon ben Zoma, Chanan HaMitzri, and Chananya ben Chachinai — who died young [and remained students their whole lives]. Accordingly, although they were great scholars whose opinions are

[36] **משניות מעשר שני / פרק ב: מעשר שני**

בִּשְׁלֹשָׁה דִינָרֵי כֶסֶף וְדִינַר מָעוֹת. רַבִּי עֲקִיבָא אוֹמֵר, שְׁלֹשָׁה דִינָרִין כֶּסֶף, וּרְבִיעִית מָעוֹת. רַבִּי טַרְפוֹן אוֹמֵר, אַרְבַּע אַסְפְּרֵי כֶסֶף. שַׁמַּאי אוֹמֵר, יַנִּיחֶנָּה בַחֲנוּת וְיֹאכַל כְּנֶגְדָּהּ.

— רע"ב —

בשלשה דינרין בסף ובדינר מעות. הסלע הוא ד' דינרים, וכשבא להחליף הסלע לא יקח אלא בדינר ח' פרוטות ושלשה דינרים יהיו כסף: רביעית בסף ברביעית

מעות. בדינר רביעי של כסף לא יקח אלא ברביעיתו מעות של נחשת, וג' חלקים כסף. שנמצא לוקח מעות אחד משמונה עשר בסלע בלבד: ארבעה אספרי בסף. הדינר ה' אספרי, ומטבע הוא בארץ יון ועד היום קורין לו אספרי. נמצא הסלע עשרים אספרים. וכשהוא מחלל הדינר יחלננו על ד' אספרי כסף ואספר א' נחשת. נמצא לוקח מעות א' מעשרים בסלע בלבד: יניחנה בחנות ויאכל בנגדה. לא יחלל כלל על פרוטות שמא ישכח ויעשה אותן חולין, אלא יניח הסלע אצל החנווני ויאכל כנגדה עד שתכלה. ואין הלכה אלא כדברי בית הלל בלבד:

בִּשְׁלֹשָׁה דִינָרֵי כֶסֶף — He must take change **for three** *dinars'* **worth** (¾ of the *sela*) **in silver coins,** **וְדִינַר מָעוֹת** — **and** he may take change for one *dinar's* **worth** (¼ of the *sela*) **in copper coins.**

רַבִּי עֲקִיבָא אוֹמֵר — R' Akiva says: **שְׁלֹשָׁה דִינָרִין כֶּסֶף** — He must take change for **three** *dinars'* **worth in silver coins,** and out of the fourth *dinar's* worth of the *sela,* he may take change for **וּרְבִיעִית מָעוֹת** — **one-quarter** of it in copper **coins,** but he must take change for the rest of it in silver coins. In other words, he may exchange only ¼ of a *dinar* (¹⁄₁₆ of the *sela*) for copper coins.

רַבִּי טַרְפוֹן אוֹמֵר — R' Tarfon says: He must take change for three *dinars'* worth of the *sela* in silver coins, and out of the fourth *dinar,* **אַרְבַּע אַסְפְּרֵי כֶסֶף** — he must take **four** *aspers'* **worth** (⁴⁄₅ of a *dinar*)[4] in **silver** coins; he may exchange only one *asper's* worth (¹⁄₂₀ of the original *sela*) for copper coins.

Another opinion:

שַׁמַּאי אוֹמֵר — **Shammai says:** He may not exchange silver for copper coins at all; **יַנִּיחֶנָּה בַחֲנוּת וְיֹאכַל בְּנֶגְדָּהּ** — Rather, **he deposits [the silver** *sela***] in a store** with the storekeeper **and,** over time, **he takes and eats** food from the store **equal to** the value of **[a** *sela***].**[5]

— NOTES —

included in the Mishnah, they are referred to as "those who debate before the Sages" (*Rav, Tos. Yom Tov*).

4. An *asper* is a Greek coin that is worth ¼ of a *dinar.* Since a *sela* is worth 4 *dinars,* 20 *aspers* equal one *sela* (*Rav*).

5. Shammai is concerned that [if someone exchanges *maaser sheni* money for copper coins that he will carry in his pocket], he might forget that the copper coins have sanctity and will use them for other purposes. Therefore, he may not exchange the *sela* for copper coins at all. Instead, he must deposit the *sela* with a storekeeper who sells food, and he will use it as credit; over time, he will take a

sela's worth of food and eat it according to the laws of *maaser sheni* (see *Rav*).

In summary, the Mishnah lists six opinions about how much of a *sela* a person may exchange for copper coins:

(1) Beis Shammai: He may exchange the entire *sela* for copper coins.
(2) Beis Hillel: He may exchange ½ of the *sela* for copper coins.
(3) Those who debate before the Sages: He may exchange ¼ of the *sela* for copper coins.
(4) R' Akiva: He may exchange ¹⁄₁₆ of the *sela* for copper coins.
(5) R' Tarfon: He may exchange ¹⁄₂₀ of the *sela* for copper coins.
(6) Shammai: He may not exchange any

― רע"ב ―

(י) מקצת בניו טמאין ומקצתן טהורים. ורוצה שישתו יחד מכד אחד, והטמאים אסורים ביין הקנוי בדמי מעשר: מניח את הסלע ואומר. מה שישתו הטהורים מן היין, לכשישתו תהא סלע זו מחוללת עליו מעכשיו. נמצא מה ששתו הטהורים היה מעשר ומה ששתו טמאים היה חולין. ואינו חולין ומעשר שני מעורבים זה בזה, שאין היין קדוש בקדושת מעשר, אלא לכשישתו חוזר היין ששתו בלבד להיות מעשר למפרע:

[י] **מִי** שֶׁהָיוּ מִקְצָת בָּנָיו טְמֵאִין וּמִקְצָתָן טְהוֹרִים, מֵנִיחַ אֶת הַסֶּלַע וְאוֹמֵר, מַה שֶׁהַטְּהוֹרִים שׁוֹתִים, סֶלַע זוֹ מְחֻלֶּלֶת עָלָיו, נִמְצְאוּ טְהוֹרִים וּטְמֵאִים שׁוֹתִים מִכַּד אֶחָד.

---

[10] *Maaser sheni* must be kept in a state of *taharah*, and may not be eaten by a person who is *tamei*. The Mishnah discusses how a person can buy a pitcher of wine with *maaser sheni* money, and yet enable *tamei* people to drink from it:

מִי שֶׁהָיוּ מִקְצָת בָּנָיו טְמֵאִין וּמִקְצָתָן טְהוֹרִים — Someone has some children who are *tamei* and some children who are *tahor*, and he wants to buy a pitcher of wine with *maaser sheni* money for his family to share. מֵנִיחַ אֶת הַסֶּלַע וְאוֹמֵר — He can put down a *sela* of *maaser sheni* and say, מַה שֶׁהַטְּהוֹרִים שׁוֹתִים סֶלַע זוֹ מְחֻלֶּלֶת עָלָיו — "This *sela* shall have its sanctity transferred to [the wine] that the *tahor* [children] will drink." This declaration takes effect: Whatever wine the *tahor* children will drink will be *maaser sheni*; the rest of the wine will be *chullin* and may be drunk by the *tamei* children.[1] נִמְצְאוּ טְהוֹרִים וּטְמֵאִים שׁוֹתִים מִכַּד אֶחָד — Thus it turns out that the *tahor* [children] and the *tamei* [children] drink from the same pitcher.[2]

NOTES

[10]

1. This does not mean that the pitcher holds a mixture of *maaser sheni* and *chullin*, for if it did, the whole mixture would have to be treated as *maaser sheni* and would be forbidden to the *tamei* children. Rather, when the *tahor* children drink their share of the wine, that wine becomes retroactively classified as *maaser*. The rest — which is drunk by the *tamei* children — remains *chullin* (*Rav*). This works by means of the principle of *bereirah*, retroactive clarification, which states that a determination made at a later time can clarify the legal status of something at an earlier time (see *Raavad, Hilchos Maaser Sheni* 8:15).

2. There are more details of this law, which depend on the type of *tumah* that the *tamei* children have. For example, if they have a type of *tumah* that contaminates whatever they touch (such as the *tumah* of a *zav*), the *tahor* children must drink their share of the wine first, because once the *tamei* children touch the pitcher all the wine will become *tamei*, and no one — not even a person who is *tamei* — may drink *maaser sheni* that is *tamei* (see *Tos. Yom Tov*).

of the *sela* for copper coins.

Chapter Three

משניות מעשר שני / פרק ג: לא יאמר

[א] לֹא יֹאמַר אָדָם לַחֲבֵרוֹ: "הַעַל אֶת הַפֵּרוֹת הָאֵלּוּ לִירוּשָׁלַיִם לְחַלֵּק", אֶלָּא אוֹמֵר לוֹ: "הַעֲלֵם שֶׁנֹּאכְלֵם וְנִשְׁתֵּם בִּירוּשָׁלַיִם"; אֲבָל נוֹתְנִים זֶה לָזֶה מַתְּנַת חִנָּם.

[ב] אֵין לוֹקְחִין תְּרוּמָה בְּכֶסֶף מַעֲשֵׂר שֵׁנִי, מִפְּנֵי שֶׁהוּא מְמַעֵט בַּאֲכִילָתוֹ;

– רע"ב –

פרק שלישי — לא יאמר. (א) לא יאמר. לחלק. שיטעול חלק בהם. לפי שעליו מוטל להביא מעשרו לירושלים, ונמצא פורע חובו ממעשר שני: **העלם שנאכלם ונשתם.** דנראה דמזמינו לאכול עמו, וזה מותר: **אבל נותנים זה לזה מתנת חנם. מפורש לעיל** בריש פרק קמא: **(ב) מפני שהוא ממעט באכילתו.** דתרומה אסורה לטבול יום ולזרים:

---

[1] A law that relates to the transportation of *maaser sheni* to Jerusalem:

הַעַל אֶת לֹא יֹאמַר אָדָם לַחֲבֵרוֹ — A person may not say to his friend: הַפֵּרוֹת הָאֵלּוּ לִירוּשָׁלַיִם לְחַלֵּק — "Bring these *maaser sheni* fruits of mine up to Jerusalem for us to divide there." Such a statement implies that the owner will give his friend some of the fruits as payment for carrying them to Jerusalem.[1] If so, the owner is essentially using *maaser sheni* produce to pay a debt, and this is forbidden. אֶלָּא אוֹמֵר לוֹ — Rather, [the owner] may say to [his friend]: הַעֲלֵם שֶׁנֹּאכְלֵם וְנִשְׁתֵּם בִּירוּשָׁלַיִם — "Bring up [the fruits] so that we may eat them and drink them together in Jerusalem." This implies that the owner is simply inviting his friend to join him in a meal of *maaser sheni*,[2] which is permitted. For, as we learned in Mishnah 1:1: אֲבָל נוֹתְנִים זֶה לָזֶה מַתְּנַת חִנָּם — But [two people] may give each other *maaser sheni* as a free gift; that is, a person may invite his friend to a meal and serve him *maaser sheni*.[3]

[2] The Mishnah cites a dispute about using *maaser sheni* funds to buy food that is *terumah*:

אֵין לוֹקְחִין תְּרוּמָה בְּכֶסֶף מַעֲשֵׂר שֵׁנִי — [A person] may not buy *terumah* with *maaser sheni* money, מִפְּנֵי שֶׁהוּא מְמַעֵט בַּאֲכִילָתוֹ — because he thereby reduces the opportunities for [the *maaser sheni*] to be eaten. If *maaser sheni* money is spent on *chullin*, it may be eaten by anyone, as long as he is in Jerusalem. *Terumah*, however, is forbidden to non-Kohanim, and even to Kohanim who are *tamei*.[1] Thus, if a person spends his *maaser sheni* money

---
NOTES

[1]

1. *Tiferes Yisrael*.

2. Since he does not mention *dividing* the produce but simply eating and drinking it, this does not seem like an offer of payment but simply an invitation to join in a meal (*Rav, Pnei Moshe*).

3. See Mishnah 1:1 with note 8. Elucidation follows *Tos. Yom Tov*.

[2]

1. Although *maaser sheni* is also forbidden to a person who is *tamei*, *terumah* is more restricted. A Kohen who is *tamei* may not eat *terumah* until he immerses in a *mikveh* and then waits until nightfall. *Maaser sheni*, though, may be eaten by a *tamei* person as soon as he immerses in a *mikveh*, even though he is not considered fully *tahor* until night falls (*Keilim* 1:5; see *Rav*).

[41] MISHNAH MAASER SHENI / Chapter 3: *Lo Yomar*

וְרַבִּי שִׁמְעוֹן מַתִּיר. אָמַר לָהֶם רַבִּי שִׁמְעוֹן: מָה, אִם הֵקֵל בְּזִבְחֵי שְׁלָמִים שֶׁהוּא מְבִיאָן לִידֵי פִגּוּל וְנוֹתָר וְטָמֵא, לֹא נָקֵל בִּתְרוּמָה? אָמְרוּ לוֹ: מָה, אִם הֵקֵל בְּזִבְחֵי שְׁלָמִים, שֶׁהֵן

– רע״ב –

ורבי שמעון מתיר. דסבר מותר להביא קדשים לבית הפסול: מה אם היקל בזבחי שלמים. שקונין שלמים בכסף מעשר שני ואעפ״י שממעט באכילתו שיכולין לבא לידי פגול ונותר וטמא, לא נקל בתרומה לקנותה בכסף מעשר שני שאין בה דין פגול ונותר ולא דין טמא, שלא כל הדברים המטמאין את הקדש מטמאין את התרומה. ואין הלכה כרבי שמעון:

on *terumah* rather than on *chullin*, fewer people may eat it and it is more likely to go to waste.[2]

The next Tanna disagrees:

וְרַבִּי שִׁמְעוֹן מַתִּיר — **But R' Shimon permits** buying *terumah* with *maaser sheni* money.[3]

R' Shimon presents an argument in support of his opinion:

אָמַר לָהֶם רַבִּי שִׁמְעוֹן — **R' Shimon said to [the Sages]:** It seems logical that *terumah* may be bought with *maaser sheni* money, מָה אִם הֵקֵל בְּזִבְחֵי שְׁלָמִים שֶׁהוּא מְבִיאָן לִידֵי פִגּוּל וְנוֹתָר וְטָמֵא — **for if [the Torah] is lenient** and permits spending *maaser sheni* money **on *shelamim* offerings,**[4] even though **that could lead to [these animals] becoming** disqualified in a number of ways, such as through *piggul, nossar*, or *tamei*,[5] לֹא נָקֵל בִּתְרוּמָה — **should we not** certainly **be lenient regarding** spending *maaser sheni* funds on *terumah*, which has fewer ways of becoming disqualified than an offering does?[6]

The Sages respond:

אָמְרוּ לוֹ — **[The Sages] said to [R' Shimon]:** That is not a valid argument. מָה אִם הֵקֵל בְּזִבְחֵי שְׁלָמִים שֶׁהֵן מֻתָּרִים לְזָרִים — **Although [the Torah] is lenient**

---- NOTES ----

2. *Mishnah Rishonah*.

3. R' Shimon holds that although a person may not waste *maaser sheni* or throw it out, he may perform a permitted action even if it might lead to the *maaser sheni* going to waste. Thus, a person may spend his *maaser sheni* funds on *terumah* even though it will then be more likely that it will go to waste than if he spends the money on ordinary food (see *Rav*). [This dispute between R' Shimon and the Sages (i.e., the Tanna Kamma) is a general dispute that applies to all sacred items (see *Zevachim* 8:3; *Sheviis* 8:7).]

4. As we learned in Mishnah 1:3. In fact, this is the preferred way of spending *maaser sheni* money (see there).

5. *Piggul, nossar*, and *tamei* are ways in which offerings can become disqualified.

Piggul refers to an offering whose service was done with intent for it to be eaten (or for its sacrificial portions to be burned) after the deadline given by the Torah. *Nossar* is meat of an offering that remains uneaten beyond the time given by the Torah. *Tamei* is meat of an offering that contracts *tumah*. Any offering that becomes *piggul, nossar*, or *tamei* is disqualified and forbidden to be eaten (*Rambam Commentary*).

6. In other words: We are allowed to use *maaser sheni* funds for an offering, even though it might become disqualified in a number of ways, and the *maaser sheni* funds will then have gone to waste. It is only logical that we should be allowed to spend *maaser sheni* funds on *terumah*, which has less risk of going to waste than an offering does.

ג/ג

מִתָּרִים לְזָרִים, נָקֵל בִּתְרוּמָה שֶׁהִיא אֲסוּרָה לְזָרִים?

[ג] מִי שֶׁהָיוּ לוֹ מָעוֹת בִּירוּשָׁלַיִם וְצָרִיךְ (לוֹ) [לָהֶם], וְלַחֲבֵרוֹ פֵּרוֹת, אוֹמֵר לַחֲבֵרוֹ: "הֲרֵי הַמָּעוֹת הָאֵלּוּ מְחֻלָּלִין עַל פֵּרוֹתֶיךָ." נִמְצָא זֶה אוֹכֵל פֵּרוֹתָיו בְּטָהֳרָה, וְהַלָּה עוֹשֶׂה צָרְכּוֹ בִּמְעוֹתָיו.

- רע"ב -

(ג) מי שהיו לו מעות של מעשר שני, וצריך לקנות מהם דברים של חולין שלא לאכילה ושתיה וסיכה: ולחבירו פירות. של חולין ורוצה לעשות עמו טובה שיתחללו מעות מעשר חבירו על פירותיו: אבל פירותיו בטהרה. שחלה קדושת מעשר על הפירות, וצריך לאכלן בטהרה:

---

and allows spending *maaser sheni* on *shelamim* offerings, that is because [*shelamim*] are permitted to be eaten by non-Kohanim as well as Kohanim,[7] just like ordinary *maaser sheni*. נָקֵל בִּתְרוּמָה שֶׁהִיא אֲסוּרָה לְזָרִים — Should we also be lenient and permit spending *maaser sheni* on *terumah*, which is forbidden to non-Kohanim and thus may be eaten by fewer people than may eat ordinary *maaser sheni*?[8]

[3] Generally, a person must use his *maaser sheni* money to buy food or drink in Jerusalem. The Mishnah discusses a way for a person to transfer the money onto produce owned by another person, without buying it:

מִי שֶׁהָיוּ לוֹ מָעוֹת בִּירוּשָׁלַיִם — Someone has *maaser sheni* coins in Jerusalem, where he must spend them on food or drink, וְצָרִיךְ לָהֶם — but he needs [the coins] to buy other things, which may not be bought with *maaser sheni* funds. וְלַחֲבֵרוֹ פֵּרוֹת — His friend has produce of *chullin* in Jerusalem[1] and allows him to transfer the *maaser sheni* coins onto that produce. אוֹמֵר לַחֲבֵרוֹ — He [the owner of the *maaser sheni* coins] may say to his friend: הֲרֵי הַמָּעוֹת הָאֵלּוּ מְחֻלָּלִין עַל פֵּרוֹתֶיךָ — "These coins should have their sanctity transferred onto your produce." The coins then become *chullin* and the produce takes on the *maaser sheni* sanctity. נִמְצָא זֶה אוֹכֵל פֵּרוֹתָיו בְּטָהֳרָה — The result is that this one [the owner of the produce] must eat his produce in a state of *taharah*, since it is now *maaser sheni*,[2] וְהַלָּה עוֹשֶׂה צָרְכּוֹ בִּמְעוֹתָיו — and that one [the

---

NOTES

7. Although some parts of a *shelamim* offering are burned on the Altar, and other parts may be eaten only by a Kohen, most of its meat may be eaten by anyone (*Tiferes Yisrael*).

8. The Sages argue that while it is true that a *shelamim* offering purchased with *maaser sheni* money might become disqualified, we are not concerned in that case with the *possibility* that the *maaser sheni* might go to waste — particularly since a person would have to transgress a Torah prohibition in order to disqualify the *shelamim*. Buying *terumah* with *maaser sheni* money, however, *definitely* reduces its opportunities to be eaten, since it immediately limits the number of people who may eat it (see *Mishnah Rishonah*).

[3]

1. *Rambam Commentary*.

2. It is forbidden for someone to eat *maaser sheni* while he is *tamei* until he immerses in a *mikveh* (*Rash*; see Mishnah 2 note 1).

[Of course, he must also eat it in Jerusalem. The Mishnah discusses only the requirement of *taharah*, to contrast it to the next case, where there is a concern that *taharah* will not be observed.]

[43] MISHNAH MAASER SHENI / Chapter 3: *Lo Yomar*

וְלֹא יֹאמַר כֵּן לְעַם הָאָרֶץ אֶלָּא בִּדְמַאי. [ד] פֵּרוֹת בִּירוּשָׁלַיִם וּמָעוֹת בַּמְּדִינָה,

- רע"ב -

ולא יאמר כן לעם הארץ. שהוא חשוד לאכול פירות מעשר בטומאה: אלא בדמאי. כגון אם היו אותן מעות מעשר שני של דמאי, אז מותר לומר כן אפילו לעם הארץ, דסמא המעות אינו מעשר:
(ד) ומעות במדינה. ומעות של מעשר שני חוץ לירושלים וצריך להן, וקא משמע לן שאע"ג שיהיו הפירות והמעות במקום אחד. ועוד אשמועינן במתניתין דאף על גב דפירות מעשר אין יכולין ליפדות בירושלים, מעות מעשר מתחללין הן בירושלים:

---

owner of the coins] **may use his coins for his** other **needs,** since the coins no longer have sanctity.[3]

The Mishnah discusses whether a person may make such a transfer to produce owned by an *am haaretz,* an unlearned person who is not careful with the laws of *maasros* and the laws of *tumah*:

וְלֹא יֹאמַר כֵּן לְעַם הָאָרֶץ — **However, [a person] may not say this** (i.e., a declaration transferring *maaser sheni* sanctity to produce) **to an *am haaretz,*** because the *am haaretz* might eat the *maaser sheni* while he is *tamei.*

The Mishnah gives an exception to the above law; it involves *demai,* which is produce that must be tithed by Rabbinic law out of concern that it was not tithed properly:

אֶלָּא בִּדְמַאי — **An exception is** if the coins have the sanctity of *maaser sheni* taken from *demai*.[4] By Torah law, *maaser sheni* does not need to be separated from *demai;* its *maaser sheni* requirement is only a Rabbinic stringency, and so certain leniencies are allowed with it. One of these leniencies is that coins with the sanctity of such *maaser sheni* may be transferred onto produce owned by an *am haaretz.*

[4] The previous Mishnah taught that a person may redeem *maaser sheni* coins onto *chullin* produce when both the coins and the produce are in Jerusalem. Our Mishnah adds that this is true even if one of them — the coins or the produce — is *outside* Jerusalem:

פֵּרוֹת בִּירוּשָׁלַיִם וּמָעוֹת בַּמְּדִינָה — **If someone has *chullin* produce in Jerusalem and *maaser sheni* coins in the provinces,** i.e., outside Jerusalem,[1] and he

---

NOTES

3. Even though the owner of the *maaser sheni* will not end up eating any of it, this exchange is permitted — as long as the *maaser sheni* will be eaten in accordance with the proper laws (see *Mishnah Rishonah*).

4. *Demai* is produce obtained from an *am haaretz.* Since some *amei haaretz* did not separate *maasros* properly, the Rabbis decreed that when a person buys produce from an *am haaretz,* he must separate certain *maasros,* including *maaser sheni* (see General Introduction to Tractate *Demai*). Our Mishnah refers to coins upon which *maaser sheni* taken from *demai* was redeemed. These coins must be brought to Jerusalem and spent on food or drink, just like ordinary *maaser sheni.* However, since *demai* is obligated to be tithed only as a stringency — for the *am haaretz* might have already tithed it, as most *amei haaretz* do tithe properly — certain leniencies apply to this *maaser sheni* that do not apply to ordinary *maaser sheni* (see *Demai* 1:2).

[4]

1. *Rambam Commentary.*

[44] משניות מעשר שני / פרק ג: לא יאמר

ג/ה

- רע"ב -

(ה) מעות. של מעשר שני:
נכנסות לירושלים ויוצאות.
שאין המחיצות קולטות מעות
כדרך שקולטות פירות:

אוֹמֵר: "הֲרֵי הַמָּעוֹת הָהֵם מְחֻלָּלִין עַל פֵּרוֹת הָאֵלּוּ". מָעוֹת בִּירוּשָׁלַיִם וּפֵרוֹת בַּמְּדִינָה, אוֹמֵר: "הֲרֵי הַמָּעוֹת הָאֵלּוּ מְחֻלָּלִין עַל פֵּרוֹת הָהֵם", וּבִלְבַד שֶׁיַּעֲלוּ הַפֵּרוֹת וְיֵאָכְלוּ בִּירוּשָׁלַיִם.

[ה] מָעוֹת נִכְנָסוֹת לִירוּשָׁלַיִם וְיוֹצְאוֹת, וּפֵרוֹת נִכְנָסִין וְאֵינָן יוֹצְאִין.

אוֹמֵר הֲרֵי הַמָּעוֹת הָהֵם — needs the coins to buy items other than food or drink, מְחֻלָּלִין עַל פֵּרוֹת הָאֵלּוּ — he may say: "Those coins outside Jerusalem should have their sanctity transferred onto this produce in Jerusalem." The produce is now *maaser sheni* and must be eaten in Jerusalem, and the coins become *chullin*.[2]

The reverse case:

מָעוֹת בִּירוּשָׁלַיִם וּפֵרוֹת בַּמְּדִינָה — If a person has *maaser sheni* coins in Jerusalem and *chullin* produce in the provinces, אוֹמֵר הֲרֵי הַמָּעוֹת הָאֵלּוּ מְחֻלָּלִין עַל פֵּרוֹת הָהֵם — he may say: "These coins in Jerusalem should have their sanctity transferred onto that produce outside Jerusalem." The coins become *chullin* and he may use them for any purpose, וּבִלְבַד שֶׁיַּעֲלוּ הַפֵּרוֹת וְיֵאָכְלוּ בִּירוּשָׁלַיִם — as long as the produce is brought up and eaten in Jerusalem, since the produce is now *maaser sheni*.[3]

[5] A law that applies to *maaser sheni* after it is brought into Jerusalem:

מָעוֹת נִכְנָסוֹת לִירוּשָׁלַיִם וְיוֹצְאוֹת — Coins of *maaser sheni* may enter and leave Jerusalem, that is, even after *maaser sheni* coins have been brought into Jerusalem, it is permitted to take them out of the city; וּפֵרוֹת נִכְנָסִין וְאֵינָן יוֹצְאִין — but produce of *maaser sheni* enters Jerusalem but may not leave. Once *maaser sheni* produce has been brought into Jerusalem, it is forbidden to take it out. Rather, it must remain in the city to be eaten.[1]

NOTES

2. Even though the produce and coins are not in the same place, the transfer is valid (*Rav*).

3. [The Mishnah mentions this point here even though it did not do so in the previous cases, to teach that] this produce may not be redeemed again onto other coins or food; it must be eaten in Jerusalem. Although produce separated as *maaser sheni* may be redeemed, food on which *maaser sheni* coins were redeemed may not be redeemed again unless the food becomes *tamei* (*Mishnah Rishonah*; see Mishnah 10).

[5]

1. This is a Rabbinic prohibition. By Torah law, although *maaser sheni* produce may be redeemed for money before it is brought to Jerusalem, once it enters the city it may no longer be redeemed. It may, however, be taken out of the city and redeemed there. As a precaution against redeeming *maaser sheni* inside Jerusalem, the Rabbis decreed that a person may not even redeem *maaser sheni* outside Jerusalem if it has once entered the city. As a further precaution, they decreed that once *maaser sheni* enters the city, it may not be taken out at all (*Mishnah Rishonah; Derech Emunah, Hilchos Maaser Sheni* 2:63). This decree, however, applies only to produce

[45] **MISHNAH MAASER SHENI** / Chapter 3: *Lo Yomar* 3/6

- רע"ב -

אַף הַפֵּירוֹת נִכְנָסִים וְיוֹצְאִים. וְדַוְקָא לְהוֹלִיאָן כְּדֵי לְטוֹחֲנָן וּלְאָפוֹתָן וּלְהַחֲזִירָן אַחַר כָּךְ לִירוּשָׁלַיִם שָׁרֵי רַבָּן שִׁמְעוֹן בֶּן גַּמְלִיאֵל, לְפִי שֶׁיּוֹתֵר הָיוּ מוֹצְאִין לִטְחוֹן וּלְאָפוֹת חוּץ לִירוּשָׁלַיִם מִבִּירוּשָׁלַיִם עַצְמָהּ. וּתְנָא קַמָּא אָסַר נַמֵּי בְּהָא. וְאֵין

רַבָּן שִׁמְעוֹן בֶּן גַּמְלִיאֵל אוֹמֵר: אַף הַפֵּרוֹת נִכְנָסִין וְיוֹצְאִין.

[ו] פֵּרוֹת שֶׁנִּגְמְרָה מְלַאכְתָּן וְעָבְרוּ בְּתוֹךְ יְרוּשָׁלַיִם, יַחֲזֹר מַעֲשֵׂר שֵׁנִי שֶׁלָּהֶן וְיֵאָכֵל בִּירוּשָׁלָיִם.

הֲלָכָה כְּרַבִּי שִׁמְעוֹן בֶּן גַּמְלִיאֵל: (ו) שֶׁנִּגְמְרָה מְלַאכְתָּן. לְמַעֲשֵׂר, כְּדִתְנַן בְּפִרְקָא קַמָּא דְּמַעַשְׂרוֹת אֵיזֶהוּ גָּרְנָן לְמַעֲשֵׂר: וְעָבְרוּ בְּתוֹךְ יְרוּשָׁלַיִם. בְּעוֹדָן טֶבֶל: יַחֲזוֹר מַעֲשֵׂר שֵׁנִי שֶׁלָּהֶן. דְּקָסָבַר מְחִיצוֹת שֶׁלֹּא הוּרְמוּ כְּמִי שֶׁהוּרְמוּ דָּמֵי, וְקָלְטוּהוּ מְחִיצוֹת לְמַעֲשֵׂר שֵׁנִי:

The next Tanna disagrees:

אַף הַפֵּרוֹת — רַבָּן שִׁמְעוֹן בֶּן גַּמְלִיאֵל אוֹמֵר — **Rabban Shimon ben Gamliel says:** נִכְנָסִין וְיוֹצְאִין — **Even** *maaser sheni* **produce may enter and leave** Jerusalem; that is, a person *is* permitted to take *maaser sheni* produce out of the city after it has been brought in.[2]

[6] Once *maaser sheni* produce enters Jerusalem, it may not be redeemed for money, but must be eaten in Jerusalem.[1] This Mishnah discusses what happens when produce from which *maaser sheni* was not yet separated is brought into Jerusalem:

פֵּרוֹת שֶׁנִּגְמְרָה מְלַאכְתָּן — **Untithed produce that was fully processed** (i.e., it reached the stage at which it becomes obligated in *maasros*),[2] וְעָבְרוּ בְּתוֹךְ יְרוּשָׁלַיִם — **which passed through Jerusalem,** and after it was taken out of the city its *maasros* (including *maaser sheni*) were separated: יַחֲזֹר מַעֲשֵׂר שֵׁנִי שֶׁלָּהֶן וְיֵאָכֵל בִּירוּשָׁלַיִם — its *maaser sheni* **must be brought back and eaten in Jerusalem.** Even though the *maaser sheni* had not yet been separated when the produce passed through Jerusalem, this *maaser sheni* is considered to

--- NOTES ---

and not to money of *maaser sheni* (*Rav*).

This concept is referred to as מְחִיצוֹת קוֹלְטוֹת, *the walls take hold*; that is, once *maaser sheni* produce enters the city, the walls of Jerusalem "take hold" of it and it may not be removed from the city or redeemed.

2. Rabban Shimon agrees that the produce may not be taken out permanently; that is, it may not be taken out and then have its sanctity transferred to other produce or money so that the original produce that was in Jerusalem will become *chullin* and be eaten elsewhere. All R' Shimon allows is taking the produce out of Jerusalem in order to prepare it for eating. Since there were more mills and ovens outside Jerusalem than there were inside, it was easier and cheaper to grind *maaser sheni* grain and bake it outside Jerusalem. Rabban Shimon ben Gamliel therefore permitted *maaser sheni* to be taken out of the city and processed, as long as it was later returned to Jerusalem to be eaten. The Tanna Kamma, however, forbids removing the produce even temporarily (*Rav, Rash*).

[6]

1. See note 1 to the previous Mishnah.

2. Produce is not obligated in *maasros* until it reaches the stage when it is considered fully processed. (See General Introduction to *Maasros* and *Maasros* 1:5-8 for more details.)

משניות מעשר שני / פרק ג: לא יאמר

וְשֶׁלֹּא נִגְמְרָה מְלַאכְתָּן: סַלֵּי עֲנָבִים לַגַּת וְסַלֵּי תְאֵנִים לַמֻּקְצָה, בֵּית שַׁמַּאי אוֹמְרִים: יַחֲזֹר מַעֲשֵׂר שֵׁנִי שֶׁלָּהֶם וְיֵאָכֵל בִּירוּשָׁלָיִם; וּבֵית הִלֵּל אוֹמְרִים: יִפָּדֶה וְיֵאָכֵל בְּכָל מָקוֹם.

– רע״ב –

ושלא נגמרה מלאכתן. כגון סלי ענבים לגת וכו׳. אבל סלי ענבים לאכילה נגמרה מלאכתן: למוקצה. מקום שטוחין בו תאנים ליבש קרוי מוקצה:

---

have already been in Jerusalem.[3] Accordingly, it may not be redeemed and must itself be eaten in Jerusalem.

The next case is subject to a dispute:

וְשֶׁלֹּא נִגְמְרָה מְלַאכְתָּן — However, regarding [produce] that was not yet processed, סַלֵּי עֲנָבִים לַגַּת וְסַלֵּי תְאֵנִים לַמֻּקְצָה — such as **baskets of grapes** headed **for the winepress or baskets of figs** headed **for the drying area,**[4] which passed through Jerusalem and were later tithed, the law is a matter of dispute: בֵּית שַׁמַּאי אוֹמְרִים — **Beis Shammai say:** יַחֲזֹר מַעֲשֵׂר שֵׁנִי שֶׁלָּהֶם וְיֵאָכֵל בִּירוּשָׁלָיִם — Its *maaser sheni* **must be returned and eaten in Jerusalem,** just as with produce that passed through Jerusalem after it was processed. וּבֵית הִלֵּל אוֹמְרִים — **But Beis Hillel say:** יִפָּדֶה וְיֵאָכֵל בְּכָל מָקוֹם — **It may be redeemed and eaten anywhere.** Since when the produce was in Jerusalem, it was not even obligated in *maaser sheni*, it cannot be said that the *maaser sheni* was in Jerusalem. Therefore, it may be redeemed.[5]

The next Tanna has a different version of the dispute between Beis Shammai and Beis Hillel:

--- NOTES ---

3. This is based on the general principle that with regard to certain laws, we consider tithes that *will* be separated as though they were already separated [מַתָּנוֹת שֶׁלֹּא הוּרְמוּ כְּמִי שֶׁהוּרְמוּ דָּמְיָין]. Thus, although this *maaser sheni* was never actually in Jerusalem — for when the produce was in Jerusalem, none of it had been designated as *maaser sheni* — it is nevertheless considered as though the *maaser sheni* was separated, and accordingly, that the *maaser sheni* entered Jerusalem (*Rav*).

[In fact, since we view this produce as containing *maaser sheni*, it is forbidden to take the produce outside Jerusalem in the first place, just as it is forbidden to take *maaser sheni* outside Jerusalem once it was brought into the city, as we learned in the previous Mishnah. Our Mishnah refers to a case where the produce was removed from Jerusalem unlawfully (*Mishnah Rishonah*).]

4. These are considered unprocessed because more work will still be done to them: the grapes will be pressed into wine, and the figs will be dried (*Rambam Commentary*). Therefore, they are not yet obligated in *maasros*.

5. According to Beis Hillel, the principle that tithes that will be separated are already considered to have been separated (see note 3) applies only once the produce has been processed and thus become obligated in *maasros*. Before it is obligated in *maasros*, the *maasros* are not considered to have been separated; therefore, it cannot be said that the *maaser sheni* of this produce was in Jerusalem (see *Beur* of *R' Chaim Kanievsky* to *Yerushalmi*).

Beis Shammai, however, hold that the principle applies even to unprocessed produce.

[47] **MISHNAH MAASER SHENI** / Chapter 3: *Lo Yomar*

– רע"ב –

רַבִּי שִׁמְעוֹן בֶּן יְהוּדָה אוֹמֵר מִשּׁוּם רַבִּי יוֹסֵי: לֹא נֶחְלְקוּ בֵית שַׁמַּאי וּבֵית הִלֵּל עַל פֵּרוֹת שֶׁלֹא נִגְמְרָה מְלַאכְתָּן, שֶׁיִּפָּדֶה מַעֲשֵׂר שֵׁנִי שֶׁלָּהֶם וְיֵאָכֵל בְּכָל מָקוֹם. וְעַל מַה נֶּחְלְקוּ? עַל פֵּרוֹת שֶׁנִּגְמְרָה מְלַאכְתָּן, שֶׁבֵּית שַׁמַּאי אוֹמְרִים, יַחֲזוֹר מַעֲשֵׂר שֵׁנִי שֶׁלָּהֶם וְיֵאָכֵל בִּירוּשָׁלַיִם; וּבֵית הִלֵּל אוֹמְרִים, יִפָּדֶה וְיֵאָכֵל בְּכָל מָקוֹם. וְהַדְּמַאי, נִכְנָס וְיוֹצֵא וְנִפְדֶּה.

רבי שמעון בן יהודה אומר וכו'. סבר דלבית הלל מתנות שלא הורמו לאו כמי שהורמו דמיין. אי נמי אפילו כמי שהורמו דמיין הני מילי [לענין] שאר דברים, אבל לענין קליטת מחיצות דרבנן, מקילין בית הלל. ואין הלכה כרבי שמעון בן יהודה, שלא נחלקו בית שמאי ובית הלל אלא על פירות שלא נגמרה מלאכתן כדברי תנא קמא. והדמאי. טבל של דמאי. נכנס. לירושלים. ויוצא ונפדה. חוץ לירושלים אחר שיצא, ואין צריך להחזיר. וכך סיפא לתנא קמא אליטריך ואליבא דבית הלל:

רַבִּי שִׁמְעוֹן בֶּן יְהוּדָה אוֹמֵר מִשּׁוּם רַבִּי יוֹסֵי — R' Shimon ben Yehudah says in the name of R' Yose: לֹא נֶחְלְקוּ בֵית שַׁמַּאי וּבֵית הִלֵּל עַל פֵּרוֹת שֶׁלֹא נִגְמְרָה מְלַאכְתָּן — Beis Shammai and Beis Hillel did *not* disagree about produce that was *not* fully processed when it passed through Jerusalem, שֶׁיִּפָּדֶה מַעֲשֵׂר שֵׁנִי שֶׁלָּהֶם וְיֵאָכֵל בְּכָל מָקוֹם — for all agree in that case that its *maaser sheni* may be redeemed and eaten anywhere.[6] וְעַל מַה נֶּחְלְקוּ — Rather, about what did they disagree? עַל פֵּרוֹת שֶׁנִּגְמְרָה מְלַאכְתָּן — About produce that *was* fully processed and then passed through Jerusalem [the Mishnah's first case]. שֶׁבֵּית שַׁמַּאי אוֹמְרִים — In that case Beis Shammai say: יַחֲזוֹר מַעֲשֵׂר שֵׁנִי שֶׁלָּהֶם וְיֵאָכֵל בִּירוּשָׁלַיִם — Its *maaser sheni* must be returned and eaten in Jerusalem, because the *maaser sheni* is considered to have been in Jerusalem. וּבֵית הִלֵּל אוֹמְרִים — And Beis Hillel say: יִפָּדֶה וְיֵאָכֵל בְּכָל מָקוֹם — [The *maaser sheni*] may be redeemed and eaten anywhere; since the *maaser sheni* was not yet separated when the produce was in Jerusalem, the *maaser sheni* is not considered to have been in Jerusalem.

All agree that the next case is an exception to the Mishnah's prohibition:

וְהַדְּמַאי נִכְנָס וְיוֹצֵא וְנִפְדֶּה — Untithed produce of *demai*,[7] even if it is fully processed, **may enter and leave** Jerusalem, **and** the *maaser sheni* later taken from it **may be redeemed** outside Jerusalem. Since *demai* is required to be tithed only as a Rabbinic stringency, its laws are more lenient than those of ordinary produce, and it is not subject to the prohibition discussed here.

NOTES

6. According to R' Shimon ben Yehudah, everyone agrees that the unseparated tithes of unprocessed produce are *not* considered as though they were separated. Thus, if produce passed through Jerusalem before it was processed, the *maaser sheni* that is later separated from that produce is not considered to have been in Jerusalem. The dispute between Beis Hillel and Beis Shammai is whether the unseparated tithes of *finished* produce are considered to have been separated: Beis Shammai hold that they are, and Beis Hillel hold that they are not (see *Rav; Beur* of R' Chaim Kanievsky).

7. See Mishnah 3 note 4.

[48] **משניות מעשר שני / פרק ג: לא יאמר** ז/ג

- רע"ב -

(ז) בפנים. מן החומה:
ונוטה לחוץ. לחומת
ירושלים: מכנגד החומה
ולפנים כלפנים. דבין
גוף ובין עיקר מכנגד
החומה ולפנים כלפנים,
ואוכלין שם מעשר שני
ולא פודין. ובין גוף ובין
עיקר מכנגד החומה ולחוץ
כלחוץ, ופודין שם מעשר

[ז] **אִילָן** שֶׁהוּא עוֹמֵד בִּפְנִים וְנוֹטֶה לַחוּץ,
אוֹ עוֹמֵד בַּחוּץ וְנוֹטֶה לִפְנִים: מִכְּנֶגֶד
הַחוֹמָה וְלִפְנִים, כְּלִפְנִים; מִכְּנֶגֶד הַחוֹמָה
וְלַחוּץ, כְּלַחוּץ. בָּתֵּי הַבַּדִּים שֶׁפִּתְחֵיהֶן לִפְנִים
וַחֲלָלָן לַחוּץ, אוֹ שֶׁפִּתְחֵיהֶן לַחוּץ וַחֲלָלָן
לִפְנִים: בֵּית שַׁמַּאי אוֹמְרִים: הַכֹּל כְּלִפְנִים;

שני ולא אוכלין. והיינו דתנן במסכת מעשרות פרק ג, ובירושלים הולך אחר הנוף. כלומר אף אחר
הנוף: **בתי הבדים.** שעוקרים בהם שמן, ורגילים היו לעשות בתים הללו בחומת המדינה: **שפתחיהן
לפנים.** מחומת ירושלים וחללן חוץ לחומת ירושלים:

---

[7] We have learned that *maaser sheni* produce may be eaten only *inside* Jerusalem, and may be redeemed only *outside* Jerusalem. For these laws, the borders of Jerusalem are the walls that surround it. This Mishnah discusses the status of trees or buildings that stand partly within the walls of Jerusalem and partly outside the walls:

אִילָן שֶׁהוּא עוֹמֵד בִּפְנִים וְנוֹטֶה לַחוּץ — Regarding **a tree that stands inside** the walls of Jerusalem **but [its branches] extend** over the wall **out of Jerusalem, אוֹ עוֹמֵד בַּחוּץ וְנוֹטֶה לִפְנִים** — **or [a tree] that stands outside** Jerusalem's walls **but [its branches] extend** over the wall **into Jerusalem,** this is its law: **מִכְּנֶגֶד הַחוֹמָה וְלִפְנִים כְּלִפְנִים** — **The part of the tree located from the wall and inward is** treated **as inside** the city; **מִכְּנֶגֶד הַחוֹמָה וְלַחוּץ כְּלַחוּץ** — the part of the tree located **from the wall and outward is** treated **as outside** the city. Thus, someone perched on the portion of the tree inside the walls[1] may eat *maaser sheni* but may not redeem it, while someone on the part of the tree outside the walls may redeem *maaser sheni* but may not eat it.[2]

The Mishnah cites a dispute about a similar case — a chamber that is built into the wall of Jerusalem, so that part is within the city and part is outside it: **בָּתֵּי הַבַּדִּים שֶׁפִּתְחֵיהֶן לִפְנִים וַחֲלָלָן לַחוּץ** — Regarding **olive presses** (chambers where olives are crushed into oil) that are built into the walls of Jerusalem: **their entrances are on the inside** of the wall (i.e., inside the city) **but their interior spaces** extend **outside** the wall, **אוֹ שֶׁפִּתְחֵיהֶן לַחוּץ וַחֲלָלָן לִפְנִים** — **or their entrances are to the outside** of the wall **but their interior spaces** extend **inside** the wall;[3] **בֵּית שַׁמַּאי אוֹמְרִים** — **Beis Shammai say: הַכֹּל כְּלִפְנִים** — **The**

NOTES
---

[7]
1. *Tiferes Yisrael.*
2. The status of both the trunk and the branches are determined by their actual location. The status of the branches does not follow the location of the trunk, nor does the status of the trunk follow the location of the branches (see *Rav*).
[*Maasros* 3:10 discusses the same law and seems to come to a different conclusion. See *Tos. Yom Tov* and *Derech Emunah, Hilchos Maaser Sheni* 2:15 for further discussion.]

3. It was common to set up olive presses in rooms built into the city walls (*Rav*). Sometimes, the entrance was inside the city and sometimes it was outside. The rooms would often extend past the wall

[49] **MISHNAH MAASER SHENI** / Chapter 3: *Lo Yomar*

וּבֵית הִלֵּל אוֹמְרִים: מִכְּנֶגֶד הַחוֹמָה וְלִפְנִים, כְּלִפְנִים; מִכְּנֶגֶד הַחוֹמָה וְלַחוּץ, כְּלַחוּץ.

[ח] הַלְּשָׁכוֹת: בְּנוּיוֹת בַּקֹּדֶשׁ וּפְתוּחוֹת לַחֹל, תּוֹכָן חֹל וְגַגּוֹתֵיהֶן

- רע"ב -

מכנגד החומה ולפנים כלפנים. ואוכלים שם מעשר שני וקדשים קלים, ואין פודין שם מעשר שני: מכנגד החומה ולחוץ כלחוץ. ואין אוכלים שם מעשר שני וקדשים,

ופודים שם מעשר שני: (ח) הלשכות בנויות בקודש. בעזרה: ופתוחות לחול. להר הבית: וגגותיהן קודש. והוא שהיו גגותיהן שווה לקרקע העזרה, כגון שהיתה הלשכה בשפוע ההר. שאם אין גגותיהן שווה לקרקע העזרה קיימא לן דעליות וגגות לא נתקדשו:

---

entire [room], even the part that is outside the city walls, **is** treated **as** if it were **inside** the city. As long as part of the press is inside the city *or* the entrance is inside the city walls, the entire press is considered part of the city, and *maaser sheni* may be eaten but not redeemed there.[4]

וּבֵית הִלֵּל אוֹמְרִים — **But Beis Hillel say:** מִכְּנֶגֶד הַחוֹמָה וְלִפְנִים כְּלִפְנִים — The section of the press located **from the wall and inward is** treated **as inside** the city; מִכְּנֶגֶד הַחוֹמָה וְלַחוּץ כְּלַחוּץ — the section of the press located **from the wall and outward is** treated **as outside** the city. Thus, someone standing in the part of the press that lies within the city walls may eat *maaser sheni* but may not redeem it, while someone standing in the part of the press that lies outside the city walls may redeem *maaser sheni* but may not eat it.

[8] Having discussed chambers built into the walls of Jerusalem, our Mishnah discusses chambers built in and around the Temple Courtyard (עֲזָרָה). The Temple Courtyard had a more sanctified status than the Temple Mount that surrounded it.[1] The Mishnah discusses the status of chambers that are located partly in the Courtyard and partly on the Temple Mount:

הַלְּשָׁכוֹת — This is the law for **the chambers** of the Temple Courtyard: בְּנוּיוֹת בַּקֹּדֶשׁ וּפְתוּחוֹת לַחֹל — **Chambers** that are **built in the sanctified area** (i.e., the Courtyard) **but open into the unsanctified area** (i.e., the rest of the Temple Mount):[2] תּוֹכָן חֹל — **Their interior spaces are not sanctified,** because the sanctity of a chamber's interior is determined by where its entrance is, and these do not open into the Courtyard.[3] וְגַגּוֹתֵיהֶן קֹדֶשׁ — **But [the**

NOTES

and protrude from the other side, into or out of the city.

4. *Tiferes Yisrael* (first explanation).

[8]

1. For example, certain types of offerings — those known as *kodshei kodashim* (*most-holy offerings,* such as *chatas* and *asham* offerings) — may be eaten only in the Courtyard and not in the rest of the Temple Mount. In addition, a person who enters the Courtyard while *tamei* is punished with *kares*.

2. These chambers were built at the edge of the sanctified Courtyard area. The interior of each chamber was located within the Courtyard but the entrance was outside the Courtyard, in the unsanctified area of the Temple Mount (*Rav*).

[Although the whole Temple Mount is sanctified to a certain degree, the Mishnah refers to it as "unsanctified," because it is less holy than the Courtyard.]

3. *Ri ben Malki Tzedek*. [This law is derived from a verse in the Torah (see *Zevachim* 56a).]

משניות מעשר שני / פרק ג: לא יאמר

קֹדֶשׁ; בְּנוּיוֹת בַּחֹל וּפְתוּחוֹת לַקֹּדֶשׁ, תּוֹכָן קֹדֶשׁ וְגַגּוֹתֵיהֶן חֹל; בְּנוּיוֹת בַּקֹּדֶשׁ וּבַחֹל וּפְתוּחוֹת לַקֹּדֶשׁ וְלַחֹל, תּוֹכָן וְגַגּוֹתֵיהֶן מִכְּנֶגֶד הַקֹּדֶשׁ וְלַקֹּדֶשׁ, קֹדֶשׁ; מִכְּנֶגֶד הַחֹל וְלַחֹל, חֹל.

- רע"ב -

תּוֹכָן קֹדֶשׁ. לִשְׁחִיטַת קָדְשֵׁי קָדָשִׁים קַלִּים, וְלַאֲכִילַת קָדְשֵׁי קָדָשִׁים, וּלְהִתְחַיֵּיב עֲלֵיהֶן מִשּׁוּם טוּמְאָה:

---

chambers'] roofs are sanctified, because the sanctity of a roof depends on where it actually is, and these roofs are located inside the Courtyard.[4] **בְּנוּיוֹת בַּחֹל וּפְתוּחוֹת לַקֹּדֶשׁ** — Chambers that are **built in the unsanctified area** (i.e., outside the Courtyard) **but open into the sanctified area** (i.e., the Courtyard): **תּוֹכָן קֹדֶשׁ** — **Their interiors are sanctified,** since their entrances are located in the Courtyard, **וְגַגּוֹתֵיהֶן חֹל** — **but their roofs are not sanctified,** since the roofs are located outside the Courtyard.

בְּנוּיוֹת בַּקֹּדֶשׁ וּבַחֹל — Chambers that are **built in** both **the sanctified and unsanctified areas,** that is, they extend through the wall of the Courtyard, so that part of the chamber is inside and part is outside, **וּפְתוּחוֹת לַקֹּדֶשׁ וְלַחֹל** — and they open into both **the sanctified and unsanctified areas,** namely, they have entrances on both sides, **תּוֹכָן וְגַגּוֹתֵיהֶן** — the law is the same for both **their interiors and roofs: מִכְּנֶגֶד הַקֹּדֶשׁ וְלַקֹּדֶשׁ קֹדֶשׁ** — The section of the chamber located **from the sanctified area** and inward, **toward the sanctified area,** i.e., the part that is in the Courtyard, **is sanctified. מִכְּנֶגֶד הַחֹל וְלַחֹל חֹל** — The section of the chamber located **from the unsanctified area** and outward, **toward the unsanctified area,** i.e., the part that is not in the Courtyard, **is not sanctified.**[5]

[9] We have learned that once *maaser sheni* produce enters the city of Jerusalem, "the walls take hold" of it, and it may neither be redeemed nor removed from the city.[1] This Mishnah discusses an exception to that rule: *maaser sheni* that became *tamei*. If *maaser sheni* becomes *tamei* in any way, it may not be eaten and may be redeemed even within the walls of Jerusalem.[2]

NOTES

4. The Mishnah refers to roofs that are level with the floor of the Courtyard. [Since the Temple Mount was a hill, it was possible for a chamber to be hollowed out of the ground beneath the Courtyard, so that it opened onto the side of the hill but its roof was at the level of the Courtyard floor.] Such roofs are considered part of the Courtyard and are sanctified. A roof that is higher than the floor of the Courtyard, though, has no sanctity, for the upper floors and roofs of the Temple rooms have no sanctity (*Rav*).

5. Since these chambers open to both sanctified and unsanctified areas, their sanctity is not determined by their openings, but by the ground upon which they are built. Thus, the law is the same for interiors and roofs: the sections built on sanctified land are sanctified; those built on unsanctified land are not sanctified.

[As in the previous cases, the roofs are sanctified only if they are at the ground level of the Courtyard. If they are higher than ground level, even the section of roof that covers the sanctified area is not sanctified (see previous note).]

[9]

1. See Mishnah 5 note 1.
2. This law is derived from *Devarim* 14:24 (*Rav*). [After the *maaser sheni* is redeemed, it loses its sanctity and becomes *chullin*, which may be eaten even though it is *tamei*.]

[ט] **מַעֲשֵׂר** שֵׁנִי שֶׁנִּכְנַס לִירוּשָׁלַיִם וְנִטְמָא, בֵּין שֶׁנִּטְמָא בְּאַב הַטֻּמְאָה בֵּין שֶׁנִּטְמָא בִּוְלַד הַטֻּמְאָה, בֵּין בִּפְנִים בֵּין בַּחוּץ, בֵּית שַׁמַּאי אוֹמְרִים: יִפָּדֶה וְיֵאָכֵל הַכֹּל בִּפְנִים, חוּץ מִשֶּׁנִּטְמָא בְּאַב הַטֻּמְאָה בַּחוּץ;

– רע"ב –

(ט) **באב הטומאה.** שרץ ונבילה וכיוצא בהן: **בולד הטומאה. הֳאִי ולד** הטומאה דתנן במתניתין לאו ולד הטומאה שנוגע באב הטומאה שהוא טמא מדאורייתא, אלא בולד הטומאה דרבנן,

כגון שנגע בכלים שנטמאו במשקין: **יפדה.** דמעשר שני שנטמא פודין אותו אפילו בירושלים, דכתיב (דברים יד) כי לא תוכל שאתו, ואין שאת אלא אכילה כדכתיב (בראשית מג) וישא משאות מאת פניו אליהם: **ויאכל הכל בפנים.** שלא יאמרו רואיו מעשר שני שנכנס לירושלים ויצא, מפני שיש קול למעשר היוצא. אבל אין לחוש כשפודים אותו שמא יאמרו רואיו מעשר שני שנפדה בירושלים, שאין קול לפדוי: **חוץ משנטמא באב הטומאה בחוץ.** שכיון שנכנס כשהוא טמא אין המחילה קולטתו:

This Mishnah cites a dispute about whether *tamei maaser sheni* may be removed from the city after it is redeemed:

מַעֲשֵׂר שֵׁנִי שֶׁנִּכְנַס לִירוּשָׁלַיִם וְנִטְמָא — If *maaser sheni* produce **entered Jerusalem and became *tamei*,** בֵּין שֶׁנִּטְמָא בְּאַב הַטֻּמְאָה — **whether it became *tamei* from** contact with **an *av hatumah*** (a primary source of *tumah*), which makes it Biblically *tamei*,[3] בֵּין שֶׁנִּטְמָא בִּוְלַד הַטֻּמְאָה — or **whether it became *tamei* from** contact with **a secondary source of *tumah*** that makes it *tamei* only by Rabbinic law,[4] בֵּין בִּפְנִים בֵּין בַּחוּץ — **whether** it became *tamei* **inside** Jerusalem **or outside,**[5] בֵּית שַׁמַּאי אוֹמְרִים — **Beis Shammai say:** יִפָּדֶה וְיֵאָכֵל הַכֹּל בִּפְנִים — In **all** these cases, [the *maaser sheni*] **should be redeemed** even though it is inside Jerusalem, **but it must be eaten inside** the city. Although this produce is now *chullin* and should really be permitted to be taken out, the Rabbis decreed that it remains forbidden to be removed from the city, out of concern that if it is removed, people who are not aware that it became *tamei* might see it being taken out of the city and will think that it is permitted to remove all *maaser sheni* from Jerusalem.[6] חוּץ מִשֶּׁנִּטְמָא בְּאַב הַטֻּמְאָה בַּחוּץ — **An exception is** [*maaser sheni*] **that became *tamei* from an *av hatumah* outside** Jerusalem: in that case it may be removed from the city

---

— NOTES —

3. *Av hatumah* refers to something that creates *tumah*. Examples are a *sheretz* (a carcass of one of the eight creeping animals listed in *Vayikra* 11:29-30) and a *neveilah* (the carcass of an animal that died without being properly slaughtered). Any person, utensil, or food (including *maaser sheni*) that is touched by an *av hatumah* becomes *tamei* under Biblical law (see *Rav*).

4. A secondary source of *tumah* (וְלַד הַטֻּמְאָה) is a category that refers to anything that became *tamei* from an *av hatumah*. Some secondary sources of *tumah* are *tamei* under Biblical law, and some are *tamei* only under Rabbinic law. Our Mishnah refers only to items that are *tamei* under Rabbinic law. An example is a utensil that touched *tamei* liquid (*Rav*).

5. That is, whether the *maaser sheni* became *tamei* after being brought into Jerusalem, or whether it became *tamei* while still outside Jerusalem and was then brought into the city (*Tiferes Yisrael*).

6. However, he may redeem the *maaser sheni* without concern of what people will think, because redeeming is generally done privately and other people will not find out about it (*Rav*).

וּבֵית הִלֵּל אוֹמְרִים: הַכֹּל יִפָּדֶה וְיֵאָכֵל בַּחוּץ, חוּץ מִשֶּׁנִּטְמָא בִּוְלַד הַטֻּמְאָה בִּפְנִים.

- רע"ב -

חוץ משנטמא בולד הטומאה בפנים. אבל נטמא בולד הטומאה בחוץ אף על פי שבולד הטומאה של דבריהם נטמא, ומן התורה טהור הוא, יאכל בחוץ. ובירושלמי מוקי לה כגון שהכניסו על מנת שלא יקלטוהו מחיצות, אבל אם לא התנה, הואיל ונכנס והרי הוא טהור דאורייתא יאכל בפנים:

---

and redeemed and eaten outside. There is no concern that people will see it taken out and draw the wrong conclusion, because when *maaser sheni* that is so severely *tamei* enters Jerusalem, that fact is widely known, and everyone will know that this *maaser sheni* is being removed from Jerusalem because it is *tamei*.[7]

וּבֵית הִלֵּל אוֹמְרִים — **But Beis Hillel say:** הַכֹּל יִפָּדֶה וְיֵאָכֵל בַּחוּץ — **In all** these cases, [the *maaser sheni*] **may be redeemed and eaten** even **outside** Jerusalem. Beis Hillel do not share Beis Shammai's concern that people will mistakenly think that *maaser sheni* may be removed from Jerusalem. Thus, there is no reason to forbid removing the produce from Jerusalem after it has been redeemed and is no longer sanctified. חוּץ מִשֶּׁנִּטְמָא בִּוְלַד הַטֻּמְאָה בִּפְנִים — **An exception,** though, **is** [*maaser sheni*] **that became *tamei* from a secondary *tumah* inside** Jerusalem; in that case it may not be removed from the city. Here, there is another concern: Since the *maaser sheni* entered Jerusalem when it was *tahor*, the walls "took hold" of it and forbade its removal from Jerusalem. That "hold" was never released, and thus the produce may not be taken out even though it became *tamei*.[8]

NOTES

7. See *Mishnah Rishonah*; see *Derech Emunah, Hilchos Maaser Sheni* 2:89.

8. As we learned, when *maaser sheni* enters Jerusalem, the walls of Jerusalem "take hold" of it and it becomes forbidden to be taken out of the city. This "hold" remains a concern in one of the Mishnah's four cases: where the produce became *tamei* from secondary *tumah* inside Jerusalem. It is not a concern in the other cases, as follows: If the produce became *tamei* from an *av hatumah* outside Jerusalem, the walls never take hold of it at all, since they do not take hold of *maaser sheni* that is unfit to eat. And if it becomes *tamei* from an *av hatumah* while in Jerusalem, although the walls took hold of it when it entered the city, this "hold" is released when it becomes unfit to eat. However, when it becomes *tamei* inside Jerusalem from a secondary *tumah*, the walls took hold when it entered (since it was *tahor* at the time) and, since it became *tamei* only by Rabbinic law and thus is still *tahor* and fit to be eaten by Torah law, they do not release their hold. Consequently, Beis Hillel rule that in such a case, the produce may not be removed from the city.

As for the fourth case — produce that became *tamei* outside Jerusalem from a secondary *tumah* — in truth, the hold of the walls should still apply. Although the walls do not take hold of *maaser sheni* that is unfit to eat, this *maaser sheni* is *tamei* only on a Rabbinic level and is *tahor* and fit to be eaten by Torah law; therefore, the walls should really take hold of it when it enters the city and forbid its removal. Beis Hillel, who said that such produce *may* be taken out of Jerusalem, refer to a case where, when the owner brought the *maaser sheni* into Jerusalem, he made a stipulation that the walls not take hold of it. In such a case, the Rabbis relaxed the walls' "hold" and the produce may be removed from the city (*Rav*, from *Yerushalmi*).

In summary, the Mishnah presents four cases: (a) *Maaser sheni* became

[53] **MISHNAH MAASER SHENI** / Chapter 3: *Lo Yomar*

- רע"ב -

(י) הלקוח בכסף מעשר שני. פירות שנקנו מדמי מעשר שני: **יקבר.** הואיל ונגמרה מצותו וקנה פירות ממעות מעשר שני שוב לא יפדה:

[י] הַלָּקוּחַ בְּכֶסֶף מַעֲשֵׂר שֵׁנִי שֶׁנִּטְמָא, יִפָּדֶה; רַבִּי יְהוּדָה אוֹמֵר: יִקָּבֵר. אָמְרוּ לוֹ לְרַבִּי יְהוּדָה: וּמָה, אִם מַעֲשֵׂר שֵׁנִי עַצְמוֹ שֶׁנִּטְמָא הֲרֵי הוּא נִפְדֶּה, הַלָּקוּחַ בְּכֶסֶף מַעֲשֵׂר שֵׁנִי שֶׁנִּטְמָא אֵינוֹ דִין שֶׁיִּפָּדֶה?!

---

[10] The previous Mishnah taught that *maaser sheni* produce that became *tamei* may be redeemed in Jerusalem. This Mishnah cites a dispute about whether this is also true if food that was bought with *maaser sheni* money became *tamei* in Jerusalem:[1]

הַלָּקוּחַ בְּכֶסֶף מַעֲשֵׂר שֵׁנִי שֶׁנִּטְמָא — If [food] bought with *maaser sheni* money became *tamei,* יִפָּדֶה — it may be redeemed, even in Jerusalem, just as actual *maaser sheni* may be redeemed when *tamei.* רַבִּי יְהוּדָה אוֹמֵר — But R' Yehudah says: יִקָּבֵר — It may not be redeemed; rather, it must be buried. According to R' Yehudah, once *maaser sheni* funds have been used to buy food, the *maaser sheni* sanctity may not be transferred another time.[2] If the food cannot be eaten because it is *tamei,* it must be buried.[3]

The Sages (i.e., the Tanna Kamma) challenge R' Yehudah's opinion:

אָמְרוּ לוֹ לְרַבִּי יְהוּדָה — [The Sages] said to R' Yehudah: It is logical to say that the purchased food may be redeemed if it becomes *tamei.* וּמָה אִם מַעֲשֵׂר שֵׁנִי עַצְמוֹ שֶׁנִּטְמָא הֲרֵי הוּא נִפְדֶּה — For if actual *maaser sheni* that became *tamei* may be redeemed, as we learned in the previous Mishnah, הַלָּקוּחַ בְּכֶסֶף מַעֲשֵׂר שֵׁנִי שֶׁנִּטְמָא אֵינוֹ דִין שֶׁיִּפָּדֶה — is it not logical that if [food]

--- NOTES ---

tamei from an *av hatumah* while outside Jerusalem; (b) from an *av hatumah* inside Jerusalem; (c) from a secondary *tumah* outside Jerusalem; and (d) from a secondary *tumah* inside Jerusalem. Beis Shammai rule that in cases (b), (c), and (d), the *maaser sheni* must be redeemed and eaten in Jerusalem, while in case (a) it may be redeemed and eaten anywhere. Beis Hillel rule that in cases (a), (b), and (c), the *maaser sheni* may be redeemed and eaten even outside of Jerusalem [in case (c) this applies only where, when the owner brought it into the city, he stipulated that he be allowed to remove it]; while in case (d) it must be redeemed and eaten in Jerusalem.

[10]

1. In general, food bought with *maaser sheni* money has the same status as *maaser sheni* produce. Thus, as long as the purchased food is *tahor,* it may not be redeemed in Jerusalem, just as *maaser sheni* produce may not be redeemed in Jerusalem. If the purchased food becomes *tamei,* though, there is a dispute what is to be done with it.

2. The Torah says that *maaser sheni* produce may be redeemed for money and that money used to buy food. Once that has been done, maintains R' Yehudah, the mitzvah has been completed. The Torah does not allow for the sanctity to be transferred another time (*Rav*).

3. Since the food may not be eaten (because it is *tamei*), nor may it be redeemed, it is of no use at all. R' Yehudah fears that if it were simply left to rot, someone might accidentally eat it. To prevent this, they decreed that it must be buried (see *Mishnah Rishonah*).

אָמַר לָהֶם: לֹא! אִם אֲמַרְתֶּם בְּמַעֲשֵׂר שֵׁנִי עַצְמוֹ, שֶׁכֵּן הוּא נִפְדֶּה בְּטָהוֹר בְּרָחוֹק מָקוֹם; תֹּאמְרוּ בְּלָקוּחַ בְּכֶסֶף מַעֲשֵׂר, שֶׁאֵינוֹ נִפְדֶּה בְּטָהוֹר בְּרָחוֹק מָקוֹם?

[יא] **צְבִי** שֶׁלְּקָחוֹ בְּכֶסֶף מַעֲשֵׂר, וָמֵת,

— רע"ב —

שֶׁכֵּן נִפְדָה טָהוֹר בְּרָחוֹק מָקוֹם. שֶׁמַּעֲשֵׂר שֵׁנִי פּוֹדִין אוֹתוֹ כְּשֶׁהוּא טָהוֹר חוּץ לִירוּשָׁלַיִם, כִּדְכְתִיב (דברים יד) וְכִי יִרְחַק מִמְּךָ הַמָּקוֹם וְגוֹ׳. אֲבָל הַלָּקוּחַ בְּכֶסֶף מַעֲשֵׂר אֵינוֹ נִפְדֶּה חוּץ לִירוּשָׁלַיִם כְּשֶׁהוּא טָהוֹר, דְּתַנַן לְעֵיל בַּפֶּרֶק קַמָּא מֵבִיא וְאוֹכְלוֹ בַּמָּקוֹם. וְאֵין הֲלָכָה כְּרַבִּי יְהוּדָה:

---

bought with *maaser sheni* **money became** *tamei,* **it may be redeemed?** In other words, it makes sense to say that actual *maaser sheni* produce has stricter laws than food that got its sanctity by being bought with money on which such produce was redeemed.[4] Since the actual produce may be redeemed if *tamei,* is it not logical that the purchased food may be redeemed if *tamei?*

R' Yehudah rejects the Sages' argument:

אָמַר לָהֶם — **[R' Yehudah] said to them:** לֹא — **No, that is not a valid argument.** אִם אֲמַרְתֶּם בְּמַעֲשֵׂר שֵׁנִי עַצְמוֹ — **Although you say that actual** *maaser sheni* **may be redeemed when it is** *tamei,* **it also has another leniency with regard to its redemption; namely,** שֶׁכֵּן הוּא נִפְדֶּה בְּטָהוֹר בְּרָחוֹק מָקוֹם — **that it may be redeemed when it is** *tahor* **if it is at a distance from "the place"** (i.e., before it arrives in Jerusalem).[5] תֹּאמְרוּ בְּלָקוּחַ בְּכֶסֶף מַעֲשֵׂר שֶׁאֵינוֹ נִפְדֶה בְּטָהוֹר בְּרָחוֹק מָקוֹם — **Will you say** that the same laws apply **to [food] that was bought with** *maaser sheni* **money,** which does not have this leniency; namely, it **may** *not* **be redeemed when** it is ***tahor*** **if it is at a distance from "the place"?**[6] In other words, with regard to redemption, *maaser sheni* produce is in fact treated more leniently than food purchased with *maaser sheni* funds. Therefore, it is likely that here too — with regard to redeeming *tamei maaser sheni* in Jerusalem — *maaser sheni* produce is treated more leniently than food purchased with *maaser sheni* funds.

[11] Having cited a dispute about food bought with *maaser sheni* money, the Mishnah cites three disputes concerning an animal bought with *maaser sheni* money. The first dispute:

צְבִי שֶׁלְּקָחוֹ בְּכֶסֶף מַעֲשֵׂר וָמֵת — **If a deer was bought with** *maaser sheni* **money**

NOTES

4. See *Meleches Shlomo.*

5. "The place" refers to Jerusalem; see Mishnah 1:5 note 4.

6. As we learned in Mishnah 1:5, *maaser sheni* funds may not be spent on food outside Jerusalem but only in Jerusalem. Thus, with regard to redeeming food for money, *maaser sheni* produce is treated more leniently: produce may be exchanged for money outside Jerusalem, while food bought with such money may be purchased only in Jerusalem.

[55] MISHNAH MAASER SHENI / Chapter 3: Lo Yomar

- רע״ב -

(יא) על ידי עורו. עס
עורו: רבי שמעון אומר
יפדה. ובהא קמיפלגי,
דתנא קמא סבר אין
פודין את הקדשים

יִקָּבֵר עַל יְדֵי עוֹרוֹ. רַבִּי שִׁמְעוֹן אוֹמֵר: יִפָּדֶה.
לְקָחוּ חַי וּשְׁחָטוֹ, וְנִטְמָא, יִפָּדֶה; רַבִּי יוֹסֵי
אוֹמֵר: יִקָּבֵר.

להאכילן לכלבים, ורבי שמעון סבר פודין את הקדשים להאכילן לכלבים. ואין הלכה כרבי שמעון:
לקחו חי ושחטו ונטמא יפדה. הכא לא פליג רבי יהודה כדפליג לעיל בפירות הלקוחים בכסף
מעשר ונטמאו, דכיון דלקחו חי אין לו ריחוק מקום לפי שיכול להוליכו לכל מקום שירצה, הלכך
הוי כמעשר שני עצמו. ונפדה כשנטמא, כדרך שנפדה מעשר שני כשנטמא: **רבי יוסי אומר יקבר.**
דמחמיר טפי מרבי יהודה, וסבר דאף על פי שקנאו חי דינו כפירות הלקוחים בכסף מעשר:

יִקָּבֵר עַל יְדֵי עוֹרוֹ — it must be buried together with its hide. **and it died,**
Since the deer died without being properly slaughtered, it is forbidden to be eaten and is suitable only to be fed to dogs. Since we have a principle that sacred items (such as meat bought with *maaser sheni* money) may not be redeemed if they will then be fed to animals, the carcass of the deer may not be redeemed but must be buried.[1] **רַבִּי שִׁמְעוֹן אוֹמֵר** — But **R' Shimon says: יִפָּדֶה** — It may be redeemed. In R' Shimon's opinion, it is permitted to redeem a sacred item even if it will then be fed to animals, and thus the carcass may be redeemed.

The second dispute:

לְקָחוּ חַי וּשְׁחָטוֹ וְנִטְמָא — If someone bought [a deer] live and then slaughtered it, and [its meat] became *tamei*,[2] **יִפָּדֶה** — it may be redeemed. Since the deer was slaughtered and thus fit to be eaten when it became *tamei*, it has the same law as food bought with *maaser sheni* money that became *tamei*, which may be redeemed.[3] **רַבִּי יוֹסֵי אוֹמֵר** — But **R' Yose says: יִקָּבֵר** — It must be buried, because in R' Yose's opinion, any food bought with *maaser sheni* money that became *tamei* may not be redeemed, but must be buried.[4]

NOTES

[11]

1. The animal's meat and its hide have *maaser sheni* sanctity. Since the meat may not be eaten or redeemed, it must be buried (see note 3 to the previous Mishnah). The hide must be buried too, because the hide of a *maaser sheni* animal is permitted for use only after the animal is eaten properly. Since this animal cannot be eaten, its hide will never be permitted for use and must be buried (see *Derech Emunah, Hilchos Maaser Sheni* 8:46).

[Although we learned in Mishnah 1:3 that when a deer is bought with *maaser sheni* funds, its hide does not take on sanctity, that is only when the meat is eaten. When the meat is not eaten, as in this Mishnah's case, the hide does take on sanctity; see Mishnah 1:6 note 3;

Derech Emunah, Hilchos Maaser Sheni 8:6, *Beur HaHalachah* ד״ה יקבר בעורו.]

2. [This can happen only after it is slaughtered, because a living animal cannot become *tamei*. It can only become *tamei* once its meat takes on the status of food, which happens after it is slaughtered (*Rambam, Hilchos Tumas Ochalin* 2:6).]

3. The previous Mishnah cited a dispute about this law. The Tanna Kamma follows the opinion of the Sages there, that such food may be redeemed.

4. In the previous Mishnah, R' Yehudah ruled that food bought with *maaser sheni* funds may not be redeemed in Jerusalem if it becomes *tamei*. R' Yose essentially holds like R' Yehudah's opinion and thus the meat of this deer may not be redeemed. However, in this particular

[56] **משניות מעשר שני / פרק ג: לא יאמר**

לָקְחוּ שָׁחוּט, וְנִטְמָא, הֲרֵי הוּא כְּפֵרוֹת.

[יב] הַמַּשְׁאִיל קַנְקַנִּין לְמַעֲשֵׂר שֵׁנִי, אַף עַל פִּי שֶׁגְּפָנָן, לֹא קָנָה מַעֲשֵׂר. זָלַף לְתוֹכָן סְתָם, עַד שֶׁלֹּא גָפָן, לֹא קָנָה מַעֲשֵׂר. מִשֶּׁגְּפָנָן, קָנָה מַעֲשֵׂר.

— רע"ב —

לקחו שחוט ונטמא הרי הוא כפיר ת. וכי היכי דאיפליגו תנא קמא ורבי יהודה לעיל בפירות הלקוחים בכסף מעשר, הכי נמי אפליגו בהא: (יב) המשאיל קנקנים למעשר שני. מי שמשאיל קנקניו להכניס בהן יין שקרא

לו כבר שם מעשר שני: אף על פי שגפנן. שסתם פיהן במגופה אחר שמלאן: לא קנה מעשר. לא נתפס הקנקן בקדושת מעשר: זלף לתוכן סתם. שהכניס לתוכן יין של טבל קודם שקרא לו שם מעשר: עד שלא גפן. אם קרא לו שם מעשר קודם שסתמן במגופה: אם משגפנן: אם לאחר שסתמן במגופה קרא שם מעשר: קנה מעשר. נתפס הקנקן בקדושת מעשר, וטעון חלול כמו היין, אם בא לחללו על הכסף:

The third dispute:

לָקְחוּ שָׁחוּט וְנִטְמָא — **If someone bought [a deer] that was already slaughtered and [its meat] then became** *tamei,* הֲרֵי הוּא כְּפֵרוֹת — **it is like** any **produce** or food bought with *maaser sheni* money, which is subject to the dispute of the previous Mishnah: according to the Sages, it may be redeemed; according to R' Yehudah, it must be buried. Since he bought the deer after it was slaughtered, it is simply considered meat, and is treated like any other food.

[12] The Mishnah discusses whether a container filled with *maaser sheni* takes on *maaser sheni* sanctity:

הַמַּשְׁאִיל קַנְקַנִּין לְמַעֲשֵׂר שֵׁנִי — **Someone lends his containers for** the storage of *maaser sheni* wine, and the containers are filled with wine. אַף עַל פִּי שֶׁגְּפָנָן — **Even though he closed [the containers]** after filling them, לֹא קָנָה מַעֲשֵׂר — the *maaser sheni* **does not acquire** the containers, that is, the containers do not take on *maaser sheni* sanctity.[1]
זָלַף לְתוֹכָן סְתָם — If, however, **someone poured ordinary** (i.e., untithed) **wine into [the containers],** and then designated the wine as *maaser sheni,* the status of the containers depends on the following: עַד שֶׁלֹּא גָפָן — **If he designated** the wine as *maaser sheni* **before he closed [the containers],** לֹא קָנָה מַעֲשֵׂר — the *maaser sheni* **does not acquire** the containers and they remain *chullin.* מִשֶּׁגְּפָנָן — **But if he designated** the wine as *maaser sheni* **after he closed [the containers],** קָנָה מַעֲשֵׂר — the *maaser sheni* **does acquire** the containers,

---
NOTES
---

case, R' Yehudah actually disagrees with R' Yose and holds like the Tanna Kamma of our Mishnah. This is because R' Yehudah holds, based on his interpretation of a verse in the Torah, that when *maaser sheni* money is spent on a live animal, its meat may always be redeemed (see *Rav;* but see *Meleches Shlomo*).

There are thus three opinions regarding food, purchased with *maaser sheni* money, which became *tamei:* (a) The Sages hold that in all cases, the food may be redeemed. (b) R' Yehudah holds that all food must be buried, with the exception of meat from an animal bought live. If a live animal was bought, slaughtered, and then became *tamei,* its meat may be redeemed. (c) R' Yose holds that in all cases, the *tamei* food must be buried.

[12]
1. See the following note.

[57] MISHNAH MAASER SHENI / Chapter 3: Lo Yomar

עוֹלוֹת בְּאֶחָד וּמֵאָה.   עַד שֶׁלֹּא גָפָן, עוֹלוֹת בְּאֶחָד וּמֵאָה. וּמִשֶּׁגְּפָן,
בְּשֶׁל תְּרוּמָה אַיְירֵי,
אִם נִתְעָרֵב קַנְקַן   מְקֻדָּשׁוֹת בְּכָל שֶׁהֵן.
שֶׁל תְּרוּמָה בְּמֵאָה

קַנְקַנִּים שֶׁל חוּלִּין, וְלֹא הָיָה פִּיהֶן סָתוּם בִּמְגוּפָה, תֵּשָׁבֵין לְהוֹ כְּאִילּוּ כּוּלָן מְעוֹרָבוֹת זוֹ בָּזוּ, וְעוֹלוֹת בְּאֶחָד וּמֵאָה כְּדִין תְּרוּמָה שֶׁנִּתְעָרְבָה בְּחוּלִּין: **מִשֶּׁגְפָן מְקֻדָּשׁוֹת בְּכָל שֶׁהֵן.** וַאֲפִילוּ אֶחָד בְּאֶלֶף אֵינָן עוֹלוֹת, וְיִמָּכְרוּ כּוּלָן לַכֹּהֵן בִּדְמֵי תְּרוּמָה, חוּץ מֵאַחַת שֶׁבָּהֶן שֶׁנּוֹטְלָהּ הַכֹּהֵן בְּלֹא דָמִים:

---

and they take on *maaser sheni* sanctity along with the wine inside them. Once the containers are closed, the wine and its container are considered a single unit, with the container subordinate to the wine. Accordingly, when the wine becomes *maaser sheni,* the container takes on sanctity as well.[2]

The Mishnah turns to other laws involving containers filled with consecrated liquids, where the status of the containers depends on whether they are open or closed. The first case involves jugs of *terumah* wine that became mixed up with jugs of ordinary wine. As a rule, if *terumah* becomes mixed up with *chullin,* the entire mixture must be treated as *terumah* unless there is 100 times more *chullin* than *terumah.*[3] If there is 100 times more *chullin* than *terumah,* the *terumah* becomes nullified and the entire mixture is treated as *chullin.* The Mishnah discusses how this relates to a situation where a container of *terumah* wine became mixed up with containers of *chullin* wine:

עַד שֶׁלֹּא גָפָן — If containers of *terumah* wine became lost among *chullin* containers **before he closed [the containers],** עוֹלוֹת בְּאֶחָד וּמֵאָה — [the *terumah* containers] **are nullified in** a proportion of **one hundred to one;** that is, if there are one hundred parts of *chullin* wine to one part of *terumah* wine, the *terumah* is nullified and all the containers are permitted to a non-Kohen. וּמִשֶּׁגְּפָן — **But** if the *terumah* containers were lost among the *chullin* containers **after he closed them,** מְקֻדָּשׁוֹת בְּכָל שֶׁהֵן — [the *terumah* containers] **prohibit** the entire mixture **even in the smallest amount.** Even if one closed barrel of *terumah* wine is mixed up with one thousand barrels of *chullin* wine, the entire mixture must be treated as *terumah.* This is because a closed container of wine is considered an important object, and an important object can never be nullified, no matter how much *chullin* it is mixed up with.[4]

--- NOTES ---

2. Thus, if he wants to redeem the *maaser sheni* wine, he must redeem the value of its container as well (*Rav*). For example, if the wine is worth 10 *shekels* and the container is worth 5 *shekels,* he must redeem them for 15 *shekels,* which he will spend on food in Jerusalem. [If he chooses instead to bring the wine to Jerusalem and drink it there, the containers remain sanctified until the wine is consumed, and then they automatically return to *chullin* status (*Meleches Shlomo*).]

In the Mishnah's first case, though, a person poured wine into a container after the wine was already designated as *maaser sheni.* In that case, the container does not take on *maaser sheni* sanctity, even if he later closes it. The container can take on sanctity only if the wine is consecrated as *maaser sheni* when the container is subordinate to it.

3. See *Terumos* 4:7.

4. If the containers are open, the container and the wine are each considered a separate item. Therefore, the wine is treated like any other *terumah* wine that was mixed with *chullin* wine; that is, it is nullified if there is a proportion of 100 to

משניות מעשר שני / פרק ג: לא יאמר

עַד שֶׁלֹּא גֵפָן, תּוֹרֵם מֵאַחַת עַל הַכֹּל. וּמִשֶּׁגֵּפָן, תּוֹרֵם מִכָּל אַחַת וְאֶחָת.

[יג] **בֵּית** שַׁמַּאי אוֹמְרִים, מִפְתֵּחַ וּמְעָרֶה לַגַּת. וּבֵית הִלֵּל אוֹמְרִים,

- רע"ב -

עד שלא גפן תורם מאחת על הכל. דחשיב מוקף: (יג) מפתח ומערה לגת. אם בא לתרום מאחת על הכל אחר שגפן, צריך לערותן לגת:

In the next case, a person has several containers of *tevel* (untithed) wine, and he wishes to separate *terumah* from them. The rule is that when a person separates part of his produce as *terumah,* that *terumah* must be touching or near the produce for which it is being designated.[5] The Mishnah discusses how this applies to containers of wine:

עַד שֶׁלֹּא גֵפָן — **Before someone closes [his containers of wine],** תּוֹרֵם מֵאַחַת עַל הַכֹּל — **he may separate** *terumah* **from one** container **for all** the others. If the containers are open, the wine inside them is considered "near" all the other wine in the room, and the *terumah* can be taken from one barrel for all the rest. וּמִשֶּׁגֵּפָן — **However, after he closes [the containers],** תּוֹרֵם מִכָּל אַחַת וְאֶחָת — **he must separate** *terumah* **from each [container]** separately. Once the barrels are closed, each barrel is considered its own unit, unconnected to any other barrels in the room, and thus *terumah* cannot be taken from one barrel for another.

[13] The previous Mishnah taught that a person may not separate *terumah* from the wine in one closed container on behalf of wine in another closed container. This Mishnah discusses a case where a person has already closed his barrels of wine and now wishes to separate *terumah* from one barrel on behalf of the others:

בֵּית שַׁמַּאי אוֹמְרִים — **Beis Shammai say:** If someone closed his barrels of wine but now wished to separate *terumah* from the wine in one barrel on behalf of the wine in the others, מִפְתֵּחַ וּמְעָרֶה לַגַּת — **he must open** all the barrels **and pour** the wine back **into the winepress.** It is not enough to merely reopen the containers; he must combine all the wine into a single vat; only then may he separate one portion of *terumah* for all the wine.[1] וּבֵית הִלֵּל אוֹמְרִים — **But**

--- NOTES ---

one. If the containers are closed, though, the container and wine are considered a single unit. Such a unit of container and wine is regarded as an important object [דָּבָר חָשׁוּב], and an important object can never be nullified, no matter how much *chullin* it is mixed up with (*Orlah* 3:7). Therefore, all the containers must be treated as *terumah* and may be used only by a Kohen (*Rav, Rash*).

5. For example, a person has two piles of grain. If the piles are next to each other, he may separate *terumah* from one pile on behalf of the produce in both piles.

If, however, the piles are not near each other, *terumah* taken from one pile cannot satisfy the *terumah* obligation of the other pile. *Terumah* must be separated from each pile (see further, *Challah* 1:9; *Bikkurim* 2:5).

[13]

1. After the containers are closed, the wine in each container is not considered "near" the wine in the other containers (see the previous Mishnah). Beis Shammai hold that in order to restore the state of "nearness," all the wine must be poured into a single vat.

[59] MISHNAH MAASER SHENI / Chapter 3: Lo Yomar

- רע״ב -

מְפַתֵּחַ וְאֵינוֹ צָרִיךְ לְעָרוֹת. בַּמֶּה דְבָרִים אֲמוּרִים, בִּמְקוֹם שֶׁדַּרְכָּן לִמְכֹּר סְתוּמוֹת. אֲבָל בִּמְקוֹם שֶׁדַּרְכָּן לִמְכֹּר פְּתוּחוֹת, לֹא יָצָא קַנְקַן לְחֻלִּין.

ואינו צריך לערות. דסגי להו בפתיחה כדמפרש קרא: במה דברים אמורים. דאם לאחר שגפן קרא שם, קנה מעשר את הקנקנים: במקום שדרכן למכור סתומות. דכי האי גוונא בירושלים הקנקן טפלה ליין כדתנן לעיל בפרק קמא, הלכך בגבולין נמי קנה מעשר: אבל במקום שדרכן למכור פתוחות לא יצא הקנקן לחולין. בירושלים, [ובגבולין] הלכך, נמי לא קנה מעשר:

Beis Hillel say: מְפַתֵּחַ וְאֵינוֹ צָרִיךְ לְעָרוֹת — **He may** just **open the containers; he does not need to pour** all the wine back into the winepress.[2]

The Mishnah returns to the laws about containers that are filled with *maaser sheni* wine. The previous Mishnah taught that if someone designated *tevel* wine as *maaser sheni* after its container was closed, the container itself also becomes sanctified as *maaser sheni*. This Mishnah now limits that ruling:

בַּמֶּה דְבָרִים אֲמוּרִים — **When were these words said?** When do containers of *maaser sheni* become sanctified along with their contents (if designated as *maaser sheni* after the container is closed)? בִּמְקוֹם שֶׁדַּרְכָּן לִמְכֹּר סְתוּמוֹת — **In a place where it is common to sell** wine in **closed [containers].** In such a place, a container is generally included in a sale of wine, and therefore, a wine's container is considered subordinate to the wine. Because of this, the container can take on *maaser sheni* sanctity along with the wine.

The Mishnah now discusses when the above rule does not apply. To do so, the Mishnah repeats a law stated in Mishnah 1:4, with regard to a person who uses *maaser sheni* funds to buy wine in a container. The Mishnah there discussed whether the container takes on *maaser sheni* sanctity:

אֲבָל בִּמְקוֹם שֶׁדַּרְכָּן לִמְכֹּר פְּתוּחוֹת — **But in a place where it is common to sell** wine in **open [containers],** that is, the wine is usually measured out and sold without a container, if a person uses *maaser sheni* funds to buy wine with its container לֹא יָצָא קַנְקַן לְחֻלִּין — **the container does not become *chullin*,** that is, it takes on *maaser sheni* sanctity. Since a container is not usually included in a sale of wine and this sale does include a jug, it is as though the jug is being purchased separately with part of the *maaser sheni* money; since it is bought with *maaser sheni* money, it takes on *maaser sheni* sanctity. This law demonstrates that in such a place, a wine's container is *not* considered subordinate to the wine.[3] Accordingly, in our case — where a person designated wine in a closed container as *maaser sheni* — the container does not take on sanctity with the wine.

Having reviewed the rule that where wine is sold in open containers, the

---
NOTES

2. Beis Hillel hold that once the containers are opened, the wine in each container is once again considered "near" the wine in the other containers.

3. If it were subordinate to the wine, it would not be regarded as being purchased separately but would rather be included in the sale of the wine; the ramifications of this are discussed in Mishnahs 1:3-4.

משניות מעשר שני / פרק ג: לא יאמר [60]

— רע״ב —

אֲבָל אִם רָצָה לְהַחֲמִיר עַל עַצְמוֹ לִמְכּוֹר בְּמִדָּה, יָצָא קַנְקַנּוֹ לְחֻלִּין. רַבִּי שִׁמְעוֹן אוֹמֵר, אַף הָאוֹמֵר לַחֲבֵרוֹ (חָבִית זוֹ) [יַיִן זֶה] אֲנִי מוֹכֵר לָךְ, חוּץ (מִקַּנְקַנִּים) [מִקַּנְקַנָּהּ], יָצָא קַנְקַנּוֹ לְחֻלִּין:

אבל אם רצה להחמיר על עצמו למכור במדה. הקונה יין ממעות מעשר שני בירושלים, וכשבא המוכר למכור רצה לדקדק על עצמו ואמר כך וכך יין במדה אני מוכר לך בכך וכך מעות: יצא קנקן לחולין. ואפילו הקנקנים סתומות: הכי גרסינן. רבי שמעון אומר אף האומר לחבירו יין זה אני מוכר לך חוץ מקנקנים יצא קנקן לחולין. ובירושלמי מפרש לה דרבי שמעון קאי אהא דתנא לעיל דאם משגפן קרא שם מעשר קנה מעשר. ואשמעינן רבי שמעון דוקא שקרא שם מעשר לכל היין שבקנקן, אבל אם אמר כל היין מעשר חוץ מרביעית, אף על פי שכשבא למדוד לחבירו אותו רביעית, אמר לו יין זה אני מוכר לך חוץ מן הקנקן שאני רוצה לשייר בשביל מעשר שבתוכה, אפילו הכי לא נעשית הקנקן טפלה למעשר, ויצא קנקן לחולין ולא קנה מעשר:

---

purchase of a container is viewed as its own purchase and the container takes on *maaser sheni* sanctity, the Mishnah gives an exception to that rule:

אֲבָל אִם רָצָה לְהַחֲמִיר עַל עַצְמוֹ לִמְכּוֹר בְּמִדָּה — **But if [the seller] wishes to conduct himself** more **precisely** and sell the wine by exact **measure** rather than by the container,[4] יָצָא קַנְקַנּוֹ לְחֻלִּין — **the container becomes** *chullin*, i.e., it is not sanctified as *maaser sheni*. Since the seller specifies a price for the exact measure of wine in the container, he implies that the container itself is not included in the sale. If he gives the buyer the container, it is as a free gift in addition to his purchase of wine. Since it was not bought with the *maaser sheni* money, it does not take on sanctity.

The next Tanna returns to the previous subject and teaches another exception to the rule stated in Mishnah 12 (that when wine in a closed container is sanctified as *maaser sheni*, the container becomes sanctified as well):

רַבִּי שִׁמְעוֹן אוֹמֵר — **R' Shimon says:** A person designated most of the wine in a closed container as *maaser sheni*, but left over some wine as *chullin*.[5] (חָבִית זוֹ) אַף הָאוֹמֵר לַחֲבֵרוֹ — **Even if [this person] says to his friend,** [יַיִן זֶה] אֲנִי מוֹכֵר לָךְ, חוּץ (מִקַּנְקַנִּים) [מִקַּנְקַנָּהּ] — **"I am selling you this** *chullin* **wine without its container,**[6] since I need the container to hold the *maaser sheni* wine that remains in it," יָצָא קַנְקַנּוֹ לְחֻלִּין — **the container becomes** *chullin*, i.e., it is not sanctified as *maaser sheni*. Even though the seller specified that he is keeping the container for the exclusive use of the *maaser sheni* wine, the container does not become sanctified as *maaser sheni*, because when he designated the wine as *maaser sheni*, the container also held *chullin* wine. Only a closed container that holds nothing but *maaser sheni* wine can take on *maaser sheni* sanctity along with its contents.

NOTES

4. Generally, wine was sold by the jug or barrel. This seller sells it by a more precise measurement: by exact amounts, for example, 10 ounces for a *dinar* (see *Rav*).

5. He designated the wine in his closed container as *maaser sheni* but stipulated that a small portion of the wine should remain *chullin*. The container thus holds both *chullin* wine and *maaser sheni* wine (*Rav*).

6. [*Rav* changes the text of the Mishnah from חָבִית זוֹ, *this barrel*, to יַיִן זֶה, *this wine*; and מְקַנְקַנִּים, *containers*, to מִקַּנְקַנָּהּ, *its container*.]

Chapter Four

משניות מעשר שני / פרק ד: המוליך

[א] הַמּוֹלִיךְ פֵּרוֹת מַעֲשֵׂר שֵׁנִי מִמְּקוֹם הַיֹּקֶר לִמְקוֹם הַזּוֹל, אוֹ מִמְּקוֹם הַזּוֹל לִמְקוֹם הַיֹּקֶר, פּוֹדֵהוּ כְּשַׁעַר מְקוֹמוֹ. הַמֵּבִיא פֵּרוֹת מִן הַגֹּרֶן לָעִיר, וְכַדֵּי יַיִן מִן הַגַּת לָעִיר, הַשֶּׁבַח לַשֵּׁנִי וִיצִיאוֹת מִבֵּיתוֹ.

— רע"ב —

פרק רביעי. המוליך. (א) המוליך. דוקא עבר והוליך, דלכתחילה אסור להוליכו ממקום למקום, אלא פודהו במקומו או מעלהו לירושלים: **בשער מקומו.** כשער המקום שהוא בשעת פדיון בין לקולא בין לחומרא: **השבח לשני.** מה שׁשוין בעיר יותר, הריוח של מעשר שני. ומה שהוליא להביאן מן השדה לעיר ישלם מביתו:

---

[1] Most of this chapter discusses the redemption of *maaser sheni* produce, that is, exchanging the produce for money. The produce becomes *chullin*, while the money takes on *maaser sheni* sanctity and must be spent on food in Jerusalem. When a person redeems his *maaser sheni* produce, he must redeem it for its market price.[1] This Mishnah discusses how to determine that price if the produce is moved between different places in which the market price is not the same:

הַמּוֹלִיךְ פֵּרוֹת מַעֲשֵׂר שֵׁנִי מִמְּקוֹם הַיֹּקֶר לִמְקוֹם הַזּוֹל — **If someone takes** *maaser sheni* **produce from a place where [that produce] is expensive to a place where it is cheap,**[2] אוֹ מִמְּקוֹם הַזּוֹל לִמְקוֹם הַיֹּקֶר — **or from a place where it is cheap to a place where it is expensive,** פּוֹדֵהוּ כְּשַׁעַר מְקוֹמוֹ — **he redeems it for the market price in its** current **location;** that is, the location where he performs the redemption, whether that price is high or low.[3]

הַמֵּבִיא פֵּרוֹת מִן הַגֹּרֶן לָעִיר — **Similarly, someone brings** *maaser sheni* **produce from the threshing floor,** where it was processed, **to the city,** where it will be stored; וְכַדֵּי יַיִן מִן הַגַּת לָעִיר — **or, someone brings jugs of** *maaser sheni* **wine from the winepress,** where it was processed, **to the city,** where it will be stored. Since food sells for a higher price in the city than at the fields or winepresses,[4] הַשֶּׁבַח לַשֵּׁנִי — **the additional value** that it has in the city is added **to the** *maaser sheni;* in other words, it must be redeemed at the city price. וִיצִיאוֹת מִבֵּיתוֹ — **And the expense** of bringing it to the city is paid **from [the owner's] assets;** he may not deduct this expense from the value of the produce when he redeems it.[5]

NOTES
---

[1]

1. Sometimes, an added fee is necessary as well, as we will learn in Mishnah 3.

2. Ideally, a person should not carry *maaser sheni* from place to place [because doing so gives the impression that he is searching for the cheapest place to redeem it (*Derech Emunah, Hilchos Maaser Sheni* 4:144)]. He should either redeem it in its original place, or bring it to Jerusalem. The Mishnah refers to a person who moved it unlawfully from one place to another (*Rav*).

3. If the produce is in one location and the money is in another (see Mishnah 3:4), it is redeemed for the market price where the produce is (*Rosh*).

4. *Rambam Commentary.*

5. Even though he caused the produce to go up in value by bringing it to the city, he may not deduct the expenses of bringing it there from its redemption price. It must be redeemed for its full city value.

He may not deduct his expenses even though it is permissible and necessary to transfer the produce to the city for

[63] **MISHNAH MAASER SHENI** / Chapter 4: *Hamolich* 4/2

- רע״ב -

[ב] **פּוֹדִין** מַעֲשֵׂר שֵׁנִי כְּשַׁעַר הַזּוֹל, כְּמוֹת שֶׁהַחֶנְוָנִי לוֹקֵחַ, לֹא כְמוֹת שֶׁהוּא מוֹכֵר. כְּמוֹת שֶׁהַשֻּׁלְחָנִי פּוֹרֵט, וְלֹא כְּמוֹת שֶׁהוּא מְצָרֵף.

(ב) פודין מעשר שני. יכול לפדות אם ירצה כשער הזול, כדמפרש ואזיל: **כמות שהחנווני לוקח.** שהוא לוקח בזול כדי להשתכר: **לא כמות שהוא מוכר.** שהוא מוכר ביוקר ביותר ממה שקנה: **כמות שהשולחני פורט.** הבא לחלל פרוטות של מעשר על סלע, מחשב הסלע בפרוטות הרבה, כשולחני הזה כשבא ליקח פרוטות מבני אדם ונותן להם סלע לוקח פרוטות הרבה: **ולא כמות שהוא מצרף.** כשמצרף השולחני פרוטות לתת לבני אדם בחלוף הסלע, נותן להם פחות:

---

[2] Even in a single location, the wholesale price for produce will be less than its retail price. The Mishnah specifies which price is used when redeeming *maaser sheni*:

פּוֹדִין מַעֲשֵׂר שֵׁנִי כְּשַׁעַר הַזּוֹל — One may redeem *maaser sheni* produce at the cheap rate, **כְּמוֹת שֶׁהַחֶנְוָנִי לוֹקֵחַ** — that is, the lower, wholesale price that the merchant pays to buy goods from his suppliers; **לֹא כְמוֹת שֶׁהוּא מוֹכֵר** — one need not redeem the *maaser sheni* at the higher, retail price at which [the merchant] sells goods to his customers.[1]

A similar leniency applies when a person transfers the sanctity of *maaser sheni* coins of one denomination onto coins of another denomination:[2]

כְּמוֹת שֶׁהַשֻּׁלְחָנִי פּוֹרֵט — A person may exchange his *maaser sheni* coins at the rate that the moneychanger uses when he takes change, that is, when he takes a number of small coins and gives a larger one in exchange, **וְלֹא כְּמוֹת שֶׁהוּא מְצָרֵף** — and not at the rate that [the moneychanger] uses when he combines coins, that is, when he gives a number of small coins in exchange for a larger one. For example, a moneychanger might charge 25 *maos* (small silver coins) for a *sela*, but when he gives *maos* in exchange for a *sela*, he will give only 24 *maos* for one *sela*.[3] A person who exchanges his *maaser sheni* coins may use the higher rate of 25 *maos* per *sela*.[4]

--- NOTES ---

storage. He certainly may not deduct expenses in the Mishnah's first case, where he was not allowed to transfer the produce in the first place (*Tos. Yom Tov*).

[2]

1. This law is derived from the Torah's reference to *maaser sheni* as the product of blessing (*Devarim* 14:24). This reference implies that *maaser sheni* may be redeemed for the cheapest available price, since when produce is blessed, it is abundant and therefore inexpensive (*Yerushalmi*, as explained by *Rash Sirilio*).

2. If a person transferred his *maaser sheni* to small coins, he might want to exchange them for larger coins, so he will

have fewer coins to carry to Jerusalem (see Mishnah 2:8). The Mishnah explains how to determine the rate of exchange.

3. A *sela* is worth 24 *maos* (*Kiddushin* 12a). However, when a moneychanger "buys" *maos* (that is, when he takes a customer's *maos* in exchange for a *sela*), he charges an extra coin as his fee, thus taking 25 *maos* per *sela*. When he "sells" *maos* (that is, when he gives *maos* in exchange for a *sela*), he charges their true value: 24 *maos* per *sela* (see *Rambam Commentary*; *Derech Emunah, Hilchos Maaser Sheni* 4:115; see also *Rash Sirilio*).

4. This is a leniency, since he may exchange 25 *maos* of *maaser sheni* for a single *sela*. If he would use the lower

משניות מעשר שני / פרק ד: המוליך [64]

וְאֵין פּוֹדִין מַעֲשֵׂר שֵׁנִי אַכְסָרָה. אֶת שֶׁדָּמָיו יְדוּעִים, יִפָּדֶה עַל פִּי עֵד אֶחָד. וְאֶת שֶׁאֵין דָּמָיו יְדוּעִים, יִפָּדֶה עַל פִּי שְׁלֹשָׁה, כְּגוֹן הַיַּיִן שֶׁקָּרַם וּפֵרוֹת שֶׁהִרְקִיבוּ וּמָעוֹת שֶׁהֶחֱלִיאוּ.

– רע״ב –

אכסרה. בְּלֹא מִדָּה וּבְלֹא מִשְׁקָל, אֶלָּא כַּמָּה אַתָּה נוֹתֵן בְּכְרִי זֶה אוֹ בִּמְלוֹא חָפְנַיִם הַלָּלוּ: על פי א׳. בְּשׁוּמַת לוֹקֵחַ אֶחָד: על פי ג׳. שַׁמָּאִים בְּקִיאִין, וַאֲפִלּוּ א׳ מֵהֶן עוֹבֵד כּוֹכָבִים

ד/ב

וַאֲפִלּוּ אֶחָד מֵהֶן בְּעָלִים: קרם. הִתְחִיל לְהַחֲמִיץ, וְגִירְסָא אַחֶרֶת שֶׁקָּסַם. וְדוּגְמָתוֹ בְּבָבָא בַתְרָא (דף נג, ב) מְקַבֵּל עָלָיו עֶשֶׂר קוּסְסוֹת לְמָאָה:

Some more laws about how a person may determine the value of his *maaser sheni*:

וְאֵין פּוֹדִין מַעֲשֵׂר שֵׁנִי אַכְסָרָה — **One may not redeem** *maaser sheni* **by estimating** its value.[5] אֶת שֶׁדָּמָיו יְדוּעִים יִפָּדֶה עַל פִּי עֵד אֶחָד — **Rather, [produce] that has a known value** in the market **must be redeemed based on** the precise assessment of **one witness,** that is, the word of a merchant who is familiar with the market prices.[6] וְאֶת שֶׁאֵין דָּמָיו יְדוּעִים יִפָּדֶה עַל פִּי שְׁלֹשָׁה — **And [produce] that has no known value** in the market, for which additional expertise is needed to assess its value, **must be redeemed based on** the precise assessment of **three** merchants. כְּגוֹן הַיַּיִן שֶׁקָּרַם — **Examples** of items that haves no known value **are wine that** began **to sour,** וּפֵרוֹת שֶׁהִרְקִיבוּ — **or fruits that** began **to rot,** וּמָעוֹת שֶׁהֶחֱלִיאוּ — **or coins that** began **to corrode.** These have no readily known market value and thus must be assessed by three merchants.[7]

――――― NOTES ―――――

rate, he would have to provide a *sela* for every 24 *maos,* and it would thus cost him more *sela'im*. [The Mishnah refers to a person who exchanges his *maos* for his own *sela'im* (see *Rav*). If he goes to a moneychanger, he will have to use whatever the going rate is.]

When a person arrives in Jerusalem with large coins of *maaser sheni,* he exchanges them again — this time for smaller coins to buy food with (as we discussed in Mishnahs 2:8-9). Here too, he may use the more lenient rate of exchange. That is, he may go to a moneychanger to get smaller coins, even though the moneychanger will give him a lower rate than he originally used when he transferred his *maaser sheni* to these coins: he originally transferred 25 *maos* onto each *sela,* and now the moneychanger will give him only 24 *maos* for each *sela* (see *Rash;* see *Derech Emunah, Hilchos Maaser Sheni* 4:115).

5. Even though *maaser sheni* may be redeemed for the lower of two possible prices, that price must be determined precisely, not by estimate. If a person has an unknown quantity of *maaser sheni* produce, he may not determine its price by simply asking a storekeeper: "How much would you pay for this basket of produce?" (*Rav*). Similarly, when a person exchanges *maaser sheni* coins for coins of another denomination, he must determine the exact price for the number of coins he holds.

6. An expert merchant must verify the market price for this produce (*Rav, Tos. Yom Tov*). The owner then counts or weighs the produce and thus arrives at an exact price.

7. Produce, wine, or coins that have started to go bad do not have a standard price in the market, because their value depends on how much they have deteriorated. Clarifying this is not simple and thus requires three experts (*Rambam Commentary, Rash*).

[65] **MISHNAH MAASER SHENI** / Chapter 4: *Hamolich*   4/3

- רע״ב -

[ג] **בַּעַל** הַבַּיִת אוֹמֵר בְּסֶלַע וְאַחֵר אוֹמֵר בְּסֶלַע, בַּעַל הַבַּיִת קוֹדֵם, מִפְּנֵי שֶׁהוּא מוֹסִיף חֹמֶשׁ. בַּעַל הַבַּיִת אוֹמֵר בְּסֶלַע וְאַחֵר אוֹמֵר בְּסֶלַע וְאִסָּר, אֶת שֶׁל סֶלַע וְאִסָּר קוֹדֵם, מִפְּנֵי שֶׁהוּא מוֹסִיף עַל הַקֶּרֶן.

(ג) מפני שהוא מוסיף חומש. כדכתיב (ויקרא כז) ואם גאול יגאל איש ממעשרו, על שלו מוסיף חומש ולא על של חבירו: בסלע ואיסר. האיסר הוא א׳ ממשה ותשעים בסלע: מפני שהוא מוסיף על הקרן. ותוספת כל שהוא דקרן עדיפא, מפני שעל החומש יכול להערים כדתנן לקמן:

---

[3] When a person uses his own money to redeem his *maaser sheni*, the Torah states (*Vayikra* 27:31) that he must add a fee of one-fifth to its redemption price.[1] Sometimes, though, *maaser sheni* is redeemed by a person who is not the owner.[2] In that case, no fee is added. This Mishnah discusses a case where two people — the owner and a stranger — offer to redeem *maaser sheni*; who has precedence?

בַּעַל הַבַּיִת אוֹמֵר בְּסֶלַע — **If the owner says** that he will redeem his *maaser sheni* **for a** *sela*, וְאַחֵר אוֹמֵר בְּסֶלַע — **and someone else says** that he, too, will redeem it **for a** *sela*, בַּעַל הַבַּיִת קוֹדֵם — **the owner has priority** to redeem it, מִפְּנֵי שֶׁהוּא מוֹסִיף חֹמֶשׁ — **because he adds a fifth** to its redemption price. Thus, if the owner redeems it, more money will end up as *maaser sheni*. בַּעַל הַבַּיִת אוֹמֵר בְּסֶלַע — **However, if the owner says** that he will redeem the *maaser sheni* **for a** *sela*, וְאַחֵר אוֹמֵר בְּסֶלַע וְאִסָּר — **and someone else says** that he will redeem it **for a** *sela* **and an** *issar*, אֶת שֶׁל סֶלַע וְאִסָּר קוֹדֵם — **the one** who made the offer **of a** *sela* **and an** *issar* **has priority** to redeem it, מִפְּנֵי שֶׁהוּא מוֹסִיף עַל הַקֶּרֶן — **because he adds an** *issar* **to the principal,** i.e., to the *maaser sheni* itself. Although the owner adds a fifth — and ⅕ of a *sela* is much more than one *issar*[3] — that is only an additional fee and he might avoid paying it, while the other person will certainly pay the extra *issar* because he added it to the actual price of the *maaser sheni*.[4]

The Mishnah now explains who is considered an owner of *maaser sheni* with regard to adding a fifth:

--- NOTES ---

[3]

1. This "one-fifth" is ⅕ of the total after the fifth is added. For example, if the *maaser sheni* is worth 4 *dinars*, he redeems it for 5 *dinars*. The extra *dinar* is ⅕ of the total — although it is ¼ of the *maaser sheni's* value (*Tiferes Yisrael; Bava Metzia* 54a).

2. For example, someone uses his own money to redeem *maaser sheni* that belongs to someone else. (The owner of the *maaser sheni* must give the other person permission to do so.) The redeemed produce, which is now *chullin*, goes to the one who redeemed it; the coins, which are now *maaser sheni*, remain his as well and he must spend them on food in Jerusalem (*Derech Emunah, Hilchos Maaser Sheni* 5:37, 44, 46).

3. A *sela* is worth 96 *issars* (*Rav*). The owner, who adds a fifth, will end up paying 1 *sela* and 24 *issars*, while the other person will pay only 1 *sela* and 1 *issar*.

4. As we will learn in the next two Mishnahs, there are ways by which a person can avoid paying the extra fifth when redeeming his *maaser sheni*. [The other person, on the other hand, must pay the full amount that he bid] (*Rav*).

ד/ד

- רע"ב -

ובין שנתן לו במתנה. הטבל, קודם שהפריש ממנו מעשר נתן לו במתנה. דאילו מעשר שני לאחר שהופרש, קיימא לן כמאן דאמר ממון גבוה הוא ואינו ניתן במתנה: (ד) לעבדו ולשפחתו העברים. שאין גופו קנוי: ופדה לך. בהן מעשר שני לעצמך:

הַפּוֹדֶה מַעֲשֵׂר שֵׁנִי שֶׁלּוֹ, מוֹסִיף עָלָיו חֲמִישִׁית, בֵּין שֶׁהוּא שֶׁלּוֹ וּבֵין שֶׁנִּתַּן לוֹ בְּמַתָּנָה.

[ד] **מַעֲרִימִין** עַל מַעֲשֵׂר שֵׁנִי. כֵּיצַד. אוֹמֵר אָדָם לִבְנוֹ וּלְבִתּוֹ הַגְּדוֹלִים, לְעַבְדּוֹ וּלְשִׁפְחָתוֹ הָעִבְרִים, הֵילָךְ מָעוֹת אֵלּוּ וּפְדֵה לָךְ מַעֲשֵׂר שֵׁנִי זֶה.

מוֹסִיף הַפּוֹדֶה מַעֲשֵׂר שֵׁנִי שֶׁלּוֹ — One who redeems his own *maaser sheni* עָלָיו חֲמִישִׁית — adds a fifth to [its value], בֵּין שֶׁהוּא שֶׁלּוֹ — whether it is produce that was always his, וּבֵין שֶׁנִּתַּן לוֹ בְּמַתָּנָה — or whether it is produce that was given to him as a gift.[5]

[4] This Mishnah describes a legal loophole by which a person can redeem his own *maaser sheni* without having to add a fifth:[1]

מַעֲרִימִין עַל מַעֲשֵׂר שֵׁנִי — One may use a trick with *maaser sheni* in order to avoid adding a fifth. כֵּיצַד — How so? אוֹמֵר אָדָם לִבְנוֹ וּלְבִתּוֹ הַגְּדוֹלִים — A person may say to his adult son or daughter,[2] לְעַבְדּוֹ וּלְשִׁפְחָתוֹ הָעִבְרִים — or to his Hebrew servant or maidservant,[3] הֵילָךְ מָעוֹת אֵלּוּ — "Here are these coins; וּפְדֵה לָךְ מַעֲשֵׂר שֵׁנִי זֶה — use them to redeem this *maaser sheni* for yourself." Since the child or servant is redeeming *maaser sheni* that is not his, he does not have to add a fifth.[4]

---- NOTES ----

5. That is, he received untithed produce as a gift and then separated its *maaser sheni*, and he wants to redeem it. The Mishnah cannot refer to a person who received *maaser sheni* as a gift after it was separated, because *maaser sheni* cannot be given as a gift, as we learned in Mishnah 1:1 (*Rav;* see note 8 there).

[4]

1. Although the Torah states that a person must add a fifth when redeeming his *maaser sheni*, the Rabbis allowed a person to use a loophole to avoid this charge, based on the Torah's reference to *maaser sheni* as a blessing, which implies that a person may redeem it as cheaply as possible (*Tos. Yom Tov;* see Mishnah 2 note 1).

2. That is, a son who is older than 13, or a daughter who is older than 12½ (see *Bava Metzia* 12a, with *Rashi*). The tactic described in the Mishnah works only with someone who is financially independent (see note 5), and a boy under 13 or a girl under 12½ is financially dependent on his or her father (see *Bava Metzia* 12a).

3. A Hebrew servant is a Jew bought as a servant by another Jew for a specific period of time — usually six years (see *Shemos* 21:2-6; *Kiddushin* 1:2). Although he must work for his master, he is not his master's property. The servant remains financially independent and can make monetary transactions of his own, without his master's involvement (in contrast to a Canaanite slave; see note 5).

4. This can work in either of two ways: (1) The owner gives the money as a gift to the other person, so that the other person is using money that is now his to redeem *maaser sheni* that belongs to the owner. (2) The owner lets the other person use the money but it still belongs to the owner; however, the other person redeems the *maaser sheni* for himself, that is, he acquires the produce for his own when he redeems it. In this case he is redeeming *maaser sheni* for his own use with money that belongs to the owner.

[67] **MISHNAH MAASER SHENI** / Chapter 4: *Hamolich*   4/5

אֲבָל לֹא יֹאמַר כֵּן לִבְנוֹ וּלְבִתּוֹ הַקְּטַנִּים וּלְעַבְדּוֹ וּלְשִׁפְחָתוֹ הַכְּנַעֲנִים, מִפְּנֵי שֶׁיָּדָן כְּיָדוֹ.

[ה] **הָיָה** עוֹמֵד בַּגֹּרֶן וְאֵין בְּיָדוֹ מָעוֹת, אוֹמֵר לַחֲבֵרוֹ, הֲרֵי הַפֵּרוֹת הָאֵלּוּ נְתוּנִים לְךָ בְּמַתָּנָה. חוֹזֵר וְאוֹמֵר, הֲרֵי אֵלּוּ מְחֻלָּלִין עַל מָעוֹת שֶׁבַּבַּיִת.

— רע״ב —

מפני שידן כידו. דמה שקנה עבד קנה רבו. ובנו קטן נמי זכייתו לאביו דמליאת קטן לאביו: (ה) היה עומד בגורן. ורוצה לפטור ולפדות מעשר שני בלא חומש: ואין בידו מעות. כדי שיתנם לחברו, שיפדה בהן המעשר בלא חומש: הרי הפירות האלו נתונים לך במתנה. ודוקא שנתן אותם לו בטבלן קודם שיפריש מעשר שני, כדפרשינן לעיל:

This tactic would not work, though, with the following people: **אֲבָל לֹא יֹאמַר כֵּן לִבְנוֹ וּלְבִתּוֹ הַקְּטַנִּים** — But [a person] cannot say this to his son or daughter who are minors, **וּלְעַבְדּוֹ וּלְשִׁפְחָתוֹ הַכְּנַעֲנִים** — or to his Canaanite slave or slavewoman, and thereby avoid adding a fifth, **מִפְּנֵי שֶׁיָּדָן כְּיָדוֹ** — because their hand is considered like his hand, that is, they do not have their own property rights; whatever they acquire belongs to their father or master. Therefore, if they take his money or produce to redeem it, it is as though he himself is redeeming it; accordingly, a fifth must be added.[5]

[5] Another tactic that a person can use to redeem his *maaser sheni* without adding a fifth:

הָיָה עוֹמֵד בַּגֹּרֶן — If [the owner] of the produce **was standing at the threshing floor** **וְאֵין בְּיָדוֹ מָעוֹת** — **and did not have** any **coins in his hand** with which to perform the tactic described in the previous Mishnah, **אוֹמֵר לַחֲבֵרוֹ** — he **may say to his friend** who is with him: **הֲרֵי הַפֵּרוֹת הָאֵלּוּ נְתוּנִים לְךָ בְּמַתָּנָה** — "This produce is hereby given to you as a gift."[1] **חוֹזֵר וְאוֹמֵר** — He then says to [his friend], **הֲרֵי אֵלּוּ מְחֻלָּלִין עַל מָעוֹת שֶׁבַּבַּיִת** — "This produce is hereby redeemed upon coins that I have in my house."[2] Since the produce

--- NOTES ---

Since in either case the money and the produce do not belong to the same person, a fifth does not need to be added (see *Rash, Yerushalmi*).

[This can also be done with a total stranger. Our Mishnah gives the example of a child or servant to teach that even if a person uses his child or servant — on whom he can rely to give back the money and produce after the redemption — the redemption is effective and permitted (*Tiferes Yisrael, Hilchasa Gevirasa*).]

5. Redemption is exempt from a fifth only if the money and produce do not belong to the same person (see note 4). However, whatever a Canaanite slave or minor child (i.e., a boy younger than 13 or a girl younger than 12 ½) acquires belongs to his master or father. Thus, whether the owner's slave or child acquires the money or the produce, it will still belong to the owner. If the slave or child redeems the *maaser sheni*, he will thus be redeeming the owner's *maaser sheni* with money that belongs to the owner. Since the redemption money and the *maaser sheni* belong to the same person, a fifth must be added (see *Rav; Derech Emunah, Hilchos Maaser Sheni* 5:54).

[5]

1. That is, he gives him the untithed produce as a gift before he separates the *maaser sheni*; see Mishnah 3 note 5 (*Rav*).

2. A person may redeem *maaser sheni* produce that is in one place upon coins that are located in another place, as

[68] משניות מעשר שני / פרק ד: המוליך

- רע"ב -

(ו) משך ממנו מעשר בסלע. המוכר מעשר שני, כדי שיתחלל על דמי המכירה ויהיו המעות נתפסים בקדושת מעשר,

[ו] **מָשַׁךְ** מִמֶּנּוּ מַעֲשֵׂר בְּסֶלַע וְלֹא הִסְפִּיק לִפְדּוֹתוֹ עַד שֶׁעָמַד בִּשְׁתַּיִם, נוֹתֵן לוֹ סֶלַע, וּמִשְׂתַּכֵּר בְּסֶלַע, וּמַעֲשֵׂר שֵׁנִי שֶׁלּוֹ.

דבכי האי גוונא שרי למכרו. והא דתנן בפרק קמא אין מוכרין אותו, היינו להוליכו לירושלים ולא שיהיו המעות נתפסים בקדושת מעשר. וכשמשך המעשר לקנותו היה שוה סלע ולא הספיק ליתן הדמים עד שעמד בשתים, שהמתעשר לא יצא לחולין עד שיתן דמיו למוכר: **נותן לו סלע.** לפי שקנאו במשיכה, ומרויח הלוקח סלע שנתייקר. וצריך לפדותו כשער של עכשיו בשתי סלעים, שהמתעשר לא יצא לחולין עד שיתן דמיו למוכר. והסלע אחד של מעשר שני שלו ואוכלו בירושלים:

---

now belongs to his friend, the original owner can redeem it with his own coins without having to add a fifth.

[6] This Mishnah discusses a person who redeems his *maaser sheni* produce by selling it. The buyer pays for the produce and the *maaser sheni* sanctity transfers to that money; the produce, now owned by the buyer, becomes *chullin*.[1] Two things are therefore happening here: a sale (i.e., a transfer of ownership from seller to buyer) and a redemption (i.e., a transfer of *maaser sheni* sanctity from produce to money). The sale takes place when the buyer takes the produce for himself;[2] at that time, the purchase price is set. However, the redemption does not take place until the buyer pays the money. The Mishnah discusses cases where the value of the produce changes between the time that the buyer takes it and the time that he pays for it:

מָשַׁךְ מִמֶּנּוּ מַעֲשֵׂר בְּסֶלַע — **If [the buyer] drew *maaser sheni* produce from [the seller] when it was worth one *sela*,** and the sale price was thus set at one *sela*, וְלֹא הִסְפִּיק לִפְדּוֹתוֹ עַד שֶׁעָמַד בִּשְׁתַּיִם — **but he did not have a chance to redeem it,** that is, to pay for it, **until its price rose, so that it is now worth two *sela'im*,** the redemption price is set at two *sela'im*, since that is what it is now worth. נוֹתֵן לוֹ סֶלַע — **Therefore, [the buyer] gives [the seller] a *sela*** as payment וּמִשְׂתַּכֵּר בְּסֶלַע — **and [the buyer] thus gains a *sela*,** since he paid one *sela* for produce that is now worth two *sela'im*. But since the redemption price is two *sela'im*, the *sela* that the buyer paid serves only as a partial redemption for the *maaser sheni*. The buyer must complete the redemption, by designating another *sela* as *maaser sheni*. The first *maaser sheni sela* [i.e., the one paid for the produce] belongs to the seller, וּמַעֲשֵׂר שֵׁנִי שֶׁלּוֹ — **and the**

NOTES

we learned in Mishnah 3:4 (*Tos. Yom Tov*).

Here, as in the previous Mishnah, the owner relies on his friend to give back the produce after he redeems it (*Tos. Yom Tov*). Nevertheless, this tactic is effective and permitted.

[6]

1. This is the only way *maaser sheni* produce may be sold; a person may not sell it on condition that the produce simply transfer to the buyer's possession but keep its *maaser sheni* sanctity. See Mishnah 1:1 note 2 (*Rav*).

2. When an object is sold, the buyer does not take ownership of it when he pays for it, but rather when he performs an act of ownership, known as a *kinyan*. Our Mishnah will assume that the buyer does the *kinyan* most commonly used for movable objects, which is known as *meshichah*, and consists of the buyer drawing the object toward himself.

[69] MISHNAH MAASER SHENI / Chapter 4: *Hamolich*   4/6

– רע״ב –

עַד שֶׁיַּעֲמֹד בְּסֶלַע. וְצָרִיךְ לִיתֵּן לַמּוֹכֵר שְׁנֵי סְלָעִים שֶׁקִּנְּאוֹ בִּמְשִׁיכָה, וְהוּא נִפְדָּה בְּסֶלַע אֶחָד כְּשַׁעַר שֶׁל עַכְשָׁיו. הִלְכָּךְ נוֹתֵן לוֹ

מָשַׁךְ מִמֶּנּוּ מַעֲשֵׂר בִּשְׁתַּיִם וְלֹא הִסְפִּיק לִפְדּוֹתוֹ עַד שֶׁעָמַד בְּסֶלַע, נוֹתֵן לוֹ סֶלַע מֵחֻלִּין וְסֶלַע שֶׁל מַעֲשֵׂר שֵׁנִי שֶׁלּוֹ.

דְּמֵי סֶלַע מִדְּמֵי חֻלִּין שֶׁלּוֹ, וּבוֹ נִפְדָּה הַמַּעֲשֵׂר, וְהַסֶּלַע הַשֵּׁנִי נוֹתֵן לוֹ מִדְּמֵי מַעֲשֵׂר שֵׁנִי שֶׁלּוֹ. וְאֵין זֶה כְּפוֹרֵעַ חוֹבוֹ מִמַּעֲשֵׂר שֵׁנִי, לְפִי שֶׁבִּתְחִלַּת הַמִּקָּח הָיָה עוֹמֵד לְכָךְ שֶׁיֹּאכַל הַמּוֹכֵר שְׁתֵּי סְלָעִים בִּירוּשָׁלַיִם אִם לֹא הוּזַל:

---

second *maaser sheni sela*, with which the buyer completed the redemption, **belongs to [the buyer].**[3]

The Mishnah discusses the reverse case — where the value of the produce *decreases* after the sale price is set:

מָשַׁךְ מִמֶּנּוּ מַעֲשֵׂר בִּשְׁתַּיִם — **If [the buyer] drew** *maaser sheni* **produce from [the seller] when** it was worth **two** *sela'im,* and the sale price was thus set at two *sela'im,* וְלֹא הִסְפִּיק לִפְדּוֹתוֹ עַד שֶׁעָמַד בְּסֶלַע — **but he did not have a chance to redeem it,** that is, to pay for it, **until** its price decreased so **it is worth** only one *sela,* the redemption price is set at one *sela.* נוֹתֵן לוֹ סֶלַע מֵחֻלִּין — **Therefore, [the buyer] gives [the seller] one** *sela,* which is half of the purchase payment, **from his** *chullin* money,[4] and since the redemption price is only one *sela,* this money redeems all the produce. וְסֶלַע שֶׁל מַעֲשֵׂר שֵׁנִי שֶׁלּוֹ — **And he may pay the** other *sela,* that is, the other half of the purchase payment, **from his own** *maaser sheni* money. Since the *maaser sheni* is already fully redeemed, this second coin is not being used for redemption; therefore, he may use a coin that is already *maaser sheni* to pay for it.[5]

--- NOTES ---

3. Since the sale price is only one *sela,* that is all the seller is entitled to receive. The produce now belongs to the buyer, but it is only half redeemed. Therefore, the buyer must designate another *sela* to redeem the rest of it. Both *sela'im* take on *maaser sheni* sanctity and the result is that the seller and buyer each have a *sela* of *maaser sheni* that they must spend in Jerusalem (see *Rav, Rash*).

[If he does not want to redeem it, the buyer can simply bring the produce to Jerusalem to eat (see *Ri ben Malki Tzedek; Derech Emunah, Hilchos Maaser Sheni* 8:60).]

4. Since this *sela* will redeem the *maaser sheni,* it must be a *sela* of *chullin,* for *maaser sheni* can be redeemed only with money that is *chullin,* and not with money that already has *maaser sheni* sanctity.

5. At this point, the buyer does not have to redeem the other *sela's* worth of produce; he just needs to pay for it. Therefore, he does not have to use *chullin* money for the purchase. He may give the seller a *sela* with *maaser sheni* sanctity, and the seller will have to use it in Jerusalem.

Although we learned (Mishnahs 1:7, 3:1) that a person may not use *maaser sheni* money to pay a debt, this buyer may pay for the second half of the purchase with a *maaser sheni* coin. This is because when the buyer took possession of the produce (when it was worth two *sela'im*), he became responsible for a debt of two *sela'im* of *maaser sheni* — for had the price not gone down, both *sela'im* that he paid would have become *maaser sheni*. Since this was the original debt, he may pay the second *sela* with *maaser sheni* money, so that the seller ends up with two *sela'im* of *maaser sheni,* just as he would have received had the price not gone down (*Rav;* see *Chidushei Maharich*).

ד/ז

[70] משניות מעשר שני / פרק ד: המוליך

אִם הָיָה עִם הָאָרֶץ, נוֹתֵן לוֹ מִדְּמַאי.

[ז] **הַפּוֹדֶה** מַעֲשֵׂר שֵׁנִי וְלֹא קָרָא שֵׁם, רַבִּי יוֹסֵי אוֹמֵר, דַּיּוֹ. רַבִּי יְהוּדָה אוֹמֵר, צָרִיךְ לְפָרֵשׁ. הָיָה מְדַבֵּר עִם הָאִשָּׁה עַל עִסְקֵי גִטָּהּ וְקִדּוּשֶׁיהָ, וְנָתַן לָהּ גִּטָּהּ וְקִדּוּשֶׁיהָ

- רע"ב -

אם היה עם הארץ נותן לו מדמיו. ואם היה המוכר עם הארץ נותן לו שני הסלעים מדמי החולין שלו, לפי שאין מוסרין דמי מעשר לעם הארץ ואית דגרסי מדמאי אם יש לו דמי מעשר של דמאי נותן לו סלע אחד מאותן דמים, דמוסרין דמי דמאי לעם הארץ: (ז) **ולא קרא שם.** לא אמר זה פדיון מעשר שני: **צריך לפרש.** ולומר זה פדיונו. והלכה כר' יוסי:

Having said that in the previous case, the buyer may pay for half the purchase with *maaser sheni* money, the Mishnah gives an exception to that law:

אִם הָיָה עִם הָאָרֶץ — **If [the seller] was an *am haaretz*,** who cannot be trusted to treat *maaser sheni* properly, the buyer may not pay him with *maaser sheni* money,[6] נוֹתֵן לוֹ מִדְּמַאי — **but [the buyer] may give him** the second *sela* from money with the sanctity of *maaser sheni* of **demai,** which may be given to an *am haaretz*.[7]

[7] The Mishnah discusses whether redeeming *maaser sheni* requires a verbal declaration:

הַפּוֹדֶה מַעֲשֵׂר שֵׁנִי וְלֹא קָרָא שֵׁם — **If someone redeems** produce of **maaser sheni** by setting aside coins that correspond to its value, **but he did not call the coins "the redemption money of *maaser sheni*" by name,** that is, he did not declare when he set aside the coins, "This is the redemption for this *maaser sheni* produce," רַבִּי יוֹסֵי אוֹמֵר דַּיּוֹ — **R' Yose says: It is enough** that he set aside the coins, and the *maaser sheni* is redeemed.[1] רַבִּי יְהוּדָה אוֹמֵר צָרִיךְ לְפָרֵשׁ — **But R' Yehudah says: He must specify** verbally that the coins are the redemption money for the *maaser sheni* produce. And if he did not, the redemption does not take effect.

R' Yose and R' Yehudah have the same dispute with regard to divorce and marriage:

הָיָה מְדַבֵּר עִם הָאִשָּׁה עַל עִסְקֵי גִטָּהּ וְקִדּוּשֶׁיהָ — **If someone was talking with a woman about the subject of her divorce** from him **or her marriage** to him, so that it was clear that he meant to divorce her (in the case of his wife) or to marry her (in the case of an unmarried woman) וְנָתַן לָהּ גִּטָּהּ וְקִדּוּשֶׁיהָ

NOTES
---

6. As we learned in Mishnah 3:3, it is forbidden to give *maaser sheni* to an *am haaretz*, out of concern that he might eat it when he is *tamei*.

Even though the first *sela* will take on *maaser sheni* sanctity when the seller takes it, there is no problem with giving it to a seller who is an *am haaretz*, because that *sela* simply replaces the *maaser sheni* produce that the *am haaretz* originally had. It is only forbidden to give him *maaser sheni* that he did not have previously (*Mishnah Rishonah*).

7. As we learned in Mishnah 3:3.

[7]

1. R' Yose holds that since it is clear from the circumstances that his intent is to redeem the *maaser sheni*, the redemption is valid even if he does not express that intent verbally (*Rambam Commentary*; see also *Tos. Yom Tov*).

[71] **MISHNAH MAASER SHENI** / Chapter 4: *Hamolich*

― רע״ב ―

וְלֹא פֵרֵשׁ, רַבִּי יוֹסֵי אוֹמֵר, דַּיּוֹ. רַבִּי יְהוּדָה אוֹמֵר, צָרִיךְ לְפָרֵשׁ.

[ח] הַמַּנִּיחַ אִסָּר וְאָכַל עָלָיו חֶצְיוֹ, וְהָלַךְ לְמָקוֹם אַחֵר וַהֲרֵי הוּא יוֹצֵא

ולא פירש. לא אמר הרי זה גיטך או הרי את מקודשת: רבי יוסי אומר דיו. כיון שעסוקים באותו ענין ומתוך אותן הדברים עמד וגירש או קדש אין צריך לפרש. והלכה כרבי יוסי: (ח) המניח איסר. להיות מחלל עליו פירות מעשר שני. וכבר חלל. ואכל עליו עד חציו והלך למקום אחר. והוליך האיסר עמו, ושם הוא שוה פונדיון, ובתחלה לא היה יוצא אלא בחצי פונדיון, שהפונדיון ב׳ איסרין נמצא מלא לפי מה שהוא עכשיו יוצא בו איסר של שנשאר חולין ולפיכך אוכל עליו עוד איסר:

וְלֹא פֵרֵשׁ — and he immediately **handed her** *get* **to her** (in the case of his wife)[2] **or he handed her something that could effect marriage**[3] **but he did not specify** verbally that "this is your *get*" or "you are hereby betrothed to me," **רַבִּי יוֹסֵי אוֹמֵר דַּיּוֹ** — **R' Yose says: It is enough** that he handed it to her silently, and the divorce or the betrothal is valid.[4] **רַבִּי יְהוּדָה אוֹמֵר צָרִיךְ לְפָרֵשׁ** — **But R' Yehudah says: He must specify** verbally that he wants this act to effect a divorce or a betrothal, and if he did not, it is not valid.[5]

[8] The Mishnah continues its discussion of transferring the sanctity of *maaser sheni* produce to a coin (see beginning of the last Mishnah). Such transfers may be done little by little. Let us say that a coin can buy eight figs, and a person has eight figs of *maaser sheni*. He does not have to redeem all eight figs on the coin at once. Rather, he can redeem them one or more at a time and fill the coin with *maaser sheni* sanctity bit by bit. Our Mishnah deals with a case in which a redemption coin changed in value before it was completely filled with sanctity:

הַמַּנִּיחַ אִסָּר — **Someone set aside an** *issar* **coin to redeem** *maaser sheni* **produce onto it,** **וְאָכַל עָלָיו חֶצְיוֹ** — **and he ate against it** *maaser sheni* **fruits of half its value.** That is, he redeemed half an *issar's* worth of *maaser sheni* onto this coin so that he could eat those fruits outside of Jerusalem.[1] Now the *issar* coin is half *maaser sheni* and half unsanctified. **וְהָלַךְ לְמָקוֹם אַחֵר וַהֲרֵי הוּא יוֹצֵא בְּפֻנְדְיוֹן** — **He then went** with this *issar* coin **to another place where** the

--- NOTES ---

2. A *get* is a document that contains the name of the husband and wife and the statement that he is now divorcing her. The Torah states that a husband divorces his wife by handing her such a document (see *Devarim* 24:1).
3. The usual way of effecting marriage is by handing the woman something of value in order to "acquire" her in marriage (see *Kiddushin* 1:1).
4. Here, too, R' Yose holds that since it is clear from their discussion that he is handing her the *get* in order to divorce her or the money in order to marry her,

these take effect just by his handing them to her, even if he does not declare anything verbally at that time.
5. R' Yehudah holds that unless the man verbally specifies that what he is handing her should effect divorce or marriage, it is not valid.

[8]

1. A silver *issar* is generally worth 8 copper *perutahs*. Let us say that a fig costs a *perutah*. He redeemed four figs on the *issar*, and the *issar* still has "room" in it to redeem another four.

ד/ח

בְּפֻנְדְּיוֹן, אוֹכֵל עָלָיו עוֹד אִסָּר. הַמֵּנִיחַ פֻּנְדְּיוֹן וְאָכַל עָלָיו חֶצְיוֹ, וְהָלַךְ לְמָקוֹם אַחֵר וַהֲרֵי הוּא יוֹצֵא בְּאִסָּר, אוֹכֵל עָלָיו עוֹד פֶּלַג.

— רע״ב —

אוכל עליו עוד פלג. חלי איסר, ולא אמרינן כיון שאינו שוה אלא איסר הרי אכלו כולו:

value of an *issar* is higher so that **it buys** as much **as a *pundyon*,** which is twice as much as an *issar*.[2] **אוֹכֵל עָלָיו עוֹד אִיסָּר** — The law is that **he may** now redeem and **eat against** the unsanctified value left in **it another *issar*** of *maaser sheni*.[3]

The Mishnah now deals with the opposite case: where a coin that was only half *maaser sheni* then *decreased* in value:

הַמֵּנִיחַ פֻּנְדְּיוֹן — **Someone set aside a *pundyon*** coin to redeem *maaser sheni* produce onto it, **וְאָכַל עָלָיו חֶצְיוֹ** — **and he ate against it** *maaser sheni* fruits of **half its value.** That is, he redeemed an *issar*'s worth (half a *pundyon*) of *maaser sheni* on this coin so that he could eat that produce outside of Jerusalem. Now the *pundyon* coin is half *maaser sheni* and half unsanctified. **וְהָלַךְ לְמָקוֹם אַחֵר וַהֲרֵי הוּא יוֹצֵא בְּאִסָּר** — **He then went** with this *pundyon* coin **to another place where it buys** only as much **as an *issar*.**[4] **אוֹכֵל עָלָיו עוֹד פֶּלַג** — The law is that **he may** now redeem and **eat against** the unsanctified value left in **it another half** an *issar*'s worth of *maaser sheni* fruits.[5]

Coins onto which *maaser sheni* was redeemed are brought to Jerusalem, where they are used to buy food to eat there. However, instead of actually buying the food with these coins, the person can simply take food corresponding to their value and intend that the sanctity of the *maaser sheni* coins be

---
NOTES
---

2. It might be that in this place there is a great demand for *issars*, so their value is double what it was in his original location (see *Rash*); in such a place, an *issar* is worth 16 *perutahs* and can buy sixteen figs.

3. That is, another 8 *perutahs*' worth [which is the usual value of a whole *issar*], or another eight figs. [When the *issar* doubled in value, the value of its unsanctified half doubled from 4 to 8 *perutahs*. So he can now redeem another eight figs onto the coin.]

Had the Mishnah not taught us this, one might have thought that since the *issar* originally had only 4 *perutahs* of *maaser sheni* in it, and the *issar* is now worth 16 *perutahs*, there is now room on it to redeem another 12 *perutahs* of *maaser sheni*. The Mishnah teaches us otherwise: Both the *maaser sheni* half and the unsanctified half doubled their value, leaving only half the coin still available for additional redemption (*Tos. Yom Tov*).

4. A *pundyon* is generally worth 16 *perutahs*. In its original location, the *pundyon* contained 8 *perutahs* of *maaser sheni* and 8 *perutahs* of unsanctified value. In the new place, where it is worth half as much, it now contains 4 *perutahs* of *maaser sheni* and 4 *perutahs* of unsanctified value.

5. That is, 4 *perutahs*' worth. Since the unsanctified part of the *pundyon* decreased in value from 8 *perutahs* to 4 *perutahs*, he can now redeem another four figs onto the *pundyon*.

Had the Mishnah not taught us this, one might have thought that since the *pundyon* originally had 8 *perutahs*' worth of *maaser sheni* in it, now that the entire *pundyon* is worth only 8 *perutahs*, it should be considered a full coin of *maaser sheni* with nothing left in it to use for additional redemption (*Rav*). The Mishnah teaches us otherwise: Both the *maaser sheni* half and the unsanctified half lost half their value, leaving half the coin still available for additional redemption.

[73] **MISHNAH MAASER SHENI** / Chapter 4: *Hamolich*   4/8

– רע"ב –

המניח איסר של מעשר שני. להיות אוכל עליו חולין שלו בקדושת מעשר, ואוכל עליו עד אחד עשר באיסר, ומחח ממאה באיסר, יצא כל האיסר לחולין. פירוש אם היה אותו איסר ממעות מעשר שני של דמאי ואכל עליו עשרה חלקים מאחד עשר חלקים שבו, כגון שאחד עשר רמונים שוין איסר, ואכל עליו עשרה רמונים ונשאר בו עדיין חלק מאחד עשר בקדושת מעשר, יצא כולו לחולין. ואם היה האיסר ממעות מעשר שני של ודאי ואכל עליו עד שנשאר בו אחד ממאה, כגון שמאה תאנים נמכרים באיסר, ואכל עליו תשעים ותשעה, יצא כולו לחולין:

המניח אסר של מעשר שני, אוכל עליו אחד עשר באסר ואחד ממאה באסר.

---

transferred to the food, which he then eats in Jerusalem. This taking of "corresponding food" can be done little by little, so that the coins are deconsecrated bit by bit, depleting their sanctity until their value is used up. This next part of the Mishnah teaches that there is a point at which the sanctity of the *maaser sheni* coins is so depleted by the successive taking of corresponding food against them that they cease to be sacred altogether.

הַמַּנִּיחַ אִסָּר שֶׁל מַעֲשֵׂר שֵׁנִי — **One who sets aside an** *issar* **coin of** *maaser sheni* to deconsecrate it little by little by eating against it corresponding food in Jerusalem אוֹכֵל עָלָיו אַחַד עָשָׂר בְּאִסָּר — **eats against it** until **one-eleventh** of the sanctity is left **in the** *issar*,[6] וְאֶחָד מִמֵּאָה בְּאִסָּר — **or** in some cases until **one-hundredth** of the sanctity is left **in the** *issar*.[7] At that point the remaining sanctity in the *issar* disappears automatically.[8] Obviously, these two different amounts (one-eleventh and one-hundredth) cannot refer to the same case. Rather, the smaller amount (one-hundredth) applies in the case of an *issar* used to redeem definite *maaser sheni,* while the larger amount (one-eleventh) applies in the case of an *issar* used to redeem *maaser sheni* of *demai*.[9]

---------- NOTES ----------

6. For example, the *issar* can buy 11 pomegranates. After the person eats 10 pomegranates against this *issar* of *maaser sheni,* only one-eleventh of its sanctity is left (*Rav*).

7. For example, the *issar* can buy 100 figs. After the person eats 99 figs against this *issar* of *maaser sheni,* only one-hundredth of its sanctity is left (*Rav*).

8. The reason the remaining sanctity disappears will be explained in the next note.

9. As explained earlier (see above, 3:3 note 4), *demai* is produce bought from an *am haaretz*. Even though the *am haaretz* has probably tithed the produce properly, the Rabbis decreed that the buyer must remove some of the tithes, including *maaser sheni*. Since *maaser sheni* of *demai* has sanctity only by Rabbinic decree, it has the leniency that the remaining sanctity of its *issar* coin disappears even if one-eleventh is left. In the case of Biblical *maaser sheni,* however, the remaining sanctity of its coins does not disappear until only one-hundredth is left (*Rav*).

Why does the last one-hundredth of *maaser sheni* sanctity disappear from the coin of Biblical *maaser sheni*? Tos. Yom Tov suggests that this is because that last hundredth becomes nullified in the rest of the coin, as follows: Biblically, an unrecognizable minority becomes nullied by the majority in a mixture. In the case of *terumah* that became mixed with *chullin,* the Rabbis decreed that the *terumah* does not become nullified until the *chullin* majority is 100 times the *terumah* (see *Terumos* 4:7). Our Tanna holds that in the case of *maaser sheni,* which is less stringent than *terumah,* we are slightly more lenient and allow the *maaser sheni* part of the coin to become nullified even if the unsanctified part of the coin is only 99 times as large.

[In the case of *demai,* however, whose

בֵּית שַׁמַּאי אוֹמְרִים, הַכֹּל עֲשָׂרָה. וּבֵית הִלֵּל אוֹמְרִים, בְּוַדַּאי אֶחָד עָשָׂר, וּבִדְמַאי עֲשָׂרָה.

- רע"ב -

בית שמאי אומרים הכל עשרה. אחד ודאי ואחד דמאי כשלא נשאר באיסר אלא עשיריתו יצא לחולין. כגון שהיו עשרה

רמונים נמכרין באיסר, ואכל עליו תשעה יצא לחולין. ואם נשאר בו יותר, כגון שלא אכל אלא שמנה צריך לאכול כנגדו: **ובית הלל אומרים בודאי אחד עשר, ובדמאי עשרה**. אם נשאר על האיסר של ודאי אחד מעשרה חייב לאכול עליו עוד [אחד], לפי שכל מה שהוא פחות משוה פרוטה אין חוששין לו, לא לענין גזל, ולא לענין נהנה מן ההקדש. ופרוטה היא אחד משמנה באיסר האיטלקי נמלא עשירית האיסר הוא שמנה עשיריות של פרוטה דהיינו פרוטה פחות חומש, נמלא כשתוסיף עליו חומש דהוא רביע מלגו היינו חומשא מלבר יהיה [בין] הכל פרוטה, ולפיכך חושבים לה, ואם יהיה פחות מעשיריתו אין חושבים לו שאפילו עם תוספת החומש יהיה בו פחות משוה פרוטה. ולפיכך אמרו בודאי אחד עשר, ובדמאי עשרה, לפי שאין חייבין חומש על הדמאי, ועשיריתו הוא פחות משוה פרוטה, והלכה כבית הלל:

The Mishnah presents other views in this matter:

בֵּית שַׁמַּאי אוֹמְרִים — **Beis Shammai say:** הַכֹּל עֲשָׂרָה — There is no difference between definite *maaser sheni* and that of *demai.* In all cases, whether the *maaser sheni* is definite or *demai,* one-tenth is the point at which the remaining sanctity in the *issar* disappears.[10] וּבֵית הִלֵּל אוֹמְרִים — But Beis Hillel say it does make a difference: בְּוַדַּאי אֶחָד עָשָׂר — In the case of definite *maaser sheni,* one-eleventh is the point at which the remaining sanctity in the *issar* disappears; וּבִדְמַאי עֲשָׂרָה — but in the case of *maaser sheni* of *demai,* one-tenth is the point at which the remaining sanctity in the *issar* disappears.[11]

NOTES

maaser sheni is sacred only Rabbinically, this Tanna holds that even one-eleventh of the *issar* ceases to be sacred — as Beis Hillel hold below with regard to Biblical *maaser sheni;* see there for the explanation.]

10. In many areas of Torah law, a *perutah* is the minimum amount of money that is considered significant. An *issar* is worth eight *perutahs* (see note 1 above). A tenth of an *issar,* then, is $8/10$ of a *perutah.* Therefore, Beis Shammai hold that when the *maaser sheni* portion of an *issar* falls to one-tenth, which is less than a *perutah,* the *maaser sheni* portion loses its monetary significance, and the coin ceases to have *maaser sheni* sanctity altogether (see *Rav* from *Rambam Commentary*). [Actually, even at one-ninth (which is larger than one-tenth), the *maaser sheni* content would be slightly less than a *perutah* ($1/9 \times 8 = 8/9$) and should be considered insignificant (see *Rashash*).]

11. Beis Hillel hold that in the case of definite *maaser sheni,* the *issar* remains sacred even at one-tenth ($8/10$ of a *perutah*). This is because one who redeems his definite *maaser sheni* must add "a fifth" of the total, which is a quarter of the *maaser sheni*'s original value (see above, Mishnah 3; see also *Rambam, Hilchos Maaser Sheni* 5:2-3). Accordingly, even $8/10$ of a *perutah* of *maaser sheni* is significant, because together with the added quarter ($2/10$) it amounts to a complete *perutah.* Only when the *maaser sheni* value of the *issar* falls to one-eleventh is it insignificant, since even with the extra quarter it is still less than a *perutah.* In the case of *maaser sheni* of *demai,* however, Beis Hillel agree with Beis Shammai that the *issar*'s sanctity is lost at one-tenth, since the law is that one does *not* add a fifth when redeeming his *maaser sheni* of *demai* [as taught in *Demai* 1:2] (*Rav,* from *Rambam Commentary*).

[75] **MISHNAH MAASER SHENI** / Chapter 4: *Hamolich* 4/9

- רע״ב -

(ט) כל המעות הנמצאים. בכל מקום בין ברגל בין בשאר ימות השנה. ובירושלים בשאר ימות השנה חוץ מימות הרגל: הרי אלו חולין. ואין חוששין להם שמא

[ט] **כָּל** הַמָּעוֹת הַנִּמְצָאִים, הֲרֵי אֵלּוּ חֻלִּין, אֲפִלּוּ דִּינַר זָהָב עִם הַכֶּסֶף וְעִם הַמָּעוֹת. מָצָא בְתוֹכָן חֶרֶשׂ וְכָתוּב עָלָיו מַעֲשֵׂר, הֲרֵי זֶה מַעֲשֵׂר.

מעות של מעשר שני הם: אפילו דינר זהב עם הכסף ועם המעות. שאין דרך לערבן יחד, ואיכא למימר הללו מעות של מעשר שני שרגילין לחלל המעשר על דינרי זהב והנשאר שאינו מגיע לדינר זהב מחללו על הכסף והמותר על מעות של נחשת ומערבין אותן יחד, אפילו הכי לא חיישינן: מצא בתוכן. בתוך הכיס או הארנק שהמעות נתונים בתוכו:

---

[9] The Mishnah considers whether one who finds a coin must be concerned that it might be a redemption coin of *maaser sheni* and must therefore be used for food in Jerusalem:

כָּל הַמָּעוֹת הַנִּמְצָאִים הֲרֵי אֵלּוּ חֻלִּין — **All coins that are found are** assumed to be **unsanctified,** because most coins are unsanctified.[1] **אֲפִלּוּ דִּינַר זָהָב עִם הַכֶּסֶף וְעִם הַמָּעוֹת** — And this applies **even** if one found **a gold dinar** together **with one of silver and with** copper **coins** in the same pouch, which might suggest that they are *maaser sheni* coins that were being kept together.[2]

The Mishnah states an exception to this rule:

מָצָא בְתוֹכָן חֶרֶשׂ וְכָתוּב עָלָיו מַעֲשֵׂר — But if **one found among them** in the pouch **a piece of pottery with** the word **"maaser" written on it,** **הֲרֵי זֶה מַעֲשֵׂר** — **then it is** assumed that these are indeed *maaser sheni* coins.[3]

NOTES
---

[9]

1. Most coins in the world are *not* redemption coins of *maaser sheni*. Any coins that we find are assumed to come from the majority and are therefore unsanctified (*Rashi* to *Pesachim* 7a ד״ה בהר הבית).

2. A person does not not usually put gold, silver, and copper coins in the same pouch. How, then, are we to explain the fact that these different coins were found together? A likely explanation would seem to be that they are *maaser sheni* coins. That is, a person had a large amount of *maaser sheni* produce to redeem. So he redeemed most of it onto the gold *dinar*. The remainder was too little to fill another gold *dinar,* so he redeemed it onto silver coins, and the little bit left over was too small to redeem even onto a silver coin so he redeemed it onto copper coins. He then kept all his *maaser sheni* coins together in the same pouch. Still, the Mishnah teaches that we do not have to be concerned that this is what happened (*Rav*). Because if they were indeed *maaser sheni* coins, the owner would probably have put some sort of note in the pouch to indicate that they are *maaser sheni* coins. Since no such note is found, we once again can assume that they are not *maaser sheni* coins, and they are permitted (*Tos. Yom Tov*).

3. Even though it is possible that this pottery note was written for a different container of *maaser* and was put in this pouch by mistake (*Rambam Commentary*). ["Maaser" is the shorthand someone would use for *maaser sheni* coins, since no other *maaser* would be in the form of coins.]

Another exception to our Mishnah's rule is where coins are found in the streets of Jerusalem during one of the Three Festivals, when people flock to Jerusalem from all over Eretz Yisrael to fulfill the mitzvah of *aliyah laregel* (coming to the Temple three times a year with

[76] משניות מעשר שני / פרק ד: המוליך

ד/י

- רע"ב -

(י) הוּא חוּלִין. שֶׁאֵין דֶּרֶךְ בְּנֵי אָדָם לְהַקְדִּישׁ חַרְסִין לְבֶדֶק הַבַּיִת, וְעַל שֵׁם מַה שֶּׁבְּתוֹכוֹ נִכְתַּב: הוּא קָרְבָּן. כְּלוֹמַר הַקֹּדֶשׁ: חוּלִין לְתוֹךְ קָרְבָּן. וְהַכֹּל קָרְבָּן. וְלֹא אֲפִלּוּ רַבָּנָן עָלֶיהָ דְרַבִּי יְהוּדָה אֶלָּא בְּשֶׁל

[י] הַמּוֹצֵא כְּלִי וְכָתוּב עָלָיו קָרְבָּן, רַבִּי יְהוּדָה אוֹמֵר, אִם הָיָה שֶׁל חֶרֶס, הוּא חֻלִּין וּמַה שֶּׁבְּתוֹכוֹ קָרְבָּן. וְאִם הָיָה שֶׁל מַתֶּכֶת, הוּא קָרְבָּן וּמַה שֶּׁבְּתוֹכוֹ חֻלִּין. אָמְרוּ לוֹ, אֵין דֶּרֶךְ בְּנֵי אָדָם לִהְיוֹת כּוֹנְסִין חֻלִּין לַקָּרְבָּן.

מַתֶּכֶת בִּלְבַד, דִּבְשֶׁל חֶרֶס מוֹדוּ שֶׁהוּא חוּלִין וּמַה שֶּׁבְּתוֹכוֹ קָרְבָּן. וַהֲלָכָה כַּחֲכָמִים:

---

[10] The last Mishnah spoke about a pouch of coins that contain a note on which *"maaser"* is written. The Mishnah now discusses similar cases:

הַמּוֹצֵא כְּלִי וְכָתוּב עָלָיו קָרְבָּן — **If someone finds a container on which** the word *"korban"* **is written**,[1] רַבִּי יְהוּדָה אוֹמֵר — **R' Yehudah says** the law depends on what the container was made of: אִם הָיָה שֶׁל חֶרֶס — **If it was** made of **pottery** הוּא חֻלִּין וּמַה שֶּׁבְּתוֹכוֹ קָרְבָּן — then **it is assumed to be non-sacred, but its contents** are assumed to be **sacred**.[2] וְאִם הָיָה שֶׁל מַתֶּכֶת — **But, if it was** made of **metal**, which people sometimes sanctify for the Temple, הוּא קָרְבָּן וּמַה שֶּׁבְּתוֹכוֹ חֻלִּין — then **it is** assumed to be **sacred, but its contents are** are assumed to be **non-sacred**.[3]

The Sages argue with R' Yehudah:

אָמְרוּ לוֹ — **They said to him:** אֵין דֶּרֶךְ בְּנֵי אָדָם לִהְיוֹת כּוֹנְסִין חֻלִּין לַקָּרְבָּן — **It is not usual for people to place non-sacred items into sacred vessels**.[4] Therefore, we must treat both the metal container *and* its contents as sacred.[5]

NOTES
---

offerings) and bring along their *maaser sheni* to eat there (*Rav*). At that time, most of the coins that are found in Jerusalem *are* coins of *maaser sheni*. Furthermore, the streets of Jerusalem were swept every day, so any coins lying there from before the festival would already have been swept away (see *Shekalim* 7:2).

[10]

1. The word *korban* (literally, *sacrifice*) usually refers to sacrificial offerings, but can be used to refer to *hekdesh* (items sanctified for the Temple) in general (see *Rav* and *Tos. Yom Tov*).

2. Earthenware containers are cheap and people do not usually sanctify them for the Temple. Therefore, R' Yehudah says, we may assume that the word *"korban"* on it was meant to label its contents,

not the container itself (*Rav*).

3. The word *"korban"* is assumed to identify the container on which it is actually written, rather than the separate contents inside. Therefore, the container is sacred, but the contents are assumed to be like the majority of things, which are not sacred.

4. Because it is forbidden to use sacred items for personal use [*me'ilah*] (*Tiferes Yisrael*). [R' Yehudah, however, holds that it might very well be that the owner inadvertently put non-sacred items into the sacred container (see *Tiferes Yisrael*.)]

5. *Rav*. In the case of an earthenware container, however, the Sages agree with R' Yehudah that we assume only that the contents are sacred, not the container itself (ibid.).

[77] **MISHNAH MAASER SHENI** / Chapter 4: *Hamolich* 4/11

- רע״ב -

[יא] **הַמּוֹצֵא** כְּלִי וְכָתוּב עָלָיו קוּ״ף, קָרְבָּן.
מ׳, מַעֲשֵׂר. ד׳, דְּמַאי. ט׳, טֶבֶל.
ת׳, תְּרוּמָה, שֶׁבִּשְׁעַת סַכָּנָה הָיוּ כוֹתְבִין ת׳
תַּחַת תְּרוּמָה.
רַבִּי יוֹסֵי אוֹמֵר, כֻּלָּם שְׁמוֹת בְּנֵי אָדָם הֵם,

(יא) קוף קרבן. הקדם:
ד׳ דמאי. לקוח מעם
הארץ: בשעת הסכנה.
שגזרו שלא לקיים המצוות:
שמות בני אדם הן.
אותיות של ראשי שמות,
קוף קהת, ד׳ דניאל,
ט׳ טוביה. והכל חולין:

---

[11] The Mishnah now teaches the laws that apply when a single letter rather than a whole word is written on the container:

הַמּוֹצֵא כְּלִי וְכָתוּב עָלָיו קוּ״ף — **If someone found a container with** the letter *"kuf"* **written on it,** קָרְבָּן — we assume that *kuf* stands for *korban,* and the law is the same as discussed in the previous Mishnah. מ׳ מַעֲשֵׂר — **If** the letter *"mem"* is written on the container, we assume that it stands for *maaser,* and the contents are *maaser sheni.*[1] ד׳ דְּמַאי — **If the letter *"dalet"* is written on the container, we assume that it stands for *demai* and the contents are *demai.*[2] ט׳ טֶבֶל — **If the letter *"tes"* is written on the container, we** assume that it stands for *tevel* and the contents are *tevel.*[3] ת׳ תְּרוּמָה — **If the letter *"tav"* is written on it, we assume that it stands for *terumah* and the contents are *terumah.*[4] Why do we assume that these letters are short for those words? שֶׁבִּשְׁעַת סַכָּנָה הָיוּ כוֹתְבִין ת׳ תַּחַת תְּרוּמָה — **Because in times of danger,** when the non-Jewish authorities in Eretz Yisrael decreed that the Jews shall not perform the mitzvos, **they would write** the letter *"tav"* **instead of *"terumah"*** on their *terumah* containers to hide their mitzvah observance from their persecutors.[5]

Another Tanna disagrees:

רַבִּי יוֹסֵי אוֹמֵר — **R' Yose says:** כֻּלָּם שְׁמוֹת בְּנֵי אָדָם הֵם — **All of these** letters **are** possibly abbreviations of **people's names;** for example, *kuf* stands for

--- NOTES ---

[11]
1. Actually, מ׳ might also stand for *maaser rishon* or *maasar ani.* However, since neither of these has any sanctity, it is more reasonable to say that the *"maaser"* label was meant to prevent people from eating the sacred *maaser sheni* outside of Jerusalem (*Tiferes Yisrael*).

In this case (as well as in the remaining cases of the Mishnah), the label certainly refers to the contents rather than to the container, since the container itself cannot be *maaser* (or any of the other things — *tevel, demai,* and *terumah* — mentioned further). It is only in the case of *korban* that the label might refer to the container itself (*Aruch HaShulchan HeAsid* 128:21).

2. *Demai* is produce bought from an *am haaretz,* and the Rabbis decreed that one may not eat it until he separates *maaser rishon* and *maaser sheni* from it (see above, Mishnah 6).

3. *Tevel* is produce that was definitely not yet tithed.

4. Which may be eaten only by a Kohen who is *tahor.*

5. And similarly, they would write all the other one-letter abbreviations listed in the Mishnah. The Tanna uses the example of *terumah* because that was the last one mentioned (*Tos. Yom Tov*). Even after the danger passed and these decrees were removed, the custom of using these abbreviations remained (*Meleches Shlomo*).

משניות מעשר שני / פרק ד: המוליך [78]

אָמַר רַבִּי יוֹסֵי, אֲפִלּוּ מָצָא חָבִית וְהִיא מְלֵאָה פֵרוֹת וְכָתוּב עָלֶיהָ תְּרוּמָה, הֲרֵי אֵלּוּ חֻלִּין, שֶׁאֲנִי אוֹמֵר אֶשְׁתָּקַד הָיְתָה מְלֵאָה פֵרוֹת תְּרוּמָה, וּפִנָּהּ.

[יב] **הָאוֹמֵר** לִבְנוֹ מַעֲשֵׂר שֵׁנִי בְּזָוִית זוֹ, וּמָצָא בְּזָוִית אַחֶרֶת, הֲרֵי אֵלּוּ חֻלִּין.

Kehas, *mem* for Moshe, *dalet* for Daniel, *tes* for Toviah, and *tav* for Tanchum. Therefore, we may assume that the letters were meant to mark the name of the container's owner, and the contents have no sanctity at all.[6] אָמַר רַבִּי יוֹסֵי — Moreover, R' Yose said: אֲפִלּוּ מָצָא חָבִית וְהִיא מְלֵאָה פֵרוֹת — Even if someone found a barrel full of produce וְכָתוּב עָלֶיהָ תְּרוּמָה — with the entire word *"terumah"* written on it, הֲרֵי אֵלּוּ חֻלִּין — these contents are assumed to be ordinary, **non-sanctified** produce, שֶׁאֲנִי אוֹמֵר — **because I may assume and say:** אֶשְׁתָּקַד הָיְתָה מְלֵאָה פֵרוֹת תְּרוּמָה וּפִנָּה — **Last year it was full of** *terumah* **produce,** which is why the owner labeled the barrel *terumah,* but he then **emptied it** and refilled it with non-sanctified produce this year and neglected to erase the mark.[7]

[12] This Mishnah discusses other cases of coins that seem to be identified as *maaser sheni*:

הָאוֹמֵר לִבְנוֹ מַעֲשֵׂר שֵׁנִי בְּזָוִית זוֹ — **If someone says to his son, "I left a bag of** *maaser sheni* **coins in one** particular **corner** of the house," וּמָצָא בְּזָוִית אַחֶרֶת — and [the son] went **and found** a bag of coins, but only **in a different corner,** הֲרֵי אֵלּוּ חֻלִּין — **these** coins that he found **are non-sacred,** because we may assume that they are not the *maaser sheni* coins to which the father referred.[1]

NOTES

6. *Rav* and *Rambam Commentary*. R' Yose holds that since such a label does not prove that the contents are sacred, we are allowed to assume that they are from the majority of all produce, which is *not* sacred (*Mishnah Rishonah* ד״ה שבשעת הסכנה). [The Tanna Kamma, however, holds that it is unlikely that the letter stands for the owner's name, because a single letter is a weak way of identifying who he is, since it might stand for *any* name that starts with that letter. Therefore, we must assume that it stands for *terumah,* etc. (ibid.).]

7. Unless the label proves that the present contents are *terumah,* we may follow the majority of all produce, which is not sacred (see previous note). R' Yose holds that the *terumah* label does not prove anything. Therefore, he rules that the contents are not sacred.

The Sages, however, hold that if the person would have refilled the container marked *"terumah"* with ordinary produce, he certainly would have erased the *terumah* mark (*Rav*). Therefore, they hold that the mark proves that the contents are *terumah.*

[12]

1. We do not assume that these are the coins the father meant, but he forgot which corner he left them in, or that someone moved them to a different corner (*Mahari Korkos, Hil. Maaser*

[79] MISHNAH MAASER SHENI / Chapter 4: *Hamolich* — 4/12

- רע״ב -

הָיָה שָׁם מָנֶה וּמָצָא מָאתַיִם, הַשְּׁאָר חֻלִּין. מָאתַיִם וּמָצָא מָנֶה, הַכֹּל מַעֲשֵׂר.

היה שם מנה. אמר לו אביו הרי שם מנה של מעשר שני ומצא מאתים, מנה מעשר ומנה חולין.

ולא אמרינן המנה של מעשר נטל ואלו אחרים הן: מאתים ומצא מנה. אמר לו אביו הרי שם מאתים ומלא מנה המנה שמלא מעשר:

Another case:

הָיָה שָׁם מָנֶה וּמָצָא מָאתַיִם — If the father told his son, "**A** *maneh* (100 *zuz*) of *maaser sheni* coins **is there** in that place," **and [the son]** went and **found two hundred** *zuz* there, **הַשְּׁאָר חֻלִּין** — one hundred are *maaser sheni* and **the rest are non-sacred.**[2]

Yet another case:

מָאתַיִם וּמָצָא מָנֶה — If the father told his son, "**Two hundred** *zuz* of *maaser sheni* coins are there in that place," **and [the son]** went and **found** there only **one** *maneh* (100 *zuz*), **הַכֹּל מַעֲשֵׂר** — **all** the coins that he found **are** *maaser sheni*, because we assume that they are the coins to which the father referred.[3]

NOTES

Sheni 6:3). Rather, since the coins were not found where the father said he left them, we may assume that these are different coins, and the *maaser sheni* coins that the father left in the house were taken by someone else (*Rav*). Therefore, it is like any other time a person finds unidentified coins: He may assume that they are from the majority, which have no sanctity.

2. Here, where the numbers do not match (because he found more than the father said he would find), we do not assume that the old coins were removed and these are completely different, non-sacred coins. Rather, we assume that the original *maaser sheni* coins are still there, except that someone added to them another 100 *zuz* of ordinary coins (*Rav*). [The Mishnah above, 2:6, teaches what we should do with a mixture of ordinary and *maaser sheni* coins.]

3. Here too, we do not assume that because the numbers do not match (because he found less than the father said he would find) all the old coins were removed and these are completely different, non-sacred coins. Rather, we assume that someone removed only some of the original *maaser sheni* coins and these are what remain (*Rambam Commentary*).

The Mishnah thus teaches that where the coins are not in the same *place*, we assume that they are entirely different coins. Where the coins are in the same place but have the wrong *amount*, we assume that they *are* the original *maaser sheni* coins but that some were added or removed.

Chapter Five

[82] משניות מעשר שני / פרק ה: כרם רבעי ה/א

- רע"ב -

פרק חמישי (א) כרם רבעי מציינין אותו. בונים אצלו ציון וסימן, שיכירו שהוא כרם

[א] **כֶּרֶם רְבָעִי, מְצַיְּנִין אוֹתוֹ בְּקוֹזְזוֹת אֲדָמָה, וְשֶׁל עָרְלָה בְּחַרְסִית, וְשֶׁל קְבָרוֹת בְּסִיד, וּמְמַחֶה וְשׁוֹפֵךְ.**

רבעי וטעון פדיון: **בקוזזות.** גבשושית ורגבי אדמה. סימנא כאדמה, מה אדמה דאיכא הנאה מינה שהיא עושה פירות אף האי נמי כי מפרקי שרי לאתהנויי מיניה: **ושל ערלה בחרסית.** באדמה שעושים ממנו כלי חרס. סימנא כחרסית זו דלית בה הנאה דכשזורעים בה אינה מוציאה כדי נפילה אף זו אין בה הנאה: **ושל קברות.** שלא יכנס שם כהן ונזיר: **בסיד.** סימנא שהסיד לבן כעצמות: **וממחה ושופך.** ממחה את הסיד במים כדי שיתלבן יותר, ושופך על הקבר.

[1] The first five Mishnahs of this chapter are not about *maaser sheni*, but about the laws of *reva'i*, the fruit of the fourth year of a tree. These are discussed here because of their similarity to the laws of *maaser sheni*.[1]

The Torah states (*Vayikra* 19:23) that when a fruit tree is planted, the fruits produced during its first three years are forbidden. These are known as עָרְלָה, *orlah* (whose laws are discussed in Tractate *Orlah*). The Torah further states (ibid. v. 24) that the fruit of the fourth year should be treated as קֹדֶשׁ, *holy*. This means that the fruit of this year should be brought to Jerusalem and eaten there like *maaser sheni*, or it should be redeemed with money and the money should be taken to Jerusalem and used to buy food to eat there. The fourth-year fruit is called רְבָעִי, *reva'i*.

Since it is not obvious to anyone besides the owner which trees are *orlah* and *reva'i*, the Rabbis were concerned that people might take fruit from them and eat it without realizing that the fruits were prohibited. The Rabbis therefore decreed that these trees should be marked in certain ways to make their status clear to everyone. The Mishnah describes these markings. In passing, it also describes how graves were marked to prevent Kohanim from becoming *tamei* from them:

כֶּרֶם רְבָעִי מְצַיְּנִין אוֹתוֹ בְּקוֹזְזוֹת אֲדָמָה — **A fourth-year vineyard**[2] **is marked with clumps of earth,** which are placed next to the vineyard;[3] וְשֶׁל עָרְלָה בְּחַרְסִית — **an orchard of** *orlah* **is marked with clay** (the type of earth from which earthenware utensils are made);[4] וְשֶׁל קְבָרוֹת בְּסִיד וּמְמַחֶה וְשׁוֹפֵךְ — **and graves**

NOTES

[1]
1. *Tos. Yom Tov, Meleches Shlomo.*
2. The Mishnah's ruling (here and in the coming Mishnahs) applies to all types of fruit trees, not just vineyards (see *Rav* to *Peah* 7:6 and *Eduyos* 4:5).

[The Gemara in *Berachos* 35a cites a dispute whether our Mishnah should read כֶּרֶם רְבָעִי, *fourth-year vineyard*, or נֶטַע רְבָעִי, *fourth-year saplings*, which refers to all fruit trees. Since the halachah follows the view that it applies to all fruit trees, *Rav* explains the Mishnah according to this reading. Indeed, the standard texts of Mishnah have the reading כֶּרֶם רְבָעִי,

fourth-year vineyard, in the first three Mishnahs of the chapter but then switch to the reading of נֶטַע רְבָעִי, *fourth-year saplings*, in the following two Mishnahs (*Tos. Yom Tov* to *Peah* 7:6).]

3. The Rabbis chose clumps of earth to mark *reva'i* because earth is similar to *reva'i* in the following way: It cannot be eaten in its present state, but it can be a source of later benefit, when we plow it, plant it, and then harvest its crop. So too with *reva'i*; although we cannot eat it as it is, we can benefit from it by redeeming its fruit (*Rav*, from *Bava Kamma* 69a).

4. Clay is a form of earth that is of no use

[83] **MISHNAH MAASER SHENI** / Chapter 5: *Kerem Reva'i*   5/1

אָמַר רַבָּן שִׁמְעוֹן בֶּן גַּמְלִיאֵל, בַּמֶּה דְבָרִים אֲמוּרִים, בַּשְּׁבִיעִית. וְהַצְּנוּעִים מַנִּיחִין אֶת הַמָּעוֹת וְאוֹמְרִים, כָּל הַנִּלְקָט מִזֶּה, יְהֵא מְחֻלָּל עַל הַמָּעוֹת הָאֵלּוּ.

- רע״ב -

במה דברים אמורים.
דעבדי הכירא לכרם רבעי
ולערלה: בשביעית. שהכל
הפקר ונוטלים בהיתר.
אבל בשאר שני שבוע
שבתים לגזול, הלעיטהו
לרשע וימות ויקחום לאכול באיסור: והצנועים. המדקדקים על עצמם, כשהיה להם כרם רבעי
בשביעית היו מניחין המעות קודם לקיטה, ואומרים כל הנלקט לכשיהיה נלקט יהא מחולל על זה:

are marked **with lime, which is mixed** with water **and poured** over the graves.[5]

According to the first Tanna, the owner of *reva'i* and *orlah* trees must mark them to prevent passersby from eating their prohibited fruit.[6] Although someone who takes the fruit without the owner's permission is a thief, the owner is required to prevent even a thief from sinning more by eating unredeemed *reva'i* or *orlah*. The next Tanna disagrees:

בַּמֶּה דְבָרִים אָמַר רַבָּן שִׁמְעוֹן בֶּן גַּמְלִיאֵל — **Rabban Shimon ben Gamliel said:** אֲמוּרִים — **When were these words said,** that *reva'i* and *orlah* trees must be marked? בַּשְּׁבִיעִית — **During the Shemittah year,** when the produce of Eretz Yisrael is ownerless and anyone is allowed to enter another person's field and take some of the fruits growing there to eat.[7] But in other years, when it is forbidden to take someone else's fruits without permission, there is no obligation to mark *reva'i* and *orlah* trees, because we are not responsible for protecting a thief from the consequences of his crime.[8]

Everyone agrees that, at least during *Shemittah*, these trees had to be marked to prevent people from sinning. The Mishnah records the practice of certain pious people who owned *reva'i* trees during *Shemittah*:

וְהַצְּנוּעִים — **And the "modest ones"** (pious people who wished to prevent people from sinning) did not rely on just marking their *reva'i*,[9] rather, מַנִּיחִין כָּל הַנִּלְקָט מִזֶּה אֶת הַמָּעוֹת וְאוֹמְרִים — **they would set aside coins and say:** יְהֵא מְחֻלָּל עַל הַמָּעוֹת הָאֵלּוּ — **"Any *reva'i* that is picked from this** orchard **shall be redeemed onto these coins."**[10] In this way, any fruits eventually taken from the orchard were redeemed and thus permitted to be eaten.

NOTES

to a farmer, since crops hardly grow in it. So too *orlah* is of no benefit, since it can never be used (*Rav*).

5. A person who touches a grave or steps over it becomes *tamei* (*Bamidbar* 19:17). Graves were therefore marked to warn Kohanim and *nezirim*, who are forbidden to become *tamei* from a corpse or grave, not to walk near the grave or over it (*Rav* here and *Shekalim* 1:1).

   Lime was chosen to identify a grave because lime is white and resembles bones. The lime was dissolved in hot water in order to make it even whiter (*Rav, Rambam Commentary*).

6. The owner knows which are the forbidden trees and has no need to mark them for himself.

7. *Vayikra* 25:6.

8. *Rav,* from *Bava Kamma* 69a.

9. They were concerned that people might not realize that the marker identifies the fruit as *reva'i* or they might not see the marker (*Meiri* and *Pnei Yehoshua* to *Bava Kamma* 69a).

10. The "modest ones" set aside coins before any produce was picked, and declared that, as soon as produce is picked, it should be redeemed onto these coins.

ה/ב

משניות מעשר שני / פרק ה: כרם רבעי [84]

- רע"ב -

(ב) כרם רבעי. יש לו דין מעשר שני, וצריך להעלות הפירות לירושלים ולאכלן שם, הם או פדיונם, ותקנו חכמים שמהלך יום [אחד] כל סביבות ירושלים יעלו הפירות [עצמם] לירושלים, כדי לעטר שוקי ירושלים בפירות, מתוך שיאכל כל אדם

[ב] **כֶּרֶם רְבָעִי הָיָה עוֹלֶה לִירוּשָׁלַיִם מַהֲלַךְ יוֹם אֶחָד לְכָל צַד. וְאֵי זוֹ הִיא תְחוּמָהּ, אֵילַת מִן הַדָּרוֹם וְעַקְרַבַּת מִן הַצָּפוֹן, לֹד מִן הַמַּעֲרָב וְהַיַּרְדֵּן מִן הַמִּזְרָח. וּמִשֶּׁרַבּוּ הַפֵּרוֹת, הִתְקִינוּ שֶׁיְּהֵא נִפְדֶּה סָמוּךְ לַחוֹמָה. וּתְנַאי הָיָה הַדָּבָר,**

נטע רבעי שלו יתמלא השוק שאר פירות: **שיהא נפדה סמוך לחומה.** אפילו כרם הסמוך לחומה:

---

[2] Generally, the owner of *reva'i* fruits has the option of either bringing them to Jerusalem to eat there, or to redeem them and bring the money to Jerusalem. However, the Rabbis decreed that in certain places the *reva'i* fruits themselves must be brought to Jerusalem and may not be redeemed:

כֶּרֶם רְבָעִי הָיָה עוֹלֶה לִירוּשָׁלַיִם — The produce of **a fourth-year vineyard would be brought up to Jerusalem** and not be redeemed **מַהֲלַךְ יוֹם אֶחָד לְכָל צַד** — if it grew within **one day's travel** of Jerusalem **in any direction**. The Rabbis made this decree so that the markets of Jerusalem would be well-supplied with fruit.[1] **וְאֵי זוֹ הִיא תְחוּמָהּ** — What are the boundaries of [this area]? **אֵילַת מִן הַדָּרוֹם** — Eilas from the south,[2] **וְעַקְרַבַּת מִן הַצָּפוֹן** — Akrabas from the north, **לֹד מִן הַמַּעֲרָב** — Lod from the west, **וְהַיַּרְדֵּן מִן הַמִּזְרָח** — and the Jordan River from the east. Any place within these four points is within a day's travel of Jerusalem, and the produce growing there had to be brought to Jerusalem.

This decree was later canceled:

וּמִשֶּׁרַבּוּ הַפֵּרוֹת — But when fruit became plentiful in the markets of Jerusalem and it was no longer necessary for *reva'i* to be brought to the city to ensure a large supply of fruit, **הִתְקִינוּ שֶׁיְּהֵא נִפְדֶּה סָמוּךְ לַחוֹמָה** — [the Rabbis] canceled the original decree and **decreed that [*reva'i* fruit] may be redeemed** even **close to** (i.e., just outside) **the wall** of Jerusalem. **וּתְנַאי הָיָה הַדָּבָר** — However, there was a condition attached to the [new decree]; namely,

---
NOTES

They did this only during the *Shemittah* year [when it was permitted for anyone to take fruits growing in another person's property] (*Rav*).

[2]

1. Since those traveling to Jerusalem from within a day's journey would bring their own fruit to eat, they would not need to buy any in Jerusalem, and there would be more fruit there for everyone else. However, the Rabbis did not want to put people to the trouble of bringing fruit to Jerusalem if it took more than a day's travel to reach the city (*Derech Emunah, Hilchos Maaser Sheni* 9:37). This decree applied to all types of fruit trees, not just vineyards (*Rav*, as explained by *Tos. Yom Tov*; see note 2 of the previous Mishnah).

2. This is not the same as present-day Eilat, which is more than a day's travel from Jerusalem, and was not part of Eretz Yisrael in Biblical or Mishnaic times (*Tos. Anshei Shem; Tziyun HaHalachah* 9:133).

[85] **MISHNAH MAASER SHENI** / Chapter 5: *Kerem Reva'i* 5/3

- רע"ב -

שֶׁאֵימָתַי שֶׁיִּרְצוּ, יַחֲזֹר הַדָּבָר לִכְמוֹת שֶׁהָיָה. רַבִּי יוֹסֵי אוֹמֵר, מִשֶּׁחָרַב בֵּית הַמִּקְדָּשׁ, הָיָה הַתְּנַאי הַזֶּה. וּתְנַאי הָיָה, אֵימָתַי שֶׁיִּבָּנֶה בֵּית הַמִּקְדָּשׁ, יַחֲזֹר הַדָּבָר לִכְמוֹת שֶׁהָיָה.

[ג] **כֶּרֶם** רְבָעִי, בֵּית שַׁמַּאי אוֹמְרִים, אֵין

שאימתי שירצו. אם יתמעטו הפירות משחרב בית המקדש היה התנאי. לא לפי שרבו הפירות כדאמרת, אלא משחרב בית המקדש והיתה ירושלים ביד האויבים ולא היו חוששין לעטר שוקי ירושלים בפירות: (ג) אין לו חומש. אין הבעלים צריכין להוסיף חומש כשפודים אותו:

שֶׁאֵימָתַי שֶׁיִּרְצוּ יַחֲזֹר הַדָּבָר לִכְמוֹת שֶׁהָיָה — **that whenever they** [the Rabbis of a later generation] **would want** to restore the original practice, **the law should return to what it was** before. The Rabbis who canceled the original decree were concerned that at some future time there might again be a shortage of fruit in Jerusalem's markets. They therefore made a condition that their new decree should not be considered permanent, so that it could be withdrawn whenever the need arose.[3]

The next Tanna has a different view about the change in the decree and the condition to reinstate it:

רַבִּי יוֹסֵי אוֹמֵר — **R' Yose says:** The decree was not canceled at a time when there was a plentiful supply of fruit in Jerusalem; מִשֶּׁחָרַב בֵּית הַמִּקְדָּשׁ הָיָה הַתְּנַאי הַזֶּה — rather, **it was after the Beis HaMikdash was destroyed that** the Rabbis canceled the decree[4] and added **this condition.** וּתְנַאי הָיָה אֵימָתַי שֶׁיִּבָּנֶה בֵּית הַמִּקְדָּשׁ יַחֲזֹר הַדָּבָר לִכְמוֹת שֶׁהָיָה — **And the condition was that when the Beis HaMikdash will be rebuilt, the law will return to what it was** before, when fruit within a day's travel of Jerusalem had to be brought there. According to R' Yose, the decree will not be reinstated by a later court; rather, it will automatically return when the Beis HaMikdash is rebuilt and it will again be appropriate to have Jerusalem's markets full of fruit.

[3] As mentioned above, *reva'i* is similar to *maaser sheni* in that it must either be eaten in Jerusalem or be redeemed. This Mishnah, which also appears in *Peah* 7:6 and *Eduyos* 4:5, cites two disputes between Beis Shammai and Beis Hillel about how far the similarity between *reva'i* and *maaser sheni* extends. The first dispute:

כֶּרֶם רְבָעִי — **The produce of the fourth year of a vineyard:** בֵּית שַׁמַּאי אוֹמְרִים — **Beis Shammai say:** אֵין לוֹ חֹמֶשׁ — **It is not subject to** the law of **a fifth**

— NOTES —

3. *Rav, Rash.* This condition was necessary because the decree of one court cannot be overturned by another court unless the second court is greater in both wisdom and numbers (*Eduyos* 1:5). Since a later court might not be greater than the one making this new decree, they placed a condition in their new decree, allowing even a lesser court to bring back the original decree if necessary (*Tiferes Yisrael*).

4. After the Beis HaMikdash was destroyed and Jerusalem was occupied by our enemies, there was no reason to keep its markets well-stocked with fruit (*Rav*).

לוֹ חֹמֶשׁ וְאֵין לוֹ בִעוּר. וּבֵית הִלֵּל אוֹמְרִים, יֵשׁ לוֹ. בֵּית שַׁמַּאי אוֹמְרִים, יֵשׁ לוֹ פֶּרֶט וְיֵשׁ לוֹ עוֹלֵלוֹת, וְהָעֲנִיִּים פּוֹדִין לְעַצְמָן.

– רע״ב –

וְאֵין לוֹ בִעוּר. בשנה שלישית וששית [וכ״ח:] רביעית ושביעית שהמעשרות מתבערין, דחומש וביעור לא נאמרו בכרם רבעי אלא במעשר. ומיהו מודו בית שמאי דפדיון מיהא אית ליה, ואף על גב דלא נאמר פדיון במקרא דכרם רבעי, דילפי ליה מדכתיב (ויקרא יט) קדש הלולים, קרי ביה הלולים אחליה והדר אכליה: וּבֵית הִלֵּל אוֹמְרִים יֵשׁ לוֹ. דילפי קדש קדש ממעשר, ליתן לו כל דין מעשר: יֵשׁ לוֹ פֶּרֶט וְיֵשׁ לוֹ עוֹלֵלוֹת. דסברי ממון בעלים הוא ולא ממון גבוה חייב הלכך בפרט ובעוללות ככל כרם דעלמא. והטעמייס שמלקטים הפרט והעוללות מכרם רבעי, פודין לעצמן ואוכלין הפדיון בירושלים:

(the law that a person must add a fifth when he redeems his own produce),[1] וְאֵין לוֹ בִעוּר — and it is not subject to the law of **removal** in the fourth and seventh years of the *Shemittah* cycle.[2] This is because the Torah mentions these laws only in connection with *maaser sheni*, not *reva'i*. וּבֵית הִלֵּל אוֹמְרִים — But Beis Hillel say: יֵשׁ לוֹ — [*Reva'i*] **is** subject to both the law of a fifth and the law of removal, just like *maaser sheni*, because the law of *reva'i* is learned from the law of *maaser sheni*.[3]

The second dispute:

יֵשׁ לוֹ פֶּרֶט וְיֵשׁ לוֹ עוֹלֵלוֹת — [The fruit of a fourth-year vineyard] **is subject to** the law of *peret* and the law of *oleilos* (two kinds of grapes that must be left for the poor to take),[4] בֵּית שַׁמַּאי אוֹמְרִים — Beis Shammai say: וְהָעֲנִיִּים פּוֹדִין לְעַצְמָן — **and the poor people** who take the *peret* or *oleilos* from the *reva'i* trees **must redeem** them **for themselves** and bring the money to Jerusalem (if they choose not to bring the grapes to Jerusalem).

NOTES

[3]

1. We learned in Mishnah 4:3 that if someone redeems his own *maaser sheni* produce, he must add a fifth to its value. Beis Shammai hold that this law does not apply to someone redeeming his *reva'i* (*Rav*).

2. The Mishnah below will teach that *maaser sheni* is subject to the law of *biur* (removal of *maasros*). This means that a person must eat all his *maaser sheni* produce and use up all his *maaser sheni* money before Pesach of the fourth and seventh years of the *Shemittah* cycle. Any *maaser sheni* or redemption money still left at that time must be destroyed (see Mishnah 6).

Beis Shammai hold that the law of removal does not apply to *reva'i*. Thus, someone who has *reva'i* in his possession at Pesach of the fourth or seventh years of the cycle does not have to destroy it; rather, he can take it to Jerusalem or redeem it even afterward (see *Rav, Rambam Commentary*).

3. The Torah refers to both *reva'i* and *maaser sheni* as קֹדֶשׁ, *sanctified* (see *Vayikra* 19:24 and 27:30). These words create a *gezeirah shavah* between *reva'i* and *maaser sheni*, teaching us to learn the laws of one from the other (*Rav, Rash* from *Kiddushin* 54b).

4. *Peret* refers to grapes that fall off a cluster as it is being picked; *oleilos* are undeveloped clusters (see *Peah* 7:3-4). The Torah requires the owner to leave *peret* and *oleilos* for the poor to take (*Vayikra* 19:10).

According to Beis Shammai, *reva'i* is considered sanctified only in that it must be eaten in Jerusalem (or redeemed), but otherwise it is מָמוֹן הֶדְיוֹט, *property of a commoner* (i.e., the personal property of the owner). Therefore, *reva'i* is subject to *peret* and *oleilos* like all other grapes (*Rav, Rash* to *Peah* 7:6).

[87] **MISHNAH MAASER SHENI** / Chapter 5: *Kerem Reva'i*   5/4

- רע״ב -

וּבֵית הִלֵּל אוֹמְרִים, כֻּלּוֹ לַגַּת.

[ד] **כֵּיצַד** פּוֹדִין נֶטַע רְבָעִי, מַנִּיחַ אֶת הַסַּל עַל פִּי שְׁלֹשָׁה, וְאוֹמֵר, כַּמָּה אָדָם רוֹצֶה לִפְדּוֹת לוֹ בְּסֶלַע

בית הלל אומרים כולו לגת. דסברי ממון גבוה הוא כמו מעשר, הלכך אין לו פרט ועוללות, אלא דורכים אותו כולו כאחת ומעלה ואוכל בירושלים, או פודהו ומעלה הדמים לירושלים: (ד) מניח את הסל על פי שלשה. בקיאין בשומא, דסתם נטע רבעי אין דמיו ידועים לפי שצריך לחשב היליאות כדתנן הכא: לפדות בסלע. כלומר ליקח בסלע במחובר לקרקע:

וּבֵית הִלֵּל אוֹמְרִים — **But Beis Hillel say:** כֻּלּוֹ לַגַּת — **All of [the** *reva'i* **grapes],** including the *peret* and *oleilos*, **goes to the winepress** of the owner; the poor do not have any right to them.[5]

[4] The following Mishnah describes the procedure for redeeming *reva'i*. We learned in Mishnah 4:2 that before we redeem *maaser sheni*, we must first determine its value. A similar requirement applies to *reva'i*:

כֵּיצַד פּוֹדִין נֶטַע רְבָעִי — **How do we redeem** the produce of **a fourth-year tree?** מַנִּיחַ אֶת הַסַּל עַל פִּי שְׁלֹשָׁה — **[The owner] puts down a basket** of *reva'i* fruit to have its value assessed **by three** experts.[1] Whatever price they set for this basket is then used for the rest of the *reva'i* fruit.[2] וְאוֹמֵר כַּמָּה אָדָם רוֹצֶה לִפְדּוֹת לוֹ בְּסֶלַע — **He** then **says** to the three experts: "**How many** baskets of such fruit **would a person be willing to buy for a** *sela*[3] while the fruits are still

---

NOTES

5. Beis Hillel hold that *reva'i* is like *maaser sheni*, and they also hold that *maaser sheni* is not considered the owner's personal property but rather מָמוֹן גָּבֹהַּ, property of Heaven (see Mishnah 1:1). Therefore, *reva'i* is exempt from all the gifts to the poor, as is the case with all sanctified property [see *Peah* 7:8]. The owner may thus gather the entire crop, press it into wine, and bring it to Jerusalem to drink there, or he may redeem it and take the money to Jerusalem (*Rav, Rambam Commentary*).

Beis Hillel state "all of it goes to the winepress" (and not "to the *owner*") to teach that it is preferable to press the grapes into wine and drink the wine in Jerusalem, rather than to bring the grapes to Jerusalem or redeem them and bring the money. Wine makes a person happy and better able to praise God for the fruits. This fulfills the verse regarding *reva'i*: קֹדֶשׁ הִלּוּלִים לַה׳, holy for giving praise to Hashem (*Meleches Shlomo* to *Peah* 7:6).

[4]

1. The redemption price of *reva'i* is never easy to know because the assessment must take into account the expenses the owner has in growing the fruit (as the Mishnah will soon explain). It must therefore always be evaluated by three experts. This makes it different from *maaser sheni*, where the owner's expenses are *not* subtracted from the redemption price (see Mishnah 4:1), making its value easy to know. *Maaser sheni* can therefore be evaluated by just one person unless it has begun to spoil. Since it is hard to determine the value of spoiling produce, it must be evaluated by three experts even in the case of *maaser*, as we learned in Mishnah 4:2 (*Rav, Tos. Yom Tov*).

Therefore, as long as the produce did not begin to spoil, its value is known (*Beur HaGra*).

2. It is not necessary to have each basket evaluated separately, because we can assume that all the fruit has the same value (*Derech Emunah, Hil. Maaser Sheni* 9:47).

3. A *sela* is a large coin, which is worth four *dinars*. A number of baskets of fruit can be bought for a *sela*. The Mishnah

עַל מְנָת לְהוֹצִיא יְצִיאוֹת מִבֵּיתוֹ. וּמַנִּיחַ אֶת הַמָּעוֹת, וְאוֹמֵר, כָּל הַנִּלְקָט מִזֶּה, מְחֻלָּל עַל הַמָּעוֹת הָאֵלּוּ בְּכָךְ וְכָךְ סַלִּים בְּסֶלַע.

- רע"ב -

על מנת להוציא יציאות מביתו. שכר פעולת הכרם משעה שנקרא פרי, כגון שכר שמירה וכך סלים בסלע:

וטידור: **וּמַנִּיחַ אֶת הַמָּעוֹת.** לְפִי הַשּׁוּמָא, לְאַחַר שֶׁשָּׁמוּ כָּךְ וְכָךְ סַלִּים בְּסֶלַע:

attached to the tree, עַל מְנָת לְהוֹצִיא יְצִיאוֹת מִבֵּיתוֹ — **with the understanding that he will pay from his own pocket the expenses** of taking care of the fruit until they are picked?"[4] This means, in effect, that the value of the fruit is assessed in such a way as to allow the owner to subtract the cost of taking care of the fruit until it is picked.[5] This lower price is what he must pay to redeem the *reva'i* fruit. וּמַנִּיחַ אֶת הַמָּעוֹת וְאוֹמֵר — **He** (the owner) **then puts down coins** equal to the amount of produce he wants to redeem, **and says:** כָּל הַנִּלְקָט מִזֶּה מְחֻלָּל עַל הַמָּעוֹת הָאֵלּוּ בְּכָךְ וְכָךְ סַלִּים בְּסֶלַע — **"Any** fruit **that is picked from this** tree **is** hereby **redeemed onto these coins, at** the rate of **such-and-such** a number of **baskets for a** *sela*" (the rate established by the experts).[6]

[5] The previous Mishnah taught that we calculate the redemption price in a way that subtracts the owner's expenses from the value of the fruit. This Mishnah teaches that there is a case in which these expenses are *not* subtracted:

---- NOTES ----

mentions this coin only as an example, but any amount of money can be used for this calculation (*Derech Emunah* there 9:49).

4. These expenses include hoeing around the tree, guarding the fruit against thieves (*Rav, Rosh*), and picking the fruit (*Rash*).

[For example, if a person would pay a *sela* for four baskets of this kind of fruit after it is picked (a *dinar* a basket), he will pay a *sela* only for *five* baskets of the same fruit if he buys it when it is still growing and he has to pay to finish it himself. The reason is that it costs him an extra *dinar* to pay for that work. *Reva'i* fruit that has already been picked is therefore assessed at the rate of five baskets a *sela*, not four. In this way, the owner is compensated for the *dinar* of expenses he had in finishing the fruit.]

5. However, the only expenses that can be taken into account are the ones he has from the time the fruit became big enough to be considered a fruit. The ones he has before this time are not

considered (*Rav, Rosh*). The reason for this is that *reva'i* becomes sanctified while it is still attached to the tree, from the time it becomes large enough to be considered a fruit. Since it is sanctified, the owner has no obligation to care for it or pick it and take it to Jerusalem [as he does in the case of *maaser sheni*]. Thus, if he does care for it and pick it, he is doing so for the sake of the *reva'i* fruit, and we therefore calculate the price of the fruit in such a way as to allow him to subtract these expenses from the redemption price (*Derech Emunah* 9:50).

6. *Reva'i* fruit cannot be redeemed while it is still attached to the tree. He therefore puts aside the money and leaves it available for the redemption to take effect whenever the rest of the fruit is picked (*Meleches Shlomo*).

Since he is redeeming his own fruit, he will have to add an extra "fifth" to the total, according to Beis Hillel in the previous Mishnah. [See above, Mishnah 4:3, for how this "fifth" is calculated.]

[ה] **וּבַשְּׁבִיעִית**, פּוֹדֵהוּ בְּשָׁוְיוֹ. וְאִם הָיָה הַכֹּל מֻפְקָר, אֵין לוֹ אֶלָּא שְׂכַר לְקִיטָה. הַפּוֹדֶה נֶטַע רְבָעִי שֶׁלּוֹ, מוֹסִיף עָלָיו חֲמִישִׁיתוֹ, בֵּין שֶׁהוּא שֶׁלּוֹ וּבֵין שֶׁנִּתַּן לוֹ בְּמַתָּנָה.

– רע"ב –

(ה) ובשביעית. שאין שכר שמירה ולא עבודת קרקע, פודהו בשוויו: אם היה הכל מופקר. אם הפקירו הבעלים נטע רבעי שלהם, אין הזוכה בו מנכה אלא שכר לקיטה, ומעלה הפירות לירושלים או פודה ומעלה הדמים. ולא אמרינן כיון דמהפקירא קא זכי אין דין רבעי נוהג בו. ובשביעית אינו מנכה שכר לקיטה שכל אדם מלקט לעצמו: מוסיף עליו חומש. סתם מתניתין כבית הלל דילפי קדש קדש ממעשר: ובין שניתן לו במתנה. כשהוא סמדר, דאילו לאחר שנגמר בשוויו הא סברי בית הלל דממון גבוה הוא כמעשר ואין יכולים ליתן אותו במתנה:

וּבַשְּׁבִיעִית — However, if someone redeems *reva'i* produce that grew **during the *Shemittah* year,** **פּוֹדֵהוּ בְּשָׁוְיוֹ** — he redeems it for its **full value**, and not according to the method described in the previous Mishnah.[1]

The Mishnah now teaches about a case where even in an ordinary (non-*Shemittah*) year, we allow for only some expenses:

וְאִם הָיָה הַכֹּל מֻפְקָר — **And if** all the *reva'i* **was ownerless,** i.e., the owner declared his *reva'i* trees ownerless and then someone acquired them and wishes to redeem the fruit,[2] **אֵין לוֹ אֶלָּא שְׂכַר לְקִיטָה** — he does not have a right to any reduction in the redemption price **except for the cost of picking the fruit.** The other work, however, was not done by him, so there is no reason to allow him any reduction for it.[3]

A final ruling about redeeming *reva'i*:

הַפּוֹדֶה נֶטַע רְבָעִי שֶׁלּוֹ מוֹסִיף עָלָיו חֲמִישִׁיתוֹ — **Someone who redeems** the produce of **his own fourth-year tree must add a fifth to it,**[4] **בֵּין שֶׁהוּא שֶׁלּוֹ** — whether [the fruit] was always **his,** **וּבֵין שֶׁנִּתַּן לוֹ בְּמַתָּנָה** — **or whether it was given to him as a gift.**[5]

NOTES

[5]

1. Since it is forbidden to work a field or guard it during *Shemittah,* the owner of a *reva'i* tree does not have any expenses in that year. Therefore, he must redeem the fruit at full value. Nor do people hire workers to pick for them in *Shemittah;* rather, they pick the fruit themselves (*Rav*). [Since each person may pick only the small amount he needs for his own family, there is no need for him to hire workers to pick all the fruit in the orchard; rather, he picks what he needs himself.] Moreover, workers were reluctant to hire themselves out to pick *Shemittah* fruit because their wages could become subject to the laws of *Shemittah* produce, which has many restrictions (*Tos. Yom Tov,* based on *Sheviis* 8:4).]

2. *Rav, Rosh.* The person who acquired the fruits must now either bring them to Jerusalem or redeem them and bring the money to Jerusalem. The Mishnah teaches that the law of *reva'i* applies even to fruit acquired from *hefker* (*Rav, Rosh*).

3. [The Mishnah is speaking of a case in which the new owner acquired the trees when the fruit was ready to be picked, so that he did not have any expenses other than picking (see *Mishnah Rishonah*).]

4. This follows the opinion of Beis Hillel in Mishnah 3 (*Rav*).

5. The Mishnah refers to fruit that was given as a gift while in a very early stage of its development known as סְמָדַר, which is when the blossoms fall off and the little

[90] משניות מעשר שני / פרק ה: כרם רבעי

ה/ו

- רע"ב -

(ו) ערב יום טוב הראשון של פסח וכו'. דכתיב (דברים יד) מקצה שלש שנים תוציא את כל

[ו] עֶרֶב יוֹם טוֹב הָרִאשׁוֹן שֶׁל פֶּסַח שֶׁל רְבִיעִית וְשֶׁל שְׁבִיעִית, הָיָה בְעוּר.

מַעֲשֵׂר תְּבוּאָתְךָ, וְנֶאֱמַר לְהַלָּן (שם לא) מִקֵּץ שֶׁבַע שָׁנִים בְּמוֹעֵד שְׁנַת הַשְּׁמִטָּה בְּחַג הַסֻּכּוֹת, מַה לְּהַלָּן רֶגֶל אַף כָּאן רֶגֶל. אִי מַה לְּהַלָּן חַג הַסֻּכּוֹת אַף כָּאן חַג הַסֻּכּוֹת ת"ל (שם כו) כִּי תְכַלֶּה לַעְשֵׂר, רֶגֶל שֶׁכָּל מַעַשְׂרוֹת כָּלִין בּוֹ, הֱוֵי אוֹמֵר זֶה פֶּסַח שֶׁאֵין פֵּירוֹת שֶׁל שָׁנָה שְׁלִישִׁית נִגְמָרִים לִהְיוֹת נִלְקָטִים כֻּלָּן עַד שֶׁיָּבֹא פֶּסַח שֶׁל שָׁנָה הָרְבִיעִית, וְכֵן שֶׁל שָׁנָה שִׁשִּׁית עַד שֶׁיָּבֹא פֶּסַח שֶׁל שָׁנָה שְׁבִיעִית:

---

[6] From here through the end of the tractate, the Mishnah discusses the laws of בְּעוּר מַעֲשֵׂר, *biur maaser* (*removal of tithes*), and וִדּוּי מַעֲשֵׂר, *viduy maaser* (*the maaser confession*). Often, a person would designate tithes and keep them for a while, and only much later give them to their proper recipients or, in the case of *maaser sheni,* eat it in Jerusalem. The Torah fixes a deadline by which all tithes must be removed from one's possession (*Devarim* 14:28, 26:12). This removal is known as *biur maaser,* or just *biur.* After *biur* is performed, the Torah commands the owner to make a statement called *viduy maaser* (*the maaser confession*), in which he declares that he properly fulfilled the laws of tithing (26:12-15 there). The next four Mishnahs discuss *biur,* and Mishnahs 10-15 deal with *viduy maaser.*

There are actually two forms of *biur* (removal): Some tithes are removed from one's possession by giving them to their proper recipients, while others are removed through being destroyed (either by burning them or throwing them into the sea).[1] Our Mishnah states the latest time when *biur* must be performed and how the different tithes are to be removed:

עֶרֶב יוֹם טוֹב הָרִאשׁוֹן שֶׁל פֶּסַח שֶׁל רְבִיעִית וְשֶׁל שְׁבִיעִית הָיָה בְעוּר — **On Erev Pesach** (the day before the first day of Pesach) **of the fourth and seventh** years of the seven-year *Shemittah* cycle, **the removal** of tithes **was** performed; that is, someone who has tithes in his possession must remove them before Pesach of the fourth year and before Pesach of the seventh year. On Erev Pesach of the fourth year he removes the tithes remaining from the first three years of the *Shemittah* cycle, and on Erev Pesach of the seventh year (i.e., *Shemittah* itself) he removes the tithes remaining from years four through six.[2]

NOTES
---

balls of fruit first become visible (see *Rashi, Gittin* 31a ד"ה הוצאת סמדר). At this stage the undeveloped fruit is not yet considered fruit, and it therefore does not yet have the sanctity of *reva'i.* It is therefore still the owner's property and he may give it away as a gift. However, once the fruit passes this stage and grows to the point where it is considered a fruit, it becomes sanctified as *reva'i* and can no longer be given as a gift. This is because the *reva'i* fruit is now considered the property of Heaven and not the owner's personal property [see Mishnah 3 note 4] (*Rav*).

[Although *reva'i* produce is the pro-

perty of Heaven, the "owner" of the produce must add a fifth when redeeming it because the Torah considers it to be his with respect to the law of a fifth. However, he cannot transfer this "ownership" to someone else (by giving it as a gift), since it is not actually his (*Bava Kamma* 69a).]

[6]

1. *Rambam, Hilchos Maaser Sheni* 11:8.

2. The Torah states that *biur* is to be done after three years (*Devarim* 14:28), which is understood to mean that *biur* is required on every fourth year of the

[91] **MISHNAH MAASER SHENI** / Chapter 5: *Kerem Reva'i* — 5/6

- רע"ב -

כֵּיצַד הָיָה בְעוּר, נוֹתְנִין תְּרוּמָה וּתְרוּמַת מַעֲשֵׂר לַבְּעָלִים, וּמַעֲשֵׂר רִאשׁוֹן לִבְעָלָיו, וּמַעֲשַׂר עָנִי לִבְעָלָיו. וּמַעֲשֵׂר שֵׁנִי וְהַבִּכּוּרִים מִתְבַּעֲרִים בְּכָל מָקוֹם.

תְּרוּמָה וּתְרוּמַת מַעֲשֵׂר לַבְּעָלִים, לַכֹּהֲנִים, שֶׁהִסְתְּרוּמָה שֶׁלָּהֶם: וּמַעֲשֵׂר רִאשׁוֹן לִבְעָלָיו. לַלְוִיִּם: וּמַעֲשֵׂר עָנִי לִבְעָלָיו. לְעַנִיִּים: מִתְבַּעֲרִים בְּכָל מָקוֹם. צָרִיךְ לְבַעֲרָם וּלְאַבְּדָם מִן הָעוֹלָם:

נוֹתְנִין תְּרוּמָה וּתְרוּמַת מַעֲשֵׂר — **How was** *biur* **performed?** כֵּיצַד הָיָה בְעוּר לַבְּעָלִים — **They would give** *terumah* **and** *terumas maaser*[3] **to their owners, the Kohanim,** וּמַעֲשֵׂר רִאשׁוֹן לִבְעָלָיו — **and** *maaser rishon* **to its owners, the Leviim,** וּמַעֲשַׂר עָנִי לִבְעָלָיו — **and** *maasar ani* **to its owners, the poor.**[4] וּמַעֲשֵׂר שֵׁנִי וְהַבִּכּוּרִים מִתְבַּעֲרִים בְּכָל מָקוֹם — **However,** *maaser sheni* **and** *bikkurim*[5] **must be removed from every place; that is, they must be destroyed. If there is not enough time to take** *maaser sheni* **and** *bikkurim* **to Jerusalem and eat them there before the** *biur* **deadline, one has to destroy them.**[6]

---— NOTES ---—

Shemittah cycle (for the produce of years one through three) and on every seventh year (for the produce of years four through sixth). Produce of the *Shemittah* year itself is not subject to tithing.

It is derived from another verse that *biur* is performed during Pesach (see *Rav*). Under Biblical law, *biur* may be done anytime during the festival, even shortly before the end of the last day. However, the Rabbis moved up the deadline to the day *before* Pesach (see *Tos. Yom Tov*).

3. After a Levi receives *maaser rishon*, he separates a tenth and gives that tenth to a Kohen. This tithe is called *terumas maaser* (see *Bamidbar* 18:25-32). The Mishnah teaches here that not only must the original owner give his *terumah* and *maasros* to their proper recipients before the deadline, but so must a Levi give his *terumas maaser* to a Kohen (*Gur Aryeh*, *Devarim* 2:13).

4. One fulfills his obligation to remove *terumah, terumas maaser, maaser rishon,* and *maasar ani* by giving them to their recipients. (He does not destroy these tithes.) The Kohen, Levi, and poor person who receive these portions may eat them after the *biur* deadline (*Meleches Shlomo*).

5. Someone who grows any of the seven species (wheat, barley, grapes, figs, pomegranates, olives, and dates) in Eretz Yisrael has to set aside the first fruits that begin to ripen each year, bring them to the Temple, and give them to a Kohen (*Devarim* 26:1-11). These fruits are called *bikkurim*.

6. The Torah states regarding *biur* (*Devarim* 26:13): בִּעַרְתִּי הַקֹּדֶשׁ מִן הַבַּיִת וְגַם נְתַתִּיו לַלֵּוִי וְלַגֵּר לַיָּתוֹם וְלָאַלְמָנָה, *I have removed the holy [things] from the house and I have also given it to the Levi, to the convert, to the orphan, and to the widow*. The verse has two clauses: *I have removed the holy [things] ... and I have given ...* The Sages interpret the first clause, *I have removed the holy [things]*, as referring to *maaser sheni* and *bikkurim* (which are called "holy" in *Vayikra* 27:30 and 19:24), and the second clause, *I have given*, as referring to *terumah, maaser rishon, maaser sheni,* and *maasar ani* (see Mishnah 10). Thus, *maaser sheni* and *bikkurim* must be "removed" (which, in this context, means *destroyed*), while the other portions need only be "given" to the required recipients (*Mishnah Rishonah*).

When our Mishnah says that *maaser sheni* and *bikkurim* must be destroyed, it does not refer to food one will eat during the festival. On the day before Pesach, one reckons how much *maaser sheni* (for example) he will eat on Pesach, sets that amount aside, and destroys the rest. Although the Sages established that *biur* must be done on the day before Pesach, they made an exception for food that will be eaten on the festival itself. The Sages had the authority to do this, because

‎- רע"ב -‎

הבכורים נתנים לכהנים בתרומה. ואין צריך לבערס מן העולם משום דתרומה [וקרינהו] רחמנא, דאמר מר ותרומת ידך אלו הבכורים דכתיב בהו (דברים כו) ולקח הכהן הטנא מידך. ואין הלכה

רַבִּי שִׁמְעוֹן אוֹמֵר, הַבִּכּוּרִים נִתָּנִין לַכֹּהֲנִים בִּתְרוּמָה. הַתַּבְשִׁיל, בֵּית שַׁמַּאי אוֹמְרִים, צָרִיךְ לְבַעֵר. וּבֵית הִלֵּל אוֹמְרִים, הֲרֵי הוּא כִמְבֹעָר.

[ז] מִי שֶׁהָיוּ לוֹ פֵרוֹת בַּזְּמַן הַזֶּה וְהִגִּיעָה שְׁעַת

כרבי שמעון: התבשיל. שיש בו מפירות שביעית, או מעשר שני בשעת הביעור: הרי הוא כמבוער. כיון דאין ממשן ניכר: (ז) בזמן הזה. שאין בית המקדש קיים:

A differing opinion regarding *bikkurim*:

רַבִּי שִׁמְעוֹן אוֹמֵר — **R' Shimon says:** הַבִּכּוּרִים נִתָּנִין לַכֹּהֲנִים בִּתְרוּמָה — **Bik-kurim** are not destroyed; rather, they **are given to the Kohanim,** just like **terumah.**[7]

The Mishnah cites a dispute about a cooked food that contains both *maaser sheni* and *chullin,* but the *maaser sheni* ingredients cannot easily be seen in it:[8]

הַתַּבְשִׁיל — If someone has a **cooked food** that contains some *maaser sheni,* and he does not have enough time to take it to Jerusalem and eat it there before the *biur* deadline, בֵּית שַׁמַּאי אוֹמְרִים — **Beis Shammai say:** צָרִיךְ לְבַעֵר — **He must remove** (i.e., destroy) **it,** because it contains *maaser sheni,* which must be destroyed. וּבֵית הִלֵּל אוֹמְרִים — **But Beis Hillel say:** הֲרֵי הוּא כִמְבֹעָר — We view the *maaser sheni* **as though it were** already **removed,** that is, since the *maaser sheni* cannot easily be seen in the cooked food, there is no need to destroy it. Rather, one may keep the cooked food and eat it in Jerusalem even after the *biur* deadline.

[7] The following Mishnah presents another dispute between Beis Shammai and Beis Hillel regarding *biur:*

מִי שֶׁהָיוּ לוֹ פֵרוֹת בַּזְּמַן הַזֶּה — If **someone has produce** of *maaser sheni* **nowadays,** when the Temple is not standing, and *maaser sheni* may not be eaten even in Jerusalem,[1] וְהִגִּיעָה שְׁעַת הַבִּעוּר — **and the time for** *biur* **arrived,**

NOTES

Biblical law does not require *biur* until the end of the festival, as stated in note 2 (*Tos. Yom Tov,* from *Yerushalmi; Rav* to Mishnah 10).

According to Beis Hillel, *reva'i* of the previous three years must also be destroyed at this time (see Mishnahs 3 and 10; *Rambam, Hilchos Maaser Sheni* 11:8; *Derech Emunah* there §35).

7. R' Shimon holds that since the Torah refers to *bikkurim* as *terumah* (*Devarim* 12:17), the laws of *bikkurim* are similar to those of *terumah.* Therefore, just as

the *biur* of *terumah* is fulfilled by giving it to a Kohen (and not by destroying it), so too the *biur* of *bikkurim* is fulfilled by giving them to a Kohen (*Rav,* from *Yevamos* 73b).

8. Since the *maaser sheni* was cooked (along with the other ingredients), it is not easily noticeable (*Derech Emunah, Hilchos Maaser Sheni* 11:49).

[7]

1. See *Rambam, Hilchos Maaser Sheni* 2:1.

[93] **MISHNAH MAASER SHENI** / Chapter 5: *Kerem Reva'i*   5/8

- רע״ב -

צָרִיךְ לְחַלְּלָן עַל הַכֶּסֶף. דכתיב (שם יד) וְצַרְתָּ הַכֶּסֶף בְּיָדְךָ, הַכֶּסֶף בלבד מטלין: אֶחָד שֶׁהֵן כֶּסֶף וְאֶחָד שֶׁהֵן פֵּרוֹת. טעונים גניזה, ומה מועיל החלול: (ח) מִהֲרוּ וְתִקְּנוּ אֶת פֵּרוֹתֵיכֶם. תרומות ומעשרות לתת אותן לראוי להן, ומעשר שני להעלותו ולאכלו בירושלים: שֶׁלֹּא הִגִּיעוּ לְעוֹנַת הַמַּעַשְׂרוֹת. כל פרי ופרי כמו שמפורש בפרק קמא דמעשרות:

הַבְּעוּר, בֵּית שַׁמַּאי אוֹמְרִים, צָרִיךְ לְחַלְּלָן עַל הַכֶּסֶף. וּבֵית הִלֵּל אוֹמְרִים, אֶחָד שֶׁהֵן כֶּסֶף וְאֶחָד שֶׁהֵן פֵּרוֹת.

[ח] **אָמַר** רַבִּי יְהוּדָה, בָּרִאשׁוֹנָה הָיוּ שׁוֹלְחִין אֵצֶל בַּעֲלֵי בָתִּים שֶׁבַּמְּדִינוֹת, מַהֲרוּ וְתִקְּנוּ אֶת פֵּרוֹתֵיכֶם עַד שֶׁלֹּא

He must — צָרִיךְ לְחַלְּלָן עַל הַכֶּסֶף — בֵּית שַׁמַּאי אוֹמְרִים — Beis Shammai say: transfer sanctity from [the produce] to money, bring the money to Jerusalem, and destroy it there.[2] וּבֵית הִלֵּל אוֹמְרִים — But Beis Hillel say: אֶחָד שֶׁהֵן כֶּסֶף וְאֶחָד שֶׁהֵן פֵּרוֹת — Whether [the *maaser sheni*] is money or whether it is the original **produce**, it has no permissible use nowadays, because not only *maaser sheni* itself, but also food bought with *money* of *maaser sheni* may not be eaten anywhere. There is nothing gained, then, by redeeming the produce with money. Rather, one may leave the produce unredeemed and destroy the produce itself.[3]

[8] The law of *biur* applies not only to tithes that have already been separated from the crop, but also to produce that has not yet been tithed (*tevel*). A farmer who has untithed produce must separate the tithes and give them to their proper recipients (or, in the case of *maaser sheni*, eat it in Jerusalem) before the *biur* deadline.[1] The Mishnah elaborates upon this law:

בָּרִאשׁוֹנָה הָיוּ שׁוֹלְחִין אֵצֶל בַּעֲלֵי בָתִּים — אָמַר רַבִּי יְהוּדָה — R' Yehudah said: שֶׁבַּמְּדִינוֹת — **Originally,** as the deadline for *biur* approached, **[the Rabbis] would send** the following message **to householders in the provinces** (i.e., the parts of Eretz Yisrael outside Jerusalem): מַהֲרוּ וְתִקְּנוּ אֶת פֵּרוֹתֵיכֶם עַד שֶׁלֹּא

NOTES

2. Beis Shammai derive from a verse in the Torah that when there is no Temple, the owner performs the *biur* of *maaser sheni* by redeeming it with money and destroying the money in Jerusalem (see *Tos. Yom Tov*).

He may destroy the coins by grinding them up and tossing the shreds into a river (*Tiferes Yisrael*), or he may throw the whole coins into the ocean (*Derech Emunah* there 11:36).

3. According to Beis Hillel, it is illogical to interpret the verse as meaning that one must redeem his *maaser sheni* with money, since nowadays the produce and the money are equally useless.

Thus, in their opinion, it is also possible to fulfill the mitzvah of *biur* with the produce itself. This can be done by hiding the produce away and letting it rot (*Rash; Melechas Shlomo,* from *Rash Sirilio*).

[8]

1. The Torah states in reference to *biur* (*Devarim* 26:13): בִּעַרְתִּי הַקֹּדֶשׁ מִן הַבַּיִת, *I have removed the holy [things] from the house.* By using the word "holy," the verse extends the law of *biur* to untithed produce (*tevel*), which is "holy" on account of the sacred portions (such as *terumah*) within it that have yet to be removed (*Rash,* from *Yerushalmi*).

משניות מעשר שני / פרק ה: כרם רבעי [94]

תַּגִּיעַ שְׁעַת הַבִּעוּר. עַד שֶׁבָּא רַבִּי עֲקִיבָא וְלִמֵּד, שֶׁכָּל הַפֵּרוֹת שֶׁלֹּא בָאוּ לְעוֹנַת הַמַּעַשְׂרוֹת, פְּטוּרִים מִן הַבִּעוּר.

[ט] **מִי** שֶׁהָיוּ פֵרוֹתָיו רְחוֹקִים מִמֶּנּוּ,

- רע"ב -

פטורים מן הבעור. ובראשונה היו אומרים דקודם עונת המעשרות נמי זקוק לבער. והלכה כרבי עקיבא:
(ט) **מי שהיו פירותיו רחוקים ממנו**. וכבר נתקנו והגיע זמן הביעור:

תַּגִּיעַ שְׁעַת הַבִּעוּר — **"Hurry and prepare** (i.e., process) **your produce before the time for** *biur* **arrives."** At first, the Rabbis held that untithed produce is subject to *biur* even before it has been fully processed.[2] They therefore sent messengers warning owners to finish processing their produce, so that they could tithe it, and then send the tithes to the proper recipients (or, in the case of *maaser sheni,* eat it in Jerusalem) before the *biur* deadline.[3] עַד שֶׁבָּא רַבִּי עֲקִיבָא וְלִמֵּד שֶׁכָּל הַפֵּרוֹת שֶׁלֹּא בָאוּ לְעוֹנַת הַמַּעַשְׂרוֹת פְּטוּרִים מִן הַבִּעוּר — This practice of sending messengers continued **until R' Akiva came and taught that any produce that has not reached the tithing stage** (i.e., its processing is not complete)[4] **is exempt from** *biur*. That is, the law of *biur* does not apply to unprocessed produce; thus, someone who has unprocessed produce does not have to do anything with it before the *biur* deadline.[5]

[9] This Mishnah speaks of someone who will not have access to his tithes before the *biur* deadline:

מִי שֶׁהָיוּ פֵרוֹתָיו רְחוֹקִים מִמֶּנּוּ — **If someone's produce is far away from him** and thus he cannot deliver the tithes to their proper recipients before the *biur*

---- NOTES ----

2. *Rambam Commentary,* Kafich edition.

[The completion of processing (גְּמַר מְלָאכָה) is different for each species of produce. The processing of grain, for example, is complete when the farmer stacks the kernels of grain into a pile and smooths down the pile.]

3. Produce may not be tithed before it has been fully processed. However, if someone breaks this law and tithes unprocessed produce, the tithes would be valid [provided that the produce is ripe enough to be edible] (*Terumos* 1:10). The Rabbis originally thought that since it is possible to remove tithes from unprocessed produce, it can be viewed as produce that "contains" sacred tithes. Thus, it is holy produce, which requires *biur,* as stated in note 1 (*Rash,* as explained by *Asvan D'Oraisa* 25). Therefore, if a farmer has unprocessed produce, he would have to

process it (because otherwise tithing it would be forbidden), then remove the tithes, and then deliver the tithes to the proper recipients. To make sure that all this got done before the deadline for *biur,* the Rabbis sent out messengers to warn the farmers that the deadline was approaching.

4. In this context, the term עוֹנַת הַמַּעַשְׂרוֹת, *tithing stage,* does not carry its usual meaning (namely, the point of growth at which produce becomes edible); rather, it refers to the completion of processing [גְּמַר מְלָאכָה] (*Meleches Shlomo,* from *Rash Sirilio*).

5. R' Akiva ruled that since it is forbidden to tithe unprocessed produce, such produce cannot be called holy. It attains the status of holy produce only after its processing has been completed, and its tithing is permitted (*Asvan D'Oraisa* there).

[95] **MISHNAH MAASER SHENI** / Chapter 5: *Kerem Reva'i*

- רע"ב -

צָרִיךְ לִקְרוֹת לָהֶם שֵׁם. מַעֲשֶׂה בְּרַבָּן גַּמְלִיאֵל וְהַזְּקֵנִים שֶׁהָיוּ בָאִין בִּסְפִינָה, אָמַר רַבָּן גַּמְלִיאֵל, עִשּׂוּר שֶׁאֲנִי עָתִיד לָמֹד, נָתוּן לִיהוֹשֻׁעַ וּמְקוֹמוֹ מֻשְׂכָּר לוֹ. עִשּׂוּר אַחֵר שֶׁאֲנִי עָתִיד לָמֹד,

צריך לקרות להם שם. לזכות אותן לבעלים, כך עובדא דרבן גמליאל וזקנים: עשור שאני עתיד למוד. מעשר ראשון שאני עתיד ליתן

מפירות שיש לי בבית: **נתון ליהושע.** לוי היה. ותרומה גדולה לא נתן עתה דמשום דתרומה מפרישין אותה בגורן, [וכדתנינא] שאי אפשר לגורן שתעקר אלא אם כן נתרמה תרומה גדולה וכבר הפריש הפירות אותה בגורן: **ומקומו מושכר לו. ומקום המעשר מושכר לו, ויקנה המעשר אגב קרקע: עשור אחר.** מעשר עני:

---

deadline, צָרִיךְ לִקְרוֹת לָהֶם שֵׁם — **he must name [their recipients],** that is, he must name the people (Kohen, Levi, poor person) to whom he wants to give the tithes, and transfer ownership of the tithes to them. He thus fulfills the obligation of *biur* even though the recipient does not yet have the tithes in his hand.[1]

The Mishnah relates an incident to show how this can be done:

מַעֲשֶׂה בְּרַבָּן גַּמְלִיאֵל וְהַזְּקֵנִים — There was **an incident** that took place **with Rabban Gamliel and the Elders,** namely, R' Yehoshua, R' Akiva, and R' Elazar ben Azaryah, שֶׁהָיוּ בָאִין בִּסְפִינָה — **who were traveling on a ship** when Rabban Gamliel realized that the deadline for *biur* was approaching and he not yet fulfilled his tithing obligations. אָמַר רַבָּן גַּמְלִיאֵל — **So Rabban Gamliel said:** עִשּׂוּר שֶׁאֲנִי עָתִיד לָמֹד נָתוּן לִיהוֹשֻׁעַ — "**The tenth** of my produce **that I will measure out** as *maaser rishon*[2] **is** hereby **given to Yehoshua,** who is a Levi, וּמְקוֹמוֹ מֻשְׂכָּר לוֹ — **and its place** (i.e., the land on which the *maaser rishon* lies) **is rented to him,** so that he can acquire the *maaser rishon* by paying for the ground beneath it.[3] עִשּׂוּר אַחֵר שֶׁאֲנִי עָתִיד לָמֹד

NOTES

[9]

1. This method works for *terumah, maaser rishon,* and *maasar ani,* because the obligation of *biur* is fulfilled in the case of these tithes by giving them to their required recipients (as taught in Mishnah 6). Regarding *maaser sheni* and *bikkurim,* however, which must be destroyed, the owner has no choice but to wait until he comes home and then destroy them (*Hilchasa Gevirasa*).

The Mishnah's ruling applies not only to tithes that have already been separated, but also to *untithed* produce, which likewise requires *biur* (as taught in the previous Mishnah). In that case, the owner must first designate the tithes, which he can do by identifying the location of each tithe (for example, he says that the *terumah* is in the northern section of a particular pile of produce). He then names the recipients and transfers ownership of the tithe to them (*Rash; Maharsha, Kiddushin* 27a).

2. Rabban Gamliel had already designated his tithes (either at home or when he was on the ship), but he had not yet physically separated them from the rest of his produce (see previous note). When he said, "that I will measure out," he was referring to the physical act of separation that he intended to perform later, after returning home (*Maharam, Bava Metzia* 11a).

3. In order to acquire something, an official act of acquisition (*kinyan*) is necessary. There is a difference in this regard between land and movable objects. One can acquire land simply by paying for it, but one cannot acquire movable objects in this manner (rather, the recipient must use a different method, such as הַגְבָּהָה,

[96] **משניות מעשר שני / פרק ה: כרם רבעי** ה/ט

נָתוּן לַעֲקִיבָא בֶּן יוֹסֵף שֶׁיִּזְכֶּה בּוֹ לָעֲנִיִּים, וּמְקוֹמוֹ מֻשְׂכָּר לוֹ. אָמַר רַבִּי יְהוֹשֻׁעַ, עָשׂוּר שֶׁאֲנִי עָתִיד לָמֹד נָתוּן לְאֶלְעָזָר בֶּן עֲזַרְיָה, וּמְקוֹמוֹ מֻשְׂכָּר לוֹ. וְנִתְקַבְּלוּ זֶה מִזֶּה שָׂכָר.

— רע״ב —

נתון לעקיבא בן יוסף. גבאי של עניים היה: עשור שאני עתיד למוד. מעשר מן המעשר, שאני צריך ליתן לכהן מן המעשר שנתן לי רבן גמליאל: נתון לאלעזר

בן עזריה. כהן היה, והוא עשירי לטוהרה: ונתקבלו שכר זה מזה. רבן גמליאל קבל שכר מקומו של מעשר ראשון מרבי יהושע, ושכר מקומו של מעשר עני מרבי עקיבא. ורבי יהושע קבל שכר מקום מעשר מן המעשר מרבי אלעזר בן עזריה, וקנה לכל אחד מקום המעשר הראוי לו בכסף שנתן למשכיר, ששכירות קרקע נקנית בכסף:

נָתוּן לַעֲקִיבָא בֶּן יוֹסֵף — **Another tenth** of my produce that I will measure out as *maasar ani* is hereby **given to Akiva ben Yosef,** who is a treasurer of a charity for the poor, **שֶׁיִּזְכֶּה בּוֹ לָעֲנִיִּים** — **so that he will acquire it on behalf of the poor, וּמְקוֹמוֹ מֻשְׂכָּר לוֹ** — **and [the** *maasar ani's***] place is rented to him,** so that he can acquire the *maasar ani* by paying for the ground beneath it." In this way, Rabban Gamliel gave his *maaser rishon* and *maaser ani* to their appropriate recipients.[4] R' Yehoshua (the Levi) was then required to separate *terumas maaser* from the *maaser rishon* he had just received and give the *terumas maaser* to a Kohen. **אָמַר רַבִּי יְהוֹשֻׁעַ** — **So R' Yehoshua said:** **עָשׂוּר שֶׁאֲנִי עָתִיד לָמֹד נָתוּן לְאֶלְעָזָר בֶּן עֲזַרְיָה** — "**The tenth** of my *maaser rishon* **that I will measure out** as *terumas maaser* is hereby **given to Elazar ben Azaryah,** who is a Kohen, **וּמְקוֹמוֹ מֻשְׂכָּר לוֹ** — **and [the** *terumas maaser's***] place is rented to him,** so that he can acquire the *terumas maaser* by paying for the ground beneath it."[5] **וְנִתְקַבְּלוּ זֶה מִזֶּה שָׂכָר** — **After** stating to whom they would give their tithes, **they received the rent payment from each other;** that is, Rabban Gamliel received payment from R' Yehoshua for the place of the *maaser rishon*, and another payment from R' Akiva for the place of the *maasar ani*. R' Yehoshua received payment from R' Elazar ben Azaryah for the place of the *terumas maaser*.

--- NOTES ---

lifting up, or מְשִׁיכָה, drawing close). However, if there are movable objects on the land being acquired, the act of acquisition performed for the land can work for the objects as well [קִנְיָן אַגַּב] (see *Kiddushin* 1:4-5). In the Mishnah's case, therefore, Rabban Gamliel rented out the land beneath the *maaser rishon* to R' Yehoshua, so that, by paying for the land, R' Yehoshua would also acquire the *maaser rishon* (see *Rav*).

[It is also possible to acquire a movable object through the act of חֲלִיפִין, *chalifin* (exchange), where the recipient hands one of his possessions to the owner and, in exchange, he acquires the movable object. Although this method is effective even if

the movable object is far away, it was not used in this circumstance, because Torah forbids using *chalifin* for the acquisition of tithes (see *Bava Metzia* 11b).]

4. The Mishnah does not say what Rabban Gamliel did with his *terumah*. Presumably, he separated his *terumah* before he left home and gave it to a Kohen then, because it was the custom to separate *terumah* as soon as possible (*Rash*).

5. R' Yehoshua received *maaser rishon*, which, before the separation of *terumas maaser*, is the equivalent of untithed produce (*tevel*). Therefore, he must have designated the *terumas maaser* before he transferred its ownership to R' Elazar ben Azaryah (see note 1).

[97] **MISHNAH MAASER SHENI** / Chapter 5: *Kerem Reva'i*

- רע״ב -

(י) ביום טוב האחרון
היו מתודין. ולא היו
מתודין בי״ט ראשון
מיד אחר הביעור, כדי
שיהיה לו מה יאכל ברגל. הלכך ערב יום טוב ראשון היה מבער ומשייר עד יום אחרון:

[י] **בְּמִנְחָה** בְּיוֹם טוֹב הָאַחֲרוֹן הָיוּ מִתְוַדִּין. כֵּיצַד הָיָה הַוִּדּוּי,

[10] The rest of the chapter discusses the mitzvah of *viduy maaser* (the *maaser* declaration). The Torah commands that after one has performed *biur* with his tithes, he must recite the *viduy maaser,* in which he declares that he has separated his tithes and dealt with them in the required manner.[1] This is the text of the declaration (*Devarim* 26:13-15):[2]

בִּעַרְתִּי הַקֹּדֶשׁ מִן הַבַּיִת וְגַם נְתַתִּיו לַלֵּוִי וְלַגֵּר לַיָּתוֹם וְלָאַלְמָנָה כְּכָל מִצְוָתְךָ אֲשֶׁר צִוִּיתָנִי לֹא עָבַרְתִּי מִמִּצְוֹתֶיךָ וְלֹא שָׁכָחְתִּי, *I have removed the holy [things] from the house, and I have also given it to the Levi, to the convert, to the orphan, and to the widow, according to Your entire commandment that You commanded me; I have not transgressed Your commandments and I did not forget.*

לֹא אָכַלְתִּי בְאֹנִי מִמֶּנּוּ וְלֹא בִעַרְתִּי מִמֶּנּוּ בְּטָמֵא וְלֹא נָתַתִּי מִמֶּנּוּ לְמֵת שָׁמַעְתִּי בְּקוֹל ה׳ אֱלֹהָי עָשִׂיתִי כְּכֹל אֲשֶׁר צִוִּיתָנִי, *I did not eat from it when I was an onein,*[3] *I did not remove it in a state of tumah, and I did not give of it for [the needs of] the dead; I listened to the voice of Hashem, my God; I have acted according to everything that You have commanded me.*

הַשְׁקִיפָה מִמְּעוֹן קָדְשְׁךָ מִן הַשָּׁמַיִם וּבָרֵךְ אֶת עַמְּךָ אֶת יִשְׂרָאֵל וְאֵת הָאֲדָמָה אֲשֶׁר נָתַתָּה לָנוּ כַּאֲשֶׁר נִשְׁבַּעְתָּ לַאֲבוֹתֵינוּ אֶרֶץ זָבַת חָלָב וּדְבָשׁ, *Gaze down from Your holy place, from the heavens, and bless Your nation, Israel, and the Land that You have given us, as You swore to our forefathers, a land flowing with milk and honey.*

The following four Mishnahs interpret the entire *viduy maaser,* phrase by phrase:

בְּמִנְחָה בְּיוֹם טוֹב הָאַחֲרוֹן הָיוּ מִתְוַדִּין — **On the afternoon of the last day of the Yom Tov of Pesach, the *viduy* would be recited.**[4] כֵּיצַד הָיָה הַוִּדּוּי — **What**

NOTES

[10]

1. This declaration is called *viduy,* which literally means *confession,* for the following reason: Originally, the firstborn son of each family was supposed to serve God in the Temple, and thus a father would have given most of his tithes (*terumah, maaser rishon,* etc.) to his firstborn son. Accordingly, these tithes would have remained in his house. After the sin of the Golden Calf, however, the duty of the Temple service was transferred to the Kohanim and Leviim and the tithes were then given to them. Thus, it was due to the sin of the Golden Calf that one must remove his tithes from his house and give them to the Kohanim and Leviim. When one recites the phrase, "I have removed the holy [things] from the house," he is confessing that his forefathers sinned and thereby caused the holy things, i.e., *terumah* and *maaser,* to be removed from his house (*Sforno* to *Devarim* 26:13, cited by *Tos. Yom Tov*).

2. The *viduy* does not have to be recited in Hebrew, but may be said in any language (*Sotah* 7:1).

3. Literally, *in my grieving.* See Mishnah 12.

4. We have learned that according to Biblical law, one may perform *biur* and recite the *viduy* until the end of the last day of Pesach, but the Sages moved *biur* forward to the day before Pesach (see Mishnah 6). Nevertheless, they did not require that *viduy* be recited immediately after *biur*

ה/י

בִּעַרְתִּי הַקֹּדֶשׁ מִן הַבַּיִת, זֶה מַעֲשֵׂר שֵׁנִי וְנֶטַע רְבָעִי. נְתַתִּיו לַלֵּוִי, זֶה מַעֲשַׂר לֵוִי. וְגַם נְתַתִּיו, זוֹ תְרוּמָה וּתְרוּמַת מַעֲשֵׂר. לַגֵּר לַיָּתוֹם וְלָאַלְמָנָה, זֶה מַעֲשַׂר עָנִי, הַלֶּקֶט וְהַשִּׁכְחָה וְהַפֵּאָה,

- רע"ב -

זה מעשר שני ונטע רבעי. שנקראו קדש: זה מעשר לוי. כלומר מעשר ראשון: וגם נתתיו זו תרומה גדולה. וגם, תוספת הוא, משמע וגם נתתיו ללוי חוץ ממה שנתתי לכהן:

---

is the meaning of **the** *viduy*? To which tithes and to which laws of tithing does it refer?   "בִּעַרְתִּי הַקֹּדֶשׁ מִן הַבַּיִת" זֶה מַעֲשֵׂר שֵׁנִי וְנֶטַע רְבָעִי" — The term *holy things* in the opening phrase, **I have removed the holy [things] from the house,** refers to **maaser sheni** and **neta reva'i**. These must be "removed ... from the house" either by being taken to Jerusalem and eaten there, or — if that is not possible — destroyed in accordance with the law of *biur*.[5]   "נְתַתִּיו לַלֵּוִי זֶה מַעֲשַׂר לֵוִי" — The next words, **I have given it to the Levi,** refer to **the maaser of the Levi** (i.e., *maaser rishon*), which must be given to a Levi.   "וְגַם נְתַתִּיו זוֹ תְרוּמָה וּתְרוּמַת מַעֲשֵׂר" — The word *also* in the phrase, **and I have also given it,** indicates to us that the declaration includes **terumah** and **terumas maaser,** which must be given to a Kohen.[6]   "לַגֵּר לַיָּתוֹם וְלָאַלְמָנָה זֶה מַעֲשַׂר עָנִי הַלֶּקֶט וְהַשִּׁכְחָה וְהַפֵּאָה" — The next words, **to the convert, to the orphan, and to the widow,** refer to **maasar ani, leket, shich'chah, and peah,** which are given to the poor.[7]

--- NOTES ---

because of the following consideration: Someone who performs *biur* on the day before Pesach may set aside as much *maaser sheni* or *reva'i* as he needs for the festival (see note 6 there). Thus, he cannot recite the *viduy* on that day, because the *viduy* implies that all one's *maaser sheni* and *reva'i* have already been removed (i.e., eaten in Jerusalem or destroyed). On the afternoon of the festival's last day, however, by which time he will have finished all his *maaser sheni* and *reva'i*, he can indeed declare that he has removed them completely (see *Rav, Tos. Yom Tov*).

5. The word קֹדֶשׁ, *holy,* is interpreted as referring to *maaser sheni* and *reva'i,* because the Torah describes them as such in *Vayikra* 27:30, 19:24 (*Rav*).

In the context of *maaser sheni*, "removal" includes the obligation to *destroy* what had not been eaten by the *biur* deadline. Therefore, our Mishnah, which mentions *reva'i* here, must be following Beis Hillel, who maintain that *reva'i* is subject to destruction, and not Beis Shammai, who hold that *reva'i* is eaten, as taught in Mishnah 3 (*Tiferes Yisrael*).

The Mishnah does not mention *bikkurim* in this clause, together with *maaser sheni* and *reva'i*. In this, it follows the opinion of R' Shimon, who holds that, unlike *maaser sheni* and *reva'i*, *bikkurim* are not destroyed but are given to a Kohen (Mishnah 6). Had the Mishnah been following the opinion of the Sages, who require *bikkurim* to be destroyed, it would have listed *bikkurim* here (*Rash*, from *Yerushalmi*).

6. The verse thus means: "I have *also* given to a Levi, besides what I gave to a Kohen" (*Rav*).

According to R' Shimon, who holds that *bikkurim* are not destroyed (see previous note), the word גַּם, *also,* includes not only *terumah* and *terumas maaser,* but *bikkurim* as well, since all of these portions must be given to the Kohen, as opposed to being destroyed. The Mishnah does not need to mention *bikkurim* separately, because the term "*terumah*" can include *bikkurim*, as we find in *Devarim* 12:6 (*Rash*).

7. *Leket* refers to one or two stalks that fell during the harvest, *shich'chah* refers

[99] **MISHNAH MAASER SHENI** / Chapter 5: *Kerem Reva'i*

- רע״ב -

מן הבית זו חלה. שהיא נתרמה מן העיסה בתוך הבית:

אַף עַל פִּי שֶׁאֵינָן מְעַכְּבִין אֶת הַוִּדּוּי. מִן הַבַּיִת, זוֹ חַלָּה.

[יא] בְּכָל מִצְוָתְךָ אֲשֶׁר צִוִּיתָנִי, הָא אִם הִקְדִּים

אַף עַל פִּי שֶׁאֵינָן מְעַכְּבִין אֶת הַוִּדּוּי — *Leket, shich'chah,* and *peah* are included in the *viduy* **even though they do not prevent the *viduy*** from being recited (that is, someone who transgressed the law and took these portions for himself may still recite the *viduy*).[8] מִן הַבַּיִת״ זוֹ חַלָּה — The words *from the house* (in the opening phrase, *I have removed the holy things from the house*) refer to **challah**, the portion of dough that must be given to a Kohen.[9]

[11] This Mishnah explains the second half of the first verse of the *viduy* (*Devarim* 26:13): בְּכָל מִצְוָתְךָ אֲשֶׁר צִוִּיתָנִי לֹא עָבַרְתִּי מִמִּצְוֹתֶיךָ וְלֹא שָׁכָחְתִּי, *according to Your entire commandment that You commanded me; I have not transgressed Your commandments, and I did not forget.* Each phrase refers to a different law:

״בְּכָל מִצְוָתְךָ אֲשֶׁר צִוִּיתָנִי״ — The phrase, *according to Your entire commandment that You commanded me,* refers to the obligation to separate the tithes in their proper order (that is, *bikkurim, terumah, maaser rishon, maaser sheni/ ani*).[1] Therefore, if one followed this order, he recites the *viduy,* הָא אִם הִקְדִּים

― NOTES ―

to sheaves or stalks that were forgotten in the field, and *peah* is a portion of the standing crop that must be left unharvested (see *Vayikra* 19:9, 23:22; *Devarim* 24:19).

8. Generally, if someone failed to separate even one of the portions listed in the Mishnah, he is forbidden to say any part of the *viduy maaser* (*Rambam, Hilchos Maaser Sheni* 11:12). However, *leket, shich'chah,* or *peah* are an exception to this rule. Even if one did not leave these portions for the poor but kept them for himself, he may recite the *viduy.* This is because the text of the *viduy* states: *I have given* etc., which, according to its plain meaning, refers only to the portions that are *given,* such as *maasar ani,* and not to *leket, shich'chah,* and *peah,* which need not actually be given to the poor, but may be left in the field for the poor to take themselves, as the Torah states: לֶעָנִי וְלַגֵּר תַּעֲזֹב אֹתָם , *For the poor man and the convert you shall leave them* (*Vayikra* 19:10; 23:22). Therefore, even if the owner kept the *leket, shich'chah,* and *peah* for himself, he can say: *I have given it … to the convert, to the orphan, and to the widow,* because this would not be a lie, since it would refer to *maasar ani* (*Meleches Shlomo,* citing *Rabbeinu Yehosef*).

It emerges that if the owner did leave *leket, shich'chah,* and *peah* for the poor, then when he says *to the convert, to the orphan, and to the widow,* he may also have these three portions in mind. But if he did not leave these portions for the poor, he may have only *maasar ani* in mind (*Tosefos Anshei Shem* to Mishnah 12, citing *Hon Ashir*).

9. *The house* alludes to *challah,* because *challah* is separated from dough, which is prepared in the house (*Rav*). This is in contrast to the other tithes, which may be separated in the field, before the produce is brought inside (*Derech Emunah, Hilchos Maaser Sheni* 11:67).

[11]

1. One who did not follow this sequence has transgressed a negative commandment, but his tithes are valid after the fact (*Terumos* 3:6).

משניות מעשר שני / פרק ה: כרם רבעי

מַעֲשֵׂר שֵׁנִי לָרִאשׁוֹן, אֵינוֹ יָכוֹל לְהִתְוַדּוֹת. לֹא עָבַרְתִּי מִמִּצְוֹתֶיךָ, לֹא הִפְרַשְׁתִּי מִמִּין עַל שֶׁאֵינוֹ מִינוֹ, וְלֹא מִן הַתָּלוּשׁ עַל הַמְחֻבָּר, וְלֹא מִן הַמְחֻבָּר עַל הַתָּלוּשׁ, וְלֹא מִן הֶחָדָשׁ עַל הַיָּשָׁן, וְלֹא מִן הַיָּשָׁן עַל הֶחָדָשׁ. וְלֹא שָׁכַחְתִּי,

- רע"ב -

(יא) ולא מן התלוש על המחובר וכו'. דהיינו מן החיוב על הפטור ומן הפטור על החיוב: ולא מן החדש על הישן. דכתיב (דברים יד) היוצא השדה שנה שנה, ולא משנה זו על של חברתה:

מַעֲשֵׂר שֵׁנִי לָרִאשׁוֹן אֵינוֹ יָכוֹל לְהִתְוַדּוֹת — **but if he** reversed the order, for example,[2] **he separated** *maaser sheni* **before** *maaser rishon*, **he may not recite the** *viduy*.

"לֹא עָבַרְתִּי מִמִּצְוֹתֶיךָ" — **The next phrase,** *I have not transgressed any of Your commandments,* **means:** לֹא הִפְרַשְׁתִּי מִמִּין עַל שֶׁאֵינוֹ מִינוֹ — **I did not separate** tithes **from one species** of produce **for a different species** of produce (for example, from wheat for barley),[3] וְלֹא מִן הַתָּלוּשׁ עַל הַמְחֻבָּר — **and not from produce that is detached** from the ground **for produce that is still attached** to the ground, וְלֹא מִן הַמְחֻבָּר עַל הַתָּלוּשׁ — **and not from attached produce for detached produce,**[4] וְלֹא מִן הֶחָדָשׁ עַל הַיָּשָׁן — **and not from the new** crop **for the old** crop, וְלֹא מִן הַיָּשָׁן עַל הֶחָדָשׁ — **and not from the old** crop **for the new** crop.[5]

"וְלֹא שָׁכַחְתִּי" — **The verse's final phrase,** *and I did not forget,* **means:**

— NOTES —

2. *Rashi* to *Devarim* 26:13.

3. The Torah forbids designating one species of produce as *terumah* or *maaser* for another species of produce. If one did make such a designation, it has no effect — the produce remains *tevel,* as it was before (*Terumos* 2:4).

4. It is a basic rule that produce exempt from tithing cannot be designated as *terumah* or *maaser* for produce subject to tithing, or the other way around. Therefore, one cannot designate detached produce as *terumah* or *maaser* for attached produce, or vice versa, because detached produce is subject to tithing, whereas attached produce is not. Such designations are ineffective even after the fact (*Rav;* see *Terumos* 1:5).

5. The "new crop" refers to produce grown in the current year, and the "old crop" is produce grown in an earlier year. The Torah disqualifies tithes that were separated from the produce of one year for the produce of another year (*Rav; Terumos* there).

Although the Mishnah does not mention this point, the law is that if someone designated tithes in any of the ways just listed (for example, from one species for another, or from detached produce for attached produce), he is forbidden to recite the *viduy maaser*. The Mishnah did not have to state this law here (as it did above regarding a designation made out of sequence), for since these designations are not effective, it is obvious that the *viduy maaser* may not be recited (*Mishnah Rishonah*).

The phrase that was discussed earlier, *[I acted] according to Your "entire" commandment,* implies that not only are the person's tithes valid, but he also designated them in the manner required by the Torah. It is thus interpreted as excluding someone who separated tithes in the wrong order, in which case, although he failed to designate his tithes properly, they are still valid. This is in contrast to the next phrase, *I did not transgress,* which excludes designations that are completely ineffective, such as separating tithes from one species for another, etc. (*Tiferes Yaakov*).

[101] **MISHNAH MAASER SHENI** / Chapter 5: *Kerem Reva'i*

לֹא שָׁכַחְתִּי מִלְּבָרֶכְךָ וּמִלְּהַזְכִּיר שִׁמְךָ עָלָיו.
[יב] לֹא אָכַלְתִּי בְאֹנִי מִמֶּנּוּ, הָא אִם אֲכָלוֹ

– רע״ב –

ולא שכחתי מלברכך ומלהזכיר שמך עליו. לפי שמברכים להפריש תרומה. וכן על מעשר ראשון ושני ומעשר עני, ולפדיון מעשר שני, ולחלה, על כולן מברכים: (יב) לא אבלתי באוני. כל יום המיתה הויא אנינות דאורייתא ואפילו לאחר קבורה. ולילה שלאחר יום המיתה הויא אנינות דרבנן, וכן יום קבורה שאינו יום המיתה הויא אנינות דרבנן:

לֹא שָׁכַחְתִּי מִלְּבָרֶכְךָ וּמִלְּהַזְכִּיר שִׁמְךָ עָלָיו — **I did not forget to bless You and to mention Your Name on it;** that is, I did not forget to recite the blessings (which include the Name of God) that must be said before separating tithes and redeeming *maaser sheni*.[6]

[12] This Mishnah explains the second verse of *viduy maaser* (*Devarim* 26:14): לֹא אָכַלְתִּי בְאֹנִי מִמֶּנּוּ וְלֹא בִעַרְתִּי מִמֶּנּוּ בְּטָמֵא וְלֹא נָתַתִּי מִמֶּנּוּ לְמֵת שָׁמַעְתִּי בְּקוֹל ה׳ אֱלֹהָי עָשִׂיתִי כְּכֹל אֲשֶׁר צִוִּיתָנִי, *I did not eat from it in when I was an onein, I did not remove it in a state of tumah, and I did not give of it for [the needs of] the dead; I listened to the voice of Hashem, my God; I have acted according to everything that You commanded me.* Whereas the laws of the previous Mishnah apply to all tithes, this Mishnah refers mainly to *maaser sheni*:[1]

״לֹא אָכַלְתִּי בְאֹנִי מִמֶּנּוּ״ — The verse begins: *I did not eat from it when I was an onein.*[2] If the owner avoided eating *maaser sheni* when he was an *onein* (which is forbidden), he recites the *viduy*, הָא אִם אֲכָלוֹ

NOTES

6. Separating tithes and redeeming *maaser sheni* are mitzvos. Therefore, before doing any of these activities, one must recite the blessing for a mitzvah. The blessing for separating *terumah* is as follows: בָּרוּךְ אַתָּה ה׳ אֱלֹהֵינוּ מֶלֶךְ הָעוֹלָם אֲשֶׁר קִדְּשָׁנוּ בְּמִצְוֹתָיו וְצִוָּנוּ לְהַפְרִישׁ תְּרוּמָה, *Blessed are You, Hashem, our God, King of the universe, Who has sanctified us with His mitzvos and commanded us to separate terumah.* The blessings for separating the other tithes and redeeming *maaser sheni* are similar but each has its appropriate ending (*Rav*).

The obligation to recite blessings is Rabbinic. Accordingly, this interpretation of the verse must be an *asmachta*, a support for a Rabbinic law (*Tos. Yom Tov*).

Although someone who forgot to recite the blessing has sinned only at the Rabbinic level, he is disqualified from fulfilling the Biblical obligation of reciting the *viduy maaser*. Since the Torah commands us to follow the rulings of the Sages (*Devarim* 17:11), he cannot honestly say, *I have acted according to everything that You have commanded me* (see *Beur HaHalachah, Hilchos Maaser Sheni* 11:15 ד״ה ולא שכחתי).

[12]
1. The Mishnah will show how each phrase refers to a certain law or laws. However, a person is disqualified from reciting the *viduy maaser* not only if he transgressed one of the particular laws listed in the Mishnah, but also if he transgressed any of the many other laws that apply to *terumos, maasros,* and the other portions (*Derech Emunah, Hilchos Maaser Sheni* 11:99).

2. Upon the death of one of a person's seven closest relatives (father, mother, brother, sister, son, daughter, spouse), he becomes an אוֹנֵן, *onein* (plural, *oneinim*). An *onein* is forbidden to eat *maaser sheni, reva'i,* or *bikkurim* (see *Derech Emunah* there).

According to Biblical law, he is an *onein* the entire day of death, even after the burial, until nightfall. The Rabbis, however, extended this period through the night following the death. They also decreed that if the relative was buried after the day of death, the person remains an *onein* through the day of burial (*Rav; Rambam, Hilchos Maaser Sheni* 3:6).

משניות מעשר שני / פרק ה: כרם רבעי [102]

בַּאֲנִינָה אֵינוֹ יָכוֹל לְהִתְוַדּוֹת. וְלֹא בִעַרְתִּי מִמֶּנּוּ בְּטָמֵא, הָא אִם הִפְרִישׁוֹ בְּטֻמְאָה אֵינוֹ יָכוֹל לְהִתְוַדּוֹת. וְלֹא נָתַתִּי מִמֶּנּוּ לְמֵת, לֹא לָקַחְתִּי מִמֶּנּוּ אָרוֹן וְתַכְרִיכִים לְמֵת, וְלֹא נְתַתִּיו לְאוֹנְנִים אֲחֵרִים.

- רע"ב -

לא לקחתי ממנו ארון ותכריכין למת. וכהאי גוונא אפילו לחי אסור, שהרי אסור לקנות מלבוש וכיוצא בזה ממעשר שני, כדתנן לעיל סוף פרק קמא כל שהוא חוץ לאכילה ושתיה וסיכה אם לקח יאכל כנגדו. ולא נקט

הכא ארון ותכריכים אלא לאשמועינן דלא מיבעיא אם סך ממנו למת שאינו יכול להתודות, דכתיב ממנו, מגופו של מעשר, אלא אפילו קנה ארון ותכריכים דלא נתן מגופו של מעשר על מת, אינו יכול להתודות:

בַּאֲנִינָה אֵינוֹ יָכוֹל לְהִתְוַדּוֹת — **but if he did eat it when he was an *onein*, he may not recite the *viduy*.**[3]

"וְלֹא בִעַרְתִּי מִמֶּנּוּ בְּטָמֵא" — The verse continues: ***And I did not remove*** (i.e., perform *biur* with) ***it in a state of tumah;*** that is, he did not separate *maaser sheni* (for the sake of *biur*) when he was *tamei*, and thus cause it to become *tamei*. In that case, he may recite the *viduy*, הָא אִם הִפְרִישׁוֹ בְּטֻמְאָה אֵינוֹ יָכוֹל לְהִתְוַדּוֹת — **but if he did separate it when he was in a state of *tumah*, thereby making it *tamei*, he may not recite the *viduy*.**[4]

"וְלֹא נָתַתִּי מִמֶּנּוּ לְמֵת" — The verse then states: ***And I did not give of it for [the needs of] the dead.*** לֹא לָקַחְתִּי מִמֶּנּוּ אָרוֹן וְתַכְרִיכִים לְמֵת — This means: I did not use [money of *maaser sheni*] to buy a coffin or shrouds for a dead person,[5] וְלֹא נְתַתִּיו לְאוֹנְנִים אֲחֵרִים — and I did not give [*maaser sheni*] to other *onenim*, who are forbidden to eat it.[6]

---- NOTES ----

3. This ruling applies to both a Biblical *onein* and a Rabbinic *onein* (*Derech Emunah* there 11:99; see note 6 on the previous Mishnah).

4. To fulfill the mitzvah of *biur* with *maaser sheni* that has not yet been separated from untithed produce, one must first separate the *maaser sheni* and then destroy it. This may not be done by a person who is *tamei*, because he will cause the *maaser sheni* to become *tamei* when he touches it (*Meleches Shlomo, Tiferes Yisrael*). [The Mishnah speaks of separating *maaser sheni* while *tamei* merely as an example. Any other way of causing *tumah* to *maaser sheni* — such as eating it while *tamei* — is also forbidden and disqualifies the person from reciting *viduy maaser*.]

5. Although the Mishnah specifies the case of buying a coffin and shrouds for a dead person, it does not mean to imply that buying similar items (such as clothing) for a living person is permitted, for, in fact, any use of *maaser sheni* other than eating, drinking, and applying to one's skin is forbidden (Mishnahs 1:7, 2:1). Rather, the Mishnah is making the following point: The verse's words, וְלֹא נָתַתִּי מִמֶּנּוּ לְמֵת, *I did not give of it to the dead*, refer to *maaser sheni* itself (as opposed to *money* of *maaser sheni*). Thus, it could have been thought that a person is disqualified from reciting the *viduy* only if he used *maaser sheni* itself for a dead person (for example, to apply oil of *maaser sheni* to his skin), and not if he used *money* of *maaser sheni* (for example, to buy him a coffin or shrouds). The Mishnah therefore teaches that even someone who used *money* of *maaser sheni* for a dead person may not recite the *viduy* (*Rav*).

6. The phrase *I did not give* cannot refer to giving to a dead person, because a dead person is incapable of receiving a gift. Instead, it is interpreted as meaning that the owner of *maaser sheni* did not give it to the *relatives* of a dead person, i.e., *onenim* (*Meleches Shlomo*). [The verse

[103] **MISHNAH MAASER SHENI** / Chapter 5: *Kerem Reva'i*

שָׁמַעְתִּי בְקוֹל ה' אֱלֹהָי, הֲבֵאתִיו לְבֵית הַבְּחִירָה. עָשִׂיתִי בְּכֹל אֲשֶׁר צִוִּיתָנִי, שָׂמַחְתִּי וְשִׂמַּחְתִּי בּוֹ.

[יג] **הַשְׁקִיפָה** מִמְּעוֹן קָדְשְׁךָ מִן הַשָּׁמַיִם, עָשִׂינוּ מַה שֶׁגָּזַרְתָּ עָלֵינוּ, אַף אַתָּה עֲשֵׂה מַה שֶׁהִבְטַחְתָּנוּ, הַשְׁקִיפָה מִמְּעוֹן קָדְשְׁךָ מִן הַשָּׁמַיִם וּבָרֵךְ אֶת עַמְּךָ אֶת יִשְׂרָאֵל.

"שָׁמַעְתִּי בְקוֹל ה' אֱלֹהָי" — The verse continues: *I listened to the voice of Hashem, my God.* הֲבֵאתִיו לְבֵית הַבְּחִירָה — This means: **I brought it to the Temple.**[7]

"עָשִׂיתִי בְּכֹל אֲשֶׁר צִוִּיתָנִי" — The verse concludes: *I have acted according to everything that You have commanded me.* שָׂמַחְתִּי וְשִׂמַּחְתִּי בּוֹ — This means: **I rejoiced and brought joy to others with it**; that is, I ate my *maaser sheni* in a state of joy and I brought joy to others by sharing it with them.[8]

[13] The Mishnah explains the final verse of the *viduy maaser* (*Devarim* 26:15), which is a prayer: הַשְׁקִיפָה מִמְּעוֹן קָדְשְׁךָ מִן הַשָּׁמַיִם וּבָרֵךְ אֶת עַמְּךָ אֶת יִשְׂרָאֵל וְאֶת הָאֲדָמָה אֲשֶׁר נָתַתָּה לָנוּ כַּאֲשֶׁר נִשְׁבַּעְתָּ לַאֲבֹתֵינוּ אֶרֶץ זָבַת חָלָב וּדְבָשׁ, *Gaze down from Your holy place, from the heavens, and bless Your nation, Israel, and the Land that You have given us, as You swore to our forefathers, a land flowing with milk and honey*:

"הַשְׁקִיפָה מִמְּעוֹן קָדְשְׁךָ מִן הַשָּׁמַיִם" — The *viduy* ends with a prayer: *Gaze down from Your holy place, from the heavens, and bless Your nation,* etc. By concluding the *viduy* in this way, it is as though we are saying: עָשִׂינוּ מַה שֶׁגָּזַרְתָּ עָלֵינוּ — **We have fulfilled what You decreed upon us** (that is, we fulfilled the laws of tithing); אַף אַתָּה עֲשֵׂה מַה שֶׁהִבְטַחְתָּנוּ — so **You, too, fulfill what You promised us.**

The Mishnah identifies the specific blessings to which this prayer refers:

"הַשְׁקִיפָה מִמְּעוֹן קָדְשְׁךָ מִן הַשָּׁמַיִם וּבָרֵךְ אֶת עַמְּךָ אֶת יִשְׂרָאֵל" — *Gaze down from*

NOTES

is understood as follows: *I did not give* maaser sheni *(to onenim, and I did not use money of* maaser sheni *to buy a coffin and shrouds) for the dead.*]

7. The word אֱלֹהָי, *My God,* alludes to the Temple, where God "resides" (see *Shenos Eliyahu*).

The Mishnah refers to the mitzvah of bringing *bikkurim* to the Temple (*Mishnah Rishonah, Tiferes Yisrael*). However, when the owner says this phrase, he also means that he brought *maaser sheni* (and *reva'i*) to Jerusalem (*Derech Emunah, Hilchos Maaser Sheni* 11:106; see *Tosefos Anshei Shem*).

8. Regarding *maaser sheni,* the Torah states (*Devarim* 12:18): *Only before Hashem, your God, shall you eat it, in the place that Hashem, your God, will choose — you and your son and your daughter and your servant and your maidservant, and the Levi who is in your cities — and you shall rejoice before Hashem, your God* (*Derech Emunah* there §107).

This part of the *viduy* can also refer to *bikkurim,* because the Torah commands with respect to *bikkurim* (*Devarim* 26:11): *You shall rejoice in all the good that Hashem, your God, has given you and your household — you and the Levi and the stranger who is in your midst* (*Mishnah Rishonah*).

[104] **משניות מעשר שני / פרק ה: כרם רבעי** ה/יד

בְּבָנִים וּבִבְנוֹת. וְאֶת הָאֲדָמָה אֲשֶׁר נָתַתָּה לָנוּ, בְּטַל וּמָטָר וּבְוַלְדוֹת בְּהֵמָה. כַּאֲשֶׁר נִשְׁבַּעְתָּ לַאֲבוֹתֵינוּ אֶרֶץ זָבַת חָלָב וּדְבָשׁ, כְּדֵי שֶׁתִּתֵּן טַעַם בַּפֵּרוֹת.

- רע"ב -
(יד) מכאן אמרו. מדכתיב ואת האדמה אשר נתת לנו:

[יד] **מִכָּאן** אָמְרוּ, יִשְׂרָאֵל וּמַמְזֵרִים מִתְוַדִּים, אֲבָל לֹא גֵרִים וְלֹא עֲבָדִים מְשֻׁחְרָרִים, שֶׁאֵין לָהֶם חֵלֶק בָּאָרֶץ.

Your holy place, from the heavens, and bless Your nation, Israel; that is, "וְאֶת הָאֲדָמָה אֲשֶׁר נָתַתָּה — bless us **with sons and daughters.** בְּבָנִים וּבִבְנוֹת בְּטַל וּמָטָר וּבְוַלְדוֹת בְּהֵמָה — לָנוּ" — ... *and the Land that You have given us;* that is, bless us **with dew and rain, and with the offspring of animals.**[1] "כַּאֲשֶׁר נִשְׁבַּעְתָּ לַאֲבוֹתֵינוּ אֶרֶץ זָבַת חָלָב וּדְבָשׁ כְּדֵי שֶׁתִּתֵּן טַעַם בַּפֵּרוֹת — ... *as You swore to our forefathers, a land flowing with milk and honey;* that is, bless us that **You will put taste into the produce.**[2]

[14] The Mishnah teaches who is eligible to recite the *viduy maaser*.

מִכָּאן אָמְרוּ — **Based on here,** i.e., the last verse of the *viduy,* which states, *the Land that You have given us,* [the Sages] said: יִשְׂרָאֵל וּמַמְזֵרִים מִתְוַדִּים — **Yisraelim and** *mamzerim*[1] **may recite the** *viduy,* אֲבָל לֹא גֵרִים וְלֹא עֲבָדִים מְשֻׁחְרָרִים — **but converts and freed slaves**[2] **may not recite it,** שֶׁאֵין לָהֶם חֵלֶק בָּאָרֶץ — **because they do not have a share in the Land** of Israel and thus cannot say *the Land that You have given us.*[3]

NOTES

[13]
1. Animals are included in the blessing of the land, because animals receive their nourishment from the ground (see *Eruvin* 27b).

God promised these particular blessings if we observe His commandments. The blessings for children and for the offspring of animals appear in *Devarim* 28:1,4: *It shall be that if you listen to the voice of Hashem, your God ... blessed shall be the fruit of your womb... and the fruit of your animals.* The blessing for rain is found in verses 11:13-14 there: *It shall be that if you listen to My commandments ... I shall provide rain for your Land* (*Mishnah Rishonah*).

2. We ask God to make our fruit sweet and rich (*Rambam Commentary*), as well as nutritious (see *Tiferes Yisrael, Sotah* 9:12).

[14]
1. A *mamzer* (plural, *mamzerim*) is the child of certain forbidden unions or the child of another *mamzer* (see *Yevamos* 4:13). Although he is forbidden to marry an ordinary Jew (*Devarim* 23:3), he is a Jew in every other respect.

2. When a Canaanite slave is acquired by a Jew, he has to undergo a partial conversion (that is, he must be circumcised and he must immerse in a *mikveh*), because he is required to observe some of the mitzvos. Upon being freed, he must complete his conversion by immersing in a *mikveh* again, because he then becomes obligated to keep all the mitzvos (*Rambam, Hilchos Issurei Bi'ah* 12:11, 13:11-12). Accordingly, a freed Canaanite slave is a Jew with a status similar to that of a convert.

3. Converts and freed slaves may not say *the Land that You have given us,* because if they had lived when Eretz Yisrael was distributed among the Jewish people in the time of Joshua, they would not have received a share. Other Jews, though, may recite the phrase (although they did not participate in Joshua's distribution of the Land), because they would have received shares had they been alive then. They are also the direct descendants of

[105] **MISHNAH MAASER SHENI** / Chapter 5: *Kerem Reva'i* 5/15

- רע״ב -

רַבִּי מֵאִיר אוֹמֵר, אַף לֹא כֹהֲנִים וּלְוִיִּם, שֶׁלֹּא נָטְלוּ חֵלֶק בָּאָרֶץ. רַבִּי יוֹסֵי אוֹמֵר, יֵשׁ לָהֶם עָרֵי מִגְרָשׁ.

[טו] **יוֹחָנָן** כֹּהֵן גָּדוֹל הֶעֱבִיר הוֹדָיוֹת הַמַּעֲשֵׂר. אַף הוּא בִּטֵּל אֶת הַמְעוֹרְרִים

יש להם ערי מגרש. ויכולים להתודות על המעשרות שמביאין ממגרש הערים שלהן. והלכה כר׳׳י: (טו) **יוחנן** כהן גדול. שמש בכהונה גדולה אחר שמעון הצדיק: העביר הודיות המעשר. לפי שעזרא קנס את הלוים שלא יתנו להם מעשר, כשעלה מן הגולה ובני לוי לא עלו עמו, ונוה שיתנו המעשר לכהנים. ויוחנן כהן גדול בטל בטל הוידוי, כיון שאינו יכול לומר ונם נתתיו ללוי: **בטל את המעוררים**. שהיו הלוים אומרים בכל יום על הדוכן עורה למה תישן ה׳. אמר להם וכי יש שינה לפני המקום, עמד וביטלו:

The Mishnah cites a dispute as to whether Kohanim and Leviim may recite the *viduy*:

רַבִּי מֵאִיר אוֹמֵר — **R' Meir says**: אַף לֹא כֹהֲנִים וּלְוִיִּם — **Also, Kohanim and Leviim may not recite the** *viduy*, שֶׁלֹּא נָטְלוּ חֵלֶק בָּאָרֶץ — **because they did not take a share in the Land** of Israel; hence, they too cannot say *the Land that You have given us*.[4] רַבִּי יוֹסֵי אוֹמֵר — **But R' Yose says**: יֵשׁ לָהֶם עָרֵי מִגְרָשׁ — **[Kohanim and Leviim] have the open cities**, which suffices for them to be able to recite the *viduy*.[5]

[15] The final Mishnah of the tractate (which also appears in *Sotah* 9:10) lists various decrees of Yochanan Kohen Gadol,[1] the first of which involves *viduy maaser*:

יוֹחָנָן כֹּהֵן גָּדוֹל הֶעֱבִיר הוֹדָיוֹת הַמַּעֲשֵׂר — **Yochanan Kohen Gadol brought an end to the recitation of *viduy maaser*.**[2] אַף הוּא בִּטֵּל אֶת הַמְעוֹרְרִים — **He also**

--- NOTES ---

those who *did* receive shares at that time (see *Rav*).

4. The land was apportioned only to the Yisraelim, and not to the Kohanim or Leviim, as stated in *Bamidbar* 18:20, 23-24.

5. Although Eretz Yisrael was divided among all the tribes except Levi, the tribes were commanded to give forty-eight cities in their own territories to the Kohanim and Leviim (*Bamidbar* 35:1-8; see *Derech Emunah* 11:115). These cities are called "open" because each was surrounded by an open ring of land, in which building and farming was forbidden (*Rashi* on verse 2 there).

R' Yose holds that the Kohanim and Leviim enjoyed full rights of ownership to these cities. He therefore rules that they can recite the *viduy maaser* because they can honestly say, *the Land that You have given us*. According to R' Meir, though, the Kohanim and Leviim may not say the

viduy maaser on account of these cities, because they did not actually own them; they were merely granted the right to live there (*Yerushalmi*; see *Makkos* 2:8).

[15]

1. Yochanan was the Kohen Gadol after Shimon HaTzaddik [who served at the beginning of the Second Temple era] (*Rav*; see *Avos* 1:2).

2. Ezra the Scribe punished the Leviim for not joining him when he went up to Eretz Yisrael from the Babylonian exile. He decreed that *maaser rishon* should be given not to the Leviim but to the Kohanim. Therefore, it was no longer appropriate to say the *maaser* confession, because it includes the words: *I have given it [maaser rishon] to the Levi* (*Rav*, from *Sotah* 47b-48a).

From the time of Ezra until Yochanan Kohen Gadol, people still recited the *viduy maaser*, because there are verses

משניות מעשר שני / פרק ה: כרם רבעי

וְאֶת הַנּוֹקְפִים. וְעַד יָמָיו הָיָה פַּטִּישׁ מַכֶּה בִּירוּשָׁלַיִם, וּבְיָמָיו אֵין אָדָם צָרִיךְ לִשְׁאֹל עַל הַדְּמַאי.

— רע״ב —

אֶת הַנּוֹקְפִים. שֶׁהָיוּ מְשָׂרְטִין לָעֵגֶל שֶׁל קָרְבָּן בֵּין קַרְנָיו כְּדֵי שֶׁיִּפֹּל לוֹ דָּם בְּעֵינָיו כְּדֵי שֶׁלֹּא יִרְאֶה וִיהֵא נוֹחַ לְכָפְתוֹ וּלְשָׁחֳטוֹ.

וְעָמַד הוּא וּבִטְּלוֹ, שֶׁנִּרְאֶה כְּבַעַל מוּם וְהִתְקִין לָהֶם טַבָּעוֹת בַּקַּרְקַע לְהַכְנִיס לָהֶם צַוַּאר הַבְּהֵמָה לְתוֹכָהּ. נוֹקְפִים, מַכִּין, וְדוּגְמָתוֹ אֵין אָדָם נוֹקֵף אֶצְבָּעוֹ מִלְּמַטָּה (חולין דף ז:): הָיָה פַּטִּישׁ מַכֶּה בִּירוּשָׁלַיִם. חָרָשֵׁי נְחֹשֶׁת וּבַרְזֶל הָיוּ מַכִּין בַּפַּטִּישׁ לַעֲשׂוֹת מְלֶאכֶת הָאֻמָּן שֶׁהִיא מֻתֶּרֶת בַּמּוֹעֵד. וְעָמַד הוּא וּבִטְּלָהּ, מִשּׁוּם דְּאוֹשָׁא מְלָאכָה טוֹבָא וְאִיכָּא זִלְזוּל מוֹעֵד: וּבְיָמָיו אֵין אָדָם צָרִיךְ לִשְׁאֹל עַל הַדְּמַאי. שֶׁהוּא אָמַר לִבְנֵי דוֹרוֹ כְּשֵׁם שֶׁתְּרוּמָה גְּדוֹלָה עֲוֹן מִיתָה כָּךְ תְּרוּמַת מַעֲשֵׂר וְטֶבֶל עֲוֹן מִיתָה. וְתִקֵּן שֶׁיּוֹצִיאוּ מִן הַדְּמַאי תְּרוּמַת מַעֲשֵׂר וּמַעֲשֵׂר שֵׁנִי בִּלְבַד, וְלֹא יוֹצִיאוּ מִמֶּנּוּ מַעֲשֵׂר רִאשׁוֹן וְלֹא מַעֲשֵׂר עָנִי, שֶׁיְּכוֹלִים לוֹמַר לַלֵּוִי אוֹ לֶעָנִי הָבֵא רְאָיָה שֶׁהוּא טֶבֶל וְטוֹל. וּמִתַּקָּנָה זוֹ וְאֵילָךְ הַלּוֹקֵחַ פֵּרוֹת מִן הַשּׁוּק לֹא הָיָה שׁוֹאֵל אִם הֵם מְתֻקָּנִים אִם לָאו, אֶלָּא מִיָּד מַפְרִישׁ מֵהֶן תְּרוּמַת מַעֲשֵׂר וּמַעֲשֵׂר שֵׁנִי וְאוֹכֵל אֶת הַשְּׁאָר, שֶׁכָּל הַלּוֹקֵחַ פֵּרוֹת מֵעַם הָאָרֶץ הֵם בְּחֶזְקַת דְּמַאי:

וְאֶת **abolished the "wakers,"** i.e., the practice of the Leviim in the Temple to recite the verse: *Awaken, why do You sleep, Hashem?* (*Psalms* 44:24),[3] הַנּוֹקְפִים **— and the "strikers,"** i.e., the practice in the Temple to make a cut in an offering's head right before it was slaughtered.[4] וְעַד יָמָיו הָיָה פַּטִּישׁ מַכֶּה בִּירוּשָׁלַיִם **— Until his days, the hammer would bang in Jerusalem** during Chol HaMoed, i.e., blacksmiths would work on Chol HaMoed, and he stopped them from doing so.[5] וּבְיָמָיו אֵין אָדָם צָרִיךְ לִשְׁאֹל עַל הַדְּמַאי **— And in his days, it was not necessary for anyone to ask whether** tithes had to be separated from *demai* (i.e., produce received from an *am haaretz*),[6] because he decreed that tithes must always be separated from such produce.[7]

NOTES

in the Torah where Kohanim are called Leviim. However, Yochanan Kohen Gadol argued that since the verse discussed here, *I have given it to the Levi,* refers to a Levi specifically, the *viduy* should not be said (*Tiferes Yisrael* to *Sotah* 9:10).

3. The Leviim would stand on their platform in the Temple each day and cry out the verse, *Awaken, why do You sleep, Hashem?* (*Psalms* 44:24). Yochanan put an end to this practice because there is no such thing as God being asleep (*Rav*). The verse refers to times of exile, when God seems to ignore our suffering and appears as if He is "asleep." But it was not proper for the Leviim to recite this verse in the time of Yochanan, when the Temple was standing (*Sotah* 48a with *Maharsha*).

4. Before an animal was slaughtered as an offering, they would cut it between its horns, causing blood to run into its eyes. This would temporarily blind the calf and make it easier to restrain it for the slaughter. Yochanan abolished this practice, because the wound looked like a disqualifying blemish (מוּם), and people might mistakenly think that a blemished animal is fit for the Altar. Instead, Yochanan installed large rings in the floor of the Temple, which would hold the animal's neck in place during the slaughter (*Rav*, from *Sotah* 48a).

5. Although work (*melachah*) is generally forbidden on Chol HaMoed, work needed to prevent a loss [דְּבַר הָאָבֵד] is permitted. The blacksmiths mentioned here were allowed to work on Chol HaMoed to prevent a loss. Yochanan Kohen Gadol, however, forbade them to work then, because their hammering was very noisy and brought disrespect to the festival (*Rav*).

6. An *am haaretz* (plural, *amei haaretz*) is an unlearned person, who is not careful in his observance of certain laws.

7. The Mishnah refers to the Rabbinic prohibition of eating *demai* before tithing

[107] **MISHNAH MAASER SHENI** / Chapter 5: *Kerem Reva'i*

―――――――――――――― NOTES ――――――――――――――

it (see Mishnah 3:3 note 4). This decree was enacted by Yochanan Kohen Gadol and his court.

According to Biblical law, one is allowed to eat the produce of an *am haaretz* without tithing it first. One need not be concerned that it might be *tevel,* for since most *amei haaretz* tithe their produce, it can be assumed that he did too. Some people, however, went beyond the letter of the law and avoided eating *demai* before asking the *am haaretz* whether it had indeed been tithed (*Tos. Yom Tov, Mishnah Rishonah*). When Yochanan became the Kohen Gadol, he made an investigation and discovered that a significant minority of *amei haaretz* separated only *terumah,* and not the other tithes, from their produce (*Sotah* 48a). Although this did not affect the Biblical law, because the majority of *amei haaretz* did separate all the necessary tithes, Yochanan and his court decreed that their produce is prohibited before it has been tithed (see *Rav* for the method of tithing *demai*). After the decree was passed, people stopped asking the *am haaretz* whether his produce has been tithed, because he may no longer be believed and they would have to tithe it in any event (*Rav*).

מסכת חלה
TRACTATE CHALLAH

General Introduction

וַיְדַבֵּר ה' אֶל מֹשֶׁה לֵּאמֹר. דַּבֵּר אֶל בְּנֵי יִשְׂרָאֵל וְאָמַרְתָּ אֲלֵהֶם בְּבֹאֲכֶם אֶל הָאָרֶץ אֲשֶׁר אֲנִי מֵבִיא אֶתְכֶם שָׁמָּה. וְהָיָה בַּאֲכָלְכֶם מִלֶּחֶם הָאָרֶץ תָּרִימוּ תְרוּמָה לַה'. רֵאשִׁית עֲרִסֹתֵכֶם חַלָּה תָּרִימוּ תְרוּמָה כִּתְרוּמַת גֹּרֶן כֵּן תָּרִימוּ אֹתָהּ. מֵרֵאשִׁית עֲרִסֹתֵיכֶם תִּתְּנוּ לַה' תְּרוּמָה לְדֹרֹתֵיכֶם.

And Hashem spoke to Moses, saying: Speak to the Children of Israel and say to them: When you come to the Land to which I am bringing you, and it shall be when you eat from the bread of the Land, you shall separate terumah for Hashem. The first of your doughs, a loaf, you shall separate as terumah, like the terumah of the threshing-floor, so shall you separate it. From the first of your doughs shall you give to Hashem terumah, for your generations (Bamidbar 15:17-21).

The Torah teaches that one who is preparing bread must separate a portion of the dough and give it to a Kohen. This portion is known as *"challah"* [literally, *a small loaf*].[1]

I.

⇨§ The *Challah* Obligation

A. Dough Subject to *Challah*

The *challah* obligation applies to dough made of flour milled from any of five species of grain: wheat, barley, spelt, oats, and rye (see Mishnah 1:1).[2]

The dough must be fit for human consumption. Dough fit for consumption only by animals is not subject to *challah* (see Mishnah 1:8).[3]

The dough must be the property of a Jew. Dough belonging to a non-Jew

---
NOTES

1. See *Rashi* to the verse, with *Targum HaLaaz* there.

2. The obligation applies when the dough is kneaded with water, wine, oil, or bee's honey (see *Rambam, Hilchos Bikkurim* 6:12). According to some authorities, the obligation also applies to a dough kneaded with other fruit juices or with eggs. Nevertheless, this should be avoided if the grain has not come into contact with any water. See *Derech Emunah* there §84 for discussion. See Mishnah 2:2.

3. According to one view, even dough fit for humans is exempt from *challah* if it is intended solely for consumption by animals (see *Rambam, Hilchos Bikkurim* 6:8 with *Derech Emunah* §57).

or that has been consecrated to the Temple is not subject to *challah* (see Mishnah 3:3, 3:5).[4]

B. Minimum Measure of Dough

For a dough to be subject to *challah* it must contain the volume of at least 43.2 average-size hen's eggs, which is 1¼ *kavs* of flour. These are referred to throughout the tractate as "five *reva'im*," i.e., *five-fourths* [of a *kav*].[5]

C. The Requirement of "Bread"

Dough is not subject to *challah* unless it falls under the classification of "bread," which includes all doughs that are baked, but excludes those that are cooked or fried (see Mishnah 1:5; *Rambam, Hilchos Bikkurim* 6:12).

According to some, a thick, kneaded dough is considered bread even if it is intended for frying, not baking [e.g., doughnuts] (see *Rabbeinu Tam, Sefer HaYashar* §344; *Tosafos, Pesachim* 37b ד"ה דכולי עלמא). Others say that even a thick dough is exempt from *challah* if the intention when it was kneaded was that it be cooked or fried. This view is adopted as halachah (see *Shulchan Aruch, Yoreh Deah* 329:3). All agree, however, that a thick dough that was originally intended for baking is subject to *challah* even if later cooked or fried (see Mishnah 1:5; *Shulchan Aruch* ibid.).

D. When the Obligation Takes Effect

The obligation to separate *challah* takes effect when the dough is thoroughly kneaded and made into a single mass (see *Rav* to Mishnah 3:1; but see *Rambam, Hilchos Bikkurim* 8:4 with *Derech Emunah* §10). If one did not separate *challah* until after the bread has been baked, it must be separated after the baking (*Rambam* ibid. 8:3). [In the case of thin batters that are mixed, rather than kneaded (such as those used in cakes), the obligation takes effect with the baking, and *challah* is separated after it has been baked (see Mishnah 1:5).]

Although the obligation to separate *challah* does not take effect until the dough is kneaded, if *challah* was separated earlier, after the flour was mixed with water, it is valid. However, under Biblical law one should not separate

---

NOTES

4. *Terumah*, too, is exempt from the *challah* obligation (see *Rav*, end of Mishnah 1:4).

5. The authorities disagree regarding the conversion of these measures to contemporary measures. Due to a discrepancy between different methods of measure given by the Talmud, as well as other doubts, two measurements are given — a smaller measure from which *challah* is removed, but, due to the uncertainty, no blessing is recited, and a larger measurement from which *challah* is separated with a blessing (see *Tzlach, Pesachim* 116b ד"ה והואיל וחביבא; *R' Avraham Chaim Na'eh, Sefer Shiurei Torah*, pp. 1-32). The corresponding measurements, converted from volume to weight, are:

According to *Chazon Ish*, if the dough contains close to five pounds [2.25 kg.] of wheat flour, one separates *challah* and recites a blessing. If it weighs less than that, but more than 2 lbs., 10.3 oz. [1.2 kg.], *challah* is separated without a blessing. According to *R' Avraham Chaim Na'eh*, the appropriate weight for reciting with a blessing is 3 lbs., 11 oz. [1.67 kg.]. If it weighs less than that, but more than 2 lbs., 12 oz. [1.25 kg.], *challah* is separated without a blessing. If one kneads a dough with less than the smaller amount, there is no *challah* requirement at all.

[5] **MISHNAH CHALLAH** / General Introduction

challah before the *challah* obligation takes effect (see Mishnah 1:9). Nevertheless, the Rabbis enacted that when preparing a *tahor* dough, one should *initially* separate *challah* when he pours water into the flour. The Rabbis were concerned that if one would wait to take *challah* until the obligation takes effect, the dough would become *tamei* in the meantime, and its *challah* would have to be burned (see Mishnah 3:1). Nowadays, though, this Rabbinic enactment is no longer relevant, for it is not possible to prepare a *tahor* dough, since we are all presumed to be *tamei meis* (i.e., *tamei* through contact with a corpse), and do not possess the means to purify ourselves from this type of *tumah*. Thus, it is preferable to wait to separate *challah* until the *challah* obligation takes effect (*Shulchan Aruch, Yoreh Deah* 327:3 with *Shach* §6).

◆§ The *Tevel* Prohibition

Once the dough is thoroughly kneaded and the *challah* obligation takes effect, the dough is *tevel,* and is Biblically prohibited for consumption.[6] One who eats the *tevel* dough is liable to מִיתָה בִּידֵי שָׁמַיִם, *death at the hands of Heaven* (see *Sanhedrin* 83a; *Rambam, Hilchos Maachalos Asuros* 10:19,20).

E. Who Is Obligated?

The owner of the dough is obligated to separate *challah*. Nevertheless, it is the specific responsibility of the woman of the household to perform this mitzvah (see *Rav, Shabbos* 2:6; *Or Zarua, Hilchos Challah* §225). For this reason, many of the Mishnahs in this tractate discuss cases of women who were separating *challah* (see *Tos. Anshei Shem* 1:7 and 4:1 ד"ה שתי נשים).

II.

◆§ The *Challah* Portion

A. The Size of the *Challah* Portion

The Torah does not require that a specific amount be separated for the *challah* portion; one may separate a portion as large or as small as he wishes, as long as he does not designate the *entire* dough as *challah* (see Mishnah 1:6; *Rambam* ibid. 5:1). The Rabbis, however, set a minimum measure of 1/24 of the dough for one who is baking for himself, and 1/48 of the dough for someone who bakes to sell the bread (see Mishnah 2:3; *Rambam* ibid. 5:2).[7]

B. Separating *Challah*

Many of the laws governing the separation of *terumah* apply also to *challah*.[8]

NOTES

6. [This term, *tevel*, is the same term used for produce that was not tithed.] Before the point that the dough is fully kneaded, it is permitted by Biblical law. However, under Rabbinic law, it may not be eaten in a set manner [אֲכִילַת קֶבַע], only as a snack [אֲכִילַת עֲרָאי] (see Mishnah 3:1).

7. These Rabbinic measures apply only when the dough is *tahor.* When it is *tamei,* even a householder need take no more than 1/48. Since the *challah* will be burned in any case, the Rabbis did not require a larger amount (see Mishnah 2:7; *Rambam, Hilchos Bikkurim* 5:4). For the custom nowadays, see below, note 16.

8. The connection between *challah* and

[6] **משניות חלה** / הקדמה

For example, like *terumah*, *challah* may be designated only for dough that is close by [מִן הַמֻּקָּף] (see Mishnah 1:9; see also *Rambam, Hilchos Bikkurim* 5:13,14, and *Hilchos Terumos* 15:20).

When separating *challah*, one recites the blessing "Blessed are You ... Who has consecrated us with His mitzvos, and commanded us to separate *terumah*" (*Shulchan Aruch, Yoreh Deah* 328:1) or "... to separate *challah*" (*Rama* there; see *Rambam* ibid. 15:11 and *Hasagos HaRaavad* there; see *Kesef Mishneh* there, and *Beur HaGra, Yoreh Deah* 328:2).[9] Others have the custom to say both: "...to separate *terumah challah*" (see *Shach* there §1).[10]

C. What Is Done With *Challah*

Like *terumah*, the *challah* portion is given to the Kohen. In general, the laws pertaining to eating *terumah* pertain to *challah* as well (see *Rambam, Hilchos Bikkurim* 5:14). Thus, *challah* may be eaten only by a Kohen and the members of his household; namely, his wife, his sons (who are Kohanim themselves), his unmarried daughters, and his Canaanite slaves.

1. Prohibited Consumption

A non-Kohen who intentionally eats *challah* is liable to מִיתָה בִּידֵי שָׁמַיִם, *death at the hands of Heaven*. A non-Kohen who eats *challah* by mistake must replace it with a portion of dough equivalent in value to the *challah* he ate, plus an additional "fifth" (see Mishnah 1:9).[11]

A Kohen who is *tamei* may not eat *challah*. If a Kohen who is *tamei* intentionally eats *challah*, he is liable to מִיתָה בִּידֵי שָׁמַיִם, *death at the hands of Heaven* (see *Vayikra* 22:9; *Sanhedrin* 83a).

2. *Challah* That Became *Tamei*

Like *terumah* that became *tamei*, *challah* that became *tamei* may not be eaten (see *Vayikra* 22:7 and *Yerushalmi Bikkurim* 2:1; see also *Bavli Yevamos* 73b). Nevertheless, it is given to the Kohen, who is obligated to burn it. The Kohen may benefit from its burning, for example, by using it as fuel for a fire (see *Shabbos* 25a).[12]

— NOTES —

terumah derives from *Bamidbar* 15:20, which refers to the *challah* portion as "*terumah*" (see *Rambam, Hilchos Bikkurim* 5:13,14, and *Hilchos Terumos* 15:20; *Rambam, Rash*, and *Rosh* to Mishnah 1:9; *Bavli Me'ilah* 15b). Furthermore, the Torah describes both *challah* and *terumah* as רֵאשִׁית, *first* (see *Bamidbar* ibid.; *Devarim* 18:4); the shared wording constitutes a *gezeirah shavah* linking these two mitzvos (see *Chullin* 135b, *Menachos* 67a). See *Toras HaAretz* (4:15 ff.) for further discussion.

9. Some add the words מִן הָעִסָּה, *from the dough*, at the end of the blessing (see *Rash* to 2:3; *Mahari ben Malki Tzedek* there; but see *Taz, Yoreh Deah* 328:1).

10. The custom in many Sefardic communities is to say "... to separate *challah terumah*" (see *Ben Ish Chai, Shanah Rishonah, Tzav* §19; *Kaf HaChaim, Orach Chaim* 457:9).

11. Whenever the Torah requires adding "one-fifth," it actually means one-fifth of the *total* amount paid, including the surcharge; i.e., a fourth of the principal. For example, if the principal was four *zuz*, the surcharge would be one *zuz*, making for a total payment of five *zuz*. The surcharge is thus one-fifth of the payment.

12. A non-Kohen may not benefit from its burning. Today, however, Kohanim do not have definite proof of their lineage. Therefore, the *challah* is not given to a Kohen to burn (*Derech Emunah, Hilchos Bikkurim* 5:24 from *Chazon Ish*).

[7]   **MISHNAH CHALLAH** / General Introduction

D. Safeguarding the *Challah* Portion

We are obligated to safeguard *challah* from all forms of destruction or *tumah*. This is known from the verse (*Bamidbar* 18:8): וַאֲנִי הִנֵּה נָתַתִּי לְךָ אֶת מִשְׁמֶרֶת תְּרוּמֹתָי, *Behold! I have given "to you" the safeguard of My terumos*, and from the verse (*Vayikra* 12:4): בְּכָל קֹדֶשׁ לֹא תִגָּע, *any holy food she shall not touch* (see *Yevamos* 75a and *Bechoros* 34a; *Rambam, Hilchos Terumos* 12:1).

III.

◈§ *Challah* Inside and Outside Eretz Yisrael

The Biblical *challah* obligation applies only in Eretz Yisrael, not outside the Land (see *Rambam, Hilchos Bikkurim* 5:5).[13] Nevertheless, the Rabbis instituted that *challah* be separated even outside the Land.[14] The actual Rabbinic institution is to separate two *challah* portions, one of which is burned, the other given to the Kohen, who may eat it even if he is *tamei*.[15] Nowadays, though, when even in Eretz Yisrael *challah* is not eaten due to *tumah*, the custom even outside of the Land is to separate only a single portion of *challah*, which is burned (see *Rash* to 4:8; *Rama, Yoreh Deah* 322:5; but see *Shulchan Aruch* there and *Rambam, Hilchos Bikkurim* 5:9).[16]

The *challah* obligation outside of Eretz Yisrael is subject to a number of leniencies. For example, while a Kohen may not eat *challah* of Eretz Yisrael if either he or the *challah* is *tamei*, the Rabbis permitted a Kohen (or a member of his household) to eat the *challah* of outside of Eretz Yisrael (that is, the portion of *challah* that would otherwise be burned) even though it is *tamei* as a result of the Rabbinically decreed state of *tumah* that exists outside

--- NOTES ---

13. The obligation does not depend on where the grain was grown. Rather, it depends on where the dough is located when the *challah* obligation takes effect (for example, when a wheat dough is fully kneaded). A dough kneaded of imported flour inside Eretz Yisrael is subject to *challah*; one kneaded outside the Land made of flour from Eretz Yisrael is exempt, even if the flour is from Eretz Yisrael (see Mishnah 2:1; *Rambam, Hilchos Bikkurim* 8:6).

14. According to most Rishonim, the Rabbinic obligation requiring the separation of *challah* outside Eretz Yisrael is in force throughout the world. This is the view accepted in *Shulchan Aruch* (*Yoreh Deah* 322:4). There are, however, some Rishonim who say that this Rabbinic obligation was instituted only with respect to certain countries surrounding Eretz Yisrael (*Sefer Halttur, Hilchos Matzah*

U'Maror; see also *Ran, Pesachim* fol. 14b ד"ה וכתב הרב אלפסי ז"ל; *Nimukei Yosef*, *Yevamos* fol. 25b-26a סד"ה ואמרינן בגמרא; *Meiri* and *Ritva, Yevamos* 82b).

15. [The reasons behind the double separation are dealt with in Mishnah 4:8.] There are differences, with respect to the law of *challah*, between different areas. The boundaries of these areas, and the differences in their laws, are discussed in Mishnah 4:8; see also, *Rambam, Hilchos Bikkurim* 5:7,8.

16. As far as the amount that is to be separated, the accepted practice is to follow the view of those who hold that since *challah* is not eaten in our times, any amount may be separated as *challah* (see *Derech Emunah, Hilchos Bikkurim* 5:75 with *Tziyun HaHalachah* §131). Ashkenazic custom is to separate a *kezayis* [i.e., an amount the size of an olive] (*Rama, Yoreh Deah* 322:5).

[8] **משניות חלה** / הקדמה

the Land.[17] Moreover, they allowed even a Kohen who is *tamei* to eat this portion, as long as he is not *tamei* with a type of *tumah* generated by a bodily emission (e.g., a seminal emission or *niddah*). Some authorities maintain, however, that in practice one should not give *challah* to a Kohen to eat, because it is not possible to definitively establish his lineage as a Kohen (see *Taz, Yoreh Deah* 322:5; *Shach* ad loc. 9; see also *Rama, Orach Chaim* 457:2). This has become the accepted custom (see *Mishnah Berurah* ad loc. 22).[18]

According to most authorities, even in Eretz Yisrael, the Biblical obligation applies only when the majority of the Jewish nation is residing in Eretz Yisrael. That has not been the case since the destruction of the First Temple. Therefore, even in Eretz Yisrael, the obligation to separate *challah* in our times is Rabbinic (see *Rambam* ibid. with *Derech Emunah* §31; see *Tziyun HaHalachah* there §73).

IV.

❧ The Merit of the Mitzvah

The Gemara teaches (*Shabbos* 32b) that if people keep the *challah* obligation, their stored produce will be blessed, as the verse states (*Ezekiel* 44:30): וְרֵאשִׁית עֲרִיסוֹתֵיכֶם תִּתְּנוּ לַכֹּהֵן לְהָנִיחַ בְּרָכָה אֶל בֵּיתֶךָ, *You shall give the first of your doughs to the Kohen, so that a blessing will rest in your house.* The reward corresponds with his fulfillment of the mitzvah. By sanctifying a portion of the finished dough, he is rewarded with a blessing bestowed upon his finished produce (see *Maharal, Chidushei Aggados* ad loc.).

A full observance of the *challah* obligation must wait for the coming of the Messiah and the ingathering of our exile. It is our prayer that in the merit of the study of this tractate, that we soon be privileged to see the coming of that long-awaited Redemption.

NOTES
---

17. Some maintain that this leniency applies only in those areas that are far removed from Eretz Yisrael; for example, Babylonia. In areas that are close to Eretz Yisrael, however, it is forbidden to eat that *challah* portion because of its *tamei* status, and it must be burned in all cases (*Tosafos, Bechoros* 27a ד"ה פסק; see also *Rash* to Mishnah 4:8).

18. Another leniency regarding *challah* of outside of Eretz Yisrael pertains to the prohibition of eating the dough or bread as long as *challah* has not been separated, due to its status as *tevel*. Because of this prohibition, if someone did not separate *challah* before Shabbos, he may not eat the bread on Shabbos, since *challah* may not be separated on Shabbos (see *Orach Chaim* 339:4). This law applies even nowadays in Eretz Yisrael (even though the obligation is Rabbinic; see further in this Introduction). However, outside of Eretz Yisrael, the law is more lenient — the bread may be eaten, and some of it left over, from which *challah* is separated after Shabbos (see *Beitzah* 9a).

Chapter One

א/א

פרק ראשון — חמשה דברים. (א) חמשה דברים חייבים בחלה. דגמרינן חלה מפסח, נאמר בפסח (דברים טז,ג) מצות לחם עוני, ונאמר לחם בחלה

[א] חֲמִשָּׁה דְבָרִים חַיָּבִים בַּחַלָּה: הַחִטִּים וְהַשְּׂעוֹרִים וְהַכֻּסְּמִין וְשִׁבֹּלֶת שׁוּעָל וְשִׁיפוֹן. הֲרֵי אֵלּוּ חַיָּבִין בַּחַלָּה, וּמִצְטָרְפִין זֶה עִם זֶה, וַאֲסוּרִין בֶּחָדָשׁ מִלִּפְנֵי

(במדבר טו,יט) והיה באכלכם מלחם הארץ, מה לחם האמור בפסח דבר הבא לידי חמוץ, אף לחם האמור בחלה דבר הבא לידי חמוץ, ואין לך בא לידי חמוץ אלא אלו חמשת המינים בלבד: **ומצטרפין זה עם זה.** להשלים שיעור העסה החייבת בחלה. ולא שיצטרפו כולן יחד, דמין בשאינו מינו אינו מצטרף, כדתנן לקמן ריש פרק ד, אלא החטים מצטרפים עם הכוסמין בלבד, מפני שהם מינן, והשעורים מצטרפים עם הכל חוץ מן החטין. ואף על גב דכוסמין מין חטין הם, לאו מין חטין דוקא אלא מין שעורים ואף מין חטים, ומצטרפין עם החטים והשעורים. ובירושלמי משמע, דאם נלושו יחד, מצטרפין אפילו מין בשאינו מינו, אבל אם לא נלושו יחד, אלא שאחר כך היו נוגעין העסות זו בזו, מין במינו מצטרפין, שלא במינו אין מצטרפין:

---

[1] When one kneads dough in order to make bread, he must separate a portion of the dough and give it to a Kohen. This portion is called "*challah.*" The Mishnah teaches that only certain types of grain are subject to this obligation:

חֲמִשָּׁה דְבָרִים חַיָּבִים בַּחַלָּה — **The following five types** of grain **are subject to the obligation of** *challah:* הַחִטִּים וְהַשְּׂעוֹרִים וְהַכֻּסְּמִין וְשִׁבֹּלֶת שׁוּעָל וְשִׁיפוֹן — **Wheat, barley, spelt, oats, and rye.** Dough made of any other type of grain is not subject to *challah.*[1]

Having taught that only these five grains are subject to the *challah* obligation, this Mishnah and the one that follows discuss a number of other laws that apply only to these species. Here, the Mishnah discusses the law of the new crop of grain (*chadash*), which may not be eaten until the *omer* offering is brought on the second day of Pesach (see *Vayikra* 23:10-14).[2] It is even prohibited to harvest the new crop of grain before the barley for the *omer* offering is harvested.[3] First, however, the Mishnah reviews the law just discussed and teaches another law about *challah:*

הֲרֵי אֵלּוּ חַיָּבִין בַּחַלָּה — **These** species **are all obligated in** *challah,* as we have just learned, וּמִצְטָרְפִין זֶה עִם זֶה — **and they join with one another** to reach the minimum amount needed for the *challah* obligation.[4] וַאֲסוּרִין בֶּחָדָשׁ מִלִּפְנֵי

NOTES

[1]

1. For example, dough made of rice or millet flour is not subject to the *challah* obligation (see *Tos. Anshei Shem* ד"ה הרי; see also Mishnah 4 below). This is learned from a verse (see *Rav*).

2. The *omer* is a *minchah* offering made from barley of the new crop. The barley for this offering was usually harvested on the night before the second day of Pesach (see *Menachos* 10:3).

3. The prohibition to harvest the new grain before harvesting the barley for the *omer* is derived from the words of the verse (*Vayikra* 23:10), which describe the *omer* as רֵאשִׁית קְצִירְכֶם, the "first" of your harvest.

4. It will be taught in Mishnah 4 that if dough is made from less than 1¼ *kav* of flour, it is not subject to the obligation of *challah.* The Mishnah here teaches that a dough that was kneaded with 1¼ *kav* of flour made from a combination of different types of the five species of grain is obligated in *challah.* For example, if the

[11] **MISHNAH CHALLAH** / Chapter 1: *Chamishah Devarim*

– רע"ב –

הַפֶּסַח, וּמִלִּקְצוֹר מִלִּפְנֵי הָעֹמֶר. וְאִם הִשְׁרִישׁוּ קֹדֶם לָעֹמֶר, הָעֹמֶר מַתִּירָן; וְאִם לָאו, אֲסוּרִין עַד שֶׁיָּבוֹא הָעֹמֶר הַבָּא.

וַאֲסוּרִים בֶּחָדָשׁ. כדכתיב (ויקרא כג,יד) ולחם וקלי וכרמל לא תאכלו עד עצם היום הזה, וגמרינן לחם לחם מפסח:

וּמִלִּקְצוֹר מִלִּפְנֵי הַפֶּסַח. שאסור לקצור מחמשת המינים קודם קצירת העומר, דכתיב בעומר (שם פסוק י) ראשית קצירכם, שתהא תחלה לכל הנקצרים, ואתיא ראשית ראשית מחלה, כתיב התם (במדבר טו,כ) ראשית עריסותיכם, וכתיב הכא ראשית קצירכם, מה להלן מחמשת המינים אף כאן מחמשת המינים: **וְאִם הִשְׁרִישׁוּ.** אחד מחמשת המינים הללו, קודם קצירת העומר: **הָעֹמֶר מַתִּירָן.** ומותר לקצרו אחר קצירת העומר, דכתיב (שמות כג,טז) אשר תזרע בשדה, משעה שנזרע ונשרש בשדה: **וְאִם לָאו.** שלא השרישו אלא אחר קצירת העומר: אסורים עד שיבא עומר הבא. של שנה הבאה:

הַפֶּסַח — **They are all subject to the prohibition of eating *chadash* before Pesach.** That is, the new crop of any of the five species may not be eaten before Pesach.[5] וּמִלִּקְצוֹר מִלִּפְנֵי הָעֹמֶר — **And** the new crop of any of the five species may not be **harvested before** the grain for **the *omer* offering is harvested.**[6]

The Mishnah explains what is considered the "new" crop with regard to the prohibition of harvesting it before the *omer*:

וְאִם הִשְׁרִישׁוּ קֹדֶם לָעֹמֶר — **If [these species] took root before the *omer*** was **harvested,** הָעֹמֶר מַתִּירָן — **the *omer* permits them** for harvesting (and eating). וְאִם לָאו — **But if not,** i.e., if they did not take root until after the harvesting of the *omer*, אֲסוּרִין עַד שֶׁיָּבוֹא הָעֹמֶר הַבָּא — **they are forbidden until next** year's ***omer* arrives.** That is, they may not be harvested (or eaten) until the next year's *omer* is harvested.[7]

NOTES
---

dough was made from wheat and spelt, *challah* must be separated (see *Rav*). However, if part of the 1¼ *kav* of flour was made from a type of grain that is not one of the five species, for example, some of it was millet flour, there is no *challah* obligation (see Mishnah 3:7 for an exception).

[It should be noted, though, that the law that all five species combine applies only when they were kneaded together as a single dough. However, if they were kneaded separately, and afterward were joined together, not all of the species combine. For example, wheat can combine with spelt, but not with barley, oats, or rye; see Mishnah 4:2 (*Rav*, as explained by *Mishnah Rishonah; Tiferes Yisrael*).]

5. We learn from a verse that this prohibition applies to any of the five species of grain (see *Rav*). It does not, however, apply to other types of grain, such as rice (see *Rashi* to *Menachos* 70b ד"ה לחם).

Although the Mishnah seems to imply that the *chadash* prohibition applies only until Pesach, it actually extends until the second day of the festival, when the *omer* is brought. [Indeed, this is stated clearly in the next case of the Mishnah, with regard to the prohibition of harvesting the grain. For why the Mishnah presents these cases differently, see *Rashash, Menachos* 70b. See also *Rav* and *Tos. Yom Tov*.]

6. This is also derived from a verse (see *Rav*).

7. Whether grain is considered *chadash* depends on when it took root. If it took root before the *omer* was harvested, i.e., before the night of the second day of Pesach (see previous note), it is considered part of the earlier year's crop. Therefore, it is permissible to harvest such grain. However, grain that took root after the *omer* was harvested is considered part of the following year's crop, and is thus *chadash*. Therefore, the owner must wait until the next year's *omer* to harvest it. This law is learned from a verse (see *Rav*).

[ב] הָאוֹכֵל מֵהֶם כְּזַיִת מַצָּה בַּפֶּסַח, יָצָא יְדֵי חוֹבָתוֹ; כַּזַיִת חָמֵץ, חַיָּב בְּהִכָּרֵת. נִתְעָרֵב אֶחָד מֵהֶם בְּכָל הַמִּינִים, הֲרֵי זֶה עוֹבֵר בַּפֶּסַח.

– רע"ב –

(ב) יצא ידי חובתו. דכתיב (דברים טז,ג) לא תאכל עליו חמץ שבעת ימים תאכל עליו מצות, דברים הבאים לידי חמוץ אדם יוצא בהן ידי חובת מצה. נתערב אחד מהן בכל המינים. נתערב אחד מחמשת המינים הללו בשאר תערובות, כגון כותח הבבלי ושכר המדי: הֲרֵי זֶה עוֹבֵר בַּפֶּסַח. על בל יראה ובל ימצא, אם הניחו ברשותו.

---

[2] This Mishnah continues to list laws that apply only to the five species of grain listed in the previous Mishnah. It begins with several laws relating to Pesach. The Torah obligates each person to eat matzah (unleavened bread, made of flour and water) on the first night of Pesach. Another Biblical law prohibits eating *chametz*[1] on Pesach. The Mishnah discusses these laws:

הָאוֹכֵל מֵהֶם כְּזַיִת מַצָּה בַּפֶּסַח — **Someone who eats a *kezayis* (the volume of an olive)**[2] **of matzah** made from any of **[these five species] on** the first night of **Pesach** יָצָא יְדֵי חוֹבָתוֹ — **has fulfilled his obligation** to eat matzah. However, if he eats matzah made from other species of grain he has not fulfilled his obligation.[3] כַּזַיִת חָמֵץ חַיָּב בְּהִכָּרֵת — Similarly, someone who eats a ***kezayis* of *chametz*** of these grains **is liable to *kares*.** But other leavened grains are not prohibited, since they are not considered *chametz*.[4] נִתְעָרֵב אֶחָד מֵהֶם בְּכָל הַמִּינִים — **If one of [the five species]** became *chametz* and **became mixed with any** other type of food,[5] הֲרֵי זֶה עוֹבֵר בַּפֶּסַח — **one who** owns this mixture **on Pesach transgresses** the Torah prohibition of having *chametz* in one's possession.[6]

The Mishnah now discusses which types of grain are included when one makes a *neder* (vow) that prohibits bread or grain:

NOTES

[2]

1. *Chametz* is grain that was allowed to ferment ("leaven") — for example, dough that was allowed to rise.

2. Generally, in order to fulfill a mitzvah that requires eating, one must eat a minimum of a *kezayis*. Similarly, someone who eats something prohibited by the Torah is liable to punishment only if he eats at least a *kezayis*.

3. We learn from a verse that matzah can be made only from grain that can become *chametz*. The Mishnah will soon teach that only the five species of grain can become *chametz* if left to rise. Therefore, only these species can be used for the mitzvah of matzah (see *Rav*). Other species, such as rice, cannot be used (see *Pesachim* 35a).

4. One who eats a *kezayis* of *chametz* on Pesach is punished with *kares* (see *Shemos* 12:19). Dough of any of the five species can become *chametz*, and are subject to this prohibition. Other grains, such as rice or millet, cannot become *chametz*. Even if they were mixed with water and fermented, that is not considered leavening, but rather spoilage (*Meleches Shlomo*; see also *Rambam Commentary*).

5. For example, one of the five grains was used to make Babylonian *kutach*, a dip made from sour milk and moldy bread crumbs (see *Rav*; see also *Pesachim* 3:1).

6. The prohibition of having *chametz* in one's possession is learned from verses in the Torah (see *Shemos* 12:19 and 13:7). [Even *chametz* that is mixed with a different food is subject to this prohibition (see *Meleches Shlomo*).]

[13] **MISHNAH CHALLAH** / Chapter 1: *Chamishah Devarim* 1/2

— רע"ב —

הַנּוֹדֵר מִן הַפַּת וּמִן הַתְּבוּאָה, אָסוּר בָּהֶם, דִּבְרֵי רַבִּי מֵאִיר. וַחֲכָמִים אוֹמְרִים: הַנּוֹדֵר מִן הַדָּגָן אֵינוֹ אָסוּר אֶלָּא מֵהֶן. וְחַיָּבִין בַּחַלָּה וּבַמַּעַשְׂרוֹת.

הנודר מן הדגן אסור בכל המינים. דדגן כל דמידגן משמט, וקטנית וחרעים מידי דמידגן הוא: אינו אסור אלא בהן. דדגן ותבואה אחד הוא. והלכה כחכמים: וחייבים בחלה ובמעשרות. אייידי דבעי למיתני אלו חייבים בחלה ופטורים

הַנּוֹדֵר מִן הַפַּת וּמִן הַתְּבוּאָה — **One who makes a** *neder* **prohibiting himself from** eating **"bread"** or from eating **"***tevuah***"** (grain) אָסוּר בָּהֶם — **is forbidden** to eat bread or grain of [the five species]. That is, if he made a *neder* prohibiting bread he may not eat bread of the five species, and if he made a *neder* prohibiting grain he may not eat grain of the five species. He is permitted, however, to eat bread or grain of other species, because when people say "bread" or *"tevuah"* they refer only to the five species of grain.[7] דִּבְרֵי רַבִּי מֵאִיר — These are **the words of R' Meir**.

Another term used to describe grain is *dagan*, literally, *pile*. Since R' Meir did not mention the case of a *neder* prohibiting *dagan*, it is evident that he holds that such a *neder* includes *all* types of grain, even those not of the five species.[8] The Sages disagree:

וַחֲכָמִים אוֹמְרִים — **But the Sages say:** הַנּוֹדֵר מִן הַדָּגָן אֵינוֹ אָסוּר אֶלָּא מֵהֶן — **Someone who makes a** *neder* **prohibiting himself from eating** *dagan* **is forbidden** to eat only **[the five species]**, but is permitted to eat other species of grain. According to the Sages, people use the term *dagan* in the same way they use the term *tevuah*. Thus, when people say the word *dagan* they mean only the five species.

Another ruling that involves the five species of grain relates to *challah* and *maasros*:[9]

וְחַיָּבִין בַּחַלָּה וּבַמַּעַשְׂרוֹת — **And [the five species] are subject to the obligations of** both *challah* and *maasros*.[10]

―――――――――― NOTES ――――――――――

7. As a rule, the meaning of a *neder* is determined by how people commonly speak. Now, while there are many types of bread, when people say "bread" without specifying which type, they mean bread made from any of the five species [in a place where bread is made from all of these species (see *Yerushalmi*, cited by *Meleches Shlomo*)]. Bread made from other species, however, is not included. This is because bread from other species, such as rice or corn, is not known simply as "bread," but rather as "rice bread" or "corn bread." Therefore, if someone made a *neder* prohibiting "bread," it includes only these five species.

Similarly, when people say *"tevuah"* they refer only to the five species. Therefore, a *neder* made with this word is also limited to these species (see *Beur of R' Chaim Kanievski* to *Yerushalmi* 8b).

8. See *Tos. Yom Tov.*

R' Meir holds that since the word *"dagan"* means "pile," it is used by people to refer to any produce that is stored in piles. Since beans and seeds (and certainly rice and millet) are stored in piles, they are included in the term *"dagan"* (see *Rav* ד"ה הנודר).

[In *Rav*'s version of the Mishnah, R' Meir is explicitly quoted as saying that a *neder* made with the word *"dagan"* includes all species.]

9. *Maasros* are the tithes that must be separated from produce grown in Eretz Yisrael. See next Mishnah, note 1.

10. That is, only these species can be

[14] משניות חלה / פרק א: חמשה דברים

א/ג

— רע"ב —

מן המעשרות (משנה ג), ואלו חייבים במעשרות ופטורים מן החלה (משנה ד), תנא הכא וחייבים

[ג] **אֵלוּ** חַיָּבִין בַּחַלָּה וּפְטוּרִים מִן הַמַּעַשְׂרוֹת: הַלֶּקֶט, וְהַשִּׁכְחָה, וְהַפֵּאָה, וְהַהֶפְקֵר,

בחלה ובמעשרות: (ג) **הלקט והשבחה והפאה וההפקר.** פטורים מן המעשרות, דכתיב (דברים יד, כט) ובא הלוי כי אין לו חלק ונחלה עמך, ממה שיש לך ואין לו אתה חייב ליתן לו, יצאו אלו שיש לו עמך:

---

[3] The previous Mishnah taught that the five species of grain are subject to both the *challah* and *maasros* obligations. This Mishnah lists cases where produce of the five species have a *challah* obligation but do not have a *maaser* obligation:

אֵלוּ חַיָּבִין בַּחַלָּה וּפְטוּרִים מִן הַמַּעַשְׂרוֹת — **The following are subject to *challah* but exempt from *maasros*:**[1] הַלֶּקֶט וְהַשִּׁכְחָה וְהַפֵּאָה — the gifts to the poor of *leket*, *shich'chah*, *peah*,[2] וְהַהֶפְקֵר — **and ownerless [grain].**[3] These are exempt from *maaser* because the *maaser* obligation applies only to produce

--- NOTES ---

subject to *both* obligations. However, other species are certainly subject to the *maaser* obligation, as explained in Mishnah 4. [In addition, produce of the five species are not *always* subject to both obligations, as will be detailed in the next Mishnah.]

The Mishnah mentions this here in order to contrast this with the cases that will be mentioned in the next two Mishnahs, where there is only either a *challah* or a *maaser* obligation (see *Rav*; *Tiferes Yisrael*).

[3]

1. The Torah requires that a number of tithes be separated from produce. These are: (1) תְּרוּמָה גְדוֹלָה, *terumah gedolah* (the greater *terumah*), which is given to a Kohen. By Biblical law, there is no minimum amount that must be given as *terumah*. [The Rabbis, however, did set a minimum amount (typically one-fiftieth of the produce).] (2) מַעֲשֵׂר רִאשׁוֹן, *maaser rishon* (the first tithe), one-tenth of the remaining produce, which is given to a Levi; (3) תְּרוּמַת מַעֲשֵׂר, *terumas maaser*, one-tenth of *maaser rishon*, which the Levi separates and gives to a Kohen; (4) מַעֲשֵׂר שֵׁנִי, *maaser sheni* (the second tithe), one-tenth of the crop remaining after *terumah* and *maaser rishon* were separated. *Maaser sheni* is separated from crops of the first, second, fourth, and fifth years of the seven-year *Shemittah* cycle, and is eaten in Jerusalem; and (5) מַעֲשַׂר עָנִי, *maasar ani* (the tithe of the poor), one-tenth of the crop, separated (instead of *maaser sheni*) from crops of the third and sixth years of the *Shemittah* cycle, and given to the poor.

[Technically, the word *maasros* (tithes) applies only to gifts that are 1/10 of the produce. In practice, however, the term is commonly used when referring to any of these gifts (see *Tos. Yom Tov, Demai* 4:1).]

2. *Leket* (gatherings) refers to one or two stalks that fall down as the grain is harvested. These stalks must be left in the field for the poor (see *Vayikra* 19:19). *Shich'chah* (forgotten) refers to sheaves of grain that the owner forgot in the field. These must also be left for the poor (see *Devarim* 24:19). *Peah* (literally, *end*) is the section of the field that the field owner must leave for the poor to harvest (see *Vayikra* there). The Mishnah teaches that if one of the five types of grain was collected as *leket*, *shich'chah*, or *peah*, *challah* must be separated from them (when kneading them into dough) but not *maasros*.

3. For example, if someone declared his grain ownerless, even if the grain was then acquired by another person, it is exempt from *maasros*.

[This applies only if the grain was made ownerless before it was completely processed (i.e., before it was smoothed into a pile). If, however, it was declared ownerless after that time, it is subject to tithing; see *Peah* 1:6 (*Mishnah Rishonah*).]

[15] MISHNAH CHALLAH / Chapter 1: *Chamishah Devarim*

– רע"ב –

וּמוֹתָר הָעוֹמֶר. שֶׁהִסְפּוּמֶר
הָיָה בָּא מִשָּׁלֹשׁ סְאִין, וּמוֹלִיאִין
מִמֶּנּוּ עִשָּׂרוֹן סֹלֶת מְנֻפָּה
בִּשְׁלֹשׁ עֶשְׂרֵה נָפָה, וְהַשְּׁאָר
נִפְדֶּה וְנֶאֱכָל לְכָל אָדָם. וְחַיָּב בְּחַלָּה, וּפָטוּר מִמַּעֲשֵׂר, לְפִי שֶׁבְּשַׁעַת מֵרוּחַ הָיָה שֶׁל הֶקְדֵּם:

וּמַעֲשֵׂר רִאשׁוֹן שֶׁנִּטְּלָה תְרוּמָתוֹ, וּמַעֲשֵׂר שֵׁנִי וְהֶקְדֵּשׁ שֶׁנִּפְדּוּ, וּמוֹתָר

---

that has an owner and that a Levi has no right to take. Since these gifts *may* be taken by a Levi, they are not subject to the *maaser* obligation.[4] Nevertheless, they are subject to the *challah* obligation.[5] **וּמַעֲשֵׂר רִאשׁוֹן שֶׁנִּטְּלָה תְרוּמָתוֹ** — Also subject to *challah* but exempt from *maaser* is **maaser rishon** whose **terumah** (i.e., *terumas maaser*) **was taken,** but *terumah gedolah* was not separated by the owner.[6] That is, the Levi separated *terumas maaser* from the *maaser rishon*. This is speaking of when *maaser rishon* was separated before the grain became obligated in *terumah gedolah*.[7] **וּמַעֲשֵׂר שֵׁנִי וְהֶקְדֵּשׁ שֶׁנִּפְדּוּ** — **Maaser sheni and hekdesh that were redeemed are also** subject to *challah* but exempt from *maaser*.[8] *Maaser sheni* that was redeemed

--- NOTES ---

4. We learn from a verse (*Devarim* 14:29) that *maaser rishon* is given to a Levi only from produce that the Levi would not be otherwise allowed to take for himself. *Leket, shich'chah,* and *peah,* however, may be taken by a poor Levi, and ownerless grain may be taken by any Levi. Therefore, they are exempt from *maaser* (see *Rav*). They remain exempt even if someone later acquires them, and even if he does so before the grain is processed.

5. We learn from a verse that the exemption of *leket, shich'chah,* and *peah,* and ownerless grain does not apply to *challah* (see *Sifrei* to *Bamidbar* 15:20 with *Emek HaNetziv* ד"ה ראשית). [However, they are subject to *challah* only if someone acquired the grain before it was made into dough, which is when the *challah* obligation takes effect. If the dough was ownerless at the time that it was kneaded, it is not subject to the obligation of *challah* (see *Shulchan Aruch, Yoreh Deah* 330:7).]

6. That is, the Levi separated *terumas maaser* from the *maaser rishon*. The Mishnah teaches that the remaining *maaser* is exempt from tithing but is obligated in *challah*. The reason for this exemption will be explained in the next note.

7. The Mishnah is discussing a case where the Yisrael separated *maaser rishon* from his unprocessed grain before he separated *terumah gedolah*. The law is that produce becomes subject to the obligation of *terumah* and *maaser* only after it is fully processed (see *Maasros* 1:5). Had the Yisrael separated *maaser rishon* after the grain was processed (without first separating *terumas maaser*), the Levi would have been obligated to separate *terumah gedolah,* since, in that case, the *terumah gedolah* requirement had already come into effect, and was not yet fulfilled. Here, however, the Yisrael separated *maaser* before the grain was processed (see *Tos. Yom Tov*). We learn from a verse that if *maaser rishon* was separated from grain that was not yet subject to *terumah gedolah,* it never becomes subject to *terumah gedolah*. Therefore, even when the Levi later finishes processing the *maaser rishon,* he need not separate *terumah gedolah* (see *Rash;* see also *Pesachim* 35b and *Rashi* there ד"ה האי לא).

The verse that exempts *maaser rishon* that was separated from unprocessed grain is speaking only with regard to *maasros*. Therefore, it is subject to *challah*.

8. *Maaser sheni* must be brought to Jerusalem and eaten there (see note 1). It can also be redeemed with money, which is brought to Jerusalem, and used to buy food. Once *maaser sheni* is redeemed, the produce no longer has sanctity, and it may be eaten even outside of Jerusalem.

הָעֹמֶר, וּתְבוּאָה שֶׁלֹּא הֵבִיאָה שְׁלִישׁ. וּתְבוּאָה שֶׁלֹּא הֵבִיאָה
שְׁלִישׁ. חַיֶּבֶת בְּחַלָּה, שֶׁאַף
הִיא בָּאָה לִידֵי מָמוֹן, וְכָל דָּבָר הַבָּא לִידֵי מָמוֹן לֶחֶם אִקְרִי וְחַיָּב בְּחַלָּה. וּפְטוּרָה מִן הַמַּעַשְׂרוֹת,
דְּבְמַעַשְׂרוֹת כְּתִיב (שם פסוק כב) תְּבוּאַת זַרְעֶךָ, דָּבָר שֶׁזּוֹרְעִים אוֹתוֹ וְצוֹמֵחַ, וְהַאי אִי זַרְעֵי לֵיהּ לֹא צָמַח:

─────────

is speaking of a case where it was separated before the grain was obligated in *maasros*.[9] *Hekdesh* that was redeemed is exempt because it did not belong to the owner when the *maaser* obligation took effect.[10] וּמוֹתַר הָעֹמֶר — Also subject to *challah* but exempt from *maaser* are **the leftovers of the *omer*** offering.[11] וּתְבוּאָה שֶׁלֹּא הֵבִיאָה שְׁלִישׁ — Also subject to *challah* but exempt from *maaser* is **grain that did not grow a third** of its full growth. Only grain that has grown enough that it will grow if replanted is obligated in *maasros*. Since grain

─────────── NOTES ───────────

Hekdesh refers to items consecrated to the Temple. When *hekdesh* is redeemed, its sanctity is removed. The Mishnah teaches that once they are redeemed, *maaser sheni* and *hekdesh* are exempt from *maasros*, but are subject to *challah*. See further.

9. The case of *maaser sheni* is similar to the previous case of *maaser rishon*: Instead of separating *maaser sheni* from the processed grain after *terumah gedolah* and *maaser rishon* were separated, as required, the owner separated *maaser sheni* from the unprocessed grain, before *terumah gedolah* and *maaser rishon* were separated. Since the *maaser sheni* was separated before the grain was processed, at which time the grain had no *terumah gedolah* or *maaser rishon* obligation, the *maaser sheni* is exempt from these tithes (see *Rav* and *Tos. Yom Tov* to *Terumos* 1:5).

The exemption of *maaser sheni* that was separated while the grain was unprocessed does not apply to *challah*. [This is true only if it was redeemed before it was made into dough. However, if it was redeemed afterward, it is exempt from *challah* because *maaser sheni* is considered Divine property (*Tos. Yom Tov*; see also *Tosafos* to *Yevamos* 73a ד"ה מה).]

10. The case of *hekdesh* is also where the grain was designated as *hekdesh* before it was processed, and was then redeemed. We learn from a verse that only privately owned produce is subject to *terumos* and *maasros*; produce of *hekdesh* is not subject to *terumos* and *maasros* (see *Rav* to

Mishnah 3:4 ד"ה בשעת). Although the *hekdesh* was later redeemed, it remains exempt. This is because it was owned by *hekdesh* at the time when the tithing obligation takes effect, which is when the processing of the grain was complete (see *Tos. Yom Tov*). [Note that unlike the earlier cases (see note 7), in the case of *hekdesh*, it is exempt from *terumos* and *maasros* only if it was redeemed *after* it was processed.]

Hekdesh that was redeemed is subject to *challah*. [Actually, the exemption of *hekdesh* does apply to *challah* (see Mishnah 6 note 6). However, our Mishnah refers to a case where the grain of *hekdesh* was redeemed before it was made into dough. Since the *challah* obligation takes effect on dough, not on grain, when the *challah* obligation took effect it was no longer *hekdesh*, and it is subject to *challah* (see *Tos. Yom Tov*).]

11. This refers to the extra flour that remained after the *omer* offering was prepared. The *omer* was made from very fine barley flour. Therefore, a large amount of barley would be bought with money of *hekdesh*. The barley would be ground, and then sifted many times until a small amount of very fine flour was produced. This leftover flour was redeemed, thus permitting it for other use. Now, the barley for the *omer* was bought (and became *hekdesh*) while it was still unprocessed, and was still owned by *hekdesh* when its processing was completed. Essentially then, the leftovers of the *omer* are *hekdesh* that was redeemed. Therefore, they are exempt from *maasros*, but subject to *challah* (see *Rav*).

[17] MISHNAH CHALLAH / Chapter 1: *Chamishah Devarim*

רַבִּי אֱלִיעֶזֶר אוֹמֵר: תְּבוּאָה שֶׁלֹּא הֵבִיאָה שְׁלִישׁ, פְּטוּרָה מִן הַחַלָּה.

[ד] **אֵלּוּ** חַיָּבִין בַּמַּעַשְׂרוֹת וּפְטוּרִים מִן הַחַלָּה: הָאֹרֶז, וְהַדֹּחַן, וְהַפְּרָגִים, וְהַשֻּׁמְשְׁמִין, וְהַקִּטְנִיּוֹת, וּפָחוֹת מֵחֲמֵשֶׁת רְבָעִים בַּתְּבוּאָה.

– רע"ב –

תְּבוּאָה שֶׁלֹּא הֵבִיאָה שְׁלִישׁ פְּטוּרָה מִן הַחַלָּה. דִּכְתִיב (במדבר טו,כ) כִּתְרוּמַת גֹּרֶן כֵּן תָּרִימוּ אוֹתָהּ, מַה תְּרוּמָה אֵינָהּ בָּאָה מִתְּבוּאָה שֶׁלֹּא הֵבִיאָה שְׁלִישׁ, אַף חַלָּה אֵינָהּ בָּאָה מִתְּבוּאָה שֶׁלֹּא הֵבִיאָה שְׁלִישׁ. וְאֵין הֲלָכָה כְּרַבִּי אֱלִיעֶזֶר: (ד) וּפְרָגִין. קוֹרִין לוֹ בְּעַרְבִי כשכ"א, ובלט"ז פפאוו"ר: וּפָחוֹת מֵחֲמֵשֶׁת רְבָעִים בַּתְּבוּאָה. תְּבוּאָה שֶׁטּוֹחֲנָהּ פָּחוֹת מֵחֲמֵשֶׁת רְבִיעִים קֶמַח, חַיֶּבֶת בְּמַעַשְׂרוֹת, וְהִיסָּה שֶׁנִּילוֹשָׁה מִן הַקֶּמַח הַהוּא, פְּטוּרָה מִן הַחַלָּה, לְפִי שֶׁשִּׁיעוּר הָעִיסָּה לְהִתְחַיֵּיב בְּחַלָּה הִיא חֲמֵשֶׁת רְבִיעִים קֶמַח, וְעוֹד, כְּלוֹמַר מְעַט יוֹתֵר מֵחֲמֵשֶׁת רְבִיעִים:

---

that has grown less than a third will not grow if replanted, it is exempt from *maasros*.[12] However, with regard to *challah*, this exemption does not apply.[13]

The next Tanna disagrees with regard to grain that grew less than a third:

תְּבוּאָה שֶׁלֹּא הֵבִיאָה שְׁלִישׁ פְּטוּרָה מִן הַחַלָּה — R' Eliezer says: רַבִּי אֱלִיעֶזֶר אוֹמֵר — Grain that did not grow a third is exempt from *challah*. R' Eliezer learns from a verse that the laws of *challah* are compared to the laws of *terumah*. Thus, just as grain that did not grow a third is exempt from *terumah*, it is also exempt from *challah*.[14]

[4] Having listed items that are subject to the *challah* obligation but are not subject to the *maaser* obligation, the Mishnah now lists items that are subject to the *maaser* obligation but are not subject to the *challah* obligation:

אֵלּוּ חַיָּבִין בַּמַּעַשְׂרוֹת וּפְטוּרִים מִן הַחַלָּה — The following items are subject to *maasros* but exempt from *challah*: הָאֹרֶז וְהַדֹּחַן וְהַפְּרָגִים וְהַשֻּׁמְשְׁמִין וְהַקִּטְנִיּוֹת — dough made from rice, millet, poppy, sesame, and legumes. All of these are subject to the obligation of *maasros*, because *maaser* applies to any edible produce, not just the five species.[1] However, dough from these species is not subject to the obligation of *challah* because only the five species are obligated in *challah* (see Mishnah 1). וּפָחוֹת מֵחֲמֵשֶׁת רְבָעִים

NOTES

12. This law is learned from a verse (see *Rav*; see also *Maasros* 1:3).

13. The *challah* obligation applies even if the grain is not suitable for replanting, for as long as grain can ferment it is subject to the *challah* obligation. And even grain that grew less than a third can ferment (*Rav*).

14. See *Rav*. R' Eliezer agrees that all the other exemptions of the Mishnah do not apply to *challah*. This is because the verse compares *challah* to *terumah* only with regard to exemptions that relate to the produce itself, such as in our case where it did not grow enough. However, the other exemptions to *terumos* and *maasros* are because of the ownership of the produce, or in the case of *maaser rishon* and *maaser sheni*, because the produce they were separated from was not processed. Therefore, those exemptions do not apply to *challah* (*Mishnah Rishonah*).

[4]

1. See *Maasros* 1:1. [Basically, all types of produce except for the five species of grain are obligated in *maasros* but exempt from *challah*. The Mishnah lists specifically these types since it is common to make dough from them (*Tiferes Yisrael*).]

[18] משניות חלה / פרק א: חמשה דברים

בַּתְּבוּאָה. הַסְּפְגָּנִין, וְהַדֻּבְשָׁנִין, וְהָאִסְקְרִיטִין, וְחַלַּת הַמַּשְׂרֶת, וְהַמְדֻמָּע, פְּטוּרִין מִן הַחַלָּה.

- רע"ב -
הסופגנין. לחס שבלילתו רכה וְעשוי כספוג. פירוש אחר, רקיקים דקים, תרגום ורקיקי

מצות (שמות כט, ב), ואספוגין: **הדובשנים**. מטוגנים בדבש. פירוש אחר, מי נמי, נילושים בדבש: **האסקריטין**. תרגום לפתיחה (שמות טז, יד), אסקריטון, משריתא: **וחלת המשרת**. חלה חלוטה במחבת. תרגום מחבת (ויקרא ו, יד), משריתא: **המדומע**. סאה של תרומה שנפלה לפחות ממאה סאין של חולין, ונעשו כולן מדומע, ואסורים לזרים. ופטור מן החלה, דכתיב (במדבר טו, יט) תרימו תרומה, ולא שכבר נתרמה:

בַּתְּבוּאָה — Also subject to *maasros* but not to *challah* is dough made from **less than five *reva'im*** (i.e., one and a quarter *kav*)[2] **of grain** flour, even if it was made from the five species. Dough made from less than five *reva'im* of flour is subject to *maasros*, because *maasros* apply to any amount. Yet it is exempt from *challah* because it is derived from a verse that the minimum amount of flour that is subject to the *challah* obligation is five *reva'im*.[3]

The Mishnah list several other items that are exempt from *challah*:

הַסְּפְגָּנִין — *Sufganin* (a sponge-like bread, made by mixing flour and water into a batter instead of a thick dough),[4] **וְהַדֻּבְשָׁנִין** — *duvshanin* (made by mixing flour and water into a batter and frying it in honey),[5] **וְהָאִסְקְרִיטִין** — wafers (made from a very thin batter), **וְחַלַּת הַמַּשְׂרֶת** — pan loaf (made by pouring hot water over dough),[6] **וְהַמְדֻמָּע** — and bread made from *meduma* flour (a mixture of *chullin* and *terumah* flour),[7] **פְּטוּרִין מִן הַחַלָּה** — are all **exempt from *challah*.** Sufganin, duvshanin, wafers, and pan loaf are exempt because they are not considered "bread."[8] Bread made from *meduma* flour

--- NOTES ---

2. A *rova* (pl. *reva'im*) is a quarter of a *kav*. Thus, five *reva'im* are 1¼ *kavs* (see General Introduction for the contemporary equivalent of this measure).

3. See below, Mishnah 2:6. [Actually, the exact amount that is subject to the *challah* obligation is a matter of dispute. *Rav* follows the opinion that the amount is *slightly more* than 1¼ *kavs*, and understands that this is actually what our Mishnah means. Thus, if the amount of flour is *exactly* 1¼ *kavs*, it is also exempt. See, however, Mishnah 2:5 with *Rav* (see *Tos. Yom Tov*).]

4. *Rav*, first interpretation. In addition, it was fried in oil and honey or cooked in water, rather than baked in an oven (see *Rav* to next Mishnah and *Tiferes Yisrael* there).

5. *Rav*, first interpretation; see *Mishnah Rishonah*.

6. The dough was placed in a pan, and hot water was poured over it (*Rav*).

7. Biblically, if *terumah* and *chullin* of the same type become mixed together the mixture is permitted, as long as the *chullin* makes up the majority of the mixture. The Rabbis, however, decreed that if even one part of *terumah* gets mixed into less than 100 parts of *chullin*, it is treated as *terumah*. Such a mixture is known as *meduma*; see *Terumos* 4:7. See note 9.

8. The Torah uses the word "bread" when discussing the *challah* obligation (see *Bamidbar* 15:19; see also *Rashi* to *Pesachim* 37a ד"ה פטורין).

All of these are not considered bread since they are made from a thin batter and not baked in the regular manner. However, if they were made from regular dough or baked in an oven they would be subject to the *challah* obligation, as we will see in the next Mishnah (see *Rav* there ד"ה תחילתה עיסה; see also *Tosafos* to *Pesachim* 36b ד"ה פרט לחלוט; *Maharam Chalavah, Pesachim* 37a).

[ה] עָשָׂה שֶׁתְּחִלָּתָהּ סֻפְגָּנִין וְסוֹפָהּ סֻפְגָּנִין, פְּטוּרָה מִן הַחַלָּה; תְּחִלָּתָהּ עִסָּה וְסוֹפָהּ סֻפְגָּנִין, תְּחִלָּתָהּ סֻפְגָּנִין וְסוֹפָהּ עִסָּה, חַיֶּבֶת בַּחַלָּה;

- רע"ב -

(ה) עסה שתחלתה סופגנין. כגון עסה שבלילתה רכה: וסופה סופגנין. שמטגנים אותה בשמן ודבש, או מבשלה במים: תחלתה עסה וסופה סופגנין. שבלילתה עבה, ואחר כך מטגנים אותה בשמן ודבש או מבשלה במים: בלילתה רכה, וסופה אותה בתנור:

is exempt because it is treated as *terumah,* and *terumah* is exempt from the *challah* obligation.[9]

[5] The previous Mishnah taught that *sufganin* are exempt from *challah.* The Mishnah elaborates on this ruling:

עָשָׂה שֶׁתְּחִלָּתָהּ סֻפְגָּנִין — **If a dough was** made **as** *sufganin* **at its beginning,** i.e., it was made as a thin batter, rather than a thick dough, וְסוֹפָהּ סֻפְגָּנִין **— and as** *sufganin* **at its end,** i.e., it was fried in oil or cooked in water,[1] פְּטוּרָה מִן הַחַלָּה — **it is exempt from the** *challah* **obligation.** תְּחִלָּתָהּ עִסָּה וְסוֹפָהּ סֻפְגָּנִין — However, if **it was** made **as dough at its beginning** (it was made as a thick dough, not a thin batter), **and as** *sufganin* **at its end** (it was fried or cooked), תְּחִלָּתָהּ סֻפְגָּנִין וְסוֹפָהּ עִסָּה — **or it was made as** *sufganin* **at its beginning** (it was made from a thin batter), **and as dough at its end** (i.e., it was baked in an oven, without liquid), חַיֶּבֶת בַּחַלָּה — **it is obligated in** *challah.* That is, in order for something to be subject to the *challah* obligation, it must either be made with the type of dough that is normally used for bread (that is, a thick dough as opposed to a batter) even though the final product is not bread, or baked in an oven in the manner that bread is baked, even if it was originally prepared as a batter.[2]

---- NOTES ----

9. We learn from a verse that we are not obligated to separate *challah* from *terumah.* Now, the Rabbis decreed that *meduma* must be treated as *terumah.* Therefore, such a mixture is considered entirely *terumah* with regard to the *challah* obligation, and the entire mixture (even the *chullin* part) is exempt from *challah* (see *Rav;* see also *Tosafos* to *Niddah* 47a ד"ה אתי). [If there are 100 parts of *chullin* for each part of *terumah,* the *terumah* is nullified, and the dough *is* subject to *challah.*]

The law applies only nowadays, when the *challah* obligation is Rabbinic (see General Introduction). In earlier times, however, the *challah* obligation was of Biblical origin. In those times, *meduma* would be subject to the *challah* obligation, since the Rabbinic prohibition of *meduma* could not override the Biblical obligation of *challah* (see *Tos. Yom Tov*).

[5]

1. See *Rav.* [*Sufganin* were prepared from a thin batter fried in oil and honey or cooked in water, rather than baked in an oven. See note 8 to the previous Mishnah.]

As will be explained further in the Mishnah, there are two ways that something can become subject to the *challah* obligation. One is when it is kneaded as a thick, regular dough, even if the final product will not be bread. A second way is if the final product is considered bread, even if it was made from a batter, rather than a dough. The Mishnah teaches that if *sufganin* were made from a thin batter that was then fried or cooked, they are exempt from *challah,* because neither condition was fulfilled.

2. [It should be noted that we have

- רע"ב -

קנובקעות. לחם שמחזירים אותו לסלתו, וטוחנים ממנו מאכל לתינוקות:
(ו) המעיסה. קמח על גבי מים רותחים: החליטה. מים רותחים על גבי קמח.

וְכֵן הַקְּנוּבְקָאוֹת חַיָּבוֹת.

[ו] הַמְּעִיסָה, בֵּית שַׁמַּאי פּוֹטְרִין, וּבֵית הִלֵּל מְחַיְּבִין. הַחֲלִיטָה,

ומפורש בגמרא (פסחים לז, ב) דתרי תנאי נינהו, ומי ששנה זו לא שנה זו, דתנא אחד תנא מעיסה והוא הדין חליטה, וסבר בין מעיסה בין חליטה בית שמאי פוטרין ובית הלל מחייבין, ואידך תנא חליטה והוא הדין מעיסה, וסבר בין חליטה בין מעיסה בית שמאי מחייבים ובית הלל פוטרים. ולענין פסק הלכה, בין מעיסה בין חליטה, אם נאפות בתנור, חייבות בחלה, ואם במרחשת או במחבת וכל דבר שהאור עוברת תחתיו, פטורות מן החלה:

Having taught that dough is subject to the *challah* obligation even though the final product is not bread, the Mishnah mentions something else that is subject to the *challah* obligation even though the end product is not bread:

וְכֵן הַקְּנוּבְקָאוֹת חַיָּבוֹת — **And, similarly,** *kenuvkaos* (a type of baby food made from ground-up bread) **are subject to the *challah* obligation,** since at one point they were bread.

[6] Having taught that dough cooked in water is exempt from *challah*, the Mishnah deals with cases in which dough was first cooked and then baked:

הַמְּעִיסָה — **Regarding a *me'isah*** (a bread made by pouring flour into hot water, and then baking the mixture):[1] בֵּית שַׁמַּאי פּוֹטְרִין — **Beis Shammai exempt** it from *challah,* because such bread is considered cooked, not baked, and cooked bread is exempt from *challah*.[2] וּבֵית הִלֵּל מְחַיְּבִין — **But Beis Hillel obligate** it in *challah*. They hold that since *me'isah* is baked at the end, it is considered a baked item, which is subject to *challah*.[3]

The Mishnah discusses the law of another type of bread that is first cooked and then baked:

הַחֲלִיטָה — **Regarding a *chalitah*** (a bread made by pouring hot water onto

---- NOTES ----

followed *Rav*, who holds that something prepared as a thick dough is subject to *challah* regardless of how it will be baked. However, most authorities disagree with this. They hold that if one made a thick dough intending to cook or fry it, it is exempt from *challah* (see *Meleches Shlomo;* see also *Shulchan Aruch, Yoreh Deah* 329:3).]

[6]

1. See *Rav*; see also *Raavad* to *Eduyos* 5:2.
2. When flour is mixed in hot water, it becomes cooked. Beis Shammai hold

that "bread" made from cooked dough is not considered bread. Therefore, it is not subject to *challah* (see *Tosafos* to *Zevachim* 95b).

[In the previous Mishnah, we learned that once flour and water were made into a dough, the dough is subject to *challah*, even if it is later cooked. Here, however, the cooking took place before the dough was finished. Therefore, it is not considered bread (see *Rosh Yosef, Pesachim* 37a ד"ה תי"ק.]

3. Beis Hillel hold that bread made from cooked dough is considered bread. Therefore, it is obligated in *challah*.

[21] MISHNAH CHALLAH / Chapter 1: *Chamishah Devarim*

בֵּית שַׁמַּאי מְחַיְּבִין, וּבֵית הִלֵּל פּוֹטְרִין. חַלּוֹת תּוֹדָה וּרְקִיקֵי נָזִיר, עֲשָׂאָן לְעַצְמוֹ, פָּטוּר; לִמְכּוֹר בַּשּׁוּק, חַיָּב.

– רע"ב –

עשאן לעצמו. לצורך תודתו ונזירותו: פטור. כיון דגלגלן לקדשן, דכתיב (במדבר טו, כ) עריסותיכם, ולא עסת הקדש: למכור בשוק. לבני אדם שצריכים לחלות תודה ורקיקי נזיר: חייב. דכל לשוק אימלוכי ממליך,

flour, and then baking it): **בֵּית שַׁמַּאי מְחַיְּבִין** — **Beis Shammai obligate** it in *challah,* because it is baked at the end, and it is thus considered a baked item. **וּבֵית הִלֵּל פּוֹטְרִין** — **But Beis Hillel exempt** it, because it was originally cooked. Therefore, it is considered cooked bread, which is exempt from *challah.*[4]

The Mishnah now begins a new discussion. A person who is saved from a dangerous situation brings an animal as a *todah* offering. When a *nazir* (someone who accepts a certain type of vow that forbids him in wine, grapes, and various other things) completes his term of *nezirus,* he brings certain animal offerings. The Torah requires someone bringing either a *todah* or *nazir* offering to bring various types of breads along with the animal offering. These breads come in two basic categories — "loaves," and "wafers" (see *Vayikra* 7:12-13 and *Bamidbar* 6:13). The Mishnah discusses the *challah* obligation of these breads: **חַלּוֹת תּוֹדָה וּרְקִיקֵי נָזִיר** — Regarding **the loaves of a *todah*** offering **and the wafers of the *nazir's*** offering, the law is as follows:[5] **עֲשָׂאָן לְעַצְמוֹ פָּטוּר** — If **one made them for himself,** that is, he prepared the breads for his own *todah* or *nazir* offering, **he is exempt** from separating *challah.* The bread is considered bread of *hekdesh,* which is exempt from *challah.*[6] **לִמְכּוֹר בַּשּׁוּק חַיָּב** — However, if he made them **to sell in the marketplace** to people who

---- NOTES ----

4. *Me'isah* and *chalitah* are essentially the same. Both are made by mixing flour with hot water and then baking it. The only difference is that *me'isah* is made by pouring the flour into the hot water, while *chalitah* is made by pouring the hot water onto the flour. Thus, the same law should apply to both. Yet Beis Shammai exempt *me'isah* from the *challah* obligation but obligate *chalitah.* On the other hand, Beis Hillel obligate *me'isah,* but exempt *chalitah.* The Gemara (*Pesachim* 37b) explains that this is actually not the case. In actuality, these two disputes are two different versions of the dispute between Beis Shammai and Beis Hillel. According to the first version, Beis Shammai exempt *me'isah* from *challah* because it was cooked first, while Beis Hillel obligate it. However, *me'isah* is mentioned only as an example; the same applies to *chalitah* as well. The second version of the dispute discusses *chalitah,* and has the opinions reversed: Beis Shammai obligate it in *challah* even though it was cooked, while Beis Hillel exempt it since it was previously cooked. Here too, the dispute is with regard to *both chalitah* and *me'isah* (*Rav*).

5. [Actually the Torah requires both the person bringing a *todah* offering and the person bringing the *nazir* offering to bring both loaves *and* wafers. For the reason why the Mishnah mentioned only the loaves of the *todah* and wafers of the *nazir* offering, see *Tos. Yom Tov* and other commentaries.]

6. The Torah describes *challah* as *the first of "your" doughs* (*Bamidbar* 15:20). The term "your doughs" implies that only privately owned dough is obligated in *challah,* not dough of *hekdesh* (*Rav*). Even though the owner did not actually consecrate the dough, it is still exempt. Since the owner intended at the time of the kneading to use the dough for his offering, it is exempt as if it were already *hekdesh* (*Rash,* second explanation).

[22] משניות חלה / פרק א: חמשה דברים

[ז] נַחְתּוֹם שֶׁעָשָׂה שְׂאוֹר לְחַלֵּק, חַיָּב בַּחַלָּה. נָשִׁים שֶׁנָּתְנוּ לְנַחְתּוֹם לַעֲשׂוֹת לָהֶן שְׂאוֹר, אִם אֵין בְּשֶׁל אַחַת מֵהֶן כַּשִּׁעוּר,

– רע"ב –

(ז) נחתום שעשה שאור לחלק. ויש בו כדי חיוב חלה, אלא שדעתו למכרו לבני אדם לחלקו לכמה עיסות, ואין בכל חלק וחלק כשיעור: חייב בחלה. שדעתו אם לא ימצא קונים, שיעשנו עיסה ויאפה אותה כולה כאחת:

אי מזבינגא מזבינגא, ואי לא, אכילגא להו אנא:

NOTES

need them for their *todah* or *nazir* offerings, **he is obligated** to separate *challah*. Since the seller knows that he might not find any buyers for his breads, he realizes that he may end up keeping the breads for his own use, rather than bringing them as an offering. Therefore, the breads are *not* considered *hekdesh* and are subject to *challah*.

[7] The Mishnah deals with cases in which one kneaded an amount of dough that is obligated in *challah*, but had in mind to divide the dough into portions that will *not* have a *challah* obligation:

נַחְתּוֹם שֶׁעָשָׂה שְׂאוֹר לְחַלֵּק — **If a baker made a sourdough** that was large enough to have a *challah* obligation,[1] but had in mind **to divide** the dough into portions less than the minimum *challah* amount,[2] and to sell those portions to his customers, חַיָּב בַּחַלָּה — the law is that **he is obligated in *challah*.** The baker knows that he might not be able to sell the sourdough, and has in mind that if this happens, he will bake the dough as one big bread.[3] Since he may bake the amount that is subject to *challah*, he must separate *challah*.[4] נָשִׁים שֶׁנָּתְנוּ לְנַחְתּוֹם לַעֲשׂוֹת לָהֶן שְׂאוֹר — **But in the case of women who** each gave a portion of flour[5] **to a baker to make sourdough for them,** and the baker made one big dough out of all the flour, large enough to be subject to *challah*,[6] אִם אֵין בְּשֶׁל אַחַת מֵהֶן כַּשִּׁעוּר — the law is that **if none of**

---

[7]
1. I.e., it was made from at least 1¼ *kav* of flour (see Mishnah 4). [Sourdough is made by leaving dough to ferment. It is added to regular dough in order to help it rise.]
2. I.e., each of the portions was less than 1¼ *kav*.
3. After kneading the dough, before letting it ferment into sourdough, the baker checks to see if he has enough customers interested in buying sourdough. If he cannot find enough customers, he does not make it into sourdough, but bakes it as bread. Once he makes it into bread, it is always possible that he will make it into one large bread. Thus, when the baker makes the dough originally, he knows that he might not end up dividing the dough (see *Rav*).
4. If at the time of kneading one has definite plans to divide the dough, it is

exempt from *challah*, as we will learn in the next case of the Mishnah. The Mishnah teaches that in this case the baker knows that he might not divide it, and therefore it is obligated in *challah*.

[While the Mishnah discusses sourdough, its ruling certainly applies where the baker intended to sell the portions as regular bread. Since in any case he is making bread, he is certainly open to the possibility of making one large bread (even if he prefers making smaller loaves). The Mishnah teaches that even in a case where the baker planned on making sourdough, and did not plan on using the dough for bread at all, he still has in mind that he might make it into one big bread (see *Tos. Anshei Shem*).]

5. *Tiferes Yisrael*.
6. Instead of kneading each portion individually, the baker kneaded all the flour

[23] MISHNAH CHALLAH / Chapter 1: *Chamishah Devarim*

- רע״ב -

(ח) עסת כלבים.
נעשית מקמח, ומורסן
הרבה מעורב בה: בזמן
שהרועים אוכלים
ממנה. שלא נתערב בה
מורסן כל כך: חייבת
בחלה. דכיון דחזיא לרועים, לחם קרינן בה: ומערבין בה. ערובי חצרות, להוציא מן הבתים לחצר:

[ח] **עִסַּת הַכְּלָבִים,** בִּזְמַן שֶׁהָרוֹעִים אוֹכְלִין מִמֶּנָּה, חַיֶּבֶת בַּחַלָּה, וּמְעָרְבִין בָּהּ, **פְּטוּרָה מִן הַחַלָּה.**

[the women's] portions **was the amount** that is obligated in *challah*,[7] **פְּטוּרָה מִן הַחַלָּה** — [the dough] is exempt from *challah*. In this case, the baker must divide the dough in order to return to each woman her portion.[8] Thus, he is certain that he will divide the dough into pieces that are not obligated in *challah*, and it is therefore not subject to the obligation of *challah*.[9]

[8] The following Mishnah deals with a type of bread that is primarily used as animal food. This bread was baked from dough, known as "dogs' dough," which had a large amount of bran mixed into the flour. This dough was used mainly as dog food, and would not be eaten by most people. However, if it did not have too much bran, it was somewhat edible, and shepherds [who could not get other bread easily] would eat some of it. Sometimes, however, the bread would have so much bran that it was practically inedible, in which case even the shepherds would not eat it. The Mishnah discusses the law of this bread with regard to *challah*, as well as regarding various other laws:

עִסַּת הַכְּלָבִים — Regarding **dogs' dough,** **בִּזְמַן שֶׁהָרוֹעִים אוֹכְלִין מִמֶּנָּה** — the following laws apply **when the shepherds eat from it** (that is, if the bread does not have so much bran that would make it almost inedible): **חַיֶּבֶת בַּחַלָּה** — **It is subject to the obligation of** *challah*, which applies only to bread. Since the shepherds eat it, it is considered bread. **וּמְעָרְבִין בָּהּ** — **We may make an** *eruv chatzeiros* **with it.** An *eruv chatzeiros* is made by putting bread into one of the houses in a courtyard, in order to permit carrying between a house and a courtyard on Shabbos.[1]

--- NOTES ---

together as one big dough. And all the flour together measured 1¼ *kav* (see *Meleches Shlomo* ד״ה אם).

7. I.e., none of the women gave a portion larger than 1¼ *kav*. [If even only one of the women gave this amount, the entire dough is subject to the obligation of *challah*, even the part that came from the other women. Since it is all combined into one dough, and part of the dough is obligated in *challah*, the whole dough is subject to *challah* (see *Meleches Shlomo*).]

8. Unlike the previous case, in which the dough belonged to the baker, here the dough belongs to the women who gave him the flour. Therefore, he does not have

the option of making the dough into one large bread (see *Derech Emunah, Hilchos Bikkurim* 6:167).

9. Since he plans on dividing the dough, it is considered as though it is already divided, and does not have the minimum amount that is subject to the *challah* obligation (*Meiri*).

[8]

1. The Rabbis prohibited carrying on Shabbos between a house and a courtyard that has more than one house opening into it. However, the Rabbis permitted carrying if an *eruv chatzeiros* is made, by collecting bread from each of the homeowners and placing the bread in one of the houses. [An *eruv chatzeiros* must be

משניות חלה / פרק א: חמשה דברים

וּמִשְׁתַּתְּפִין בָּהּ, וּמְבָרְכִין עָלֶיהָ, וּמְזַמְּנִין עָלֶיהָ, וְנַעֲשֵׂית בְּיוֹם טוֹב, וְיוֹצֵא בָהּ אָדָם יְדֵי חוֹבָתוֹ בַּפֶּסַח; אִם אֵין הָרוֹעִים אוֹכְלִין מִמֶּנָּה, אֵינָהּ חַיֶּבֶת בַּחַלָּה, וְאֵין מְעָרְבִין בָּהּ,

- רע״ב -

ומשתתפין בה. שתופי מבואות, להוציא מן החצרות למבוי: ומברכין עליה. ברכת המוציא: ומזמנין עליה. שלשה שאכלו ממנה כאחת, חייבים לזמן: ונאפית ביום טוב. משום חלק רועים: ואדם יוצא בה ידי חובתו בפסח. לילה ראשונה, שחייב לאכול כזית מצה: אינה חייבת בחלה. דכתיב (במדבר טו, כ) ראשית עריסותיכם, שלכס חייבת ולא של חיה:

וּמִשְׁתַּתְּפִין בָּהּ — **We may make** *shitufei mevo'os* **with it.** *Shitufei mevo'os*, which can be made with any food, permits carrying from a courtyard to an alleyway on Shabbos.[2] **וּמְבָרְכִין עָלֶיהָ** — **We recite the blessing** of *HaMotzi* **on it,** **וּמְזַמְּנִין עָלֶיהָ** — **and we join in a** *zimun* **on it.** That is, if three people eat this bread they are obligated in the *zimun* blessing, since it is considered bread.[3] **וְנַעֲשֵׂית בְּיוֹם טוֹב** — **It may be made** (i.e., baked) **on Yom Tov,** even though it is forbidden to bake food for animals on Yom Tov.[4] Since some of the bread will be eaten by the shepherds, it is considered baking for people, not animals.[5] **וְיוֹצֵא בָהּ אָדָם יְדֵי חוֹבָתוֹ בַּפֶּסַח** — **A person may fulfill his obligation with it on Pesach.** That is, if such bread is baked as matzah, one can eat it on the first night of Pesach to fulfill his matzah obligation. Since it is considered bread, it can be made into matzah, which must also be "bread."[6] **אִם אֵין הָרוֹעִים אוֹכְלִין מִמֶּנָּה** — However, **if the shepherds do not eat from [the dogs' bread]** because it contains a large amount of bran, the following laws apply: **אֵינָהּ חַיֶּבֶת בַּחַלָּה** — **It is not subject to the** *challah* **obligation.** Since it is eaten only by animals it is considered animal food.[7] **וְאֵין מְעָרְבִין בָּהּ** — We

---

— NOTES —

made with bread; other types of food cannot be used (see *Eruvin* 7:10 with note 2 there).]

2. Just as the Rabbis forbade carrying from a private house to a communal courtyard, they forbade carrying from a courtyard to an alleyway that has several courtyards opening into it. To permit such carrying, a *shituf mevo'os* must be made. This is done by collecting food from all the residents of the courtyards, and placing the food in one of the courtyards (see *Eruvin* 7:10).

3. When three or more people eat bread together, they recite a certain blessing (called the *zimun* blessing) before beginning *Bircas HaMazon*. The Mishnah teaches that if three people eat this type of dogs' bread they must recite this blessing (*Rav*).

4. Although it is permitted to bake food on Yom Tov, this applies only to food that will be eaten by people, not food that will be fed to animals (see *Beitzah* 21a-b).

5. *Rav*. [Although the shepherds eat only part of the bread, it is nevertheless permitted to bake all the bread. The entire bread is considered being baked for the shepherds, since, if they wish, they can eat the entire bread, and give the dogs an animal carcass instead (see *Rambam, Hilchos Yom Tov* 1:14 with *Maggid Mishneh*).]

6. The Torah calls matzah the "bread" of affliction. Thus, matzah must be considered "bread" to be eligible for the mitzvah of matzah (*Meiri*, second explanation; see also *Rash Sirilio* 12a ד״ה כל). Here too, since the shepherds eat such dogs' bread it is considered bread, and therefore qualifies as "bread of affliction" when made into matzah.

7. The verse (*Bamidbar* 15:20) describes the *challah* as *the first of "your" doughs*. The word "*your*" implies that it must be suitable for people to eat (see *Rav*).

[25] **MISHNAH CHALLAH** / Chapter 1: *Chamishah Devarim*

וְאֵין מִשְׁתַּתְּפִין בָּהּ, וְאֵין מְבָרְכִין עָלֶיהָ,
וְאֵין מְזַמְּנִין עָלֶיהָ, וְאֵינָהּ נַעֲשֵׂית בְּיוֹם
טוֹב, וְאֵין אָדָם יוֹצֵא בָהּ יְדֵי חוֹבָתוֹ בַּפֶּסַח;
בֵּין כָּךְ וּבֵין כָּךְ, מִטַּמְּאָה טֻמְאַת אֳכָלִין.
[ט] **הַחַלָּה** וְהַתְּרוּמָה, חַיָּבִין עֲלֵיהֶן
מִיתָה וְחֹמֶשׁ, וַאֲסוּרִים

- רע"ב -

מטמאה טומאת אוכלין. כיון דעל ידי הדחק נאכלת לאדם, מטמאה, עד שתפסל מלאכול לכלב: (ט) חייבין עליהן מיתה. זר האוכלן מזיד חייב מיתה בידי שמים, דחלה אקרייא תרומה, ובתרומה כתיב (ויקרא כב, ט) ומתו בו כי יחללוהו. וחומש. האוכלן שוגג, משלם קרן לבעלים, וחומש לכל כהן שירצה:

וְאֵין מִשְׁתַּתְּפִין בָּהּ **— and we may not make an *eruvei* [*chatzeiros*] with it,** may not make *shitufei mevo'os* with it. Since such bread is eaten only by animals, it is not considered food at all, and thus it cannot be used even for *shitufei mevo'os*.[8] וְאֵין מְבָרְכִין עָלֶיהָ **— We do not recite the blessing of** *HaMotzi* **on it,**[9] וְאֵין מְזַמְּנִין עָלֶיהָ **— and we do not join in a *zimun* because of it,** since it is not bread.[10] וְאֵינָהּ נַעֲשֵׂית בְּיוֹם טוֹב **— It may not be made** (baked) **on Yom Tov,** because it is forbidden to do *melachah* (certain types of labor) on Yom Tov to prepare food for animals.[11] וְאֵין אָדָם יוֹצֵא בָהּ יְדֵי חוֹבָתוֹ בַּפֶּסַח **— A person cannot fulfill his** matzah **obligation with it on Pesach.** The reason for this is that this type of dogs' bread is not considered bread, and matzah must be "bread."[12]

The Mishnah concludes with a law that applies to both types of dogs' bread: בֵּין כָּךְ וּבֵין כָּךְ מִטַּמְּאָה טֻמְאַת אֳכָלִין **— In either case,** i.e., whether the bread is eaten by shepherds or not, **it can become** *tamei* **under the law of *tumah* of foods.**[13] In a case of pressing need, even dogs' bread that is not normally eaten by shepherds will be eaten by humans. Therefore, with regard to the laws of *tumah* it *is* considered food.[14]

[9] *Challah* and *terumah* (i.e., the portion of one's produce that must be given to a Kohen) share many laws. The Mishnah lists these laws:

הַחַלָּה וְהַתְּרוּמָה **— Both *challah* and *terumah* are subject to the following laws:** חַיָּבִין עֲלֵיהֶן מִיתָה וְחֹמֶשׁ **— [Non-Kohanim] are liable to** the penalty of **death**

NOTES
---

8. Although a *shitufei mevo'os* does not require bread, it must at least be a food. Since even shepherds do not eat this type of dogs' bread, it is not considered food with regard to this law.

9. Someone who eats it would nevertheless recite the blessing of *shehakol* (*Tiferes Yisrael*).

10. [Just as someone who eats it does not recite the blessing of *HaMotzi* beforehand, he does not recite *Bircas HaMazon* afterward, since these blessings are recited only on bread. Certainly then, three

people who eat such bread would not join in *zimun*, which is performed only when *Bircas HaMazon* is recited.]

11. See above, note 4.

12. See above, note 6.

13. Food that comes in contact with certain types of *tamei* items can become *tamei* (*Vayikra* 11:34).

14. Regarding the laws of *tumah*, anything that is eaten by people, under any circumstances, is considered food (see *Rav*).

[26] **משניות חלה / פרק א: חמשה דברים**

לַזָּרִים, וְהֵם נִכְסֵי כֹהֵן, וְעוֹלִין בְּאֶחָד וּמֵאָה, וּטְעוּנִין רְחִיצַת יָדַיִם וְהַעֲרֵב שָׁמֶשׁ,

– רע"ב –
וַאֲסוּרִים לַזָּרִים. בְּחֵנֶק הִיא שְׁנוּיָה, דְּכֵיוָן שֶׁחַיָּבִים הַזָּרִים עֲלֵיהֶם מִיתָה וְחוֹמֶשׁ, פְּשִׁיטָא

דַּאֲסוּרִים לַזָּרִים. וְלְרַבִּי יוֹחָנָן דְּאָמַר חֲלִי שִׁעוּר מִדְּאוֹרַיְתָא, מָצִינוּ לְמֵימַר דְּתַנָּא דְּמַתְנִיתִין אֲסוּרִים לַזָּרִים לְחֲלִי שִׁעוּר, שֶׁאֵין בּוֹ לֹא מִיתָה וְלֹא חוֹמֶשׁ, אֲבָל אִסוּרָא דְּאוֹרַיְתָא מִיהָא אִיכָּא: **וְהֵן נִכְסֵי כֹהֵן.** שֶׁיָּכוֹל לְמָכְרָן וְלִיקַח בָּהֶן עֲבָדִים וְקַרְקָעוֹת וּבְהֵמָה טְמֵאָה: **וְעוֹלִין בְּאֶחָד וּמֵאָה.** אִם נִתְעָרְבוּ בְּמֵאָה שֶׁל חוּלִּין: **וּטְעוּנִים רְחִיצַת יָדַיִם.** הַבָּא לִיגַּע בָּהֶן צָרִיךְ לִיטוֹל יָדָיו תְּחִלָּה, שֶׁסְּתָם יָדַיִם פּוֹסְלוֹת אֶת הַתְּרוּמָה, וְאֶת הַחַלָּה, שֶׁאַף הִיא נִקְרֵאת תְּרוּמָה: **וְהַעֲרֵב שָׁמֶשׁ.** טָמֵא שֶׁטָּבַל, אֵינוֹ אוֹכֵל בַּתְּרוּמָה עַד שֶׁיַּעֲרִיב שִׁמְשׁוֹ, כְּדִכְתִיב (ויקרא כב, ז) וּבָא הַשֶּׁמֶשׁ וְטָהֵר וְאַחַר יֹאכַל מִן הַקֳּדָשִׁים, וְהוּא הַדִּין לְחַלָּה:

for eating them if they did so intentionally, **and** to the penalty of a "fifth" if they ate them unintentionally.[1] **וַאֲסוּרִים לַזָּרִים** — [Both] are forbidden to non-Kohanim.[2] **וְהֵם נִכְסֵי כֹהֵן** — They are the personal property of the Kohen.[3] **וְעוֹלִין בְּאֶחָד וּמֵאָה** — They become nullified in one hundred and one, if they get mixed together with *chullin*.[4] That is, they become nullified only if there are one hundred parts of *chullin* for each part of *challah* or *terumah*.[5] **וּטְעוּנִין רְחִיצַת יָדַיִם** — They require hand-washing, that is, one must wash his hands before touching *challah* or *terumah*.[6] **וְהַעֲרֵב שָׁמֶשׁ** — They

―――― NOTES ――――

[9]
1. We learn from a verse that if a non-Kohen eats *terumah* intentionally, he is punished with "death at the hands of Heaven" [מִיתָה בִּידֵי שָׁמַיִם] (see *Rav*; see also *Tos. Yom Tov*). This law also applies to *challah*, because the Torah (*Bamidbar* 15:19-21) refers to *challah* as *terumah* (see *Rav*).
  If a non-Kohen eats *terumah* by mistake, the Torah obligates him to pay back the principal plus an additional "fifth" (see *Vayikra* 22:14). [Actually, the penalty is one-quarter of the principal, which is one-fifth of the *final* payment.] And the same is true for a non-Kohen who eats *challah*, since *challah* has the same law as *terumah* (see *Rav*).
2. This Mishnah has already taught that a non-Kohen is punished for eating *challah* or *terumah*. That law, however, applies only when he eats a *kezayis* (an olive's volume). Here, the Mishnah teaches that even if a non-Kohen eats less than a *kezayis* (an olive's volume) of *challah* or *terumah* (in which case he is not liable to any punishment) he has transgressed a Biblical prohibition (*Rav*).
3. The Kohen may sell his *challah* and *terumah*, and use the money to buy anything he wants (*Rav; Tiferes Yisrael*).

4. Literally, *they become raised in one hundred and one.* The Mishnah uses the term "raised" because the law is that before the mixture can be permitted one must remove ("raise") from the mixture an amount equal to the *challah* or *terumah* that got mixed in, and give this portion to a Kohen. Once this is done, a non-Kohen may eat the rest of the mixture (see *Tos. Anshei Shem*).

5. [When the Mishnah says that they are "nullified in one hundred and one" it refers to the entire mixture, including the *challah* or *terumah*. Thus, it is nullified when the mixture contains 100 parts of *chullin* and one part of *challah* or *terumah* (see *Rav* to *Terumos* 4:7 ד"ה תרומה).]
  Normally, a prohibited substance that is mixed with a permitted substance of the same type is nullified either if the permitted is the majority, or is sixty times more than the prohibited substance, depending on the case (see *Chullin* 99b and 97b). With regard to *challah* and *terumah*, however, the Rabbis decreed that if *challah* and *terumah* of the same type become mixed together, there must be 100 times more *chullin* in order to nullify the *terumah* (see *Tos. Yom Tov* ד"ה אסורה לזרים).

6. The Rabbis decreed that unwashed hands are considered *tamei*. Thus, if one

[27] **MISHNAH CHALLAH** / Chapter 1: *Chamishah Devarim*

– רע״ב –

וְאֵינָן נִטָּלִין מִן הַטָּהוֹר עַל הַטָּמֵא, אֶלָּא מִן הַמֻּקָּף וּמִן הַדָּבָר הַגָּמוּר.

ואינו ניטלים מן הטהור על הטמא. גזרה שמא יתרום שלא מן המוקף, משום דמסתפי שמא יגע הטמא בטהור ויטמאנו, ואין בעינן שהתורם יתרום מן המוקף כדתנן בסמוך: ואין ניטלין אלא מן המוקף. גרסינן. ופירוש: מן הדבר הגמור. שנגמרה מלאכתן. וחלה, משתתגלגל העיסה:

both require **nightfall**. That is, if a Kohen became *tamei* and immersed in a *mikveh*, he must wait until nightfall to eat *challah* or *terumah*.[7] וְאֵינָן נִטָּלִין מִן הַטָּהוֹר עַל הַטָּמֵא — **They may not be taken from** something that is **tahor** **for** something that is **tamei**. That is, one may not designate a *tahor* piece of dough as *challah* for *tamei* dough, or designate *tahor* produce as *terumah* for *tamei* produce;[8] אֶלָּא מִן הַמֻּקָּף — **and they are taken only from** something **that is close by**,[9] that is, the *challah* or *terumah* are to be close to the rest of the dough or produce when they are being designated;[10] וּמִן הַדָּבָר הַגָּמוּר — **and they are taken only from something that is finished,** that is, in the case of *challah* the dough must already be made before designating *challah*, and in the case of *terumah* the produce must be fully processed.[11]

---- NOTES ----

touches *terumah* with such hands, the *terumah* becomes *tamei*. Since a Kohen may not eat *terumah* that became *tamei*, the Rabbis required us to wash our hands (in the same manner that we wash for bread) before touching *terumah*. Since *challah* has the same laws as *terumah*, one must also wash his hands before touching *challah* (see *Rav*).

7. The Mishnah teaches that even after a Kohen immerses in a *mikveh*, he is not considered *tahor* with regard to eating *terumah* until nightfall following his immersion. We learn this law from a verse. Similarly, the Kohen must wait until nightfall to eat *challah*, since *challah* has the same laws as *terumah* (see *Rav*).

[It should be noted that all the laws listed until this point apply to *terumas maaser* as well.]

8. This law is a Rabbinic decree. The Rabbis were concerned that if one would use *tahor* produce as *terumah* for *tamei* produce, he might specifically keep the *terumah* at a distance from the rest of the produce so that the *terumah* should not touch the produce and become *tamei*. [*Terumah* that is *tamei* may not be eaten (see above note 6).] And the law is that when separating *terumah*, the *terumah* must be close to the rest of the produce (as the Mishnah will soon

teach). Therefore, to prevent people from separating *terumah* incorrectly, the Rabbis decreed that one may not use *tahor* produce as *terumah* for *tamei* produce; rather, he should use only *tamei* produce for the *terumah* (see *Rav*). This decree applies to *challah* as well, since (as the Mishnah will teach) *challah* must also be next to the rest of the dough when it is separated.

9. Literally, *from that which is surrounded*, i.e., from something that is in the same area.

10. This law is learned from a verse (see *Yerushalmi Terumos* 2:1).

[There are many rules governing what is considered "close" to the rest of the produce. See *Rambam, Hilchos Terumos* 3:17-19).]

11. We learn from a verse that *terumah* is to be separated only after the produce is processed (see *Rav* to *Terumos* 1:10 ד״ה על). The exact stage at which produce is considered processed depends on the type of produce (see *Maasros* 1:4-5). For example, grain is considered processed when it is smoothed into a pile. Thus, one should not separate *terumah* from grain before this point.

We learn from a different verse that *challah* is compared to *terumah* regarding this law. Thus, *challah* is also not

א/ט

הָאוֹמֵר כָּל גָּרְנִי תְרוּמָה וְכָל עִסָּתִי חַלָּה, לֹא אָמַר כְּלוּם, עַד שֶׁיְּשַׁיֵּר מִקְצָת.

- רע"ב -

עד שישייר מקצת. דחלה ותרומה כתיב בהו ראשית (במדבר טו, כ; דברים יח, ד), ובעינן שיהו שיריהן ניכרים:

The Mishnah concludes with a final law that applies to both *terumah* and *challah*:

הָאוֹמֵר כָּל גָּרְנִי תְרוּמָה — **If someone says, "All [the grain in] my silo is *terumah*,"** וְכָל עִסָּתִי חַלָּה — **or, "My entire dough is *challah*,"** לֹא אָמַר כְּלוּם — **he has not said anything**, i.e., the *terumah* or *challah* does not take effect, עַד שֶׁיְּשַׁיֵּר מִקְצָת — **unless he leaves over a part** that is not *terumah* or *challah*. Only a portion of the produce or dough is to be separated as *terumah* or *challah*, not all of it.[12]

NOTES

to be separated until the dough is "processed" (see *Rambam Commentary*), which is after it is kneaded (*Rav*).

[It should be noted, though, that in some cases the Rabbis instituted that *challah* must be separated *before* the kneading is complete (see Mishnah 3:1).]

12. The Torah calls *terumah* "the first of your grain" (*Devarim* 18:4). This implies that there must be another portion that is not *terumah*. Thus, if one designates all his produce as *terumah,* it does not take effect, and the produce remains *tevel*, unless he leaves over some produce that will not be *terumah*.

Similarly, *challah* is called "the first of your doughs" (*Bamidbar* 15:20). Therefore, there must be one part of the dough that is *challah* and another part that is not (see *Rav*).

Chapter Two

משניות חלה / פרק ב: פרות

- רע"ב -

פרק שני — פירות.
(א) פירות חוצה לארץ שנכנסו לארץ חייבין בחלה. דכתיב (במדבר טו,יח) אל הארץ אשר אני מביא אתכם שמה, שמה אתם חייבים בין בפירות

[א] פֵּרוֹת חוּצָה לָאָרֶץ שֶׁנִּכְנְסוּ לָאָרֶץ, חַיָּבִים בַּחַלָּה.
יָצְאוּ מִכָּאן לְשָׁם, רַבִּי אֱלִיעֶזֶר מְחַיֵּב, וְרַבִּי עֲקִיבָא פּוֹטֵר.

הארץ בין בפירות חולה לארץ: **מכאן לשם**. מחרן ישראל לחוץ לארץ: **רבי אליעזר מחייב**. דכתיב (שם, פסוק יט) והיה באכלכם מלחם הארץ, בין שאתם אוכלים אותו בארץ, בין שאתם אוכלים אותו בחולה לארץ, הואיל ולחם הארץ הוא, חייב בחלה. **ורבי עקיבא פוטר**. דשמה משמע ליה מיעוטא, שמה אתם חייבים, ואין אתם חייבים בחולה לארץ, אף על פי שאתם אוכלים מלחם הארץ. והלכה כרבי עקיבא:

---

[1] Biblically, the *challah* obligation applies only in Eretz Yisrael. The Mishnah discusses the law of grain that was grown outside of Eretz Yisrael, but was made into bread in Eretz Yisrael:

פֵּרוֹת חוּצָה לָאָרֶץ שֶׁנִּכְנְסוּ לָאָרֶץ — **Produce** (i.e., grain) grown **outside of Eretz Yisrael that entered Eretz Yisrael** and was then made into dough there חַיָּבִים בַּחַלָּה — **is subject to the *challah* obligation.** The requirement to separate *challah* depends on whether the dough was in Eretz Yisrael at the time when the *challah* obligation takes effect (which is the time when it is made into dough). Since this produce was in Eretz Yisrael at that time, it is subject to *challah*.[1]

The Mishnah now discusses the law of grain that was grown in Eretz Yisrael, but was then made into bread outside Eretz Yisrael:

יָצְאוּ מִכָּאן לְשָׁם — If the grain **went out from here** (Eretz Yisrael) **to there** (outside of Eretz Yisrael),[2] and was then made into dough outside of Eretz Yisrael, רַבִּי אֱלִיעֶזֶר מְחַיֵּב — **R' Eliezer obligates** it in *challah* on the Biblical level. R' Eliezer holds that grain that grows in Eretz Yisrael is subject to *challah*, even if it was not in Eretz Yisrael at the time when the actual *challah* obligation takes effect (i.e., when it is made into dough).[3] וְרַבִּי עֲקִיבָא פּוֹטֵר — **But R' Akiva**

--- NOTES ---

[1]
1. The verse teaches that even produce of outside of Eretz Yisrael is subject to the *challah* obligation on the Biblical level if it is in Eretz Yisrael when the *challah* obligation takes effect (see *Rav*). The obligation to separate *challah* takes effect at the time of the kneading (Mishnah 3:6; see there for another opinion). Thus, dough kneaded in Eretz Yisrael is subject to *challah* on the Biblical level, whether the grain grew in Eretz Yisrael or outside of Eretz Yisrael.

[Rabbinically, however, even bread made entirely outside of Eretz Yisrael is subject to the *challah* obligation; see Mishnah 4:8 (see *Meleches Shlomo*).]

2. The Tannaim of the Mishnah lived in Eretz Yisrael. They therefore referred to Eretz Yisrael as "here," and to areas outside of Eretz Yisrael as "there" (see *Tos. Anshei Shem*).

3. The verse states with regard to *challah* (Bamidbar 15:19): *And it shall be when you eat of the bread of the Land, you shall set aside a portion for Hashem.* This implies that as long as it is "bread of the Land" (that is, it is made from grain grown in Eretz Yisrael) it is subject to *challah*, regardless of where the bread is [finished and] eaten. Thus, even if it was kneaded outside of Eretz Yisrael, it is nevertheless subject to the *challah* obligation (see *Rav*).

[31] **MISHNAH CHALLAH** / Chapter 2: *Peiros*

- רע״ב -

[ב] **עָפָר** חוּצָה לָאָרֶץ שֶׁבָּא בַסְּפִינָה לָאָרֶץ, חַיָּב בַּמַּעַשְׂרוֹת וּבַשְּׁבִיעִית.

(ב) עפר חוצה לארץ הבא בספינה לארץ. בספינה נקובה איירי, ורגבי האדמה סותמין את הנקב שאין המים נכנסים בה: חייבת במעשרות. אם זרע ולמחו הזרעים בעפר שבתוך הספינה. ואף על פי שמעפר חולה לארץ הוא, הואיל והיא נקובה, הזרע יונק מלחות עפרה של ארץ ישראל:

exempts. R' Akiva holds that the place where the grain grows is not a factor in creating a *challah* obligation. Rather, it depends on where it became dough. Since it was made into dough outside of Eretz Yisrael, there is no Biblical obligation to separate *challah*.[4]

[2] The previous Mishnah taught that grain grown outside of Eretz Yisrael becomes obligated in *challah* once it is brought into Eretz Yisrael and made into dough there. This Mishnah discusses another case of something that was brought into Eretz Yisrael:

עָפָר חוּצָה לָאָרֶץ שֶׁבָּא בַסְּפִינָה לָאָרֶץ — **If soil from outside of Eretz Yisrael came on a boat into** a river or lake in **Eretz Yisrael,**[1] חַיָּב בַּמַּעַשְׂרוֹת וּבַשְּׁבִיעִית — the produce that grows in that soil in the boat **is subject to the obligations of** *maasros* **and** *Shemittah*.[2] This is because the produce receives nourishment from the ground under the water. Therefore, it is considered produce grown in Eretz Yisrael, which is subject to the laws of *maaser* and *Shemittah*.[3]

---- NOTES ----

4. According to R' Akiva, the verse teaches that any dough that has reached the stage of *challah* obligation outside of Eretz Yisrael is not subject to the requirement of *challah* (see *Rav*). Thus, dough that was kneaded outside of Eretz Yisrael is exempt even if it later came into Eretz Yisrael, since the time of kneading is when the *challah* obligation comes into effect. If, however, the dough was kneaded in Eretz Yisrael, it remains subject to the *challah* obligation even if it left Eretz Yisrael afterward (*Mishneh LaMelech,* cited by *Tos. R' Akiva Eiger* and *Mishnah Rishonah*).

[As noted earlier, the discussion of the Mishnah is only with regard to the Biblical obligation of *challah.* On the Rabbinic level, however, even bread of grain that grew outside of Eretz Yisrael, that was made in its entirety outside of Eretz Yisrael, is subject to the law of *challah* (see *Meleches Shlomo;* see also *Rambam, Hilchos Bikkurim* 5:7).]

[2]

1. A boat containing a load of soil from outside Eretz Yisrael was traveling in a river or lake inside Eretz Yisrael (*Meiri*).

2. *Maasros* are the tithes that a person must separate from his produce — see Mishnah 1:3 note 1. Produce that grows during the year of *Shemittah* (which is observed every seven years) is subject to certain restrictions. For example, *Shemittah* produce is considered ownerless, and must be left in the fields for anyone to take (see *Rambam, Hilchos Sheviis* 4:24). Generally, both *maaser* and *Shemittah* apply only to produce grown in Eretz Yisrael. The Mishnah teaches that in our case the produce is considered to have grown in Eretz Yisrael, and is therefore subject to these laws.

3. Although the actual soil in which the produce grows is not from Eretz Yisrael, it is considered produce of Eretz Yisrael since it gets nourishment from the ground of Eretz Yisrael.

This applies only if the boat has a hole in it. [The hole is filled with clods of earth to prevent the water from coming in.] In such a case, the nutrients of the riverbed pass through the hole and reach the produce. However, if there is no hole, the produce is exempt from *maaser* and *Shemittah,* because the hull of the boat prevents the nutrients from reaching the produce (see *Rav*).

אָמַר רַבִּי יְהוּדָה: אֵימָתַי? בִּזְמַן שֶׁהַסְּפִינָה גּוֹשֶׁשֶׁת.

עִסָּה שֶׁנִּלּוֹשָׁה בְּמֵי פֵרוֹת, חַיֶּבֶת בַּחַלָּה,

- רע"ב -

אימתי בזמן שהספינה גוששת. נוגעת בגוּשֵׁי העפר, כלומר שהיא דבוּקה בארץ: עיסה שנילושה במי פירות חייבת בחלה. בירושלמי (הלכה א') מוכיח הלכה קלת, שאין הלכה כסתם משנה זו, ועיסה שנילושה במי פירות פטוּרה מחלה. הלכך אין ללוש עיסה שיש בה שיעוּר חלה, במי ביצים או במי פירות לבדם, בלא תערוֹבת מים, הואיל ולא אתברי הלכה מי חייבת בחלה או פטוּרה:

The next Tanna limits this ruling to a certain case:

אֵימָתַי — **When** does this ruling apply? אָמַר רַבִּי יְהוּדָה — **R' Yehudah says:** בִּזְמַן שֶׁהַסְּפִינָה גּוֹשֶׁשֶׁת — Only **when the** bottom of the **boat is touching the ground** beneath the water.[4] In such a case, the produce in the boat draws nourishment from the ground. However, if the bottom of the boat is not touching the ground, the produce does not draw nourishment from the ground. In such a case, it is not considered to be growing in Eretz Yisrael. Therefore, it is exempt from the laws of *maaser* and *Shemittah*.[5]

The Mishnah returns to the laws of *challah*. It discusses the law of dough made with fruit juice:

עִסָּה שֶׁנִּלּוֹשָׁה בְּמֵי פֵרוֹת — **Dough that was kneaded with fruit juice** (for example, apple juice)[6] חַיֶּבֶת בַּחַלָּה — **is subject to the *challah* obligation,** because fruit juice can bond the separate pieces of flour together to form dough.[7]

NOTES
---

4. I.e., the boat is in very shallow water and thus its bottom scrapes against the riverbed (*Rash Sirilio*).

5. See *Rashi, Gittin* 8a ד"ה כולי עלמא.

The Tanna Kamma, however, disagrees, and holds that the produce draws nourishment even though the boat is not touching the ground. Therefore, the produce *is* subject to the laws of *maaser* and *Shemittah* (*Tos. Yom Tov,* from *Rash*).

6. "Fruit juice" refers to any juice except the seven liquids listed in *Machshirin* 6:4 (*Meleches Shlomo; Mishnah Rishonah*). [These seven liquids are: dew, water, wine, olive oil, blood, milk, and bees' honey.]

7. The Mishnah in *Tevul Yom* (3:4) cites a dispute concerning the status of dough made with fruit juice. R' Akiva holds that such dough is not considered one entity but a collection of many particles of flour. His reason is that fruit juice lacks significance and therefore the separate pieces of flour are not considered to be combined into one entity (see *Rav* there ד"ה לא). R' Elazar ben Yehudah, however, holds that fruit juice *can* combine the flour into dough. While the Mishnah there deals with the laws of *tumah,* this dispute affects the laws of *challah* as well, since only dough is subject to *challah*. Therefore, according to R' Akiva, dough made with fruit juice is exempt from *challah* because it is not considered "dough," but separate pieces of flour. On the other hand, according to R' Elazar, it *is* considered dough and is therefore obligated in *challah*. Our Mishnah sides with the opinion of R' Elazar that such dough is obligated in *challah* (see *Tos. R' Akiva Eiger* in explanation of *Rav;* see also *Meleches Shlomo*).

[*Shulchan Aruch* (*Yoreh Deah* 329:10), however, writes that, nowadays, one should avoid kneading a dough purely of fruit juice. Since, in our times, *challah* is not eaten by Kohanim, we are faced with the question of how to dispose of the *challah*. Now, when the *challah* is *tamei* (as is normally the case in our times), the law is that it is burned. However, food can become *tamei* only if at some point it was made wet with one of the seven liquids listed in note 6. *Challah* made of pure

[33] **MISHNAH CHALLAH** / Chapter 2: *Peiros*

– רע״ב –

ונאכלת בידים מסואבות. שאין אוכל מוכשר לקבל טומאה, עד שיבואו עליו מים, או אחד משבעה משקין, [ומה] שלא הוכשר לקבל טומאה,

וְנֶאֱכֶלֶת בְּיָדַיִם מְסוֹאָבוֹת.

[ג] הָאִשָּׁה יוֹשֶׁבֶת וְקוֹצָה חַלָּתָהּ עֲרֻמָּה, מִפְּנֵי שֶׁהִיא יְכוֹלָה לְכַסּוֹת עַצְמָהּ; אֲבָל לֹא הָאִישׁ.

אין הידים מסואבות פוסלות אותה. מפרשת חלה ומברכת על הפרשתה, והוא שפניה של מטה טוחות בקרקע וכל ערותה מכוסה, והטנגבות אין בהן משום ערוה לענין ברכה. אבל האיש אינו יכול לברך ערום, שאי אפשר לו לכסות ערותו, שבולטים הביצים והגיד:

וְנֶאֱכֶלֶת בְּיָדַיִם מְסוֹאָבוֹת — **And** [*challah*] **that is taken from this dough may be eaten with unclean hands,** i.e., unwashed hands,[8] because dough made with fruit juice cannot become *tamei*.[9]

[3] Before separating *challah,* we are required to recite a blessing.[1] One whose *ervah* (private parts) is uncovered may not recite a blessing.[2] The Mishnah discusses whether an unclothed person may separate *challah*:

הָאִשָּׁה יוֹשֶׁבֶת וְקוֹצָה חַלָּתָהּ עֲרֻמָּה — **A woman may sit** on the ground **and separate her** *challah* **while unclothed,** מִפְּנֵי שֶׁהִיא יְכוֹלָה לְכַסּוֹת עַצְמָהּ — **because she is able to cover herself.** That is, she can sit in a way that her *ervah* is covered.[3] Therefore, she can recite the blessing, and separate *challah*.[4] אֲבָל לֹא הָאִישׁ — **But** this is **not** the case with **a man.** That is, a man may not separate *challah* while unclothed even if he is sitting on the ground. This is because a man's private area is exposed even when he sits in this way,[5] which

— NOTES —

fruit juice, however, does not become *tamei,* and may not be burned. Therefore, in order to avoid this issue, some water (or another one of the seven liquids) should be added to the dough.]

8. We have learned in Mishnah 1:9 that before touching (or eating) *challah* one must wash his hands. This is because the Rabbis decreed that unwashed hands are considered *tamei.* Therefore, if someone touches *challah* without washing his hands, the *challah* becomes *tamei,* and may not be eaten (see note 6 there). The Mishnah teaches that in our case there is no requirement to wash one's hands before eating the *challah* (*Rash Sirilio*). See next note.

9. Food can become *tamei* only if at some point it was made wet with one of the seven liquids listed in *Machshirin* 6:4 (see above, note 6). Thus, if someone who did not wash his hands eats the *challah* of this dough it does *not* become *tamei,* since it was kneaded with fruit juice (*Rav*). Since there is no concern of

the *challah* becoming *tamei,* the Kohen does not need to wash his hands before eating it.

[3]

1. The customary wording of the blessing is: *Blessed are You ... Who has sanctified us with His mitzvos, and has commanded us to separate challah* (*Derech Emunah, Hilchos Bikkurim* 5:100).

2. See *Rav* to *Terumos* 1:6 ד״ה האלם; see also *Rash Sirilio* (ד״ה אבל).

3. The Mishnah refers to a case where the woman presses her *ervah* into the ground, so that it is completely covered (*Rav;* see *Meleches Shlomo*).

4. A person who is unclothed may not separate *challah,* since he will not be able to make the required blessing. The Mishnah teaches that an unclothed woman may separate *challah,* as long as she sits in the manner described in the previous note, because her *ervah* is not exposed.

5. Because a man's private parts protrude from his body (see *Rav*).

[34] **משניות חלה / פרק ב: פרות**

מִי שֶׁאֵינוֹ יָכוֹל לַעֲשׂוֹת עִסָּתוֹ בְּטָהֳרָה, יַעֲשֶׂנָּה קַבִּין, וְאַל יַעֲשֶׂנָּה בְּטֻמְאָה. וְרַבִּי עֲקִיבָא אוֹמֵר: יַעֲשֶׂנָּה בְּטֻמְאָה, וְאַל יַעֲשֶׂנָּה קַבִּים; שֶׁכְּשֵׁם שֶׁהוּא קוֹרֵא לַטְּהוֹרָה, כָּךְ הוּא קוֹרֵא לַטְּמֵאָה, לָזוֹ קוֹרֵא

— רע"ב —

מי שאינו יכול לעשות עסתו בטהרה. כגון שהוא טמא, ואין שם מרחץ סמוך שיטבול בהן: יעשנה קבין. יעשה כל עיסתו קב קב, כדי שלא תתחייב בחלה ויטרך להפריש בטומאה. דהכי עדיף טפי ממה שיפטור עסתו מן החלה, ולא יהיה בה חלק לשם. ואין הלכה כרבי עקיבא:

יעשנה בטומאה:

prohibits him from reciting the blessing on the mitzvah of separating *challah*. Therefore, he may not separate *challah* in such a case.

When kneading dough that will have a *challah* obligation, one must take care that it should not become *tamei*. The reason for this is that if the dough becomes *tamei*, *challah* taken from it will also be *tamei*, and it is forbidden to cause *challah* to become *tamei*.[6] The Mishnah discusses a case where the person kneading the dough is *tamei* and has no way to purify himself:

מִי שֶׁאֵינוֹ יָכוֹל לַעֲשׂוֹת עִסָּתוֹ בְּטָהֳרָה — **Someone who cannot make his dough in a state of *taharah*,** because he is *tamei* and there is no *mikveh* available in which he can immerse,[7] יַעֲשֶׂנָּה קַבִּין — **should make [the dough] in *kav* portions.** Each portion is thus smaller than the minimum amount subject to the *challah* obligation.[8] וְאַל יַעֲשֶׂנָּה בְּטֻמְאָה — **He may not make [the dough] in a state of *tumah*.** That is, he may not knead a dough that is large enough to be subject to the *challah* obligation, and separate *challah* from it. This is prohibited because that dough will be *tamei*, and as a result, he will be obligated to separate *challah* even though he will make it *tamei*. Since it is forbidden to cause *challah* to become *tamei*, he must avoid the *challah* obligation entirely by making the dough in smaller portions.[9]

The next Tanna disagrees:

וְרַבִּי עֲקִיבָא אוֹמֵר — **But R' Akiva says:** יַעֲשֶׂנָּה בְּטֻמְאָה וְאַל יַעֲשֶׂנָּה קַבִּים — **He should make it in a state of *tumah*** (i.e., he should make it as a large dough, and separate *challah* that will be *tamei*), **but he may not make it in *kav* portions** to exempt the dough from the *challah* obligation; שֶׁכְּשֵׁם שֶׁהוּא קוֹרֵא לַטְּהוֹרָה כָּךְ הוּא קוֹרֵא לַטְּמֵאָה — **for just as one designates *challah* for a *tahor* dough, so too one designates *challah* for a *tamei* dough.** לָזוֹ קוֹרֵא

─────────── NOTES ───────────

6. This is prohibited because *challah* that is *tamei* may not be eaten, and must be burned (see *Mishnah Rishonah*).

7. If the *tamei* person touches the dough it becomes *tamei*. He is therefore obligated to immerse in a *mikveh* before kneading the dough, so that the dough and its *challah* should remain *tahor*. In our case, however, there is no *mikveh* available. Thus, the dough he kneads will be *tamei* (see *Rav*).

8. A dough containing only a *kav* of flour is not subject to the laws of *challah*, since it contains less than the minimum 1¼ *kav* of flour that is subject to the *challah* obligation (Mishnah 1:4).

9. Normally, however, one may not divide dough into smaller parts in order to exempt himself from taking *challah* (see *Yerushami* 25a-b). Nevertheless, in this case it is permitted to do so in order to avoid the prohibition of causing *challah* to become *tamei*.

[35] **MISHNAH CHALLAH** / Chapter 2: *Peiros*

חַלָּה בַּשֵּׁם וְלָזוֹ קוֹרֵא חַלָּה בַּשֵּׁם, אֲבָל קַבִּים אֵין לָהֶם חֵלֶק בַּשֵּׁם.

[ד] **הָעוֹשֶׂה** עִסָּתוֹ קַבִּים וְנָגְעוּ זֶה בָזֶה, פְּטוּרִים מִן הַחַלָּה עַד שֶׁיִּשּׁוֹכוּ.

– רע"ב –
(ד) קבים. קב קב בפני עצמו: ונגעו זה בזה. אין הנגיעה מצרפתן להתחייב בחלה: עד שישוכו. שיתדבקו זה בזה כל כך, שאם בא להפרידם נתלש מזה לזו:

חַלָּה בַּשֵּׁם וְלָזוֹ קוֹרֵא חַלָּה בַּשֵּׁם — **That is, regarding this one** (*tahor* dough) **he assigns the name** *"challah"* **to the portion separated, and regarding that one** (*tamei* dough) **he assigns the name** *"challah"* **to the portion separated.**[10] We thus see that just as *challah* separated from *tahor* dough has sanctity, so too *challah* separated from *tamei* dough has sanctity.[11] אֲבָל קַבִּים אֵין לָהֶם חֵלֶק בַּשֵּׁם — *Kav* **portions,** on the other hand, **do not have a portion** that is assigned **the name** *"challah."* That is, no *challah* is separated from them. And it is more important to have a portion of one's dough sanctified for Hashem than to prevent *challah* from becoming *tamei*. Therefore, he should make one large dough even though the *challah* will be *tamei*, because by doing so there will be a portion that is sanctified.

[4] The Mishnah discusses the law in a case where two doughs, each one smaller than the minimum amount subject to *challah*, are touching each other:

הָעוֹשֶׂה עִסָּתוֹ קַבִּים — **If someone makes his dough in** *kav* **portions** (i.e., he makes two separate doughs, and each one measures only a *kav*, which is less than the 1¼-*kav* minimum that is subject to the *challah* obligation), וְנָגְעוּ זֶה בָזֶה — **and [the two doughs] touched each other,** and together they have the minimum amount that is subject to the *challah* obligation,[1] פְּטוּרִים מִן הַחַלָּה — the law is that **they are exempt from** the obligation of *challah*, עַד שֶׁיִּשּׁוֹכוּ — **until** they **"bite" each other.** That is, they are exempt from the obligation of *challah*, unless they are pressed so firmly together that if one would separate the two doughs, a piece of one dough would be pulled along with the other dough. Doughs that are merely touching each other, however, do not combine to form one dough. Since each dough by itself is exempt from *challah*, the doughs remain exempt from *challah*.

The next Tanna adds another way that the two doughs can combine to create a *challah* obligation:

───────── NOTES ─────────

10. That is, the method for separating *challah* is the same whether the *challah* is *tahor* or *tamei*. In either case, the owner separates a piece of dough and declares, "This is hereby *challah*" (see *Meleches Shlomo*).

11. The Torah refers to *challah* as *a portion for Hashem* (*Bamidbar* 5:19), which shows that *challah* has sanctity. Since *challah* that is *tamei* is also separated by calling it *"challah,"* it too has this sanctity (see *Rav*).

[4]

1. The minimum amount that is obligated in *challah* is 1¼ *kavs*. Since each dough is only a *kav*, each one by itself is exempt. However, the two doughs combined equal two *kavs*, which is more than the 1¼-*kav* minimum.

משניות חלה / פרק ב: פרות [36]

רַבִּי אֱלִיעֶזֶר אוֹמֵר: אַף הָרוֹדֶה וְנוֹתֵן לַסַּל, הַסַּל מְצָרְפָן לַחַלָּה.

[ה] הַמַּפְרִישׁ חַלָּתוֹ קֶמַח, אֵינָהּ חַלָּה, וְגָזֵל בְּיַד כֹּהֵן.

— רע"ב —

אַף הָרוֹדֶה וְנוֹתֵן לַסַּל. הרודה חלות מן התנור לאחר שנאפו, ונותנם בסל: הַסַּל מְצָרְפָן לַחַלָּה. ואף על פי שאין נושכות. והלכה כרבי אליעזר. והא דמצרכי רבנן נשיכה ורבי

אליעזר נגיעה, הני מילי לגרף שני טיסנים יחד שאין בכל אחת כשיעור, אבל לענין לתרום [מן] המוקף, אף נגיעה לא בעי, רק שיהיו סמוכים זה לזה. ובשילהי פרקין (משנה ח) דאמר רבי אליעזר נותן פחות מכביצה באמצע כדי לתרום מן המוקף, אלמא בעינן נגיעה לענין מוקף, טהורה וטמאה שאני, מפני שהוא דבר שמקפיד על תערובתו, אין הכלי מצרף: **(ה) אֵינָהּ חַלָּה.** דבראשית עריסותיכם כתיב (במדבר טו,כ): **וְגָזֵל בְּיַד כֹּהֵן.** וצריך להחזירה לבעלים, שאם תאחר בידו, יהיה סבור שעיסתו פטורה:

אַף הָרוֹדֶה וְנוֹתֵן לַסַּל — **Also, if one bakes the two kav-sized doughs and removes them from the oven, and then places the finished breads in a basket,**[2] הַסַּל מְצָרְפָן לַחַלָּה — **the basket combines them to be subject to the requirement of** *challah*.[3] Since both breads together contain the amount necessary to be obligated in *challah*, they are subject to *challah*.[4]

[5] The requirement to separate *challah* does not take effect until the dough is kneaded. The Mishnah discusses the law where someone separated *challah* from flour before it was kneaded:

הַמַּפְרִישׁ חַלָּתוֹ קֶמַח אֵינָהּ חַלָּה — **If someone separates his** *challah* **from flour,** the law is that **it is not** *challah*, because *challah* must be taken from dough, not flour.[1] וְגָזֵל בְּיַד כֹּהֵן — If he gives this "*challah*" to a Kohen, **it is considered stolen goods in the hands of the Kohen,** and the Kohen must return it.[2]

NOTES
---

2. Or, if one places the two doughs into one basket before they are baked (see *Mishnah Rishonah*).

3. Even though they are not "biting" each other, the fact that they are in one basket combines them. R' Eliezer learns this law from a verse (see *Tos. Yom Tov*). [However, even according to R' Eliezer, the breads must at least be touching each other. If not, the basket does not combine them (see *Rav*).]

The Tanna Kamma, however, disagrees, and holds that only doughs that "bite" each other can combine. However, being in the same basket does not combine them, even if they are touching each other (see *Rav*).

4. See *Rambam, Hilchos Bikkurim* 6:16. [Although *challah* should normally be separated before the dough is baked, it can also be separated once the dough is made into bread (see *Shulchan Aruch,*

Orach Chaim 457:1 with *Magen Avraham* 2).]

[5]

1. The Torah calls *challah* "the first of your *doughs*" (*Bamidbar* 15:20). This teaches that only *challah* taken from dough is considered *challah*, not *challah* taken from flour.

2. In actuality, on the Biblical level, the Kohen is not required to return the flour. Although this *challah* is invalid, and the owner must separate *challah* again (as the Mishnah will soon teach), the Kohen can claim that the owner gave it to him as a gift (*Kiddushin* 46b, as explained by *Pnei Yehoshua* there ד"ה ותהוי). However, the Rabbis were concerned that the owner might think that he fulfilled his *challah* obligation with the flour. Therefore, to make it clear that the *challah* was invalid, they required the Kohen to return it to the owner (*Rav*). [However, as we will see

[37] **MISHNAH CHALLAH** / Chapter 2: *Peiros*   2/5

– רע״ב –

הָעִסָּה עַצְמָהּ חַיֶּבֶת בַּחַלָּה; וְהַקֶּמַח, אִם יֵשׁ בּוֹ כַּשִּׁעוּר, חַיֶּבֶת בַּחַלָּה, וַאֲסוּרָה לַזָּרִים. דִּבְרֵי רַבִּי יְהוֹשֻׁעַ. אָמְרוּ לוֹ: מַעֲשֶׂה וּקְפָשָׂהּ זָקֵן זָר.

הָעִסָּה עַצְמָהּ. שֶׁהִפְרִישׁ חַלָּתָהּ קֶמַח, חַיֶּבֶת בְּחַלָּה: **וְהַקֶּמַח.** שֶׁבָּא לְיַד כֹּהֵן בְּתוֹרַת חַלָּה: **אִם יֵשׁ בּוֹ בַשִּׁעוּר.** חֲמֵשֶׁת רְבִיעִית קֶמַח, חַיֶּבֶת בְּחַלָּה. וַאֲסוּרָה לַזָּרִים, כָּל הַקֶּמַח שֶׁבָּא לְיַד כֹּהֵן. וְחוּמְרָא בְעָלְמָא הוּא, לְפִי שֶׁרָאוּהוּ שֶׁבָּא לְיַד כֹּהֵן, שֶׁלֹּא יֹאמְרוּ רוֹאֵינוּ זָר אוֹכֵל חַלּוֹת: **וּקְפָשָׂהּ זָקֵן זָר.** חֲטָפָהּ זָקֵן זָר, וַאֲכָלָהּ.

The Mishnah addresses the law of the rest of the flour:

הָעִסָּה עַצְמָהּ חַיֶּבֶת בַּחַלָּה — **The dough itself** that the owner kneads from the rest of the flour **is** still **subject to the obligation of** *challah*, since the *challah* separated from the flour was invalid. Thus, the owner must separate another *challah* portion from the dough.

The Mishnah now returns to the laws of the flour that the owner gave as *challah*:

וְהַקֶּמַח — **And** regarding the *"challah"* **flour** that was given to the Kohen, אִם יֵשׁ בּוֹ כַּשִּׁעוּר — **if it has the** minimum **amount** that is subject to *challah* (1¼ *kavs*),[3] חַיֶּבֶת בַּחַלָּה — **it is subject to** *challah.* Although there is normally no obligation to separate *challah* from the portion of *challah* given to a Kohen, here the flour is not actual *challah*. Therefore, the dough kneaded from this flour is subject to the *challah* obligation like other flour.[4] וַאֲסוּרָה לַזָּרִים — **And all** the flour that was originally given to the Kohen as *challah* **is forbidden to non-Kohanim**.[5] Although the flour is not *challah*, the Rabbis forbade it to non-Kohanim as if it were *challah*.[6] דִּבְרֵי רַבִּי יְהוֹשֻׁעַ — **These** are the **words of R' Yehoshua**.

The Sages disagree with this last ruling:

אָמְרוּ לוֹ — **The Sages said to him:** מַעֲשֶׂה וּקְפָשָׂהּ זָקֵן זָר — **There was an incident** in which *challah* was separated from flour, **and an elder** (i.e., a Torah

--- NOTES ---

later in the Mishnah, the owner may not eat the flour; rather, he sells it to a Kohen (*Tiferes Yisrael*).]

3. That is, the owner had originally given the Kohen 1¼ *kavs* of flour as *challah* (see *Rav*). The Kohen then returned this flour to the owner as he is required to do (see *Derech Emunah, Hilchos Bikkurim* 8:6), and the owner made it into dough.

4. However, if the flour is less than 1¼ *kavs* it is exempt from *challah*. This is because the flour was separated from the rest of the flour when the owner gave it to the Kohen. Therefore, it must have the minimum *challah* amount by itself in order to be obligated in *challah*.

5. The Mishnah previously ruled that the flour must be returned to the owner. Nevertheless, he may *not* eat it, since it may be eaten only by a Kohen. The purpose of returning it is so that the owner may now sell the flour to a Kohen (see *Tiferes Yisrael* 22).

6. The Rabbis were concerned that since the flour was given to a Kohen as *challah*, people will mistakenly think that it really is *challah*. [Although the Rabbis required the Kohen to return it to the owner in order to show that it is not *challah* (see above, note 2), there might still be some people who think that it is *challah* since they saw it being given to a Kohen (see *Tos. Anshei Shem*).] If the flour would be permitted to non-Kohanim, these people will think that non-Kohanim may eat *challah*. Therefore, in order to prevent this mistake, the Rabbis forbade non-Kohanim from eating it (*Rav*).

משניות חלה / פרק ב: פרות [38]

אָמַר לָהֶם: אַף הוּא קִלְקֵל לְעַצְמוֹ וְתִקֵּן לַאֲחֵרִים.

[ו] **חֲמֵשֶׁת** רְבָעִים קֶמַח חַיָּבִים בַּחַלָּה.

– רע"ב –

קלקל לעצמו. דאכלה ואיענש: ותיקן לאחרים. שאחרים אוכלין ותולין בו, ומוגלאים פתח להתיר לפי שראוהו שאכל: (ו) חמשת רביעים. של

קב חייבין בחלה, דכתיב (במדבר טו,כ) ראשית עריסותיכם, ועשה מדבר היתה טומר לגלגולת, והטומר עשירית האיפה הוא (שמות טז,לו), האיפה שלש סאין, והסאה שש קבין, הרי שמונה עשר קבין באיפה, והקב ארבעת לוגין. עשירית שבטים, שבטה לוגין. עשירית ועשירית שני לוגין הוא ביצה וחומש ביצה, שהלוג הוא שש ביצים. כשבאו לירושלים והוסיפו שתות על המדות, נמלא שש לוגין [הם] חמשה, ולוג (השביעי) [הוא] חמשה בילים, שכל שש נעשים חמשה, ובילה וחומש בילה נעשית בילה. נמלא הטומר שהיה במדבר שבעה לוגין ובילה וחומש בילה, נעשים בירושלם שש לוגין. כשבאו לציפורי והוסיפו שתות על המדות של ירושלם, נעשו השש לוגין חמשה. והיינו חמשת רביעים קמח. ונקראו הלוגין רביעים, לפי שהלוג הוא רובע הקב, שהקב ארבעה לוגין:

---

scholar)[7] **who was a non-Kohen grabbed it** and ate it.[8] This proves that non-Kohanim *may* eat such *challah*.

R' Yehoshua responds:

אָמַר לָהֶם — **He said to them:** אַף הוּא קִלְקֵל לְעַצְמוֹ — [**The Torah scholar] in fact ruined matters for himself;** that is, the Torah scholar actually committed a sin by eating the *challah* and was punished for it.[9] וְתִקֵּן לַאֲחֵרִים — **Nevertheless, he did fix matters for others** who eat such *challah*, because they base their actions on the Torah scholar to do this act. Thus, their sin is unintentional.[10] At any rate, the Torah scholar acted incorrectly, and thus no proof can be brought from his actions.[11]

[6] The Mishnah elaborates on the minimum amount of flour that has a *challah* obligation:

חֲמֵשֶׁת רְבָעִים קֶמַח חַיָּבִים בַּחַלָּה — **Five *reva'im*** (1¼ *kavs*) **of flour are subject to the *challah* obligation.**[1]

NOTES

7. See *Tos. Yom Tov*.

8. The owner of the flour had separated the flour as *challah* and given it to a Kohen. Since the Mishnah ruled previously that the Kohen must return such *challah*, the Torah scholar had the right to grab it. [This is evidently speaking of a case where the Torah scholar himself was the original owner, or he grabbed it with the owner's permission.]

9. R' Yehoshua responded that while the scholar was a learned person and could be relied on for halachic matters, in this particular case he made a mistake, and thought that it is permitted to eat the flour separated as *challah*. However, in truth it is forbidden (*Tos. Yom Tov* ד"ה ותקן).

10. *Tos. Yom Tov, Tiferes Yisrael*; see also *Or Same'ach, Hil. Geirushin* 1:17.

11. [R' Yehoshua's main point is that the scholar himself sinned. However, once he mentions how the act affected the scholar himself, he explains how it affected others.]

[6]

1. [A *rova* (pl. *reva'im*) is a quarter of a *kav*. Thus, five *reva'im* are 1¼ *kavs*.]

The Torah (*Bamidbar* 15:20) refers to *challah* as *the first of your doughs*. This teaches that only an amount that is considered *your* dough is subject to the obligation of *challah*. Since this mitzvah was told to the Jews while they were in the Wilderness, the phrase *your dough* refers to their daily meal at that time,

[39] **MISHNAH CHALLAH** / Chapter 2: *Peiros*

הֵם וּשְׂאוֹרָן וְסֻבָּן וּמֻרְסָנָן חֲמֵשֶׁת רְבָעִים, חַיָּבִין. נִטַּל מֻרְסָנָן מִתּוֹכָן וְחָזַר לְתוֹכָן, הֲרֵי אֵלּוּ פְּטוּרִין.

– רע״ב –

הן ושאורן. השאור שנותנין לתוכן: וסובן. הוא הדק: מורסנן. הוא הגס. כולן מצטרפין עם הקמח להשלים השיעור, שכן עני אוכל פתו בעיסה מעורבת, עם סובין ומורסן: ניטל מורסן מתוכן וחזר לתוכן הרי אלו פטורים. שאין דרך עיסה להחזיר מורסן לתוכה לאחר שנטל ממנה.

The Mishnah discusses what components of the dough count toward this amount:

הֵם וּשְׂאוֹרָן וְסֻבָּן וּמֻרְסָנָן חֲמֵשֶׁת רְבָעִים — If the flour, its sourdough, fine bran, and coarse bran equal five *reva'im*, חַיָּבִין — it is subject to the *challah* obligation. Sourdough counts toward the *challah* minimum because it is a normal ingredient added to dough.[2] Fine and coarse bran count because they are found in bread eaten by poor people. Therefore, they too are considered part of the dough.[3] נִטַּל מֻרְסָנָן מִתּוֹכָן וְחָזַר לְתוֹכָן — However, if the coarse bran was removed from [these five *reva'im*] of flour and then put back in, הֲרֵי אֵלּוּ פְּטוּרִין — they are exempt from the *challah* obligation, because even poor people do not add bran to their dough when making bread. Thus, such bran is not a normal ingredient of the dough, and cannot count toward the *challah* minimum.[4]

[7] The previous Mishnah discussed the minimum amount of dough that is subject to the *challah* obligation. This Mishnah discusses how much of the dough is separated as *challah*:

— NOTES —

which was a portion of manna (מָן). Accordingly, the amount that is obligated in *challah* is the same amount as the daily portion of manna. Now, the Torah states elsewhere (*Shemos* 16:16,36) that the amount of daily manna was one-tenth of an *eiphah*. An *eiphah* equals 18 *kavs*. A tenth of that, 1 ⅘ *kavs*, is the amount that is subject to the obligation of *challah*.

These measurements, however, are given in "Wilderness units." That is, the units of measurement used in the Wilderness. In the times of the Mishnah, though, the size of standard measures was increased. According to the new measurements (known as "Tzippori units"), 1 ⅘ *kavs* of Wilderness *kavs* were now 1 ¼ *kavs*. Therefore, the Mishnah states that the minimum amount for *challah* is 1 ¼ (Tzippori) *kavs* (see *Rav*; see also *Eduyos* 1:2 with notes 5, 6, and 7). The weight of this amount of flour in contemporary measures ranges from 3 ⅔ to 5 pounds [1 ⅔ to 2 ¼ kg.],

depending on the opinion followed (see *Middos V'Shiurei Torah* Ch. 17). [See also General Introduction.]

2. Sourdough on its own is exempt from *challah* because it is inedible (see note 1 to Mishnah 1:7). Nevertheless, when combined with other dough it can contribute to the *challah* minimum, because sourdough is added to dough to help it rise. Therefore, it is considered part of the dough (see *Chesed L'Avraham*).

3. The bran discussed here is not eaten on its own. Thus, like sourdough, it is exempt from *challah*. However, it can combine with the dough to create a *challah* obligation, because some people eat bread that contains bran. It is therefore considered a normal ingredient of dough (see *Rav*).

4. Since even poor people do not add bran to their dough, the bran cannot be considered part of the dough to create a *challah* obligation (see *Rav*).

משניות חלה / פרק ב: פרות [40]

[ז] שִׁעוּר הַחַלָּה, אֶחָד מֵעֶשְׂרִים וְאַרְבָּעָה. הָעוֹשֶׂה עִסָּה לְעַצְמוֹ, וְהָעוֹשָׂה לְמִשְׁתֵּה בְנוֹ, אֶחָד מֵעֶשְׂרִים וְאַרְבָּעָה. נַחְתּוֹם שֶׁהוּא עוֹשֶׂה לִמְכֹּר בַּשּׁוּק, וְכֵן הָאִשָּׁה שֶׁהִיא עוֹשָׂה לִמְכֹּר בַּשּׁוּק, אֶחָד מֵאַרְבָּעִים וּשְׁמוֹנָה.

— רע"ב —

(ז) אחד מעשרים וארבעה. לפי שבעל הבית עסתו מטועט, ובפחות מאחד מעשרים וארבעה אין בה כדי מתנה, והתורה אמרה (במדבר טו,כא) תתנו, שיהא בו כדי נתינה: והעושה למשתה בנו. אף על פי שעוסה עסה מרובה, לא פלוג בעסת בעל הבית: נחתום העושה למכור בשוק. עסתו מרובה, ובאחד מארבעים ושמונה יש בה כדי מתנה: וכן האשה העושה למכור. אף על פי שעסתה מטועט, לא פלוג בפת העשוי למכור:

שִׁעוּר הַחַלָּה אֶחָד מֵעֶשְׂרִים וְאַרְבָּעָה — **The** minimum **amount** that a private person must give **as** *challah* **is one twenty-fourth** of the dough. This is because the portion one gives as *challah* must be a significant amount,[1] and less than one twenty-fourth of a small dough is not significant. הָעוֹשֶׂה עִסָּה לְעַצְמוֹ וְהָעוֹשָׂה לְמִשְׁתֵּה בְנוֹ — Moreover, whether **one makes** a small amount of **dough for himself or** a large amount of dough **for his son's** wedding **feast,** אֶחָד מֵעֶשְׂרִים וְאַרְבָּעָה — he must separate **one twenty-fourth** as *challah.* Since a private person generally makes a small dough,[2] the Rabbis established the amount of one twenty-fourth for *all* privately made dough. Thus, even if a private person prepares a large amount of dough, he must still separate one twenty-fourth.[3]

The Mishnah discusses the amount that is given as *challah* by one who is selling bread:

נַחְתּוֹם שֶׁהוּא עוֹשֶׂה לִמְכֹּר בַּשּׁוּק — **A baker who makes** a dough **to sell in the market,** וְכֵן הָאִשָּׁה שֶׁהִיא עוֹשָׂה לִמְכֹּר בַּשּׁוּק — **and, likewise, a woman who makes** a dough **to sell in the market,** אֶחָד מֵאַרְבָּעִים וּשְׁמוֹנָה — separates **one forty-eighth** of the dough as *challah.* A baker usually makes a large amount of dough. Therefore, even one forty-eighth of such a dough is a significant gift. Even a woman who makes a smaller dough to sell may separate only one forty-eighth, because the Rabbis set this as the minimum for all dough made to be sold.[4]

The Mishnah discusses the amount given as *challah* if the dough became *tamei:*

NOTES

[7]

1. The Torah (*Bamidbar* 15:21) states that one must "give" *challah.* This implies that one should give an amount that is considered a respectable gift (*Rav*).

2. That is, a dough made from the minimum amount of flour subject to the *challah* obligation (1¼ *kav*) or somewhat more (see *Rambam* Commentary).

3. The Rabbis wanted to establish one uniform amount for all dough made by private people. They chose ¹⁄₂₄ since ¹⁄₂₄ of a dough made from 1¼ *kavs* of flour is considered a respectable gift (*Rav*).

4. Since dough made to be sold is *usually* made in larger amounts, the Rabbis fixed the amount of *challah* as one forty-eighth for *all* dough intended for sale (*Rav*).

[41] MISHNAH CHALLAH / Chapter 2: *Peiros*

- רע״ב -

נִטְמֵאת עִסָּתָהּ שׁוֹגֶגֶת אוֹ אֲנוּסָה, אֶחָד מֵאַרְבָּעִים וּשְׁמוֹנָה. נִטְמֵאת מְזִידָה, אֶחָד מֵעֶשְׂרִים וְאַרְבָּעָה, כְּדֵי שֶׁלֹּא יְהֵא חוֹטֵא נִשְׂכָּר.

נטמאת. הואיל ולשריפה עומדת אחד מארבעים ושמונה: (ח) נטלת מן הטהור על הטמא. ולא חייישין שמא יגעו זה בזה:

[ח] **רַבִּי אֱלִיעֶזֶר** אוֹמֵר: נִטֶּלֶת מִן הַטָּהוֹר עַל הַטָּמֵא.

נִטְמֵאת עִסָּתָהּ שׁוֹגֶגֶת אוֹ אֲנוּסָה — If a woman was making bread for her household, and **her dough became** *tamei* either **by accident** (for example, she mistakenly used a utensil that was *tamei* to make the dough) **or because of an unavoidable circumstance** (for example, she became a *niddah* while making the dough),[5] אֶחָד מֵאַרְבָּעִים וּשְׁמוֹנָה — she separates **one forty-eighth** of the dough, instead of the usual one twenty-fourth.[6] This is because *challah* that is *tamei* may not be eaten, but must be burned. Therefore, the Rabbis were lenient and allowed her to separate the smaller amount set for *challah*. נִטְמֵאת מְזִידָה — However, if [the dough] became *tamei* intentionally, rather than by mistake, אֶחָד מֵעֶשְׂרִים וְאַרְבָּעָה — she must separate **one twenty-fourth** as *challah*, כְּדֵי שֶׁלֹּא יְהֵא חוֹטֵא נִשְׂכָּר — **so that the sinner** (i.e., this woman) **should not gain** because of her sin.[7] Had she not sinned, the dough would have been *tahor*, and *tahor* dough made for private use is subject to the amount of one twenty-fourth. Thus, she would have been obligated to give one twenty-fourth as *challah*. Therefore, although the dough is now *tamei*, she must still separate one twenty-fourth, so that she should not benefit because of the sin.

[8] Dough being designated as *challah* must be close to the dough for which it is being designated.[1] For this reason, *tahor* dough may not be designated as *challah* for *tamei* dough. The Rabbis were concerned that someone who designates *tahor* dough as *challah* for *tamei* dough might not bring the dough being designated as *challah* close to the *tamei* dough. Therefore, they decreed that it is forbidden to designate *tahor* dough as *challah* for *tamei* dough (see Mishnah 1:9).

Our Mishnah records another view on this issue:

נִטֶּלֶת מִן הַטָּהוֹר עַל הַטָּמֵא — [*Challah*] רַבִּי אֱלִיעֶזֶר אוֹמֵר — R' Eliezer says: may be taken from *tahor* dough for *tamei* dough. We are not concerned that people will be afraid that the *challah* will become *tamei*, and not bring the dough being designated as *challah* close to the *tamei* dough.[2]

— NOTES —

5. See *Tos. Anshei Shem.*

6. The woman was making the dough for personal use, not to sell. As the Mishnah just taught, the amount of *challah* for privately made dough is normally one twenty-fourth.

7. It is forbidden to cause dough that has a *challah* obligation to become *tamei*,

as we have learned in Mishnah 3.

[8]

1. Normally, this means that they must be in the same area (such as in the same room). [Here, however, the requirement would be somewhat more stringent, as will be explained below (see note 3).]

2. R' Eliezer holds that people are

משניות חלה / פרק ב: פרות [42]

בֵּיצַד? עָשָׂה טְהוֹרָה וְעָשָׂה טְמֵאָה, נוֹטֵל כְּדֵי חַלָּה מֵעִסָּה שֶׁלֹּא הוּרְמָה חַלָּתָהּ, וְנוֹתֵן פָּחוֹת מִכַּבֵּיצָה בָּאֶמְצַע,

– רע"ב –
נוטל כדי חלה. שעור חלה שצריך ליטול מן הטהור והטמא, נוטל מאותה עיסה הטהורה שלא הורמה חלתה:

ונותן פחות מכביצה באמצע. בין הטמאה והטהורה, דפחות מכביצה אינו מטמא. ומניח החלה על מותו פחות מכביצה המחבר בין הטמאה והטהורה, שאין החלה מקבלת טומאה בכך:

Normally it suffices if the dough that is being designated as *challah* is near the dough for which it is designated, and they need not touch each other. However, when *tahor* dough is separated as *challah* for *tamei* dough, the two pieces must be touching each other.[3] R' Eliezer details how the two doughs can touch without the *challah* becoming *tamei*:

בֵּיצַד — **How**, in fact, **is** this *challah* separated without it becoming *tamei*?[4] עָשָׂה טְהוֹרָה וְעָשָׂה טְמֵאָה — **If** someone has **a *tahor* dough and a *tamei* dough**, and wants to designate a portion of the *tahor* dough as *challah* for both doughs, he does the following: נוֹטֵל כְּדֵי חַלָּה — **He takes** a portion of dough **that is** large **enough to be *challah*** for both doughs מֵעִסָּה שֶׁלֹּא הוּרְמָה חַלָּתָהּ — **from** the *tahor* **dough, if it has not** yet **had *challah* separated from it**.[5] וְנוֹתֵן פָּחוֹת מִכַּבֵּיצָה בָּאֶמְצַע — **He then places** a different piece of the *tahor* dough,[6] that is **less than an egg's volume**,[7] **between** the two doughs, touching both of them. This piece of dough acts as a "bridge," connecting the two doughs. Then he places the portion of dough that will be designated as *challah*

NOTES

generally not afraid that the dough being designated as *challah* will touch the *tamei* dough. Therefore, they *will* put the dough being designated as *challah* near the dough as required (see *Rav* below ד"ה וחכמים, as explained by *Tos. Anshei Shem*). [The exact procedure will be described below in the Mishnah.]

3. This is because of a general rule that it suffices for the dough that is being designated as *challah* to be close to the dough for which it is being separated only as long as the owner does not mind if the two doughs would touch. If, however, for some reason he is careful to keep the two doughs separate, the law is that they must be touching when *challah* is taken. Therefore here, where the owner is careful that the *tahor* dough should be kept apart from the *tamei* dough (so that the *tahor* dough should not become *tamei*), they must be (at least indirectly) touching each

other (see *Rav* to Mishnah 4 ד"ה הסל). The Mishnah will go on to explain how the dough being designated as *challah* can "touch" the *tamei* dough without the *challah* becoming *tamei*.

4. As we have learned in Mishnah 3, it is forbidden to cause *challah* to become *tamei*. If the *challah* dough directly touches the other dough it will become *tamei*. How is it possible to separate the *challah* properly and avoid the prohibition of making it *tamei*? (See *Rashi, Sotah* 30a ד"ה רבי אליעזר.)

5. [See *Derech Emunah, Hilchos Bikkurim* 7:96.] Dough that is exempt from *challah* cannot itself serve as *challah*. Therefore, if *challah* had already been separated from the *tahor* dough, it would not be possible to take a portion of it and use it as *challah* for the *tamei* dough (see *Tos. Anshei Shem*).

6. *Tiferes Yisrael*.

7. [The reason why it must be this size will be explained below (note 10).]

[43] MISHNAH CHALLAH / Chapter 2: Peiros

- רע"ב -

כְּדֵי שִׁיטּוּל מִן הַמֻּקָּף. וַחֲכָמִים אוֹסְרִין.

כדי שיטול מן המוקף.
שתהיה הטמאה מחוברת
לטהורה על ידי אותו פחות מכביצה, וכאילו הטמאה וטהורה טיסה אחת: וחכמים אוסרין. ליטול
מן הטהורה על הטמאה, דחיישינן שמא יגע זו בזו. אלא נוטל מן הטהור לעצמו, ומן הטמא לעצמו.
והלכה כחכמים:

---

on the bridge,[8] **כְּדֵי שִׁיטּוּל מִן הַמֻּקָּף** — so that he will be taking *challah* **from something that is close** to the doughs. Since the bridge joins the *tahor* and *tamei* doughs together, the *challah* is considered to be close to (and actually touching) the *tamei* dough.[9] Nevertheless, the *challah* does not become *tamei*, because it is touching the bridge, not the *tamei* dough.[10]

וַחֲכָמִים אוֹסְרִין — **But the Sages forbid** separating *tahor* dough as *challah* for *tamei* dough even with a bridge. The Sages hold that people might be afraid that the *tahor* dough will touch the *tamei* dough directly and become *tamei*, and they would therefore designate *challah* without setting up a bridge. Therefore, the Sages required that *challah* be separated from the *tamei* dough itself.[11]

— NOTES —

8. See diagram.

[Diagram: TAHOR DOUGH | CHALLAH-DESIGNATE / BRIDGE | TAMEI DOUGH]
© 2017, MPL. Reproduction prohibited.

9. Since all three doughs (the *tahor* dough, the bridge, and the *tamei* dough) are touching one another, they are all considered one dough regarding the laws of *challah*.

10. Although the bridge itself is touching the *tamei* dough, and becomes *tamei* from the *tamei* dough, it does not transmit *tumah* to the *challah*. This is because the bridge is less than the size of an egg, and *tamei* food that is less than the size of an egg does not transmit *tumah* (see *Rav* ד"ה ונותן). [However, a bridge the size of an egg or larger may not be used, because then the bridge, which can transmit *tumah*, would cause the *challah* to become *tamei*.]

11. R' Eliezer, however, holds that the concern that the *challah* will become *tamei* does not stop people from using such a bridge.

Chapter Three

משניות חלה / פרק ג: אוכלין

[א] **אוֹכְלִין** עֲרַאי מִן הָעִסָּה עַד שֶׁתִּתְגַּלְגֵּל בְּחִטִּים וְתִטַּמְטֵם בִּשְׂעוֹרִים.

– רע"ב –

פרק שלישי — אוכלין עראי. (א) אוכלין עראי עד שתתגלגל. שתתערב יפה, לפי שאין שם עסה עליה קודם גלגול: **ותטמטם בשעורים.** לפי שעסת השעורים מתפררת, ואינה מתערבת יפה כעסה של חטים, אלא מטמטם ביד:

---

[1] There are two stages in the dough-making process with regard to the *challah* obligation. The first stage is reached when the flour is mixed with water, as we will see in this Mishnah. Before that point, there is no requirement to separate *challah*, and the grain may be eaten without restrictions.[1] Once that stage is reached, separating *challah* is effective, even though there is still no *obligation* to separate *challah*. In addition, after it has reached the first stage, due to a Rabbinic law it may be eaten only in a casual manner. The dough may be eaten in that manner until the second stage, גְּמַר מְלָאכָה, *completion of processing*, has been reached (the exact point will be defined in the Mishnah). Once the second stage is reached, the obligation to separate *challah* takes effect, and the dough is considered *tevel*, which may not be eaten in any manner.[2] The Mishnah begins by defining when dough that has reached the first stage is considered to have reached the *completion of processing*, which is the second stage:

עַד שֶׁתִּתְגַּלְגֵּל אוֹכְלִין עֲרַאי מִן הָעִסָּה — **We may eat casually from a dough** בְּחִטִּים — **until it is completely kneaded, in the case of wheat** dough,[3] וְתִטַּמְטֵם בִּשְׂעוֹרִים — **or until it is packed** together, **in the case of barley** dough.[4]

NOTES
---

[1]

1. In fact, if *challah* is separated at that point, it is ineffective (Mishnah 2:5).

2. [This term, *tevel*, is the same term used for produce that was not tithed.] The two stages of the *challah* obligation parallel two stages that apply regarding the tithing of produce. There, the first stage, עוֹנַת הַמַּעַשְׂרוֹת, the stage of *maasros* (tithing), is reached when the produce has reached the stage that it begins to become edible (see *Maasros* 1:2-4). After that point, the produce may be eaten only in a casual manner until *maasros* are separated. The גְּמַר מְלָאכָה, *completion of processing*, is reached when the produce has been fully processed. At that point, the produce is *tevel*, which may not be eaten at all until *maasros* are separated (see *Maasros* 1:5-8). [Regarding *maasros*, an additional condition, known as רְאִיַּת פְּנֵי הַבַּיִת, *seeing the face of the house*, may also apply, depending on the circumstances (see General

Introduction to *Maasros*, Section II, for further discussion).]

3. Dough made from wheat flour is considered to be processed completely when it has been thoroughly kneaded and joined together into a single mass (see *Rash*). Before the kneading is complete, the mixture is not considered a dough. It is therefore permitted for eating in a casual manner (*Rav*).

[While dough is not usually eaten raw, the same law applies if a person bakes the dough before eating it: The bread may be eaten (in a casual manner), since it was produced from "unfinished" dough (see *Mishnah Rishonah* ד"ה עראי).]

4. Dough made from barley flour has a crumbly texture, and cannot be kneaded well. Instead, it is packed down firmly by hand, and left as is (*Rav; Rash*). Once a barley dough is packed down, its processing is considered "finished," and it is classified as *tevel*.

[47] MISHNAH CHALLAH / Chapter 3: *Ochlin*

גִּלְגְּלָה בְּחִטִּים וְטִמְטְמָה בִּשְׂעוֹרִים, הָאוֹכֵל מִמֶּנָּה חַיָּב מִיתָה.
כֵּיוָן שֶׁהִיא נוֹתֶנֶת אֶת הַמַּיִם, מַגְבַּהַת חַלָּתָהּ, וּבִלְבַד שֶׁלֹּא יְהֵא שָׁם חֲמִשָּׁה רְבָעֵי קֶמַח.

— רע"ב —

חייב מיתה. דגמרה מלאכתה, וטבל הוא
במיתה: מגבהת חלתה. תקנת חכמים היא בעסה טהורה, למהר להפריש חלה בטהרה, שמא תטמא העיסה, דעיקר מצוה היא להמתין עד אחר גמר לישה: ובלבד שיהא שם חמשת רביעים קמח. שנתערבו במים, דבפחות מהן לא הגיעה העסה לכלל חיוב חלה. ואית ספרים דגרסי, ובלבד שלא יהיה שם חמשת רביעית קמת, כלומר שלא ישארו חמשת רביעית קמח שלא נתערבו במים. דאם נשארו חמשת רביעית, לא נפטרו בחלה שהפריש קודם שנתגלגלו. ובירושלמי מוכיח, שאם אמר, הרי זה חלה על השאור ועל העסה ועל הקמח הנשאר, לכשתתגלגל העסה כולה, תתקדש זו שבידי לשם חלה, הרי זה מותר. וכן ילמד אדם בתוך ביתו לנשים לומר כן, כשמפרישות חלה מיד אחר גלגול העסה, קודם עריכת הלחם:

גִּלְגְּלָה בְּחִטִּים וְטִמְטְמָה בִּשְׂעוֹרִים — **However, once she has completed its kneading in** the case of **wheat** dough, **or packed it together in** the case of **barley dough,** הָאוֹכֵל מִמֶּנָּה חַיָּב מִיתָה — **one who eats from it** without first separating *challah* **is liable to death** at the hands of Heaven. Once the wheat dough is completely kneaded or the barley dough is packed together, it is "finished," and is thus subject to the *challah* obligation. Someone who eats dough that has been "finished" without first separating *challah* is liable to death at the hand of Heaven.

The Mishnah now identifies when the first stage is reached, and *challah* can be separated (even though the *challah* obligation has not yet taken effect):

כֵּיוָן שֶׁהִיא נוֹתֶנֶת אֶת הַמַּיִם — **As soon as she puts the water** into the flour in the kneading basin, מַגְבַּהַת חַלָּתָהּ — **she separates**[5] its *challah,* even for the flour that did not yet mix with the water,[6] וּבִלְבַד שֶׁלֹּא יְהֵא שָׁם חֲמִשָּׁה — **and as long as there are not five** *reva'im* רְבָעֵי קֶמַח **of** dry **flour** (the minimum amount that is subject to the *challah* obligation)[7] remaining **there in the kneading basin.** That is, if the amount of flour that has not yet mixed with

---

— NOTES —

5. Literally, *lifts up.*

6. There is no obligation to separate *challah* until the dough is kneaded into a single mass (when the dough becomes *tevel*). Nevertheless, *challah* can be separated as soon as water is poured into the flour and they have begun mixing together. Now, normally, separating *challah* for dry flour is invalid — see Mishnah 2:5. The Mishnah here teaches that the woman may separate *challah* from the portion of the flour that has mixed with the water, and this separation is effective even for the flour in the basin that has not yet been mixed with water (*Meiri*).

In fact, it was *preferable* to separate *challah* once the water and flour have begun mixing, rather than wait until all the flour and water have been mixed and kneaded into dough. The Sages preferred this because they wanted *challah* to be *tahor* when it is separated. The earlier *challah* is separated, the less of a chance there is for the dough to become *tamei* (*Rav*).

[Nowadays that we are all *tamei*, this preference does not apply. We therefore follow the Torah law and do not separate *challah* until after the dough is completely kneaded (*Shulchan Aruch, Yoreh Deah* 327:3 with *Shach* §6).]

7. See Mishnahs 1:4 and 2:6.

[48] **משניות חלה / פרק ג: אוכלין**

ג/ב

[ב] נִדְמְעָה עִסָּתָהּ עַד שֶׁלֹּא גִלְגְּלָהּ, פְּטוּרָה, שֶׁהַמְדֻמָּע פָּטוּר; וּמִשֶּׁגִּלְגְּלָהּ, חַיֶּבֶת.

— רע"ב —

(ב) נדמעה עסתה. נתערב בה תרומה בפחות ממאה חולין: משגלגלה חייבת. דכיון דנתחייבה בחלה כבר,

---

water is less than five *reva'im*, the *challah* separation is effective not only for the flour that has already been mixed with water but also for any unmixed flour in the kneading basin.[8]

[2] *Terumah* produce is exempt from *challah* (see *Sifrei* to *Bamidbar* 15:21).

A mixture of *terumah* and non-*terumah* containing less than 100 parts of non-*terumah* for each part of *terumah* is known as *meduma*.[1] Such a mixture is treated as *terumah*, and is exempt from *challah*. The Mishnah discusses a case of *meduma*, and explains that whether it is subject to the laws of *challah* depends on the stage in the process that the dough has reached when it became *meduma*:

נִדְמְעָה עִסָּתָהּ עַד שֶׁלֹּא גִלְגְּלָהּ — **If her dough became *meduma*** (by produce of *terumah* becoming mixed into it) **before she completed** its **kneading**, i.e., before the dough became subject to the obligation of *challah*,[2] **פְּטוּרָה** — then even after she completes kneading it, **it [remains] exempt** from *challah*. **שֶׁהַמְדֻמָּע פָּטוּר** — This is **because *meduma* is exempt from the obligation of *challah*.**[3] **וּמִשֶּׁגִּלְגְּלָהּ** — **But** if her dough became *meduma* **after she completed** its **kneading**, which is after it already became subject to *challah*, **חַיֶּבֶת** — **it** remains **subject** to *challah* even though it is now *meduma*. Since it had already become obligated in *challah*, it remains obligated.

It is forbidden to cause *challah* to become *tamei*. This prohibition is learned from the verse, *Behold, I have given you the safeguard of My terumos* (*Bamidbar* 18:18). Because of this, it is even prohibited to cause dough that is *subject* to *challah* (from which *challah* has not yet been separated) to become *tamei*.[4] Causing dough to become *tamei* even *before* it is subject to *challah* is

---

NOTES

8. This is because the dry flour is not considered to have its own significance, and is considered subordinate to the rest. Therefore, all of the flour is treated as if it were mixed with water. If, however, the amount of unmixed flour in the basin is five *reva'im* or more, then that flour is viewed by itself. Since *challah* separation is not effective for dry flour, it is therefore not effective for the unmixed portion (*Meiri*).

[2]

1. Biblically, if *terumah* became mixed with non-*terumah* of the same type, the mixture is not treated as *terumah* (and may be eaten by a non-Kohen) as long as there is a majority of non-*terumah* in the mixture. By Rabbinic law, however, *terumah* is not nullified, and is considered

meduma unless there are 100 parts of non-*terumah* for each part of *terumah*.

2. The Mishnah uses an example of wheat dough, which becomes obligated in *challah* when its kneading is completed, as was taught in the previous Mishnah.

3. See Mishnah 1:4 note 9. This leniency is based on the fact that the *challah* obligation in our days is Rabbinic in nature (see *Kesubos* 25a and *Niddah* 47a; see General Introduction). The Rabbis, who established this *challah* obligation, did not apply it to *meduma* (*Rash, Rosh*).

4. Once a dough becomes obligated in *challah*, the unseparated *challah* portion is viewed as present within the dough (see *Niddah* 6b-7a with *Tosafos*). See further.

[49] **MISHNAH CHALLAH** / Chapter 3: *Ochlin*

- רע״ב -

תו לא פקע על ידי דמוע: **עד שלא גלגלה תעשה בטומאה.** כיון דאפילו אם תעשה בטהרה, אין הכהן רשאי לאכלה מפני ספק שנולד בה, יכול לטמאתה מיד קודם גלגול:

נוֹלַד לָהּ סָפֵק טְמֵאָה עַד שֶׁלֹּא גִלְגְּלָהּ, תֵּעָשֶׂה בְטֻמְאָה; וּמִשֶּׁגִּלְגְּלָהּ, תֵּעָשֶׂה בְטָהֳרָה.

[ג] **הִקְדִּישָׁה** עִסָּתָהּ עַד שֶׁלֹּא גִלְגְּלָהּ, וּפְדָאַתָּה, חַיֶּבֶת. מִשֶּׁגִּלְגְּלָהּ

משגלגלה תעשה בטהרה. אם נולד בה ספק לאחר הגלגול, אסור לטמאתה. דחולין הטבולים לחלה כחלה דמו, ותרומה תלויה צריכה שמור: (ג) **עד שלא גלגלה ופדאתה.** ולאחר שפדאתה גלגלה, חייבת, כיון דבשעת הגלגול לא היתה הקדש:

---

forbidden as well, but for a different reason: If the dough is *tamei*, the *challah* that will eventually be separated from it will also be *tamei*. This will cause a loss to the Kohen who will receive the *challah*, for he will be forbidden to eat it.[5] The Mishnah now discusses the law in a case of doubt:

נוֹלַד לָהּ סָפֵק טְמֵאָה — If there **arose a doubt** that perhaps **[the dough] became** *tamei*, **it depends on the following:** עַד שֶׁלֹּא גִלְגְּלָהּ — **If the doubt arose before she completed** its **kneading**, i.e., before it became subject to *challah,* תֵּעָשֶׂה בְטֻמְאָה — **it may** then **be prepared** (that is, its kneading may be completed) **in** *tumah,* i.e., in a way that it will become *definitely tamei* (for example, by preparing it with *tamei* utensils).[6] וּמִשֶּׁגִּלְגְּלָהּ — **But if the doubt arose after she completed** its **kneading,** i.e., when it had already become obligated in *challah*, תֵּעָשֶׂה בְטָהֳרָה — **it must be prepared in** *taharah,* i.e., she must continue to make sure that it does not have any contact with *tumah*.[7] Although the dough was already possibly *tamei,* it is forbidden to make it definitely *tamei* once it has become subject to the *challah* obligation.[8]

[3] Produce that is *hekdesh* (consecrated to the Temple) is not subject to the obligation of *challah*.[1] The Mishnah explains how that law too depends on the stage in the process that the dough has reached when it was consecrated: הִקְדִּישָׁה עִסָּתָהּ עַד שֶׁלֹּא גִלְגְּלָהּ — **If she consecrated her dough** to the Temple **before she completed** its **kneading**, that is, before the point when it becomes subject to *challah*,[2] וּפְדָאַתָּה — **and she redeemed it** right away, before completing its kneading, חַיֶּבֶת — **it is subject to the** *challah* **obligation** when she completes its kneading. Even though dough that is *hekdesh* is exempt from *challah*, this dough was no longer *hekdesh* when its kneading was completed. Thus, it became subject to the *challah* obligation. מִשֶּׁגִּלְגְּלָהּ — So

---

NOTES

5. See Mishnah 2:3.
6. Here, the prohibition based on the verse, *Behold, I have given you the safeguard of My terumos,* does not apply because this dough was not yet subject to *challah*. And the prohibition to cause a loss to the Kohen also does not apply, because the Kohen was already forbidden to eat the dough when it was possibly *tamei*. Therefore, the Kohen does not lose anything when the dough becomes definitely *tamei* (*Rash*; see also *Rav*; *Rashi* to *Niddah* 6b ד״ה תעשה בטומאה).

7. *Rashi* there.
8. This prohibition, too, is based on the verse, *Behold, I have given you the safeguard of My terumos* (see *Rash*).

[3]
1. See Mishnah 1:6 note 7.
2. The Mishnah is discussing a dough made of wheat flour; see Mishnah 1.

וּפְדָאַתָה, חַיֶּבֶת. הִקְדִּישַׁתָּה עַד שֶׁלֹּא גִלְגְּלָה, וְגִלְגְּלָהּ הַגִּזְבָּר, וְאַחַר כָּךְ פְּדָאַתָּה, פְּטוּרָה, שֶׁבִּשְׁעַת חוֹבָתָהּ הָיְתָה פְּטוּרָה.

[ד] **כַּיּוֹצֵא** בּוֹ, הַמַּקְדִּישׁ פֵּרוֹתָיו עַד שֶׁלֹּא בָּאוּ לְעוֹנַת הַמַּעַשְׂרוֹת, וּפְדָאָן, חַיָּבִין. וּמִשֶּׁבָּאוּ לְעוֹנַת הַמַּעַשְׂרוֹת, וּפְדָאָן,

– רע"ב –

שֶׁבְּשַׁעַת חוֹבָתָהּ הָיְתָה פְּטוּרָה. דְּגִלְגּוּל הַקְדֵּשׁ פּוֹטֵר, דִּכְתִיב (במדבר לו,כא) טרימותיכם, ולא עִסַּת הַקְדֵּשׁ: (ד) עַד שֶׁלֹּא בָּאוּ לְעוֹנַת הַמַּעַשְׂרוֹת. כָּל אֶחָד כְּמִשְׁפָּט הַמְפוֹרָשׁ בְּפֶרֶק קַמָּא דְמַעַשְׂרוֹת:

---

too, if she consecrated the dough only **after she completed its kneading,** in which case it had already become subject to *challah,* וּפְדָאַתָה — **and she then redeemed it,** חַיֶּבֶת — **it remains subject to the** *challah* **obligation.**[3] הִקְדִּישַׁתָּה עַד שֶׁלֹּא גִלְגְּלָה — **However, if she consecrated it before she completed its kneading,** i.e., before it became subject to the *challah* obligation, וְגִלְגְּלָהּ הַגִּזְבָּר — **and the** Temple **treasurer completed** its **kneading,** וְאַחַר כָּךְ פְּדָאַתָּה — **and then she redeemed it,** פְּטוּרָה — **it is exempt** from *challah.* שֶׁבִּשְׁעַת חוֹבָתָהּ הָיְתָה פְּטוּרָה — The reason for this is **because at the time of its obligation** (that is, the time when the kneading was completed and the obligation would have taken effect) **it was exempt,** since it belonged to *hekdesh.* Since the dough was exempt from *challah* when its kneading was completed, it remains exempt even after it is redeemed.

[4] The previous Mishnah explained that whether *hekdesh* is subject to the obligation of *challah* is dependent on the stage in the process that the dough reached when it was consecrated. Now, *hekdesh* is also not subject to the obligation of *maasros* (tithing). This Mishnah explains that this exemption, too, depends on when the produce was consecrated:

כַּיּוֹצֵא בּוֹ — **Similarly,** הַמַּקְדִּישׁ פֵּרוֹתָיו עַד שֶׁלֹּא בָּאוּ לְעוֹנַת הַמַּעַשְׂרוֹת — if **someone consecrated his fruits before they reached the time of** *maasros,*[1] וּפְדָאָן — **and then redeemed them,** while they have still not reached the time of *maasros,* חַיָּבִין — **they are subject to the** *maaser* **obligation,** because when the *maaser* obligation took effect they were no longer *hekdesh.* וּמִשֶּׁבָּאוּ לְעוֹנַת הַמַּעַשְׂרוֹת וּפְדָאָן — **So too,** if he consecrated them **after they reached**

NOTES

3. Once a dough becomes subject to the obligation of *challah,* it remains obligated even if it is later consecrated (*Rash*). [Although the Mishnah speaks of a case where it was redeemed, the *hekdesh* produce remains obligated in *maasros* even if it was not redeemed, since the obligation took effect before it was consecrated (see *Meleches Shlomo, Peah* 4:8 ד"ה משבאו).]

[4]

1. That is, before the produce has been fully processed, and thus becomes fully obligated in *maasros;* see Mishnah 1 note 2. [As explained there, the term עוֹנַת הַמַּעַשְׂרוֹת is usually used when referring to a totally different time — when the growing produce reaches the point when it begins becoming edible. The Mishnah here is actually referring to the *completion of processing,* which is generally referred to as גְּמַר מְלָאכָה. Later, the Mishnah will indeed use the expression נִגְמְרוּ, *it was finished,* and is referring to the same stage as it is here — the completion of processing (see *Meleches Shomo*).]

[51] **MISHNAH CHALLAH** / Chapter 3: *Ochlin*

חַיָּבִין. הִקְדִּישָׁן עַד שֶׁלֹּא נִגְמְרוּ, וּגְמָרָן הַגִּזְבָּר, וְאַחַר כָּךְ פְּדָאָן, פְּטוּרִין, שֶׁבִּשְׁעַת חוֹבָתָן הָיוּ פְטוּרִין.

[ה] **עוֹבֵד** כּוֹכָבִים שֶׁנָּתַן לְיִשְׂרָאֵל לַעֲשׂוֹת לוֹ עִסָּה, פְּטוּרָה מִן הַחַלָּה. נְתָנָהּ לוֹ מַתָּנָה, עַד שֶׁלֹּא גִלְגֵּל, חַיָּב; וּמִשֶּׁגִּלְגֵּל, פָּטוּר.

– רע"ב –

וּגְמָרָן הַגִּזְבָּר. שֶׁנִּגְמְרוּ בְּעוֹדָן תַּחַת יַד הַגִּזְבָּר: **שֶׁבִּשְׁעַת חוֹבָתָן הָיוּ פְטוּרִים.** דִּכְתִיב (דברים יח,ד) דְּגָנְךָ, וְלֹא דְגַן הֶקְדֵּשׁ: (ה) **פְּטוּרָה מִן הַחַלָּה.** שֶׁאֵין גִּלְגּוּלוֹ שֶׁל יִשְׂרָאֵל מְחַיֵּיב עִסָּה שֶׁל עוֹבֵד כּוֹכָבִים. וְכֵן עִסָּה שֶׁל יִשְׂרָאֵל, אֵין גִּלְגּוּל הָעוֹבֵד כּוֹכָבִים פּוֹטֶרֶת:

---

the time of *maasros,* and then redeemed them, חַיָּבִין — **they are subject to the** *maaser* **obligation,** because, here too, the produce was not *hekdesh* when the processing was completed. Thus, it became subject to the *maaser* obligation. That obligation remains in effect even if the produce was then consecrated and redeemed.[2] הִקְדִּישָׁן עַד שֶׁלֹּא נִגְמְרוּ וּגְמָרָן הַגִּזְבָּר — **If, however, he consecrated them before their processing was complete, and the Temple official completed their** processing,[3] וְאַחַר כָּךְ פְּדָאָן פְּטוּרִין — **and [the owner] then redeemed them, they are exempt** from *maasros,* שֶׁבִּשְׁעַת חוֹבָתָן הָיוּ פְטוּרִין — **because at the time of their obligation** (i.e., at the time the tithing obligation would ordinarily take effect) **they were** consecrated and thus **exempt** from *maasros.* Therefore, even if they are then redeemed, they remain exempt from *maasros.*

[5] The Torah (*Bamidbar* 15:21) uses the term עֲרִסֹתֵיכֶם, *"your" doughs,* to describe the dough from which *challah* must be taken. The Gemara (*Menachos* 67a) teaches that this term excludes dough that belongs to a non-Jew. The Mishnah discusses a number of cases relating to this law: עוֹבֵד כּוֹכָבִים שֶׁנָּתַן לְיִשְׂרָאֵל לַעֲשׂוֹת לוֹ עִסָּה — **If a non-Jew gave flour**[1] **to a Jew to make a dough for [the non-Jew],** פְּטוּרָה מִן הַחַלָּה — **[the dough] is exempt from the** *challah* **obligation** because it belongs to the non-Jew. נְתָנָהּ לוֹ מַתָּנָה — **If [the non-Jew] gave [this dough] as a gift to [the Jew]** who was preparing the dough, the law depends on the following: עַד שֶׁלֹּא גִלְגֵּל — **If the** non-Jew gave the dough to the Jew **before [the Jew] completed kneading** the dough, חַיָּב — **[the Jew] is obligated** to separate *challah* when he completes kneading the dough, because the dough is owned by a Jew when the *challah* obligation takes effect. וּמִשֶּׁגִּלְגֵּל — **However, if** the non-Jew gave the dough to a Jew **after he completed kneading** the dough, פָּטוּר — then **he is exempt** from *challah,* because it still belonged to the non-Jew at the time the *challah* obligation took effect.[2]

NOTES

2. [As in the previous Mishnah, even if it was *not* redeemed, the obligation remains in effect, since the obligation already took effect before it was consecrated (see *Meleches Shlomo*).]

3. That is, the processing was completed while it was still *hekdesh* and under the control of the Temple official in charge of *hekdesh* (*Rav*).

[5]

1. *Rash; Ri ben Malki Tzedek.*
2. *Ri ben Malki Tzedek.*

[52] משניות חלה / פרק ג: אוכלין

הָעוֹשֶׂה עִסָּה עִם הָעוֹבֵד כּוֹכָבִים, אִם אֵין בְּשֶׁל יִשְׂרָאֵל כְּשִׁעוּר חַלָּה, פְּטוּרָה מִן הַחַלָּה.

[ו] גֵּר שֶׁנִּתְגַּיֵּר וְהָיְתָה לוֹ עִסָּה, נַעֲשֵׂית עַד שֶׁלֹּא נִתְגַּיֵּר, פָּטוּר; וּמִשֶּׁנִּתְגַּיֵּר, חַיָּב. וְאִם סָפֵק, חַיָּב, וְאֵין חַיָּבִין עָלֶיהָ חֹמֶשׁ.

- רע"ב -

אם אין בשל ישראל כשיעור. שחייבין להפריש ממנה חלה, שהן חמשה רביעיות: (ו) ספק חייב. משום דהוי ספק איסורא, ולחומרא, ומפריש חלה ומוכרה לכהן: ואין חייבין עליה חומש. זר האוכלה אינו משלם את החומש, אבל הקרן משלם, דתשלומי תרומה כפרה נינהו. הלכך מפריש תשלומין ומכפרים מספק, ומוכרן לכהן:

Only a dough containing at least five *reva'im* of flour is subject to the *challah* obligation (see Mishnah 2:6). The Mishnah discusses a case in which a dough is owned partly by a Jew and partly by a non-Jew:

הָעוֹשֶׂה עִסָּה עִם הָעוֹבֵד כּוֹכָבִים — **If [a Jew] makes a dough together with a non-Jew,** that is, each one owns part of the dough, אִם אֵין בְּשֶׁל יִשְׂרָאֵל כְּשִׁעוּר חַלָּה — the law is that **if the portion owned by the Jew does not contain the minimum measure subject to the *challah* obligation** (five *reva'im* of flour), פְּטוּרָה מִן הַחַלָּה — **[the dough] is exempt from the *challah* obligation.** Although the entire dough contains five *reva'im* of flour, the portion of the dough that is owned by the non-Jew is not counted toward the minimum measure subject to *challah*. Since the portion owned by the Jew by itself does not contain the minimum measure for the *challah* obligation, it is not subject to the *challah* obligation.[3]

[6] Continuing the discussion of the previous Mishnah regarding dough of a non-Jew, our Mishnah discusses a case in which the non-Jewish owner of a dough converted to Judaism:

גֵּר שֶׁנִּתְגַּיֵּר — **If someone converted to Judaism** וְהָיְתָה לוֹ עִסָּה — **and he owned a dough,** the law is as follows: נַעֲשֵׂית עַד שֶׁלֹּא נִתְגַּיֵּר — **If it was completed**[1] **before he converted,** פָּטוּר — **he is exempt** from separating *challah* from it, because it belonged to a non-Jew when the *challah* obligation took effect. וּמִשֶּׁנִּתְגַּיֵּר — **However, if the dough was completed after he converted,** חַיָּב — **he is obligated** to separate *challah* from it, because he was a Jew when the *challah* obligation took effect. וְאִם סָפֵק — **If it is uncertain** whether the dough was made before he converted or afterward, חַיָּב — **he is obligated** to separate *challah* from it. Since there is a doubt whether the dough is subject to the *challah* obligation, we must deal with it strictly and separate *challah*.[2] וְאֵין חַיָּבִין עָלֶיהָ חֹמֶשׁ — **However, if [non-Kohanim] unlawfully**

NOTES

3. *Pnei Moshe*. [The Mishnah implies that if the Jew owns five *reva'im* of the flour, the dough *is* subject to the *challah* obligation. The fact that a non-Jew owns part of the dough is not a reason to exempt the Jew's portion (see *Rash*).]

[6]

1. That is, wheat dough that was completely kneaded or barley dough that was packed together; see Mishnah 1 (*Rambam* Commentary).

2. The *challah* that is separated is "doubtful *challah.*" Since the dough may have been owned by a Jew when the *challah* obligation took effect, the portion separated as *challah* may be

[53] MISHNAH CHALLAH / Chapter 3: *Ochlin*

- רע״ב -

אחר הקרימה בתנור. דסבר רבי עקיבא, אין גמר מלאכתה של חלה עד שיקרמו פני הפת בתנור, וזו היא טונתה לחלה. הלכך אם נתגייר קודם שיקרמו פני הפת בתנור, חייב בחלה. ואין הלכה כרבי עקיבא:

רַבִּי עֲקִיבָא אוֹמֵר: הַכֹּל הוֹלֵךְ אַחַר הַקְּרִימָה בַתַּנּוּר.

---

ate this *challah* that was separated only out of doubt, they **are not obligated to pay an added "fifth" on account of** eating **it**. Normally, a non-Kohen who mistakenly eats *challah* must replace it with produce of the same value as an atonement, and also pay the Kohen an added penalty, which amounts to a "fifth" of the total amount that he is paying (see *Vayikra* 22:14).[3] In a case of doubt, however, the non-Kohen is not obligated to separate the added "fifth."[4]

The Mishnah quotes a Tanna who disagrees with the Tanna Kamma regarding the stage upon which the law is dependent:

הַכֹּל הוֹלֵךְ אַחַר הַקְּרִימָה בַתַּנּוּר — It is — **רַבִּי עֲקִיבָא אוֹמֵר — R' Akiva says: entirely dependent on** the time of **the formation of a crust in the oven.** That is, whether the convert is obligated to separate *challah* from his dough does not depend on whether he was Jewish at the time of the kneading of the dough. Rather, it depends on when the dough formed a crust in the oven.[5]

NOTES

actual *challah* that may not be eaten by non-Kohanim. On the other hand, since it may have been owned by a non-Jew at that time, it may not be *challah*. Therefore, based on the principle that הַמּוֹצִיא מֵחֲבֵרוֹ עָלָיו הָרְאָיָה, *the [burden of] proof is on the one seeking to take from his fellow*, the Kohen has no legal claim to the *challah*, since he cannot prove that he has a right to it. Nevertheless, since only a Kohen can eat it, the owner will have no choice other than to give it to a Kohen to eat. However, the owner may charge the Kohen money for it (*Rav; Rosh*).

3. That is, one-quarter of the principal (see Mishnah 1:9 note 1).

4. In order for the Kohen to have a legal claim to the "fifth" paid as a penalty, he would have to prove that the non-Kohen definitely ate *challah*. Here, however, he is not able to do so, for no one knows whether the dough from which the "*challah*" was separated was subject to *challah* or not. The non-Kohen is therefore not obligated to pay the "fifth" (*Rambam Commentary*).

In fact, this same logic tells us that the non-Kohen is also not obligated to repay the principal. As to how he gains atonement for having eaten doubtful *challah*, it is sufficient to simply take produce that has the value of the doubtful *challah* that was eaten, and *designate* it as *challah* (see *Tosafos, Kesubos* 30b ד״ה זר שאכל תרומה). [After designating it, he does not need to give it to the Kohen for free, because as just explained, the Kohen cannot prove that the non-Kohen ate actual *challah* (*Rav*).]

The "fifth," however, need not even be *designated*, because the atonement is not dependent on the "fifth" (*Mishnah Rishonah*). Therefore, the "fifth" does not need to be paid in cases of doubt such as ours, where it is possible that the non-Kohen did not commit any sin at all.

5. According to R' Akiva, the dough becomes subject to *challah* when a crust has formed on the bread, not when the dough was completed. In fact, the same applies to the other cases discussed in this chapter until this point. R' Akiva holds that all the laws taught will depend on when the dough develops a crust, rather than on when the dough is completely kneaded (see *Rav*; see also *Tos. Yom Tov*).

[54] משניות חלה / פרק ג: אוכלין

- רע"ב -

[ז] **הָעוֹשָׂה** עִסָּה מִן הַחִטִּים וּמִן הָאֹרֶז,
אִם יֵשׁ בָּהּ טַעַם דָּגָן, חַיֶּבֶת
בַּחַלָּה, וְיוֹצֵא בָהּ אָדָם יְדֵי חוֹבָתוֹ בַּפֶּסַח.
וְאִם אֵין בָּהּ טַעַם דָּגָן, אֵינָהּ חַיֶּבֶת בַּחַלָּה.

(ז) אורז. לאו מין דגן הוא. וכל שאינו מין דגן פטור מן החלה, ואין אדם יוצא בו ידי חובתו בפסח: אם יש בה טעם דגן חייב בחלה. ואף על גב דאין בדגן כשיעור חלה:

---

[7] We have learned (Mishnah 1:1) that the *challah* obligation applies only to dough made from one of five species of grain: wheat, barley, spelt, oats, and rye. Similarly, only these five species can be used to bake matzah to fulfill the obligation to eat matzah on the first night of Pesach (Mishnah 1:2). Dough made from any other grain, such as rice, is exempt from *challah,* and may not be used to fulfill the mitzvah of matzah.[1] The Mishnah will now discuss the status of dough made from a mixture of one of these five species of grain and another species of grain, with regard to both of these laws:

הָעוֹשָׂה עִסָּה מִן הַחִטִּים וּמִן הָאָרֶץ — If a person made a dough from a mixture of wheat flour and rice flour, the law is as follows: אִם יֵשׁ בָּהּ טַעַם דָּגָן — If the flavor of the wheat grain can be tasted in [the dough], חַיֶּבֶת בַּחַלָּה — it is subject to *challah*.[2] וְיוֹצֵא בָהּ אָדָם יְדֵי חוֹבָתוֹ בַּפֶּסַח — Similarly, a person can fulfill his obligation to eat matzah on Pesach with matzah made from it.[3] וְאִם אֵין בָּהּ טַעַם דָּגָן — But if the flavor of the wheat grain cannot be tasted in [the dough], אֵינָהּ חַיֶּבֶת בַּחַלָּה — it is not subject to the *challah* obligation,

---
NOTES

[7]

1. The Gemara (*Pesachim* 35a) derives from a verse that the matzah obligation can be fulfilled only with matzah made from grain that has the ability to become *chametz* ("leavened"). Now, only grain of the five species can become *chametz*. Other species of grain, however, do not become *chametz* when they ferment; they simply become spoiled. Therefore, they cannot be used to fulfill the mitzvah of matzah.

2. If the wheat flour can be tasted in the dough, one must separate *challah* from it, even if there is more rice flour in the dough than wheat flour (*Zevachim* 78a). In fact, *challah* must be separated even if the amount of wheat flour on its own is less than five *reva'im,* the minimum amount of flour needed to create a *challah* obligation (see Mishnah 2:6). As long as the wheat flour and rice flour *together* total at least five *reva'im,* and the flavor of wheat can be tasted in the dough, the dough is subject to *challah* (see *Rav*).

Generally, we determine the halachic status of a mixture by the part that makes up its majority. In a case such as ours, however, we apply the principle of טַעַם כְּעִקָּר, *flavor is the equivalent of substance,* and give consideration even to something that makes up a small part of a mixture if its flavor can be detected. Thus, our Mishnah teaches, if the flavor of the wheat can be tasted in the dough, the entire dough is regarded as if it were made of wheat (see *Zevachim* 78a-b).

3. That is, if matzah was made from this dough, it is suitable for the mitzvah. Just as we apply the principle of טַעַם כְּעִקָּר, *flavor is the equivalent of substance,* to teach that dough made from rice and wheat flour is subject to *challah* when the wheat can be tasted, so too it teaches that such a dough can be used to fulfill the matzah obligation. In fact, even the rice portion of the matzah counts toward the required minimum measure of a *kezayis* (an olive-sized portion) of matzah (*Rosh, Chullin* 7:31).

[55] **MISHNAH CHALLAH** / Chapter 3: *Ochlin*　　　　　　　　　　3/8

- רע"ב -

וְאֵין אָדָם יוֹצֵא בָהּ יְדֵי חוֹבָתוֹ בַּפֶּסַח.

[ח] הַנּוֹטֵל שְׂאֹר מֵעִסָּה שֶׁלֹּא הוּרְמָה חַלָּתָהּ וְנוֹתֵן לְתוֹךְ עִסָּה שֶׁהוּרְמָה חַלָּתָהּ, אִם יֶשׁ לוֹ פַּרְנָסָה מִמָּקוֹם אַחֵר,

(ח) אם יש לו פרנסה ממקום אחר. אם יש לו קמח אחר חוץ מעיסה זו, מביא קמח כשיעור שאם יצרפנו לשאור זה שחייב בחלה יהיה בו חמשת רביעית, שהוא שיעור חלה, ולש עיסה, ומערב עם העיסה שיש בה השאור, ומוציא ממנה כשיעור חלה שצריך להפריש מחמשת רביעית:

וְאֵין אָדָם יוֹצֵא בָהּ יְדֵי חוֹבָתוֹ בַּפֶּסַח — and a person cannot fulfill his obligation to eat matzah **on Pesach with** matzah made from it.[4]

[8] The Mishnah discusses a case in which a person mixes some dough from which *challah* has not been separated (*tevel*) into dough from which *challah* has already been separated:

הַנּוֹטֵל שְׂאֹר מֵעִסָּה שֶׁלֹּא הוּרְמָה חַלָּתָהּ — If someone takes a piece of **sourdough from a dough whose** *challah* **has not** yet **been separated, וְנוֹתֵן לְתוֹךְ עִסָּה שֶׁהוּרְמָה חַלָּתָהּ** — and mistakenly **puts** that sourdough **into a dough whose** *challah* **has** already **been separated,** thus creating a mixture of dough of *chullin* (i.e., dough from which *challah* has been separated) and dough of *tevel*,[1] he should do as follows:[2] **אִם יֶשׁ לוֹ פַּרְנָסָה מִמָּקוֹם אַחֵר** — **If he has a batch**

NOTES

4. If the flavor of the wheat flour cannot be tasted, we follow the general rule that the minority ingredient is nullified in a mixture. Thus, the wheat, which is the minority ingredient, is nullified in the mixture, and the dough is viewed as if it is made entirely of rice. The entire dough is therefore exempt from *challah,* even if it contains five *reva'im* of wheat flour (*Tos. Anshei Shem*). Similarly, one cannot fulfill the mitzvah of matzah with this dough.

[8]

1. Sourdough is made by leaving dough to ferment. It is added to regular dough in order to make it rise. Our Mishnah is discussing a person who placed a small piece of sourdough into a dough from which *challah* had been separated, not realizing that *challah* had not yet been separated from the sourdough (*Meiri*). [The Mishnah discusses a common case. The same law would apply to a case where *dough* (rather than sourdough) that was *tevel* was mixed into dough from which *challah* has already been separated (*Tiferes Yisrael; Derech Emunah, Hil. Bikkurim* 7:79).]

2. Under Biblical law, the minority of *tevel* sourdough is nullified in the majority of non-*tevel* dough. Nevertheless, the Rabbis prohibited even the smallest amount of *tevel* in a mixture of like kinds of permissible and prohibited foods [מִין בְּמִינוֹ, *a kind in its own kind*]; see Mishnah 10 with note 4. [Sourdough and regular dough are considered to be of one kind (see *Meleches Shlomo* and *Tos. R' Akiva Eiger* to *Orlah* 2:6, cited in note 4 there).]

In order to permit the dough, we must separate *challah* for the sourdough and thus remove its *tevel* status. But this is not so simple. We cannot separate *challah* directly from the sourdough, because the sourdough is thoroughly mixed with the *chullin* (non-*tevel*) dough and is not identifiable. Nor can we separate *challah* for the sourdough from the dough from which it came. This is because the Gemara (*Menachos* 31a) teaches that the separation of *challah* from one dough for another is valid only if both doughs have the same level of obligation — that is, they are both either Biblically obligated or both Rabbinically obligated. Here, however, the sourdough (which is nullified on the Biblical level) is only Rabbinic *tevel,* while the other dough is Biblical *tevel* (*Mishnah Rishonah* ד"ה פרנסה ממקום אחר). The Mishnah will now discuss how this issue can be resolved.

משניות חלה / פרק ג: אוכלין [56]

- רע"ב -

מוֹצִיא לְפִי חֶשְׁבּוֹן; וְאִם לָאו, מוֹצִיא חַלָּה אַחַת עַל הַכֹּל.

ואם לאו. שאין לו קמח, מוציא חלה, אחת מעשרים וארבעה כולה טבולה לחלה:

על כל העסה. דטבל חוסר בכל שהוא במינו, ונעשית כולה טבולה לחלה:

---

of flour to bring **from somewhere else**, which together with the sourdough contains the minimum five *reva'im* measure of flour that is subject to *challah*, he kneads that flour into dough and joins the two batches of dough together.[3] **מוֹצִיא לְפִי חֶשְׁבּוֹן** — Then, **he separates** an amount of *challah* from the new dough **in proportion** to the amount of *tevel* in both doughs together. That is, he calculates the total amount of *tevel* in the two doughs, and separates 1/24 of that amount[4] from the new dough. By doing so, he exempts the sourdough and removes its *tevel* status. The original dough will now be permitted in its entirety. **וְאִם לָאו** — **But if** he does **not** have another batch of flour from which to make a new dough, **מוֹצִיא חַלָּה אַחַת עַל הַכֹּל** — he must separate **one** full measure of **challah** (i.e., one twenty-fourth) from within the dough and sourdough mixture itself **for the entire** mixture of dough and sourdough.[5]

[9] Having discussed how the law of *challah* applies to a dough partly containing *tevel*, the Mishnah discusses a similar situation with regard to the laws of *terumos* and *maasros*.[1] As a rule, the laws of *terumos* and *maasros*

NOTES
---

3. The new dough is placed so that it touches the dough and sourdough mixture, thus connecting the two batches. When the two batches are combined they contain the minimum five *reva'im* of flour. The new batch of dough on its own, however, contains less than five *reva'im* of flour (*Rav*, as emended by *Tos. Anshei Shem; Meleches Shlomo*).

The reason why the new batch of dough must contain less than five *reva'im* of flour is as follows: As explained in note 2, on the Biblical level, the sourdough is nullified. It is subject to *challah* only on the Rabbinic level. Therefore, as explained there, when *challah* is separated for the sourdough, it may be separated only from dough that is also Rabbinically subject to *challah*. Had the new dough contained five *reva'im* on its own, it would have been Biblically obligated. Therefore, we take a dough that contains less than the required amount, which is not subject to the obligation on its own at all. When the new dough is joined with the original dough, it will be subject to the *challah* obligation only because it is combined with the original dough. Since the original dough is subject to the obligation only on the Rabbinic level (since the sourdough is nullified on the Biblical level), the obligation of the new dough is also Rabbinic, since the level of its obligation (which is entirely a result of its combination with the original dough) cannot be greater than that of the original dough (*Mishnah Rishonah*).

4. [Or, 1/48 of the dough if it is being baked for sale; see Mishnah 2:7.] Since the *challah* is being separated only for the *tevel*, not for the entire dough, it is sufficient to separate an amount equal to 1/24 of the *tevel*. Thus, if only one-third of the dough is *tevel*, he need declare only 1/24 of one-third of the entire dough as *challah*.

5. In this case, where the *challah* is being separated from the mixture itself, the entire mixture is treated as *tevel*. Therefore, he must separate an amount equal to 1/24 of the entire mixture (see *Shach, Yoreh Deah* 324:18).

[9]

1. The Torah requires that certain tithes be separated from produce. These are: (1) תְּרוּמָה גְּדוֹלָה, *terumah gedolah* (*the greater terumah*), which is given to a Kohen. By Biblical law, there is no minimum amount that must be given as *terumah*. [The Rabbis, however, did set a

[57] **MISHNAH CHALLAH** / Chapter 3: *Ochlin*

- רע״ב -

[ט] **כַּיּוֹצֵא** בּוֹ, זֵיתֵי מָסִיק שֶׁנִּתְעָרְבוּ עִם זֵיתֵי נִקּוּף, עִנְּבֵי בָצִיר עִם עִנְּבֵי עוֹלֵלוֹת, אִם יֶשׁ לוֹ פַּרְנָסָה מִמָּקוֹם אַחֵר, מוֹצִיא לְפִי חֶשְׁבּוֹן. וְאִם לָאו,

(ט) זיתים מסיק. זיתים שבטל הבית מלקט. ולקיטת הזיתים קרויה מסיקה: זיתי נקוף. זיתים שנוגעין מלקטים. כמה דאת אומר (ישעיה יז,ו) כנוקף זית שנים שלשה גרגרים. והם פטורים מן המעשר: ענבי בציר. שחייבים במעשר: עם ענבי עוללות. שפטורים מן המעשר: אם יש לו. טבל אחר כיוצא בזה. מוציא ממנו לפי חשבון כשיעור מה שצריך להוציא מזיתי מסיק, או מענבי בציר שחייבים במעשר: ואם לאו. אם אין לו טבל אחר, רואים אותו כאילו כולו טבל, ומוציא תרומה ותרומת מעשר על הכל:

---

do not apply to gifts that the Torah awards to the poor [see Mishnah 1:3]. The Mishnah discusses a case where such gifts became mixed with other produce that is subject to *maasros*:

כַּיּוֹצֵא בּוֹ זֵיתֵי מָסִיק שֶׁנִּתְעָרְבוּ עִם זֵיתֵי נִקּוּף — Similarly, with regard to **harvested olives** (that is, regular olives that are *tevel*) **that became mixed with picked olives** (i.e., olives that must be left as gifts to be picked by the poor, and are thus not subject to *maasros*),[2] **עִנְּבֵי בָצִיר עִם עִנְּבֵי עוֹלֵלוֹת** — or **harvested grapes,** that are *tevel,* that became mixed **with** *oleilos* **grapes** (i.e., grapes that are left as gifts for the poor, and are thus not subject to *maasros*),[3] he can do as follows, in order to permit the mixture: **אִם יֶשׁ לוֹ פַּרְנָסָה מִמָּקוֹם אַחֵר** — **If he has a batch** of *tevel* of the same type of produce that he can bring **from somewhere else,**[4] **מוֹצִיא לְפִי חֶשְׁבּוֹן** — **he may separate** an amount of *maasros* from that batch of *tevel* **in proportion to the amount of** *tevel* **in the mixture. וְאִם לָאו** — **But if he does not** have another batch of

--- NOTES ---

minimum amount (typically one-fiftieth of the produce).] (2) מַעֲשֵׂר רִאשׁוֹן, *maaser rishon* (*the first tithe*), one-tenth of the remaining produce, which is given to a Levi. (3) תְּרוּמַת מַעֲשֵׂר, *terumas maaser,* one-tenth of *maaser rishon,* which the Levi separates and gives to a Kohen. (4) מַעֲשֵׂר שֵׁנִי, *maaser sheni* (*the second tithe*), one-tenth of the crop remaining after *terumah* and *maaser rishon* were separated. *Maaser sheni* is separated from crops of the first, second, fourth, and fifth years of the seven-year *Shemittah* cycle, and is eaten in Jerusalem. (5) מַעֲשֵׂר עָנִי, *maasar ani* (*the tithe of the poor*), one-tenth of the crop, separated (instead of *maaser sheni*) from crops of the third and sixth years of the *Shemittah* cycle, and given to the poor.
  Terumah and *terumas maaser* may not be eaten by a non-Kohen. *Maaser rishon* and *maasar ani* may be eaten by all. The only reason why these portions cannot be eaten by someone other than a Levi or poor person is because, if he does

so, he is stealing from the Leviim and poor people to whom the Torah awarded them. However, the Levi or poor person may give or sell his portions to whomever he wishes, and the one who receives it may eat it.

2. "Harvested olives" are olives that the farmer harvests for himself and are thus subject to *maasros*. "Picked olives" are those olives that he is required to leave on the tree for the poor [namely, *shich'chah* and *pe'ah* — see *Rash Sirilio*]. Picked olives are thus exempt from *maasros;* see Introduction to Mishnah (*Rav*).

3. *Oleilos* are clusters of grapes that have not developed normally (as described in *Peah* 7:4). The Torah awards *oleilos* to the poor (see *Vayikra* 19:10; *Devarim* 24:21). Thus, they too are exempt from *maasros* (*Rash; Rambam Commentary*).

4. Separating *maasros* from one species for another is invalid. Therefore, the other *tevel* produce must be the same species as the mixture (see *Terumos* 2:4).

משניות חלה / פרק ג: אוכלין

מוֹצִיא תְּרוּמָה וּתְרוּמַת מַעֲשֵׂר לַכֹּל, וְהַשְּׁאָר מַעֲשֵׂר וּמַעֲשֵׂר שֵׁנִי לְפִי חֶשְׁבּוֹן.

— רע"ב —

והשאר מעשר ראשון ומעשר שני. או מעשר עני, אין מוציא אלא לפי חשבון. ולא שלא יפריש

אלא לפי חשבון, דהא אי אפשר להפריש תרומת מעשר, עד שיפריש תחלה מעשר על הכל, ועוד אי אפשר מפריש מעשר על הכל, הרי כל מה שמעשר יש בהן חולין לפי חשבון, ונמצא מפריש מן הפטור על החיוב, אלא כל המעשרות צריך להפריש על הכל, אבל אינו צריך ליתן ללוי ולעני אלא לפי חשבון, והשאר מעורב עם פירותיו, וכן מעשר שני אין צריך לפדות אלא לפי חשבון. אבל תרומה ותרומת מעשר שהן במיתה, כשמפריש על הכל, נמצאו חולין שבהן מדומעין, וצריך שיתן הכל לכהן:

מוֹצִיא — *tevel* from which to separate *maasros* for the *tevel* in this mixture, **תְּרוּמָה וּתְרוּמַת מַעֲשֵׂר לַכֹּל** — he must separate the amount of *terumah* and *terumas maaser* necessary for the entire mixture and give those portions to the Kohen.[5] **וְהַשְּׁאָר מַעֲשֵׂר וּמַעֲשֵׂר שֵׁנִי לְפִי חֶשְׁבּוֹן** — And, as for the remaining *maasros* of **maaser rishon** and **maaser sheni** (or *maasar ani*, when applicable), the amount of fruit he treats as *maaser* is **in proportion** to the amount of *tevel* in the olives or grapes mixture. As with *terumah,* he must designate an amount of *maasros* that is sufficient for the entire mixture. Nevertheless, unlike *terumah,* he is not obligated to give all the fruits he designated as *maaser rishon* to a Levi or give the entire *maasar ani* to the poor. Nor is he required to redeem the entire *maaser sheni*. Rather, he gives or redeems only the amount of *maaser* that corresponds to the amount of *tevel* in the mixture.[6]

NOTES
---

5. First, he separates *terumah gedolah.* Then, he separates one-tenth as *maaser rishon,* which must be separated before *terumas maaser.* [See further in the Mishnah for what is done with the *maaser rishon.*] Afterward, he separates one-tenth of the *maaser rishon* as *terumas maaser,* and gives the *terumah gedolah* and *terumas maaser* to a Kohen (*Rav*).

Although the Mishnah states, "he must separate *terumah* and *terumas maaser* for the entire mixture," it does not mean that the other *maasros* need not be designated for the *entire* mixture. In actuality, other *maasros* must also be designated for the entire mixture. However, only part of those *maasros* is treated as *maaser.* The portions separated as *terumah* and *terumas maaser,* on the other hand, must be treated entirely as *terumah* and given in their entirety to the Kohen (*Rav*). See further.

6. For example, the mixture contains 600 *tevel* fruits and 400 *chullin* fruits (that is, fruits that he must leave for the poor, which are not subject to *maasros*). When *maaser rishon* is being separated, the owner must separate 10 percent of the entire 1,000-fruit mixture (100 fruits) as *maaser rishon.* Nevertheless, since only 600 fruits in the mixture are *tevel,* he gives the Levi only 60 of those fruits. Similarly, when separating *maasar ani* or *maaser sheni* from the remaining 900 fruits, he separates 90 fruits, which he designates as *maasar ani* or *maaser sheni.* Yet, since only sixty percent of the fruits (540 fruits) are *tevel,* he needs to take only 54 of those 90 fruits, and give them to the poor (if they are *maasar ani*) or redeem them (if they are *maaser sheni*). He may keep the rest for himself.

The portions designated as *terumah* and *terumas maaser,* however, must be given in their *entirety* to a Kohen. The difference between them is as follows:

Terumah and *terumas maaser,* besides belonging to the Kohanim, are *forbidden* to non-Kohanim. The owner is now faced with the following predicament: He *owes* the Kohen only the *terumah* and *terumas maaser* fruits that are in the mixture that he separated, which in our case make up 60 percent of the mixture. But if he gives the Kohen only 60 percent of the mixture (the percentage assumed to be

[59] **MISHNAH CHALLAH** / Chapter 3: *Ochlin*　　　3/10

- רע״ב -

[י] **הַנּוֹטֵל** שְׂאֹר מֵעִסַּת חִטִּים וְנוֹתֵן לְתוֹךְ עִסַּת אֹרֶז, אִם יֵשׁ בָּהּ טַעַם דָּגָן, חַיֶּבֶת בְּחַלָּה; וְאִם לָאו, פְּטוּרָה. אִם כֵּן, לָמָה אָמְרוּ הַטֶּבֶל אוֹסֵר כָּל שֶׁהוּא?

(י) הנוטל שאור מעסת חטין. שלא הורמה חלתה: ואם לאו פטורה. דאין הטבל אוסרה, כיון דליכא טעם: אם כן למה אמרו הטבל אוסר בכל שהוא. דאמרן לעיל (משנה ח) כשאין לו פרנסה שמביא על הכל. הני מילי במינו, אבל שלא במינו כי האי דחטין

---

[10] The Mishnah discusses another case in which a person mixed a dough of *tevel* (dough which is subject to *challah* from which *challah* has not been separated) into dough that is not subject to *challah*:

הַנּוֹטֵל שְׂאֹר מֵעִסַּת חִטִּים — **If someone takes** a piece of **sourdough from a wheat dough** of *tevel* וְנוֹתֵן לְתוֹךְ עִסַּת אֹרֶז — **and places it into a rice dough,** which is not subject to *challah*,[1] the law is as follows: אִם יֵשׁ בָּהּ טַעַם דָּגָן — **If the flavor of the** wheat **grain can be tasted in [the dough],** חַיֶּבֶת בְּחַלָּה — **[the entire mixture] is subject to the obligation of** *challah*.[2] וְאִם לָאו — **But if the flavor of the wheat grain cannot** be tasted in the dough, פְּטוּרָה — **it is exempt** from *challah*. The sourdough is nullified in the majority of *chullin* rice dough, and there is no requirement at all to separate *challah*.[3]

The Mishnah above (Mishnah 8) teaches that when *tevel* sourdough is placed into *chullin* dough, the entire dough becomes forbidden no matter how little *tevel* the mixture contains. The Mishnah addresses the difference between the ruling of that Mishnah and this one:

אִם כֵּן — **If it is so,** as we have just said, that the *tevel* sourdough forbids the rice dough only if the flavor of the sourdough can be tasted, לָמָה אָמְרוּ הַטֶּבֶל — **regarding what** case **did [the Sages] say that** *tevel* **forbids a**

NOTES

terumah), many of the fruits he gives the Kohen will likely be *chullin*, and many of the fruits that remain in his possession will likely be *terumah*, and forbidden to a non-Kohen! His only solution is to give all of the fruits separated to a Kohen. And, as for the *chullin* fruits (40 percent of the fruits) that he gave the Kohen, to which the Kohen is not entitled, he can request payment from the Kohen for them.

Maaser rishon, on the other hand, is not forbidden to non-Leviim. Therefore, the owner may simply give the Levi 60 fruits, which is the amount to which the Levi is entitled. The fact that many of the fruits that he gives to the Levi will be *chullin,* and many of the fruits that remain in his possession will be *maaser,* does not present a problem. Since he has given the Levi the *amount* of fruit to which he is entitled, he may keep and eat the rest.

The same reasoning applies to *maaser ani.* By giving the poor the *amount* of fruit to which they are entitled, he has fulfilled his obligation. And regarding *maaser sheni,* he has fulfilled his obligation by redeeming the fruit that require to be tithed, even if he cannot identify them (*Rav*). [This is because it is never necessary to identify the *maaser sheni* fruits in order to redeem them; one can simply declare that wherever the fruits that are *maaser sheni* are located, they are redeemed with the redemption money.]

[10]
1. See Mishnah 1:1.
2. If the flavor of the *tevel* sourdough can be tasted in the mixture, the entire mixture becomes subject to *challah,* even though most of the dough is not subject to *challah.* See Mishnah 7 note 2.
3. *Rash.*

משניות חלה / פרק ג: אוכלין

מִין בְּמִינוֹ; וְשֶׁלֹּא בְמִינוֹ, בְּנוֹתֵן טַעַם.

— רע"ב —

באחר, בנותן טעם. דטעמא דטבל בכל שהוא, משום דכהתירו דחטה אחת פוטרת את הכרי כך איסורו, והאי טעמא לא שייך אלא מין במינו:

מִין **בְּמִינוֹ** — They said it regarding a mixture of a food of **one kind with its own kind**, as is the case in Mishnah 8, where both the sourdough and dough are made of wheat. In that case the mixture is prohibited even if the *tevel* cannot be tasted. **וְשֶׁלֹּא בְמִינוֹ** — But regarding a mixture of a food of one kind **with an unlike** (i.e., a different) **kind**, such as the case in our Mishnah, of wheat and rice, **בְּנוֹתֵן טַעַם** — the law is that *tevel* prohibits only **when it gives taste** to the mixture.[4]

NOTES

4. The Gemara (*Avodah Zarah* 73b) explains: Under Biblical law, even a single kernel of grain may be separated as *terumah*, no matter how much grain there is in the pile. [The requirement to separate approximately 1/50 is a Rabbinic enactment.] Therefore, the Rabbis decreed that just as a single kernel of grain may be separated as *terumah*, so too a single kernel of *tevel* is significant enough to make an entire pile of *chullin* forbidden. This applies, however, only if the *tevel* and the *chullin* are of the same species of produce [מִין בְּמִינוֹ]. Since one species cannot be designated as *terumah* for a different species (*Terumos* 2:4), *tevel* of a different species does not prohibit the mixture (*Rav*).

Chapter Four

ד/א

- רע"ב -

פרק רביעי — שתי נשים. (א) שתי נשים. אפילו הן ממין אחד פטור. ואין נשיכה ועירוף סל מצרפן, כיון שמקפידות.

[א] שְׁתֵּי נָשִׁים שֶׁעָשׂוּ שְׁנֵי קַבִּין, וְנָגְעוּ זֶה בָזֶה, אֲפִלּוּ הֵם מִמִּין אֶחָד, פְּטוּרִים. וּבִזְמַן שֶׁהֵם שֶׁל אִשָּׁה אַחַת, מִין בְּמִינוֹ, חַיָּב.

ואפילו לשו שני קבין כאחד, כיון דסופן ליחלק, פטורות. וסתם מתניתין כבית הלל דאמר (עדיות א,ב) קביים לחלה, ואינה הלכה, דקיימא לן דחמשה רביעים הוא שיעור חלה: ובזמן שהן של אשה אחת. סתם אשה אחת אינה מקפדת אם העסות נוגעות זו בזו: מין במינו חייב. בנשיכה או בצרוף סל:

---

[1] Two portions of dough, each of which is too small to be subject to the obligation of *challah,* but together *are* large enough to be subject to *challah,* can, under certain circumstances, combine into a single *challah*-liable dough. Earlier (Mishnah 2:4), the Tanna cited a dispute regarding how they must be attached for them to combine. According to the Sages, the two doughs must "bite" into each other, meaning that they must stick to each other so firmly that some of one dough would remain attached to the other if they were to be pulled apart. According to R' Eliezer, if the two doughs are placed touching each other in one basket they combine.

This Mishnah notes other conditions that must be met for the combined dough to be subject to *challah*:

שְׁתֵּי נָשִׁים שֶׁעָשׂוּ שְׁנֵי קַבִּין — **If two women made two** doughs of **one** *kav* **each,**[1] וְנָגְעוּ זֶה בָזֶה — **and the two doughs touched each other,** forming a combined dough large enough to be subject to *challah,*[2] אֲפִלּוּ הֵם מִמִּין אֶחָד פְּטוּרִים — the law is that **even if [the two doughs] were** made **from the same kind** of flour, **they are exempt** from a *challah* obligation. This is because the combined doughs of different people are not viewed as a single dough.[3] וּבִזְמַן שֶׁהֵם שֶׁל אִשָּׁה אַחַת — **But when [the two doughs] belong to one woman,** the law is as follows: מִין בְּמִינוֹ חַיָּב — **If one kind** of dough is joined **with its own kind** of dough (for example, if both doughs are made of wheat flour), the combined

--- NOTES ---

[1]
1. Each dough did not contain the minimum amount of flour that is subject to *challah*. [This Mishnah, which discusses a case where the doughs together contain two *kavs* of flour, is following the opinion (*Eduyos* 1:2) that a dough is not subject to the *challah* obligation unless it was made with a minimum of two *kavs* of flour. The halachah, however, follows the view that there is a *challah* obligation as long as the dough was made with 1¼ *kavs* of flour (*Rav*). See also Mishnah 1:4 note 3.]

[Although the Mishnah discusses women, the rulings of this Mishnah apply equally to men as well. Women are mentioned because they bear the main responsibility for fulfilling the mitzvah of *challah* (*Tos. Anshei Shem;* see *Shabbos* 2:6 with *Rav*).]

2. According to R' Eliezer the doughs touched while in the same basket; according to the Sages, they stuck to each other so firmly that some of one dough would remain attached to the other if they were to be pulled apart.

3. Since each woman is careful to keep her portions separate, each dough is considered on its own. In fact, even if the women would knead their portions together into a single large dough, but they plan to bake each portion separately, the doughs of the two women are viewed as being separate (*Rav,* as explained by *Mishnah Rishonah*).

[63] **MISHNAH CHALLAH** / Chapter 4: *Shtei Nashim* 4/2

– רע״ב –

(ב) הַחִטִּים אֵינָן מִצְטָרְפוֹת עִם הַכֹּל. אִם הָיוּ שְׁתֵּי עִסּוֹת, אַחַת שֶׁל חִטִּים וְאַחַת שֶׁל מִין אַחֵר מֵחֲמֵשֶׁת הַמִּינִים, וְאֵין בְּאַחַת מֵהֶן שִׁעוּר חַלָּה, וְנוֹשְׁכוֹת זוֹ בָזוֹ: הַשְּׂעוֹרִים מִצְטָרְפוֹת עִם הַכֹּל. אַף עִם הַכֻּסְּמִין, וְאַף עַל גַּב דְּמִין חִטִּים הֵן, לָאו דַּוְקָא מִין חִטִּים, אֶלָּא מִין שְׂעוֹרִים וְאַף מִין חִטִּים, וְהָכִי פָּרֵישְׁנָא לָהּ בְּרֵישׁ פֶּרֶק קַמָּא:

וְשֶׁלֹּא בְמִינוֹ, פָּטוּר.

[ב] אֵיזֶה הוּא מִין בְּמִינוֹ? הַחִטִּים אֵינָן מִצְטָרְפוֹת עִם הַכֹּל, אֶלָּא עִם הַכֻּסְּמִין. הַשְּׂעוֹרִים מִצְטָרְפוֹת עִם הַכֹּל חוּץ מִן הַחִטִּים. רַבִּי יוֹחָנָן בֶּן נוּרִי אוֹמֵר:

dough is **subject to** *challah*.[4]   וְשֶׁלֹּא בְמִינוֹ פָּטוּר — However, if one **kind** of dough is joined **with another kind** of dough (for example, wheat dough with barley dough), the combined dough is **exempt** from the *challah* obligation.[5]

[2] The previous Mishnah stated that two small portions of dough that are touching combine into a single *challah*-liable dough if the two portions are made from the same kind of flour. There are five types of grain that are subject to the *challah* obligation: wheat, barley, spelt, oats, and rye. This Mishnah discusses which of these types of grain are considered "the same kind," and combine with one another to become a single *challah*-liable dough:

אֵיזֶה הוּא מִין בְּמִינוֹ — **Which** grains are similar enough to be viewed as "**a kind** of grain combined **with its** own **kind**" with regard to combining into a single *challah*-liable dough?   הַחִטִּים אֵינָן מִצְטָרְפוֹת עִם הַכֹּל אֶלָּא עִם הַכֻּסְּמִין — **Wheat does not combine with any** grain **other than spelt**. Wheat is not similar to barley, rye, or oats. Thus, it does not combine with those grains. But wheat *is* similar to spelt, and those two grains will thus combine.[1]   הַשְּׂעוֹרִים מִצְטָרְפוֹת עִם הַכֹּל חוּץ מִן הַחִטִּים — **Barley**, on the other hand, **combines with every** grain **except for wheat**. Barley is similar to spelt, rye, and oats, but is not similar to wheat. Thus, barley combines with spelt, rye, or oats, but not with wheat.[2]   רַבִּי יוֹחָנָן בֶּן נוּרִי אוֹמֵר — **R' Yochanan ben Nuri says:**

─────────────── NOTES ───────────────

4. Typically, a woman does not mind if her own doughs touch each other [or join together (see *Challas Lechem, Sheyarei Berachah,* end of 5:16)]. Therefore, when they join together they are considered one large dough, as long as they are made from the same type of flour (*Rav*).

5. Normally, when a woman makes two doughs from different kinds of flour, she is careful to keep them separate (*Meiri* to Mishnah 2:3; see *Tiferes Yisrael*). [Nevertheless, if a single dough is kneaded from a mixture of different kinds of flour, the varieties do combine to establish a *challah* obligation; see Mishnah 1:1 (*Meleches Shlomo*).]

[2]

1. Thus, a wheat dough and a spelt dough combine to form a single large dough that is subject to *challah* (*Rav*). However, a wheat dough and a dough made from any of the other three species are viewed as separate, and both are exempt from *challah*.

This, however, applies only to *separate* doughs that were joined. As was taught earlier (Mishnah 1:1), when flour of two or more of the five grains are kneaded together, they combine into a single large *challah*-liable dough — regardless of whether the types of flour are similar or not (*Rambam Commentary*).

2. Spelt is unique in that it shares characteristics with both wheat and barley. Therefore, it combines with either one (*Rav*). Rye and oats, however, share characteristics (and thus combine) only with barley, not with wheat.

משניות חלה / פרק ד: שתי נשים

- רע"ב -

שאר המינים מצטרפין זה עם זה. כגון כוסמין ושבולת שועל ושיפון. והלכה כרבי יוחנן בן נורי: (ג) שני קבין: של אחד מחמשת המינים שחייבין בחלה: וקב אורז או תרומה. באמצע: אין מצטרפין. להתחייב בחלה:

משנה

[ג] **שְׁנֵי** קַבִּים, וְקַב אֹרֶז אוֹ קַב תְּרוּמָה בָּאֶמְצַע, אֵינָן מִצְטָרְפִין.

שְׁאָר הַמִּינִים מִצְטָרְפִין זֶה עִם זֶה.

שְׁאָר הַמִּינִים מִצְטָרְפִין זֶה עִם זֶה — **The other kinds** of grain besides wheat and barley, namely, spelt, oats, and rye, all **combine with one another.**[3]

[3] Having discussed how two attached doughs can combine into a single *challah*-obligated dough, the Mishnah discusses when doughs that are not directly attached to each other can combine:

שְׁנֵי קַבִּים — If someone made **two** doughs of one *kav* each, **וְקַב אֹרֶז אוֹ קַב תְּרוּמָה בָּאֶמְצַע** — **and** a dough made from **a** *kav* **of rice** flour **or** from **a** *kav* **of** *terumah* (which are not subject to *challah*) **is between** the two doughs, connecting them,[1] **אֵינָן מִצְטָרְפִין** — the two [doughs] **do not combine** into a single *challah*-liable dough, because they are not connected with a dough that is subject to the obligation of *challah*.[2]

---- NOTES ----

3. R' Yochanan ben Nuri is not disputing the Tanna Kamma. Rather, he is providing information about spelt, rye, and oats not explicitly taught by the Tanna Kamma. The Tanna Kamma has defined the status of wheat and barley, but not the status of spelt, rye, and oats. Nonetheless, we already know that according to the Tanna Kamma, spelt combines with either wheat or barley, while rye and oats combine with barley, but not with wheat. We do not know, however, whether these three grains combine with one another. Accordingly, R' Yochanan ben Nuri now explains that the Tanna Kamma maintains that these three grains *do* combine with one another (*Rambam*, according to *Kesef Mishneh, Hilchos Bikkurim* 7:3).

In summary: (1) Wheat combines only with spelt. (2) Spelt combines with everything. (3) Barley, rye, and oats combine with each other and with spelt, but not with wheat. See chart.

[3]

1. In this case, *chullin* (non-*terumah*) flour of any of the five types of grain that are subject to the obligation of *challah* was used to make two doughs containing only one *kav* of flour each (*Rav*). A third dough made from rice or *terumah* flour (both of which are exempt from *challah*; see Mishnah 1:4 and note 9 there) was then attached to the sides of the wheat doughs. The dough stuck so firmly that some of one dough would remain attached to the other if they were to be pulled apart (*Rambam Commentary*).

2. *Challah*-exempt dough cannot serve as a "bridge" to combine two small wheat doughs into a single *challah*-obligated dough. [Thus, even a rice dough or *terumah* dough made with *two kavs* of flour would not serve to combine the small doughs, since it is exempt from the *challah* obligation regardless of its

	WHEAT	BARLEY	SPELT	OATS	RYE
WHEAT	--	No	Yes	No	No
BARLEY	No	--	Yes	Yes	Yes
SPELT	Yes	Yes	--	Yes	Yes
OATS	No	Yes	Yes	--	Yes
RYE	No	Yes	Yes	Yes	--

[65] **MISHNAH CHALLAH** / Chapter 4: *Shtei Nashim* 4/4

– רע״ב –

(ד) יטול מן האמצע. ממקום שנושכין זה את זה, נמלא מפריש משתיהן: וחכמים אוסרים. שהרווחה סבור שמותר לתרוס ולעשר מן החדש על הישן ומן הישן על החדש. והלכה כחכמים:

דָּבָר שֶׁנִּטְּלָה חַלָּתוֹ בָּאֶמְצַע, מִצְטָרְפִין, שֶׁכְּבָר נִתְחַיֵּב בְּחַלָּה.

[ד] **קַב** חָדָשׁ וְקַב יָשָׁן שֶׁנָּשְׁכוּ זֶה בָזֶה, רַבִּי יִשְׁמָעֵאל אוֹמֵר: יִטּוֹל מִן הָאֶמְצַע, וַחֲכָמִים אוֹסְרִים.

דָּבָר שֶׁנִּטְּלָה חַלָּתוֹ בָּאֶמְצַע מִצְטָרְפִין — However, if **something** (i.e., a dough that was subject to the *challah* obligation) **whose** *challah* **has** already **been separated is between** the two doughs, the two [doughs] **do combine.** שֶׁכְּבָר נִתְחַיֵּב בְּחַלָּה — The reason for this is **because** [the connecting dough] **has been previously subject to** *challah.* Unlike a dough of rice flour or *terumah,* a dough from which *challah* has been separated *was* subject to a *challah* obligation at one point. Therefore, it can serve to combine the two other doughs into one *challah*-liable dough. [3]

[4] Dough made with flour of one year's grain cannot be designated as *challah* for dough made with flour of another year's grain (*Rambam Commentary,* based on *Terumos* 1:5).[1] This Mishnah discusses a case where dough made from the flour of one year's grain was joined with dough made with flour of another year's grain:

קַב חָדָשׁ וְקַב יָשָׁן שֶׁנָּשְׁכוּ זֶה בָזֶה — **If a dough made from a *kav* of new** flour (i.e., flour of this year's grain) **and** a dough made from **a *kav* of old** flour (i.e., flour of last year's grain) were firmly attached, so **that they "bite" into one another,** the law is as follows: רַבִּי יִשְׁמָעֵאל אוֹמֵר — **R' Yishmael says:** יִטּוֹל מִן הָאֶמְצַע — **One separates** *challah* **from the middle** point (i.e., the point where the two doughs are joined), so that he is separating the *challah* from both doughs.[2] וַחֲכָמִים אוֹסְרִים — **But the Sages forbid** doing so.[3]

─────────── NOTES ───────────

size (*Derech Emunah, Hilchos Bikkurim* 7:41).]

3. Any dough that could be subject to *challah* can cause the other doughs to combine. In fact, this is true even if the connecting dough is made from barley, and the other doughs are made from wheat, which normally do not combine (see previous Mishnah). Nevertheless, since the dough is made from a grain that is subject to a *challah* obligation, it can serve as a bridge to connect the two doughs into a single *challah*-obligated dough (*Rash*).

[4]

1. For the purposes of *challah,* grain "belongs" to the year in which its kernels were formed. Thus, flour made from kernels of grain that formed in the current year is known as "new flour," while flour made from kernels formed in a previous year is known as "old flour." See Mishnah 1:3 (where another opinion is cited) and *Yerushalmi* there.

2. *Yerushalmi* explains that R' Yishmael derives the law that dough from two different years combine by means of a *kal vachomer* [a type of logical argument] (*Rash*).

3. The Sages agree that according to Biblical law, the new and old doughs combine to become a single two-*kav* dough that is subject to *challah*. Nevertheless, they were concerned that if people would separate *challah* in the way presented by R' Yishmael, they

ד/ה

משניות חלה / פרק ד: שתי נשים [66]

- רע"ב -

מן הקב. שאין בו שיעור חלה: רבי עקיבא אומר חלה. והוא שהשלים על העסה אחר כך כשיעור חלה, דכיון שנשלם השיעור הוייא חלה למפרע: אינה חלה. כיון שבשעה שהפרישה היתה העסה פטורה.

הַנּוֹטֵל חַלָּה מִן הַקַּב, רַבִּי עֲקִיבָא אוֹמֵר: חַלָּה, וַחֲכָמִים אוֹמְרִים: אֵינָהּ חַלָּה.

[ה] **שְׁנֵי** קַבִּין שֶׁנִּטְּלָה חַלָּתוֹ שֶׁל זֶה בִּפְנֵי עַצְמוֹ וְשֶׁל זֶה בִּפְנֵי עַצְמוֹ, חָזַר וַעֲשָׂאָן עִסָּה אַחַת, רַבִּי עֲקִיבָא פּוֹטֵר,

והלכה כחכמים: (ה) **רבי עקיבא פוטר**. ואזדא לטעמיה דהדרא והויא חלה למפרע:

The Mishnah turns to discuss a case where *challah* was separated from a dough that was made with less than the minimum amount that is subject to the *challah* obligation:

הַנּוֹטֵל חַלָּה מִן הַקַּב — Regarding **someone who separates** *challah* **from a** dough made with only **a** *kav* of flour, and later adds enough dough to make it large enough to be subject to *challah*, רַבִּי עֲקִיבָא אוֹמֵר — **R' Akiva says:** חַלָּה — What he separated is considered *challah* retroactively.[4] וַחֲכָמִים אוֹמְרִים — **But the Sages say:** אֵינָהּ חַלָּה — **It is not** *challah*, since it was separated before the dough became subject to the *challah* obligation.[5]

[5] The Mishnah presents another dispute between R' Akiva and the Sages, which is dependent on the dispute of the previous Mishnah:

שְׁנֵי קַבִּין — **If someone made two** doughs of one *kav* each, שֶׁנִּטְּלָה חַלָּתוֹ שֶׁל זֶה בִּפְנֵי עַצְמוֹ וְשֶׁל זֶה בִּפְנֵי עַצְמוֹ — **and the** *challah* **of this dough was separated by itself, and the** *challah* **of this dough was separated by itself,** חָזַר וַעֲשָׂאָן עִסָּה אַחַת — **and he then went and combined [the doughs] into a single** two-*kav* **dough,** רַבִּי עֲקִיבָא פּוֹטֵר — **R' Akiva exempts** the combined dough from a *challah* obligation, because *challah* was already separated. This ruling is in line with R' Akiva's position in the previous Mishnah, where he rules that if *challah* was separated for a dough containing less than the minimum amount of flour it is valid, as long as the final size of the dough was large enough to

---

NOTES

might mistakenly conclude that *terumos* and *maasros* too may be separated from new produce for old produce and vice versa, when in fact it is forbidden (*Rav*). The only solution in this case is that *challah* be taken from two other obligated doughs — from a new dough for the *kav* of new dough, and from an old dough for the *kav* of old dough in the mixture (*Rash*).

4. R' Akiva agrees with the other Tannaim who hold that dough made from a *kav* of flour is not subject to the *challah* obligation, as we see from his ruling in

Mishnah 2:3 (*Tos. Yom Tov*). Nevertheless, he holds that once the dough is large enough to become subject to the *challah* obligation, it is viewed as having been obligated originally as well — from the time the first *kav* was kneaded. Thus, the *challah* that was originally separated is valid (*Rav*).

5. Since at the time when *challah* was separated the dough did not contain enough flour to be subject to the *challah* obligation, the Sages maintain that the separation is not valid, and it was never considered *challah* (*Rav*).

[67] **MISHNAH CHALLAH** / Chapter 4: *Shtei Nashim* 4/5

- רע"ב -

נִמְצָא חוּמְרוֹ קוּלוֹ. וַחֲכָמִים מְחַיְּבִין. נִמְצָא חֻמְרוֹ קֻלּוֹ.

חוּמְרוֹ שֶׁל רַבִּי עֲקִיבָא

דְּאָמַר לְעֵיל (מִשְׁנָה ד) בְּנוֹטֵל חַלָּה מִקַּב דְּהָוְיָא חַלָּה וְקֹדֶשׁ, גּוֹרֵס לוֹ לְהָקֵל וְלִפְטוֹר בִּשְׁנֵי קַבִּים שֶׁנָּטְלָה חַלָּתוֹ שֶׁל זֶה בִּפְנֵי עַצְמוֹ וְשֶׁל זֶה בִּפְנֵי עַצְמוֹ:

---

be subject to the obligation. וַחֲכָמִים מְחַיְּבִין — **But the Sages require** that *challah* be separated. In their opinion, the original *challah* separation was not valid, since each dough contained less than the minimum amount of flour. Therefore, since the combined dough *does* contain the minimum amount of flour, it is necessary to separate *challah* from the combined dough.

The Mishnah links this to the previous Mishnah:

נִמְצָא חֻמְרוֹ קֻלּוֹ — **It** thus **emerges that [R' Akiva's] stringency** in the previous Mishnah, where he rules that the *challah* initially separated has the sanctity of *challah*, **leads to his leniency** in this Mishnah, where he exempts the combined dough from *challah*.[1]

[6] The Mishnah discusses a situation where there is a doubt whether *challah* has been separated from a dough. The Mishnah refers to such dough as "dough of *demai*." Normally, *challah* may be separated either from the dough itself, or from other dough that is subject to *challah*. This discussion pertains to designating a dough from which *challah* has not been separated as *challah* for dough of *demai* that is *tamei*:[1]

NOTES

[5]

1. R' Akiva's lenient ruling in this Mishnah, regarding the combined dough, is based on his stringent ruling in the previous Mishnah, regarding the original *challah* separation. Since the initial *challah* separation is effective, there is no need to separate *challah* again after the doughs are combined (*Rav*). On the other hand, the Sages' leniency regarding the original *challah* separation leads to their stringent ruling regarding the combined dough. Since the initial *challah* separation never took effect, the doughs become subject to the *challah* obligation now, when they are combined (*Rash*).

[6]

1. See *Rambam, Hilchos Bikkurim* 7:13.

Normally, the term *demai* is used in the context of *maasros* (tithes), in reference to produce purchased from an *am haaretz* ("unlearned person"; pl. *amei haaretz*). The Rabbis decreed that the purchaser must tithe such produce, since there was a significant minority of *amei haaretz* who neglected to tithe their produce. Here, however, we are not discussing dough that was made from produce purchased from an *am haaretz*, since there was no requirement for the *am haaretz* to separate *challah* from such produce (because the obligation does not take effect until it is kneaded). Moreover, even if dough or bread itself was purchased from an *am haaretz*, we may, in fact, trust an *am haaretz* that *challah* was separated, since we do not find that *amei haaretz* were lax about separating *challah*. Rather, dough of *demai* refers to dough whose status is in doubt for some other reason — such as if there are contradictory testimonies whether *challah* was separated from it. The term *demai* is used in a borrowed sense to describe dough whose obligation for *challah* is in doubt (*Mishnah Rishonah*).

Commentators offer various explanations to this Mishnah (referred to by *Tiferes Yisrael* as "a difficult Mishnah"). Each explanation, though, has its difficulties. We have followed the approach taken by *Rambam* (*Hilchos Bikkurim* 7:13). [*Rav*, however, explains the Mishnah as referring to actual produce of an *am haaretz*. See *Tos. Yom Tov* and other commentaries for further discussion.]

משניות חלה / פרק ד: שתי נשים [68]

[ו] **נוֹטֵל** אָדָם כְּדֵי חַלָּה מֵעִסָּה שֶׁלֹּא הוּרְמָה חַלָּתָהּ, לַעֲשׂוֹתָהּ בְּטָהֳרָה, לִהְיוֹת מַפְרִישׁ עָלֶיהָ וְהוֹלֵךְ חַלַּת דְּמַאי עַד שֶׁתִּסָּרַח, שֶׁחַלַּת דְּמַאי נִטֶּלֶת מִן הַטָּהוֹר עַל הַטָּמֵא וְשֶׁלֹּא מִן הַמֻּקָּף.

– רע"ב –

(ו) נוטל אדם כדי חלה וכו'. הרולה ללוש כמה עסות של דמאי טמא, יכול לקבוע חלתן מעסה טהורה שלא הורמה חלתה, ותהיה זאת העסה הטהורה קבועה לחלה על כל

עסות שילוש מן הדמאי הטמא: **עד שתסרח**. עסה זו ולא תהיה ראויה למאכל אדם, שבדמאי הקילו לתרום מן הטהור על הטמא ושלא מן המוקף, והקלו נמי לתרום מן הרע על היפה. וחלת דמאי הייינו הלוקח תבואה מעם הארץ ומאכילה לעניים ולאכסניא, כדתנן (דמאי ג,א) מאכילין את העניים דמאי ואת האכסניא דמאי, וחלה שמפרישים ממנה היא חלת דמאי:

נוֹטֵל אָדָם כְּדֵי חַלָּה מֵעִסָּה שֶׁלֹּא הוּרְמָה חַלָּתָהּ — A person may separate an amount that can be used as *challah* from a *tahor* dough whose *challah* has not yet been separated,[2] לַעֲשׂוֹתָהּ בְּטָהֳרָה — and take care to keep it in a state of *taharah*, לִהְיוֹת מַפְרִישׁ עָלֶיהָ וְהוֹלֵךְ חַלַּת דְּמַאי — in order to continually designate portions of it as *challah* for doughs of *demai* that are *tamei*.[3] עַד שֶׁתִּסָּרַח — He may continue designating *challah* from the dough he has separated **until it becomes spoiled** to the point that it is no longer fit for human consumption. At that point, it is not considered food, and can no longer be designated as *challah*.

Ordinarily, the portion one wishes to separate as *terumah* or *challah* must be in close proximity to the produce that it comes to permit. In addition, the Rabbis decreed that one may not designate produce that is *tahor* as *terumah* or *challah* for *tamei* produce (see Mishnah 1:9). The Mishnah explains why these restrictions do not apply here:

שֶׁחַלַּת דְּמַאי נִטֶּלֶת מִן הַטָּהוֹר עַל הַטָּמֵא וְשֶׁלֹּא מִן הַמֻּקָּף — It is permissible here to designate *tahor* dough as *challah* for *tamei* dough and to designate a dough that is not close by as *challah*, **because *challah* for *demai* may be taken from *tahor* dough for *tamei* dough, and from a dough that is not close by.** The restrictions on designating *tahor* dough as *challah* for *tamei* dough and on designating a dough that is not close by as *challah* do not apply to *demai*.

─────────────── NOTES ───────────────

2. A person expects to be kneading a number of doughs of *demai* that are *tamei*. Instead of separating *challah* from each of those doughs [which will be *tamei*, and may not be eaten], he may set aside a large piece of non-*demai* dough that is *tahor*, from which he will designate small portions as *challah* for the doughs of *demai* that are *tamei* (Rambam Commentary; Rav).

The piece of *tahor* dough must come from dough that is still subject to the *challah* obligation, since *challah*-exempt dough cannot be designated as *challah*. Therefore, the owner separates a large piece of dough that is still subject to the *challah* obligation, and then designates *part* of that piece as *challah* for the dough from which it was separated. The rest of the piece — which remains *challah*-obligated — may be designated as *challah* for other doughs.

3. The Mishnah will soon explain why this is permitted even though it is ordinarily forbidden to designate dough that is *tahor* as *challah* for dough that is *tamei*.

[69] **MISHNAH CHALLAH** / Chapter 4: *Shtei Nashim*

– רע"ב –

(ז) בסוריא. ארצות שכבש דוד, ואינה קדושה כקדושת ארץ ישראל: רבי אליעזר מחייב וכו'. קסבר עשו סוריא כארץ ישראל לענין מעשרות ושביעית: ורבן גמליאל פוטר. דסבר לא עשו סוריא כארץ ישראל, ואינו חייב במעשרות בסוריא אלא בזמן שהקרקע של ישראל ואין לעובד כוכבים חלק בו:

[ז] **יִשְׂרָאֵל** שֶׁהָיוּ אֲרִיסִין לְעוֹבְדֵי כּוֹכָבִים בְּסוּרְיָא, רַבִּי אֱלִיעֶזֶר מְחַיֵּב פֵּרוֹתֵיהֶם בַּמַּעְשְׂרוֹת וּבַשְּׁבִיעִית, וְרַבָּן גַּמְלִיאֵל פּוֹטֵר.

[7] Surya (a country that was located in what is now the northern part of Syria, along the banks of the Euphrates River) was conquered and added to Eretz Yisrael by King David. Since the conquest of Surya took place before the entirety of Eretz Yisrael proper was completely conquered and divided, Surya does not have the status of Eretz Yisrael according to Biblical law. This Mishnah records two disputes (one of which pertains to *challah*), regarding the status of the produce of Surya:

יִשְׂרָאֵל שֶׁהָיוּ אֲרִיסִין לְעוֹבְדֵי כּוֹכָבִים בְּסוּרְיָא — Regarding **Jews who were sharecroppers** in the fields **of idolaters in Surya**,[1] רַבִּי אֱלִיעֶזֶר מְחַיֵּב פֵּרוֹתֵיהֶם בַּמַּעְשְׂרוֹת וּבַשְּׁבִיעִית — **R' Eliezer** rules that **their produce** is Rabbinically subject to the laws of *maasros* and *Shemittah*, because Rabbinic law equates Surya with Eretz Yisrael with regard to the laws of *maasros* and *Shemittah*.[2] וְרַבָּן גַּמְלִיאֵל פּוֹטֵר — **But Rabban Gamliel** rules that it is **exempt** from these laws. In his view, the Rabbinic obligations of *maasros* and *Shemittah* in Surya are limited to produce grown on land owned entirely by Jews.[3]

We will see in the next Mishnah that although there is no Biblical obligation outside of Eretz Yisrael to separate *challah*, the Rabbis decreed that, in fact, *two* portions of *challah* are separated — one is burned and the other is given to a Kohen.[4] In Eretz Yisrael, however, only one portion is separated.

────── NOTES ──────

[7]
1. A sharecropper is not paid a set amount for his work; rather, he receives a percentage of the harvested crop from the owner of the land.

2. Produce grown in Eretz Yisrael on land owned by an idolater is subject to *maasros* and *Shemittah* (see *Gittin* 47a and *Menachos* 66b with *Tos.* ד"ה מירוח for discussion of the opinions on this matter). In R' Eliezer's opinion, the same is true for produce grown on an idolater's land in Surya. The sharecropper must therefore tithe his share of the produce during the first six years of the *Shemittah* cycle, and treat the produce of the seventh year with the holiness of *Shemittah* produce.

3. Thus, according to Rabban Gamliel, if an idolater owns any share of the land in Surya [such as where an idolater and a Jew are partners or, where a Jew works as a sharecropper on an idolater's land], the produce is not subject to the laws of *maasros* and *Shemittah* (*Rav*).

4. This is due to a Rabbinic decree that assigns *tumah* to lands outside Eretz Yisrael because of the unmarked graves located there. [Idolaters did not always bury their dead in marked graves or cemeteries. Therefore, any place in their lands might be a gravesite (*Rambam Commentary, Oholos* 2:3).] Rabbinically, *challah* is separated outside of Eretz Yisrael. However, that *challah* is *tamei* because of the *tumah* of the lands outside Eretz Yisrael. Therefore, such *challah* may not be eaten and must be burned. The Rabbis decreed, however, that an additional portion of dough should be separated outside of Eretz Yisrael and given to a Kohen to

[70] משניות חלה / פרק ד: שתי נשים

ד/ז

רַבָּן גַּמְלִיאֵל אוֹמֵר: שְׁתֵּי חַלּוֹת בְּסוּרְיָא. וְרַבִּי אֱלִיעֶזֶר אוֹמֵר: חַלָּה אֶחָת. אָחֲזוּ קֻלּוֹ שֶׁל רַבָּן גַּמְלִיאֵל וְקֻלּוֹ שֶׁל רַבִּי אֱלִיעֶזֶר. חָזְרוּ לִנְהֹג כְּדִבְרֵי רַבָּן גַּמְלִיאֵל בִּשְׁתֵּי דְרָכִים.

— רע״ב —

רבן גמליאל אומר שתי חלות בסוריא. כדרך שמפרישים שתי חלות בחולה לארץ, האחת נשרפת, מפני שהיא טמאה בטומאת ארץ העמים, והשניה תנתן לכהן, כדי שלא תשתכח תורת חלה מישראל: ורבי אליעזר אומר חלה אחת. רבי אליעזר לטעמיה דאמר עשו סוריא כארץ ישראל ואין עפרה מטמא כעפר ארץ העמים, הלכך חלה אחת ותו לא: אחזו קולו של רבן גמליאל. דפוטר סוריא ממעשרות ושביעית: וקולו של רבי אליעזר. דאומר בסוריא חלה אחת. ואנן קיימא לן (עירובין ו,ב) שטועשה כקולי דמר וכקולי דמר רשע, הלכך חזרו לעשות כרבן גמליאל בשתי דרכים, שאין סוריא כארץ ישראל, לא לענין מעשרות ושביעית כשיש לעובד כוכבים חלק בקרקע, ולא לענין חלה. וכן הלכה:

The Mishnah discusses how many portions of *challah* are separated in Surya:

רַבָּן גַּמְלִיאֵל אוֹמֵר — **Rabban Gamliel says:** שְׁתֵּי חַלּוֹת בְּסוּרְיָא — **Two** portions of *challah* are separated from dough **in Surya,** since it is outside of Eretz Yisrael. וְרַבִּי אֱלִיעֶזֶר אוֹמֵר — **But R' Eliezer says:** חַלָּה אֶחָת — **Only one** portion of *challah* is separated in Surya, because Surya is treated like Eretz Yisrael.[5]

The Mishnah concludes:

אָחֲזוּ קֻלּוֹ שֶׁל רַבָּן גַּמְלִיאֵל וְקֻלּוֹ שֶׁל רַבִּי אֱלִיעֶזֶר — **Originally, [the people] took hold** of both **the leniency of Rabban Gamliel** regarding *maasros* and *Shemittah* **and the leniency of R' Eliezer** regarding *challah.* Thus, Jewish sharecroppers in Surya did not observe the laws of *Shemittah* and *maasros,* yet they separated only a single *challah* portion from dough of Surya. חָזְרוּ לִנְהֹג כְּדִבְרֵי רַבָּן גַּמְלִיאֵל בִּשְׁתֵּי דְרָכִים — When they were made aware of the inconsistency of this approach, **they changed** their practice **to follow the words of Rabban Gamliel** (who did not equate Surya with Eretz Yisrael) **in both matters.**[6] Thus,

--- NOTES ---

eat [even if he is *tamei*], so that people living there will not forget that *challah* actually belongs to the Kohanim (*Rav*).

5. According to Rabban Gamliel, Surya was included in the decree that assigned *tumah* to lands outside Eretz Yisrael. Therefore, two portions of *challah* must be separated from dough of Surya for the same reason that this is done outside Eretz Yisrael (see previous note).

R' Eliezer, on the other hand, follows his previously stated view that the Rabbis equated Surya with Eretz Yisrael. Therefore, the Rabbinic *tumah* imposed on lands outside of Eretz Yisrael does not apply to Surya. As such, only one portion of *challah* is separated from dough in Surya (*Rav*).

6. Both disputes of R' Eliezer and Rabban Gamliel center on whether Surya has the status of Eretz Yisrael proper. Rabban Gamliel maintains that Surya is more similar to lands outside of Eretz Yisrael (even though the Rabbis applied *some* of the laws of Eretz Yisrael to Surya). Therefore, he exempts the produce of a Jewish sharecropper grown on an idolater's land in Surya from *maasros* and *Shemittah.* Similarly, he maintains that Surya is included in the Rabbinic decree of *tumah* on lands outside of Eretz Yisrael. Thus, two *challah* portions must be separated from dough of Surya. R' Eliezer, on the other hand, maintains that the Rabbis fully equated Surya with Eretz Yisrael. Produce of Surya is thus subject to the laws of *maasros* and *Shemittah,* and only one *challah* portion is taken there (*Rambam Commentary*).

Since each Tanna uses the same

[71] **MISHNAH CHALLAH** / Chapter 4: *Shtei Nashim* 4/8

[ח] **רַבָּן** גַּמְלִיאֵל אוֹמֵר: שָׁלֹשׁ אֲרָצוֹת לַחַלָּה. מֵאֶרֶץ יִשְׂרָאֵל וְעַד כְּזִיב, חַלָּה אֶחָת,

– רע״ב –

(ח) שלש ארצות. חלוקות בדין חלה: מארץ ישראל ועד כזיב. כלומר כל ארץ ישראל עד כזיב, שהיא רצועה היוצאה מטכו לצד צפון, וכבשוה עולי בבל וקדשה קדושה שניה:

the sharecroppers of Surya did not observe the laws of *maasros* and *Shemittah*, but *did* separate two *challah* portions from the dough of Surya.

[8] Biblically, the mitzvah of *challah* applies only in Eretz Yisrael, and only when most of the Jewish people are living there. However, the Rabbis required that *challah* be separated even nowadays, and even outside of Eretz Yisrael (see General Introduction). Nevertheless, different areas have different laws, based on the following:

When Joshua conquered Eretz Yisrael after the Exodus from Egypt, he sanctified the lands that he conquered. However, this sanctification ended when the First Temple was destroyed and the Jews were exiled to Babylonia (*Rambam, Hilchos Terumos* 1:5). Seventy years later, the Babylonian exiles returned to Eretz Yisrael under the leadership of Ezra. They reconquered much — but not all — of the Land, and sanctified their areas of conquest. This second sanctification, according to the view that will be followed in this Mishnah, remains in effect even today.

There are thus three regions regarding *challah*: (a) The areas sanctified by Joshua and resanctified by Ezra, which are still holy today; (b) the areas sanctified only by Joshua, which were holy until the First Temple was destroyed but are no longer holy; (c) lands that were conquered neither by Joshua nor by Ezra, and were thus never holy. The Mishnah describes how *challah* is separated in each region:

רַבָּן גַּמְלִיאֵל אוֹמֵר — **Rabban Gamliel says:** שָׁלֹשׁ אֲרָצוֹת לַחַלָּה — There are **three regions with respect to** the laws of *challah*.

The first region, the part of Eretz Yisrael resanctified by Ezra, which is still holy today:

מֵאֶרֶץ יִשְׂרָאֵל וְעַד כְּזִיב חַלָּה אֶחָת — **In the area of Eretz Yisrael until** the city of **Keziv**[1] **one** portion of *challah* is separated, which is given to a Kohen, and is eaten by him or an eligible member of his household, while he or she is *tahor*.[2]

─────────── NOTES ───────────

reasoning in both disputes, it is contradictory to follow the leniencies of both Rabban Gamliel and R' Eliezer. The practice was therefore changed to follow both the lenient and stringent rulings of Rabban Gamliel (*Rav*).

[The reason for accepting Rabban Gamliel's positions rather than those of R' Eliezer is that R' Eliezer was a disciple of Shammai, whose views are generally not accepted as halachah (*Meleches Shlomo*).]

[8]
1. Keziv was the northernmost city to be conquered and resanctified by the Jews who returned from Babylonia. Although the main northern border established by Ezra runs parallel to the town of Acco, which is *south* of Keziv, a strip of land extending northward from Acco to Keziv was also conquered and sanctified (*Rav*).

2. This area is sanctified even today, according to the view followed by this Mishnah. Nevertheless, in our times,

[72] **משניות חלה** / פרק ד: שתי נשים

ד/ח

מִכְּזִיב וְעַד הַנָּהָר וְעַד אֲמָנָה, שְׁתֵּי חַלּוֹת, אַחַת לָאוּר וְאַחַת לַכֹּהֵן. שֶׁל אוּר יֵשׁ לָהּ שִׁעוּר,

– רע"ב –

מפרישים חלה אחת ונתנת לכהן ואוכלה בטהרה: **מכזיב ועד הנהר.** לצד מזרח, ומכזיב ועד אמנה לצד מערב. ואמנה ארץ ישראל ממש לפי, שכבשוה עולי מצרים ולא כבשוה עולי בבל, וקדושה ראשונה לא קדשה לעתיד לבא. מפרישין שתי חלות, הראשונה נשרפת לפי שהיא טמאה בטומאת ארץ העמים, כיון שלא כבשוה עולי בבל, והשניה נאכלת, לפי שאין טומאת החלה הראשונה מפורסמת, שהרי אינה ארץ העמים גמורה, ואם לא היו מפרישין חלה שניה הנאכלת, יאמרו תרומה טהורה נשרפת, אבל כשמפרישין חלה שניה ונאכלת, הרואה נותן על לבו להבין טעם הדבר, או שואל לחכמים ואומרים לו: **של אור יש לה שיעור.** מפני שזאת הארץ היתה קדושה כבר, נראית חלתה כשל תורה, הלכך יפריש כשיעור שמפרישים מעיסה טמאה, אחד מעשרים וארבעה או מארבעים ושמונה:

The second region, which was conquered and sanctified by Joshua but not by Ezra:

מִכְּזִיב וְעַד הַנָּהָר וְעַד אֲמָנָה שְׁתֵּי חַלּוֹת — In the area **from Keziv** eastward **until the river, and** from Keziv westward **until the mountains of Amanah,**[3] which was originally part of Eretz Yisrael, but not conquered by Ezra, **two** *challah* **portions are separated.** אַחַת לָאוּר — **One is to be burned in the fire,** since this area is *tamei* from the *tumah* of lands outside Eretz Yisrael,[4] וְאַחַת לַכֹּהֵן — **and one is to be given to the Kohen,** so that people should understand that the one that is burned in the fire is burned because of *tumah*.[5] שֶׁל אוּר יֵשׁ לָהּ שִׁעוּר — **The one** burned **in the fire must have a** minimum **measure,**

--- NOTES ---

when the majority of the Jewish people do not live on the Land, the requirement of *challah* is Rabbinic (see introduction to this Mishnah).

As in the time when the obligation was Biblical, the Rabbis required someone who is baking for personal use to separate at least ¹⁄₂₄ of the dough as *challah*. Someone who is baking bread to sell is required to separate ¹⁄₄₈ of the dough (as set forth in Mishnah 2:7).

3. It is unclear exactly which river the Mishnah is referring to; see *Ramban*, *Gittin* 7b; *Maharit* I:84; *Tevuas HaAretz* 7a. Amanah is a mountain, or a group of mountains, in the northwestern corner of Eretz Yisrael (*Targum Yerushalmi, Bamidbar* 34:7).

4. This region, which was not resanctified by Ezra, is subject to the Rabbinic decree assigning

tumah to lands outside Eretz Yisrael (as explained in the previous Mishnah note 4). *Challah* separated in this region is therefore *tamei*, and must be burned.

5. Many people do not realize that this region is *tamei*, since it had once been part of Eretz Yisrael. Burning the *challah* of this region may thus lead people to think that *challah* that is *tahor* may be burned. The Rabbis therefore required that an additional portion of *challah* be separated, which does not have sanctity. This portion is given to a Kohen and eaten by him even if he is *tamei*. People will understand that there must be a reason why the first portion was burned and not also given to a Kohen. They will thus realize on their own [or it will be explained to them] that the first portion is burned because of the *tumah* of the lands outside Eretz Yisrael (see *Rav*).

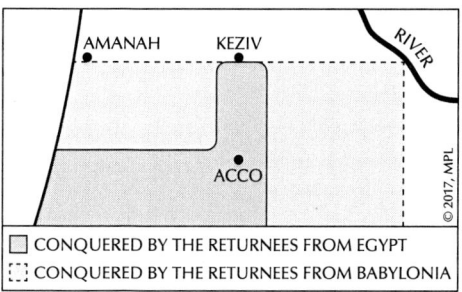

[73] **MISHNAH CHALLAH** / Chapter 4: *Shtei Nashim*

וְשֶׁל כֹּהֵן אֵין לָהּ שִׁעוּר. מִן הַנָּהָר (וְעַד) [וּמִן] אֲמָנָה וְלִפְנִים, שְׁתֵּי חַלּוֹת, אַחַת לָאוּר וְאַחַת לַכֹּהֵן. שֶׁל אוּר אֵין לָהּ שִׁעוּר, וְשֶׁל כֹּהֵן יֵשׁ לָהּ שִׁעוּר, וּטְבוּל יוֹם אוֹכְלָהּ.

– רע״ב –

ושל כהן אין לה שיעור. לפי שהיא מדברי סופרים: מן הנהר ומן אמנה ולפנים. כלומר מתחלת הנהר ולפנים ממנו, וכן מתחלת אמנה ולפנים ממנו, חולה לארץ ממש, ומפרישין שתי חלות.

ושתיהן מדברי סופרים: אחת לאור. שהיא טמאה בטומאת ארץ העמים ממש: ואחת לכהן. כדי שלא תשתכח תורת חלה שנתנת לכהן: של אור אין לה שיעור. הואיל ושתיהן מדברי סופרים, מוטב להרבות באותה שנותנין לכהן שנאכלת ולא בנשרפת: וטבול יום אוכלה. לחלת האור של חולה לארץ ותבול יום דקאמר הכא הוא כהן שטבל לקריו, שאין חלת האור של חולה לארץ אסורה אלא למי

וְשֶׁל כֹּהֵן אֵין לָהּ שִׁעוּר — while the one of the Kohen has no minimum measure.[6]

The third region was never conquered, and thus was never part of Eretz Yisrael:

מִן הַנָּהָר (וְעַד) [וּמִן] אֲמָנָה וְלִפְנִים שְׁתֵּי חַלּוֹת — **From the river**bank **and from** the foot of the **Amanah** mountains **inward** toward the river eastward and toward the mountains westward (that is, the entire area from the riverbank into the river and beyond, and from the foot of the mountains into the mountains and beyond),[7] two *challah* portions are separated: אַחַת לָאוּר — **One is to be burned in the fire,** since this area is *tamei* from the *tumah* of lands outside Eretz Yisrael, וְאַחַת לַכֹּהֵן — **and one is to be** given **to the Kohen,** so that the law that *challah* is given to a Kohen not be forgotten. שֶׁל אוּר אֵין לָהּ שִׁעוּר — **The one burned in the fire has no minimum measure,** וְשֶׁל כֹּהֵן יֵשׁ לָהּ שִׁעוּר — **while the one of the Kohen must have a minimum measure.**[8]

The Mishnah presents a situation where a single portion suffices in this third region:

וּטְבוּל יוֹם אוֹכְלָהּ — **But** a Kohen or a member of his household who is **a *tevul***

NOTES
---

6. As in the region of Eretz Yisrael that was resanctified by Ezra, a portion of *challah* that is at least ¹⁄₂₄ or ¹⁄₄₈ of the dough (depending on whether it is for private use or for sale) is separated in this region, which was not resanctified. Here, however, where two portions are separated, this requirement applies to only one of them. The Rabbis applied the requirement to the portion of *challah* that is burned, which is similar to Biblical *challah*, since it is burned because it is *tamei*. The portion given to the Kohen, however, is completely Rabbinic in origin (see *Rav;* see also *Tos. Yom Tov*).

7. *Rav.* The river itself and the Amanah mountains (and beyond) are entirely outside of Eretz Yisrael.

8. *Challah* separated in this region (which was never part of Eretz Yisrael) is not at all similar to the Biblical *challah* of Eretz Yisrael. Thus, both portions that are separated here are clearly Rabbinic in origin. Therefore, the Rabbis preferred applying the requirement to separate the minimum amount to the portion given to the Kohen, which will be eaten, rather than to the portion that will be burned.

In this case, the minimum amount of *challah* required for the portion that will be eaten by the Kohen is ¹⁄₄₈ of the dough (regardless of whether it is being made for personal use or for sale). This is the amount separated from any dough that became *tamei* unintentionally; see Mishnah 2:7 (see *Rav*). [For a discussion of why this law does not apply in the second region, see *Tos. Yom Tov*.]

משניות חלה / פרק ד: שתי נשים

רַבִּי יוֹסֵי אוֹמֵר: אֵינוֹ צָרִיךְ טְבִילָה. וַאֲסוּרָה לַזָּבִים וְלַזָּבוֹת, לַנִּדָּה וְלַיּוֹלְדוֹת,

- רע"ב -

שטומאה יוצאה עליו מגופו, אבל טמא בשאר טומאות מותר בה. הלכך בחולה לארץ היכא דאיכא כהן קטן שלא ראה קרי מימיו, או כהן גדול בשנים שטבל לקריו, מפריש חלה אחת בלבד ונותנה לכהן. ואי ליכא כהן קטן או כהן שטבל לקריו, ואיכא כהן בעל קרי, מפריש שתי חלות, אחת לאור ואין לה שיעור, ואחת לכהן ויש לה שיעור, אחד מארבעים ושמנה, כדין כל עסה שנטומאה באונס, דטומאת ארץ העמים טומאת אונס היא, ואוכלה הכהן בקריו, כדי שלא תשתכח תורת חלה מישראל: **אינו צריך טבילה.** ובעל קרי מותר בחלת חוץ לארץ. ואין הלכה כרבי יוסי: **ואסורה לזבים ולזבות.** רבנן קאמרי לה, דאילו לרבי יוסי שרי לזבים ולזבות כי היכי דשרי לבעל קרי:

yom may eat [the *challah*] that otherwise would have been burned in the fire.[9] That is, we must burn the first portion of *challah* and give a second portion to the Kohen only when there is no Kohen available who has immersed to purify himself from a bodily emission. If a Kohen who has immersed is present, the portion that would have been burned is given to him to eat, and there is no need to separate a second portion.[10]

The Mishnah presents a more lenient view:

רַבִּי יוֹסֵי אוֹמֵר — R' Yose says: אֵינוֹ צָרִיךְ טְבִילָה — He does not need to have immersed in order to eat *challah* of outside Eretz Yisrael.[11]

The Mishnah returns to the Tanna Kamma's position:

וַאֲסוּרָה לַזָּבִים וְלַזָּבוֹת לַנִּדָּה וְלַיּוֹלְדוֹת — [*Challah*] separated outside Eretz Yisrael (i.e., the portion that is separated to be burned) **is forbidden to** a Kohen or a

---- NOTES ----

9. *Tevul yom* here refers to a man who immersed in a *mikveh* to purify himself after a seminal discharge. Even after immersing, a *tevul yom* retains a trace of *tumah* for the rest of the day, and thus may not eat Biblical *challah* until nightfall. But since *challah* outside Eretz Yisrael is Rabbinic in origin, the Rabbis permitted a *tevul yom* to eat it. Moreover, a Kohen who became *tamei* from an external source, such as by touching a *neveilah* (animal carcass) or dead *sheretz*, may eat *challah* from outside Eretz Yisrael, even if he has not immersed. Only Kohanim who became *tamei* through bodily discharge (a relatively severe form of *tumah*) and have not yet immersed are forbidden to eat this *challah* (*Rav*). [This discussion pertains to the "first" portion, i.e., the one that would otherwise be burned. The second portion, which is given to a Kohen when the first portion is burned, may be eaten by him even if he is *tamei* with a severe type of *tumah*.]

10. The law stated previously in the Mishnah, that requires that two portions be separated, applies only if the only Kohanim available to receive the *challah* were *tamei* through bodily discharge. Since these Kohanim may not eat the first portion of *challah*, that portion is burned. A second portion is then separated and given to a Kohen (to remind people that *challah* of Eretz Yisrael belongs to Kohanim). This portion may be eaten even by a Kohen who is *tamei* with a severe type of *tumah*. However, when there is a Kohen available who has immersed in a *mikveh* (even if he is a *tevul yom*) or if there is a Kohen available who is under the age of nine (whose discharge does not render him *tamei*), a single portion of *challah* (measuring ¹⁄₄₈ of the dough) is given to him to eat, and there is no need to separate a second portion (*Rav*).

11. R' Yose maintains that since *challah* outside Eretz Yisrael is Rabbinic in origin, it may be eaten even by a Kohen who is *tamei* due to a bodily discharge. See note 13.

[75] **MISHNAH CHALLAH** / Chapter 4: *Shtei Nashim*

– רע"ב –

וְנֶאֱכֶלֶת עִם הַזָּר עַל הַשֻּׁלְחָן, וְנִתֶּנֶת לְכָל כֹּהֵן. ונאבלת עם הזר על השלחן. דלא גזרינן העלמה אטו אכילה: ונתנת לבל בהן. בין לכהן חבר בין לכהן עם הארץ, כך פירש רמב"ס. ואין שיטת הגמרא מוכחת כן, אלא בין לכהן שאוכל חוליו בטהרה, בין לכהן שאינו אוכל חוליו בטהרה, אבל לעם הארץ אין נותנין שום מתנה ממתנות כהונה, דכתיב (דברי הימים-ב לא,ד) לתת מנת הכהנים והלוים למען יחזקו בתורת ה', אין נותנין מנה אלא לכהנים המחזיקים בתורת ה'. וכן הא דתנן לקמן (משנה ט) אלו נתנין לכל כהן, לאו לכהן עם הארץ, אלא לכל כהן אף על פי שאינו אוכל חוליו בטהרה:

member of his household who is **a** *zav, zavah, niddah*,[12] **or a woman who has given birth.** Therefore, if the only available Kohanim (or members of their household) are *tamei* with such types of *tumah*, two portions of *challah* must be set aside; one portion is burned, and the other portion may be eaten even by Kohanim who are *tamei* with such types of *tumah*.[13]

Challah of Eretz Yisrael is subject to a number of restrictions. A Kohen may not eat *challah* of Eretz Yisrael on a table where a non-Kohen is eating, out of concern that the non-Kohen may end up eating the *challah*. It is also forbidden to give the *challah* of Eretz Yisrael to a Kohen who is not careful to observe the practice of eating *chullin* only under conditions of *taharah*. This is due to the concern that he might be careless with the *challah* and allow it to become *tamei*. The Mishnah explains that these prohibitions do not apply to the Kohen's portion of *challah* outside Eretz Yisrael:

וְנֶאֱכֶלֶת עִם הַזָּר עַל הַשֻּׁלְחָן — **It may be eaten** by a Kohen along with **a non-Kohen at one table.** The Rabbis did not forbid this due to the concern that the non-Kohen may eat the *challah*. וְנִתֶּנֶת לְכָל כֹּהֵן — **And it may be given to any Kohen,** even to one who is not careful to eat *chullin* only under conditions of *taharah*.[14]

NOTES

12. A *niddah* is a woman who experienced a menstrual discharge. On the Biblical level, she is *tamei* for seven days, after which she immerses in a *mikveh*. [Rabbinically, there are further laws and particulars to the purification process.] A *zavah* is a woman who had a discharge of blood during the eleven days that follow the seven-day *niddah* period. A *zav* is a man who had a type of semen-like discharge. They too must follow a specific purification process.

13. This is the view of the Tanna Kamma, who allows only a *baal keri* who is a *tevul yom* to eat the portion of *challah* of outside of Eretz Yisrael that otherwise would have been burned in the fire — not a *baal keri* who has not immersed in a *mikveh*. R' Yose, however, treats a *zav, zavah, niddah*, or a woman who has given birth in the same manner that he treats a *baal keri*. In his view, they may all eat *challah* of outside of Eretz Yisrael (*Rav*; see *Tos. Yom Tov*). [It would thus seem that a single portion of *challah* would always suffice according to R' Yose, even if the only Kohanim available are *tamei* (see *Tos. Yom Tov*).]

14. Although we are normally concerned that such a Kohen might make the *challah tamei*, this concern does not exist outside Eretz Yisrael, where the *challah* is already *tamei* due to the Rabbinic *tumah* of the land.

It is absolutely forbidden, however, to give *challah* to a Kohen who is an *am haaretz* (an unlearned person who is not meticulous in his mitzvah observance) even outside Eretz Yisrael. This prohibition is based on a verse in *II Divrei HaYamim* 31:4, which implies that the Kohanic gifts are to be given only to those who will use them to "hold strongly to the Torah of Hashem" (*Rav*).

משניות חלה / פרק ד: שתי נשים

[ט] וְאֵלּוּ נִתָּנִין לְכָל כֹּהֵן: הַחֲרָמִים, וְהַבְּכוֹרוֹת, וּפִדְיוֹן הַבֵּן, וּפִדְיוֹן פֶּטֶר חֲמוֹר, וְהַזְּרוֹעַ, וְהַלְּחָיַיִם, וְהַקֵּבָה,

- רע"ב -

(ט) החרמים. לכהנים, כדכתיב (במדבר יח, יד) כל חרם בישראל לך יהיה: והבכורות. אי תם הוא, הרי זה קדשי מקדם, ואי בעל מום הוא, כתיב (דברים יב, טו) הטמא והטהור יאכלנו: ופדיון פטר חמור. פודהו בשה ואין בו קדושה:

---

[9] Having taught the law of the portion of *challah* from outside Eretz Yisrael that may be given to any Kohen (that is, even to a Kohen who is not careful to eat *chullin* only under conditions of *taharah*), the Mishnah lists other Kohanic gifts that may be given to any Kohen:[1]

וְאֵלּוּ נִתָּנִין לְכָל כֹּהֵן — **These, too, may be given to any Kohen,** even one who is not careful to eat *chullin* only under conditions of *taharah*: הַחֲרָמִים — *Charamim* vows;[2] וְהַבְּכוֹרוֹת — **the firstborn animal offerings;**[3] וּפִדְיוֹן הַבֵּן — **redemption money of the firstborn son;**[4] וּפִדְיוֹן פֶּטֶר חֲמוֹר — **the redemption sheep of the firstborn donkey;**[5] וְהַזְּרוֹעַ וְהַלְּחָיַיִם וְהַקֵּבָה — **the foreleg, jaws, and abomasum** (the fourth stomach) of a kosher animal;[6]

--- NOTES ---

[9]

1. The expression "any Kohen" refers to a Kohen who observes mitzvos properly, even if he does not observe the practice of eating *chullin* only under conditions of *taharah*. Since he is not careful to protect the *taharah* of his *chullin,* the Rabbis were concerned that he might also not properly protect his *terumah,* resulting in it becoming *tamei.* Therefore, we may not give him *challah* or *terumah* of Eretz Yisrael.

This concern does not apply to the Kohanic gifts listed below for one of two reasons. Either they are not holy at all and may therefore be eaten when *tamei,* or they are so holy that they must be brought to the Temple. Even a Kohen who might be careless about *tumah* will make sure that he is *tahor* before entering the Temple (*Rav*).

2. If someone declares, "This property is *cherem,*" it is divided among the Kohanim (*Rav,* from *Bamidbar* 18:14). The property becomes, and remains, holy for as long as it is in the owner's possession, As soon as it is given to the Kohanim, however, it becomes *chullin* (*Arachin* 29a). There is thus no need to keep it *tahor,* and it may be given even to a Kohen who is not careful about eating *chullin* while *tahor.*

3. A male calf, sheep, or goat that is the firstborn (*bechor*) of its mother is holy at birth and must be given to a Kohen. If it is unblemished, he brings it as an offering in the Temple (*Bamidbar* 18:17-18). Its meat may be eaten only by a Kohen or the members of his household, when they are *tahor* (*Zevachim* 5:8). Now, even a Kohen who is not careful about protecting *terumah* will make sure that he is *tahor* before entering the Temple. Since an unblemished *bechor* is offered in the Temple, it may be given to any Kohen.

If the *bechor* has a blemish and may thus not be offered, it must still be given to a Kohen. However, it is treated as *chullin* and may be eaten by anyone, even while *tamei*; *Devarim* 15:22 (*Rav*). As such, it too may be given to any Kohen to eat.

4. A boy who is his mother's firstborn must be redeemed by giving five *shekalim* to a Kohen (*Bamidbar* 18:15-16).

5. The male firstborn of a Jewish-owned donkey must be redeemed with a sheep or goat that is given to a Kohen (*Bamidbar* 18:15).

6. When someone slaughters a kosher animal that is *chullin,* he is required to give these three portions to a Kohen (*Devarim* 18:3).

[77] **MISHNAH CHALLAH** / Chapter 4: *Shtei Nashim* 4/9

– רע"ב –

וְרֵאשִׁית הַגֵּז, וְשֶׁמֶן שְׂרֵפָה, וְקָדְשֵׁי הַמִּקְדָּשׁ, וְהַבִּכּוּרִים; רַבִּי יְהוּדָה אוֹסֵר בַּבִּכּוּרִים. כַּרְשִׁינֵי תְרוּמָה, רַבִּי עֲקִיבָא מַתִּיר וַחֲכָמִים אוֹסְרִים.

ראשית הגז. דכתיב (שם יח, ד) וראשית גז צאנך תתן לו: ושמן שרפה. שמן תרומה שנטמאה: וקדשי מקדש. דלא אסרו לתת לכהן שאינו נזהר בטומאה, אלא דבר שיש בו איסור טומאה בגבולין, כגון תרומה ותרומת מעשר וחלה, אבל קדשי מקדש ובכורים שמביאין אותם לעזרה, לא חששו, דטהורי מטהר נפשיה: רבי יהודה אוסר בבכורים. דחייש דלמא לא מזדהר בהו, הואיל ואין עושין בהן עבודה. ואין הלכה כרבי יהודה: רבי עקיבא מתיר. רבי עקיבא לטעמיה, דאמר בפרק שני דמעשר שני (משנה ד) דכרשינין כל מעשיהן בטומאה, דלא חשיבי אוכל: וחכמים אוסרים. דחשיבי להו אוכל, הואיל והן נאכלין בשנות רעבון. והלכה כחכמים:

וְרֵאשִׁית הַגֵּז — the **first of the fleece;**[7] וְשֶׁמֶן שְׂרֵפָה — **oil** of *terumah* that must be **burned** because it became *tamei*;[8] וְקָדְשֵׁי הַמִּקְדָּשׁ — the Kohen's portion of **holy** offerings **of the Temple;**[9] וְהַבִּכּוּרִים — **and** *bikkurim,* which are brought to the Temple.[10]

A different opinion about the last item in the list:

רַבִּי יְהוּדָה אוֹסֵר בַּבִּכּוּרִים — **R' Yehudah forbids** giving *bikkurim* to a Kohen who is not careful about *tumah*.[11]

The next case is also the subject of dispute:

כַּרְשִׁינֵי תְרוּמָה — Regarding **vetch** (a type of herb) **of** *terumah,* which is used as feed for animals, רַבִּי עֲקִיבָא מַתִּיר — **R' Akiva permits** giving it to any Kohen, even one who is not careful to eat *chullin* only under conditions of *taharah*.[12] וַחֲכָמִים אוֹסְרִים — **But the Sages forbid** doing so. Since people

---
NOTES
---

7. Someone who shears his sheep must give part of the fleece to a Kohen (*Devarim* 18:4).

The last four gifts — the redemption money of a firstborn boy; the redemption sheep of a firstborn donkey; the foreleg, jaws, and abomasum; and the first of the fleece — are not holy. They may thus be given even to a Kohen who is not careful to eat *chullin* only under conditions of *taharah*.

8. Although *terumah* that is *tamei* must be burned, it is still given to a Kohen (*Rambam, Hilchos Terumos* 2:14), who may use it as fuel or otherwise benefit from its burning (*Shabbos* 25a). Once *terumah* is *tamei,* there is obviously no point in restricting it to a Kohen who is careful about *taharah*.

9. Kohanim are entitled to a portion of most offerings after their sacrificial service has been performed. Since this portion is distributed in the Temple Courtyard, it may be given to any Kohen,

because all Kohanim make sure to purify themselves before entering the Temple (*Rav*).

10. *Bikkurim* are the first-ripening fruits of the seven species for which the Torah praises Eretz Yisrael. They are brought to the Temple for a ceremony described in *Devarim* 26:1-12, after which they are given to the Kohanim (*Bamidbar* 18:13). *Bikkurim* may be given to any Kohen because they are distributed in the Temple Courtyard, where even a Kohen who is not careful to protect the *taharah* of his *chullin* is sure to be *tahor* (*Rav*).

11. *Bikkurim* are not offered on the Altar. R' Yehudah therefore treats *bikkurim* like the *challah* and *terumah* of Eretz Yisrael, which may be given only to a Kohen who is careful to protect the *taharah* of his *chullin* (*Rav*).

12. Animal feed of *terumah* does not need to be safeguarded from *tumah*. Therefore, R' Akiva holds that vetch, which is ordinarily used for animal feed,

ד/י

- רע״ב -

שם מביתר. (י) שֶׁם מִבֵּיתָר: מָקוֹם בְּחוּצָה לָאָרֶץ: וְלֹא קִבְּלוּ מִמֶּנּוּ. דְּלֵאְכֹל אִי אֶפְשָׁר, שֶׁהֲרֵי נִטְמְאוּ בָאָרֶץ

[י] נִתַּאי אִישׁ תְּקוֹעַ הֵבִיא חַלּוֹת מִבֵּיתָר, וְלֹא קִבְּלוּ מִמֶּנּוּ. אַנְשֵׁי אֲלֶכְּסַנְדְּרִיָּא הֵבִיאוּ חַלּוֹתֵיהֶן מֵאֲלֶכְּסַנְדְּרִיָּא, וְלֹא קִבְּלוּ מֵהֶם.

הַטְּמֵאִים, וְלִשְׂרְפָן אִי אֶפְשָׁר, לְפִי שֶׁאֵין טוֹמְאִין זוֹ יְדוּעָה, שֶׁמָּא יֹאמְרוּ רָאִינוּ תְרוּמָה טְהוֹרָה נִשְׂרֶפֶת. לְהַחֲזִירָן לִמְקוֹמָן אִי אֶפְשָׁר, שֶׁלֹּא יֹאמְרוּ תְרוּמָה יוֹצְאָה מֵאֶרֶץ יִשְׂרָאֵל לְחוּצָה לָאָרֶץ, אֶלָּא מַנִּיחָן עַד עֶרֶב פֶּסַח וְשׂוֹרְפָן:

---

eat vetch during a famine, the Sages classify it as human food and thus it must be safeguarded from *tumah*. Therefore, it may be given only to a Kohen who can be trusted to protect the *terumah* from *tumah*.

[10] Having discussed, in Mishnah 8, the laws of separating *challah* both in and out of Eretz Yisrael, the Mishnah now discusses how *challah* from outside Eretz Yisrael is treated if it is brought to Eretz Yisrael:

נִתַּאי אִישׁ תְּקוֹעַ הֵבִיא חַלּוֹת מִבֵּיתָר — **Nitai, a resident of Tekoa** (a town in Eretz Yisrael),[1] **brought** *challah* portions to Eretz Yisrael **from Beisar,** a town outside Eretz Yisrael that he had been visiting, in order to distribute them to the Kohanim of Tekoa.[2] וְלֹא קִבְּלוּ מִמֶּנּוּ — **But they did not accept** these *challah* portions **from him,** because *challah* separated outside Eretz Yisrael is *tamei* due to the Rabbinically imposed *tumah* on the lands outside Eretz Yisrael. Instead, they instructed Nitai to save the *challah* and burn it with his *chametz* before Pesach.[3] אַנְשֵׁי אֲלֶכְּסַנְדְּרִיָּא הֵבִיאוּ חַלּוֹתֵיהֶן מֵאֲלֶכְּסַנְדְּרִיָּא — In a similar incident, **residents of Alexandria brought their** *challah* portions to Eretz Yisrael **from Alexandria,**[4] וְלֹא קִבְּלוּ מֵהֶם — **but**

--- NOTES ---

need not be safeguarded from *tumah* (*Rav*, from *Maaser Sheni* 2:4). Obviously, then, it may be given even to Kohanim who are not careful about *taharah*.

[10]
1. See *Amos* 1:1 (*Meleches Shlomo*).
2. *Tos. Anshei Shem*. [Beisar should not be confused with the famous city known as Beitar, which was located in Eretz Yisrael, and destroyed by Hadrian's Roman legions fifty-two years after the destruction of the Second Temple. Rather, this Mishnah is discussing a town outside Eretz Yisrael with the same or a similar name (see *Pnei Moshe*).]
3. The Sages did not allow Nitai to distribute the *challah* to the Kohanim of Tekoa, since it was *tamei*. Although ordinarily *challah* that is *tamei* is burned, the Sages did not allow Nitai to burn this *challah*, because people would not necessarily be aware that the *challah* came from a land that was *tamei*. Thus, if he would burn it, people may assume that the *challah*

was *tahor*, and think that it is permissible to burn *challah* that is *tahor* (*Rav*, as explained by *Tos. Yom Tov*). The Sages therefore forbade burning any *challah* brought into Eretz Yisrael from outside the Land.

The Sages did not let Nitai return the *challah* to Beisar for a similar reason. *Challah* of Eretz Yisrael may not be sent elsewhere, where the land, which is *tamei*, would cause the *challah* to become *tamei* (see *Sheviis* 6:5 with *Mishnah Rishonah*). Although Nitai's *challah* — having been separated outside the Land — was already *tamei*, the Sages were concerned that people would not be aware of its *tumah*. Thus, if he sent this *challah* out of the Land, they might wrongly conclude that any *challah* — even that of Eretz Yisrael — may also be sent out. To avoid these issues, the *challah* was set aside until Erev Pesach, to be burned along with the *chametz* [when burning it would not attract attention] (*Rav*).

4. This refers either to the Egyptian city of Alexandria (*Tos. Yom Tov*), or to a city

[79] **MISHNAH CHALLAH** / Chapter 4: *Shtei Nashim* 4/11

— רע״ב —

אַנְשֵׁי הַר צְבוֹעִים הֵבִיאוּ בִכּוּרֵיהֶם קֹדֶם עֲצֶרֶת, וְלֹא קִבְּלוּ מֵהֶם, מִפְּנֵי הַכָּתוּב שֶׁבַּתּוֹרָה: "וְחַג הַקָּצִיר בִּכּוּרֵי מַעֲשֶׂיךָ אֲשֶׁר תִּזְרַע בַּשָּׂדֶה".

[יא] **בֶּן** אַנְטִינוֹס הֶעֱלָה בְכוֹרוֹת מִבָּבֶל,

וחג הקציר בכורי מעשיך. דשתי הלחם אקרו בכורים, ומתירין את החדש במקדש (יא) העלה בכורות מבבל ולא קבלו ממנו. דכתיב (דברים יד, כג) ואכלת לפני ה׳ אלהיך מעשר דגנך תירושך ויצהרך ובכורות בקרך וצאנך, ממקום שאתה מביא מעשר דגן אתה מביא בכורות, מחוצה לארץ שאי אתה מביא מעשר דגן אין אתה מביא בכורות:

---

they did not accept the *challah* **from them** either.

Having recorded two incidents in which the Sages of Eretz Yisrael rejected *challah* from outside the Land, the Mishnah (here and in the Mishnah that follows) goes on to discuss other Kohanic gifts and animal offerings that were refused for a variety of reasons. The first case pertains to *bikkurim,* the first-ripening fruits of the seven species for which the Torah praises Eretz Yisrael, which are to be brought to the Temple from the produce of the Land:

אַנְשֵׁי הַר צְבוֹעִים הֵבִיאוּ בִכּוּרֵיהֶם קֹדֶם עֲצֶרֶת — **The residents of Mount Tzevoim** once **brought their** *bikkurim* **to the Temple before the festival of Shavuos.** וְלֹא קִבְּלוּ מֵהֶם — **But they did not accept** the *bikkurim* **from them,**[5] מִפְּנֵי הַכָּתוּב שֶׁבַּתּוֹרָה — **because of [the verse] that is written in the Torah** (*Shemos* 23:16) regarding the Two Loaves offering of Shavuos: "וְחַג הַקָּצִיר בִּכּוּרֵי מַעֲשֶׂיךָ אֲשֶׁר תִּזְרַע בַּשָּׂדֶה" — **And the Festival of the Harvest** (Shavuos), **the first fruits of your labors** (i.e., the offering of the Two Loaves on Shavuos)[6] **that you plant in the field.** By referring to the Two Loaves as *the first fruits,* the verse teaches that *bikkurim* may not be brought until the Two Loaves are offered on Shavuos.

[11] This Mishnah records other incidents where the Sages of Eretz Yisrael rejected Kohanic gifts. The first incident discusses a *bechor* — a male calf, sheep, or goat that is the firstborn of its mother. It is holy from birth, and its owner is obligated to give it to a Kohen, who brings it as an offering, and is entitled to eat its meat:

בֶּן אַנְטִינוֹס הֶעֱלָה בְכוֹרוֹת מִבָּבֶל — **Ben Antinos brought** *bechoros* (firstborn

---
NOTES

with the same name on the Syrian coast (*Tos. Anshei Shem*). Either way, the *challah* was separated outside Eretz Yisrael.

5. They returned the *bikkurim* to the residents of Mount Tzevoim [and told them to return after Shavuos] (*Tos. Yom Tov*). [Fruit grown outside Eretz Yisrael are not subject to the obligation of *bikkurim* (see next Mishnah). However, this is not an issue here, since Mount Tzevoim was located in Eretz Yisrael (*Meleches*

Shlomo, from *I Shmuel* 13:18).]

6. On Shavuos, two loaves of bread from the new wheat crop are offered on the Altar (*Vayikra* 23:16-17). This is known as the offering of the "Two Loaves." Here, the Torah refers to them as the *first fruits* to teach that they must be the first produce offering of the year; no other produce may be brought from the new crop until after the Two Loaves of Shavuos have been offered (*Rav*).

ד/יא

[80] **משניות חלה** / פרק ד: שתי נשים

וְלֹא קִבְּלוּ מִמֶּנּוּ. יוֹסֵף הַכֹּהֵן הֵבִיא בִּכּוּרֵי יַיִן וְשֶׁמֶן, וְלֹא קִבְּלוּ מִמֶּנּוּ. אַף הוּא הֶעֱלָה אֶת בָּנָיו וּבְנֵי בֵיתוֹ לַעֲשׂוֹת פֶּסַח קָטָן בִּירוּשָׁלַיִם, וְהֶחֱזִירוּהוּ, שֶׁלֹּא יִקָּבַע הַדָּבָר חוֹבָה.

– רע"ב –
הביא בכורים יין ושמן ולא קבלו ממנו. לפי שלא בלרום מתחלה לכך, דאילו בלרום מתחלה לכך שרי, דהכי תנן פרק בתרא דתרומות (משנה ג) אין

מביאין בכורים משקה אלא היוצא מן הזיתים וענבים בלבד: **פסח קטן**. ובניו קטנים היו, ובפסח ראשון בלבד הן חייבים, שהכל חייבים בראייה, כדכתיב (שמות כג, יז) יראה כל זכורך, אבל לא בפסח שני:

---

animals) from Babylonia to Eretz Yisrael for the Kohanim to offer upon the Altar. וְלֹא קִבְּלוּ מִמֶּנּוּ — **But they did not accept** them from him, because only a *bechor* born in Eretz Yisrael may be offered upon the Altar.[1]

The next incident involves *bikkurim*:

יוֹסֵף הַכֹּהֵן הֵבִיא בִּכּוּרֵי יַיִן וְשֶׁמֶן — **Yosef the Kohen brought his** first-ripening grapes and olives that grew in Eretz Yisrael as *bikkurim* in the form of **wine and oil.** וְלֹא קִבְּלוּ מִמֶּנּוּ — **But they did not accept** them from him, since the fruits themselves must be brought as *bikkurim,* not their juice.[2]

There is a mitzvah to bring the *pesach* offering on the 14th of Nissan. If someone was *tamei* or too far from Jerusalem on that day, he is required to bring the offering one month later on Pesach Sheni, the 14th of Iyar (*Bamidbar* 9:9-14). In the next incident, Yosef the Kohen came with his family to offer a *pesach sheni* :

אַף הוּא הֶעֱלָה אֶת בָּנָיו וּבְנֵי בֵיתוֹ לַעֲשׂוֹת פֶּסַח קָטָן בִּירוּשָׁלַיִם — **He also brought his** minor **sons and the members of his household to offer a** *pesach sheni* **on the fourteenth of Iyar in Jerusalem.**[3] וְהֶחֱזִירוּהוּ — **But they turned him back,** preventing him from offering a *pesach sheni* on behalf of his sons, שֶׁלֹּא יִקָּבַע הַדָּבָר חוֹבָה — **so that the matter** of having minor children

---
NOTES
---

[11]
1. [Although a *bechor* born outside the Land cannot be offered on the Altar, it is still holy. It is therefore given to a Kohen and sent out to pasture until it develops a blemish, after which it may be slaughtered and eaten, as ordinary *chullin* (see *Tiferes Yisrael*).]
2. The Sages based their rejection on *Devarim* 26:2, which states that *bikkurim* are to be brought *from the first of every "fruit" of the ground* — implying that the *bikkurim* ceremony may be performed only with the fruit itself — not with the juice extracted from it (*Meleches Shlomo,* from *Rash Sirilio*).
The wine and oil were rejected only because Yosef the Kohen had intended at the time of the harvest to bring the grapes and olives themselves as *bikkurim,* but afterward changed his mind and decided

to press them. Had he harvested his fruits with the intention of pressing them, then the wine and oil would have been eligible for the *bikkurim* ceremonies (*Rav,* based on *Terumos* 11:3).
3. Yosef and his family were unable to bring the *pesach* offering in Nissan since they were *tamei* (*Rash Sirilio* based on *Zevachim* 100a), so they brought a *pesach* offering to the Temple on Pesach Sheni.
[The Mishnah refers to the second *pesach* offering as the "small *pesach*," because it is celebrated on a smaller scale than the actual Festival of Pesach. The Festival of Pesach is celebrated Biblically for seven days, while Pesach Sheni is observed for only one day. Moreover, most people bring their *pesach* offering on Pesach, and only a small number of people who could not bring it then would offer it on Pesach Sheni (*Tos. Anshei Shem*).]

[81] **MISHNAH CHALLAH** / Chapter 4: *Shtei Nashim*   4/11

– רע"ב –

אֲרִיסְטוֹן הֵבִיא בִכּוּרָיו מֵאַפַּמְיָא, וְקִבְּלוּ מִמֶּנּוּ, מִפְּנֵי שֶׁאָמְרוּ: הַקּוֹנֶה בְסוּרְיָא, כְּקוֹנֶה בְּפַרְוָר שֶׁבִּירוּשָׁלָיִם.

מאפמיא. גרסינן,
בסוריא: כקונה
בפרוורי ירושלים.
מגרשי ירושלים
וכפרים שסביבותיה. תרגום מגרשיה פרווהא:

והוא שם מקום
כקונה
בפרוורי ירושלים.
מגרשי ירושלים

participate in *pesach sheni* should not be established as a requirement.[4]

The verse (*Devarim* 26:2) states: *You shall take of the first of every fruit of the ground that you bring in from your land.* The term *from your land* excludes fruit grown outside Eretz Yisrael from the obligation of *bikkurim* (*Bava Basra* 81a). The Mishnah cites an incident in which the Sages accepted *bikkurim* from outside of Eretz Yisrael:

אֲרִיסְטוֹן הֵבִיא בִכּוּרָיו מֵאַפַּמְיָא — Ariston brought his *bikkurim* to the Temple in Jerusalem **from Apamya,** a city in Surya that was outside the Biblical borders of Eretz Yisrael,[5] וְקִבְּלוּ מִמֶּנּוּ — **and they accepted** the *bikkurim* **from him,** and performed the *bikkurim* ceremony in the Temple, even though *bikkurim* are not brought from lands outside Eretz Yisrael, מִפְּנֵי שֶׁאָמְרוּ — **because [the Sages] said:** הַקּוֹנֶה בְסוּרְיָא כְּקוֹנֶה בְּפַרְוָר שֶׁבִּירוּשָׁלָיִם — **One who purchases** land **in Surya is like one who purchases [land] in the very outskirts of Jerusalem.** That is, the Sages decreed that *bikkurim* must be brought from produce grown in Surya, just as it must be brought from produce grown in the outskirts of Jerusalem.[6]

NOTES

4. A person includes his minor children in the celebration of the first *pesach* offering, since he is obligated to appear with his children in the Temple for Pesach, Shavuos, and Succos (*Shemos* 23:17). However, there is no requirement to include them in the second *pesach* offering (*Rav;* see *Tos. Anshei Shem*).

5. Surya (ancient Syria), a land that bordered Eretz Yisrael, was conquered and annexed by King David. It does not have the status of Eretz Yisrael according to Biblical law (see introduction to Mishnah 7). Nevertheless, the Sages granted it the status of Eretz Yisrael with regard to certain laws.

6. Even though they did not require (or even permit) that *bikkurim* be brought from other lands, the Sages decreed that *bikkurim* be brought from Surya, because it has the Rabbinic status of Eretz Yisrael.

מסכת ערלה
TRACTATE ORLAH

MISHNAH ORLAH / General Introduction

General Introduction

וְכִי תָבֹאוּ אֶל הָאָרֶץ וּנְטַעְתֶּם כָּל עֵץ מַאֲכָל וַעֲרַלְתֶּם עָרְלָתוֹ אֶת פִּרְיוֹ שָׁלֹשׁ שָׁנִים יִהְיֶה לָכֶם עֲרֵלִים לֹא יֵאָכֵל. וּבַשָּׁנָה הָרְבִיעִת יִהְיֶה כָּל פִּרְיוֹ קֹדֶשׁ הִלּוּלִים לַה׳. וּבַשָּׁנָה הַחֲמִישִׁת תֹּאכְלוּ אֶת פִּרְיוֹ לְהוֹסִיף לָכֶם תְּבוּאָתוֹ אֲנִי ה׳ אֱלֹהֵיכֶם.

When you shall come to the Land, and you shall plant any food tree, you shall treat as closed its orlah, its fruit; for three years it shall be closed for you, it shall not be eaten. And in the fourth year, all its fruit shall be sanctified to praise Hashem. And in the fifth year you may eat its fruit — so that it will increase its crop for you — I am Hashem, your God (Vayikra 19:23-25).

I.

◈§ The Torah's Commandment

The Torah commands that for the first three years of a tree, its fruit is forbidden as *orlah*. The fruit of the fourth year (called *reva'i*) is holy, which means that it must be consumed in Jerusalem. From the fifth year and on, the fruit is like any other produce.

Tractate *Orlah* discusses the laws that apply to the fruit of the first three years. [There are also some references in this tractate to *reva'i* (the holy fruit of the fourth year) but its laws are discussed mainly in the last chapter of Tractate *Maaser Sheni*, since *reva'i* has the same laws as *maaser sheni*.]

II.

◈§ The Meaning of the Word "*Orlah*"

As we have translated in the verse above, the word עָרֵל means "closed" or "blocked" (*Rashi* to the verse). So, too, a male who is uncircumcised is called an עָרֵל, because the covering that is cut away during circumcision has not been removed and he is thus still "closed." The *orlah* fruit is "closed," meaning it cannot be used at all, neither as food nor for any other purpose (see below, section V).

III.

❧ To What Species Does *Orlah* Apply?

Since the verse specifies that the laws of *orlah* apply to an עֵץ, *tree,* they apply to any produce that grows on trees, but not to grains, vegetables, and the like.

IV.

❧ Counting the Three Years

How the three years of a tree's *orlah* are counted is not discussed in this tractate but in Tractate *Rosh Hashanah* (9b-10a). The basic rule is that we do not follow the tree's "birthday," but rather Rosh Hashanah. That is, as long as a tree began to grow thirty days before Rosh Hashanah, the day of Rosh Hashanah begins the second year, and the following Rosh Hashanah begins the third year. Whether the third year ends with the third Rosh Hashanah or extends until Tu B'Shevat might depend on how long the tree grew during the first "year." See *Shulchan Aruch, Yoreh Deah* 294:4-5.

V.

❧ The Extent of the *Orlah* Prohibition

As will be explained in the Mishnah and as indicated in the verse, only the fruit of the *orlah* tree is forbidden, not its wood or leaves. The prohibition of the fruit, though, is not only for eating but for any benefit. Thus, the fruit may not be eaten, fed to animals, sold, used for fuel, or planted.

VI.

❧ The Disposal of *Orlah*

The Mishnah in *Temurah* 7:5 (33b) lists *orlah* among the prohibited items that must be burned (unless it has been made into a liquid, such as wine or oil, in which case it is buried in the ground — see ibid. 34a). This law is also evident in the first few Mishnayos of the third chapter of our tractate. There is a question whether this "burning" requirement is Biblical[1] or Rabbinic.[2]

NOTES

1. See *Rashi* to *Temurah* 33b ד"ה כלאי הכרם and *Tosafos* to *Succah* 35a ד"ה לפי and *Chazon Ish, Dinei Orlah* §40.
2. See *Ritva* to *Succah* 35a ד"ה והנכון;

Aruch HaShulchan, Yoreh Deah 293:3; see also *Teshuvos Chasam Sofer, Orach Chaim* §104,180 and *Yoreh Deah* §286.

[5] **MISHNAH ORLAH** / General Introduction

VII.

~§ *Orlah* Outside the Land of Israel

Unlike most of the agricultural laws, *orlah* applies even to trees that grow outside the Land of Israel. This application of *orlah* outside the Land of Israel is not recorded in the Written Torah, but is a הֲלָכָה לְמֹשֶׁה מִסִּינַי, *an oral law given to Moses at Sinai*. That oral law, however, contains a lenient provision; namely, that outside the Land only definite *orlah* is forbidden. If, however, there exists any doubt — even a remote doubt — that the fruit growing outside the Land might not be *orlah,* that fruit is permitted (see Mishnah 3:7 and *Kiddushin* 38b-39a).

VIII.

~§ Nullification [בִּטוּל] of *Orlah*

According to Biblical law, a forbidden food that becomes mixed unrecognizably with a majority of permitted food is considered nullified, and the entire mixture may be eaten. The Rabbis decreed, however, that *orlah* shall not become nullified unless the permitted content of the mixture is two hundred times the *orlah*. (See Chapter 2 for details.)

IX.

~§ The Chapters of This Tractate

Only the first chapter and part of the third chapter of the tractate deal specifically with the laws of *orlah*. The entire second chapter and much of the third chapter, however, deal also with general laws concerning the nullification of prohibited substances in a mixture.

Chapter One

[8] משניות ערלה / פרק א: הנוטע

א/א-ב

– רע"ב –

פרק ראשון — הנוטע.
(א) הנוטע לסייג. שיהיה האילן גדר לכרם: ולקורות. לגדל עצים לעשות מהן קורות לבנין, ואין עיקר נטיעתו לאכול הפירות: פטור מן הערלה. דכתיב (ויקרא יט, כג) ונטעתם כל עץ מאכל, את שהוא למאכל חייב, לסייג ולקורות

[א] **הַנּוֹטֵעַ** לִסְיָג וּלְקוֹרוֹת, פָּטוּר מִן הָעָרְלָה. רַבִּי יוֹסֵי אוֹמֵר: אֲפִלּוּ אָמַר הַפְּנִימִי לְמַאֲכָל וְהַחִיצוֹן לִסְיָג, הַפְּנִימִי חַיָּב, וְהַחִיצוֹן פָּטוּר.

[ב] **עֵת** שֶׁבָּאוּ אֲבוֹתֵינוּ לָאָרֶץ, מָצְאוּ נָטוּעַ, פָּטוּר. נָטְעוּ, אַף עַל פִּי שֶׁלֹּא כָבְשׁוּ,

ולעלים פטור: **הפנימי למאכל.** נתכוין שיחזור פנימי יהיה למאכל ויחזור החיצון לסייג, אף על פי שהכל אילן אחד, החיצון פטור. ואין הלכה כרבי יוסי: (ב) **ומצאו נטוע פטור.** דכתיב (שם) כי תבואו אל

---

[1] The Torah commands the law of *orlah* with the words: *When you shall come to the Land and you shall plant any food tree, you shall treat its fruit as closed* (forbidden); *for three years it shall be closed* (forbidden) *to you, it shall not be eaten* (*Vayikra* 19:23). The first two Mishnahs of this tractate explain what we can learn from the way the Torah words this commandment. First the Mishnah discusses what the Torah means by specifying that *orlah* applies to a *"food" tree*:

הַנּוֹטֵעַ לִסְיָג וּלְקוֹרוֹת — **If someone plants** a fruit tree **to be part of a fence, or** to use its wood **for beams,**[1] פָּטוּר מִן הָעָרְלָה — **it is exempt from** the law of *orlah*, and one may eat the fruit of that tree even during the first three years.[2] רַבִּי יוֹסֵי אוֹמֵר — **R' Yose says:** אֲפִלּוּ אָמַר הַפְּנִימִי לְמַאֲכָל וְהַחִיצוֹן לִסְיָג — **Even if he said** when he planted the tree, "I will use **the part that faces the inside** of my property **for food and** the part that faces **the outside for a fence,"** הַפְּנִימִי חַיָּב וְהַחִיצוֹן פָּטוּר — the fruit that grows from the part facing **the inside is subject** to *orlah*, but the fruit that grows from the part facing **the outside is exempt** from *orlah*.[3]

[2] This Mishnah now discusses what we can learn from the words *"When you shall come to the Land and you shall plant any"* food tree (see introductory paragraph to the previous Mishnah):

עֵת שֶׁבָּאוּ אֲבוֹתֵינוּ לָאָרֶץ — **At the time that our forefathers,** led by Joshua, **entered the Land** of Israel, מָצְאוּ נָטוּעַ — **if they found** a tree already **planted,** even if it was not yet three years old, פָּטוּר — **it was exempt** from *orlah*.[1] נָטְעוּ אַף עַל פִּי שֶׁלֹּא כָבְשׁוּ — **If they planted** a tree after they entered the Land,

— NOTES —

[1]
1. In either case, the planter's main intent is not to grow fruit (*Rav*).
2. The Torah states that *orlah* applies to any *"food" tree*. A fruit tree that is planted for a purpose other than fruit is not considered a "food" tree, so its fruit does not become *orlah* (*Rav*).
3. The part facing the inside was intended for fruit, so it is subject to *orlah*. The part facing the outside was *not* intended for fruit, so it is *not* subject to *orlah*. According to R' Yose, even though it is all one tree and part of it is a "food tree" planted for its fruit, the part that was not intended for its fruit is exempt from *orlah* (*Rav*).

[2]
1. The Torah says that *orlah* will apply *when you shall come to the Land and you shall plant*. This excludes any fruit tree planted before you came to the Land (*Rav*).

[9] MISHNAH ORLAH / Chapter 1: *Hanotei'a* 1/2

- רע"ב -

חַיָּב. הַנּוֹטֵעַ לָרַבִּים, חַיָּב; רַבִּי יְהוּדָה פּוֹטֵר. הַנּוֹטֵעַ בִּרְשׁוּת הָרַבִּים, וְהָעוֹבֵד כּוֹכָבִים שֶׁנָּטַע,

האָרֶץ ונטעתם, פרט לנטעו עובדי כוכבים עד שלא בָּאוּ לארץ: נָטְעוּ. בֵּין ישׂראל בין עובדי כוכבים, לאחר שֶׁבָּאוּ לארץ, אף על פי שלא כבשו ישראל את הארץ, חַיָּב, דכתיב (שם) כל עץ, בין נטעו ישראל בין נטעו עובד כוכבים. שנטע ברשותו לצורך רבים: חַיָּב. דכתיב (שם) יהיה לכם ערלים, להביא הנטוע לצורך רבים: וְרַבִּי יְהוּדָה פּוֹטֵר. סבר ונטעתם נמי משמע לרבים, ואין רבוי אחר רבוי אלא למעט. ורבנן סברי, ונטעתם כל אחד לטעמו משמע. ואין הלכה כרבי יהודה: וְהַנּוֹטֵעַ בִּרְשׁוּת הָרַבִּים: וְהָעוֹבֵד כּוֹכָבִים שֶׁנָּטַע. לְצוֹרֶךְ עַצְמוֹ. בִּשְׂדֵה שֶׁל יִשְׂרָאֵל:

even before conquering all of it, **חַיָּב** — [the tree] was subject to *orlah*.[2]

The Mishnah discusses other laws that can be seen from the verse:

הַנּוֹטֵעַ לָרַבִּים חַיָּב — **If someone plants** a tree in his own property **for the public** to use the fruit,[3] **it is subject** to *orlah*;[4] **רַבִּי יְהוּדָה פּוֹטֵר** — **R' Yehudah,** however, **exempts** it from *orlah*.[5]

The Mishnah concludes with other cases in which *orlah* applies:

הַנּוֹטֵעַ בִּרְשׁוּת הָרַבִּים — **If someone plants** a tree **in the public domain** for his own use,[6] **וְהָעוֹבֵד כּוֹכָבִים שֶׁנָּטַע** — **or if an idolater planted** a tree,[7]

──────── NOTES ────────

2. [Whereas many other mitzvos of Eretz Yisrael did not go into effect until after Joshua conquered the entire Land and divided it among the Israelites (a process that took fourteen years), the *orlah* obligation took effect as soon as they entered the Land.] This is because the Torah states *when you shall come to the Land and you shall plant "any" food tree*. The extra word "any" comes to include any tree that is planted after you come to the Land — even if it was planted by a non-Jew, and even if it was planted before the entire Land was conquered and divided (*Rav*).

3. *Rav, Rambam Commentary, Rosh.*

4. Understood simply, the Torah's expression *and you shall plant* refers to the usual type of planting, which is where an individual person plants [on his own land] for his own use (see *Rashi* to *Pesachim* 23a ונטעתם ליחיד משמע ד"ה). However, the verse goes on to say about the *orlah* fruits that *for three years it shall be forbidden "to you"* [לָכֶם] (plural), [an extra expression] that comes to expand the law to include even a tree planted on private property for *public* use of the fruit (*Rav*).

5. R' Yehudah holds that even the verse's first expression, וּנְטַעְתֶּם, *and "you"* (plural) *shall plant,* implies a broadening of the law to include public use of the fruit. If so, the later expression, *shall be forbidden "to you"* (plural), which once again broadens the law to include public use of the fruit, makes this a case of "a broadening after a broadening" [רִבּוּי אַחַר רִבּוּי] and the rule is that a broadening after a broadening means only to *restrict* the law [לְמַעֵט]. In this case, it restricts the law only to where the tree is planted for *private* use of the fruit (*Rav*, from *Pesachim* 23a). [See *Tos. Yom Tov* here for an explanation of the rule אֵין רִבּוּי אַחַר רִבּוּי אֶלָּא לְמַעֵט, *a broadening after a broadening comes only to restrict.*]

[The Tanna Kamma, though, holds that the plural is used in the first part of the verse because the verse speaks to the entire nation — if *any one of you* plants (*Rav*). This is the more reasonable way to understand the verse, since planting is usually done by individuals (see *Rashi* cited above in note 4).]

6. *Rav.* This is like a "normal" planting in that it is done by an individual for his own use (see above, note 4). Therefore, the law of *orlah* applies to it. (See *Mishnah Rishonah* and *Tos. Chadashim* here, and *Derishah* to *Yoreh Deah* 294.)

7. This applies whether he planted it on a Jew's property (*Rav*) or even if he did

משניות ערלה / פרק א: הנוטע

וְהַגַּזְלָן שֶׁנָּטַע, וְהַנּוֹטֵעַ בַּסְּפִינָה, וְהָעוֹלָה מֵאֵלָיו, חַיָּב בָּעָרְלָה.

[ג] **אִילָן** שֶׁנֶּעֱקַר וְהַסֶּלַע עִמּוֹ, שְׁטָפוֹ נָהָר וְהַסֶּלַע עִמּוֹ, אִם יָכֹל לִחְיוֹת, פָּטוּר,

- רע״ב -

וְהַגַּזְלָן. שֶׁגָּזַל קַרְקַע וּנְטָעָהּ, וּנְתִיאֲשׁוּ הַבְּעָלִים מִמֶּנָּה: **וְהַנּוֹטֵעַ בַּסְּפִינָה.** אַף עַל פִּי שֶׁאֵינָהּ נְקוּבָה, אִם הִיא שֶׁל חֶרֶס, לְפִי שֶׁאֵין כְּלֵי חֶרֶס עוֹמֵד בִּפְנֵי הַשָּׁרָשִׁים, וְהֵן מְפַטְפְּטִין דֶּרֶךְ הַחֶרֶס וְיוֹנְקִים מִן הַקַּרְקַע, אֲבָל שֶׁל עֵץ בָּעֵי נְקִיבָה: **וְהָעוֹלָה מֵאֵלָיו.** וְדַוְקָא בִּמְקוֹם יִשּׁוּב, אֲבָל בִּמְקוֹם יְעָרִים וּמִדְבָּרוֹת לֹא: **(ג) אִילָן שֶׁנֶּעֱקַר.** שֶׁעֲקָרַתּוּ הָרוּחַ, אוֹ שְׁטָפוֹ נָהָר, וְהוֹלִיכוּ לְמָקוֹם אַחֵר: **וְהַסֶּלַע עִמּוֹ.** הֶעָפָר שֶׁסָּבִיב הַשָּׁרָשִׁים קָרוּי סֶלַע, לְפִי שֶׁהוּא נַעֲשֶׂה שָׁם קָשֶׁה כְּסֶלַע. וְקָאָמַר שֶׁאִם הָיָה אוֹתוֹ עָפָר עִמּוֹ, וְהוֹסִיף עָלָיו עָפָר וְנִשְׁרַשׁ שָׁם בָּאָרֶץ, רְוָחִים, אִם יָכוֹל לִחְיוֹת מִן הֶעָפָר שֶׁבָּא עִמּוֹ, בְּלֹא תּוֹסֶפֶת עָפָר אַחֵר, [הֲרֵי] הוּא כִּנְטוּעַ בִּמְקוֹמוֹ הָרִאשׁוֹן וּפָטוּר מִן הָעָרְלָה, וְאִם לָאו הֲרֵי הוּא כְּאִילוּ הָעוֹלָה מֵאֵלָיו וְחַיָּב:

וְהַגַּזְלָן שֶׁנָּטַע — **or if a robber** stole land and **planted** a tree on it,[8] וְהַנּוֹטֵעַ בַּסְּפִינָה — **or if someone plants** a tree **in a boat**,[9] וְהָעוֹלָה מֵאֵלָיו — **or if [a tree] sprouted on its own** in a private domain,[10] חַיָּב בָּעָרְלָה — **in all these cases, the tree is subject to *orlah*.**

[3] The Mishnah discusses a tree that was uprooted and replanted. When is this considered a new "planting" that requires a new counting of three years of *orlah*?

אִילָן שֶׁנֶּעֱקַר וְהַסֶּלַע עִמּוֹ — **If a tree** that was more than three years old **was uprooted** (such as in a storm) **together with the soil-rock**[1] and became replanted in the ground, שְׁטָפוֹ נָהָר וְהַסֶּלַע עִמּוֹ — **or if a river swept it away together with the soil-rock** and the tree became replanted in a new location, the law is as follows: אִם יָכֹל לִחְיוֹת פָּטוּר — **If it could have survived** by drawing nourishment from just that soil-rock with no additional earth, **it is exempt**

NOTES

so on his own property (see *Rambam Commentary*, Kafich ed., and *Rambam, Hilchos Maaser Sheni* 10:5). As mentioned above (end of note 2), the extra word *"any" food tree* comes to include even one that was planted by an idolater.

8. Even though the Mishnah already taught that a tree planted in the public domain is subject to *orlah*, it still had to teach that the same applies to a tree planted on stolen property. Otherwise, one might have thought that the law of *orlah* is extended only to a tree planted in the public domain, since the planter, like everyone else, has a share in the public domain. But planting on stolen property is perhaps altogether different, since the planter does not own the property at all. Therefore, the Mishnah had to teach that *orlah* applies even in the case of a robber who plants on stolen property (*Tos. Yom Tov*).

9. This refers to planting a tree in an earthenware boat filled with earth. Since the boat is made of earthenware, the tree's roots will eventually puncture the bottom of the boat and draw nourishment from the ground underneath. The tree is therefore treated as though it were growing from the ground, and is subject to *orlah* (*Rav; Rash*).

10. *Rambam Commentary* (see also *Mishnah Rishonah*; see *Derech Emunah, Hil. Maaser Sheni* 10:5 §41). [Although this tree was not "planted" at all, it is similar to usual planting in that it grows in an individual's domain and will be used by him.]

[3]

1. This is the clump of earth that hardens around the roots of a tree (*Rav*) and remains stuck to the roots when the tree is pulled from the ground.

[11] **MISHNAH ORLAH** / Chapter 1: *Hanotei'a*

וְאִם לָאו, חַיָּב. נֶעֱקַר הַסֶּלַע מִצִּדּוֹ, אוֹ שֶׁזְּעָזַעֲתוּ הַמַּחֲרֵשָׁה, אוֹ שֶׁזִּעְזְעוֹ וַעֲשָׂאוֹ כֶּעָפָר, אִם יָכוֹל לִחְיוֹת, פָּטוּר, וְאִם לָאו, חַיָּב. [ד] **אִילָן** שֶׁנֶּעֱקַר וְנִשְׁתַּיֵּר בּוֹ שֹׁרֶשׁ,

— רע״ב —

זִעְזְעַתוּ הַמַּחֲרֵשָׁה וְנִתְפַּזֵּר מִמֶּנּוּ הֶעָפָר וְנִתְגַּלּוּ הַשָּׁרָשִׁים: (ד) וְנִשְׁתַּיֵּר בּוֹ שֹׁרֶשׁ. מְחֻבָּר לַקַּרְקַע שֶׁלֹּא נֶעֱקַר:

---

from *orlah*, because it is as if it was never uprooted from the earth in which it was growing.[2] **וְאִם לָאו חַיָּב** — **But if** it could **not** have survived without the additional earth in which it was replanted, then **it** is considered to have been uprooted and is **subject** to three years of *orlah* once more.[3]

The Mishnah now applies these laws to where a tree that was more than three years old became "uprooted" without moving from its place at all: **נֶעֱקַר הַסֶּלַע מִצִּדּוֹ** — **If** some of **the soil-rock became separated from [the tree's] side**,[4] **אוֹ שֶׁזִּעְזַעְתּוּ הַמַּחֲרֵשָׁה** — **or** **if a plow** hit and **shook it,** causing some of the soil-rock to separate from the tree, **אוֹ שֶׁזִּעְזְעוֹ וַעֲשָׂאוֹ כֶּעָפָר** — **or** if he shook it until he made [the soil-rock] like loose earth;[5] and he then repacked the soil around the roots. In any of these cases, the law is as follows: **אִם יָכוֹל לִחְיוֹת פָּטוּר** — **If [the tree] could have survived** as is, without the additional earth that was repacked around it, then **it is exempt** from *orlah*, because it is as if it was never uprooted from the earth in which it was growing. **וְאִם לָאו חַיָּב** — **But if** it could **not** have survived without the additional earth that was repacked around it, **it is subject** to a new count of *orlah*, because it is considered to be a tree that was uprooted and then replanted.[6]

[4] Our Mishnah continues the discussion, begun in the previous Mishnah, of a tree that was partially uprooted: **אִילָן שֶׁנֶּעֱקַר וְנִשְׁתַּיֵּר בּוֹ שֹׁרֶשׁ** — **If a tree** that was more than three years old

--- NOTES ---

2. If the soil-rock that remained attached to the tree is large enough by itself to sustain the tree, then the tree has never been separated from "the earth in which it was growing" and it is as if the tree was never uprooted (*Rav, Rambam Commentary*). [According to *Chazon Ish*, the soil-rock does not have to be able to sustain the tree for three years, but only until the tree is able to strike new roots in its new location (see *Derech Emunah, Hil. Maaser Sheni* 10:88).]

3. It is like a tree that "sprouted on its own" in the new location, which, as taught in the previous Mishnah, is subject to *orlah* (*Rav*).

4. By a storm or floodwaters (*Tos. Yom Tov*) [or because the ground shifted for some other reason]. The tree itself was not "uprooted," but part of its soil-rock became separated from it, so that it no longer draws nourishment from the separated part.

5. [*Tiferes Yisrael, Rashash*; see also *Chazon Ish, Orlah* 2:10.] This loosened earth does not nourish the tree as well as the soil-rock (*Rashash*).

6. Most commentators (*Rambam Commentary, Rosh, Rash, Rash Sirilio, Meleches Shlomo, Tos. Yom Tov*, and apparently *Rav* as well) have a slightly different reading in our Mishnah: וַעֲשָׂאוֹ בֶּעָפָר, *and he made* [i.e., restored] *it "with" earth*. That is, the storm or shaking dislodged some of the soil-rock, thereby exposing the roots, and the person then covered and packed them with earth. If the tree could have survived without the new earth, it is not considered to have been replanted.

משניות ערלה / פרק א: הנוטע [12]

פָּטוּר. וְכַמָּה יְהֵא הַשֹּׁרֶשׁ? רַבָּן גַּמְלִיאֵל אוֹמֵר מִשּׁוּם רַבִּי אֶלְעָזָר בֶּן יְהוּדָה אִישׁ בַּרְתּוֹתָא: כְּמַחַט שֶׁל מִתוּן.

[ה] **אִילָן** שֶׁנֶּעֱקַר וּבוֹ בְרֵכָה, וְהוּא חָיֶה מִמֶּנָּה, חָזְרָה הַזְּקֵנָה לִהְיוֹת

- רע"ב -

במחט של מתוח. גרסינן, כלומר שיעור עובי השורש כמחט שהאורגים מותחים בו הבגד אחר שארגוהו, להשיטו ולהרחיבו: (ה) **ובו בריכה.** מנהג עובדי אדמה שחופרים גומא, ולוקחים יחור אחד מן האילן וטומנין אותו באותו גומא, ויוצא שורש היחור מצד אחד ונעשה שם אילן, וראש היחור נשאר מחובר באילן. ואין דין ערלה נוהג בו בעודו מחובר לאילן ויונק, ממנו אף על פי שהוא יונק גם מן הקרקע. ואם נעקר אילן הזקן מן הקרקע, ונמצא שכל חיותו ויניקתו עתה מן הבריכה: **חזרה הזקנה להיות כבריכה.** ושניהם, הזקנה

---

was uprooted almost entirely, **but there remained in it** a single root that was still firmly connected to the ground as before,[1] **פָּטוּר** — **[the tree] remains exempt** from *orlah*.[2] **וְכַמָּה יְהֵא הַשֹּׁרֶשׁ** — **And how thick must this** single root be? **רַבָּן גַּמְלִיאֵל אוֹמֵר מִשּׁוּם רַבִּי אֶלְעָזָר בֶּן יְהוּדָה אִישׁ בַּרְתּוֹתָא** — **Rabban Gamliel says in the name of R' Elazar ben Yehudah the man of Bartosa:** **כְּמַחַט שֶׁל מִתוּן** — **Like** the thickness of **a stretching needle.**[3]

[5] Our Mishnah continues the discussion of a tree that was older than three years but is then uprooted.

The first part of our Mishnah deals with a case of "layering." One of the branches of a fruit tree, say a grapevine, is bent down to the ground, where the middle of that branch is then buried so that it will develop its own roots. One end of the branch remains connected to the original vine (the "parent") and the other, free end rises from the ground as if it were a separate vine. When the new roots are sufficiently developed, the branch is severed from the parent, at which point the layered branch becomes a completely separate grapevine.[1]

אִילָן שֶׁנֶּעֱקַר וּבוֹ בְרֵכָה — **If a tree** that was more than three years old **was uprooted** from the ground, **but had a layered branch** still attached to it **וְהוּא חָיֶה מִמֶּנָּה** — **from which [the tree] could be sustained,**[2] **חָזְרָה הַזְּקֵנָה לִהְיוֹת**

--- NOTES ---

[4]

1. *Rav*; *Chazon Ish*, *Orlah* 2:10.

2. Because the tree could survive with that single connected root alone. Thus, the tree has never been "uprooted," and it remains exempt from *orlah* even if the rest of the roots are then reinserted into the ground (*Rosh*).

3. Weavers would insert needles at the edges of newly woven fabric to stretch it across a board (*Tos. Yom Tov*, from *Aruch*). These needles had a standard thickness, and that is the thickness a single root must have in order to sustain a tree (see *Rosh*). [*Chazon Ish* (*Orlah* 2:14) explains that our Mishnah is speaking specifically of a grapevine. It is for this "tree" that a root as thick as a stretching needle is enough. Other trees, however, might need a thicker root to sustain them (see *Derech Emunah*, *Maaser Sheni* 10:92).]

[5]

1. As long as the layered branch remains connected to the parent, it is considered part of the parent (even if the branch is also drawing nourishment from its own roots). Therefore, if the parent is "old" (more than three years old), even the branch's fruits are not subject to *orlah* (*Rav*).

2. [Originally, the layered branch was

[13] **MISHNAH ORLAH** / Chapter 1: *Hanotei'a* 1/5

- רע"ב -

כַּבְּרֵכָה. הִבְרִיכָהּ שָׁנָה אַחַר שָׁנָה, וְנִפְסְקָה, מוֹנֶה מִשָּׁעָה שֶׁנִּפְסְקָה.

והבריכה, הוו כאילו נטעו עתה, ומונים להם שלש שנים משעה שנעקר האילן: **הבריכה שנה אחר שנה.** לאחר שהגדילה בריכה ראשונה, לקח ממנו יחור והבריכו בארץ, וכן עשה כמה פעמים זה אחר זה: **מונה.** לכולן שני ערלה, משנפסקה הבריכה הראשונה מן האילן:

כַּבְּרֵכָה — **the old tree now changes to be like a branch** of the rooted layer, and the rooted layer is now like the main tree, and both begin a three-year *orlah* count from that moment.[3] הִבְרִיכָהּ שָׁנָה אַחַר שָׁנָה — **If he layered [the old tree] year after year,** drawing each year's layered branch from the branch that was layered the previous year, so that now after several years he has a series of layered branches, the later ones connected through the earlier ones all the way back to the parent,[4] וְנִפְסְקָה — **and it** [the first layered-branch] **was** then **severed** from the original parent, making the tree that grew from that branch — as well as all the trees that came after it (and are still connected to one another) — independent of the original parent, מוֹנֶה מִשָּׁעָה שֶׁנִּפְסְקָה — **he counts a** new three-year *orlah* period for all the trees that grew from all the layered branches **from the time [the first layered branch] was severed** from the parent.[5]

Another cultivation technique is "grafting." The planter takes a branch from one tree and grafts that branch onto a different tree (called the "rootstock"). The grafted branch (the "scion") then draws nourishment from the rootstock. The Mishnah now discusses a special case of grafting; namely, where the scion is grafted onto the rootstock but remains attached as well to its original tree:

─── NOTES ───

drawing nourishment from the old tree. But now that the old tree's roots have been pulled up, it is the old tree that is surviving by drawing nourishment from the layered branch and *its* roots.]

3. As we will learn further in the Mishnah (see below, note 5), when a layered branch's connection to the parent is severed, the branch is considered a separate tree that has now been planted in the place of its own roots, starting its own three-year *orlah* count. The Mishnah now teaches that the same thing happens when the connection is not actually severed but the parent is *uprooted*. The branch is now considered to be newly planted in the place of its own roots, starting its own three-year *orlah* count. And moreover, since the roles have been reversed and the uprooted parent is now like part of the branch whose roots now sustain it, the parent, too, is considered to be newly planted in the place of the branch's roots, and begins the same

three-year *orlah* as the branch (see *Rav, Rambam Commentary,* and *Rash Sirilio*).

4. See illustration. At this point, none of the layered branches is subject to *orlah* since all are ultimately still connected to the parent, which is more than three years old (*Rambam Commentary*).

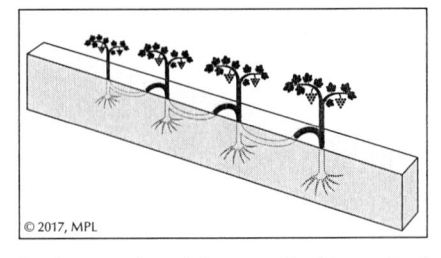

© 2017, MPL

5. As mentioned in note 3, this part of the Mishnah teaches that when a layered branch's connection to the parent is severed, the branch is considered a separate tree that has now been planted in the place of its own roots, starting its own three-year *orlah* count.

משניות ערלה / פרק א: הנוטע [14]

סִפּוּק הַגְּפָנִים, וְסִפּוּק עַל גַּבֵּי סִפּוּק, אַף עַל פִּי שֶׁהִבְרִיכָן בָּאָרֶץ, מֻתָּר. רַבִּי מֵאִיר אוֹמֵר: מָקוֹם שֶׁכֹּחָהּ יָפֶה, מֻתָּר, וּמָקוֹם שֶׁכֹּחָהּ רַע, אָסוּר.

— רע״ב —

סִפּוּק גְּפָנִים. דֶּרֶךְ עוֹבְדֵי אֲדָמָה שֶׁלּוֹקְחִים זְמוֹרָה אֲרוּכָּה מִגֶּפֶן זוֹ, וּמוֹשְׁכִים אוֹתָהּ לְגֶפֶן שֶׁבְּצִדָּהּ וּמַרְכִּיבִין הַזְּמוֹרָה בַּגֶּפֶן וְזֶהוּ הַנִּקְרָא סִפּוּק, וּפָטוּר מִן הָעָרְלָה. וְהָא דִּתְנַן (ראש השנה ט, ב) אֶחָד הַנּוֹטֵעַ וְאֶחָד הַמַּבְרִיךְ וְאֶחָד הַמַּרְכִּיב חַיָּב בְּעָרְלָה, הָתָם מַיְירֵי כְּשֶׁחֲתָכְךָ הַזְּמוֹרָה מִן הַגֶּפֶן, אוֹ הַיִּחוּר מִן הָאִילָן, וְאַחַר כָּךְ הִבְרִיכָן אוֹ הִרְכִּיבָן: **מָקוֹם שֶׁכֹּחָהּ יָפָה מֻתָּר.** אִם הַזְּמוֹרָה שֶׁהִבְרִיכוּהָ בַּגֶּפֶן כֹּחָהּ יָפָה וְיוֹנֶקֶת מִן הַגֶּפֶן אֲשֶׁר מִמֶּנָּה לוּקְחָה, מֻתָּר וּפָטוּר מִן הָעָרְלָה, וְאִם כֹּחָהּ רַע חַיֶּיבֶת בְּעָרְלָה. וְאֵין הֲלָכָה כְּרַבִּי מֵאִיר:

סִפּוּק הַגְּפָנִים — **In the case of extension of a grapevine,** where a vine is stretched and then grafted onto another grapevine, while remaining attached to its original grapevine,[6] וְסִפּוּק עַל גַּבֵּי סִפּוּק — **and an extension upon an extension,**[7] אַף עַל פִּי שֶׁהִבְרִיכָן בָּאָרֶץ — **even if he** also **layered [the extensions] in the ground,** so that in addition to "replanting" them into another grapevine, he also "replanted" them into the ground, the law is that מֻתָּר — **it is permitted** to eat the fruits that grow from these vines, if the original grapevines are past the years of *orlah*. The "grafting" and "layering" of these extended vines is not considered a new planting, since these extended vines were never severed from their original place of growth. The Mishnah now quotes a Tanna who says that this is not always the case:

רַבִּי מֵאִיר אוֹמֵר — **R' Meir says:** מָקוֹם שֶׁכֹּחָהּ יָפֶה מֻתָּר — **Where the strength of [the extended vine] is strong** so that it still draws most of its nourishment from the parent to which it is still connected, **it is permitted** to eat its fruits, as the first Tanna said, because the extended vine is still considered to be a part of its parent. וּמָקוֹם שֶׁכֹּחָהּ רַע אָסוּר — **But where the strength [of the extended vine] is weak** so that it does not draw its main nourishment from the parent, **it is forbidden** to eat the fruits that will now grow from the vine, because it is considered replanted in the rootstock onto which it has been grafted, even though it is still connected to its parent.[8]

The Mishnah gives another case of replanting where the fruits are forbidden:

— NOTES —

6. *Rav* and *Rambam Commentary*. [This is called סִפּוּק, extension (or "lengthening"), because the vine becomes "longer" by being attached to a second vine (*Tos. Yom Tov,* from *Rash*).]

7. That is, in addition to a vine from the first grapevine being extended and grafted onto the second, a vine from the second grapevine is in turn also extended back and grafted onto the first. In that way, each grapevine has a vine from the other one grafted onto it (*Rambam Commentary*).

8. [*Rambam Commentary*; see also *Rav.*]

The first Tanna, however, holds that whenever the extended vine remains attached to its parent, it is not considered to be replanted in the rootstock onto which it has been grafted. [According to *Yerushalmi*, the first Tanna holds this way only where we have no *proof* that the extended vine is drawing its main nourishment from the rootstock onto which it has been grafted. But where we do have such proof, he agrees with R' Meir that the extended vine is considered replanted in the rootstock (*Tos. Yom Tov*).]

[15] **MISHNAH ORLAH** / Chapter 1: *Hanotei'a* 1/6

- רע"ב -

וְהִיא מְלֵאָה פֵּירוֹת. אִם תְּלָשָׁן מִיָּד, הֵן מוּתָּרִין מִפְּנֵי שֶׁגָּדְלוּ בְּהֶיתֵּר. וְאִם הִנִּיחָן בְּאִילָן, וְגָדְלוּ לְאַחַר שֶׁנִּפְסְקָה, וְאֵין בְּפֵירוֹת שֶׁגָּדְלוּ כְּבָר מָאתַיִם לְבַטֵּל הַתּוֹסֶפֶת, אָסוּר, דְּעָרְלָה מוֹסֶרֶת עַד מָאתַיִם. וְהוּא הַדִּין

וְכֵן בְּרֵכָה שֶׁנִּפְסְקָה וְהִיא מְלֵאָה פֵּרוֹת, אִם הוֹסִיף בְּמָאתַיִם, אָסוּר.

[ו] נְטִיעָה שֶׁל עָרְלָה וְשֶׁל כִּלְאֵי הַכֶּרֶם שֶׁנִּתְעָרְבוּ בִּנְטִיעוֹת, הֲרֵי זֶה לֹא יִלְקֹט; וְאִם לָקַט, יַעֲלֶה בְּאֶחָד וּמָאתַיִם,

בְּאִילָן זָקֵן שֶׁנֶּעֱקַר וּבוֹ פֵּירוֹת, וְחָזַר וּשְׁתָלוֹ: (ו) שֶׁנִּתְעָרְבָה בִּנְטִיעוֹת. שֶׁל הֶיתֵּר, וְאֵינוֹ מַכִּיר הַנְּטִיעָה שֶׁל עָרְלָה: וְשֶׁל כִּלְאֵי הַכֶּרֶם. כְּגוֹן שֶׁהֶעֱבִיר עָלָיו נָקוּב תַּחַת גֶּפֶן אַחַת וְנַאֲסָרָה, וְאֵינוֹ מַכִּירָה בֵּין שְׁאָר גְּפָנִים: דְּכֵיוָן שֶׁאֵינוֹ מַכִּיר אוֹתָהּ שֶׁל אִיסּוּר, כֻּלָּן אֲסוּרוֹת:

וְכֵן בְּרֵכָה שֶׁנִּפְסְקָה וְהִיא מְלֵאָה פֵּרוֹת — **And also, a layered branch that was cut** from an old tree **when the layered branch was already filled with** non-*orlah* **fruit,** אִם הוֹסִיף בְּמָאתַיִם אָסוּר — then **if it grew one two-hundredth more** from its own roots after being cut from the old tree, **it is forbidden** to eat those fruits, because the new *orlah* growth is too large to be nullified.[9]

[6] The Mishnah continues its discussion of the nullification of *orlah* "in two hundred":

נְטִיעָה שֶׁל עָרְלָה וְשֶׁל כִּלְאֵי הַכֶּרֶם שֶׁנִּתְעָרְבוּ בִּנְטִיעוֹת — **If a young tree of** *orlah* **or of** *kilayim* **of the vineyard**[1] **became mixed with other young trees** so that the grower does not know which tree is the forbidden one,[2] הֲרֵי זֶה לֹא יִלְקֹט — **one may not pick** fruit from any of the mixed trees, even if the permitted trees are two hundred times the forbidden ones.[3] וְאִם לָקַט יַעֲלֶה בְּאֶחָד וּמָאתַיִם —

NOTES

9. As we learned earlier in the Mishnah, a layered branch that is cut from its parent is considered to be newly planted in the place of its own roots, and any fruit that grows from it for the next three years is forbidden as *orlah*. The Mishnah now discusses the case in which the layered branch already had permitted fruits on it when it became newly planted. If the person were to cut those fruits from the layered branch immediately, they would remain permitted, because they did not grow from an *orlah* tree. However, if he leaves them on the "newly planted" tree and they continue to grow, their new growth *will* be forbidden as *orlah,* and the fruits will therefore contain a "mixture" of *orlah* and non-*orlah*. Now, the law is that *orlah* that became mixed with permitted fruits becomes nullified if the permitted fruits are at least 200 times the *orlah* (below, 2:1). In our Mishnah's case as well, as long as the original fruit is at least 200 times the new growth in the fruit, the *orlah* portion is nullified and the fruit remains permitted. But if the new growth is more than one part in 200, that new growth is too large to be nullified in the original fruit, which therefore becomes forbidden because of the *orlah* that it contains (*Rav*).

[6]

1. If grain or the like is planted near a grapevine, both the grain and the vine become "*kilayim* of the vineyard" and are forbidden for all benefit (see *Devarim* 22:9 and *Kilayim* 8:1), just like *orlah* fruits. And like *orlah* fruits, *kilayim* of the vineyard becomes nullified in a mixture if the permitted part is at least 200 times the forbidden part.

2. In the case of *orlah*, the grower forgot which tree was less than three years old. In the case of *kilayim* of the vineyard, the grain was later removed and the farmer cannot tell near which vine it grew (see *Rav*).

3. The law is that "something significant"

משניות ערלה / פרק א: הנוטע

וּבִלְבַד שֶׁלֹּא יִתְכַּוֵּן לִלְקֹט. רַבִּי יוֹסֵי אוֹמֵר: אַף יִתְכַּוֵּן לִלְקֹט וְיַעֲלוּ בְּאֶחָד וּמָאתָיִם.

- רע"ב -

אף יתבוין וילקוט. דחזקה אין אדם אוסר כרמו בנטיעה אחת, ולא חיישינן דלמא אתי לערב הנטיעה לכתחלה. ואף על גב דבעלמא אין מבטלין איסור לכתחלה, הכא מלתא דלא שכיחא היא ולא גזור. ואין הלכה כרבי יוסי:

But if he *did* pick some fruit, **it becomes nullified in two hundred and one**, i.e., if there are two hundred times as many permitted fruit as there are forbidden fruit,[4] **וּבִלְבַד שֶׁלֹּא יִתְכַּוֵּן לִלְקֹט** — **provided that he did not intend to pick** the fruits in order to cause them to become nullified.[5] **רַבִּי יוֹסֵי אוֹמֵר** — **R' Yose says:** **אַף יִתְכַּוֵּן לִלְקֹט וְיַעֲלוּ בְּאֶחָד וּמָאתָיִם** — **He may even intend to pick them and they will become nullifed in two hundred and one.**[6]

NOTES

[דָּבָר חָשׁוּב] does not become nullified. Something connected to the ground is considered "significant" in this regard. Accordingly, the forbidden tree and its fruits do not become nullified among the permitted trees and their fruits even if there are 200 times as many (see *Rav, Mishnah Rishonah,* and *Rashi* to *Gittin* 54b ד"ה הרי זה לא ילקט). Therefore the Mishnah says that one may not pick any of the fruits to eat them, because where there is no nullification the entire "mixture" is forbidden (see *Rav*). [Something is called a "mixture" even if each piece is separate, as long as we do not know which piece is which.]

Now (as we will see in the next part of the Mishnah), if one *would* pick some of the fruit, that fruit should really become nullified in the majority of fruits, because it is no longer attached and thus no longer significant. However, the law is that one may not purposely nullify a forbidden thing in a mixture [אֵין מְבַטְּלִין אִסּוּר לְכַתְּחִלָּה]. That is why the Mishnah here rules "one may not pick" any of the fruit.

4. Where there are 200 times as much permitted fruit, the forbidden fruit should really become nullified while still on the tree, except for the fact that the attached fruit is significant and cannot become nullified (see preceding note). Now that a fruit was picked and is no longer attached, it can and does become nullified, even it is from the forbidden tree (see *Yoreh Deah* 101:7).

5. [See note 3.] If someone purposely nullifies a forbidden thing in a mixture, the Rabbis decreed that he may not eat the mixture even though the forbidden thing is now technically nullified (see *Gittin* 54b). Therefore, the Mishnah says that the picked fruit is permitted only if the person did not intend to nullify it by picking it, such as where he mistakenly thought that the forbidden fruit was nullified in 200 even while still on the tree (*Meleches Shlomo,* from *Rashi* to *Gittin* 54b). But if he picked it knowing that this would make it nullified, it remains forbidden.

6. R' Yose holds that the usual Rabbinic prohibition against intentional nullification does not apply in this case (for reasons that will be explained in the next paragraph). Therefore, he permits the person to pick the fruit, even though this will make it nullified.

There is a general rule that the Rabbis make their decrees only for common cases. It is common for some forbidden food to become mixed indistinguishably with permitted food. For such cases, the Rabbis decreed that one may not add more permitted food to the mixture in order to nullify what is forbidden. But, R' Yose holds, it is not common for a person to forget which tree is *orlah* or *kilayim* for this could cause the surrounding trees to become forbidden. Therefore, in the rare case that a person *did* do so, the Rabbis did not decree that he may not cause the forbidden fruit to become nullified by picking the fruit (see *Rav*).

[17] MISHNAH ORLAH / Chapter 1: *Hanotei'a*

- רע"ב -

[ז] הֶעָלִים, וְהַלּוּלָבִים, וּמֵי גְפָנִים, וּסְמָדַר, מֻתָּרִים בָּעָרְלָה וּבָרְבָעִי וּבַנָּזִיר, וַאֲסוּרִים בָּאֲשֵׁרָה.

(ז) ומי גפנים. המיס היוצאים מן הגפנים כשחותכים אותם או את הזמורות בימי ניסן: והסמדר. הוא הפרח שממנו יצא הבוסר, אבל הבוסר עצמו הכל מודים שהוא פרי: מותרים בערלה. דכתיב (ויקרא יט, כג) וערלתם ערלתו את פריו, והני לאו פרי נינהו: וברבעי. נאכלין בשנה רביעית חוץ לירושלים בלא פדיון, דהיינו כל פרי קדש הלולים כתיב (שם פסוק כד), והני לא הוי פרי: ובנזיר. מותר הנזיר לאכלם, דבנזיר כתיב (במדבר ו, ד) לא יאכל, והני לאו בני אכילה נינהו: ואסורים באשרה. דכתיב (דברים יג, יח) ולא ידבק בידך מאומה מן החרם, ואשרה הוא אילן הנעבד:

---

[7] The Torah specifies in the *orlah* prohibition: וַעֲרַלְתֶּם עָרְלָתוֹ אֶת פִּרְיוֹ, *you shall treat its "fruit" as closed* (forbidden) (*Vayikra* 19:23). This teaches that only the "fruit" of an *orlah* tree is forbidden. The next Mishnah discusses which edible parts of an *orlah* tree or vine are considered "fruit":

הֶעָלִים וְהַלּוּלָבִים וּמֵי גְפָנִים וּסְמָדַר מֻתָּרִים בָּעָרְלָה — **The leaves, the shoots, the water of vines, and the buds are permitted** in the case of *orlah*,[1] וּבָרְבָעִי — and may be eaten without restriction in the case of *reva'i*[2] וּבַנָּזִיר — **and in** the case of **a** *nazir*,[3] וַאֲסוּרִים בָּאֲשֵׁרָה — **but they are forbidden in** the case **of an** *asheirah*.[4]

NOTES

[7]

1. By "leaves," the Mishnah means even leaves that are somewhat edible (*Derech Emunah, Hil. Maaser Sheni* 9:101). The "shoots" are young branches that are soft [and somewhat edible] (*Rambam Commentary*). The "water of vines" is the liquid that oozes from a vine when it is cut during the spring. The "bud" is the flower bud that will eventually develop into a grape. These are not classified as "fruits." Therefore, they are not forbidden as *orlah* (*Rav*).

2. The Torah states that while the fruit of the first three years is forbidden as *orlah*, וּבַשָּׁנָה הָרְבִיעִית יִהְיֶה כָּל פִּרְיוֹ קֹדֶשׁ הִלּוּלִים לַה׳ *And in the fourth year all its "fruit" shall be sanctified to praise Hashem* (*Vayikra* 19:24). That is, the fruit of the fourth year (or its redemption money) shall be brought to Jerusalem to be consumed there. Here, too, the Torah specifies "fruit." Therefore, the law does not apply to the fourth year's leaves, shoots, vine-water, or buds, and the Mishnah says that "they are permitted," meaning that they may be eaten anywhere without being redeemed (*Rav*).

3. The Torah says that if one becomes a *nazir*, מִיַּיִן וְשֵׁכָר יַזִּיר חֹמֶץ יַיִן וְחֹמֶץ שֵׁכָר לֹא יִשְׁתֶּה וְכָל מִשְׁרַת עֲנָבִים לֹא יִשְׁתֶּה וַעֲנָבִים לַחִים וִיבֵשִׁים לֹא יֹאכֵל. כֹּל יְמֵי נִזְרוֹ מִכֹּל אֲשֶׁר יֵעָשֶׂה מִגֶּפֶן הַיַּיִן מֵחַרְצַנִּים וְעַד זָג לֹא יֹאכֵל, *From new or aged wine he shall abstain, and he shall not drink vinegar of wine or vinegar of aged wine; anything in which grapes have been soaked he shall not drink, and fresh and dry grapes "he shall not eat." All the days of his nezirus, anything made from the grapevine, even the pits or skin, "he shall not eat"* (*Bamidbar* 6:3-4). Since the Torah gives the prohibition in terms of *he shall not eat*, it applies only to those parts of the grapevine that are normally eaten. This excludes the leaves, shoots, vine-water, and buds, which (though somewhat edible) are not normally eaten (see *Rav* and *Rambam Commentary*; see also *Meleches Shlomo*, citing *Nazir* 44b, for another derivation from the verse).

4. An *asheirah* is a tree worshiped as an idol. And the Torah commands about idols: וְלֹא יִדְבַּק בְּיָדְךָ מְאוּמָה מִן הַחֵרֶם, *And no part of the banned property may adhere to your hand* (*Devarim* 13:18); that is, you shall not derive benefit from any part of it. Thus, the prohibition applies to any part of the *asheirah*, not just to its fruit (*Rav; Rambam Commentary*).

[18] משניות ערלה / פרק א: הנוטע

א/ח

- רע"ב -

רַבִּי יוֹסֵי אוֹמֵר: הַסְמָדַר אָסוּר, מִפְּנֵי שֶׁהוּא פֶּרִי. רַבִּי אֱלִיעֶזֶר אוֹמֵר: הַמַּעֲמִיד בִּשְׂרַף הָעָרְלָה, אָסוּר. אָמַר רַבִּי יְהוֹשֻׁעַ: שָׁמַעְתִּי בְּפֵרוּשׁ, שֶׁהַמַּעֲמִיד בִּשְׂרַף הֶעָלִים, בִּשְׂרַף הֶעִקָּרִים, מֻתָּר; בִּשְׂרַף הַפַּגִּים, אָסוּר, מִפְּנֵי שֶׁהֵם פֶּרִי.

[ח] עֲנֻקוֹקְלוֹת, וְהַחַרְצַנִּים, וְהַזַּגִּים, וְהַתֶּמֶד

המעמיד בשרף הערלה. המעמיד גבינה בשרף הנוטף מעצי ערלה. שרף גומ"א בלט"ז. וסבר רבי אליעזר דשרף הוי פרי, בין באילן העושה פירות בין באילן שאינו עושה פירות. ואין הלכה כרבי יוסי ולא כרבי אליעזר: בשרף הפגים. שרף הנוטף מן הפירות שלא בשלו כל צרכן. והלכה כרבי יהושע: (ח)

ענקוקלות. לשון נוטריקון, ענבים דלקו תלת. כלומר שלקו קודם שהביאו שליש בשולן: החרצנים. גרעינים שבתוך הענבים: והזגים. הקליפות שבחוץ: תמד. שנתן מים על גבי שמרים או על החרלנים והזגין, ויש בהן טעם יין:

A different opinion regarding the buds:

רַבִּי יוֹסֵי אוֹמֵר — **R' Yose says:** הַסְמָדַר אָסוּר מִפְּנֵי שֶׁהוּא פֶּרִי — **The bud is forbidden** in all cases, even in the cases of *orlah*, *reva'i*, and *nazir*, **because it is** considered **a fruit.**[5]

The Mishnah now discusses the law regarding the *sap* of an *orlah* tree:

רַבִּי אֱלִיעֶזֶר אוֹמֵר — **R' Eliezer says:** הַמַּעֲמִיד בִּשְׂרַף הָעָרְלָה אָסוּר — **If one curdles** milk **with the sap of** *orlah*, [the cheese] is **forbidden.**[6]

Another Tanna says that not all sap is the same:

אָמַר רַבִּי יְהוֹשֻׁעַ — **R' Yehoshua said:** שָׁמַעְתִּי בְּפֵרוּשׁ שֶׁהַמַּעֲמִיד בִּשְׂרַף הֶעָלִים בִּשְׂרַף הֶעִקָּרִים מֻתָּר — **I heard explicitly that if one curdles** milk **with the sap of the leaves** of an *orlah* tree, **or with the sap of the trunk,**[7] [the cheese] is **permitted,** because such sap is not considered "fruit"; בִּשְׂרַף הַפַּגִּים אָסוּר מִפְּנֵי שֶׁהֵם פֶּרִי — **but if he curdles** milk **with the sap of the unripe fruits** [the **cheese**] **is forbidden, because they are** considered **fruit.**

[8] The Mishnah now discusses various other parts of the tree that *do* qualify as "fruit":

עֲנֻקוֹקְלוֹת — **Defective grapes,**[1] וְהַחַרְצַנִּים וְהַזַּגִּים וְהַתֶּמֶד שֶׁלָּהֶם — **grape pits,**

NOTES

5. Unlike the Tanna Kamma, who does not consider the buds to be "fruit," R' Yose does consider them to be "fruit." Therefore they are subject to all these prohibitions, just like any other fruit that is normally eaten.

6. Cheese is made by adding a curdling agent to milk, which causes the milk solids to separate from the liquid and form cheese. Tree sap can be used as a curdling agent. [Sap is a sticky substance, different from the vine-water mentioned earlier.] R' Eliezer holds that sap is considered one of the fruits of a tree, and thus is subject to the *orlah* prohibition. Therefore, if a person uses the sap of an *orlah* tree to make cheese, the cheese is forbidden (*Rav*).

7. Translation follows *Rash Sirilio, Sheviis* 7:2 ד"ה אתיא דר"ש כר' יהושע.

[8]

1. These are grapes that became damaged [and inedible] before reaching a third of their ripeness (*Rav*). Though less than one-third ripe, they had already

[19] **MISHNAH ORLAH** / Chapter 1: *Hanotei'a*

שֶׁלָּהֶם, קְלִפֵּי רִמּוֹן וְהַנֵּץ שֶׁלּוֹ, קְלִפֵּי אֱגוֹזִים, וְהַגַּרְעִינִים, אֲסוּרִים בָּעָרְלָה, וּבָאֲשֵׁרָה, וּבַנָּזִיר, וּמֻתָּרִין בְּרְבָעִי; וְהַנּוֹבְלוֹת כֻּלָּם אֲסוּרוֹת.

— רע״ב —

פרח והנץ שלהן. גבי שעל הפטמא: והגרעינין. גרעין של כל פרי, כגון הגרטינין הנמלאים בתוך התמרים והאפרסקים וכיולא בהן: אסורים בערלה. דכתיב (ויקרא יט, כג) את פריו, את הטפל לפריו: ומותרים ברבעי. שנטע רבעי אינו אסור בהנאה, אלא נאכל לבעלים בירושלים כמעשר שני, ואין מתקדש בקדושת מעשר שני אלא דבר הראוי לאכילה: נובלות. פירות הנושרין מן האילן קודם גמר בשולן: כולן אסורות. בין בערלה, בין ברבעי, בין באשרה, בין בנזיר:

קְלִפֵּי רִמּוֹן וְהַנֵּץ שֶׁלּוֹ — a pomegranate's skins and its blossom,[3] **קְלִפֵּי אֱגוֹזִים** — nut shells, **וְהַגַּרְעִינִים** — and the pits of all fruits **אֲסוּרִים בָּעָרְלָה** — are prohibited in the case of *orlah*,[4] **וּבָאֲשֵׁרָה** — and in the case of *asheirah*,[5] **וּבַנָּזִיר** — and in the case of *nazir*;[6] **וּמֻתָּרִין בְּרְבָעִי** — but they are permitted without restriction in the case of *reva'i*.[7]

The Mishnah gives the law for unripe fruit:

וְהַנּוֹבְלוֹת כֻּלָּם אֲסוּרוֹת — And fruits that fall from the tree before ripening are considered normal, edible fruit and are in all these cases prohibited — whether in the case of *asheirah* (where the entire tree is prohibited, not just its fruit), or in the cases of *orlah* and *nazir*, and they may not be eaten outside Jerusalem if they are *reva'i*.

NOTES
---

reached the stage of being a "fruit" and thus were subject to *orlah*. Therefore, their *orlah* prohibition remains even though they have since become inedible (*Chazon Ish, Orlah* 3:6).

2. *Temed* is the inferior wine made by soaking the grape pits or the grape skins in water (*Rav*). The *temed* has the same status as the pits or skins from which it was made.

3. The "blossom" is the crown that grows from the projection at the top of the pomegranate (*Rav*).

4. These are not the actual "fruit" but only secondary to the fruit. Nevertheless, the Torah says with regard to *orlah*, "אֶת פִּרְיוֹ", which can be translated "*with*" its fruit, and which comes to include in the *orlah* prohibition even things that are secondary to the fruit (see *Rav*). [This derivation is not needed for defective grapes, which were actual fruit before they became damaged (see *Mishnah Rishonah*).]

5. For *any* part of the *asheirah* tree is forbidden (see Mishnah 7 note 6).

6. That is, the defective grapes, grape pits, grape skins, and their *temed* are forbidden to a *nazir*.

[These items are not normally eaten, and thus should not be included in the *nazir* prohibition — see Mishnah 7 note 3. Nevertheless,] they are forbidden to a *nazir* because the verse specifically includes them when it says: *even the pits or skin, he shall not eat* (*Bamidbar* 6:4). [Defective grapes, too, are no different from the pits and skins of normal grapes.] And the *temed* that they produce, too, is forbidden by the verse *anything in which grapes have been soaked he shall not drink* (ibid. v. 3) (see *Rambam Commentary*).

7. As explained in the previous Mishnah (note 2) *reva'i* is not something prohibited, but rather something that is to be eaten in Jerusalem. Therefore, it applies only to fruits that are commonly eaten, and not to defective grapes, pits, or skins. And since it does not apply to these items, it does not apply to the *temed* made from them either (see *Rav* and *Rambam Commentary*).

[ט] **רַבִּי** יוֹסֵי אוֹמֵר: נוֹטְעִין יִחוּר שֶׁל עָרְלָה, וְאֵין נוֹטְעִין אֱגוֹז שֶׁל עָרְלָה, מִפְּנֵי שֶׁהוּא פֶרִי; וְאֵין מַרְכִּיבִין בְּכַפְנִיּוֹת שֶׁל עָרְלָה.

– רע"ב –

(ט) נוֹטעים יחור של ערלה. שהטען מותר בהנאה, אבל לא האגוז שהוא פרי ואסור בהנאה. ומודה רבי יוסי שאם נטע והבריך והרכיב שהוא מותר, דזה וזה גורס מותר: בכפניות. יחור שיש בו כפניות, תמרים בעודן סמדר נקראים כפניות. רבי יוסי לטעמיה דאמר (משנה ז) הסמדר אסור מפני שהוא פרי. והלכה כמותו דמותר ליטע יחור של ערלה, ואין הלכה כמותו שחוסר בכפניות:

[9] We learned in the last two Mishnahs that *orlah* applies only to "fruit." This Mishnah continues that discussion:

רַבִּי יוֹסֵי אוֹמֵר — **R' Yose says:** נוֹטְעִין יִחוּר שֶׁל עָרְלָה — **One may plant the branch of an *orlah* tree,**[1] וְאֵין נוֹטְעִין אֱגוֹז שֶׁל עָרְלָה — **but one may not plant a nut of *orlah*,** מִפְּנֵי שֶׁהוּא פֶרִי — **because** while a branch is not a fruit, [a nut] *is* a fruit, and it is forbidden to benefit from the fruit of *orlah*. וְאֵין מַרְכִּיבִין בְּכַפְנִיּוֹת שֶׁל עָרְלָה — **And** similarly, **one may not graft** a branch **with date-bud clusters of *orlah*,** because date-bud clusters, too, are considered fruit.[2]

NOTES

[9]

1. Even though the fruit of an *orlah* tree is forbidden, its branches, which are not fruit, are permitted for use (see above, Mishnah 7). Therefore, one may plant and root the branch of an *orlah* tree.

2. [A date tree produces clusters of buds, which eventually develop into clusters of dates.] R' Yose follows his opinion in Mishnah 7 above, that the buds of *orlah* are considered a fruit and are forbidden. Therefore, he rules here that one may not take a branch with date-bud clusters from an *orlah* tree and graft that branch onto another date tree (*Rav*). Although the branch itself is permitted, the clusters on it are already forbidden as *orlah* fruits. Therefore, R' Yose forbids the grafting out of concern that one will come to eat those forbidden fruits (*Rash*).

Chapter Two

משניות ערלה / פרק ב: התרומה

- רע"ב -

פרק שני — התרומה.
(א) התרומה. עולין
באחד ומאה. אם

[א] הַתְּרוּמָה וּתְרוּמַת מַעֲשֵׂר שֶׁל דְּמַאי,
הַחַלָּה וְהַבִּכּוּרִים, עוֹלִים

נפלה סאה אחת מאלו במאה סאין של חולין, בטלה, ומותרים לזרים. בפחות ממאה, הכל אסור לזרים.

---

[1] The second chapter discusses the rules of בִּטּוּל בְּרוֹב, *nullification by the majority,* as they apply to *orlah, kilei hakerem,* and holy foods (*terumah* and the meat of offerings).

Prohibited items that become mixed with permitted items become בָּטֵל, *nullified,* in a simple majority. For example, if one prohibited item falls into two permitted items, and we cannot tell which one is the prohibited one, all three may be used because the prohibited item has become "nullified" (lost its prohibited status) through its mixture with the larger number of permitted items.[1]

The situation is more complicated when it comes to food mixtures, because the prohibited food adds its forbidden flavor to the mixture as a whole.[2] Therefore, food mixtures require more than a simple majority to nullify the prohibited food in them; there must be so much more permitted food that someone eating the mixture would not taste the flavor of the prohibited food.[3] When this cannot be determined, we generally require sixty times more permitted food than prohibited food to permit the mixture (since most flavors cannot be detected in these proportions).[4] The first Mishnah teaches that there are certain kinds of holy foods and prohibited foods that are subject to a higher standard and do not become בָּטֵל, *nullified,* in a simple majority or even in a mixture of sixty to one:

הַתְּרוּמָה וּתְרוּמַת מַעֲשֵׂר שֶׁל דְּמַאי הַחַלָּה וְהַבִּכּוּרִים — *Terumah, terumas maaser of demai, challah,* and *bikkurim*[5] עוֹלִים בְּאֶחָד וּמֵאָה — all **become nullified**

--- NOTES ---

[1]
1. See *Rashi* to *Beitzah* 3b ד"ה אפילו for the Biblical source for this rule.
2. The flavor of a prohibited food is also prohibited (*Chullin* 108a). This is known as טַעַם כְּעִקָּר, *the flavor is like the main part* of the food (*Pesachim* 44b).
3. *Avodah Zarah* 5:8. See next note.
4. When the prohibited and permitted foods are both the same kind (מִין בְּמִינוֹ), for example, kosher slaughtered meat with nonkosher meat of the same kind, the taste of the prohibited food can never be detected. Nevertheless, sixty times more permitted food is needed to nullify the forbidden food (by Rabbinic decree). When the two foods are not of the same kind (מִין בְּשֶׁאֵינוֹ מִינוֹ), for example, bacon mixed with kosher meat, and there is someone who can taste it and determine whether the flavor of the nonkosher food is detectable in the mixture (for example,

there is a non-Jewish chef who can taste it and tell us), then the mixture can be permitted even with less than sixty, if he tells us that there is no taste of the nonkosher food in the mixture (*Chullin* 97b). [However, it is the practice of Ashkenazic Jews not to rely on the opinion of a non-Jewish taster (*Yoreh Deah* 98:1).]

This is the rule for foods that were blended together or cooked together [לַח בְּלַח, literally, *wet in wet*]. The rule for pieces that simply got mixed together but did not give any flavor to each other [יָבֵשׁ בְּיָבֵשׁ, literally, *dry in dry*] is somewhat different. These still need a proportion of 60:1 when they are of different kinds, but only a simple majority when they are of the same kind (see *Yoreh Deah* 109:1).

5. *Terumah* is the portion of a crop grown in Eretz Yisrael that is given to a Kohen. *Terumas maaser* is the portion separated by a Levi from *the maaser rishon* he

[23] MISHNAH ORLAH / Chapter 2: *HaTerumah*

בְּאֶחָד וּמֵאָה, וּמִצְטָרְפִין זֶה עִם זֶה, וְצָרִיךְ לְהָרִים.

- רע״ב -

ומפקינן לה מדכתיב גבי תרומת מעשר (במדבר יח, כט) אֶת מִקְדְּשׁוֹ מִמֶּנּוּ, מַה שֶׁהוּרַם מִמֶּנּוּ אִם חָזַר לְתוֹכוֹ מְקַדְּשׁוֹ, דְּהַיְינוּ תִּשְׁעִים וְתִשְׁעָה, דְּמִמֶּנּוּ הִפְרִישׁ עֲשָׂרָה לְמַעֲשֵׂר וּמֵעֲשָׂרָה אַחַת לִתְרוּמַת מַעֲשֵׂר: וּמִצְטָרְפִין זֶה עִם זֶה. אִם נָפְלָה סְאָה אַחַת מְכֻלָּן לְפָחוּת מִמֵּאָה חֻלִּין, מְקַדַּשְׁתָּן. וּבְהָא מוֹדוּ כּוּלֵי עָלְמָא דְּמִצְטָרְפִין, דְּשֵׁם אֶחָד לְכוּלְּהוּ וְכוּלְּהוּ מִקְרוּ תְּרוּמָה דְּבִתְחִלָּה כְּתִיב (שם טו, כ) חַלָּה תָּרִימוּ תְרוּמָה, וּבִכּוּרִים נַמִּי אִקְרוּ תְּרוּמָה, דְּאָמַר מַר (מכות יז, א) וּתְרוּמַת יָדֶךָ (דברים יב, יז) אֵלּוּ בִּכּוּרִים, דִּכְתִיב בְּהוּ (דברים כו, ד) וְלָקַח הַכֹּהֵן הַטֶּנֶא מִיָּדָךְ: וְצָרִיךְ לְהָרִים. הַסְּאָה שֶׁנָּפְלָה וְלָתֵת אוֹתָהּ לַכֹּהֵן, וְהַשְּׁאָר מֻתָּר לְזָרִים. וְאַף עַל גַּב דְּבְעָרְלָה וְכִלְאֵי הַכֶּרֶם דַּחֲמִירֵי טְפֵי אֵין צָרִיךְ לְהָרִים וְהַאִיסּוּר עַצְמוֹ בָּטֵל, שֶׁאֲנִי תְּרוּמָה דְּיֵשׁ לָהּ בְּעָלִים וְצָרִיךְ לְהָרִים מִפְּנֵי גֶזֶל הַשֵּׁבֶט, אֲבָל בְּכָל שְׁאָר אִיסּוּרִים דְּלָא שַׁיָּךְ בְּהוּ דִּין גֶּזֶל כְּשֶׁהֵן מִתְבַּטְּלִין אֵין צָרִיךְ לְהָרִים:

---

in a mixture of **a hundred and one** parts; i.e., a mixture containing one part of these holy foods together with 100 parts of *chullin* (ordinary food). It takes 100 parts of *chullin* to nullify one part of *terumah* or any of these other holy foods. Once they become nullified, the mixture may be eaten by anyone, even someone who is not a Kohen.[6] וּמִצְטָרְפִין זֶה עִם זֶה — **And they combine with one another** to prohibit the mixture into which they fall. If two or more of these types of holy foods fall into permitted food, they combine to prohibit the mixture to non-Kohanim unless there is 100 times as much permitted food as all the holy foods combined.[7] וְצָרִיךְ לְהָרִים — **But** even in a case where they

--- NOTES ---

receives from the crop; it too is given to a Kohen. *Challah* is the portion a person must give to a Kohen from dough that he makes. *Bikkurim* are the first fruits of the Seven Species for which Eretz Yisrael was famous; these are brought to the Temple and eventually given to a Kohen. [These terms are all explained more fully in the General Introductions to *Terumos, Maasros, Challah,* and *Bikkurim.*] All of these are referred to in the Torah as "*terumah*" (see *Bamidbar* 18:26, 15:19 and *Deuteronomy* 12:17), and they may all be eaten only by a Kohen and his family.

Terumas maaser of *demai* is the portion separated from *maaser* of *demai* and given to a Kohen. *Demai* is produce bought from an *am haaretz* (an unlearned person). When the Rabbis saw that not all *amei haaretz* separated *maasros*, they decreed that any produce bought from an *am haaretz* must be tithed even if he claims that he already did so. The strict law of nullification the Mishnah is about to teach for *terumas maaser* certainly applies to regular *terumas maaser* as well. The Mishnah speaks of *terumas maaser* of *demai* to show that it applies

even to *terumas maaser* of *demai* [which is required only by Rabbinic law] (*Tiferes Yisrael*).

6. *Rosh.* However, if there is less than 100 times as much *chullin,* only a Kohen may eat from the mixture since these foods are forbidden to non-Kohanim. [The Mishnah below will qualify this rule.]

[This is a Rabbinic decree due to the special holiness of these foods. By Biblical law, *terumah* and the other holy foods become nullified in the same proportions as any other prohibited food (see *Nedarim* 59a; *Tosafos, Bava Metzia* 53a ד״ה עולה).]

7. For example, if one part *terumah* and one part *challah* fall into 100 parts of *chullin,* the mixture is prohibited to non-Kohanim unless there are 200 parts of *chullin* (100 x 2) to nullify them.

These foods combine even according to those who say (below) that different prohibitions do *not* ordinarily combine to prohibit a mixture. Since these are all called *terumah* by the Torah (see note 5), we treat them all as one large measure of *terumah* (*Rav, Rash;* see note 13).

[24] **משניות ערלה** / פרק ב: התרומה

הָעָרְלָה וְכִלְאֵי הַכֶּרֶם, עוֹלִים בְּאֶחָד וּמָאתַיִם, וּמִצְטָרְפִין זֶה עִם זֶה, וְאֵין צָרִיךְ לְהָרִים.

– רע"ב –

עולין באחד ומאתים. דגבי תרומה כתיב מלאה, מלאתך ודמעך לא תאחר (שמות כב, כח), ובכלאי הכרם כתיב מלאה, פן תקדש המלאה (דברים כב, ט), מה מלאה האמור להלן טולה, כדילפינן מאת מקדשו ממנו (במדבר יח, כז), אף כאן טולה. ולפי שכפל אסורו, שהוא אסור בהנאה, כפלו עלייתו וצריך מאתים. וערלה ילפינן לה מכלאים, לפי שהיא אסורה בהנאה כמותן: **ומצטרפין זה עם זה.** ערלה וכלאי הכרם מצטרפין יחד שנפלו לתוך היתר, מלטרפין לאסור ביבש עד מאתים, ובלח בקדרה בנותן טעם:

---

become nullified, **he must remove** from the mixture the amount of holy food that fell in and became nullified, and give it to a Kohen. Since *terumah, terumas maaser, challah,* and *bikkurim* belong to the "tribe" of Kohanim, keeping the part that became nullified would be like stealing from the Kohanim.[8]

The Mishnah now discusses the nullification (*bitul*) of prohibited produce, specifically, *orlah* and *kilei hakerem*:

הָעָרְלָה וְכִלְאֵי הַכֶּרֶם — **Orlah and kilei hakerem** (*kilayim* of the vineyard)[9] עוֹלִים בְּאֶחָד וּמָאתַיִם — **become nullified in** a mixture of **two hundred and one;** i.e., in a mixture containing one part of these prohibited foods and 200 parts of ordinary food. It takes 200 parts of permissible food to nullify one part of *orlah* or *kilei hakerem* and permit the mixture to be eaten.[10] וּמִצְטָרְפִין זֶה עִם זֶה — **And they combine with each other** to prohibit the mixture into which they fall. If both *orlah* and *kilei hakerem* fall into permitted food, the mixture may not be eaten unless there is 200 times as much permitted food as the both of them together.[11] וְאֵין צָרִיךְ לְהָרִים — **And** in a case where they do

---

NOTES

8. For example, if a *se'ah* measure of *terumah, terumas maaser, challah,* and *bikkurim* fell into 100 *se'ahs* of *chullin,* they become nullified and the mixture can be eaten by anyone. But a *se'ah* of the mixture must still be separated and given to a Kohen (*Rav, Rash* from *Yerushalmi*). Although the holiness of the *terumah* became nullified, the property rights of the Kohanim did not.

9. The Torah prohibits planting grains or vegetables together with grapevines (see *Devarim* 22:9). If they are planted together, both the grapes and the grains or vegetables become prohibited as *kilei hakerem* — *kilayim* of the vineyard. They may not be eaten, nor may one have any benefit from them (*Kilayim* 8:1). It is similarly forbidden to eat or have any benefit from *orlah* (Mishnah below, 3:1-5).

10. This, too, is a Rabbinic decree (see *Gittin* 54b; *Tosafos, Bava Metzia* 53a ד"ה עולה). The reason the Rabbis were stricter with *orlah* and *kilei hakerem* and required a margin of 200:1 to nullify them is that their prohibitions are "twice as strict" as the prohibition of *terumah.* While a non-Kohen is forbidden to eat *terumah,* he may nevertheless have benefit from it. [For example, if he inherited *terumah* from his mother's father who was a Kohen, he may sell it to a Kohen.] In the case of *orlah* and *kilei hakerem,* however, we are forbidden to have any benefit from them. Since the prohibition is twice as strict, the Rabbis set their margin for nullification at twice as much — 200:1 instead of 100:1 (*Rav, Rash* from *Yerushalmi*).

11. According to this Tanna, *orlah* and *kilei hakerem* combine to prohibit a mixture even though they are different prohibitions. [See Mishnah 10 for a discussion of the conditions under which they combine.]

[This is true for all types of mixtures (same kind, different kind, dry, wet — see note 2), except in a case where they were

[25] MISHNAH ORLAH / Chapter 2: *HaTerumah* — 2/1

- רע״ב -

רַבִּי שִׁמְעוֹן אוֹמֵר: אֵינָן מִצְטָרְפִין. רַבִּי אֱלִיעֶזֶר אוֹמֵר: מִצְטָרְפִין בְּנוֹתֵן טַעַם,

אֵינָן מִצְטַרְפִין. אֲפִילוּ לֶאֱסוֹר הַקְּדֵרָה בְּנוֹתֵן טַעַם, כֵּיוָן דִּשְׁנֵי שֵׁמוֹת נִינְהוּ, אֶלָּא אִם יֵשׁ בַּקְּדֵרָה לְבַטֵּל טַעַם הָעָרְלָה בִּפְנֵי עַצְמָן, וְטַעַם כִּלְאֵי הַכֶּרֶם בִּפְנֵי עַצְמָן, הַכֹּל מֻתָּר: מִצְטָרְפִין בְּנוֹתֵן טַעַם. שֶׁצָּרִיךְ בַּקְּדֵרָה בְּלַח כְּדֵי לְבַטֵּל טַעַם שְׁתֵּיהֶן יַחַד:

---

become nullified, **he does not need to remove** anything from the mixture, since no one has any monetary claim to them.[12]

Another Tanna disagrees:

רַבִּי שִׁמְעוֹן אוֹמֵר — **R' Shimon says:** אֵינָן מִצְטָרְפִין — [*Orlah* and *kilei hakerem*] **do not combine, because they are different prohibitions with different names.** According to R' Shimon, only prohibitions that at least share a common name can combine with each other.[13]

According to the first Tanna, *orlah* and *kilei hakerem* combine with each other to prohibit a mixture. According to R' Shimon they do not combine to prohibit a mixture. The Mishnah now cites a third opinion. According to this next Tanna, *orlah* and *kilei hakerem* sometimes combine to prohibit and sometimes they do not. It all depends on what type of mixture they fall into:

רַבִּי אֱלִיעֶזֶר אוֹמֵר — **R' Eliezer says:** מִצְטָרְפִין בְּנוֹתֵן טַעַם — [*Orlah* and *kilei hakerem*] **combine** to prohibit a mixture **when it comes to giving flavor;** i.e., when they fall into the type of mixture in which their flavors can spread through the entire mixture and be tasted. This occurs in a "wet" mixture (for example, where wine made from *orlah* grapes and *kilei hakerem* grapes falls into water, or where *orlah* fruit and *kilei hakerem* fall into a pot of food that is being cooked).[14] In such a mixture, if the flavor of the two of them together

---

NOTES

cooked together with permitted food of a different kind (*Rav, Rosh*, as explained by *Or Gadol*). This will be explained further at the end of the Mishnah (see note 15).]

The Mishnah speaks of a case where the *orlah* and *kilei hakerem* fell into the permitted food together (*Rav*). If one fell first and then the other, the law is different, as we will see in Mishnah 3 (*Tos. Yom Tov, Tiferes Yisrael*).

12. Since there is no requirement to give *orlah* and *kilei hakerem* to anyone, there is no question of "stealing," as there was in the case of *terumah* [see note 6] (*Rosh;* see *Rav*).

13. *Rav, Rash*. Nowhere do we find the Torah referring to them as part of a single category of prohibition. Therefore, since they are different prohibitions, they do not combine to prohibit a mixture. However, *terumah, terumas maaser, challah,* and *bikkurim* are all called "*terumah*" by the Torah (see note 3). Therefore, even R' Shimon agrees in the first case of the Mishnah that they combine to prohibit a mixture to non-Kohanim (*Rash, Meleches Shlomo;* see note 7).

Since *orlah* and *kilei hakerem* do not combine according to R' Shimon, if there is 200 times more permissible food than the *orlah*, the *orlah* is nullified, and if there is 200 times more permissible food than the *kilei hakerem*, that too is nullified. As long as the permissible food is 200 times more than each of them individually, they are nullified; it does not need to be 200 times more than the *orlah* and *kilei hakerem* together (*Rav*).

14. Mixtures in which liquids or foods are blended together are known as לַח בְּלַח, literally, *wet in wet* mixtures. Foods that are cooked together are also considered "wet" mixtures (even if they are solid foods), because the liquid in which they

[26] **משניות ערלה** / פרק ב: התרומה

ב/ב

– רע"ב –
אבל לא לאסור.
ביבש, שאין צריך
שיהיה בהיתר מאתים
כנגד שתיהן. והלכה

אֲבָל לֹא לֶאֱסֹר.
[ב] הַתְּרוּמָה מַעֲלָה אֶת הָעָרְלָה, וְהָעָרְלָה אֶת

כתנא קמא: (ב) התרומה מעלה את הערלה. מנטרפת עם החולין לבטל את הערלה. וכן הערלה מנטרפת עם החולין לבטל את התרומה:

---

can be tasted, the mixture is prohibited.[15] אֲבָל לֹא לֶאֱסֹר — **But** they do **not combine to prohibit** a mixture in regard to needing 200:1 to nullify them; i.e., when they fall into the kind of mixture in which their flavor does not spread through the mixture — a "dry" mixture — *orlah* and *kilei hakerem* do *not* combine to need 200 times more permissible food to nullify both of them together. As long as there is enough to nullify each of them *separately* by a margin of 200:1, they both become nullified; it is not necessary to have 200 times more than both of them together.[16]

[2] The Mishnah teaches how one forbidden food can sometimes help nullify a different forbidden food:

הַתְּרוּמָה מַעֲלָה אֶת הָעָרְלָה וְהָעָרְלָה אֶת הַתְּרוּמָה — *Terumah* can help **nullify**

NOTES
---

are cooked causes their flavors to spread throughout the pot.

[As we will see at the end of Mishnah 7, mixtures of this kind are an exception to the 100:1 law for *terumah* or the 200:1 law for *orlah* and *kilei hakerem*. The only issue in such mixtures is whether the flavor of the prohibited food can be tasted in the mixture.]

15. According to R' Eliezer, if *orlah* and *kilei hakerem* both fall into a mixture of this kind, the mixture is not permitted as long as we can still taste the combined flavor of the two (*Rav; Rosh*). Although neither the *orlah* wine nor the *kilei hakerem* wine could flavor the mixture by itself, since the flavor of the two of them together can be tasted, they combine to prohibit the mixture.

[R' Eliezer is obviously speaking of a case where the *orlah* and *kilei hakerem* fell into a *different* kind of food (מִין בְּשֶׁאֵינוֹ מִינוֹ), for example, wine into water, or grapes cooked with vegetables or meat. If the *orlah* and *kilei hakerem* wine mixed with permissible wine, or their grapes were cooked with permissible grapes (מִין בְּמִינוֹ), there is no possibility of tasting their flavor, since all the flavors are the same. In this case, they are subject to the next rule of the Mishnah.]

[R' Eliezer holds like R' Shimon that different prohibitions do not combine to prohibit. He makes an exception only where the two combine to give a noticeable flavor to the permitted food.] R' Shimon, however, holds that even in this case the two do not combine. Although we can taste the flavor of wine in the mixture, since it is not the flavor of *orlah* by itself or the flavor of *kilei hakerem* by itself, the mixture is permitted (*Rav*).

16. In cases where *orlah* and *kilei hakerem* get mixed up with permissible food in a "dry mixture" (יָבֵשׁ בְּיָבֵשׁ), in which each piece remains separate from the others (and they are not cooked together), the prohibited food does not give any flavor to the permitted food. In mixtures of this type, the rule is that *orlah* and *kilei hakerem* do not become nullified unless there is 200 times more permissible food. In regard to *this* rule, *orlah* and *kilei hakerem* do not combine. That is, as long as there is 200 times more permissible food than each of them separately, the mixture may be eaten — even though we do not have 200 times more than *both* of them together (*Rav*, as explained by *Or Gadol*; see *Rav* to *Avodah Zarah* 5:8). [An example of this case is where a container of food made from *orlah* and a container of food made from *kilei hakerem* got mixed up with 200 containers of food made from permissible fruit.]

[27] MISHNAH ORLAH / Chapter 2: HaTerumah 2/2

- רע"ב -

שנפלה למאה. לאו דוקא מאה אלא פחות ממאה, דאילו מאה ממש, עולה ולא בטי לירוף, אלא הכי קאמר התרומה שנפלה לחולין ונעשה הכל מאה: **ואחר כך נפלו שלשה קבין של ערלה.** סתם מתניתין כרבי יהושע, דאמר בפרק (קמא) [רביעי] דתרומות (משנה ז) דתרומה עולה במאה ועוד, הלכך כשנפלה סאה של תרומה לתשעים ותשע של חולין, וחזרו ונפלו שם שלשה קבין של ערלה, ומצטרפין עם החולין, שנמלאו שם תשעים ותשע ועוד שלשה קבין חולין, הרי סאה של תרומה בטלה במאה ועוד. אי נמי מצינו לאוקמיה כרבי אליעזר דהלכתא כותיה, דאמר תרומה עולה באחד ומאה, וכגון שנפלה סאה של תרומה לתוך תשעים ותשע חלי סאה של חולין, ושלשה קבין הללו של ערלה שהוא חלי סאה מצטרפין עם החולין להשלים לשיעור מאה של חולין, כדי שתעלה באחד ומאה. **זו היא שהתרומה מעלה את הערלה.** שאותה סאה של תרומה נצטרפה עם החולין להשלים מאתים חלאי סאין, להעלות שלשה קבין של ערלה באחד ומאתים: **והערלה את התרומה.** דשלשה קבין של ערלה שהן חלי סאה נצטרפו עם החולין, לבטל סאה של תרומה באחד ומאה, דכשנפלה סאה לתוך תשעים ותשע וחלי נאסרו, וכשחזר ונפל שם שלשה קבין ערלה או כלאים, הותרו:

סָאָה תְּרוּמָה — **How so?** בֵּיצַד — If a *se'ah* of *terumah* fell into close to **a hundred** *se'ah* of *chullin*, i.e., it fell into 99½ *se'ah* of *chullin* (which is not enough to nullify *terumah*),[2] וְאַחַר כָּךְ נָפְלוּ שְׁלֹשָׁה קַבִּין עָרְלָה — **and afterward three** *kavs* (half a *se'ah*) of *orlah* fell into the *chullin* as well,[3] אוֹ שְׁלֹשָׁה קַבִּין כִּלְאֵי הַכֶּרֶם — **or three** *kavs* (half a *se'ah*) of *kilei hakerem* fell in, זוֹ הִיא שֶׁהַתְּרוּמָה מַעֲלָה אֶת הָעָרְלָה וְהָעָרְלָה אֶת הַתְּרוּמָה — **this is [the case] in which the** *terumah* **nullifies the** *orlah* **(or** *kilei hakerem***) and the** *orlah* **nullifies the** *terumah*. The mixture now contains 99½ *se'ahs* of *chullin*, one *se'ah* of *terumah*, and half a *se'ah* of *orlah* (or *kilei hakerem*). The *se'ah* of *terumah* combines with the 99½ *se'ahs* of *chullin* to form a unit of 100½ *se'ahs*, which is enough to nullify the half-*se'ah* of *orlah* by a margin of 200:1,[4] and the half-*se'ah* of *orlah* combines with the 99½ *se'ahs* of *chullin* to form a unit of 100 *se'ahs*, which is enough to nullify the *terumah* by a margin of 100:1.[5]

— NOTES —

[2]

1. That is, *terumah* can join with the *chullin* to create the 200:1 majority necessary to nullify *orlah*, and the *orlah* can join with the *chullin* to create the 100:1 majority necessary to nullify *terumah* (*Rav; Rosh*).

2. *Terumah* only becomes nullified in 100 times more *chullin*, as we learned in the previous Mishnah. Thus, the *se'ah* of *terumah* that fell in did not become nullified (*Rav and Rosh*, second explanation, based on *Yerushalmi*).

[*Se'ah* was the name of a common measure used in Mishnaic times.]

3. There are six *kavs* in a *se'ah*. Thus, three *kavs* are half a *se'ah*.

Since there are only 99½ *se'ahs* of *chullin* (or 199 half-*se'ahs*), there is not enough *chullin* to nullify the half-*se'ah* of *orlah*, which needs a margin of 200:1 to nullify it (see previous Mishnah).

4. One hundred and a half *se'ahs* equals 201 half-*se'ahs*, which is more than enough to nullify the half-*se'ah* of *orlah*.

5. The Mishnah speaks of a case where the *terumah* fell in first and then the *orlah*. If they fell in together, however, they would not combine with the *chullin* to help nullify each other. On the contrary, they

משניות ערלה / פרק ב: התרומה

[ג] **הָעָרְלָה** מַעֲלָה אֶת הַכִּלְאַיִם, וְהַכִּלְאַיִם אֶת הָעָרְלָה, וְהָעָרְלָה אֶת הָעָרְלָה. כֵּיצַד? סְאָה עָרְלָה שֶׁנָּפְלָה לְמָאתַיִם, וְאַחַר כָּךְ נָפְלָה סְאָה וְעוֹד עָרְלָה,

– רע"ב –

(ג) **והערלה את הערלה.** צריך לומר דאחד מהם נטע רבעי, שהם שני שמות, דאי אפשר לאיסור של שם אחד, שיהיה מבטל קלטו לקלטו. וקרי תנא לנטע

רבעי ערלה, שמן הערלה הוא בא. והכי קתני את הערלה ולא קתני הערלה את הכלאים, שאין בכלאים שני שמות כמו שיש בערלה: **שנפלה למאתים.** לאו למאתים דוקא, דאילו מאתים ממש לא בעי ירוק. וכשנפלה סאה ערלה לתוך מאה תשעים ותשע של היתר נאסרו, ונפל שם סאה ועוד של כלאים, מצטרפים עם המאה תשעים ותשע לבטל הערלה, וכן הערלה מצטרפת עם המאה תשעים ותשע לבטל סאה ועוד של כלאי הכרם. והיינו כרבי יהושע, דאית ליה (תרומות ה, ז) דערלה בטלה במאתים ועוד, כמו תרומה במאה ואחד, הלכך סאה של כלאים בטלה במאה תשעים ותשע ומשהו, והעוד בטל בסאה חסר משהו. וכן נמי אם נפל שם סאה ועוד של נטע רבעי, מצטרפין עם המאה תשעים ותשע לבטל את הסאה של ערלה שנפלה ואסרה הכל, וכן סאה של ערלה מצטרפת עם המאה תשעים ותשע לבטל סאה של היתר, ותשע של נטע רבעי שנפלו באחרונה:

---

[3] The previous Mishnah dealt with *terumah* helping to nullify *orlah* or *kilei hakerem*. Our Mishnah deals with *orlah* and *kilei hakerem* helping to nullify each other:

וְהָעָרְלָה מַעֲלָה אֶת הַכִּלְאַיִם — *Orlah* can help nullify *kilayim*, וְהַכִּלְאַיִם אֶת הָעָרְלָה — *kilayim* can help nullify *orlah*, וְהָעָרְלָה אֶת הָעָרְלָה — and one kind of *orlah* can help nullify another kind of *orlah*; namely, *reva'i*.[1] כֵּיצַד — How so? סְאָה עָרְלָה שֶׁנָּפְלָה לְמָאתַיִם — If a *se'ah* of *orlah* fell into close to two hundred *se'ahs* of permitted produce (which is not enough to nullify it)[2] וְאַחַר כָּךְ נָפְלָה סְאָה וְעוֹד עָרְלָה — and afterward a *se'ah* and a tiny bit more of a different type of *orlah* (i.e., of *reva'i*) fell in as well,[3]

--- NOTES ---

would combine with each other to form a larger bloc of forbidden food, which would require enough *chullin* to nullify both of them together, as we learned in Mishnah 1 [see note 9 there] (see *Tos. R' Akiva Eiger* and *Chazon Ish, Orlah* 4:4).

[3]

1. A forbidden food cannot help nullify other forbidden food of the same prohibition, even in combination with something else. Thus, *orlah* cannot nullify other *orlah*. However, there are two stages associated with the law of *orlah*. The first three years of a tree's growth, its fruit is completely prohibited and is known as *orlah*. In the fourth year, the fruit is known as *reva'i* and it is subject to a different law — it must be eaten in Jerusalem or be redeemed. It is forbidden to eat unredeemed *reva'i* outside of Jerusalem (see Mishnah 1:7 note 4). Our Mishnah teaches

that if *orlah* fell into permitted food and then unredeemed *reva'i* fell in, the unredeemed *reva'i* can help to nullify it and permit it to be eaten anywhere. Since *orlah* and unredeemed *reva'i* are prohibited by different prohibitions (שְׁנֵי שֵׁמוֹת), each can help to nullify the other (*Rav; Rosh*).

[If the *reva'i* in the mixture can be redeemed, it must be redeemed and cannot be nullified. However, the Mishnah is speaking of a case where it cannot be redeemed, for example, where it was worth less than a *perutah*, which is not enough of a value to be redeemed (*Rosh*).]

2. The permitted food was just slightly less than 200 *se'ahs*, for example, 199.9 *se'ahs*. Since *orlah* is nullified only by 200 parts of permissible food, it did not become nullified when it first fell in.

3. The *reva'i* that fell in was very slightly more than a *se'ah*, so that the total

[29] **MISHNAH ORLAH** / Chapter 2: *HaTerumah* 2/4

אוֹ סְאָה וְעוֹד שֶׁל כִּלְאֵי הַכֶּרֶם, זוֹ הִיא שֶׁהָעָרְלָה מַעֲלָה אֶת הַכִּלְאַיִם, וְהַכִּלְאַיִם אֶת הָעָרְלָה, וְהָעָרְלָה אֶת הָעָרְלָה.

[ד] **כֹּל** הַמְחַמֵּץ וְהַמְתַבֵּל וְהַמְדַמֵּעַ בַּתְּרוּמָה

– רע״ב –

(ד) כל המחמץ והמתבל וכו'. הכי קאמר, כל המחמץ והמתבל, בערלה ובכלאי הכרם אסור, והמדמע בתרומה. המחמץ את העיסה בתפוחים או בשמרי יין של ערלה ושל כלאי הכרם, והמתבל את הקדרה בתבלין של כללי הכרם או של ערלה, אסור, ואין עולין באחד ומאתים. וכן בתרומה, כיון שהחמיצה עיסה של חולין בשאור של תרומה, ונתבלה קדרה של חולין בתבלין של תרומה, נעשה הכל מדומע ואסור לזרים, ואינו עולה באחד ומאה:

אוֹ סְאָה וְעוֹד שֶׁל כִּלְאֵי הַכֶּרֶם — or a *se'ah* and a tiny bit more of *kilei hakerem* fell in,[4] **זוֹ הִיא שֶׁהָעָרְלָה מַעֲלָה אֶת הַכִּלְאַיִם** — this is [the case] in which *orlah* helps nullify *kilayim,* **וְהַכִּלְאַיִם אֶת הָעָרְלָה** — *kilayim* helps nullify *orlah,* **וְהָעָרְלָה אֶת הָעָרְלָה** — and *orlah* helps nullify a different type of *orlah* (i.e., *reva'i*).[5]

[4] The Mishnah now discusses cases in which *terumah, orlah,* and *kilei hakerem* do *not* become nullified, even when they mix with a large enough amount of permitted food. This is because their presence in the mixture can still be noticed by the effect they have on it:[1]

כֹּל הַמְחַמֵּץ וְהַמְתַבֵּל — Anything that leavens a dough (i.e., causes it to rise)[2] or that spices a dish of food,[3] if it falls into permitted food, **וְהַמְדַמֵּעַ בַּתְּרוּמָה** — in the case of *terumah,* it makes it *meduma* (a mixture of *chullin*

NOTES
---

amount of permitted food plus *orlah* (200.9 *se'ah*) was 200 times more than the *se'ah*-plus of *reva'i* (*Tos. Yom Tov,* according to *Rav's* second explanation in the previous Mishnah; *Rav* here follows his first explanation there; see note 5).

4. As we learned in Mishnah 1, *kilei hakerem* also requires a 200:1 ratio to be nullified.

5. The *se'ah* of *orlah* that fell in first combines with the 199.9 *se'ah* of permitted produce to form a bloc of 200.9, which is just enough to nullify the *se'ah* plus of *reva'i* or *kilei hakerem* that fell in afterward, by a margin of 200:1. [The extra 0.9 of a *se'ah* in the combination is 200 times more than the tiny bit we called "plus."] At the same time, the *se'ah*-plus of *reva'i* or *kilei hakerem* that fell in second combines with the 199.9 *se'ahs* of permitted produce to be more than enough to nullify the one *se'ah* of *orlah* by 200:1 (*Tos. Yom Tov,* according to *Rav's* second explanation in the previous Mishnah; *Rav* himself explains this Mishnah only according to his first explanation there).

[4]

1. *Rambam Commentary.* Because they have this noticeable effect, they cannot be considered insignificant and nullified.

2. [Dough that is left to rise on its own takes a long time to rise. To speed up the process, certain ingredients can be added to the dough to make it rise ("leaven") faster. This is usually done by adding a piece of שְׂאוֹר, sourdough (dough that was left to rise for a long time until it became highly fermented).] However, it can also be done by adding fermented apples or wine dregs to the dough. The Mishnah is speaking of a case where he leavened dough either with sourdough made from *terumah,* apples from an *orlah* tree, or wine dregs from grapes that were either *orlah* or *kilei hakerem* (*Rav*).

3. [Certain spices grow on trees and can be forbidden as *orlah.* Others grow as herbs and can become forbidden as *kilei hakerem* when they are planted in a vineyard.] Although most foods lose their flavor when they become mixed in 60

משניות ערלה / פרק ב: התרומה [30]

וּבָעָרְלָה וּבְכִלְאֵי הַכֶּרֶם, אָסוּר, בֵּית שַׁמַּאי אוֹמְרִים: אַף מְטַמֵּא; וּבֵית הִלֵּל אוֹמְרִים: לְעוֹלָם אֵינוֹ מְטַמֵּא, עַד שֶׁיְּהֵא בוֹ כַּבֵּיצָה.

— רע״ב —

בית שמאי אומרים אף מטמא. שאור טמא שהחמיץ עיסה טהורה, או תבלין טמאין שתבלו קדרה טהורה, אף על פי שאין בשאור או בתבלין כביצה, שהוא שעור טומאת אוכלין, נטמאת העיסה ונטמאת הקדרה: ובית הלל אומרים עד שיהא בו כביצה. דאין אוכל מטמא פחות מכביצה, לא שנא שאור ולא שנא שאר אוכלין:

וּבָעָרְלָה וּבְכִלְאֵי הַכֶּרֶם and *terumah* that is forbidden to a non-Kohen),[4] אָסוּר — and in the case of *orlah* and *kilei hakerem*, it makes [the mixture] **forbidden** to everyone — even if the amount of permitted food would normally be enough to nullify the forbidden item. Since the effects of the *terumah*, *orlah*, or *kilei hakerem* are still noticeable, they do not become nullified no matter how much permitted food is present in the mixture.

Having taught the effect that *forbidden* leaven and spices have on permitted food, the Mishnah now presents a dispute about the effect that *tamei* leaven and spices have on *tahor* food. Normally, only *tamei* food that is at least the size of an egg can make other food *tamei*.[5] The question here is whether *tamei* leaven and spices have a different rule:

בֵּית שַׁמַּאי אוֹמְרִים — **Beis Shammai say:** אַף מְטַמֵּא — **If [leaven or spice]** that is *tamei* was added to a dough or to a food, **it also makes** the other food ***tamei*,** even when it is smaller than the size of an egg.[6] Just as a small amount of forbidden leaven or spice does not become nullified when it has a noticeable effect on a large mixture, so too a small amount of *tamei* leaven or spice is considered significant enough to make other foods *tamei* because of the noticeable effect it has on them.[7] וּבֵית הִלֵּל אוֹמְרִים — **But Beis Hillel say:** לְעוֹלָם אֵינוֹ מְטַמֵּא עַד שֶׁיְּהֵא בוֹ כַּבֵּיצָה — **[A leaven or spice] can never make** other foods ***tamei* unless it is** at least **the size of an egg,** as is the law with ordinary food.[8]

NOTES

parts of other food (see introduction to Mishnah 1), many spices can be tasted even when they are mixed in much greater amounts of food, as a small amount of them can flavor a large dish of food.

4. The word וְהָמְדֻמָּע should be understood as if it were מְדַמֵּעַ. It is not part of the previous list of effects, but part of the ruling that follows (see *Rav; Rambam Commentary*). Indeed, Rambam's reading of the Mishnah is מְדַמֵּעַ (see *Mishnah Rishonah* and the Kafich edition of *Rambam's Commentary*).

If sourdough made from *terumah* [or wine dregs from *terumah*] fell into dough that is *chullin,* or spices that were *terumah* were added to a dish of *chullin* food and flavored it, the mixture is forbidden to non-Kohanim even though the *chullin* food is more than 100 times as much as the *terumah*. Since the effects of the *terumah* are noticeable, the *terumah* cannot become nullified (*Rav*).

5. This is learned from a verse (*Rash Sirilio*, from *Toras Kohanim*).

6. Beis Shammai hold that if leaven that was *tamei* was used in a dough that was *tahor,* or if a *tamei* spice was used to flavor a cooked dish that was *tahor,* then the dough or cooked dish becomes *tamei* even if the leaven or spice was *less* than the size of an egg (*Rav*).

7. *Rambam Commentary.*

8. [Beis Hillel hold that the egg-size needed to transmit *tumah* is a Biblical decree that was said for all foods, and is not based on the relative significance of the food.]

[31] MISHNAH ORLAH / Chapter 2: HaTerumah — 2/5-6

[ה] **דּוֹסְתַּאי** אִישׁ כְּפַר יַתְמָה, הָיָה מִתַּלְמִידֵי בֵית שַׁמַּאי, וְאָמַר: שָׁמַעְתִּי מִשַּׁמַּאי הַזָּקֵן שֶׁאָמַר: לְעוֹלָם אֵינוֹ מְטַמֵּא עַד שֶׁיְּהֵא בּוֹ כַּבֵּיצָה.

[ו] **וְלָמָּה** אָמְרוּ כָּל הַמְחַמֵּץ וְהַמְתַבֵּל וְהַמְדַמֵּעַ לְהַחֲמִיר? מִין בְּמִינוֹ;

— רע״ב —

(ו) ולמה אמרו. כמו ובמה אמרו. כלומר, באיזה ענין אמרו שהמחמץ חולין בשאור של תרומה, והמתבל קדרת חולין בתבלין של תרומה, והמדמע שמתערב [ומבטל] חולין ותרומה יחד, שאנו הולכים הכל להחמיר, ומשני מין במינו. ובמה אמרו פעמים להקל ופעמים להחמיר, במין שנתערב עם שאינו מינו. ומפרש, להחמיר כילד, שאור של תרומת חטין שנפל לתוך עסת חטין של חולין, דהיינו מין במינו, אוסר בנותני טעם אפילו יותר ממאה, ועד מאה אוסר אפילו בלא נתינת טעם:

---

[5] This Mishnah continues the discussion about *tumah* begun at the end of the last Mishnah:

דּוֹסְתַּאי אִישׁ כְּפַר יַתְמָה הָיָה מִתַּלְמִידֵי בֵית שַׁמַּאי — **Dostai, the chief of Kfar Yasmah, was among the students of Beis Shammai,** וְאָמַר — **and he said:** שָׁמַעְתִּי מִשַּׁמַּאי הַזָּקֵן שֶׁאָמַר — **I heard from Shammai the Elder, who said:** לְעוֹלָם אֵינוֹ מְטַמֵּא עַד שֶׁיְּהֵא בּוֹ כַּבֵּיצָה — **[A leaven or spice] can never make other food** *tamei* **unless it is the size of an egg.**[1]

[6] We learned in Mishnah 4 that leaven and spices of *terumah* do not become nullified even in a mixture containing 100 times more *chullin*. The Mishnah now qualifies that ruling:[1]

וְלָמָּה אָמְרוּ כָּל הַמְחַמֵּץ וְהַמְתַבֵּל וְהַמְדַמֵּעַ לְהַחֲמִיר — **In regard to what did [the Sages] say: "Any** *terumah* **that leavens dough that is** *chullin*, **or that spices a dish that is** *chullin*, **or that creates a** *meduma* **mixture of** *terumah* **and** *chullin* **(without any leavening or spicing taking place)**[2] **is always to be treated strictly"?** מִין בְּמִינוֹ — **They said it in regard to** *terumah* **of one kind of produce that mixed with** *chullin* **of the same kind.**[3]

NOTES

[5]

1. Dostai testifies here that Shammai himself (the teacher of Beis Shammai) agreed with the opinion of Beis Hillel in the previous Mishnah, that *tamei* leaven and spices are no different from other *tamei* foods: they do not make other foods *tamei* unless they are at least the size of an egg.

It seems that the other students of Shammai (Beis Shammai) argued with Beis Hillel because they had not paid close enough attention to Shammai and were therefore not aware of his opinion on the matter (*Meleches Shlomo*, citing *Rash Sirilio*; see *Sotah* 47b).

[6]

1. [The ruling of Mishnah 4 was taken from an older tradition of the Sages, which said: "Any (*terumah*) that leavens or spices or creates a *meduma* mixture is to be treated strictly (in some cases), and to be treated strictly and leniently (in other cases)."] The Mishnah will now explain the meaning of this older rule (see *Pri Chadash*, cited in *Tosefos Anshei Shem*, in explanation of *Rav*).

2. That is, ordinary *terumah* that fell into *chullin* and was cooked with it (*Rav*; *Rash*). [*Rav* explains the word וְהַמְדַמֵּעַ here differently than he did in Mishnah 4 (*Tos. Yom Tov*). See *Tosefos Anshei Shem* for the reason.]

3. Literally, *of its own kind*. The Mishnah will soon explain this.

לְהָקֵל וּלְהַחֲמִיר? מִין בְּשֶׁאֵינוֹ מִינוֹ. כֵּיצַד? שְׂאֹר שֶׁל חִטִּים שֶׁנָּפַל תּוֹךְ עִסַּת חִטִּים, וְיֵשׁ בּוֹ כְּדֵי לְחַמֵּץ, בֵּין שֶׁיֵּשׁ בּוֹ לַעֲלוֹת בְּאֶחָד וּמֵאָה וּבֵין שֶׁאֵין בּוֹ לַעֲלוֹת בְּאֶחָד וּמֵאָה, אָסוּר. אֵין בּוֹ לַעֲלוֹת בְּאֶחָד וּמֵאָה, בֵּין שֶׁיֵּשׁ בּוֹ כְּדֵי לְחַמֵּץ בֵּין שֶׁאֵין בּוֹ כְּדֵי לְחַמֵּץ, אָסוּר.

לְהָקֵל וּלְהַחֲמִיר — And in regard to what did they: "The mixture is **to be treated** sometimes **leniently** and sometimes **strictly**"? מִין בְּשֶׁאֵינוֹ מִינוֹ — They said it in regard to *terumah* of **one kind** of produce that mixed with *chullin* of **another kind** of produce.[4]

The Mishnah illustrates the first of these two rules:

כֵּיצַד — **How so?** In what way is a mixture of *terumah* and *chullin* of the *same* kind of produce always treated strictly in the case of leaven? שְׂאֹר שֶׁל חִטִּים שֶׁנָּפַל תּוֹךְ עִסַּת חִטִּים — **For example:** If **sourdough** made from *terumah* **wheat fell into a** regular **dough** made from *chullin* **wheat**[5] וְיֵשׁ בּוֹ כְּדֵי לְחַמֵּץ — **and there is enough** sourdough **to leaven** the *chullin* dough, בֵּין שֶׁיֵּשׁ בּוֹ לַעֲלוֹת בְּאֶחָד וּמֵאָה — **then whether there is enough** [*chullin*] **to nullify** *terumah* in a mixture of **a hundred and one** parts (100 parts *chullin* to one part *terumah*),[6] וּבֵין שֶׁאֵין בּוֹ לַעֲלוֹת בְּאֶחָד וּמֵאָה — **or whether there is not enough** [*chullin* dough] **to nullify** *terumah* in a mixture of **a hundred and one** parts (i.e., there are less than 100 parts of *chullin* to one part of *terumah*), אָסוּר — [the dough] **is forbidden** to non-Kohanim. Where the *terumah* leavens the *chullin*, no amount of *chullin* can nullify it because the *terumah's* effect is visible, as we learned in Mishnah 4. אֵין בּוֹ לַעֲלוֹת בְּאֶחָד וּמֵאָה — On the other hand, if **there is not enough** [*chullin*] **to nullify** the *terumah* sourdough **in a mixture of a hundred and one** parts, בֵּין שֶׁיֵּשׁ בּוֹ כְּדֵי לְחַמֵּץ בֵּין שֶׁאֵין בּוֹ כְּדֵי לְחַמֵּץ — **then whether there is enough** [*terumah* sourdough] **to leaven** the *chullin* dough **or whether there is not enough to leaven it,** אָסוּר — [the *chullin* dough] **is forbidden** to non-Kohanim. Since there are less than 100 parts of *chullin* to the one part of *terumah* sourdough, it does not matter whether the *terumah* leavens it or not; *terumah* never becomes nullified (in a mixture with the same kind) unless there are 100 parts of *chullin* to one part of *terumah*.[7]

In short, when *terumah* sourdough falls into ordinary dough of the same kind (מִין בְּמִינוֹ), we always treat it according to the stricter of its two qualities. If it can leaven the dough, we treat it with the rule for things that leaven — and

---
NOTES

4. Literally, *not of its own kind*. This rule will be explained in the next Mishnah.
5. This mixture is considered מִין בְּמִינוֹ, a *kind in the same kind* (*Rav*), even though the taste of sourdough is somewhat different from the taste of regular dough (see *Meleches Shlomo* and *Tos. R' Akiva Eiger*).
6. This is the amount usually needed to nullify *terumah*, as we learned in Mishnah 1.
7. *Rav*, as explained by *Pri Chadash*, cited in *Tosefos Anshei Shem*. [When *Rav* speaks here of "giving flavor," he means that the sourdough causes the dough to leaven and rise (see *Mishnah Rishonah* to Mishnah 15 below).]

[33] MISHNAH ORLAH / Chapter 2: HaTerumah

- רע"ב -

[ז] לְהָקֵל וּלְהַחֲמִיר? מִין בְּשֶׁאֵינוֹ מִינוֹ. כֵּיצַד? כְּגוֹן גְּרִיסִין שֶׁנִּתְבַּשְּׁלוּ עִם עֲדָשִׁים, וְיֵשׁ בָּהֶם בְּנוֹתֵן טַעַם, בֵּין שֶׁיֵּשׁ בָּהֶם לַעֲלוֹת בְּאֶחָד וּמֵאָה וּבֵין שֶׁאֵין בָּהֶם לַעֲלוֹת בְּאֶחָד וּמֵאָה, אָסוּר;

(ז) גְּרִיסִין. שֶׁל פּוּל שֶׁל תְּרוּמָה, שֶׁנִּתְבַּשְּׁלוּ עִם עֲדָשִׁים שֶׁל חוּלִין, וְנִתְנוּ בָּהֶם טַעַם, טַעֲמָא לֹא בָּטֵל אֲפִילּוּ בְּיוֹתֵר מִמֵּאָה. וּבְלֹא טַעַם, אֲפִילּוּ בְּפָחוֹת מִמֵּאָה שָׁרֵי, דְּהָא דְּבָעִינַן מֵאָה, הַיְינוּ דַּוְקָא חִטִּים בְּחִטִּים דַּהֲוֵי מִין בְּמִינוֹ, דְּאִסְמַכְתּוּהָ אַקְרָא (במדבר יח, כט) אֶת מִקְדְּשׁוֹ מִמֶּנּוּ, מַה שֶּׁאַתָּה מֵרִים מִמֶּנּוּ אִם נָפַל לְתוֹכוֹ מִקְדְּשׁוֹ, וְזֶהוּ מִין בְּמִינוֹ:

---

it never becomes nullified. If it cannot leaven the dough, we treat it with the rule for *terumah* — and it cannot become nullified unless there are 100 parts more *chullin*.[8] This is what the Sages meant when they said: "Any *terumah* that leavens ... is always to be treated strictly."[9]

[7] The Mishnah now explains the second rule of the previous Mishnah:

לְהָקֵל וּלְהַחֲמִיר — And in regard to what did they say that "a mixture of *chullin* and *terumah* is **to be treated** sometimes **leniently** and sometimes **strictly**"? **מִין בְּשֶׁאֵינוֹ מִינוֹ** — They said this in regard to *terumah* of **one kind** of produce that mixed with *chullin* of **another kind** of produce. **כֵּיצַד** — **How so?** In what way is a mixture of *terumah* and *chullin* of different kinds of produce sometimes treated leniently and sometimes treated strictly? **כְּגוֹן גְּרִיסִין שֶׁנִּתְבַּשְּׁלוּ עִם עֲדָשִׁים** — **For example:** If split *terumah* **beans**[1] were **cooked with** *chullin* **lentils,** **וְיֵשׁ בָּהֶם בְּנוֹתֵן טַעַם** — and there are enough beans to **give a flavor** to the lentils, **בֵּין שֶׁיֵּשׁ בָּהֶם לַעֲלוֹת בְּאֶחָד וּמֵאָה** — then regardless of **whether there are enough** [*chullin* lentils] **to nullify** the *terumah* beans **in a mixture of one hundred and one** (100 parts *chullin* to one part *terumah*), **וּבֵין שֶׁאֵין בָּהֶם לַעֲלוֹת בְּאֶחָד וּמֵאָה** — or **whether there are not enough** [*chullin* lentils] **to nullify** the *terumah* beans **in one hundred and one** (there are less than 100 parts *chullin* to one part *terumah*), **אָסוּר** — [the mixture] **is forbidden** to non-Kohanim. Where the flavor of the *terumah* can be tasted in the *chullin*, the mixture is forbidden to non-Kohanim no matter how much *chullin* there is. The 100:1 ratio nullifies *terumah* only when the flavor of the *terumah*

NOTES

8. See *Ri ben Malki Tzedek*.

9. [The ruling the Mishnah is explaining also referred to *terumah* spices and *meduma* (*terumah* and *chullin* that became mixed and were then cooked together). The rule for them is as follows: If they fell into *chullin* of the same kind, we always treat them strictly. If they can give flavor to more than 100 parts of *chullin* (had it been of a different kind), we judge them by their flavor and the food is forbidden to non-Kohanim. If they cannot give flavor, we judge them as *terumah* and they do not become nullified by less than 100 parts *chullin*.]

[7]

1. גְּרִיסִין are beans that have been split in two (see *Rashi, Bava Metzia* 60a ד"ה גריסין).

[The Mishnah does not use the example of sourdough to illustrate this rule, as it did in the previous Mishnah to illustrate the first rule, because this Mishnah discusses mixtures of *different* kinds, and it is not common to leaven dough with sourdough of a different kind (*Tos. Yom Tov*).]

משניות ערלה / פרק ב: התרומה [34]

- רע"ב -

אֵין בָּהֶם בְּנוֹתְנֵן טַעַם, בֵּין שֶׁיֵּשׁ בָּהֶם לַעֲלוֹת בְּאֶחָד וּמֵאָה וּבֵין שֶׁאֵין בָּהֶם לַעֲלוֹת בְּאֶחָד וּמֵאָה, מֻתָּר.

[ח] **שְׂאֹר** שֶׁל חֻלִּין שֶׁנָּפַל לְתוֹךְ עִסָּה, וְיֶשׁ בּוֹ כְּדֵי לְחַמֵּץ, וְאַחַר כָּךְ נָפַל שְׂאֹר שֶׁל תְּרוּמָה, אוֹ שְׂאֹר שֶׁל כִּלְאֵי הַכֶּרֶם, וְיֶשׁ בּוֹ כְּדֵי לְחַמֵּץ, אָסוּר.

(ח) ויש בו כדי לחמץ אסור. הא קא משמע לן, דלא אמרינן הואיל ובלא שאור זה של איסור היתה העיסה מתחמצת על ידי שאור של היתר שנפל בו תחלה, לא נחוש לשאור של איסור:

---

cannot be tasted.[2] This is the case where *terumah* mixing with *chullin* of a different kind is treated strictly (that is, the special *terumah* proportion of 100:1 is not enough to nullify what fell in).

אֵין בָּהֶם בְּנוֹתְנֵן טַעַם — If, however, [the *terumah* beans] do *not* give flavor to the lentils, בֵּין שֶׁיֵּשׁ בָּהֶם לַעֲלוֹת בְּאֶחָד וּמֵאָה — then regardless of whether there are enough [*chullin* lentils] to nullify the *terumah* beans in one hundred and one (100 parts *chullin* to one part *terumah*) וּבֵין שֶׁאֵין בָּהֶם לַעֲלוֹת בְּאֶחָד וּמֵאָה — or whether there are not enough [*chullin* lentils] to nullify the *terumah* beans in one hundred and one (there are less than 100 parts *chullin* to one part *terumah*), מֻתָּר — [the mixture] is permitted to non-Kohanim. The 100:1 ratio for nullifying *terumah* applies only to *terumah* that mixes with *chullin* of the *same* kind. When it mixes with *chullin* of a *different* kind (such as beans with lentils), the only thing that matters is whether it gives flavor to the *chullin*.[3] This is the case in which *terumah* mixing with *chullin* of a different kind is treated leniently (that is, we do not require the special *terumah* proportion of 100:1 to nullify it).

[8] The next two Mishnahs consider cases in which dough was leavened by *both* permitted and forbidden sourdoughs.

שְׂאֹר שֶׁל חֻלִּין שֶׁנָּפַל לְתוֹךְ עִסָּה — If sourdough of *chullin* (non-*terumah*) fell into *chullin* dough, וְיֶשׁ בּוֹ כְּדֵי לְחַמֵּץ — and there was enough of it to leaven the dough, וְאַחַר כָּךְ נָפַל שְׂאֹר שֶׁל תְּרוּמָה אוֹ שְׂאֹר שֶׁל כִּלְאֵי הַכֶּרֶם — and afterward, sourdough of *terumah* or of *kilei hakerem* fell into the mixture, וְיֶשׁ בּוֹ כְּדֵי לְחַמֵּץ — and there was also enough of it to leaven the dough on its own, and the two sourdoughs leavened the dough together,[1] אָסוּר — [the

---
NOTES

2. [To be nullified means to become so insignificant that the thing is considered to have disappeared. Something that can be tasted cannot be considered to have disappeared.]

3. *Rav; Rash; Rambam Commentary*.
    The 100:1 rule for nullifying *terumah*, which is Rabbinic (see Mishnah 1 note 4), was nevertheless based by the Sages on a verse (*Bamidbar* 18:29). Since that verse discusses *terumah* that fell into *chullin* of the same kind, the Sages did not decree this stricter rule except for mixtures of the same kind (*Rav, Rosh*; see *Rash* for another reason).

[8]

1. The prohibited sourdough fell in shortly after the permitted sourdough, so that the dough had not yet become leavened when the second sourdough fell in

[35] MISHNAH ORLAH / Chapter 2: *HaTerumah*

- רע"ב -

[ט] **שְׂאֹר** שֶׁל חֻלִּין שֶׁנָּפַל לְתוֹךְ עִסָּה וְחִמְּצָהּ, וְאַחַר כָּךְ נָפַל שְׂאֹר שֶׁל תְּרוּמָה, אוֹ שְׂאֹר שֶׁל כִּלְאֵי הַכֶּרֶם, וְיֵשׁ בּוֹ כְּדֵי לְחַמֵּץ, אָסוּר. רַבִּי שִׁמְעוֹן מַתִּיר.

(ט) ורבי שמעון מתיר. בריסא לא פליג רבי שמעון, כיון דנפל שאור של תרומה קודם שנתחמצה בשל חולין, והרי היא ממהרת להתחמץ על ידי שאור של תרומה. אבל בסיפא כיון דכבר נתחמצה בשל חולין, כי הדר נפיל של תרומה אינו אלא אלא פוגם. ורבנן סברי אף על גב דבטלמוד נותן טעם לפגם מותר, שאני הכא שהוא עושה אותה ראויה לחמץ בה כמה עסות אחרות. והלכה כחכמים:

---

dough] is forbidden. Although the permitted sourdough could have done the job on its own, the prohibited sourdough contributed to and indeed speeded up the leavening process.[2] Its effect is therefore considered visible and it does not become nullified.[3]

[9] This Mishnah, like the previous one, discusses a case of dough that was leavened by *both* permitted and prohibited sourdoughs. The previous Mishnah discussed a case where the prohibited sourdough fell in *before* the permitted sourdough could leaven the dough. This Mishnah discusses a case where the prohibited sourdough fell in *after* the permitted sourdough had leavened the dough:

שְׂאֹר שֶׁל חֻלִּין שֶׁנָּפַל לְתוֹךְ עִסָּה — If *chullin* (permitted) **sourdough fell into** *chullin* **dough,** וְחִמְּצָהּ — **and leavened it,** וְאַחַר כָּךְ נָפַל שְׂאֹר שֶׁל תְּרוּמָה אוֹ שְׂאֹר שֶׁל כִּלְאֵי הַכֶּרֶם — **and afterward** *terumah* **sourdough or** *kilei hakerem* **sourdough fell into the dough,**[1] וְיֵשׁ בּוֹ כְּדֵי לְחַמֵּץ — **and there was enough of it to leaven** the dough on its own had the *chullin* sourdough not already done so, אָסוּר — **[the dough] is forbidden,** because the prohibited sourdough leavens it even more. רַבִּי שִׁמְעוֹן מַתִּיר — **But R' Shimon permits** it, because this extra leavening spoils the taste of the bread made from the dough.[2]

NOTES

(*Rav, Rash* to Mishnah 9). Thus, the two sourdoughs leavened the dough together (*Rash Sirilio*).

2. *Rav, Rash* to Mishnah 9. For example, had the permitted sourdough been left to leaven the dough on its own, the leavening process would have taken two hours, while with the assistance of the *terumah* sourdough it took only an hour.

3. Thus, if the prohibited sourdough was *terumah*, the dough is prohibited to non-Kohanim; and if it was *kilei hakerem* it is prohibited to everyone.

The Mishnah says that the permitted sourdough fell in *first* to teach that even so, the contribution made by the prohibited sourdough afterward is enough to prohibit the dough (*Rav, Rambam Commentary*).

[9]

1. At this point the dough was as leavened as it needed to be. The additional sourdough, however, leavens it even more (see *Rav*).

2. There is a principle that any forbidden substance that worsens the flavor of a food [נוֹתֵן טַעַם לִפְגָם] does not prohibit it. In our case, once the dough has been fully leavened by the *chullin* sourdough, the additional leavening given by the *terumah* sourdough does not improve it but makes it worse. The dough is therefore permitted (*Rav, Rash,* from *Avodah Zarah* 68b).

The first Tanna agrees with this principle but he holds that this case is different. Since the over-leavened dough can now be used to leaven *other* doughs, and this

משניות ערלה / פרק ב: התרומה

[י] **תַּבְלִין**, שְׁנַיִם וּשְׁלֹשָׁה שֵׁמוֹת מִמִּין אֶחָד, אוֹ מִשְּׁלֹשָׁה, אָסוּר וּמִצְטָרְפִין. רַבִּי שִׁמְעוֹן אוֹמֵר: שְׁנַיִם וּשְׁלֹשָׁה שֵׁמוֹת מִמִּין אֶחָד, אוֹ שְׁנֵי מִינִין מִשֵּׁם אֶחָד, אֵינָן מִצְטָרְפִין.

- רע״ב -

(י) תבלין שנים ושלשה שמות. איסורין חלוקין זה מזה כגון קרי שלשה שמות, פלפלין של ערלה ושל אשרה ושל תרומה:

אסור ומצטרפין. כלומר מצטרפין יחד לאסור התבשיל שנתבשל בהם: **או שני מינים משם אחד.** כגון זנגביל ופלפלין, ושניהם ערלה או שניהם תרומה. ואין הלכה כרבי שמעון:

---

[10] The following Mishnah considers cases in which several prohibited spices combined to season a food. None of these spices could have seasoned the food on its own.[1]

תַּבְלִין שְׁנַיִם וּשְׁלֹשָׁה שֵׁמוֹת מִמִּין אֶחָד — **Spices** that are forbidden under **two or three** different **prohibitions**[2] (such as *terumah, orlah,* and *asheirah*) but they are all **of one kind** (for example, pepper),[3] אוֹ מִשְּׁלֹשָׁה — **or** spices made up **of three** different **[kinds]** of ingredients, but all three are forbidden under the same prohibition,[4] אָסוּר וּמִצְטָרְפִין — all **combine to prohibit** the food being flavored.[5] Although none of the individual ingredients can flavor the food by itself, the food is still prohibited if the ingredients *together* give flavor to it.[6] רַבִּי שִׁמְעוֹן אוֹמֵר — **R' Shimon says:** שְׁנַיִם וּשְׁלֹשָׁה שֵׁמוֹת מִמִּין אֶחָד — **Spices** that are forbidden under **two or three** different **prohibitions** but the spices are all **of one kind,** אוֹ שְׁנֵי מִינִין מִשֵּׁם אֶחָד — **or** spices of **two** different **kinds** but both are **of one** (the same) **prohibition,** אֵינָן מִצְטָרְפִין — **do not combine** to prohibit the food being flavored. According to R' Shimon, only spices of the same kind and of the same prohibition combine to prohibit a mixture. If they are of different kinds or are of different prohibitions, they do not combine and each one becomes nullified by itself.[7]

NOTES
---

beneficial use comes from the addition of the prohibited sourdough, the dough is forbidden (*Rav, Rash,* from *Avodah Zarah* 68b). R' Shimon disagrees because the dough was made to be eaten, and in regard to this purpose it has been spoiled (*Ritva* to *Avodah Zarah* 68a).

[10]

1. The word תַּבְלִין (spices) is used in this Mishnah to include any ingredient that is used to flavor food. Thus, for example, garlic, onions, oil, vinegar, and wine are all included here in the category of תַּבְלִין (*Rambam Commentary*).

2. Literally, *names.*

3. Some of the pepper was *terumah,* some was *orlah,* and some was from an *asheirah* tree [a tree worshiped as *avodah zarah*] (*Rav, Rash;* see *Tosafos, Shabbos* 89b ד״ה תבלין).

4. *Tiferes Yisrael;* see *Tos. Yom Tov.* For example, there was ginger, pepper, and cinnamon, all of which were forbidden as *orlah* (see *Rav* below ד״ה או שני מינים, and *Shabbos* 89b).

5. Translation follows *Rav* and *Rambam Commentary;* see *Rash* and *Tosafos, Shabbos* 89b.

6. The Mishnah speaks of a case where the tastes of all three were similar enough so that they can reinforce one another and be tasted together in the mixture (see *Avodah Zarah* 66a). Since they can be tasted, they do not become nullified in the mixture.

7. See *Mahara Fulda.* That is, as long as there is enough to nullify each ingredient by itself, each one becomes nullified and the mixture can be eaten. R' Shimon follows his view in Mishnah 1, that different prohibitions do not combine to prohibit.

[37] **MISHNAH ORLAH** / Chapter 2: *HaTerumah*

– רע"ב –

(יא) אחר אחרון אני בא. אם השאור של תרומה נפל באחרונה, העסה כולה נעשית מדומע, ואם של חולין נפל באחרונה, הכל מותר, שהאחרון הוא שעושה החמוץ. והא דשרי רבי אליעזר כשנפל אותו של חולין אחרון, היינו דוקא כשקדם וסלק את האיסור, ואף על פי שהועיל קצת שסייע לאחרון דהיתר לגמור החמוץ, אף על פי כן נתבטל טעמו ואינו חוזר וניעור, אבל לא קדם וסלק האיסור, ונתחמץ על ידי שניהם, אסור, דסבר רבי אליעזר זה וזה גורם אסור. **לעולם אינו אוסר בו עד שיהא בו כדי לחמץ.** דזה וזה גורם מותר. והלכה כחכמים:

[יא] **שְׂאוֹר** שֶׁל חֻלִּין וְשֶׁל תְּרוּמָה שֶׁנָּפְלוּ לְתוֹךְ עִסָּה, לֹא בָזֶה כְּדֵי לְחַמֵּץ וְלֹא בָזֶה כְּדֵי לְחַמֵּץ, נִצְטָרְפוּ וְחִמְּצוּ, רַבִּי אֱלִיעֶזֶר אוֹמֵר: אַחַר הָאַחֲרוֹן אֲנִי בָא; וַחֲכָמִים אוֹמְרִים: בֵּין שֶׁנָּפַל אִסּוּר בַּתְּחִלָּה, בֵּין בַּסּוֹף, לְעוֹלָם אֵינוֹ אוֹסֵר עַד שֶׁיְּהֵא בוֹ כְּדֵי לְחַמֵּץ.

[11] **The Mishnah now returns to the subject of two sourdoughs that combined to leaven dough.** In Mishnahs 8 and 9 we learned about cases in which two sourdoughs, one permitted and one prohibited, leavened dough together. In those cases, the Mishnah said that each of the sourdoughs could have done the job by itself. The Mishnah now considers a case in which neither of them could have leavened the dough by itself:

שְׂאוֹר שֶׁל חֻלִּין וְשֶׁל תְּרוּמָה שֶׁנָּפְלוּ לְתוֹךְ עִסָּה — **If sourdough of** *chullin* **and sourdough of** *terumah* **fell into a dough** of unleavened *chullin,* first one and then the other, לֹא בָזֶה כְּדֵי לְחַמֵּץ וְלֹא בָזֶה כְּדֵי לְחַמֵּץ — **and there was not enough of this one** (the *chullin* sourdough) **or of that one** (the *terumah* sourdough) **to leaven** the dough on its own, נִצְטָרְפוּ וְחִמְּצוּ — **but they combined** in the dough **and leavened** it together, there is a dispute about the law: רַבִּי אֱלִיעֶזֶר אוֹמֵר — **R' Eliezer says:** אַחַר הָאַחֲרוֹן אֲנִי בָא — **I follow the last one.** If the *terumah* sourdough was the last one to fall in, the dough is considered to have been leavened by the *terumah* and it may be eaten only by Kohanim. But if it was the *chullin* sourdough that fell in last, then the dough is considered to have been leavened by the *chullin,* and it may be eaten by anyone. Since the leavening process did not take off until the second one fell in, the second one is considered to be the one to have leavened it.[1] וַחֲכָמִים אוֹמְרִים — **But the Sages say:** בֵּין שֶׁנָּפַל אִסּוּר בַּתְּחִלָּה בֵּין בַּסּוֹף — **Whether the prohibited [sourdough] fell in first or whether** it fell in last, לְעוֹלָם אֵינוֹ אוֹסֵר עַד שֶׁיְּהֵא בוֹ כְּדֵי לְחַמֵּץ — **it never prohibits** the *chullin* dough **unless there is enough of it to leaven** the dough by itself. Therefore, in this case, where there was not enough *terumah* sourdough to leaven the dough by itself, the dough is permitted, regardless of the order in which the two sourdoughs fell in. Although the *terumah* contributed to the leavening, it is only the partial cause of it, and a partial cause is not enough to prohibit according to the Sages.[2]

— NOTES —

[11]

1. *Rav.* This will be explained further at the end of the next note.

2. Although the leavening does not take place until the second one falls in, it cannot be denied that the first one also contributes to the final result, since there is not enough of the second one to do the job by itself. According to the Sages,

[יב] **יוֹעֶזֶר** אִישׁ הַבִּירָה הָיָה מִתַּלְמִידֵי בֵית שַׁמַּאי וְאָמַר: שָׁאַלְתִּי אֶת רַבָּן גַּמְלִיאֵל הַזָּקֵן עוֹמֵד בְּשַׁעַר הַמִּזְרָח, וְאָמַר: לְעוֹלָם אֵינוֹ אוֹסֵר עַד שֶׁיְּהֵא בּוֹ כְּדֵי לְחַמֵּץ.

[12] The Mishnah cites support for the view of the Sages in the last Mishnah:[1]

יוֹעֶזֶר אִישׁ הַבִּירָה הָיָה מִתַּלְמִידֵי בֵית שַׁמַּאי וְאָמַר — Yoezer, an officer of the Temple,[2] was one of the students of Beis Shammai, and he said: שָׁאַלְתִּי אֶת רַבָּן גַּמְלִיאֵל הַזָּקֵן עוֹמֵד בְּשַׁעַר הַמִּזְרָח — I once asked Rabban Gamliel the Elder[3] what the law is while he was standing at the East Gate of the Temple Mount, וְאָמַר לְעוֹלָם אֵינוֹ אוֹסֵר עַד שֶׁיְּהֵא בּוֹ כְּדֵי לְחַמֵּץ — and he said that [terumah sourdough] never prohibits dough unless there is enough of it to leaven the dough by itself, as the Sages said in the previous Mishnah.

― NOTES ―

there is no reason to consider the second one more important than the first one. Rather, this is a case of two things working together to bring about one result.

Two factors that together cause something to happen are known as זֶה וְזֶה גּוֹרֵם, *this one and this one cause it*. The Sages hold that even if one of these is a prohibited substance, the final result is permitted (זֶה וְזֶה גּוֹרֵם מוּתָּר, *when this one and this one cause it, it is permitted*). Thus, in our case, where the *terumah* sourdough cannot leaven the dough by itself but only together with the *chullin* sourdough, the final result — the leavening of the dough — is permitted, because it was brought about by two sourdoughs, and only one of them was prohibited (*Rav*). [Since the dough itself was permitted, the partial influence of the *terumah* in leavening it is not strong enough to cause it to become prohibited.]

[However, when the prohibited sourdough *is able* to leaven the dough by itself, it does prohibit the dough, even if there is an equal amount of permitted sourdough working as well (see above, Mishnah 8). This is what the Mishnah means when it adds: "unless there is enough of it to leaven the dough by itself."]

R' Eliezer disputes this rule. In his opinion, even when two factors cause something to happen together, if one of them is prohibited, the final result is prohibited (זֶה וְזֶה גּוֹרֵם אָסוּר, *when this one and this one cause it, it is prohibited*). The only reason he permits the dough when the *chullin* falls in last is that he considers the second influence more important than the first.

However, even in this case he permits it only when the *terumah* sourdough was *removed* before the *chullin* sourdough fell in. Although the *terumah* began the leavening process, since it was removed before any leavening actually took place, its contribution became nullified. Thus, when the *chullin* falls in and completes the leavening, we "follow the last one" and permit the result. But if the *terumah* is still in the dough when the *chullin* falls in and finishes the leavening, it is considered to have done so together with the *terumah*. R' Eliezer therefore prohibits the dough because this is a case of זֶה וְזֶה גּוֹרֵם, *this one and this one cause it*, which in his opinion is prohibited (*Rav, Rambam Commentary, Rash,* from *Pesachim* 27a).

[12]

1. *Rambam Commentary.*
2. The word *birah* (literally, *palace*) is used to refer to the Temple (*Tiferes Yisrael,* from *Yoma* 2a).
3. There were several heads of the Sanhedrin who were known as Rabban Gamliel. The first of them was the grandson of Hillel, who became *Nasi* (head of the Sanhedrin) not long after his famous grandfather died. He was known as Rabban Gamliel the Elder. He lived during the time of the Second Temple.

[39] MISHNAH ORLAH / Chapter 2: HaTerumah

- רע"ב -

[יג] **כֵּלִים** שֶׁסָּכָן בְּשֶׁמֶן טָמֵא וְחָזַר וְסָכָן בְּשֶׁמֶן טָהוֹר, אוֹ שֶׁסָּכָן בְּשֶׁמֶן טָהוֹר וְחָזַר וְסָכָן בְּשֶׁמֶן טָמֵא,

(יג) בלים ששכן. כגון מנעלים ושאר כלים של עור, שסכין אותן בשמן לרככן: וחזר וסכן בשמן טהור. לאחר שנתייבש השמן הראשון, והטבילו לכלי שנטמא בשמן טמא, חזר וסכו בשמן טהור, וכשמשתמשים בכלי נפלט השמן לחוץ:

[13] The following Mishnah deals with the laws of *tumah*, not nullification.

It is included here only because of its similarity to Mishnah 11, where R' Eliezer and the Sages disagreed about whether to follow the last substance that fell in.

The Mishnah discusses the case of a leather utensil, such as a shoe, that was rubbed with oil to soften it. Much of this oil becomes absorbed into the leather and some of it comes out again when the utensil is used and pressure is applied to it; for example, when a person wears the shoe and steps down on it. In the case the Mishnah discusses, the shoe was rubbed twice, once with oil that was *tamei* and once with oil that was *tahor*. The question is, which oil came out when the person wore the shoe?

The Mishnah begins by giving two cases — one where the *tamei* oil was used first and one where it was used last:

כֵּלִים שֶׁסָּכָן בְּשֶׁמֶן טָמֵא — If leather **utensils were rubbed with *tamei* oil** to soften them,[1] thereby making them *tamei*,[2] וְחָזַר וְסָכָן בְּשֶׁמֶן טָהוֹר — **and then,** after being immersed in a *mikveh* to make them *tahor*, **they were rubbed again with oil, this time with *tahor* oil;**[3] אוֹ שֶׁסָּכָן בְּשֶׁמֶן טָהוֹר — **or the opposite: first they were rubbed with *tahor* oil** וְחָזַר וְסָכָן בְּשֶׁמֶן טָמֵא — **and then,** after the *tahor* oil had dried, **they were rubbed again with *tamei* oil,** thereby making them *tamei*, and then they were immersed in a *mikveh* to make them *tahor*;[4] and then they were used and some of the oil came out. The question is, do we assume that this was *tamei* oil that came out or do we assume that it was the *tahor* oil that came out?[5]

The ruling:

NOTES

[13]

1. Leather utensils, such as shoes, are often stiff. It was common to rub [olive] oil into them to soften the leather (*Rav; Rash*). In this case, the oil he used was *tamei*.

2. *Rav.* By Rabbinic law, a *tamei* liquid can make a utensil *tamei* (*Rambam, Avos HaTumah* 7:1). Thus, the *tamei* oil he rubbed onto the shoe made it *tamei*.

3. *Rav, Rash.* The leather utensil now has two different oils absorbed in it: the *tamei* oil (which was absorbed before it was immersed in the *mikveh*) and the *tahor* oil (which was absorbed after it was immersed in the *mikveh*). The *tamei* oil

that was absorbed in the shoe did not become *tahor* when it was immersed in the *mikveh* because foods and beverages [with the exception of water] do not become *tahor* in a *mikveh*; only people and utensils become purified this way (see *Mikvaos* 10:8 with *Rav*). Nevertheless, the *tamei* oil in the shoe does not make it *tamei* while it is absorbed in it, because a source of *tumah* that is absorbed inside something else [טֻמְאָה בְּלוּעָה] cannot transmit *tumah* (*Chullin* 71a).

4. *Tiferes Yisrael.*

5. If we assume that *tamei* oil came out, the utensil (shoe) will again become *tamei* from it.

[40] משניות ערלה / פרק ב: התרומה ב/יד

רַבִּי אֱלִיעֶזֶר אוֹמֵר: אַחַר הָרִאשׁוֹן אֲנִי בָא; וַחֲכָמִים אוֹמְרִים: אַחַר הָאַחֲרוֹן.

[יד] שְׂאֹר שֶׁל תְּרוּמָה וְשֶׁל כִּלְאֵי הַכֶּרֶם שֶׁנָּפְלוּ לְתוֹךְ עִסָּה, לֹא בָזֶה כְּדֵי לְחַמֵּץ וְלֹא בָזֶה כְּדֵי לְחַמֵּץ, וְנִצְטָרְפוּ וְחִמְּצוּ, אָסוּר לַזָּרִים וּמֻתָּר לַכֹּהֲנִים;

— רע״ב —

אחר ראשון אני בא. דסבר רבי אליעזר ראשון נפלט לחוץ: וחכמים אומרים אחר אחרון. סברי אחרון נפלט. והלכה כחכמים: (יד) אסור לזרים. רבנן לטעמייהו, דאמרי לעיל (משנה י) תבלין משנים ושלשה שמות מצטרפין לאסור הדבר הנטבל. ומותר לכהנים. דתרומה שריא להו, ואין בכלאי הכרם כדי להחמיץ:

— רַבִּי אֱלִיעֶזֶר אוֹמֵר — R' Eliezer says: אַחַר הָרִאשׁוֹן אֲנִי בָא — I follow the first oil. The oil that was absorbed first is the one that comes out.[6] Thus, in the case where the *tamei* oil was absorbed first, the utensils would be *tamei;* in the case where the *tahor* oil was absorbed first, the utensils would remain *tahor.* וַחֲכָמִים אוֹמְרִים — But the Sages say: אַחַר הָאַחֲרוֹן — We follow the last oil.[7] Thus, if the second oil was *tamei,* the utensil would be *tamei;* if the second was *tahor,* the utensil would be *tahor.*

[14] The Mishnah returns to the subject of two sourdoughs that combine to leaven permitted dough. Mishnahs 11 and 12 discussed this in a case where one of the sourdoughs was prohibited. Our Mishnah gives the law in a case where both sourdoughs were prohibited:

שְׂאֹר שֶׁל תְּרוּמָה וְשֶׁל כִּלְאֵי הַכֶּרֶם שֶׁנָּפְלוּ לְתוֹךְ עִסָּה — If sourdough of *terumah* and sourdough of *kilei hakerem* fell into permitted dough, לֹא בָזֶה כְּדֵי לְחַמֵּץ וְלֹא בָזֶה כְּדֵי לְחַמֵּץ — and there was not enough of either this one (*terumah*) or that one (*kilei hakerem*) to leaven the dough on its own, וְנִצְטָרְפוּ וְחִמְּצוּ — but they combined and leavened the dough together, אָסוּר לַזָּרִים — [the dough] is prohibited to non-Kohanim, because both the *terumah* sourdough and the *kilei hakerem* sourdough are prohibited to them,[1] וּמֻתָּר לַכֹּהֲנִים — but it is permitted to Kohanim, for whom *terumah,* at least, is permitted. Since only the *kilei hakerem* is forbidden to them, and it cannot leaven the dough by itself, the dough is permitted to them.[2]

———— NOTES ————

6. *Rav, Rash. Yerushalmi* (according to emended text of *Gra*) explains that the second oil "pushes out" the first. [That is, when the second oil is absorbed, it penetrates more deeply and pushes the first oil closer to the surface. Thus, when the leather is squeezed and some oil comes out, it is the first oil that comes out.]

7. According to the Sages, the oil that was absorbed first caused the leather to become largely saturated (and thus unable to hold much more oil). The second oil therefore remains close to the surface and is the one that gets "pushed out" (*Tiferes Yisrael;* see also *Yerushalmi,* according to emended text of *Gra*).

[14]

1. Since both sourdoughs are of the same kind, they combine to prohibit the dough even though they are each prohibited by a different prohibition. This follows the view of the Tanna Kamma in Mishnah 10.

2. A Kohen may eat this dough because *terumah* is permitted to him. The only ingredient prohibited to him here is the *kilei hakerem* — and it is not able to leaven the dough by itself (*Rav, Rash*). It therefore

[41] MISHNAH ORLAH / Chapter 2: HaTerumah

– רע"ב –

רבי שמעון מתיר לזרים, דאמר (שם) שנים או שלשה שמות ממין אחד אין מצטרפין: (טו) תבלין של תרומה ושל כלאי הכרם. בהא נמי רבנן לטעמייהו ורבי שמעון לטעמיה. ודין תבלין כדין שאור:

רַבִּי שִׁמְעוֹן מַתִּיר לַזָּרִים וְלַכֹּהֲנִים. [טו] **תַּבְלִין** שֶׁל תְּרוּמָה וְשֶׁל כִּלְאֵי הַכֶּרֶם שֶׁנָּפְלוּ בַקְּדֵרָה, לֹא בָאֵלּוּ כְּדֵי לְתַבֵּל וְלֹא בָאֵלּוּ כְּדֵי לְתַבֵּל, וְנִצְטָרְפוּ וְתִבְּלוּ, אָסוּר לַזָּרִים וּמֻתָּר לַכֹּהֲנִים; רַבִּי שִׁמְעוֹן מַתִּיר לַזָּרִים וְלַכֹּהֲנִים.

רַבִּי שִׁמְעוֹן מַתִּיר לַזָּרִים וְלַכֹּהֲנִים — **But R' Shimon permits it to both non-Kohanim and Kohanim.** Since the two pieces of leaven are not forbidden under the same prohibition, they do not combine to prohibit.[3]

[15] The Mishnah repeats the rulings of the previous Mishnah in regard to spices:

תַּבְלִין שֶׁל תְּרוּמָה וְשֶׁל כִּלְאֵי הַכֶּרֶם שֶׁנָּפְלוּ בַקְּדֵרָה — **If spices of** *terumah* **and of** *kilei hakerem* **fell into a pot** of food, לֹא בָאֵלּוּ כְּדֵי לְתַבֵּל וְלֹא בָאֵלּוּ כְּדֵי לְתַבֵּל — **and there was not enough of these** (*terumah*) **spices or of those** (*kilei hakerem*) **spices to spice** the food on their own, וְנִצְטָרְפוּ וְתִבְּלוּ — **but they combined and spiced** the food together,[1] אָסוּר לַזָּרִים — **[the food] is prohibited to non-Kohanim** וּמֻתָּר לַכֹּהֲנִים — **but it is permitted to Kohanim,** who are permitted to eat *terumah*. Since both *terumah* and *kilei hakerem* are prohibited to non-Kohanim, they combine to prohibit the food to a non-Kohen.[2] But since *terumah* is permitted to Kohanim, the *kilei hakerem* by itself does not prohibit the food to a Kohen.[3] רַבִּי שִׁמְעוֹן מַתִּיר לַזָּרִים וְלַכֹּהֲנִים — **R' Shimon permits it to both non-Kohanim and to Kohanim,** because he holds that two prohibitions do not combine to prohibit.[4]

NOTES

becomes nullified, following the view of the Sages in Mishnah 11 (*Rash; Rambam Commentary*) that when two sourdoughs are needed to leaven dough and only one of them is prohibited, we say: זֶה וָזֶה גּוֹרֵם מוּתָּר, *when this one and this one cause it, it is permitted* (*Tiferes Yisrael*).

[The Mishnah is discussing a case where there is enough dough to nullify the *terumah* by a margin of 100:1 and the *kilei hakerem* by 200:1. The only reason why they should not become nullified is that leaven does not become nullified, as we learned in Mishnah 6. Since in this case the *kilei hakerem* could not leaven the dough by itself, it becomes nullified and is permitted to Kohanim.]

3. R' Shimon is consistent with his ruling in Mishnah 10 that even two substances that are the same do not combine to prohibit if they are forbidden by different prohibitions (*Rav, Rash*).

[15]

1. Their flavors were similar, so that they reinforced each other and combined to flavor the food.

2. This ruling follows the view of the Tanna Kamma in Mishnah 10 (*Rav*), that ingredients with two different prohibitions combine with each other to prohibit a mixture.

3. Since Kohanim are allowed to eat *terumah*, the only substance prohibited here to a Kohen is the *kilei hakerem* — and it is not able to flavor the food by itself. The food is therefore permitted to Kohanim (*Rav*), according to the view of the Sages in Mishnah 11 who say that זֶה וָזֶה גּוֹרֵם מוּתָּר, *when this one and this one cause it, it is permitted* (see note 4 there).

4. R' Shimon is consistent with his ruling in Mishnah 10 above (*Rav*).

משניות ערלה / פרק ב: התרומה [42]

[טז] חֲתִיכָה שֶׁל קָדְשֵׁי קָדָשִׁים [וְ]שֶׁל פִּגּוּל וְשֶׁל נוֹתָר שֶׁנִּתְבַּשְּׁלוּ עִם הַחֲתִיכוֹת, אָסוּר לַזָּרִים וּמֻתָּר לַכֹּהֲנִים;

– רע"ב –

(טז) חתיכה של קדשי קדשים. שאסורה לזרים ומותרת לכהנים: ושל פגול ושל נותר ושל טמא. דאסירי בין לזרים בין לכהנים:

שנתבשלו עם החתיכות. של חולין, ויש בחולין כדי לבטל של קדשי קדשים בפני עצמן ושל פגול נותר וטומאה בפני עצמן: אסור לזרים. רבנן לטעמייהו, דאמרי (משנה י) שנים ושלשה שמות מצטרפין לאסור:

---

[16] The Mishnah now presents a similar ruling in regard to the permitted meat of sacrificial offerings that was cooked together with forbidden sacrificial meat.

The meat of most *korbanos* (sacrificial offerings) is eaten either by Kohanim or by the person bringing the offering and his guests, with only a small amount of it being burned on the Altar. However, certain things can happen to an offering that prohibit its meat from being eaten. If an offering is made with the intention of eating its meat beyond the time permitted for it, or with the intention of burning its sacrificial parts (*emurin*) on the Altar beyond the time permitted for placing them on the Altar, the entire offering becomes invalid and is called *piggul*.[1] Its meat may not be eaten. Also, the meat of a valid offering that was left over beyond the time allowed for eating it becomes forbidden and is called *nossar*.[2] This Mishnah discusses the case of meat from a valid offering that was cooked together with *piggul*, *nossar*, and *chullin* (ordinary, non-holy meat):

חֲתִיכָה שֶׁל קָדְשֵׁי קָדָשִׁים — If a piece of *kodshei kodashim* meat,[3] which is permitted only to a Kohen, וְשֶׁל פִּגּוּל וְשֶׁל נוֹתָר — and [a piece] of *piggul* meat and [a piece] of *nossar* meat, which are prohibited even to a Kohen, שֶׁנִּתְבַּשְּׁלוּ עִם הַחֲתִיכוֹת — were cooked together with pieces of *chullin* (non-holy) meat; and there was enough *chullin* meat to nullify the *kodshei kodashim* meat or the *piggul* and *nossar* meat, but not enough to nullify both of them together,[4] אָסוּר לַזָּרִים — [the mixture] is prohibited to non-Kohanim, because the *kodashim* meat and the *piggul* and *nossar* meat — all of which are prohibited to non-Kohanim — combine to prohibit the mixture,[5] וּמֻתָּר לַכֹּהֲנִים — but it is permitted to Kohanim, for whom the *kodashim* meat, at

---

NOTES

[16]
1. The meat is forbidden (even to Kohanim) under penalty of *kares* (*Zevachim* 2:2).

2. Like *piggul*, *nossar* may not be eaten (even by Kohanim) under penalty of *kares* (*Kereisos* 1:1).

3. The sacrificial offerings brought in the Temple fall into two groups: *Kodshei kodashim* (most-holy offerings) and *kodashim kalim* (offerings of lesser holiness). The offerings in both groups are holy, but the laws of *kodshei kodashim* are stricter than those of *kodashim kalim*.

One example of this is that the meat of *kodshei kodashim* offerings (e.g., the *chatas* and *asham*) may be eaten only by Kohanim, whereas the meat of *kodashim kalim* (e.g., *shelamim* and *todah*) may in general be eaten even by non-Kohanim. See *Zevachim* Chapter 5.

4. *Rav*; *Rash*. The meat of an offering, like *terumah*, needs 100 times as much *chullin* to nullify it (see *Yevamos* 81b; *Rambam, Maachalos Asuros* 6:23, 24).

5. [Since the prohibited items (*kodashim*, *piggul*, and *nossar*) are all the same substance (meat), they combine to prohibit the mixture, even though they are from

[43] **MISHNAH ORLAH** / Chapter 2: *HaTerumah* 2/17

- רע"ב -

רַבִּי שִׁמְעוֹן מַתִּיר לַזָּרִים וְלַכֹּהֲנִים.

[יז] **בְּשַׂר** קָדְשֵׁי קָדָשִׁים וּבְשַׂר קָדָשִׁים קַלִּים שֶׁנִּתְבַּשְּׁלוּ עִם בְּשַׂר הַתַּאֲוָה, אָסוּר לַטְּמֵאִים וּמֻתָּר לַטְּהוֹרִים.

רבי שמעון מתיר לזרים לטעמיה, דאמר (שם) שנים או שלשה שמות ממין אחד [אין] מצטרפין: (יז) בשר קדשי קדשים. אסור לזרים אפילו טהורים. בשר קדשים קלים, שרי לזרים טהורים ואסור לטמאים. ובשלן עם בשר תאוה, בשר חולין, דשרי אף לטמאים, מצטרפין לאסור לטמאים, אפילו לרבי שמעון, דקדשים וקדשים קלים שם אחד להם, כדאמרינן לעיל (משנה א) גבי תרומה וחלה וביכורים. ומותר לזרים טהורים, אפילו לרבנן, דקדשי קדשים אין בהם כדי לאסור:

least, is permitted.[6] רַבִּי שִׁמְעוֹן מַתִּיר לַזָּרִים וְלַכֹּהֲנִים — But **R' Shimon rules** [the mixture] **permitted** both **to non-Kohanim and to Kohanim.** According to R' Shimon, prohibited items do *not* combine to prohibit a mixture.[7]

[17] The Mishnah presents another case that deals with a mixture involving the meats of sacrificial offerings:

בְּשַׂר קָדְשֵׁי קָדָשִׁים וּבְשַׂר קָדָשִׁים קַלִּים — **If meat of** a *kodshei kodashim* **offering and meat of a** *kodashim kalim* **offering,**[1] neither of which may be eaten by a person who is *tamei,* שֶׁנִּתְבַּשְּׁלוּ עִם בְּשַׂר הַתַּאֲוָה — **were cooked together with ordinary** *chullin* **meat,**[2] which may be eaten even by someone *tamei,* and there is enough *chullin* meat in the mixture to nullify either the *kodshei kodashim* or the *kodashim kalim* but not both of them together,[3] אָסוּר לַטְּמֵאִים — [**the mixture**] **is prohibited to people who are** *tamei,* because the *kodshei kodashim* and *kodashim kalim* combine to prohibit the mixture to a *tamei,*[4] וּמֻתָּר לַטְּהוֹרִים — **but it is permitted to people who are** *tahor,* even

--- NOTES ---

different prohibitions.] This again follows the view of the Tanna Kamma in Mishnah 10 (*Rav, Rash*).

6. [Since the *kodshei kodashim* meat is permitted to Kohanim, the only substance prohibited here to a Kohen is the *piggul* and *nossar*. Since there is enough *chullin* to nullify the mixture, the mixture is permitted to a Kohen.] This ruling follows the view of the Sages in Mishnah 11 above (*Rav, Rosh*).

7. Here, too, R' Shimon follows his view in Mishnah 10, that two prohibitions do not combine to forbid (*Rav, Rash*).

[17]

1. *Kodshei kodashim* may be eaten only by male Kohanim; *kodashim kalim* may be eaten by anyone (see previous Mishnah, note 3). However, no *kodashim* may be eaten by someone who is *tamei.*

2. Literally, *meat of the appetite.* The expression is based on *Devarim* 12:20. It refers to ordinary *chullin* meat intended for personal food, in contrast to meat that comes from an offering (*Tos. Yom Tov*). Being *chullin,* this meat is permitted to anyone, regardless of whether the person eating is *tamei* or *tahor* (see *Devarim* 12:22).

3. *Rav, Rash.*

4. Since the two prohibited items (*kodshei kodashim* and *kodashim kalim*) are the same substance (meat), they combine to make the mixture subject to whatever prohibition is common to both of them; namely, the prohibition against eating holy food while *tamei.*

Even R' Shimon, who holds in the previous Mishnahs that two prohibitions do not combine to prohibit, agrees in this case that they do combine. This is because both *kodshei kodashim* and

non-Kohanim. Since the *kodashim kalim* meat is permitted to non-Kohanim who are *tahor,* and there is enough *chullin* meat in the mixture to nullify the *kodshei kodashim* meat by itself, it does not prohibit the mixture to them.

NOTES
---

kodashim kalim are called "*kodesh.*" This enables them to combine even according to R' Shimon, as we saw in the case of *terumah, challah,* and *bikkurim,* which are all called *terumah* [see Mishnah 2:1 note 13] (*Rav, Rash*).

Chapter Three

משניות ערלה / פרק ג: בגד [46]

- רע"ב -

פרק שלישי — בגד.
(א) בגד שצבעו בקליפי ערלה. כגון קליפי אגוזים ורמונים, דגם הקליפים אסורים בהנאה, כדדרשינן

[א] **בֶּגֶד** שֶׁצְּבָעוֹ בִּקְלִפֵּי עָרְלָה, יִדָּלֵק. נִתְעָרֵב בַּאֲחֵרִים, כֻּלָּם יִדָּלְקוּ, דִּבְרֵי רַבִּי מֵאִיר; וַחֲכָמִים אוֹמְרִים: יַעֲלֶה בְּאֶחָד וּמָאתָיִם.

(ברכות לו, ב) את פריו (ויקרא יט, כג), את הטפל לפריו: ידלק. שאסור בהנאה דכתיב (שם) וערלתם ערלתו, שלא יהנה ולא יצבע ולא ידליק בו את הנר: בולם ידלקו. רבי מאיר לטעמיה, דאמר לקמן (משנה ז) את שדרכו למנות מקדש, ובגד שלבטו שדרכו למנות הוא: וחכמים אומרים יעלה באחד ומאתים. לטעמייהו, דאמרי לקמן בפרקין (שם) אין מקדש אלא שבעה דברים בלבד. והלכה כחכמים:

[1] It is not only forbidden to eat *orlah*; it is also forbidden to have any benefit from it.[1] The first half of this chapter discusses cases in which *orlah* was used to manufacture some other item, and when this prohibits us to use that item. The first Mishnah discusses a case in which a garment was dyed with a coloring made from *orlah*:

בֶּגֶד שֶׁצְּבָעוֹ בִּקְלִפֵּי עָרְלָה — If **a garment was dyed with** coloring made from the **peels of *orlah* fruit,**[2] יִדָּלֵק — **it must be burned,** because the improved appearance of the garment is considered a benefit received from *orlah*.[3]

The Mishnah now discusses what happens if this garment gets lost among other, permitted garments:

נִתְעָרֵב בַּאֲחֵרִים — If **[the *orlah*-dyed garment] became mixed up with other [garments]** and it cannot be told apart from them, כֻּלָּם יִדָּלְקוּ — **they must all be burned** so that no one will have benefit from the prohibited garment; דִּבְרֵי רַבִּי מֵאִיר — **these are the words of R' Meir.** According to R' Meir, the prohibited garment does not become nullified, because a garment is considered something significant and a significant item does not become nullified.[4] וַחֲכָמִים אוֹמְרִים — **But the Sages say:** יַעֲלֶה בְּאֶחָד וּמָאתָיִם — **[The prohibited garment] is nullified in** a mixture of **two hundred and one,** i.e., 200 permitted garments to the one *orlah*-dyed garment. If there are two hundred permitted garments in the mix, the *orlah*-dyed one becomes nullified like any other *orlah*, and all the garments may be used. According to the Sages, a garment is not subject to the rule that significant items do not become nullified.[5]

NOTES

[1]
1. This is learned from a verse (*Rav*).
2. Dyes in ancient times were commonly made from plants, including the peels of certain fruits (such as pomegranates), and the shells of certain nuts (such as walnuts). If the pomegranates or walnuts were from an *orlah* tree, the peels and shells are also forbidden for benefit (*Rav*). This, too, is learned from a verse (see *Tos. Yom Tov*).
3. See *Meleches Shlomo*. The garment must therefore be burned, like all *orlah* (see *Temurah* 7:5). [The Mishnah is discussing a case where the dye cannot be washed out. If it can be removed, the garment is permitted once it is removed (*Mishnah Rishonah*).]
4. R' Meir prohibits all the garments in the mixture even when there are enough other garments to nullify *orlah*. This is because a garment is a דָּבָר שֶׁבְּמִנְיָן, *an item which* [on account of its importance] *is sold by the unit* [and not by estimate]. According to R' Meir, any such item is in the category of a דָּבָר חָשׁוּב, *significant item,* which is not subject to nullification [see Mishnah 7] (*Rav*; *Rash*).
5. As we will see in Mishnah 7, the Sages hold that only large items that are

[47] **MISHNAH ORLAH** / Chapter 3: *Beged*   3/2-3

- רע״ב -

(ב) מלא הסיט. הוא כדי הפסק שיש בין אמה לאצבע, כל מה שיכול להרחיבו. והפסק שיש בין הגודל לאצבע, כל מה שיוכל להרחיבו, הוא הסיט כפול, לפי שהוא כפול ממה שיש בין אמה לאצבע.

[ב] **הַצּוֹבֵעַ** מְלֹא הַסִּיט בִּקְלִפֵּי עָרְלָה, וַאֲרָגוֹ בַּבֶּגֶד, וְאֵין יָדוּעַ אֵיזֶה הוּא, רַבִּי מֵאִיר אוֹמֵר: יִדָּלֵק הַבֶּגֶד; וַחֲכָמִים אוֹמְרִים: יַעֲלֶה בְּאֶחָד וּמָאתָיִם.

[ג] **הָאוֹרֵג** מְלֹא הַסִּיט מִצֶּמֶר הַבְּכוֹר בַּבֶּגֶד,

ומלא הסיט הוא שיעור חשוב לאיסור, הלכך כשארגו בבגד, ואין ידוע איזהו, רבי מאיר אומר ידלקן, לטעמיה, וחכמים אומרים יעלו באחד ומאתיים, לטעמייהו, כפלוגתא דלעיל: (ג) מצמר הבכור. ואסור לגזוז בכור, שנאמר (דברים טו, יט) ולא תגוז בכור צאנך. ובבכור בעל מום איירי, ולהכי בעי מלא הסיט, דאילו בכור תם הרי הוא מוקדשים, ותנן ובמוקדשים מקדשים כל שהוא:

---

[2] The previous Mishnah discussed the law of a garment dyed with *orlah* dye. This Mishnah discusses the law of a single thread dyed with *orlah* dye:

הַצּוֹבֵעַ מְלֹא הַסִּיט בִּקְלִפֵּי עָרְלָה — **If someone dyes** a thread **the length of a** *sitt*[1] with coloring made from **the peels of** *orlah*, וַאֲרָגוֹ בַּבֶּגֶד — **and he wove it into a garment** וְאֵין יָדוּעַ אֵיזֶה הוּא — **and it is not known which** thread it is,[2] רַבִּי מֵאִיר אוֹמֵר — **R' Meir says:** יִדָּלֵק הַבֶּגֶד — **The garment must be burned,** because wearing it would mean having benefit from the *orlah* dye in that thread.[3] וַחֲכָמִים אוֹמְרִים — **But the Sages say:** יַעֲלֶה בְּאֶחָד וּמָאתָיִם — **[The thread] is nullified in** a mixture of **two hundred and one.** Thus, if there are at least 200 permitted threads in the garment, the *orlah*-dyed thread becomes nullified and the garment may be worn.[4]

[3] Having mentioned a case in which forbidden *orlah* thread was woven into a garment, the Mishnah now discusses several cases in which *other* forbidden threads were woven into a garment:

הָאוֹרֵג מְלֹא הַסִּיט מִצֶּמֶר הַבְּכוֹר בַּבֶּגֶד — **If someone weaves into a garment**

---- NOTES ----

considered especially important are considered a דָּבָר חָשׁוּב (*significant item*) that does not become nullified. A dyed garment is not one of these and it can therefore be nullified (*Rav; Rash;* see Mishnah 3:7). However, even according to the Sages a majority of 200:1 is required, as with all *orlah* produce (see Mishnah 2:1).

[2]

1. A *sitt* is the space between the index finger and middle finger when they are spread as far apart as possible (*Rav, Rash*).
2. If it could be identified, it could simply be removed (see *Temurah* 34a). However, in the Mishnah's case the prohibited thread is lost among the other, permitted threads.

3. R' Meir considers even a dyed thread the length of a *sitt* a דָּבָר חָשׁוּב, *significant item*, because it is a דָּבָר שֶׁבְּמִנְיָן, *something counted by the unit*. Therefore, it cannot be nullified (*Rav; Rosh;* see note 4 of the previous Mishnah). Some say that this length is considered significant because it is the measure used by the Torah to define the *melachah* of weaving on Shabbos [*Shabbos* 13:4] (*Rash Sirilio*, cited by *Meleches Shlomo*).

4. The Sages follow their view in the previous Mishnah that even a dyed garment becomes nullified. Surely, then, a dyed string becomes nullified (*Rav*). This case was taught only to show that R' Meir is strict even with a dyed *thread* (*Tos. Yom Tov*, from *Rambam*).

משניות ערלה / פרק ג: בגד [48]

יִדָּלֵק הַבֶּגֶד. וּמִשְּׂעַר הַנָּזִיר וּמִפֶּטֶר חֲמוֹר בְּשַׂק, יִדָּלֵק הַשַּׂק. וּבַמֻּקְדָּשִׁין, מְקַדְּשִׁין כָּל שֶׁהֵן.

- רע"ב -

משער הנזיר. ופטרו חמור בהנאה, שנאמר (במדבר ו, ה) קדוש יהיה גדל פרע, גדולו של פרע יהיה קדוש: ומפטר חמור. לאחר טריפה כולי עלמא מודו דאסור בהנאה, דגמרינן טריפה טריפה מעגלה ערופה: בשק. גבי למר תנא בגד, וגבי שער תנא שק, דהכי אורחיה:

---

a thread **the length of a** *sitt* that was made from **the forbidden wool of a bechor,**[1] — יִדָּלֵק הַבֶּגֶד — **the garment must be burned,** because the thread does not become nullified. Since it is forbidden to benefit from the wool of a *bechor,* the garment may not be used. וּמִשְּׂעַר הַנָּזִיר וּמִפֶּטֶר חֲמוֹר בְּשַׂק — Similarly, if someone weaves the length of a *sitt* **of the** forbidden **hair of a** *nazir*[2] or the forbidden hair **of a firstborn male donkey**[3] into a sack, יִדָּלֵק הַשַּׂק — **the sack must be burned,** because the hair does not become nullified.[4]

The Mishnah concludes:

וּבַמֻּקְדָּשִׁין — **And** if the forbidden threads woven into a garment are **from consecrated [animals],** i.e., animals designated as offerings, מְקַדְּשִׁין כָּל שֶׁהֵן — **they prohibit** the garment in **any amount,** even less than a *sitt.* Because of the special holiness of offerings, the Sages were particularly strict with them and did not allow the smallest part of them to be nullified.[5]

NOTES

1. An animal *bechor* (a firstborn male calf, sheep, or goat) is automatically sanctified at birth. It is given to a Kohen who brings it as an offering and eats its meat. If it is blemished and cannot be brought as an offering, the Kohen may slaughter it and eat its meat — but he may not cut off its wool (see *Devarim* 15:19). Even the wool of a blemished *bechor* is (Rabbinically) forbidden for use (*Rav; Rash*). See note 5.

2. A *nazir* is someone who makes a vow of *nezirus,* which prohibits him to drink wine, cut his hair, or become *tamei* from a human corpse. When the *nazir* completes the term of his *nezirus,* he must undergo a ritual that includes shaving his head (see *Bamidbar* Chapter 6). The shaved-off hair is forbidden for benefit and must be burned (see *Temurah* 34a).

3. A firstborn male donkey (פֶּטֶר חֲמוֹר) must be redeemed with a sheep or goat, which is given to a Kohen. If the owner does not want to redeem it, he must chop off the head of the donkey (*Shemos* 13:13). The carcass of the donkey is then forbidden for benefit (see *Rav* and *Bechoros* 9b).

4. This Mishnah follows the view of R' Meir in the previous two Mishnahs, who holds that a thread the length of a *sitt* does not become nullified [see note 3 in the previous Mishnah] (*Rash;* based on *Yerushalmi*).

[Animal hair and human hair are not usually woven into a garment, but they are used in making sacks. This is why the Mishnah speaks of "sacks" in their case (*Rav; Rosh*).]

5. *Rav, Rosh.* It is forbidden to have personal benefit from an animal sanctified as an offering.

[At the beginning of the Mishnah we learned that wool of a *bechor* — which is a sanctified animal — prohibits an entire garment only if it is the length of a *sitt.* The Mishnah there is discussing a blemished *bechor,* which is no longer fit to be brought as an offering. For this reason its wool does not prohibit the garment unless it is the length of a *sitt* (*Rosh; Rav* at the beginning of the Mishnah).]

[49] **MISHNAH ORLAH** / Chapter 3: *Beged* — 3/4-5

[ד] **תַּבְשִׁיל** שֶׁבִּשְּׁלוֹ בִּקְלִפֵּי עָרְלָה, יִדָּלֵק. נִתְעָרֵב בַּאֲחֵרִים, יַעֲלֶה בְּאֶחָד וּמָאתָיִם.

[ה] **תַּנּוּר** שֶׁהִסִּיקוּהוּ בִּקְלִפֵּי עָרְלָה וְאָפָה בּוֹ אֶת הַפַּת, תִּדָּלֵק הַפַּת; נִתְעָרְבָה בַּאֲחֵרוֹת, תַּעֲלֶה בְּאֶחָד וּמָאתָיִם.

– רע״ב –
(ד-ה) ידלק. דיש שבח עצים בתבשיל, וכן בפת: יעלה באחד ומאתים. ובהא מודה רבי מאיר, דאין זה מעשרה דברים דחשיב רבי מאיר דמקדשים, כדמוכח בירושלמי (הלכה ז):

[4] The Mishnah turns to address the law of food that was cooked using a fire that was fueled by *orlah*:

תַּבְשִׁיל שֶׁבִּשְּׁלוֹ בִּקְלִפֵּי עָרְלָה יִדָּלֵק — **A food that was cooked** on a fire made **from the shells of** *orlah*[1] **must be burned.** Since the food has been improved through the *orlah* shells, making use of the food is considered benefiting from *orlah*.[2] נִתְעָרֵב בַּאֲחֵרִים יַעֲלֶה בְּאֶחָד וּמָאתָיִם — **If [that food] became mixed with others, it is nullified** in a mixture of **two hundred and one,** i.e., 200 pieces of other cooked food to one piece of this *orlah*-cooked food. Food cooked over an *orlah* fire is not worse than actual *orlah*, which becomes nullified in a mixture of 200:1.[3]

[5] The Mishnah continues with a similar ruling for bread that was baked using a fire that was fueled by *orlah*:

תַּנּוּר שֶׁהִסִּיקוּהוּ בִּקְלִפֵּי עָרְלָה וְאָפָה בּוֹ אֶת הַפַּת — **If an oven was heated with** a fire made **from the shells of** *orlah* **and then he baked bread in it,** תִּדָּלֵק הַפַּת — **the bread must be burned.** Since the bread came into being through the *orlah*, using the bread is considered benefiting from *orlah*.[1] נִתְעָרְבָה בַּאֲחֵרוֹת תַּעֲלֶה בְּאֶחָד וּמָאתָיִם — **If [this bread] became mixed with others, it is nullified in** a mixture of **two hundred and one** (200 ordinary breads to one *orlah*-baked bread).[2]

— NOTES —

[4]
1. The shells were used as fuel for the fire.
2. Although the food does not contain any actual *orlah*, it *does* contain the improvement brought about by the *orlah* that was used to cook it. The Mishnah teaches that we view this improvement as if the "benefit" of the *orlah* is present in the cooked food [יֵשׁ שֶׁבַח עֵצִים בַּתַּבְשִׁיל, *the improvement of the wood* (fuel) *is contained in the food*]. Therefore, eating the food is considered having benefit from *orlah* [even though the *orlah* itself no longer exists] (*Rav, Rash* from *Pesachim* 26b-27a).
3. Even R' Meir, who holds that a garment (or even a thread) dyed with *orlah* dye cannot be nullified (see Mishnahs 1-2), agrees that food cooked with *orlah* shells can become nullified (*Rav, Rash*). This is because the food is not forbidden on its own account, but only because of the shells by which it was cooked. Since those shells were not a דָּבָר שֶׁבְּמִנְיָן, *item sold by the piece*, and could have been nullified in a mixture, the food cooked with them is not treated any more strictly. [See *Mishnah Rishonah* to Mishnah 1, who explains why a thread dyed with *orlah* is different.]

[5]
1. Here too, the improvement brought about by the *orlah* shells (being baked) is considered a benefit from *orlah* that is present in the bread [יֵשׁ שֶׁבַח עֵצִים בַּפַּת]. The bread is therefore prohibited. See previous Mishnah, note 3.
2. See note 3 of the previous Mishnah.

[50] משניות ערלה / פרק ג: בגד

ג/ו-ז

- רע"ב -

(ו) חבילי תלתן. אין חבילה פחותה מעשרים וחמשה זירים: נתערבו באחרים. גרסינן, ולא גרסינן ומתריס באחרים. ואי גרסינן לה צריך לומר שנתערבו כל אותן

[ו] **מִי** שֶׁהָיוּ לוֹ חֲבִילֵי תִלְתָּן שֶׁל כִּלְאֵי הַכֶּרֶם, יִדָּלֵקוּ. נִתְעָרְבוּ בַאֲחֵרִים, כֻּלָּם יִדָּלֵקוּ, דִּבְרֵי רַבִּי מֵאִיר. וַחֲכָמִים אוֹמְרִים: יַעֲלוּ בְאֶחָד וּמָאתָיִם.

[ז] **שֶׁהָיָה** רַבִּי מֵאִיר אוֹמֵר: אֶת שֶׁדַּרְכּוֹ לִמָּנוֹת,

אחרים באחרים, דלא הוי אלא חד ספיקא, ואשמעינן אף על גב דאיכא תרי רובי, אסירי: **כולם ידלקו**. והא דלא אמרינן ימכרו כולן חוץ מדמי איסור שבהן, כדאמר רבי שמעון בן גמליאל בפרק [בתרא] דעבודה זרה (משנה י) גבי יין נסך, משום דהכא חיישינן בכולהו שמא יחזור העובד כוכבים וימכרם לישראל, מה שאין כן ביין נסך דליכא למיחש להכי: (ז) **שדרכו למנות**. שאין אדם מוכרו אלא במנין מפני חשיבותו:

---

[6] The laws of *kilei hakerem* are similar to those of *orlah*.[1] The Mishnah now deals with nullifying bundles of *kilei hakerem*:

מִי שֶׁהָיוּ לוֹ חֲבִילֵי תִלְתָּן שֶׁל כִּלְאֵי הַכֶּרֶם יִדָּלֵקוּ — If someone has bundles of fenugreek that were forbidden as *kilei hakerem*,[2] they must be burned. נִתְעָרְבוּ בַאֲחֵרִים — If any of these [bundles] became mixed with other [bundles] of fenugreek, כֻּלָּם יִדָּלֵקוּ — they must all be burned, even if there were 200 or more bundles of permitted fenugreek; דִּבְרֵי רַבִּי מֵאִיר — these are the words of R' Meir. A bundle of fenugreek is something significant, according to R' Meir, and it therefore cannot become nullified.[3] וַחֲכָמִים אוֹמְרִים — But the Sages say: יַעֲלוּ בְאֶחָד וּמָאתָיִם — They can become nullified in a mixture of two hundred and one (200 permitted bundles to one forbidden one).[4]

[7] The Mishnah now explains the basis of the dispute between R' Meir and the Sages in the previous Mishnah:[1]

שֶׁהָיָה רַבִּי מֵאִיר אוֹמֵר אֶת שֶׁדַּרְכּוֹ לִמָּנוֹת מְקַדֵּשׁ — For R' Meir would say: **Something that is customarily counted** when it is sold and not merely

--- NOTES ---

[6]

1. Both *orlah* and *kilei hakerem* must be burned (*Temurah* 7:5), both are forbidden for benefit (Mishnah 1), and both become nullified only in a mixture of 200:1 (Mishnah 2:1 above).

2. [Fenugreek is an herb with edible leaves. Its seeds are used as a spice (see *Rashi, Beitzah* 3b ד"ה תילתן).]

The fenugreek had been planted together with, or next to, grapevines, which caused it to become forbidden as *kilei hakerem* (see Mishnah 2:1 note 7). It was then collected and tied in bundles. A bundle consists of at least twenty-five stalks (*Rav*, from *Yerushalmi*).

3. A bundle of fenugreek is a דָּבָר שֶׁבְּמִנְיָן, *an item sold by the unit,* rather than

by estimate (see *Rashi, Beitzah* 3b ד"ה כל שדרכו למנות). [People do not sell a basketful of bundles; rather, they charge separately for each bundle.] According to R' Meir, any item which, on account of its significance, is sold by the unit, cannot be nullified (*Tiferes Yisrael*; *Rav* to Mishnah 7).

4. The Sages do not consider a דָּבָר שֶׁבְּמִנְיָן, an item sold by the unit, so significant that it cannot be nullified. Therefore, even bundles of fenugreek can be nullified by a margin of 200:1 (the margin that applies to *kilei hakerem*).

[7]

1. [This explanation is also the basis of the disputes between R' Meir and the Sages in the first two Mishnahs of the chapter.]

[51] MISHNAH ORLAH / Chapter 3: *Beged*

- רע״ב -

פרך ובדן. שמות מקומות הן. ואני שמעתי, אגוזי פרך, אגוזים שקליפתן רכה ונפרכין: חֲלְפֵי תְרָדִין. עלין מללטות התרדין: קלְסֵי כְרוּב. קלחי כרוב שבארץ ישראל, שהם גדולים וטובים: של בעל הבית. שכן גדולים, אבל של נחתום קטנים הן:

מְקַדֵּשׁ. וַחֲכָמִים אוֹמְרִים: אֵינוֹ מְקַדֵּשׁ אֶלָּא שִׁשָּׁה דְבָרִים בִּלְבָד, וְרַבִּי עֲקִיבָא אוֹמֵר: שִׁבְעָה.

וְאֵלּוּ הֵם: אֱגוֹזֵי פֶרֶךְ, רִמּוֹנֵי בָדָן, וְחָבִיּוֹת סְתוּמוֹת, וְחִלְפוֹת תְּרָדִין, וְקִלְסֵי כְרוּב, וּדְלַעַת יְוָנִית; רַבִּי עֲקִיבָא אוֹמֵר: אַף כִּכָּרוֹת שֶׁל בַּעַל הַבָּיִת.

---

estimated[2] **prohibits** the mixture into which it falls.[3] וַחֲכָמִים אוֹמְרִים — **But the Sages say:** אֵינוֹ מְקַדֵּשׁ אֶלָּא שִׁשָּׁה דְבָרִים בִּלְבָד — **Only six items prohibit** the mixture into which they fall without becoming nullified. וְרַבִּי עֲקִיבָא אוֹמֵר — **And R' Akiva says:** שִׁבְעָה — **Seven items do so.**[4]

The Mishnah proceeds to list the six items referred to by the Sages, and the one added by R' Akiva:

וְאֵלּוּ הֵם — **And these are [the six items]:** אֱגוֹזֵי פֶרֶךְ — **(1) the walnuts of Perech,** רִמּוֹנֵי בָדָן — **(2) the pomegranates of Badan,**[5] וְחָבִיּוֹת סְתוּמוֹת — **(3) sealed barrels** of wine, וְחִלְפוֹת תְּרָדִין — **(4) leaves of beets,**[6] וְקִלְסֵי כְרוּב — **(5) stalks of cabbage,**[7] וּדְלַעַת יְוָנִית — **and (6) the Greek gourd.** רַבִּי עֲקִיבָא אוֹמֵר — **R' Akiva says:** אַף כִּכָּרוֹת שֶׁל בַּעַל הַבָּיִת — **Also the loaves of a householder.**[8]

If any of these seven items were forbidden and became mixed with similar items, they do not become nullified. The Mishnah explains how these seven items became forbidden:

--- NOTES ---

2. Due to its importance, people sell it by an exact count of the pieces and not merely by estimating how many there are (*Rav;* see Mishnah 6 note 3).

3. The Mishnah uses the word מְקַדֵּשׁ to mean *prohibit* based on the verse in the Torah (*Devarim* 22:9) that uses this term to describe the prohibition of *kilei hakerem*. According to *Rambam Commentary,* the Torah uses the word תִּקְדָּשׁ (literally, *sanctifies*) to indicate that the mixture must be burned.

4. [The Sages and R' Akiva disagree with R' Meir. They hold that even something sold by a precise count is not important enough to prevent it from being nullified. The item must be particularly special to qualify as a דָּבָר חָשׁוּב, *an item of significance.* The items the Mishnah will now list are large, expensive, and the most outstanding of their species (*Rashi, Zevachim* 72b ד״ה אלא ששה).

5. Perech and Badan were names of places (*Rav; Rash*).

6. *Rav.* That is, the leaves and long stalks that grow out of the beetroot (*Tos. Yom Tov,* from *Aruch*). [Certain varieties of beets have large leaves that grow from long, colorful stalks that emerge from the beetroot. These leaves and stalks are used as food.]

7. That is, the stems with their leaves [in other words, heads of cabbage] (*Rashi, Zevachim* 72b). The cabbages of Eretz Yisrael were very large and very tasty (*Rav*).

8. The loaves of a householder are larger than the loaves of a baker (*Rav; Rash*). Additionally, the householder uses finer flour, which results in a better-quality bread (*Rash Sirilio*).

‎[52]‎ ‎משניות ערלה / פרק ג: בגד‎

‎הָרָאוּי לְעָרְלָה, עָרְלָה, לְכִלְאֵי הַכֶּרֶם,‎
‎כִּלְאֵי הַכֶּרֶם.‎

‎[ח] כֵּיצַד? נִתְפַּצְעוּ הָאֱגוֹזִים, נִתְפָּרְדוּ‎
‎הָרִמּוֹנִים, נִתְפַּתְּחוּ הֶחָבִיּוֹת,‎
‎נִתְחַתְּכוּ הַדְּלוּעִים, נִתְפָּרְסוּ הַכִּכָּרוֹת, יַעֲלוּ‎
‎בְּאֶחָד וּמָאתָיִם.‎

‎- רע״ב -‎

‎הראוי לערלה.‎ ‎כגון‎
‎אגוזים ורמונים וחביות‎
‎סתומות: והראוי לכלאי‎
‎הכרם.‎ ‎כגון חלפי תרדין‎
‎וקולסי כרוב ודלעת‎
‎יונית. ואין הלכה כרבי‎
‎מאיר ולא כרבי עקיבא:‎
‎(ח) נתפצעו האגוזים.‎
‎גרסינן, ולא גרסינן כילד.‎
‎וקא משמע לן מתניתין‎
‎דדוקא שלמים לא בטילי, אבל לא שבורים ופטוטיס: נתפרסו הכברות.‎ ‎האי סתמא כרבי עקיבא‎
‎(במשנה ז), דהלכתא כוותיה:‎

הָרָאוּי לְעָרְלָה עָרְלָה — **The ones** in this list **that were fit to be** *orlah* were forbidden as *orlah;* **לְכִלְאֵי הַכֶּרֶם כִּלְאֵי הַכֶּרֶם** — **the ones that were fit to be** *kilei hakerem* were forbidden as *kilei hakerem*.[9]

[8] The previous Mishnah listed six items that do not become nullified according to the Sages, and a seventh one according to R' Akiva. That Mishnah spoke of whole items. The law is different if these items were no longer whole, as the Mishnah now explains:

כֵּיצַד — **How so;** i.e., under what conditions do these items not become nullified? When they are whole. **נִתְפַּצְעוּ הָאֱגוֹזִים** — **But if the walnuts were cracked open,** **נִתְפָּרְדוּ הָרִמּוֹנִים** — **the pomegranates were split,** **נִתְפַּתְּחוּ הֶחָבִיּוֹת** — **the barrels** of wine **were opened,** **נִתְחַתְּכוּ הַדְּלוּעִים** — **the gourds were cut,** **נִתְפָּרְסוּ הַכִּכָּרוֹת** — or **the loaves were broken,** **יַעֲלוּ בְּאֶחָד וּמָאתָיִם** — **they can become nullified in** a mixture of **two hundred and one** parts (200 permitted parts to one part *orlah* or *kilei hakerem*). The items listed in the previous Mishnah are considered to be too important to become nullified only when they are whole. Once they have been broken, they lose their special significance and they can become nullified the same as any other *orlah* or *kilei hakerem*.[1]

NOTES

9. Of the seven foods listed above, the first three (walnuts of Perech, pomegranates of Badan, the grapes for the sealed barrels of wine) are fit to be *orlah* since they grow on trees. The next three (beet leaves, heads of cabbage, Greek gourds) are vegetables and cannot be *orlah,* but they can become forbidden as *kilei hakerem* by being planted in a vineyard (see *Rav, Rash*). [*Kilei hakerem* applies only to grains and vegetables planted in a vineyard, not to fruit trees planted there (*Rambam, Hilchos Kilayim* 5:6).] Wine, which comes from grapes, can be subject to both *kilei hakerem* and *orlah*.

The seven items mentioned in our Mishnah were of special significance in Eretz Yisrael in the times of the Mishnah. Items of equal importance in other places or times are similarly not subject to nullification. The Mishnah listed these seven items because they were always considered especially important in the times of the Mishnah (*Rambam, Hilchos Maachalos Asuros* 16:9; *Yoreh Deah* 110:1).

[8]

1. *Rav.* The Mishnah is discussing cases where these special items fell into the mixture after they had already been broken. The law in a case where they fell in whole and then broke apart in the mixture is debated by Tannaim in a Baraisa (*Meleches Shlomo;* see *Gittin* 54b).

[53] MISHNAH ORLAH / Chapter 3: Beged

– רע"ב –

(ט) ספק ערלה. כגון עובד כוכבים שיש לו נטיעות של ערלה בגינתו, ובידו פירות, ואין ידוע אם משל ערלה אם משל זקנה:

[ט] סָפֵק עָרְלָה, בְּאֶרֶץ יִשְׂרָאֵל אָסוּר וּבְסוּרְיָא מֻתָּר, וּבְחוּצָה לָאָרֶץ יוֹרֵד וְלוֹקֵחַ, וּבִלְבַד שֶׁלֹּא יִרְאֶנּוּ לוֹקֵט.

[9] This final Mishnah discusses the laws of possible *orlah* and *kilei hakerem*; that is, fruit that *may* be *orlah* or *kilei hakerem*, but we do not know for sure. Generally, when there is a question whether something is prohibited, we must be strict about it if we are dealing with a Biblical prohibition, and we may be more lenient about it if we are dealing with a Rabbinic prohibition. In regard to *orlah* and *kilei hakerem* the Mishnah will teach that there is a difference between Eretz Yisrael and outside of Eretz Yisrael:

סְפֵק עָרְלָה — **Possible *orlah*** (that is, fruit that *may* have come from an *orlah* tree but we do not know for sure)[1] is subject to the following law: בְּאֶרֶץ יִשְׂרָאֵל אָסוּר — **If the fruit grew in Eretz Yisrael, it is forbidden.** Since the *orlah* prohibition is a Biblical one, when there is a doubt about it we must act strictly and prohibit it.[2] וּבְסוּרְיָא מֻתָּר — **But if the fruit grew in Surya,** which is only Rabbinically considered part of Eretz Yisrael, **it is permitted** to buy fruit that may possibly be *orlah*, as long as we do not buy it from a field that is known to contain some *orlah* trees.[3] וּבְחוּצָה לָאָרֶץ יוֹרֵד וְלוֹקֵחַ — **And outside of Eretz Yisrael,** the law is even more lenient: **[A Jew] may go down** to a field that has both *orlah* and non-*orlah* trees[4] **and buy** fruit that was already picked by a non-Jew, וּבִלְבַד שֶׁלֹּא יִרְאֶנּוּ לוֹקֵט — **as long as he does not** actually **see [the non-Jew] gathering** the fruit from the trees. Since it is not clear that the fruit came from the *orlah* trees, he may buy and eat it.[5] However, if he sees him pick the fruit he may not buy it. This is a Rabbinic stringency.[6]

— NOTES —

[9]
1. For example, a non-Jew brought fruit from his orchard. His orchard contained both *orlah* and non-*orlah* trees, and we do not know whether the fruit he brought was from an *orlah* tree or a non-*orlah* tree (*Rav; Rash*).
2. This is the general rule for all Biblical prohibitions [סְפֵקָא דְּאוֹרַיְיתָא לְחַמְרָא] (*Rav; Rosh*).
3. The Biblical prohibition of *orlah* actually applies even outside of Eretz Yisrael, as the Mishnah will say below, but only in cases where it is definitely *orlah*. Possible *orlah* is Biblically permitted outside Eretz Yisrael. The reason for this will be explained in note 11.
  Surya is Aram Tzovah [the area roughly corresponding to present-day northern Syria]. It was conquered by King David (*Rashi, Kiddushin* 38b ד"ה בסוריא). It

was not part of the Land of Israel under Biblical law, but the Rabbis decreed that it should be treated in many ways with the laws of Eretz Yisrael (see *Rashi, Gittin* 47a ד"ה בסוריא).
4. *Ran's* second explanation (*Kiddushin* 15b in *Rif*), cited by *Mishnah Rishonah* and *Meleches Shlomo* (at the end of the Mishnah).
5. However, in Surya the Rabbis did not permit this. They only permitted buying from the non-Jew if he found him with his fruit outside the field [where it is possible that the fruit was not even from this field]. Since Surya was treated by the Rabbis as part of Eretz Yisrael, the Rabbis were stricter there about buying possible *orlah* [and required a greater degree of uncertainty before permitting us to buy it] (*Rav, Rash; Tiferes Yisrael*).
6. *Ran,* cited by *Mishnah Rishonah* and

[54] משניות ערלה / פרק ג: בגד

כֶּרֶם נָטוּעַ יָרָק, וְיָרָק נִמְכָּר חוּצָה לוֹ, בְּאֶרֶץ יִשְׂרָאֵל אָסוּר, וּבְסוּרְיָא מֻתָּר, וּבְחוּצָה לָאָרֶץ יוֹרֵד וְלוֹקֵט, וּבִלְבַד שֶׁלֹּא יְלַקֵּט בְּיָד.

– רע״ב –

בארץ ישראל. דהוי ספיקא דאורייתא לחומרא: **בסוריא** מותר. דכבוש יחיד הוא ולאו שמיה כבוש,

והחמירו בו קלת: **ובחוצה לארץ יורד ולוקח.** בתוך הגינה וקונה מן העובד כוכבים מאותם שליקט כבר, ובלבד שלא יראנו לוקט: **ובחוצה לארץ יורד ולוקט.** העובד כוכבים יורד ולוקט בפני הישראל, וישראל קונה ממנו, ובלבד שלא ילקוט ישראל ביד:

The Mishnah now discusses a similar law with regard to the prohibition of *kilei hakerem*:

כֶּרֶם נָטוּעַ יָרָק — If there is **a vineyard** that was **planted** with **vegetables,** causing those vegetables to become prohibited as *kilei hakerem*,[7] וְיָרָק נִמְכָּר חוּצָה לוֹ — **and vegetables are being sold outside [the vineyard],** and we do not know if they came from this vineyard or from somewhere else, the law is as follows: בְּאֶרֶץ יִשְׂרָאֵל אָסוּר — **In Eretz Yisrael, [the vegetables] are forbidden.** Since the prohibition of *kilei hakerem* in Eretz Yisrael is a Biblical one, when there is a doubt about it we must act strictly and prohibit it. וּבְסוּרְיָא מֻתָּר — **But if the possible *kilei hakerem* vegetables grew in Surya, they are permitted,** because the prohibition of *kilei hakerem* in Surya is only Rabbinic, and when there exists a doubt involving a Rabbinic prohibition we may act leniently.[8] וּבְחוּצָה לָאָרֶץ יוֹרֵד וְלוֹקֵט — **And outside of Eretz Yisrael** the law is even more lenient: a Jew may ask **[a non-Jew] go down and gather** vegetables on his behalf, even though they may be *kilei hakerem,* וּבִלְבַד שֶׁלֹּא יְלַקֵּט בְּיָד — **provided that [the Jew] does not pick with his own hand.**[9]

NOTES

Meleches Shlomo. Where we see him picking the fruit from this field, the only question that remains is whether the tree he picked from was an *orlah* tree or a non-*orlah* tree. The Rabbis did not permit buying such fruit [since it might lead people to buy fruit from a non-Jew even when it was clearly from an *orlah* tree]. They only permitted buying fruit in that field when it had already been picked before the Jew came, so that there is still a slight chance that the fruit is not from this field at all (see *Mishnah Rishonah*).

7. *Kilei hakerem* may not be eaten, nor may we benefit from them (Mishnah, *Kilayim* 8:1).

8. *Kilei hakerem* is Biblically prohibited only in Eretz Yisrael; outside of Eretz Yisrael it is Rabbinically prohibited, as the Mishnah will say below. Therefore, we apply the general rule for all Rabbinic prohibitions that where there is a doubt, it is permitted [סְפֵיקָא דְרַבָּנָן לְקוּלָא] (see *Ran* cited above).

9. The Mishnah is discussing a case where there are vegetables in or near this vineyard that are not prohibited as *kilei hakerem*. Therefore, since it is possible that the non-Jew will give him permitted vegetables, he is allowed to ask him to go gather vegetables for him (*Mishnah Rishonah*, citing *Tur*). However, the Jew may not pick the vegetables himself, since he can see which vegetables are prohibited. Similarly, if he sees the non-Jew pick vegetables that are definitely *kilei hakerem*, he may not take them (*Ran* cited above; *Derech Emunah* 8:82; see *Rav*).

[In the case of *orlah* outside of Eretz Yisrael, we cannot ask a non-Jew to gather for us from a field that contains *orlah*; we can only buy what was already picked (see note 6). *Kilei hakerem* outside of Eretz Yisrael is treated more leniently in this respect (*Ran, Mishnah Rishonah*) because even definite *kilei hakerem* is not Biblically forbidden outside Eretz Yisrael, unlike definite *orlah*.]

[55] **MISHNAH ORLAH** / Chapter 3: *Beged*

הֶחָדָשׁ, אָסוּר מִן הַתּוֹרָה בְּכָל מָקוֹם; וְהָעָרְלָה, הֲלָכָה; וְהַכִּלְאַיִם, מִדִּבְרֵי סוֹפְרִים.

- רע"ב -

בכל מקום. ואפילו בחוצה לארץ, דכתיב (ויקרא כג, יד) ולחם וקלי וכרמל לא תאכלו וגו' בכל מושבותיכם: והערלה הלכה. למשה מסיני שאסור בחולה לארץ. ואף על פי כן ספיקה מותר, שכך נאמרה ההלכה למשה בסיני, שיהיה ספיקה מותר בחולה לארץ: והכלאים מדברי סופרים. דוקא כלאי הכרם, כיון דבארץ חמירי ואסירי בהנאה מן התורה, בחולה לארץ גזרו בהן רבנן, אבל כלאי זרעים דבארץ שרו בהנאה, בחולה לארץ לא גזרו בהו רבנן. והרכבת האילן אסורה בחולה לארץ מן התורה, דכתיב (שם יט, יט) בהמתך לא תרביע כלאים שדך לא תזרע כלאים, מה בהמתך הרבעה אף שדך הרכבה, ומה בהמתך בין בארץ בין בחולה לארץ אף שדך הרכבה בין בארץ בין בחולה לארץ:

The Mishnah now defines the law for a number of produce-related prohibitions outside Eretz Yisrael:

הֶחָדָשׁ אָסוּר מִן הַתּוֹרָה בְּכָל מָקוֹם — **Chadash is prohibited by the Torah everywhere,** even outside of Eretz Yisrael.[10] וְהָעָרְלָה הֲלָכָה — **Orlah is prohibited outside of Eretz Yisrael by a *Halachah LeMoshe MiSinai*, which has the status of a Torah law.**[11] וְהַכִּלְאַיִם מִדִּבְרֵי סוֹפְרִים — **But *kilayim* of the vineyard** (*kilei hakerem*) **is prohibited outside of Eretz Yisrael only by Rabbinic enactment.**[12]

NOTES

10. The word *chadash* means "new." The Torah states that the new crop of grain (wheat, barley, spelt, rye, and oats) may not be eaten until the *omer*-offering has been brought on the 16th day of Nissan (*Vayikra* 23:14). [Nowadays, when we do not have a Temple in which to bring the *omer*-offering, the new crop becomes permitted at the end of the day on the 16th of Nissan (see Mishnah, *Succah* 3:12).]

The Tanna of our Mishnah holds that the prohibition of *chadash* applies on the Biblical level even outside the Land of Israel. He learns this from the end of the verse about *chadash*, which states that the law applies בְּכֹל מֹשְׁבֹתֵיכֶם, *in all your dwellings* (*Rav*). Other Tannaim disagree (see *Kiddushin* 1:9).

11. *Rav*, from *Kiddushin* 38b. A *Halachah LeMoshe MiSinai* is a law given to Moshe at Mount Sinai, which was not written in the Torah itself.

The *Halachah LeMoshe MiSinai* about *orlah* included a provision that in cases where there is a doubt whether something is *orlah*, the matter should be treated leniently (even though it has the status of a Biblical prohibition). This is the reason why the Mishnah said above that possible *orlah* is treated leniently outside of Eretz Yisrael (*Rav*, from *Kiddushin* 38b and *Yerushalmi* here). See note 3 above.

12. [Literally, *by the words of the Scribes*.] Biblically, the prohibition of *kilei hakerem*, like other mitzvos dependent on the Land, applies only in Eretz Yisrael (*Kiddushin* 1:8). Nevertheless, it applies on a Rabbinic level even outside of Eretz Yisrael.

This Rabbinic prohibition applies only to *kilayim* of the vineyard. Since such *kilayim* is prohibited in Eretz Yisrael even for benefit, the Rabbis prohibited it outside of Eretz Yisrael as well. However, they did not prohibit *kilayim* of seeds (planting different kinds of vegetables and grains together) outside of Eretz Yisrael, since this kind of *kilayim* is not prohibited for benefit (or even to eat) in Eretz Yisrael (*Rav*, from *Kiddushin* 38b). Grafting different species of trees together is Biblically prohibited even outside of Eretz Yisrael (*Rav*).

מסכת ביכורים
TRACTATE BIKKURIM

זרעים
מועד
נשים
נזיקין
קדשים
טהרות

General Introduction

רֵאשִׁית בִּכּוּרֵי אַדְמָתְךָ תָּבִיא בֵּית ה' אֱלֹהֶיךָ ...

The first of the ripening [fruits] of your land you shall bring to the House of Hashem, your God ... (Shemos 23:19, 34:26).

בִּכּוּרֵי כָּל אֲשֶׁר בְּאַרְצָם אֲשֶׁר יָבִיאוּ לַה' לְךָ יִהְיֶה כָּל טָהוֹר בְּבֵיתְךָ יֹאכְלֶנּוּ.

The ripening fruits of all that is in their land, which they bring to Hashem, shall be yours, every pure person in your household may eat it (Bamidbar 18:13).

א. וְהָיָה כִּי תָבוֹא אֶל הָאָרֶץ אֲשֶׁר ה' אֱלֹהֶיךָ נֹתֵן לְךָ נַחֲלָה וִירִשְׁתָּהּ וְיָשַׁבְתָּ בָּהּ. ב. וְלָקַחְתָּ מֵרֵאשִׁית כָּל פְּרִי הָאֲדָמָה אֲשֶׁר תָּבִיא מֵאַרְצְךָ אֲשֶׁר ה' אֱלֹהֶיךָ נֹתֵן לָךְ וְשַׂמְתָּ בַטֶּנֶא וְהָלַכְתָּ אֶל הַמָּקוֹם אֲשֶׁר יִבְחַר ה' אֱלֹהֶיךָ לְשַׁכֵּן שְׁמוֹ שָׁם. ג. וּבָאתָ אֶל הַכֹּהֵן אֲשֶׁר יִהְיֶה בַּיָּמִים הָהֵם וְאָמַרְתָּ אֵלָיו הִגַּדְתִּי הַיּוֹם לַה' אֱלֹהֶיךָ כִּי בָאתִי אֶל הָאָרֶץ אֲשֶׁר נִשְׁבַּע ה' לַאֲבֹתֵינוּ לָתֶת לָנוּ. ד. וְלָקַח הַכֹּהֵן הַטֶּנֶא מִיָּדֶךָ וְהִנִּיחוֹ לִפְנֵי מִזְבַּח ה' אֱלֹהֶיךָ. ה. וְעָנִיתָ וְאָמַרְתָּ לִפְנֵי ה' אֱלֹהֶיךָ אֲרַמִּי אֹבֵד אָבִי וַיֵּרֶד מִצְרַיְמָה וַיָּגָר שָׁם בִּמְתֵי מְעָט וַיְהִי שָׁם לְגוֹי גָּדוֹל עָצוּם וָרָב. ו. וַיָּרֵעוּ אֹתָנוּ הַמִּצְרִים וַיְעַנּוּנוּ וַיִּתְּנוּ עָלֵינוּ עֲבֹדָה קָשָׁה. ז. וַנִּצְעַק אֶל ה' אֱלֹהֵי אֲבֹתֵינוּ וַיִּשְׁמַע ה' אֶת קֹלֵנוּ וַיַּרְא אֶת עָנְיֵנוּ וְאֶת עֲמָלֵנוּ וְאֶת לַחֲצֵנוּ. ח. וַיּוֹצִאֵנוּ ה' מִמִּצְרַיִם בְּיָד חֲזָקָה וּבִזְרֹעַ נְטוּיָה וּבְמֹרָא גָּדֹל וּבְאֹתוֹת וּבְמֹפְתִים. ט. וַיְבִאֵנוּ אֶל הַמָּקוֹם הַזֶּה וַיִּתֶּן לָנוּ אֶת הָאָרֶץ הַזֹּאת אֶרֶץ זָבַת חָלָב וּדְבָשׁ. י. וְעַתָּה הִנֵּה הֵבֵאתִי אֶת רֵאשִׁית פְּרִי הָאֲדָמָה אֲשֶׁר נָתַתָּה לִּי ה' וְהִנַּחְתּוֹ לִפְנֵי ה' אֱלֹהֶיךָ וְהִשְׁתַּחֲוִיתָ לִפְנֵי ה' אֱלֹהֶיךָ. יא. וְשָׂמַחְתָּ בְכָל הַטּוֹב אֲשֶׁר נָתַן לְךָ ה' אֱלֹהֶיךָ וּלְבֵיתֶךָ אַתָּה וְהַלֵּוִי וְהַגֵּר אֲשֶׁר בְּקִרְבֶּךָ.

[1] It will be when you enter the Land that Hashem, your God, gives you as an inheritance, and you possess it, and dwell in it, [2] that you shall take of the first of every fruit of the ground that you bring in from your Land that Hashem, your God, gives you, and you shall put it in a basket and go to the place that Hashem, your God, will choose, to make His Name rest there. [3] You shall come to whomever will be the Kohen in those days, and you shall say to him, "I declare today to Hashem, your God, that I have come to the Land that Hashem swore to our forefathers to give to us." [4] The Kohen shall take the basket from your hand, and lay it before the Altar of Hashem, your God. [5] Then you shall call out and say before Hashem, your God, "An Aramean tried to destroy

משניות ביכורים / הקדמה [4]

my forefather. He descended to Egypt and sojourned there, few in number, and there he became a nation — great, strong, and numerous. ⁶ The Egyptians mistreated us and afflicted us, and placed hard work upon us. ⁷ Then we cried out to Hashem, the God of our forefathers, and Hashem heard our voice and saw our affliction, our travail, and our oppression. ⁸ Hashem took us out of Egypt with a strong hand and with an outstretched arm, with great awesomeness, and with signs and with wonders. ⁹ He brought us to this place, and He gave us this Land, a Land flowing with milk and honey. ¹⁰ And now, behold! I have brought the first fruit of the ground that You have given me, Hashem!" And you shall place it before Hashem, your God, and you shall prostrate yourself before Hashem, your God. ¹¹ You shall rejoice with all the goodness that Hashem, your God, has given you and your household — you and the Levite and the stranger who is in your midst (Devarim 26:1-11).

I.

↰§ The Torah's Commandment

The Torah commands an owner of land in Eretz Yisrael to designate the first fruits that emerge each year, and then, after they have ripened, bring them to the Temple and give them to the Kohanim. These fruits are known as בִּכּוּרִים, *bikkurim* (ripening ones), based on the verse: רֵאשִׁית בִּכּוּרֵי אַדְמָתְךָ תָּבִיא בֵּית ה' אֱלֹהֶיךָ, *the first of the ripening [fruits] of your land you shall bring to the House of Hashem, your God* (*Shemos* 23:19, 34:26). At the Temple, he recites a Biblical passage (*Devarim* 26:3, 5-10), in which he thanks God for having given him the land he owns in Eretz Yisrael and the produce that grows there. He then sets down the *bikkurim* near the Altar, and they are distributed to the Kohanim serving in the Temple, to be eaten by them and their families.

The laws of *bikkurim* apply only to the seven species for which Eretz Yisrael is praised — wheat, barley, grapes, figs, pomegranates, olives, and dates. The Torah also requires that *bikkurim* fruits be of superior quality (Mishnah 1:3). One who owns such fruits, as well as the land on which they grew, is obligated to observe the laws of *bikkurim* (Mishnah 1:1).

II.

↰§ Designating *Bikkurim*

Fruits should be designated as *bikkurim* when they start ripening, as stated in Mishnah 3:1: "A person goes down into his field and sees a fig that has begun to ripen, a cluster of grapes that has begun to ripen, [or] a pomegranate that has begun to ripen, he ties it with a reed and he says, 'These are *bikkurim.*'" This is the preferred method of designating *bikkurim*. If the first-ripening fruits were not designated before they were harvested, they can

[5] **MISHNAH BIKKURIM** / General Introduction

be designated later (*Rambam, Hilchos Bikkurim* 2:19). Similarly, although it is preferable to designate the first fruits to emerge, if later-ripening fruits were designated instead, they are valid *bikkurim* (*Derech Emunah* there in *Beur HaHalachah* ד״ה כיצד).[1]

III.

∽§ Bringing *Bikkurim*

An owner of *bikkurim* is required to bring them to the Temple Courtyard, where he gives them to a Kohen. If his *bikkurim* are lost or damaged before entering the Temple Mount, he must bring others instead (Mishnah 1:8-9; *Rambam, Hilchos Bikkurim* 2:20).

The season for bringing *bikkurim* begins at Shavuos (Mishnah 1:3). Between Shavuos and Succos, one brings *bikkurim* and recites the passage. Once Succos arrives, however, the passage is not recited (Mishnah 1:6).[2] From Chanukah and on, *bikkurim* are not brought at all (*Sifri, Devarim* 26:2).

One who owns *bikkurim* could fulfill his duty by bringing them to the Temple on his own (*Yerushalmi* 22b), but this is not the preferred course of action. He should rather travel with other *bikkurim* owners (Mishnah 3:2).[3]

IV.

∽§ Reciting the *Bikkurim* Passage

The Torah commands an owner of *bikkurim* to recite a certain passage, *Devarim* 26:3,5-10. This passage gives an outline of Jewish history, including how God saved us from the slavery in Egypt and brought us to *a Land flowing with milk and honey*. It concludes: *And now, behold! I have brought the first fruit of the ground that You have given me, Hashem*. The purpose of reciting the passage is to show that Eretz Yisrael could never have been given to the Jewish people without God's miraculous intervention. By reciting the passage, the farmer shows his gratitude to God for having awarded him the land he owns in Eretz Yisrael and the produce that grew there.

--- NOTES ---

1. Mishnah 2:3 indicates that there is no minimum; one may designate even the smallest amount of each species as *bikkurim* (see *Rav* there). However, *Rambam* (*Hilchos Bikkurim* 2:17) rules that according to Rabbinic law one must designate at least one-sixtieth of the crop.

2. After recording the *bikkurim* passage, the Torah states: וְשָׂמַחְתָּ בְכָל הַטּוֹב אֲשֶׁר נָתַן לְךָ ה׳ אֱלֹהֶיךָ, *You shall rejoice with all the goodness that Hashem, your God, has given you* (*Devarim* 26:11). The gladness mentioned here refers to the months before Succos, when farmers rejoice over the crops they gather and bring indoors before the rainy season. The declaration of gratitude is therefore recited only until Succos (*Sifri, Devarim* 26:2; *Pesachim* 36b).

3. By performing the mitzvah in a large group, they honor the One Whose commandment they are observing, as taught by the verse (*Proverbs* 14:28): בְּרָב עָם הַדְרַת מֶלֶךְ, *With many people is the glory of the king* (*Rav* to Mishnah 3:2).

V.

✍ The Temple Service

Rambam (*Hilchos Bikkurim* 3:12) describes the Temple service as follows: In the Courtyard of the Temple, the owner stands with his basket[4] of *bikkurim* on his shoulder, and he says to the appointed Kohen: הִגַּדְתִּי הַיּוֹם לַה׳ אֱלֹהֶיךָ כִּי בָאתִי אֶל הָאָרֶץ אֲשֶׁר נִשְׁבַּע ה׳ לַאֲבֹתֵינוּ לָתֶת לָנוּ, *I declare today to Hashem, your God, that I have come to the Land that Hashem swore to our forefathers to give to us* (*Devarim* 26:3). He takes the basket down from his shoulder and holds it by its rim. The Kohen puts his hand underneath the basket and they move it to and fro in all four directions and up and down.[5] After this, the owner recites the second part of the passage (verses 5-10 there): אֲרַמִּי אֹבֵד אָבִי וְגוֹ׳, *An Aramean tried to destroy my forefather*, etc.[6] He puts the basket down next to the Altar, prostrates himself on the floor of the Courtyard, and takes his leave (see Mishnah 3:6).

Following the ceremony, the *bikkurim* are divided among the Kohanim serving in the Temple that week (Mishnah 3:10). *Bikkurim* are one of the twenty-four Kohanic gifts (*Bamidbar* 18:13).

An owner of *bikkurim* must also bring sacrificial offerings (Mishnah 2:4). These offerings, however, are not part of the *bikkurim* ceremony. One may offer them any time during his stay in Jerusalem (*Rashi* to *Menachos* 58a ד״ה לעטר with *Shitah Mekubetzes* there §15).

After bringing *bikkurim*, one must spend the night in Jerusalem and not travel elsewhere until the next day (Mishnah 2:4).[7]

VI.

✍ The Sanctity of *Bikkurim*

The Torah (*Devarim* 12:17) refers to *bikkurim* as תְּרוּמַת יָדֶךָ, *the terumah of your hands* (*Makkos* 17a), from which it is derived that *bikkurim* have the same sanctity as *terumah*. As such, they may be eaten only by a Kohen (and the members of his household) and only when he is *tahor*. Should a Kohen who is *tamei* or a non-Kohen eat *bikkurim*, he is liable to premature death

---
NOTES

4. *Bikkurim* must be brought into Jerusalem and presented to the Kohen in a basket (or other vessel), as is written (*Devarim* 26:2): וְשַׂמְתָּ בַטֶּנֶא, *you shall put it [the bikkurim] in a basket* (*Sifri* there).

5. This is the Biblical obligation of תְּנוּפָה, *waving*, which is derived from *Devarim* 26:4 (*Rambam, Hilchos Bikkurim* 3:12).

6. Verses 5-9, which begin: אֲרַמִּי אֹבֵד אָבִי וְגוֹ׳, *An Aramean tried to destroy my forefather*, form the basis of much of the Passover Haggadah (see *Pesachim* 10:4).

7. In fact, anyone who brings an offering to the Temple must spend that night in Jerusalem. Therefore, a *bikkurim* owner should have to stay overnight in any event, on account of his other offerings. *Yerushalmi* (2:3) teaches that even if one fails to bring the offerings (or he offered them the day before), he must still stay in Jerusalem the night after the *bikkurim* ceremony.

[7] **MISHNAH BIKKURIM** / General Introduction

at the hands of Heaven [מִיתָה בִּידֵי שָׁמַיִם] (see Mishnah 2:1; *Rambam, Hilchos Bikkurim* 3:1,5).

There is a Biblical prohibition against eating *bikkurim* outside Jerusalem. This prohibition applies even to Kohanim. Furthermore, even Kohanim are forbidden to eat *bikkurim* until they have been set down next to the Altar. These transgressions bear the penalty of *malkus* (*Rambam* there 3:3).[8]

VII.

∽§ Rejoicing

The Torah states in the context of *bikkurim* (*Devarim* 26:11): וְשָׂמַחְתָּ בְכָל הַטּוֹב אֲשֶׁר נָתַן לְךָ ה' אֱלֹהֶיךָ וגו', *You shall rejoice with all the goodness that Hashem, your God, has given you,* etc. The third chapter of this tractate relates that the groups of *bikkurim* owners traveled to the Temple with much joy and celebration. An ox with gold-covered horns and a wreath of olives on its head would walk at the head of the procession, and a flutist would play. They sang as they journeyed, a different song for each stage of the trip (*Yerushalmi* 3:2). When they neared Jerusalem, leaders of the Kohanim and officials of the Temple would go out to greet them. When they entered the city, craftsmen would stop working to stand in their honor and welcome them. And when they reached the Courtyard of the Temple, the Leviim would break out in song (Mishnahs 3:3-4).

The laws of *bikkurim* apply only when the Temple is standing (Mishnah 2:3). It is our prayer that studying this tractate will bring closer the day on which we will all rejoice with the bringing of *bikkurim* to the Third Temple.

NOTES

8. *Bikkurim* do not acquire the sanctity of *terumah* until they are brought inside Jerusalem. Nevertheless, it is Biblically forbidden for anyone (Kohen or non-Kohen) to eat *bikkurim* from the moment they are designated, though he would not be liable to a premature death or *malkus* (see *Rambam, Hilchos Bikkurim* 3:1-3; *Derech Emunah* 2:144, 3:12).

Chapter One

א/א

- רע"ב -

פרק ראשון — יש מביאין בבכורים וקורין. מקרא בכורים, מאהרמי אובד אבי (דברים כו,ה) עד סוף הפרשה (שם פסוק י): שחפר גומא והטמין יחור

[א] יֵשׁ מְבִיאִין בִּכּוּרִים וְקוֹרִין, מְבִיאִין וְלֹא קוֹרִין, וְיֵשׁ שֶׁאֵינָן מְבִיאִין. אֵלּוּ שֶׁאֵינָן מְבִיאִין: הַנּוֹטֵעַ לְתוֹךְ שֶׁלּוֹ וְהִבְרִיךְ לְתוֹךְ שֶׁל יָחִיד אוֹ שֶׁל רַבִּים, וְכֵן הַמַּבְרִיךְ מִתּוֹךְ שֶׁל יָחִיד אוֹ מִתּוֹךְ שֶׁל רַבִּים לְתוֹךְ שֶׁלּוֹ.

של אילן בתוכה וכסהו בעפר, והוציא ראש היחור לתוך שדה חבירו או ברשות הרבים, וכן אם הנטיעה עומדת בתוך של חבירו או ברשות הרבים, והוציא ראש היחור בתוך שלו, אינו מביא, כדמפרש בסמוך (משנה ב) לפי שאין כל הגדולים מאדמתו:

---

[1] When the owner of land in Eretz Yisrael sees the fruits of his land begin to ripen, he designates some as "bikkurim." After they ripen and are harvested, he brings them to the Temple and gives them to the Kohanim. At the Temple, he recites a Biblical passage in which he praises and thanks God for having giving him his land in Eretz Yisrael.[1] The obligation to bring bikkurim and the obligation to recite the passage are two separate, though related, mitzvos. This chapter lists cases in which a person is obligated to do both mitzvos, or only the mitzvah of bringing bikkurim, or neither of the mitzvos:

יֵשׁ מְבִיאִין בִּכּוּרִים וְקוֹרִין — **There are those who bring** bikkurim **and recite** the passage, מְבִיאִין וְלֹא קוֹרִין — **there are those who bring** bikkurim **but do not recite** the passage, וְיֵשׁ שֶׁאֵינָן מְבִיאִין — **and there are those who do not even bring** bikkurim.

The Mishnah illustrates the last category:[2]

אֵלּוּ שֶׁאֵינָן מְבִיאִין — **These** people **do not even bring** bikkurim: הַנּוֹטֵעַ לְתוֹךְ שֶׁלּוֹ וְהִבְרִיךְ לְתוֹךְ שֶׁל יָחִיד אוֹ שֶׁל רַבִּים — **someone who plants a tree in his own** land **and bends** a branch from it **into the private property** of another person **or** into **public property,** so that the branch grows into a new tree there;[3] וְכֵן הַמַּבְרִיךְ מִתּוֹךְ שֶׁל יָחִיד אוֹ מִתּוֹךְ שֶׁל רַבִּים לְתוֹךְ שֶׁלּוֹ — **similarly, someone who bends** a branch **from** a tree planted in the **private property** of another person **or public property into his own** land, where the branch grows into a new tree.[4]

NOTES

[1]

1. He recites: הִגַּדְתִּי הַיּוֹם לַה' אֱלֹהֶיךָ וְגו', *I declare today to Hashem, your God,* etc. (*Devarim* 26:3) and then: אֲרַמִּי אֹבֵד אָבִי וְגו', *An Aramean tried to destroy my forefather,* etc. (verses 5-10 there) (see Mishnah 3:6).

2. After making a list, it is not unusual for a Mishnah to begin its explanation with the last item on the list, since that is the one it had just mentioned (*Meleches Shlomo*, from *Nedarim* 2b-3a). The Mishnah's first and second categories are discussed later in the chapter.

3. "Bending a branch" refers to a procedure in which one digs a hole near a tree, bends a branch from the tree into the hole, covers the middle of the branch with earth, and makes the end of the branch stick out from the ground. [Over time, the protruding end takes root, grows into a new tree, and produces fruit.] The Mishnah refers to a case where someone had the tip emerge in land that did not belong to him (*Rav*).

4. In this case, he took a branch from a tree that was standing in the property of another and bent it so that its tip emerged from his own land (*Rav*).

[11] **MISHNAH BIKKURIM** / Chapter 1: *Yeish Mevi'in*

- רע״ב -

הַנּוֹטֵעַ לְתוֹךְ שֶׁלּוֹ וְהִבְרִיךְ לְתוֹךְ שֶׁלּוֹ, וְדֶרֶךְ הַיָּחִיד וְדֶרֶךְ הָרַבִּים בָּאֶמְצַע, הֲרֵי זֶה אֵינוֹ מֵבִיא; רַבִּי יְהוּדָה אוֹמֵר: כָּזֶה, מֵבִיא.

ודרך היחיד או דרך הרבים באמצע. כגון שיש לו שתי גנות משני צדי הדרכים, אינו מביא, שאין כל הגדולים מאדמתו:

בזה מביא. כיון שיש לו רשות לעשות כן, שמותר לעשות חלל תחת רשות הרבים כשאינו מזיק לרבים כלום, אדמתך (שמות כג,יט) קרינן ביה. ומכל מקום סבר רבי יהודה, שאף על פי שמביא אינו קורא. ואין הלכה כרבי יהודה:

In both cases, he cannot designate the fruit of either tree as *bikkurim,* because both trees draw some nourishment from land that is not his, and the law is that one cannot bring *bikkurim* except from the fruit of trees that grow entirely in one's own land.[5]

The law in the next case is subject to dispute:

הַנּוֹטֵעַ לְתוֹךְ שֶׁלּוֹ וְהִבְרִיךְ לְתוֹךְ שֶׁלּוֹ — **If someone plants a tree in his own** land **and bends** a branch from it **into** another part of **his own** land, וְדֶרֶךְ הַיָּחִיד וְדֶרֶךְ הָרַבִּים בָּאֶמְצַע — **but there is** a public **path or a public road**[6] **in the middle,** that is, the branch passes beneath a public path or road and it grows into a tree in his land on the other side, הֲרֵי זֶה אֵינוֹ מֵבִיא — **he does not bring** *bikkurim* from the fruit of either tree. Although both trees are in his property, he cannot designate their fruit as *bikkurim,* because the trees draw some nourishment from the earth under the public path or road, which does not belong to him. רַבִּי יְהוּדָה אוֹמֵר כָּזֶה מֵבִיא — **But R' Yehudah says** that in a situation **like this he can bring** *bikkurim* from the fruit of either tree. According to R' Yehudah, anyone has permission to dig a hole or tunnel under public property (as long as it will not harm or inconvenience the public).[7] Thus, in our case, the owner was allowed to pass the branch through the earth under the public road, which means that his trees are drawing nourishment from the ground in a permitted way. That suffices to make the fruits of the trees fit to be *bikkurim.*[8]

NOTES

5. The old tree draws nourishment not only from the land in which it stands but also from the place of the new tree, since it is connected to the new tree by means of the buried branch. Likewise, the new tree is also nourished by the land occupied by the old tree. The owner, therefore, cannot bring *bikkurim* from the fruit of either tree, since both receive at least some nourishment from land that is not his. In order for a person's fruits to be eligible as *bikkurim,* they must grow entirely from land that belongs to him. This is a Biblical law whose source is cited in the next Mishnah (*Rash*).

6. In this Mishnah, דֶּרֶךְ הַיָּחִיד (literally, *path of the individual*) refers to a public path that is relatively narrow, through which only a few people can pass at a time, while a דֶּרֶךְ הָרַבִּים (*path of the many*) is a wide road that can be used by many people (see *Tosafos Chadashim*).

7. It is permitted to dig a tunnel under a public road, provided that the surface of the road is not weakened but remains strong enough to support heavy traffic. This is also the opinion of the Tanna R' Eliezer in *Bava Basra* 3:8 (*Tos. Yom Tov*).

8. Both trees stand in the owner's land and they draw only a small amount of nourishment from the earth under the public road. In this circumstance, even though he does not actually own that earth but merely has permission to use it, the fruits of both trees are fit to be *bikkurim* (see *Mishnah Rishonah* and *Tosefos Anshei Shem*).

By just stating *he brings* (as opposed

משניות ביכורים / פרק א: יש מביאין

- רע״ב -

(ב) האריסין. מקבלין את השדה למחצה לשליש ולרביע: חבירות. מקבל את השדה בדבר קצוב, כך וכך כורים לשנה, בין שהיא עושה הרבה בין שהיא עושה מעט: סקריקון. הורג נפשות, ונותן לו קרקע כדי שלא יהרגנו. ולשון סקריקון, שם קרקע

[ב] **מֵאֵיזֶה** טַעַם אֵינוֹ מֵבִיא? מִשׁוּם שֶׁנֶּאֱמַר: "רֵאשִׁית בִּכּוּרֵי אַדְמָתְךָ", עַד שֶׁיִּהְיוּ כָּל הַגִּדּוּלִין מֵאַדְמָתְךָ. הָאֲרִיסִין, וְהֶחָכוֹרוֹת, וְהַסִּקְרִיקוֹן, וְהַגַּזְלָן, אֵין מְבִיאִין, מֵאוֹתוֹ הַטַּעַם, מִשׁוּם שֶׁנֶּאֱמַר: "רֵאשִׁית בִּכּוּרֵי אַדְמָתְךָ".

והניחני. ואף על גב דייתיב ליה לפי שעה, לא מחיל ליה, דסבר האידנא לשקול ולמחר תבעינא ליה בדינא:

---

[2] This Mishnah cites the Scriptural source for the laws taught in the previous Mishnah:

מֵאֵיזֶה טַעַם אֵינוֹ מֵבִיא — **Why does one not bring** bikkurim **from produce that draws some of its nourishment from another person's land?** מִשׁוּם שֶׁנֶּאֱמַר "רֵאשִׁית בִּכּוּרֵי אַדְמָתְךָ" — **Because it is stated** regarding bikkurim (Shemos 23:19, 34:26): *The earliest of the first fruits of your land.* עַד שֶׁיִּהְיוּ כָּל הַגִּדּוּלִין מֵאַדְמָתְךָ — By specifying "*your* land," the verse implies that you can**not bring** bikkurim from produce **unless all** of its **growths** (i.e., nourishment) **are from your land.**

Other applications of this rule:

הָאֲרִיסִין וְהֶחָכוֹרוֹת וְהַסִּקְרִיקוֹן וְהַגַּזְלָן אֵין מְבִיאִין מֵאוֹתוֹ הַטַּעַם — **Sharecroppers,**[1] **tenant farmers,**[2] **a** *sikrikon*,[3] **and a robber do not bring** bikkurim **for the same reason;** מִשׁוּם שֶׁנֶּאֱמַר "רֵאשִׁית בִּכּוּרֵי אַדְמָתְךָ" — **namely, because it is stated:** *The earliest of the first fruits of your land.* Since these people do not

--- NOTES ---

to *he brings and recites*), R' Yehudah implies that although this person brings *bikkurim,* he does not recite the passage (*Rav*). Although anyone may dig under a public road, he has no right to stop another person from using the hole or tunnel that he dug. This limited ownership is enough for the purpose of bringing *bikkurim* but not for reciting the passage [because it includes the words (*Devarim* 26:10): הָאֲדָמָה אֲשֶׁר נָתַתָּה לִי, *the land that You have given me*] (*Tos. Yom Tov*).

The Tanna Kamma, on the other hand, rules that the owner does not even bring *bikkurim,* because, in his view, it is always prohibited to use the ground under public property. [This is the opinion of the first Tanna in *Bava Basra* there.] Therefore, if someone passed a branch under a public road, the trees on both sides draw some nourishment from land he is forbidden to use, which disqualifies their fruits from being *bikkurim* (*Yerushalmi*).

[2]

1. An אָרִיס (*sharecropper*) farms the land of another person and pays the owner a share of the crop as rent (*Rav*).

2. A חָכוּר (*tenant farmer*) also farms the land of another person, but he pays the owner a fixed amount of produce each year, regardless of how much the land actually produces (*Rav*).

The Mishnah's ruling also applies to someone who rents land (*S'deh Yehoshua*).

3. A *sikrikon* is a known murderer who would steal land by threatening to kill the owner. Even though the owner tells the *sikrikon* to take the land, he does not really intend to give up its ownership, because he expects that one day he will recover it in court (*Rav*).

[13] MISHNAH BIKKURIM / Chapter 1: Yeish Mevi'in

- רע"ב -

(ג) אלא משבעת המינין. דכתיב (דברים כו,ב) מראשית, ולא כל ראשית, שאין כל הפירות חייבים בבכורים אלא שבעת המינין שנשתבחה בהן ארץ ישראל (שם ח,ח)

[ג] **אֵין** מְבִיאִין בִּכּוּרִים חוּץ מִשִּׁבְעַת הַמִּינִים. לֹא מִתְּמָרִים שֶׁבֶּהָרִים, וְלֹא מִפֵּרוֹת שֶׁבָּעֲמָקִים, וְלֹא מִזֵּיתֵי שֶׁמֶן שֶׁאֵינָם מִן הַמֻּבְחָר.

חטה ושעורה וגו', ודבש הוא דבש תמרים: מתמרים שבהרים ופירות שבעמקים. לפי שהן גרועין: ולא מזיתי שמן שאינם מן המובחר. דכתיב (שם) זית שמן, זית אגורי, שבאים עליו גשמים והוא אוגר שמנו לתוכו, והוא מובחר ומשובח:

---

own the land on which they are working or which they have taken, they cannot bring *bikkurim* from its produce.

[3] The Mishnah specifies the types of produce from which *bikkurim* are brought:

אֵין מְבִיאִין בִּכּוּרִים חוּץ מִשִּׁבְעַת הַמִּינִים — **One does not bring** *bikkurim* from produce **other than the seven species** for which Eretz Yisrael is praised; namely, wheat, barley, grapes, figs, pomegranates, olives, and dates.[1]

Furthermore, the seven species themselves are not eligible unless they are of good quality.[2] The Mishnah gives three examples of fruits that are invalid for this reason:

לֹא מִתְּמָרִים שֶׁבֶּהָרִים — *Bikkurim* are **not brought from the dates of mountains,**[3] וְלֹא מִפֵּרוֹת שֶׁבָּעֲמָקִים — **nor from the fruits of valleys,**[4] וְלֹא מִזֵּיתֵי שֶׁמֶן שֶׁאֵינָם מִן הַמֻּבְחָר — **nor from oil-olives that are not of the best quality.**[5]

The Mishnah identifies the earliest time of the year for bringing *bikkurim* to the Temple:

--- NOTES ---

[3]

1. The Torah states (*Devarim* 26:2) regarding *bikkurim*: וְלָקַחְתָּ מֵרֵאשִׁית כָּל פְּרִי הָאֲדָמָה אֲשֶׁר תָּבִיא מֵאַרְצֶךָ, *You shall take from the first of every fruit of the ground that you bring in from your land*. Since the verse commands us to take *"from the first,* etc.," it implies that only certain fruits are fit to be *bikkurim,* and not others. This limits the mitzvah of *bikkurim* to the seven species for which Eretz Yisrael is praised, which are listed in *Devarim* 8:8 (*Rav*).

2. This law is taught by the prefix *from* in the word מֵאַרְצֶךָ, *from your land* (see previous note), which indicates that not all the produce of your land is eligible; rather, only the better-quality produce is to be brought as *bikkurim* (*Menachos* 84b).

3. Dates that grow on mountains produce less honey than dates of low-lying areas. In its list of the seven species, the Torah refers to dates as דְּבַשׁ, *honey* (*Devarim* 8:8), which implies that dates are desirable because of the honey they produce. Thus, dates that produce only a small amount of honey are not fit to be *bikkurim* (*Rav* to Mishnah 10).

4. This refers to all the species except dates. Those that grow on mountains taste better than those that grow in low-lying areas (*Rav* there; *Tiferes Yisrael*).

5. Certain types of olives express their oil when rain falls on them, while others retain their oil even in the rain. By referring to olives as זֵיתֵי שֶׁמֶן, *oil-olives* (*Devarim* 8:8), the Torah stresses the oil-producing nature of the olives. Therefore, only the types of olives that retain their oil even when it rains can be designated as *bikkurim* (*Rav, Tiferes Yisrael*).

משניות ביכורים / פרק א: יש מביאין

אֵין מְבִיאִין בִּכּוּרִים קֹדֶם לָעֲצֶרֶת. אַנְשֵׁי הַר צְבוֹעִים הֵבִיאוּ בִּכּוּרֵיהֶם קֹדֶם לָעֲצֶרֶת, וְלֹא קִבְּלוּ מֵהֶם, מִפְּנֵי הַכָּתוּב שֶׁבַּתּוֹרָה: "וְחַג הַקָּצִיר בִּכּוּרֵי מַעֲשֶׂיךָ אֲשֶׁר תִּזְרַע בַּשָּׂדֶה".

[ד] **אֵלוּ** מְבִיאִין וְלֹא קוֹרִין: הַגֵּר מֵבִיא וְאֵינוֹ קוֹרֵא, שֶׁאֵינוֹ יָכוֹל לוֹמַר "אֲשֶׁר נִשְׁבַּע ה' לַאֲבוֹתֵינוּ לָתֶת לָנוּ";

— רע״ב —

אין מביאין בכורים קודם לעצרת. דשתי הלחם שמביאין בעצרת אקרו בכורים (ויקרא כג,יז), והם מתירין החדש במקדש: (ד) שאינו יכול לומר אשר נשבע לאבותינו לתת לנו. שאין אבותיו מישראל, והגרים לא נטלו חלק בארץ. ורמב״ס כתב שאין הלכה כמשנה זו, אלא הגר מביא וקורא, ומלי למימר לאבותינו לתת לנו, מפני שהארץ ניתנה לאברהם, והוא אב לגרים כמו לישראל, דכתיב (בראשית יז,ה) כי אב המון גוים נתתיך, ודרשינן ביה (ירושלמי) לשעבר היית אב לארם, מכשיו אתה אב לכל העולם. וכן כשהוא מתפלל, בין בינו לבין עצמו בין בבית הכנסת, אומר אלהי אבותינו, אפילו אין אמו מישראל:

אֵין מְבִיאִין בִּכּוּרִים קֹדֶם לָעֲצֶרֶת — One may not bring *bikkurim* before the festival of **Shavuos**. אַנְשֵׁי הַר צְבוֹעִים הֵבִיאוּ בִּכּוּרֵיהֶם קֹדֶם לָעֲצֶרֶת — The people of Mount Tzevo'im once brought their *bikkurim* before Shavuos, וְלֹא קִבְּלוּ מֵהֶם — and [the Kohanim] did not accept their *bikkurim* from them, מִפְּנֵי הַכָּתוּב שֶׁבַּתּוֹרָה — because of that which is written in the Torah (*Shemos* 23:16) regarding the offering of the *shtei halechem*, which is brought on Shavuos:[6] "וְחַג הַקָּצִיר בִּכּוּרֵי מַעֲשֶׂיךָ אֲשֶׁר תִּזְרַע בַּשָּׂדֶה" — *And the Festival of the Harvest* (i.e., Shavuos), *when you bring the first fruits of your labor that you sow in the field* (i.e., the *shtei halechem*). The verse describes the *shtei halechem* as "the *first* fruits," which teaches that the *shtei halechem* must be the first offering brought from the new crop. All other offerings from the new crop, such as *bikkurim*, may not be brought until after the *shtei halechem*. Thus, *bikkurim* are not to be brought before Shavuos.[7]

[4] This Mishnah illustrates the second category listed in Mishnah 1; namely, people who must bring *bikkurim* but do not recite the *bikkurim* passage: אֵלוּ מְבִיאִין וְלֹא קוֹרִין — **These bring** *bikkurim* **but do not recite** the passage: הַגֵּר מֵבִיא וְאֵינוֹ קוֹרֵא — **A convert** (or a descendant of converts)[1] **brings** *bikkurim*[2] **but does not recite** the passage, שֶׁאֵינוֹ יָכוֹל לוֹמַר "אֲשֶׁר נִשְׁבַּע ה' לַאֲבוֹתֵינוּ לָתֶת לָנוּ" — **because he cannot say** the verse (*Devarim* 26:3): *I have come to the land that Hashem swore to our forefathers to give to us.* It

---

NOTES

6. The *shtei halechem* (Two Loaves) was a public offering that was brought on Shavuos. It consisted of two loaves made of wheat from the new crop (*Vayikra* 23:15-18).

7. For the same reason, it is forbidden to bring *menachos* (flour offerings) from the grain of the new crop before the *shtei halechem* have been offered on Shavuos (*Menachos* 10:6).

[4]

1. *Yerushalmi*; see note 5.

2. A convert is obligated to do all the mitzvos, just like a born Jew (*Mahara Fulda*).

[15] **MISHNAH BIKKURIM** / Chapter 1: *Yeish Mevi'in*

וְאִם הָיְתָה אִמּוֹ מִיִּשְׂרָאֵל, מֵבִיא וְקוֹרֵא. וּכְשֶׁהוּא מִתְפַּלֵּל בֵּינוֹ לְבֵין עַצְמוֹ, אוֹמֵר: "אֱלֹהֵי אֲבוֹת יִשְׂרָאֵל". וּכְשֶׁהוּא בְּבֵית הַכְּנֶסֶת, אוֹמֵר: "אֱלֹהֵי אֲבוֹתֵיכֶם". וְאִם הָיְתָה אִמּוֹ מִיִּשְׂרָאֵל, אוֹמֵר: "אֱלֹהֵי אֲבוֹתֵינוּ".

[ה] **רַבִּי** אֱלִיעֶזֶר בֶּן יַעֲקֹב אוֹמֵר: אִשָּׁה בַת גֵּרִים לֹא

---

would be untruthful for him to say "*our* forefathers," since he is not descended from the forefathers of the Jewish people. וְאִם הָיְתָה אִמּוֹ מִיִּשְׂרָאֵל מֵבִיא וְקוֹרֵא — **But if his mother** or his father[3] **is an** ordinary **Jew** (i.e., one of his parents has unbroken Jewish lineage), **he brings** *bikkurim* **and recites** the passage, because he is descended from the Jewish forefathers on one side of his family.[4]

Having taught that converts and descendants of converts may not recite the *bikkurim* passage, because it states "our forefathers," the Mishnah cites a law regarding their recitation of the *Shemoneh Esrei*, which includes the words, "the God of our forefathers":

וּכְשֶׁהוּא מִתְפַּלֵּל בֵּינוֹ לְבֵין עַצְמוֹ — **And when he prays** the *Shemoneh Esrei* **by himself**, instead of saying, "the God of our forefathers," אוֹמֵר אֱלֹהֵי אֲבוֹת יִשְׂרָאֵל — **he says, "the God of the forefathers of Israel"**; וּכְשֶׁהוּא בְּבֵית הַכְּנֶסֶת — **and when he is** praying publically **in the synagogue** (i.e., he is the prayer leader, who is repeating the *Shemoneh Esrei* aloud), אוֹמֵר אֱלֹהֵי אֲבוֹתֵיכֶם — **he says, "the God of your forefathers."** וְאִם הָיְתָה אִמּוֹ מִיִּשְׂרָאֵל — **But if his mother** or his father **is an** ordinary **Jew** (i.e., one of his parents has unbroken Jewish lineage), אוֹמֵר אֱלֹהֵי אֲבוֹתֵינוּ — **he says, "the God of our forefathers."**[5]

[5] This Mishnah deals with a child of converts in regard to a different law; namely, the prohibition against a Kohen marrying a convert.[1] The Mishnah discusses whether a daughter of converts is included this prohibition:

אִשָּׁה בַת גֵּרִים לֹא — **R' Eliezer ben Yaakov says**: רַבִּי אֱלִיעֶזֶר בֶּן יַעֲקֹב אוֹמֵר

NOTES

3. See *Rambam Commentary* to the next Mishnah.

4. This suffices to give him the right to say *the land that Hashem swore to our forefathers to give to us*.

5. *Yerushalmi* cites a Tanna who disagrees with our Mishnah. In his view, a convert *may* say, "that Hashem swore to our forefathers to give to us," in the *bikkurim* passage. He may also say, "the God of our forefathers," in the *Shemoneh Esrei*. This Tanna's reason is that Abraham is considered the father of all converts, as the Torah states (*Bereishis* 17:5): *for I have made you the father of a multitude of nations*. Since Abraham taught all the nations to believe in God, a convert, who has formally adopted this belief, can correctly be described as a spiritual descendant of Abraham (*Rav, Rambam Commentary*).

[5]

1. See *Kiddushin* 4:1.

תִּנָּשֵׂא לַכְּהֻנָּה, עַד שֶׁתְּהֵא אִמָּהּ מִיִּשְׂרָאֵל. אֶחָד גֵּרִים וְאֶחָד עֲבָדִים מְשֻׁחְרָרִים, וַאֲפִלּוּ עַד עֲשָׂרָה דוֹרוֹת, עַד שֶׁתְּהֵא אִמָּן מִיִּשְׂרָאֵל.

— רע״ב —

(ה) לֹא תִנָּשֵׂא לִכְהוּנָה. דִּכְתִיב (יחזקאל מד,כב) מִזֶּרַע בֵּית יִשְׂרָאֵל יִקְחוּ לָהֶם נָשִׁים, [וּכְשֶׁאִמָּהּ] מִיִּשְׂרָאֵל קְרִינָא בָהּ מִזֶּרַע יִשְׂרָאֵל, דְּשָׁמַעְתְּ וְאָפִילוּ מִקְצָת זֶרַע. וַהֲלָכָה כְּרַבִּי אֱלִיעֶזֶר בֶּן יַעֲקֹב לִכְתְּחִלָּה, אֲבָל בְּדִיעֲבַד אִם נָשָׂא, אֵין מוֹצִיאִין אוֹתָהּ מִמֶּנּוּ, וּבָנֶיהָ כְּשֵׁרִים אֲפִלּוּ לִהְיוֹת כֹּהֲנִים גְּדוֹלִים:

תִּנָּשֵׂא לַכְּהֻנָּה — **A woman who is the daughter of converts** (or the daughter of people descended from converts) **may not be married to a Kohen,** עַד **שֶׁתְּהֵא אִמָּהּ מִיִּשְׂרָאֵל** — **unless her mother** or father **is an** ordinary **Jew,** i.e., someone of unbroken Jewish lineage.[2]

R' Eliezer ben Yaakov explains:

אֶחָד גֵּרִים וְאֶחָד עֲבָדִים מְשֻׁחְרָרִים — Regarding **both converts and freed** Canaanite **slaves,**[3] **וַאֲפִלּוּ עַד עֲשָׂרָה דוֹרוֹת** — **even if up to ten generations** have passed since they were converted or freed,[4] each of their descendants has the status of "convert" with respect to the prohibition against marrying Kohanim, i.e., a female descendant may not be married to a Kohen, עַד **שֶׁתְּהֵא אִמָּן מִיִּשְׂרָאֵל** — **unless [the descendant's] mother** or father **is an** ordinary **Jew,** i.e., someone of unbroken Jewish lineage. When someone converts to Judaism (or a Canaanite slave is freed) and marries another convert, they transmit the status of "convert" to their children, who in turn transmit it to their children, and so on.[5] This continues until someone along the line (male or female) marries an ordinary Jew. The children of this marriage do *not* have the status of "convert." Their daughter is thus permitted to a Kohen.[6]

NOTES

2. Furthermore, even if both of this woman's parents are converts or the descendants of converts, but a grandparent on either side (even many generations removed) had Jewish lineage, she is permitted to be married to a Kohen (*Rambam Commentary;* see note 5).

3. When a Canaanite slave is acquired by a Jew, he has to undergo a partial conversion (that is, he must be circumcised and he must immerse in a *mikveh*), because he is obligated to observe some of the mitzvos. Upon being freed, he must complete his conversion by immersing in a *mikveh* again, because he then becomes obligated to keep all the mitzvos (*Rambam, Hilchos Issurei Bi'ah* 12:11, 13:11-12). A freed Canaanite slave thus has the same status as a convert. As such, if the slave is female, she is forbidden to be married to a Kohen.

4. This is simply an expression that means "a very long time." The status of "convert" does not stop after ten generations, but can be passed on forever (*Tos. Yom Tov*).

5. Someone whose parents are both converts has the status of "convert," which means that if female, she is forbidden to be married to a Kohen. Despite being a Jew from birth (since she was born to a converted Jewish mother), she has "convert" status in regard to the prohibition against marrying Kohanim.

6. Thus, according to R' Eliezer ben Yaakov, a daughter of converts is forbidden to a Kohen unless she has some ancestor (even many generations in the past) who was born Jewish.

The opinion of R' Eliezer ben Yaakov is disputed by R' Yose in *Kiddushin* 4:2. According to R' Yose, the daughter of converts *is* permissible to a Kohen, even if she does not have any Jewish-born ancestors. The law is that a Kohen may not marry a woman who is descended entirely from converts, but if he did, they are not required to divorce (*Rav, Rambam Commentary*).

[17] **MISHNAH BIKKURIM** / Chapter 1: *Yeish Mevi'in*

- רע"ב -

הָאַפּוֹטְרוֹפּוֹס, וְהַשָּׁלִיחַ, וְהָעֶבֶד, וְהָאִשָּׁה, וְטוּמְטוּם, וְאַנְדְּרוֹגִינוֹס, מְבִיאִין וְלֹא קוֹרִין, שֶׁאֵינָן יְכוֹלִין לוֹמַר "אֲשֶׁר נָתַתָּה לִי ה'".

[ו] **הַקּוֹנֶה** שְׁנֵי אִילָנוֹת בְּתוֹךְ שֶׁל חֲבֵרוֹ,

הָאַפּוֹטְרוֹפּוֹס. הַמְמֻנֶּה עַל הַיְתוֹמִים, בֵּין שֶׁמִּנָּהוּ בֵּית דִּין בֵּין שֶׁמִּנָּהוּ אֲבִי יְתוֹמִים. אַפּוֹטְרוֹפּוֹס, אֲבִי הַקְּטַנִּים, בִּלְשׁוֹן רוֹמִי קוֹרִין לְאָב פָּאטֵי"ר וְלִקְטַנִּים פּוּס: וְהַשָּׁלִיחַ. שֶׁלְּקָטָן מִתְּחִלָּה לְשָׁלְחָן בְּיַד אַחֵר, אָז מָלֵי לְמַשְׁלְחַנְהוּ, אֲבָל לְקָטָן לַהֲבִיאוֹ הוּא עַצְמוֹ, לָא מָלֵי לְמַשְׁלְחַנְהוּ, שֶׁכָּל בִּכּוּרִים שֶׁגֵּרְאוּ לִקְרִיאָה אֵינָן נִתָּנִים אֶלָּא בִּקְרִיאָה: וְהָאִשָּׁה. אֲבָל אִם יֵשׁ לָהּ בַּעַל, בַּעֲלָהּ מֵבִיא וְקוֹרֵא, דִּכְתִיב (דברים כו,י') אֲשֶׁר נָתַן לִי ה' אֱלֹהֶיךָ וּלְבֵיתֶךָ, מְלַמֵּד שֶׁאָדָם מֵבִיא בִּכּוּרֵי אִשְׁתּוֹ וְקוֹרֵא: שֶׁאֵינָן יְכוֹלִין לוֹמַר אֲשֶׁר נָתַתָּ לִי. שֶׁלֹּא נִתְחַלְּקָה הָאָרֶץ לִנְקֵבוֹת, וּכְתִיב (במדבר כו,נ"ד) אִישׁ לְפִי פְקוּדָיו, עַד שֶׁיִּהְיֶה זָכָר וַדַּאי אִישׁ:

The Mishnah returns to the list, begun in the previous Mishnah, of people who bring *bikkurim* but do not recite the *bikkurim* passage:

הָאַפּוֹטְרוֹפּוֹס — **Guardians**[7] of orphans who want to bring the orphans' *bikkurim* to the Temple, וְהַשָּׁלִיחַ — **an agent** appointed by a landowner to bring his *bikkurim* to the Temple, וְהָעֶבֶד — **a freed Canaanite slave** who has *bikkurim* that grew on his own land,[8] וְהָאִשָּׁה — **a woman** who has *bikkurim* that grew in her own land, וְטוּמְטוּם — **a** *tumtum,* וְאַנְדְּרוֹגִינוֹס — **and an androgyne:**[9] מְבִיאִין וְלֹא קוֹרִין — All these **bring** *bikkurim* **but do not recite** the passage, שֶׁאֵינָן יְכוֹלִין לוֹמַר "אֲשֶׁר נָתַתָּה לִי ה'" — **because they cannot say** these words: (*Devarim* 26:10): *I have brought the first fruit of the land that You have given me, Hashem.* The guardian and the agent cannot say, "that You have given *me*," because he is bringing *bikkurim* from land that is not his. The freed slave, woman, *tumtum,* and androgyne cannot say these words either, because when Eretz Yisrael was originally divided, it was not given to people from these groups.[10]

[6] The Mishnah lists three more circumstances in which *bikkurim* are brought but the passage is not recited:

הַקּוֹנֶה שְׁנֵי אִילָנוֹת בְּתוֹךְ שֶׁל חֲבֵרוֹ — **If someone buys two** fruit **trees that are in the property of another person,** and it was not specified whether the sale

---

NOTES

7. This refers to someone who manages the affairs of orphans, having been appointed by their father (in his lifetime) or by the court (*Rav*).

8. *Rash Sirilio.*

9. A טוּמְטוּם, *tumtum,* is a person whose private parts are covered by a thick membrane, so that it is not known whether he is a male or a female. An androgyne has both male and female organs. (The laws of an androgyne are the subject of the fourth chapter.)

10. It is derived from the Torah that Eretz Yisrael was divided only among free men who were definitely male. Thus, it would be inappropriate for a woman, Canaanite slave, *tumtum,* or androgyne to say the *bikkurim* passage, which contains the words (*Devarim* 26:10): הֲבֵאתִי אֶת רֵאשִׁית פְּרִי הָאֲדָמָה אֲשֶׁר נָתַתָּה לִי ה', *I have brought the first fruit of the land that You have given me, Hashem* (*Rav*).

[In addition, as taught in the previous Mishnah regarding converts, Canaanite slaves cannot say, *the land that Hashem swore to our forefathers to give to us,* since his forefathers were not Jewish.]

[18] **משניות ביכורים** / פרק א: יש מביאין א/ו

- רע״ב -

מֵבִיא וְאֵינוֹ קוֹרֵא; רַבִּי מֵאִיר אוֹמֵר: מֵבִיא וְקוֹרֵא. יָבַשׁ הַמַּעְיָן, נִקְצַץ הָאִילָן, מֵבִיא וְאֵינוֹ קוֹרֵא; רַבִּי יְהוּדָה אוֹמֵר: מֵבִיא וְקוֹרֵא.

(ו) מביא ואינו קורא. מספקא ליה לתנא קמא אי קנה קרקע אי לא, הלכך מביא מספק, ואינו קורא מספק. ודוקא שתי

אילנות אבל שלשה אילנות כולי עלמא מודו דקנה קרקע, ומביא וקורא, כדתנן בסוף פרקין: **רבי מאיר אומר מביא וקורא.** דסבר הקונה שני אילנות נמי קנה קרקע שתחתיהם וחולה להם כמלא מורה וסלו. ואין הלכה כרבי מאיר: **יבש המעין.** שהאילן חי וגדל ממנו: **ונקצץ האילן:** והוא שיבש ונקצץ קודם שהפריש בכורים, אבל אם הפריש קודם, הואיל ונראו לקריאה ונדחו, ירקבו: **רבי יהודה אומר מביא וקורא.** כיון שהקרקע קיים לא חיים לא חייש לאילן. ואין הלכה כרבי יהודה:

[the buyer] מֵבִיא וְאֵינוֹ קוֹרֵא — includes the land on which the trees grow, brings *bikkurim* from the fruit of these trees **but does not recite** the passage. This Tanna holds that it is unclear whether the buyer acquired the land under the trees.[1] Since we do not know whether he owns this land, his obligation to bring *bikkurim* from the fruit of these trees is also in doubt (because one does not bring *bikkurim* unless he owns the land on which they grew, as taught in Mishnah 2). The rule in cases of this type is that since he *possibly* owns the land, he is obligated to bring the *bikkurim* to satisfy the doubt, but on the other hand since he possibly does *not* own the land, he does not recite the passage because it might be untruthful for him to say, *the land that You have given me*.[2] רַבִּי מֵאִיר אוֹמֵר — However, **R' Meir says:** מֵבִיא וְקוֹרֵא — He brings *bikkurim* **and recites** the passage. According to R' Meir, when two (or more) trees are sold, it is certain that the sale includes the land, even if the land was not mentioned. Therefore, the buyer is subject to all the obligations of *bikkurim*, which includes reciting the passage.

The second case:

יָבַשׁ הַמַּעְיָן — **If someone owns a tree that received its water from a spring but the spring dried up**, leaving the tree unable to produce fruit, נִקְצַץ הָאִילָן — **or the tree was cut down**, מֵבִיא וְאֵינוֹ קוֹרֵא — he brings *bikkurim* from fruit that had already begun to grow on the tree, **but he does not recite** the passage. When a tree becomes unable to bear fruit, it is as though the land itself has been destroyed and lost. The *bikkurim* passage must therefore be omitted because it includes the words, *the land that You have given me*.[3] רַבִּי יְהוּדָה אוֹמֵר — But **R' Yehudah says:** מֵבִיא וְקוֹרֵא — **He brings** *bikkurim* **and**

NOTES

[6]

1. When someone buys *three* trees, it is assumed that the sale includes the land under the trees and under their branches, the land between the trees, and an area around each tree wide enough for a harvester and his basket. This is so even if the buyer and the seller mentioned only the trees, and not the land (*Rav;* see *Bava Basra* 5:4; see below, Mishnah 11). On the other hand, when someone buys a *single* tree, this Tanna rules that the buyer acquires only the tree, without any land (see note 3 there). The buyer has the right to maintain the tree in its place as long as it lives, but, since he does not own the land beneath it, he may not plant another in its place when it dies (*Rashbam, Bava Basra* 81a ד״ה הקונה). Our Mishnah deals with someone who buys *two* trees, in which case the Tanna considers it unclear whether land is included in the sale.

2. *Bava Basra* 82a.

3. *Rambam Commentary.*

[19] **MISHNAH BIKKURIM** / Chapter 1: *Yeish Mevi'in*

מֵעֲצֶרֶת וְעַד הֶחָג, מֵבִיא וְקוֹרֵא. מִן הֶחָג וְעַד חֲנֻכָּה, מֵבִיא וְאֵינוֹ קוֹרֵא; רַבִּי יְהוּדָה בֶּן בְּתֵירָה אוֹמֵר: מֵבִיא וְקוֹרֵא.

[ז] **הַפְרִישׁ** בִּכּוּרָיו וּמָכַר שָׂדֵהוּ, מֵבִיא וְאֵינוֹ קוֹרֵא. וְהַשֵּׁנִי, מֵאוֹתוֹ הַמִּין, אֵינוֹ מֵבִיא; מִמִּין אַחֵר, מֵבִיא וְקוֹרֵא.

– רע״ב –

מן החג ועד חנוכה מביא ואינו קורא. דכתיב בפרשת ביכורים (דברים כו,יא) ושמחת בכל הטוב, אין קריאה אלא בזמן שמחה, מעצרת ועד החג, שאדם מלקט תבואתו ופירותיו ושמח בהם. ומהחג ואילך, אף על פי שהרבה פירות נלקטים עד חנוכה, מכל מקום שמחת אותה שנה כבר נגמרה בחג, הלכך מביא ואינו קורא. ומחנוכה ואילך אינו מביא כלל, דכתיב (שם, פסוק ב) אשר תביא מארצך, כל זמן שמצויין בארצך, ועד חנוכה הן מצויין: רבי יהודה אומר מביא וקורא. דלא דריש ושמחת בזמן שמחה. ואין הלכה כרבי יהודה: (ז) והשני מאותו המין אינו מביא. הקונה את השדה אינו מביא בכורים מאותה שדה מאותו המין שהביא המוכר, דכתיב (דברים כו,ג) הגדתי היום, פעם אחת מגיד ואינו מגיד שתי פעמים:

---

recites the passage because, despite the state of the tree, the land still exists.

The third case:

מֵעֲצֶרֶת וְעַד הֶחָג מֵבִיא וְקוֹרֵא — **From Shavuos until Succos, one brings** *bikkurim* **and recites the passage;**[4] מִן הֶחָג וְעַד חֲנֻכָּה מֵבִיא וְאֵינוֹ קוֹרֵא — **from Succos until Chanukah, one brings** *bikkurim* **but does not recite the passage.**[5] רַבִּי יְהוּדָה בֶּן בְּתֵירָה אוֹמֵר — **However, R' Yehudah ben Beseirah says:** מֵבִיא וְקוֹרֵא — **Even between Succos and Chanukah, he brings** *bikkurim* **and recites the passage.**[6]

[7] הִפְרִישׁ בִּכּוּרָיו וּמָכַר שָׂדֵהוּ — **If someone designated his** *bikkurim* **from some of the species in his field and then he sold his field,** מֵבִיא וְאֵינוֹ קוֹרֵא — **he brings** the *bikkurim* that he designated **but he does not recite** the passage, for since he does not own the land, he cannot say, *the land that You have given me.* וְהַשֵּׁנִי — **And the second one,** i.e., the buyer of the field, does the following: מֵאוֹתוֹ הַמִּין אֵינוֹ מֵבִיא — **From the species** that had already been designated as *bikkurim,* **he does not bring** more *bikkurim;*[1] מִמִּין אַחֵר מֵבִיא וְקוֹרֵא — **but from a different species** growing in that field,

--- NOTES ---

4. As we learned in Mishnah 3 (see note 6 there), *bikkurim* may not be brought before the *shtei halechem* are offered on Shavuos.

5. The Torah states regarding *bikkurim* (Devarim 26:11): וְשָׂמַחְתָּ בְכָל הַטּוֹב אֲשֶׁר נָתַן לְךָ ה' אֱלֹהֶיךָ, *And you shall rejoice in all the good that Hashem, your God, has given you.* This teaches that the *bikkurim* passage is to be recited only during the time of year when people rejoice over their harvest. This rejoicing lasts from Shavuos, the beginning of the harvest season (*Devarim* 16:9), until Succos, when the crops are brought indoors to protect them from the coming rain (*Rav*).

It is learned from a verse in the Torah that *bikkurim* may be brought as long as similar fruits can still be found on the land, which is the case until Chanukah but not later (*Rav*).

6. R' Yehudah ben Beseirah holds that the time of reciting the passage is not limited to the time of rejoicing. The passage is therefore recited even after Succos, when the period of rejoicing has ended (*Rav*).

[7]

1. This Tanna derives from a verse in the Torah that *bikkurim* can be brought only once from a particular species in a particular field (*Rav*).

משניות ביכורים / פרק א: יש מביאין [20]

רַבִּי יְהוּדָה אוֹמֵר: אַף מֵאוֹתוֹ הַמִּין מֵבִיא וְקוֹרֵא.

[ח] הַפְרִישׁ בִּכּוּרָיו, נִבְזְזוּ, נָמַקּוּ, נִגְנְבוּ, אָבְדוּ, אוֹ שֶׁנִּטְמְאוּ, מֵבִיא אֲחֵרִים תַּחְתֵּיהֶם וְאֵינוֹ קוֹרֵא; וְהַשְּׁנִיִּים, אֵינָם חַיָּבִים עֲלֵיהֶם חֹמֶשׁ. נִטְמְאוּ בָעֲזָרָה,

- רע"ב -

רבי יהודה אומר אף מאותו המין מביא וקורא. דהא דאמרן פטס אחת מגיד ואינו מגיד שתי פעמים, הני מילי באדם אחד, אבל בשני בני אדם מגיד וחוזר ומגיד: ואין הלכה כרבי יהודה: (ח) נמקו. נרקבו ונמסו, כמו אתם ימקו (ויקרא

כו,לט): נבזזו. נגזלו ממנו, כמו בזזנו לנו (דברים ג,לה): אין חייבים עליהם חומש. זר שאכלן אינו משלם את החומש. והך מתניתין יחידאה היא, ואינה הלכה, אלא הלכה שחייבים עליהם חומש:

— רַבִּי יְהוּדָה אוֹמֵר — However, R' Yehudah says: he does bring *bikkurim* and he recites the passage. אַף מֵאוֹתוֹ הַמִּין מֵבִיא וְקוֹרֵא — Even from that species that had already been designated as *bikkurim*, he brings more *bikkurim* and he recites the passage.[2]

[8] The Mishnah teaches what should be done if *bikkurim* become damaged or otherwise unfit to be offered:

הַפְרִישׁ בִּכּוּרָיו — If someone designated his *bikkurim* נִבְזְזוּ — and they were plundered, נָמַקּוּ — or they rotted, נִגְנְבוּ — or they were stolen,[1] אָבְדוּ — or they were lost, אוֹ שֶׁנִּטְמְאוּ — or they became *tamei*, מֵבִיא אֲחֵרִים תַּחְתֵּיהֶם — he brings others in their place,[2] וְאֵינוֹ קוֹרֵא — but he does not recite the passage. Since these are not his original *bikkurim*, it would be inappropriate for him to say that he has brought *the first fruits of the land* (*Devarim* 26:19), which is a verse in the passage.[3] וְהַשְּׁנִיִּים — And as for these second ones, i.e., the replacement *bikkurim*, אֵינָם חַיָּבִים עֲלֵיהֶם חֹמֶשׁ — one who is not a Kohen is not obligated to pay the penalty of a "fifth" for eating them by mistake.[4] נִטְמְאוּ בָעֲזָרָה — However, if the original

---

NOTES

2. According to R' Yehudah, the verse refers to land that had just one owner, in which case he cannot bring *bikkurim* more than once from a particular species. But if the land had two owners (such as a seller and a buyer), both can bring *bikkurim* from the same species (*Rav*).

[8]
1. "Plundered" refers to things seized openly, while "stolen" refers to what was taken secretly (*Rash Sirilio*).
2. The owner of *bikkurim* is obligated to bring them to the Temple Mount (see note 7). If he cannot bring the ones that he originally designated, he must bring others. The Biblical source for this law is cited in the next Mishnah.
3. *Rambam Commentary*.

4. *Bikkurim* are called *terumah* in *Devarim* 12:17. Therefore, like *terumah*, *bikkurim* may be eaten only by a Kohen and the members of his household. And if a non-Kohen ate *bikkurim* by mistake (that is, he did not know that they were *bikkurim* or he did not know that eating *bikkurim* is forbidden), he must pay a Kohen the value of what he ate plus a "fifth" (i.e., a *quarter* of the principal, which is a fifth of the final total). These laws appear in Mishnah 2:1.

Our Mishnah teaches that one who ate replacement *bikkurim* does not have to pay the "fifth," for since they are not the "first fruits of the land," they are not true *bikkurim* (*Radvaz*, *Hilchos Bikkurim* 4:9).

[21] **MISHNAH BIKKURIM** / Chapter 1: *Yeish Mevi'in*

- רע"ב -

נטמאו בעזרה נופֵץ
ואינו קורֵא. גרסינן.
כלומר מנער ומריק
הסל מן הפירות כיון
שנטמאו, והסל ניתן
לכהנים, דכתיב (שם
כו,ד) ולקח הכהן
הטנא מידך, פעמים
שאין הכהן לוקח אלא
הטנא. ואינו חייב להביא בכורים אחרים תחתיהן, דכיון שבאו להר הבית לא מחייב תו באחריותן:

נוֹפֵץ וְאֵינוֹ קוֹרֵא.

[ט] **וּמִנַּיִן** שֶׁהוּא חַיָּב בְּאַחֲרָיוּתָן עַד שֶׁיָּבִיא לְהַר הַבַּיִת? שֶׁנֶּאֱמַר: "רֵאשִׁית בִּכּוּרֵי אַדְמָתְךָ תָּבִיא בֵּית ה' אֱלֹהֶיךָ", מְלַמֵּד שֶׁחַיָּב בְּאַחֲרָיוּתָם עַד שֶׁיָּבִיא לְהַר הַבַּיִת.

---

bikkurim became *tamei* in the Temple Courtyard, he does not replace them;[5] **נוֹפֵץ** — rather, **he shakes them out** of their basket onto the floor of the Courtyard,[6] **וְאֵינוֹ קוֹרֵא** — **and he does not recite** the passage.[7]

[9] This Mishnah provides the source for the law taught in the previous Mishnah; namely, that if *bikkurim* are lost or ruined before they are brought into the Temple Mount, the owner must replace them:

וּמִנַּיִן שֶׁהוּא חַיָּב בְּאַחֲרָיוּתָן עַד שֶׁיָּבִיא לְהַר הַבַּיִת — **And from where** do we learn **that [the owner] is responsible for them until he brings them into the Temple Mount?**[1] **שֶׁנֶּאֱמַר "רֵאשִׁית בִּכּוּרֵי אַדְמָתְךָ תָּבִיא בֵּית ה' אֱלֹהֶיךָ"** — **For it is stated** in the Torah (*Shemos* 23:19): *The earliest of the first fruits of your land you shall bring to the House of Hashem, your God.* **מְלַמֵּד שֶׁחַיָּב בְּאַחֲרָיוּתָם עַד שֶׁיָּבִיא לְהַר הַבַּיִת** — **This teaches that he is responsible for them until he brings** them **into the Temple Mount.** Thus, if they become unfit before that point, he must replace them.

--- NOTES ---

5. Once the owner has brought his *bikkurim* to the Temple Mount, he has fulfilled his obligation, and he is no longer required to replace them if they are lost or ruined (*Rav*; see note 8).

6. *Bikkurim* should be brought in a basket (see Mishnah 3:6). He shakes them out of the basket to publicly demonstrate that they are *tamei* and may not be eaten (*Mahara Fulda*).

The empty basket is given to a Kohen. This is derived from the verse (*Devarim* 26:4): וְלָקַח הַכֹּהֵן הַטֶּנֶא מִיָּדֶךָ, *the Kohen shall take the basket from your hand,* which (based on its literal meaning) indicates that sometimes the Kohen takes *only* the basket, without the *bikkurim* that were inside it (*Rav*, from *Yerushalmi*).

7. In connection with the mitzvah of reciting the *bikkurim* passage, the Torah states (*Devarim* 26:11): וְשָׂמַחְתָּ בְכָל הַטּוֹב אֲשֶׁר נָתַן לְךָ ה' אֱלֹהֶיךָ, *You shall rejoice in all the good that Hashem, your God, has given to you.* This verse teaches that the passage must be recited in a state of happiness and rejoicing. Such joy is lacking when the *bikkurim* are lost or ruined (*Tos. Yom Tov*).

Although the Mishnah mentions the Courtyard, the law is that even if *bikkurim* become *tamei* upon being brought into the Temple Mount (before reaching the Courtyard), the owner has fulfilled his duty and need not replace them. This is stated explicitly in the next Mishnah. Our Mishnah mentions the Courtyard in order to teach that even if the *bikkurim* were *tahor* when they were brought into the Temple Mount, and did not become *tamei* until they reached the Courtyard, the passage should not be recited (*Tos. Yom Tov*).

[9]

1. See note 7 to the previous Mishnah.

[22] משניות ביכורים / פרק א: יש מביאין

א/י

- רע"ב -

(ט) הרי שהביא ממין אחד וקרא. לא נצרכה אלא לרבי יהודה, דאמר לעיל (משנה ז) מגיד וחוזר ומגיד, קא משמע לן דמודה רבי יהודה דאדם אחד אינו מגיד וחוזר ומגיד: (י) הכי גרסינן מפירות שבהרים ומתמרות שבעמקים ומזיתי שמן מעבר הירדן

הֲרֵי שֶׁהֵבִיא מִמִּין אֶחָד וְקָרָא, וְחָזַר וְהֵבִיא מִמִּין אַחֵר, אֵינוֹ קוֹרֵא.

[י] וְאֵלּוּ מְבִיאִין וְקוֹרִין: מִן הָעֲצֶרֶת וְעַד הֶחָג, מִשִּׁבְעַת הַמִּינִים, מִפֵּרוֹת שֶׁבֶּהָרִים, מִתְּמָרוֹת שֶׁבָּעֲמָקִים, וּמִזֵּיתֵי שֶׁמֶן מֵעֵבֶר הַיַּרְדֵּן.

רבי יוסי הגלילי אומר אין מביאין בכורים מעבר הירדן שאינה ארץ זבת חלב ודבש. והכי פירושו, פירות שבהרים הם מוטעמים יותר מפירות שבעמקים, הלכך מביאים בכורים מפירות שבהרים.

The Mishnah cites its last case in which the owner brings *bikkurim* but does not recite the passage:

הֲרֵי שֶׁהֵבִיא מִמִּין אֶחָד וְקָרָא — **If someone brought** *bikkurim* **from one species** of fruit **and recited** the passage, וְחָזַר וְהֵבִיא מִמִּין אַחֵר — **and later brought** *bikkurim* **again** that year **from a different species** (for example, first he brought grapes and later he brought figs), אֵינוֹ קוֹרֵא — **he does not recite** the passage a second time.[2]

[10] Having discussed cases in which one does not bring *bikkurim* at all (Mishnah 1-3), and cases in which one brings *bikkurim* but does not recite the passage (Mishnah 4-9), the Mishnah defines who brings *bikkurim* and recites the passage:

וְאֵלּוּ מְבִיאִין וְקוֹרִין — **These** people **bring** *bikkurim* **and recite** the passage: מִן הָעֲצֶרֶת וְעַד הֶחָג — **one who brings** *bikkurim* **from Shavuos until Succos**,[1] מִשִּׁבְעַת הַמִּינִים — **from the seven species** for which Eretz Yisrael is praised (wheat, barley, grapes, figs, pomegranates, olives, and dates),[2] מִפֵּרוֹת שֶׁבֶּהָרִים מִתְּמָרוֹת שֶׁבָּעֲמָקִים וּמִזֵּיתֵי שֶׁמֶן — **from** good-quality fruits such as **the fruits of the mountains, the dates of the valleys, and** good **oil-producing olives**,[3] מֵעֵבֶר הַיַּרְדֵּן — **and even if they are not from the main part of Eretz Yisrael, but from the east side of the Jordan**.[4]

NOTES

2. A person must bring *bikkurim* from all of the seven species that grow on his land. However, if he brings only some species first and the other species later, he recites the passage only the first time. This law is learned from the verse (*Devarim* 26:3): הִגַּדְתִּי הַיּוֹם, *I declare on this day*. By specifying "*this* day," the Torah teaches that the passage is recited no more than once (*Rambam, Hilchos Bikkurim* 4:11).

[10]

1. *Bikkurim* may not be brought before Shavuos (Mishnah 3), and the passage may not be recited after Succos (Mishnah 6).

2. See Mishnah 3 note 1.

3. See Mishnah 3 notes 2-5.

4. This is the land east of the Jordan River that was conquered by the Jewish people from Sichon, king of the Amorites, and Og, king of Bashan (*Bamidbar* 21:21-35). It was given to the tribes of Reuven and Gad and half the tribe of Menasheh (32:33 there). The produce of this area is subject to *terumos* and *maasros* and the other agricultural obligations of Eretz Yisrael. This Tanna therefore rules that its produce is also subject to *bikkurim* (*Mishnah Rishonah*).

[23] **MISHNAH BIKKURIM** / Chapter 1: *Yeish Mevi'in*

- רע"ב -

רַבִּי יוֹסֵי הַגְּלִילִי אוֹמֵר: אֵין מְבִיאִין בִּכּוּרִים מֵעֵבֶר הַיַּרְדֵּן, שֶׁאֵינָהּ אֶרֶץ זָבַת חָלָב וּדְבָשׁ.

[יא] הַקּוֹנֶה שְׁלֹשָׁה אִילָנוֹת בְּתוֹךְ שֶׁל חֲבֵרוֹ, מֵבִיא וְקוֹרֵא; רַבִּי מֵאִיר אוֹמֵר: אֲפִלּוּ שְׁנָיִם.

אֲבָל הַתְּמָרִים הֵם הֵפֶךְ זֶה, שֶׁהַתְּמָרִים שֶׁבָּעֲמָקִים הֵם יוֹתֵר מְלֵאִים מִדְּבַשׁ, וְהַגְּרָא מֵהַתְּמָרִים הוּא הַדְּבַשׁ שֶׁבָּהֶם, שֶׁהֲרֵי הַתּוֹרָה קְרָאָהּ לַתְּמָרִים דְּבָשׁ, הָלַךְ מְבִיאִין בִּכּוּרִים מִתַּמְרוֹת שֶׁבָּעֲמָקִים וְלֹא מִשֶּׁל הָרִים. וּמֵזֵיתֵי שֶׁמֶן, מֵזֵיתִים הַטּוֹעֲשִׁים שֶׁמֶן. מֵעֵבֶר הַיַּרְדֵּן, מְפֵירוֹת שֶׁל עֵבֶר הַיַּרְדֵּן נַמֵּי מְבִיאִין בִּכּוּרִים, אַף עַל פִּי שֶׁאֵינָהּ אֶרֶץ זָבַת חָלָב וּדְבָשׁ, שֶׁכֵּיוָן שֶׁנְּתָנָהּ הַקָּדוֹשׁ בָּרוּךְ הוּא לְיִשְׂרָאֵל קְרִינָא בָּהּ פְּרִי הָאֲדָמָה אֲשֶׁר נָתַתָּה לִי (דברים כו,י). וּפְלִיג רַבִּי יוֹסֵי הַגְּלִילִי וְאָמַר, אֵין מְבִיאִין בִּכּוּרִים מֵעֵבֶר הַיַּרְדֵּן. וְאֵין הֲלָכָה כְּרַבִּי יוֹסֵי הַגְּלִילִי: (יא) הַקּוֹנֶה שְׁלֹשָׁה אִילָנוֹת. בִּסְתָם, וְלֹא פֵּירַשׁ אִם קָנָה קַרְקַע אִם לָאו, מֵבִיא וְקוֹרֵא, דִּבְסְתָם, קָנָה קַרְקַע שֶׁתַּחְתֵּיהֶן וְחוּצָה לָהֶן. אֲבָל פָּחוֹת מִשְּׁלֹשָׁה אִילָנוֹת, בִּסְתָם, לֹא קָנָה קַרְקַע. וְרַבִּי מֵאִיר פְּלִיג וְאָמַר, דְּאַף שְׁנֵי אִילָנוֹת נַמֵּי קָנָה קַרְקַע. וְאֵין הֲלָכָה כְּרַבִּי מֵאִיר:

A Tanna disagrees with the last ruling:

אֵין מְבִיאִין בִּכּוּרִים מֵעֵבֶר הַיַּרְדֵּן — רַבִּי יוֹסֵי הַגְּלִילִי אוֹמֵר — R' Yose HaGlili says: שֶׁאֵינָהּ אֶרֶץ — We do not bring *bikkurim* from the east side of the Jordan, זָבַת חָלָב וּדְבָשׁ — because it is not "a land flowing with milk and honey,"[5] which is how the *bikkurim* passage describes the land where the mitzvah applies (*Devarim* 26:9).[6]

[11] Mishnah 6 cited a dispute regarding someone who bought *two* trees in the land of another person. (According to the Tanna Kamma, the buyer brings *bikkurim* but does not read the passage, but R' Meir requires him to read the passages as well.) This Mishnah states the law that applies where someone bought *three* trees:

הַקּוֹנֶה שְׁלֹשָׁה אִילָנוֹת בְּתוֹךְ שֶׁל חֲבֵרוֹ — If someone buys three trees that are in the property of another person, מֵבִיא וְקוֹרֵא — he brings *bikkurim* from their fruits **and recites** the passage. This is because a sale of three (or more) trees includes the land on which they grow (even if the land was not actually mentioned by the seller or the buyer). The buyer thus owns not only the trees but also the land beneath them, which makes him obligated in all the laws of *bikkurim*.[1] רַבִּי מֵאִיר אוֹמֵר — R' Meir says: אֲפִלּוּ שְׁנָיִם — Even if someone bought only **two** trees, he brings *bikkurim* from their fruit and recites the passage (as R' Meir himself stated in Mishnah 6), and certainly if he bought **three** trees.[2]

— NOTES —

5. This refers to the plentiful milk that flows from the goats of Eretz Yisrael and the honey that flows from its dates and figs (*Rashi* to *Shemos* 13:5).

6. The first Tanna agrees that the land east of the Jordan is not called "a land flowing with milk and honey." However, he holds that since God gave it to the Jewish people, the mitzvos of *bikkurim* apply there as well, for the *bikkurim* passage states (*Devarim* 26:10): *the fruit of the land that You have given me, Hashem* (*Rav*).

[11]

1. See Mishnah 6.

2. Although R' Meir's ruling was cited in Mishnah 6, it is repeated here. Based

[24] **משניות ביכורים** / פרק א: יש מביאין

א/יא

- רע״ב -

קָנָה אִילָן וְקַרְקָעוֹ, מֵבִיא וְקוֹרֵא. רַבִּי יְהוּדָה אוֹמֵר: אַף בַּעֲלֵי אֲרִיסוּת וְחָכוֹרוֹת מְבִיאִין וְקוֹרִין.

אף בעלי אריסות וחכירות מביאים וקוראים. דסבר רבי יהודה אריס וחוכר יש לו קנין בארץ כאילו יש לו חלק בה. ואין הלכה כרבי יהודה:

The Mishnah now deals with the purchase of a single tree:

קָנָה אִילָן וְקַרְקָעוֹ — If **someone bought a** single **tree** together with **its land**, i.e., the land was explicitly included in the sale, מֵבִיא וְקוֹרֵא — all agree that he **brings** bikkurim from that tree **and recites** the passage, since he owns the land beneath the tree.[3]

We learned in Mishnah 2 that sharecroppers and tenant farmers do not bring bikkurim at all from the produce of the land on which they work, because that land does not belong to them. This Mishnah cites a Tanna who disagrees:

אַף בַּעֲלֵי אֲרִיסוּת וְחָכוֹרוֹת מְבִיאִין וְקוֹרִין — **R' Yehudah says:** רַבִּי יְהוּדָה אוֹמֵר — **Even sharecroppers and tenant farmers bring** bikkurim **and recite** the passage. According to R' Yehudah, the right of a sharecropper or tenant farmer to take a share of the crops gives him some degree of ownership in the land. This level of ownership is enough for him to be obligated to bring bikkurim and recite the passage.[4]

---- NOTES ----

on that Mishnah alone, it could have been thought that R' Meir requires even someone who buys a *single* tree to bring bikkurim and recite the passage. R' Meir did not say so there only because that Mishnah deals exclusively with the case of buying *two* trees. Our Mishnah teaches that this is not correct. Since R' Meir says (in our Mishnah), "even two," it is clear that he requires the owner to bring bikkurim and recite the passage *only* in the case of two trees, because if he held the same in the case of one tree, he would have said, "even one" (*Tiferes Yisrael*). [Rather, in the case of one tree, R' Meir rules that the passage is not recited, as explained in the next note.]

3. However, if the land was not explicitly included in the sale, the buyer acquires only the tree, and not the land. He would therefore be exempt from having to bring bikkurim at all (*Tosefta* 1:2).

[This is the view of the Tanna Kamma. According to R' Meir, though, there is a question whether one who buys a single tree also acquires the land. Thus, he brings bikkurim but he does not recite the passage, because it might be untruthful for him to say, *the land that You have give me, Hashem* (see *Tosefta* there, Gemara *Bava Basra* 81a-b, and Mishnah 6 above).]

4. R' Yehudah refers to sharecroppers and tenant farmers who have the *exclusive* rights to work particular fields and are thus entitled to a share of the produce forever. (This is in contrast to those who are granted the right to work the land and take a share of its produce only one year at a time.) Sharecroppers and tenant farmers who have *exclusive* rights enjoy such a strong hold in the land that they are obligated to bring bikkurim from its fruit (*Rash*, from *Yerushalmi*).

Chapter Two

ב/א

משניות ביכורים / פרק ב: התרומה [26]

- רע"ב -

פרק שני — התרומה. (א) התרומה והבכורים חייבין עליהם מיתה. זר האוכלן במזיד, חייב מיתה בידי שמים, דכתיב

[א] הַתְּרוּמָה וְהַבִּכּוּרִים, חַיָּבִים עֲלֵיהֶן מִיתָה וָחֹמֶשׁ, וַאֲסוּרִים לְזָרִים, וְהֵם נִכְסֵי כֹהֵן, וְעוֹלִין בְּאֶחָד וּמֵאָה,

בתרומה (ויקרא כב,ט) ומתו בו כי יחללוהו, ובכורים אקרו תרומה, דאמר מר (מכות יז,א) ותרומת ידך (דברים יב,יז) אלו בכורים, שנאמר בהן (שם כו,ד) ולקח הכהן הטנא מידך: **וחומש.** האוכלן שוגג, משלם קרן לבעלים וחומש לכל כהן שירצה: **ואסורים לזרים.** בתנאי היא שנויה, דכיון שחייבין עליהם מיתה וחומש פשיטא שאסורים לזרים. ולרבי יוחנן דאמר (יומא עג,ב) חלי שיעור אסור מן התורה, מלינן למימר דתנן אסורים לזרים לחלי שיעור, שהוא אסור מן התורה, ואין בו לא מיתה ולא חומש: **והן נכסי כהן.** שיכול למכרן וליקח בהן עבדים וקרקעות ובהמה טמאה: **ועולים באחד ומאה.** אם נתערבו במאה של חולין:

---

[1] The first part of this chapter compares *terumah*, *bikkurim*, and *maaser sheni* with one another. It starts by listing laws that apply to both *terumah* and *bikkurim*, but not to *maaser sheni*:

הַתְּרוּמָה וְהַבִּכּוּרִים — ***Terumah* and *bikkurim*** have the following laws in common: חַיָּבִים עֲלֵיהֶן מִיתָה — **[Non-Kohanim] are liable to** an early **death** at the hands of Heaven **for** eating **them** knowingly (i.e., knowing that the food is *terumah* or *bikkurim* and knowing the severity of the sin);[1] וָחֹמֶשׁ — **and** non-Kohanim who ate them by mistake (i.e., without knowing that the food is *terumah* or *bikkurim* or without knowing the severity of the sin) must pay a Kohen the value of what they ate plus **a "fifth"** (i.e., a quarter of the value, which is a fifth of the final total);[2] וַאֲסוּרִים לְזָרִים — **and [*terumah* and *bikkurim*] are forbidden to non-Kohanim** to eat;[3] וְהֵם נִכְסֵי כֹהֵן — **and they are** completely **the property of the Kohen** to whom they are given;[4] וְעוֹלִין בְּאֶחָד וּמֵאָה — **and [*terumah* and *bikkurim*]** that become mixed with

---
NOTES

---

[1]

1. The Torah states this law in connection with *terumah* (*Vayikra* 22:9), but it is understood as applying to *bikkurim* as well, because the Torah (*Devarim* 12:17) refers to *bikkurim* as "*terumah*" (see *Rav*).

The Torah's description of *bikkurim* as "*terumah*" establishes a general link between *bikkurim* and *terumah*, from which it is learned that *bikkurim* have the same holiness as *terumah*, and are therefore subject to many of *terumah*'s laws. This is the Biblical basis for the rulings of our Mishnah. Each law taught by the Mishnah appears in the Torah in regard to *terumah*, but it is extended to *bikkurim* because *bikkurim* have a similar status (*Rambam Commentary*).

2. A non-Kohen who eats *terumah* (or *bikkurim*) pays the value of what he ate to the Kohen who owned it, and he pays the "fifth" to any Kohen he wants (*Rav*,

from *Terumos* 6:2). If the *terumah* had not yet been given to a Kohen, he also pays its basic value to any Kohen of his choosing (see *Terumos* there).

3. Since the Mishnah just taught that a non-Kohen is punished (with early death or payment of the "fifth") for eating *terumah* or *bikkurim*, it should go without saying that he is prohibited to eat them. The Mishnah adds this ruling to teach that a non-Kohen may not eat even the smallest amount of *terumah* and *bikkurim*. Although he would not be *punished* (in the ways mentioned above) unless the amount eaten was at least a *kezayis* (the size of an olive), he is *forbidden* to eat any amount (*Rav;* see *Tos. Yom Tov*).

4. That is, *terumah* and *bikkurim* become the personal property of the Kohen to whom they are given, rather than being the property of Heaven that the Kohen merely has the right to eat. As such, the Kohen may not only eat *terumah* or

[27] MISHNAH BIKKURIM / Chapter 2: *HaTerumah*

וּטְעוּנִין רְחִיצַת יָדַיִם וְהַעֲרֵב שֶׁמֶשׁ, הֲרֵי אֵלּוּ בַּתְּרוּמָה וּבְבִּכּוּרִים, מַה שֶּׁאֵין כֵּן בְּמַעֲשֵׂר.

– רע"ב –

וטעונים רחיצת ידים. הבא ליגע בהן, צריך ליטול ידיו תחלה, שסתם ידים פוסלות את התרומה, ובכורים נמי מקרו תרומה: והערב שמש. טמא שטבל, אינו אוכל בתרומה עד שיעריב שמשו, דכתיב (ויקרא כב,ז) ובא השמש וטהר ואחר יאכל מן הקדשים, והוא הדין לבכורים: מה שאין כן במעשר. דשרי לזרים, ואסור לקנות בדמי מעשר שני בהמה ועבדים וקרקעות, ובעל ברוב היכא דאין לו מתירין, והנוגע בו אין טעון רחיצת ידים, ואין צריך הערב שמש דאמרינן (פסחים לה,א) טבל ועלה אוכל במעשר:

permitted produce **are nullified in one hundred and one**, that is, if one part of *terumah* or *bikkurim* becomes mixed with one hundred parts of permitted produce, the *terumah* or *bikkurim* is "nullified," and so the mixture is permitted even to non-Kohanim;[5] וּטְעוּנִין רְחִיצַת יָדַיִם — **and they require hand washing**, that is, before a Kohen eats *terumah* or *bikkurim*, he must wash his hands;[6] וְהַעֲרֵב שֶׁמֶשׁ — **and they require sunset**, that is, after a *tamei* Kohen immerses in a *mikveh*, he must wait until nightfall before he may eat *terumah* or *bikkurim*.[7] הֲרֵי אֵלּוּ בַּתְּרוּמָה וּבְבִּכּוּרִים מַה שֶּׁאֵין כֵּן בְּמַעֲשֵׂר — **These are laws that apply to *terumah* and *bikkurim*, but not to *maaser sheni*.** Someone who ate *maaser sheni* knowingly (outside Jerusalem) is not liable to an early death at the hands of Heaven; one who ate it by mistake does not have to pay the "fifth"; *maaser sheni* may be eaten (in Jerusalem) even by non-Kohanim; *maaser sheni* does not completely belong to its owner;[8] *maaser sheni* that became mixed with permitted produce is nullified in a simple majority;[9] there

―――― NOTES ――――

bikkurim, but he may also use it for any other purpose [provided that he does not destroy or damage it] (see Mishnah 3:12).

5. Generally, if prohibited dry food becomes mixed with permitted dry food of the same type (for example, a piece of non-kosher meat becomes mixed with pieces of kosher meat), and we cannot tell them apart, a simple majority of permitted food "nullifies" the minority of forbidden food, and all the pieces are permitted. In some cases, the mixture is not permitted unless the permitted food is sixty times larger than the forbidden food. However, the Rabbis decreed that in a mixture of *terumah* (or *bikkurim*) and permitted food of the same type, the mixture is not permitted unless there are at least 100 parts of permitted food for each part of *terumah* (see *Terumos* 4:7; Rambam, *Hilchos Terumos* 13:1).

6. By Rabbinic decree, a person's hands are *sheni letumah*, secondary level of *tumah* (see *Shabbos* 14a for the reason). If a *sheni letumah* touches holy food, such as *terumah*, *bikkurim*, or sacrificial meat, it makes the holy food prohibited

to be eaten. Thus, before eating *terumah* or *bikkurim*, a Kohen must remove the *tumah* from his hands by washing them in a procedure called *netilas yadayim*, in which water is poured from a vessel onto the hands (*Rav*). [In order to get Kohanim into the habit of doing *netilas yadayim*, the Sages decreed that any Jew who eats bread (even if it is not sacred) must do *netilas yadayim* first (see *Chullin* 106a and *Mishnah Berurah* 158:1).]

7. Although immersion in a *mikveh* removes the main *tumah* immediately, a trace of the *tumah* remains until nightfall. For this reason, a Kohen who immersed must wait until nightfall before he may eat *terumah* or *bikkurim* (see *Yevamos* 74b).

8. The owner of *maaser sheni* does not have the right to use it for whatever he wants; rather, he must take it to Jerusalem and eat it there. Although the Torah allows him to redeem it with money, the money then has the sanctity of *maaser sheni*, and may be used only to buy food in Jerusalem (see *Maaser Sheni* 1:3-7).

9. See note 5.

[28] **משניות ביכורים** / פרק ב: התרומה

ב/ב

[ב] **יֵשׁ** בְּמַעֲשֵׂר וּבְבִכּוּרִים מַה שֶּׁאֵין כֵּן בִּתְרוּמָה, שֶׁהַמַּעֲשֵׂר וְהַבִּכּוּרִים טְעוּנִים הֲבָאַת מָקוֹם, וּטְעוּנִים וִדּוּי, וַאֲסוּרִין לְאוֹנֵן; וְרַבִּי שִׁמְעוֹן מַתִּיר.

— רע"ב —

(ב) **הבאת מקום.** להעלותן לירושלם, דכתיב (דברים יב,ו) והבאתם שמה עולותיכם וזבחיכם מעשרותיכם ותרומת ידכם, ודרשינן (ירושלמי)

תרומת ידכם אלו הבכורים: **וטעונים וידוי.** במעשר כתיב (שם כו,יג) ואמרת לפני ה' אלהיך בערתי הקדש מן הבית, ובבכורים כתיב (שם פסוק ה) וענית ואמרת לפני ה' אלהיך הגדתי היום לה' אלהיך. ואף על גב דתרומה נמי בעיא וידוי, כדאמרינן (מעשר שני ה,י) וגם נתתיו ללוי (שם פסוק יג) זו תרומה ותרומת מעשר, מיהו מעשר ובכורים מעשר לבדו או בכורים לבדן טעונים וידוי, ותרומה אי ליה אלא תרומה לבדה אינו טעון וידוי: **ואסורין לאונן.** במעשר כתיב (שם פסוק יד) לא אכלתי באוני ממנו. ובבכורים נאמר (שם, פסוק יא) ושמחת בכל הטוב, מלמד שאסורים לאונן: **ורבי שמעון מתיר.** בכורים לאונן, דתרומה

---

is no obligation to wash one's hands before eating *maaser sheni*;[10] and a *tamei* person who immersed in a *mikveh* may eat *maaser sheni* right away.[11]

[2] This Mishnah contrasts *maaser sheni* and *bikkurim* with *terumah*:

יֵשׁ בְּמַעֲשֵׂר וּבְבִכּוּרִים מַה שֶּׁאֵין כֵּן בִּתְרוּמָה — There are laws that apply to *maaser sheni* and *bikkurim*, but not to *terumah*: **שֶׁהַמַּעֲשֵׂר וְהַבִּכּוּרִים טְעוּנִים הֲבָאַת מָקוֹם** — *Maaser sheni* and *bikkurim* must be brought to a particular place, that is, the owner has to bring them to Jerusalem, where they must be eaten; **וּטְעוּנִים וִדּוּי** — and they require a declaration, that is, the owner declares every fourth and seventh year of the seven-year *Shemittah* cycle that he has dealt with his *maaser sheni* in the required manner,[1] and when he brings *bikkurim* to the Temple, he makes a declaration thanking God; **וַאֲסוּרִין לְאוֹנֵן** — and they are forbidden to an *onein* (i.e., someone whose close relative has died but has not yet been buried, or was buried that day).[2]

R' Shimon disagrees with the last point:

וְרַבִּי שִׁמְעוֹן מַתִּיר — But R' Shimon rules that an *onein* is allowed to eat *bikkurim*.

NOTES

10. As explained above (note 6), a person's hands are *sheni letumah*. Something with this level of *tumah* can contaminate *terumah*, *bikkurim*, and other sacred foods, but it cannot contaminate *maaser sheni*. Thus, it is not necessary to wash one's hands before eating *maaser sheni*.

11. In fact, there are other laws that apply to *terumah* and *bikkurim* but not to *maaser sheni* (for example, it is possible to redeem *maaser sheni* with money, which cannot be done with *terumah* and *bikkurim*). The Mishnah does not mean to list every difference (*Mishnah Rishonah*).

[2]

1. On the last day of Pesach of the fourth and seventh years of the seven-year *Shemittah* cycle, one says the וִדּוּי מַעֲשֵׂר, *viduy maaser*, literally, *confession of maaser* (*Devarim* 26:13-14). In it, he declares that he has properly fulfilled all his obligations with regard to *terumos* and *maasros* (see *Maaser Sheni* 5:10-13).

The text of the *viduy maaser* makes reference to both *maaser sheni* and *terumah* (see 5:10 there). When our Mishnah states that the law of *viduy maaser* does not apply to *terumah*, it means that someone who has only *terumah* (and none of the other tithes) need not say the *viduy maaser* at all. *Terumah* is included in a recitation of *viduy maaser* that was going to be made anyway, but *terumah* does not require *viduy maaser* in its own right. In this respect *terumah* is different from *maaser sheni*, because even someone who has nothing but *maaser sheni* must still recite the *viduy maaser* (*Rav*).

2. *Tiferes Yisrael*; see Rambam, *Hilchos Maaser Sheni* 3:6.

[29] MISHNAH BIKKURIM / Chapter 2: *HaTerumah*

וְחַיָּבִין בַּבִּעוּר, וְרַבִּי שִׁמְעוֹן פּוֹטֵר. וַאֲסוּרִין
כָּל שֶׁהֵן מִלֶּאֱכֹל בִּירוּשָׁלַיִם, וְגִדּוּלֵיהֶן אֲסוּרִים

- רע"ב -

קרבנו כרחמנא, ותרומה
שריא לאונן: **וחייבים
בביעור.** לבערן מן
העולם לסוף שלש שנים, כדכתיב בפרשת מעשר (שם, פסוק יג), בערתי הקדש מן הבית, ומשמע
נמי בכורים מדכתיב הקדש, הקדש האמור למעלה, אלו בכורים שנאמרו בפרשה שלמעלה: **ורבי
שמעון פוטר.** בכורים מן הביעור, אלא ינתנו לכהן, דתרומה קרנהו רחמנא, ותרומה אין צריך
לבערה מן העולם: **ואסורים.** מעשר שני ובכורים שנתערבו בחולין, אוסרים תערובתן בכל שהו,
ואין עולים באחד ומאה: **מלאכול בירושלים.** כלומר אם נתערבו המעשר שני או הבכורים בעוד
שהן בתוך ירושלים, אז אוסרים תערובתן בכל שהוא מלאכול בתורת חולין, משום דהוי דבר שיש לו
מתירין, הואיל ויכול לאכול התערובת כלה במקומה. אבל מעשר שני ובכורים שנתערבו בחולין חוץ
לירושלים, אינן אוסרים בכל שהוא, הואיל ויש טורח להעלותן, לא מקרי דבר שיש לו מתירין: **וגדוליהם
אסורים.** תערובת של מעשר ובכורים שזרעם וצמחו וגדלו, אותן הגדולים נמי אסורים לאכול
בתורת חולין, אם זרען וגדלו בירושלים, ואוסרין תערובתן בכל שהוא, כיון שיכולים ליאכל במקומה:

The first Tanna continues:

וְחַיָּבִין בַּבִּעוּר — And [*maaser sheni* and *bikkurim*] require *biur*, that is, every fourth year and seventh year of the seven-year *Shemittah* cycle, any *maaser sheni* and *bikkurim* that have not yet been eaten in Jerusalem must be destroyed.[3]

R' Shimon disagrees here, too:

וְרַבִּי שִׁמְעוֹן פּוֹטֵר — But R' Shimon rules that one is exempt from having to destroy *bikkurim*.[4]

The first Tanna continues:

וַאֲסוּרִין כָּל שֶׁהֵן מִלֶּאֱכֹל בִּירוּשָׁלַיִם — Any amount of [*maaser sheni* or *bikkurim*] that becomes mixed with permitted produce in Jerusalem may not be eaten outside Jerusalem, no matter how much permitted produce is in the mixture; instead, the entire mixture must be treated as *maaser sheni* or *bikkurim*, which may be eaten only in Jerusalem;[5] וְגִדּוּלֵיהֶן אֲסוּרִים

NOTES

3. On the day before Pesach of the fourth and seventh years of the seven-year *Shemittah* cycle, one must perform בִּעוּר מַעֲשְׂרוֹת, *removal of maasros* (Deuteronomy 14:28-29). This means that he must separate *terumos* and *maasros* from any *tevel* he still has in his possession and give them to their proper recipients; that is, he gives *terumah* to a Kohen, *maaser rishon* to a Levi, etc. If he has *maaser sheni* (or money with which *maaser sheni* was redeemed) or *bikkurim* that he cannot bring to Jerusalem that day, he must destroy it. *Terumah*, however, may not be destroyed; it must be given to a Kohen even after this day (*Maaser Sheni* 5:6).

4. R' Shimon holds that *bikkurim* are like *terumah*, which is not destroyed but is given to a Kohen, as stated in the previous note (*Rav*). R' Shimon's ruling also appears in *Maaser Sheni* 5:6.

5. We have learned that when a forbidden substance becomes mixed with enough of a permitted substance, the forbidden item is "nullified" and the entire mixture is permitted. If *maaser sheni* or *bikkurim* were nullified, the entire mixture would be permitted to be eaten outside Jerusalem. However, it is a general rule that "nullification" does not take place if the forbidden item is a דָּבָר שֶׁיֵשׁ לוֹ מַתִּירִין, *something that has permitting factors;* that is, there are easily available situations in which the forbidden item is permitted. This category includes *maaser sheni* and *bikkurim*, because they are permitted to be eaten in Jerusalem. Therefore, if either of these foods becomes mixed with

משניות ביכורים / פרק ב: התרומה

מֶאֱכָל בִּירוּשָׁלַיִם אַף לְזָרִים וְלַבְּהֵמָה, אַף לְזָרִים וְלַבְּהֵמָה. — רע"ב —

מעשר שני וביכורים שאוסרין תערובתן בכל שהוא וגדוליהן נמי דאסורין, אף לזרים ולבהמה אסורים, אם ביכורים הם אוסרין התערובת לזרים, ואם מעשר שני הוא אוסר [אֶת] התערובת לבהמה, דלא תימא דוקא לענין ליאכל חוץ לירושלם הוא דאוסרים בכל שהוא, דלהאי מלתא חשיבי דבר שיש לו מתירין, כיון שיכול לאכלן במקומם בירושלם, ואפילו באלף לא בטלי, אבל לאסור התערובת לזרים ולבהמה, דאסור זרות ובהמה אין לו מתירין, סלקא דעתך אמינא דלא יאסרו תערובתן בכל שהוא, קמשמע לן דכיון דחל על התערובת שם ביכורים ומעשר ליאסר לאכלן חוץ לירושלם, חל נמי לענין זה ליאסר לאכול לזרים אם הן ביכורים או לבהמה אם הוא מעשר:

מֶאֱכָל בִּירוּשָׁלַיִם אַף לְזָרִים וְלַבְּהֵמָה — moreover, if seeds from the prohibited mixture were planted **in Jerusalem, their growths would be forbidden to be eaten** outside Jerusalem,[6] and they would **even** be forbidden **to non-Kohanim and animals.**[7]

NOTES

permitted produce, they are not nullified, regardless of how much permitted produce is present (*Rav*).

However, this law applies only if the *maaser sheni* or *bikkurim* became mixed with the ordinary food *in* Jerusalem. In that case, the *maaser sheni* or *bikkurim* is certainly "something that has permitting factors," since it may be eaten right away in that very place. But if the mixing took place *outside* Jerusalem, the *maaser sheni* or *bikkurim* would not be considered "something that has permitting factors," because it would have to be carried to Jerusalem, which takes great effort. Thus, the usual rules of nullification would apply. As long as there is enough permitted food in the mixture, the *maaser sheni* or *bikkurim* would be nullified, and the mixture may be eaten outside Jerusalem (*Rav*).

[When the previous Mishnah said that *bikkurim* are nullified in a mixture — provided that at least 100 parts of permitted food are present — it was referring to a mixture created *outside* Jerusalem.]

6. If seeds from a mixture of *maaser sheni* and permitted produce, or seeds from a mixture of *bikkurim* and permitted produce, were planted in Jerusalem, the growths from the seeds would be treated like *maaser sheni* or *bikkurim* and may not be eaten outside the city. Even though these are new plants that do not contain any *maaser sheni* or *bikkurim*, the Rabbis decreed that since they are already in Jerusalem, they may not be taken outside the city and eaten there. The Sages applied this decree only in the case of seeds that were planted *inside* Jerusalem (see *Rav*).

7. The Mishnah taught above that if *maaser sheni* or *bikkurim* became mixed with permitted produce in Jerusalem, they are not nullified — no matter how much permitted food is present — because they have "permitting factors" (see note 5). The mixture is thus forbidden to be eaten outside Jerusalem. However, the prohibition of eating *maaser sheni* and *bikkurim* outside Jerusalem is not the only prohibition that applies to these foods. They are subject to certain other restrictions as well; namely, *bikkurim* may not be eaten by non-Kohanim and *maaser sheni* may not be fed to animals. These prohibitions do *not* have "permitting factors," for they apply in all circumstances. The usual rules of nullification should therefore apply with respect to these prohibitions. If so, it would emerge that although the mixture may not be eaten outside Jerusalem, it may be eaten by non-Kohanim (in the case of *bikkurim*) and it may be fed to animals (in the case of *maaser sheni*). The Mishnah teaches that this is not so. Rather, we say that since the mixture has the status of *bikkurim* or *maaser sheni* with respect to the prohibition against eating it outside Jerusalem, it has the same status with respect to the other prohibitions as well, and so it may not be eaten by non-Kohanim or animals (*Rav*).

[31] **MISHNAH BIKKURIM** / Chapter 2: *HaTerumah*

וְרַבִּי שִׁמְעוֹן מַתִּיר. הֲרֵי אֵלּוּ בְּמַעֲשֵׂר וּבְבִכּוּרִים, מַה שֶּׁאֵין כֵּן בִּתְרוּמָה.

[ג] יֵשׁ בִּתְרוּמָה וּמַעֲשֵׂר מַה שֶּׁאֵין כֵּן בְּבִכּוּרִים,

— רע״ב —
ורבי שמעון מתיר. אגדוליהן בלבד קאי, דסבר כבר בטלים הס, אבל בתערובת עצמה מודה רבי שמעון. ואין הלכה כרבי שמעון בכולה מתניתין: מה שאין כן בתרומה. שכל הדינים הללו אין נוהגים בתרומה:

The previous Tanna, who forbids the growths of a *mixture* of *maaser sheni* or *bikkurim* seeds and permitted seeds, would certainly forbid the growths of actual *maaser sheni* or *bikkurim*. R' Shimon, though, permits the growths even in the latter case:

וְרַבִּי שִׁמְעוֹן מַתִּיר — **But R' Shimon rules** that the growths of actual *maaser sheni* and *bikkurim* are **permitted** to be eaten outside Jerusalem, and certainly to be eaten by non-Kohanim or animals.[8]

The first Tanna continues:

הֲרֵי אֵלּוּ בְּמַעֲשֵׂר וּבְבִכּוּרִים — **All these** are laws that apply **to** *maaser sheni* and *bikkurim*, מַה שֶּׁאֵין כֵּן בִּתְרוּמָה — **but do not apply to** *terumah*. *Terumah* does not have to be brought to any specific place; it does not require a declaration of any sort;[9] it may be eaten by an *onein*; it does not require *biur*;[10] it becomes permitted when mixed with permitted produce[11] (and the growths of the mixture are certainly permitted).

[3] This Mishnah contrasts *terumah* and *maaser sheni* with *bikkurim*:

יֵשׁ בִּתְרוּמָה וּמַעֲשֵׂר מַה שֶּׁאֵין כֵּן בְּבִכּוּרִים — **There are** laws that apply **to**

NOTES

8. That is, the growths of *bikkurim* seeds that were planted may be eaten by non-Kohanim and the growths of *maaser sheni* seeds that were planted may be fed to animals. Both set of growths are permitted to be eaten even outside Jerusalem (despite the fact that they could easily be taken inside the city and eaten there). According to R' Shimon, since these growths do not contain any of the original *maaser sheni* or *bikkurim*, but are entirely new plants, they are permitted in every respect.

However, R' Shimon rules leniently only in regard to the *growths* of these forbidden foods. He agrees that *mixtures* are forbidden because they contain actual *maaser sheni* or *bikkurim*, which do not become nullified due to the reason given in note 3 (*Rav*).

9. See note 1.

10. See note 3.

11. In contrast to *maaser sheni* and *bikkurim*, which cannot be nullified (inside Jerusalem), *terumah* is nullified if one part becomes mixed with one hundred parts of permitted produce, as taught in the previous Mishnah.

This is a summary of the laws of *terumah*, *maaser sheni*, and *bikkurim* with respect to nullification:

(a) *Terumah* is nullified in a mixture that contains 100 times as much permitted produce (Mishnah 1). It makes no difference where the mixture was created.

(b) *Maaser sheni* cannot be nullified in Jerusalem, regardless of how much permitted produce is present (Mishnah 2). Outside Jerusalem, it is nullified in a mixture that contains a simple majority of permitted produce.

(c) *Bikkurim* cannot be nullified in Jerusalem, regardless of how much permitted produce is present (Mishnah 2). Outside Jerusalem it is nullified in a mixture that contains 100 times as much permitted produce (Mishnah 1).

משניות ביכורים / פרק ב: התרומה

שֶׁהַתְּרוּמָה וְהַמַּעֲשֵׂר אוֹסְרִין אֶת הַגֹּרֶן, וְיֵשׁ לָהֶם שִׁעוּר, וְנוֹהֲגִים בְּכָל הַפֵּרוֹת, בִּפְנֵי הַבַּיִת וְשֶׁלֹּא בִּפְנֵי הַבַּיִת, וּבָאֲרִיסִין וּבַחֲכוֹרוֹת וּבַסִּקְרִיקוֹן וּבַגַּזְלָן. הֲרֵי אֵלּוּ בִּתְרוּמָה וּבְמַעֲשֵׂר, מַה שֶּׁאֵין כֵּן בְּבִכּוּרִים.

- רע"ב -

(ג) אוסרין את הגרן. אסור לאכול מתבואה שבגורן עד שיפריש תרומות ומעשרות, אבל בכורים אין אוסרין: ויש להן שיעור. תרומה יש לה שיעור מדרבנן, אחד מחמשים, אבל בכורים אין להם שיעור

אפילו מדרבנן: ונוהגים בכל הפירות. מדרבנן, ובכורים אינן באין אלא משבעת המינין: בפני הבית ושלא בפני הבית. ובכורים אינן אלא בפני הבית בלבד, דכתיב בהו (דברים כו,ד) והניחו לפני מזבח ה' אלהיך, אם אין מזבח אין בכורים: ובאריסות ובחכירות: מפורש לעיל בריש פרק קמא (משנה ב) ובכורים אינן אלא ממי שהקרקע שלו מן הדין, דכתיב (שמות כג,יט) בכורי אדמתך:

שֶׁהַתְּרוּמָה וְהַמַּעֲשֵׂר אוֹסְרִין — *terumah* and *maaser sheni* but not to *bikkurim*: אֶת הַגֹּרֶן — *Terumah* and *maaser sheni* forbid produce that has been processed,[1] that is, once produce has been completely processed, eating it is forbidden until *terumos* and *maasros* (including *maaser sheni*) have been separated from it;[2] וְיֵשׁ לָהֶם שִׁעוּר — and they have a required amount: *terumah* is usually one-fiftieth of the crop[3] and *maaser sheni* is one-tenth; וְנוֹהֲגִים בְּכָל הַפֵּרוֹת — and they apply to all kinds of produce,[4] בִּפְנֵי הַבַּיִת וְשֶׁלֹּא בִּפְנֵי הַבַּיִת — when there is a Temple and when there is not a Temple;[5] וּבָאֲרִיסִין וּבַחֲכוֹרוֹת וּבַסִּקְרִיקוֹן וּבַגַּזְלָן — and they apply to the produce of sharecroppers, tenant-farmers, a *sikrikon*,[6] and a thief, although these people do not own the land on which the produce grew.[7] הֲרֵי אֵלּוּ בִּתְרוּמָה וּבְמַעֲשֵׂר מַה שֶּׁאֵין כֵּן בְּבִכּוּרִים — These are laws that apply to *terumah* and *maaser sheni* but not to *bikkurim*. Even processed produce may be eaten before *bikkurim* have been separated from it; *bikkurim* may consist of any amount, no matter how

--- NOTES ---

1. Literally, *the [produce of the] threshing floor*. This expression is borrowed from the law for grain, whose processing is completed on the threshing floor, where the farmer stacks the kernels of grain into a pile and then smooths down the pile [מֵרוּחַ] (see *Rav* and *Meleches Shlomo*).

2. Before produce has been fully processed, it may be eaten casually (that is, as a snack, rather than a meal). But once its processing is completed, it may not be eaten at all until its *terumos* and *maasros* have been designated (see *Maasros* 1:5).

3. The Torah does not set any minimum amount for *terumah*, but under Rabbinic law a generous person should designate one-fortieth of his crop as *terumah*, a miserly person may designate as little as one-sixtieth, while all other people designate a fiftieth (*Terumos* 4:3).

4. *Terumos* and *maasros* must be separated from grain, grapes, and olives according to Biblical law, and from all other types of edible produce according to Rabbinic law.

5. Even when the Temple is not standing, *terumos* and *maasros* have to be separated from crops that grew in Eretz Yisrael. However, *maaser sheni* may not be eaten (even in Jerusalem) when there is no Temple; instead, one redeems it with money and throws the money into the sea (*Rambam, Hilchos Maaser Sheni* 2:2).

6. See Mishnah 1:2 for the definitions of these terms.

7. Any produce that grew in Eretz Yisrael may not be eaten before its *terumos* and *maasros* have been separated, even if the land on which the produce grew is stolen.

[33] MISHNAH BIKKURIM / Chapter 2: *HaTerumah*

- רע"ב -

[ד] וְיֵשׁ בַּבִּכּוּרִים מַה שֶּׁאֵין כֵּן בַּתְּרוּמָה וּבַמַּעֲשֵׂר, שֶׁהַבִּכּוּרִים נִקְנִין בִּמְחֻבָּר לַקַּרְקַע, וְעוֹשֶׂה אָדָם כָּל שָׂדֵהוּ בִּכּוּרִים, וְחַיָּב בְּאַחֲרָיוּתָם, וּטְעוּנִים קָרְבָּן, וְשִׁיר, וּתְנוּפָה, וְלִינָה.

(ד) נקנין במחובר לקרקע. דכתיב (במדבר יח,יג) בכורי כל אשר בארצם, בשעה שהם מחוברים בארצם בכורים הם, והכי תנן לקמן (ג,א) יורד אדם לתוך שדהו וכו', קושרו בגמי ואומר הרי [אלו] בכורים: ועושה אדם כל שדהו בכורים. דכתיב (יחזקאל מד,ל) בכורי כל מראשית כל: וטעונים קרבן. נאמר בבכורים שמחת, ונאמר בכל הטוב (דברים כו,יא), ונאמר להלן (שם כז,ז) וזבחת שלמים ושמחת שם ואכלת שם ושמחת, מה להלן שלמים אף כאן שלמים: ושיר. נאמר כאן בכל הטוב, ונאמר להלן (יחזקאל לג,לב) כשיר עגבים יפה קול ומטיב נגן: ותנופה. כתיב הכא (דברים כו,ד) ולקח הכהן הטנא מידך, וכתיב התם (ויקרא ז,ל) ידיו תביאינה את אשי ה', מה כאן תנופה אף כאן תנופה: ולינה. שילין בירושלים כל לילה של אחר היום שהביא הבכורים, דכתיב (דברים טז,ז) ופנית בבקר והלכת לאהליך, הא כל פונות לא יהיו אלא בבקר:

---

small;[8] *bikkurim* are separated only from the "seven species";[9] *bikkurim* are brought only when there is a Temple;[10] and they are brought only by the person who owns the land on which they grew.[11]

[4] Like the previous Mishnah, this one also contrasts *terumah* and *maaser sheni* with *bikkurim*:

וְיֵשׁ בַּבִּכּוּרִים מַה שֶּׁאֵין כֵּן בַּתְּרוּמָה וּבַמַּעֲשֵׂר — **And there are** laws that apply to *bikkurim* but not to *terumah* and *maaser sheni*: שֶׁהַבִּכּוּרִים נִקְנִין בִּמְחֻבָּר לַקַּרְקַע — *Bikkurim* **can be designated**[1] while the produce is still **attached to the ground;**[2] וְעוֹשֶׂה אָדָם כָּל שָׂדֵהוּ בִּכּוּרִים — **and a person can designate all** the produce of **his field as** *bikkurim*, without leaving any for himself; וְחַיָּב בְּאַחֲרָיוּתָם — **and he is responsible for them,** that is, if one's *bikkurim* are lost or ruined before he brings them to the Temple, he must replace them with others;[3] וּטְעוּנִים קָרְבָּן — **and they require an offering,** that is, one who brings *bikkurim* to the Temple must bring an offering as well;[4] וְשִׁיר — **and they require song,** that is, the Leviim sing when *bikkurim* are brought into the Temple,[5] וּתְנוּפָה — **and they require waving,** that is, the owner of the *bikkurim* and a Kohen hold the *bikkurim* together and wave them in all directions;[6] וְלִינָה — **and**

NOTES

8. *Bikkurim* have no minimum amount even according to Rabbinic law (*Rav;* see *Derech Emunah, Hilchos Bikkurim* 2:17 in *Beur Halachah* ד"ה מדבריהם).

9. See Mishnah 1:3.

10. Since the Torah requires *bikkurim* to be placed before the Altar (*Devarim* 26:4), they are not brought except when the Temple is standing (*Rav*).

11. See Mishnah 1:2.

[4]

1. Literally, *acquired;* that is, the fruits acquire the sanctity of *bikkurim* (*Mahari Korkos, Hilchos Bikkurim* 2:19).

2. As taught below (Mishnah 3:1), the ideal procedure is that when a farmer sees fruits beginning to ripen on a tree (or the ground) he designates them as *bikkurim* (*Rav*).

3. See Mishnah 1:8-9.

4. He must bring a *shelamim* offering before leaving Jerusalem (*Rashi, Menachos* 58a ד"ה לעטר). However, if he does not bring this offering, he has still fulfilled the mitzvah of *bikkurim* (*Rambam, Hilchos Bikkurim* 3:12).

5. See Mishnah 3:4.

6. They move the basket containing the

משניות ביכורים / פרק ב: התרומה [34]

ב/ה

[ה] **תְּרוּמַת** מַעֲשֵׂר שָׁוָה לַבִּכּוּרִים בִּשְׁתֵּי דְרָכִים, וְלַתְּרוּמָה בִּשְׁתֵּי דְרָכִים: נִטֶּלֶת מִן הַטָּהוֹר עַל הַטָּמֵא, וְשֶׁלֹּא מִן הַמֻּקָּף,

- רע"ב -

(ה) נטלת מן הטהור על הטמא. דהא דאין תרומה נטלת מן הטהור על הטמא, היינו טעמא משום דבעינן מוקף, וחיישינן דלמא לא מקיף, דמסתפי דלמא נגע הטהור בטמא, והאי טעמא ליכא למימר הכא, דהא נתרמת שלא מן המוקף:

---

they require **staying overnight**, that is, when someone brings *bikkurim* to the Temple, he may not leave Jerusalem before the morning, but must spend that night in the city.[7] These laws do not apply to *terumah* or *maaser sheni*, for *terumah* and *maaser sheni* can be separated only from produce that has been picked; one cannot make his whole crop into *terumah* or *maaser sheni*, but must leave some as regular produce;[8] and if *terumah* or *maaser sheni* is lost or ruined, it need not be replaced. The remaining laws (offering, song, waving, staying in Jerusalem overnight), which are related to the Temple and its offerings, also have no relevance to *terumah* and *maaser sheni*.

[5] This Mishnah deals with *terumas maaser*, which has not been mentioned so far in this chapter. When *maaser rishon* is separated from produce and given to a Levi, the Levi separates a tenth of it and gives that tenth to a Kohen. This portion is called *terumas maaser* (*the terumah of maaser*). The Mishnah compares *terumas maaser* to *bikkurim* and *terumah*:

תְּרוּמַת מַעֲשֵׂר שָׁוָה לַבִּכּוּרִים בִּשְׁתֵּי דְרָכִים — *Terumas maaser* is similar to *bikkurim* in two ways, וְלַתְּרוּמָה בִּשְׁתֵּי דְרָכִים — and similar to *terumah* in two ways: נִטֶּלֶת מִן הַטָּהוֹר עַל הַטָּמֵא — [*Terumas maaser*] may be separated from *tahor* produce on behalf of *tamei* produce,[1] וְשֶׁלֹּא מִן הַמֻּקָּף — and it may be separated from produce that is not near the produce for which it

--- NOTES ---

bikkurim in each of the four directions of the compass, and up and down (*Menachos* 62a with *Rashi*). See Mishnah 3:6.

7. In fact, the requirement of לִינָה, *staying overnight*, applies whenever someone brings an offering to the Temple (see *Tos. Yom Tov*).

8. Furthermore, *maaser sheni* cannot be more than a tenth of the crop (see *Menachos* 54b).

[5]

1. If someone has both *tamei* and *tahor* produce, he is forbidden to separate *terumah* from the *tahor* produce for the sake of the *tamei* produce (even though *tahor* produce is superior to *tamei* produce). This is because of the "law of proximity" [מִן הַמֻּקָּף], which states that when *terumah* is designated, it must be touching or near the produce for which it is being designated (see *Rav, Challah* 2:4 ד"ה הסל מצרפן). The Sages were concerned that someone who separates *terumah* from *tahor* produce for the sake of *tamei* produce might be afraid to put the piles of produce near each other for fear that the *tamei* produce will touch the *tahor* produce, thus making it *tamei*. Accordingly, the Sages decreed that *terumah* may never be separated from *tahor* produce on behalf of *tamei* produce. However, this Rabbinic decree is relevant only to *terumah*, and not to *terumas maaser*, because the "law of proximity" applies only to *terumah*, as the Mishnah teaches next. It is thus permitted to separate *terumas maaser* from *maaser rishon* that is *tahor* for the sake of *maaser rishon* that is *tamei* (*Rav*).

[35] **MISHNAH BIKKURIM** / Chapter 2: *HaTerumah*

- רע"ב -

וְיֵשׁ לָהּ שִׁעוּר כִּתְרוּמָה.
שֶׁהַתְּרוּמָה נָתְנוּ בָּהּ חֲכָמִים
שִׁיעוּר, חֲדָא מִמְּאָה:

כְּבִכּוּרִים. וְאוֹסֶרֶת אֶת הַגֹּרֶן, וְיֵשׁ לָהּ שִׁעוּר,
כִּתְרוּמָה.

is being separated;[2] **כְּבִכּוּרִים** — in these two ways, *terumas maaser* is **like bikkurim**.[3] **וְאוֹסֶרֶת אֶת הַגֹּרֶן** — However, [*terumas maaser*] **forbids produce that has been processed**; that is, once produce is processed, eating it is forbidden until *terumas maaser* has been designated,[4] **וְיֵשׁ לָהּ שִׁעוּר** — **and it has a specific amount** (one-tenth),[5] **כִּתְרוּמָה** — in these two ways, *terumas maaser* is **like terumah**.[6]

[6] Like the first half of this chapter, the second half also compares and contrasts one item with another. However, none of these comparisons involve *bikkurim*. This Mishnah deals with laws of an *esrog*. For halachic purposes, it is necessary to identify the year to which certain produce belongs (for example, if produce started growing in the second year of the *Shemittah* cycle but is picked in the third year, we need to determine whether it is second-year produce, from which *maaser sheni* must be separated, or third-year produce, from which *maasar ani* must be separated). In general, the determining factor for *fruit* is when they start to grow,[1] but the determining factor for *vegetables* is when they are picked. [Thus, for example, if fruit and vegetables began to grow in the second year, but were picked in the third year, the fruit would be attributed to the second year, but the vegetables would be attributed to the third year.] The *esrog* is a special case. The Mishnah teaches that in some respects the year of an *esrog* is determined by when it starts to grow (like fruit) and in some respects the year is determined by when it is picked (like vegetables):[2]

――――――― NOTES ―――――――

2. See previous note.
3. The "law of proximity" does not apply to *bikkurim,* as is clear from the fact that the fruit of one tree can be designated as *bikkurim* on behalf of the fruit of other trees, even though the two groups of fruit are not next to each other. And since *bikkurim* are not subject to "the law of proximity," there is no reason to forbid designating *tahor* produce as *bikkurim* for the sake of *tamei* produce (*Mishnah Rishonah;* see note 1).
4. Once a farmer has finished processing his produce, it may not be eaten (even as a snack) until he designates its *terumah, maaser rishon,* and *maaser sheni/ani*. Although the remaining produce is now permitted to be eaten, the *maaser rishon* itself is forbidden, because it contains *terumas maaser*. Even after being given to a Levi, the *maaser rishon* remains forbidden until he separates *terumas maaser* from it.
5. *Terumas maaser* must be one-tenth of the *maaser rishon.*

6. Processed produce may not be eaten at all until *terumah* (and the other required portions) have been separated from it. *Terumah* must be a specific amount, usually, one-fiftieth of the crop (see Mishnah 3 note 3).
Bikkurim are different in both respects. Processed produce may be eaten before *bikkurim* have been separated from it (provided that the other portions have already been separated). Also, *bikkurim* can be any amount.

[6]

1. The *esrog* is basically a fruit because it grows on a tree. However, unlike other trees, the *esrog* tree cannot survive on rainwater alone, but requires water from other sources. In this sense, the *esrog* is like vegetables, which also require additional water (*Rashi* to *Succah* 39b ד"ה אתרוג; see *Tos. Yom Tov*).
2. This is the stage known as חֲנָטָה, when the blossom falls off and the fruit begins to emerge in its place (*Rashi, Bamidbar* 17:23).

[ו] אֶתְרוֹג שָׁוֶה לְאִילָן בִּשְׁלֹשָׁה דְרָכִים, וְלַיָּרָק בְּדֶרֶךְ אֶחָד: שָׁוֶה לְאִילָן בְּעָרְלָה וּבִרְבָעִי, וּבַשְּׁבִיעִית. וְלַיָּרָק בְּדֶרֶךְ אֶחָד, שֶׁבִּשְׁעַת לְקִיטָתוֹ עִשּׂוּרוֹ, דִּבְרֵי רַבָּן גַּמְלִיאֵל. רַבִּי אֱלִיעֶזֶר אוֹמֵר, שָׁוֶה לְאִילָן בְּכָל דָּבָר.

— רע"ב —

(ו) שוה לאילן. דאזלינן בתר חנטה, ומונין לו שלש לערלה משעת חנטה, וכן לרבעי, וכן לשביעית, דאם נחנט בששית ונגמר בשביעית מותר, ומכל מקום פטור מִמַּעֲשֵׂר, דְּלֵתְנִין מְעַשֵּׂר חוֹזְלִין בָּתַר לְקִיטָה כְּדִין יָרָק, וְכֵיוָן דְּנִלְקַט בַּשְּׁבִיעִית פָּטוּר מִמַּעֲשֵׂר:

אֶתְרוֹג שָׁוֶה לְאִילָן בִּשְׁלֹשָׁה דְרָכִים — An *esrog* is like the fruit of **a tree in three ways,** **וְלַיָּרָק בְּדֶרֶךְ אֶחָד** — and it is like **vegetables in one way.** **שָׁוֶה לְאִילָן בְּעָרְלָה** — It is like the fruit of **a tree with respect to** the prohibition of *orlah* (which states that the fruit of a tree's first three years may not be eaten or used for any other benefit). Thus, if an *esrog* starts to grow during a tree's first three years, it is subject to the prohibition of *orlah* even if it is picked in the fourth year, because regarding *orlah* we follow the year of the *esrog*'s growth (as is the case with fruit), and not the year in which it is picked (as is the case with vegetables). **וּבִרְבָעִי** — Similarly, an *esrog* is like the fruit of a tree **with respect to** the law of *reva'i* (which states that the fruit of a tree's fourth year must be eaten in Jerusalem). Thus, if an *esrog* starts to grow during a tree's fourth year, it must be eaten in Jerusalem even if it is picked in the fifth year, because regarding *reva'i* we follow the year of the *esrog*'s growth (like fruit), and not the year in which it is picked (like vegetables). **וּבַשְּׁבִיעִית** — Similarly, it is like the fruit of a tree **with respect to** the laws of **Shemittah** (for example, the requirement to leave *Shemittah* produce free for anyone to take, and the prohibitions against destroying *Shemittah* produce or using it for business purposes). Thus, if an *esrog* starts to grow during the sixth year of the *Shemittah* cycle, it is treated as ordinary (non-*Shemittah*) produce even if it is picked during *Shemittah*, because regarding *Shemittah* we follow the year of the *esrog*'s growth (like fruit), and not the year in which it is picked (like vegetables). **וְלַיָּרָק בְּדֶרֶךְ אֶחָד** — However, it is like **vegetables in one way,** **שֶׁבִּשְׁעַת לְקִיטָתוֹ עִשּׂוּרוֹ** — because with respect to its tithing (i.e., separating *terumos* and *maasros*), we go by **when it is picked;** thus, for example, if an *esrog* starts to grow in the second year of the seven-year *Shemittah* cycle but is picked in the third year, it is attributed to the third year, when *maasar ani* must be separated, rather than to the second year, when *maaser sheni* is separated, because regarding tithes we go by the year in which the *esrog* is picked (like vegetables), and not the year in which it starts to grow (like fruit).[3] **דִּבְרֵי רַבָּן גַּמְלִיאֵל** — These are the words of Rabban Gamliel. **רַבִּי אֱלִיעֶזֶר אוֹמֵר** — But R' Eliezer says: **שָׁוֶה לְאִילָן בְּכָל דָּבָר** — [An *esrog* tree] is similar to the fruit of **a tree in every respect,** even *terumos* and *maasros*. Therefore, an *esrog* that started to grow in the second year but was picked in the third year is attributed to the second year, and must have *maaser sheni* separated from it.

NOTES

3. *Rambam Commentary.*

[37] **MISHNAH BIKKURIM** / Chapter 2: *HaTerumah* 2/7-8

– רע"ב –

[ז] **דָּם** מְהַלְכֵי שְׁתַּיִם שָׁוֶה לְדַם בְּהֵמָה לְהַכְשִׁיר אֶת הַזְּרָעִים, וְדַם הַשֶּׁרֶץ אֵין חַיָּבִין עָלָיו.

[ח] **כּוֹי,** יֵשׁ בּוֹ דְרָכִים שָׁוֶה לְחַיָּה,

(ז) דם מהלכי שתים. היינו דם האדם, כמו דם חללין: להכשיר. [את] הזרעים לקבל טומאה, כמו דם בהמה, דכתיב ביה (דברים יב,כד) על הארץ תשפכנו כמים: ודם השרץ. כלומר ושוה דם מהלכי שתים לדם השרץ, שאין חייבין עליו משום דם. ודוקא כשהתרו בו משום דם אין חייבין על דם השרץ, אבל אם התרו בו משום שרץ, לוקה, שדם השרץ כבשרו הוא: (ח) כוי. נחלקו בו חכמי ישראל, יש אומרים שהוא חיל הבר, ויש אומרים שהוא תיש הבא על הצביה, ויש אומרים בריה בפני עצמה היא ולא הכריעו בה חכמים אם חיה היא אם בהמה:

---

[7] This Mishnah compares the laws of human blood to the laws of animal blood:

דַּם מְהַלְכֵי שְׁתַּיִם — **The blood of those who walk on two** feet, i.e., **people,**[1] **שָׁוֶה לְדַם בְּהֵמָה לְהַכְשִׁיר אֶת הַזְּרָעִים** — **is similar to animal blood in regard to making seeds** (i.e., food) **fit to become** *tamei.* The rule is that food cannot become *tamei* unless it first touched one of the "seven liquids," which include blood.[2] Thus, if food touched animal blood or human blood and later it came into contact with a source of *tumah,* it becomes *tamei.* **וְדַם הַשֶּׁרֶץ אֵין חַיָּבִין עָלָיו** — **However, human blood is similar to the blood of a** *sheretz*[3] in that **one is not liable** to the punishment of *kares* for eating it.[4] In this respect, human blood is different from animal blood, because one who eats animal blood *is* liable to *kares.*

[8] The Torah divides large animals into two groups: *beheimah* (domestic animals, i.e., species that are commonly raised by people, such as sheep, goats, cattle), and *chayah* (wild animals, i.e., species that are not commonly raised but are found in the wild, such as deer and gazelles). The following Mishnahs deal with an animal known as a *koy,* whose classification is unknown:[1]

כּוֹי יֵשׁ בּוֹ דְרָכִים שָׁוֶה לְחַיָּה — **A** *koy* **has ways** in which it is **like a** *chayah* (as

---
NOTES

[7]

1. For example, blood from a human corpse (*Rav*).
   The Mishnah uses the unusual expression "those who walk on two" instead of "people," to teach that even the blood of a living person — who can walk on two feet — is subject to the same law (*Mishnah Rishonah;* see *Machshirin* 6:5).
2. The seven liquids are listed in *Machshirin* 6:4.
3. This refers to the eight crawling animals that transmit *tumah* when dead. They are listed in *Vayikra* 11:29-30.
4. The Torah's prohibition against eating or drinking blood does not include the blood of a *sheretz* (see *Kereisos* 20b-21a) or the blood of humans (see *Rav, Rambam Commentary*). It is nevertheless forbidden to eat or drink human blood (*Kesubos* 60a).
   Consuming blood of a *sheretz* is also forbidden, as it is no different than consuming the flesh of a *sheretz;* however, the penalty is *malkus,* not *kares* (see *Rav*).

[8]

1. A *koy* is a cross between a goat (*beheimah*) and a deer (*chayah*), or it is an independent species that bears similarities to both goats and deer (*Rav,* from *Chullin* 8a; see *Mishnah Rishonah*).

משניות ביכורים / פרק ב: התרומה

וְיֵשׁ בּוֹ דְרָכִים שָׁוֶה לִבְהֵמָה, וְיֵשׁ בּוֹ דְרָכִים שָׁוֶה לִבְהֵמָה וְלַחַיָּה, וְיֵשׁ בּוֹ דְרָכִים שֶׁאֵינוֹ שָׁוֶה לֹא לִבְהֵמָה וְלֹא לְחַיָּה.

[ט] **כֵּיצַד** שָׁוֶה לְחַיָּה? דָּמוֹ טָעוּן כִּסּוּי כְּדַם חַיָּה, וְאֵין שׁוֹחֲטִין אוֹתוֹ בְּיוֹם טוֹב, וְאִם שְׁחָטוֹ, אֵין מְכַסִּין אֶת דָּמוֹ, וְחֶלְבּוֹ מְטַמֵּא בְּטֻמְאַת נְבֵלָה כְּחַיָּה,

(ויקרא ז,כד). ומשום דספק בהמה הוא וחלבו טהור, ספק חיה טמא, לפיכך טומאתו ספק:

— רע״ב —

(ט) טעון כיסוי כדם חיה. לחומרא. ואין מברכין על כסויו, כיון דספק הוא: ואין שוחטין אותו ביום טוב. לפי שאסור לכסות את דמו. ואף על גב דאפר כירה מוכן הוא, מוכן לגדי ואינו מוכן לספק: בטומאת נבילה בחיה. דחלב בהמה טהורה טהור הוא, כדילפינן (פסחים כג,א) מן וחלב נבלה וחלב טרפה יעשה לכל מלאכה

---

taught in the next Mishnah), וְיֵשׁ בּוֹ דְרָכִים שָׁוֶה לִבְהֵמָה — and it has ways in which it is **like a** *beheimah* (as taught in Mishnah 10), וְיֵשׁ בּוֹ דְרָכִים שָׁוֶה לִבְהֵמָה וְלַחַיָּה — **and it has ways** in which it is **like** both **a** *beheimah* **and a** *chayah* (as taught in Mishnah 11), וְיֵשׁ בּוֹ דְרָכִים שֶׁאֵינוֹ שָׁוֶה לֹא לִבְהֵמָה וְלֹא לְחַיָּה — **and it has ways** in which **it is not like a** *beheimah* **or a** *chayah* (as taught in Mishnah 11).

[9] כֵּיצַד שָׁוֶה לְחַיָּה — **How is [a** *koy***] like a** *chayah*? דָּמוֹ טָעוּן כִּסּוּי כְּדַם חַיָּה — **If a** *koy* is slaughtered, **its blood must be covered** with earth, **just like the blood of a** slaughtered *chayah* must be covered with earth.[1] וְאֵין שׁוֹחֲטִין אוֹתוֹ בְּיוֹם טוֹב — **One may not slaughter [a** *koy***] on Yom Tov,** וְאִם שְׁחָטוֹ אֵין מְכַסִּין אֶת דָּמוֹ — **and if one did slaughter it** on Yom Tov, **one may not cover its blood.**[2] וְחֶלְבּוֹ מְטַמֵּא בְּטֻמְאַת נְבֵלָה כְּחַיָּה — **And the**

--- NOTES ---

[9]
1. When someone slaughters a kosher *chayah* or bird, he is obligated to cover its blood with earth or similar substance (*Vayikra* 17:13). This mitzvah applies only to *chayos* and birds, and not to *beheimos*. Since a *koy* might be a *chayah*, its blood must be covered out of doubt. This is an application of the general rule: סָפֵק דְּאוֹרַיְיתָא לְחוּמְרָא, *A doubt in a case of Biblical law is decided strictly* (Rav). Many of the laws taught in this and the following two Mishnahs are based on this rule.

However, because the obligation to cover the *koy's* blood is based only on a doubt, the blessing for the mitzvah is not recited (*Rav*). [Reciting a blessing for no purpose is a transgression; thus, it is forbidden to recite blessings in cases of doubt.]

2. Although slaughtering an animal is a *melachah* (an act forbidden on Shabbos and Yom Tov), one may slaughter an animal for food on Yom Tov, because all manner of food preparation is permitted on Yom Tov. However, if someone slaughters a *chayah* or bird on Yom Tov and thereby becomes obligated to cover its blood, he may not use earth for that purpose, because moving earth is forbidden under the laws of *muktzeh*. It is permitted, though, to cover the blood with ash taken from one's oven (see *Rashi* to *Beitzah* 8a ד״ה מותר). This ash is not *muktzeh*, because it was presumably designated by the owner before Yom Tov for this very purpose of covering the blood of a slaughtered animal. Nevertheless, the ash may not be used for a *koy*, because it is assumed that the owner designated it only for a regular *chayah*, whose blood definitely needs to be covered, and not for a *koy*, whose blood needs to be covered only out of

[39] **MISHNAH BIKKURIM** / Chapter 2: *HaTerumah*

וְטֻמְאָתוֹ בְּסָפֵק, וְאֵין פּוֹדִין בּוֹ פֶּטֶר חֲמוֹר.

[י] **כֵּיצַד** שָׁוֶה לִבְהֵמָה? חֶלְבּוֹ אָסוּר כְּחֵלֶב בְּהֵמָה, וְאֵין חַיָּבִין עָלָיו כָּרֵת,

— רע״ב —

ואין פודין בו פטר חמור. שמא חיה הוא, ורחמנא אמר (שמות לד,ד) ופטר חמור תפדה בשה, והוי ספק שה ספק לבי:
(י) חלבו אסור כחלב בהמה. כחלב שור וכשב ועז: ואין חייבין עליו כרת. להביא חטאת על שגגתו, והוא הדין שאין לוקין עליו:

---

fat[3] of [a dead *koy*] transmits the *tumah* of *neveilah*, just like the fat of a dead *chayah* transmits the *tumah* of *neveilah*; וְטֻמְאָתוֹ בְּסָפֵק — but its *tumah* (i.e., the *tumah* of a dead *koy's* fat) is based on doubt, because a *koy* might be a *beheimah*, whose fat is not *tamei*.[4] וְאֵין פּוֹדִין בּוֹ פֶּטֶר חֲמוֹר — And one may not redeem a firstborn donkey with [a *koy*], because a firstborn donkey can be redeemed only with a sheep or goat, and a *koy* might be a *chayah*, rather than a sheep or goat.[5]

[10] חֶלְבּוֹ אָסוּר כְּחֵלֶב — כֵּיצַד שָׁוֶה לִבְהֵמָה — How is [a *koy*] like a *beheimah*? בְּהֵמָה — Its fat is forbidden to be eaten, like the fat of a *beheimah*,[1] וְאֵין חַיָּבִין עָלָיו כָּרֵת — but one who eats the fat of a *koy* is not liable to be

---

NOTES

doubt (see previous note). The Mishnah therefore teaches that a *koy* should not be slaughtered on Yom Tov, because one will be unable to fulfill the obligation of covering its blood. Furthermore, even if someone transgressed the law and slaughtered a *koy* on Yom Tov, its blood must be left uncovered (*Rav*).

This law does not show how a *koy* is similar to a *chayah*. To the contrary, it teaches that they are different, because slaughtering a regular *chayah* on Yom Tov is permitted, whereas slaughtering a *koy* on Yom Tov is forbidden. The Mishnah includes this point to clarify that although a *koy* is like a *chayah* in that its blood must be covered, it is different from a *chayah* in that it may not be slaughtered on Yom Tov (*Tos. Yom Tov*).

3. The term "fat" (*cheilev*) refers specifically to the layer of hard fat that surrounds the stomachs, the loins, and kidneys.

4. A *neveilah* is a dead animal (other than a kosher animal that was slaughtered through *shechitah*). A *neveilah* is a source of *tumah*, but there is a difference in this regard between the *neveilah* of a kosher *beheimah* and the *neveilah* of a kosher *chayah*. In the case of a kosher *beheimah* that died, although most of its body transmits *tumah*, its fat is not *tamei* at all (see *Pesachim* 23b). However, with regard to a kosher *chayah*, the entire body — including the fat — transmits *tumah*. The fat of a *koy* transmits *tumah*, like the fat of a *chayah*, since a *koy* might be a *chayah*. Nevertheless, its *tumah* is not certain, given the possibility that a *koy* is a *beheimah*, whose fat is not *tamei* (*Rav*).

5. The Torah commands the owner of a firstborn male child of a donkey to redeem it by giving a sheep or goat to a Kohen. Even if a *koy* is a cross between a sheep and a deer (see Mishnah 8 note 1), it may not be used for this purpose, because it might belong to the halachic category of a deer (*Rav*; see *Tosefos Anshei Shem*).

[10]

1. The term "fat" (*cheilev*) is defined in note 3 on the previous Mishnah.

The Torah prohibits eating the *cheilev* of cattle, sheep, and goats, which fall under the category of *beheimah* (*Vayikra* 7:23). It is thus forbidden to eat the *cheilev* of a *koy* out of concern that it might be a goat (*Rambam Commentary*).

משניות ביכורים / פרק ב: התרומה [40]

וְאֵינוֹ נִלְקָח בְּכֶסֶף מַעֲשֵׂר לֵאָכֵל בִּירוּשָׁלַיִם, וְחַיָּב בַּזְּרוֹעַ וּלְחָיַיִם וְקֵבָה; רַבִּי אֱלִיעֶזֶר פּוֹטֵר, שֶׁהַמּוֹצִיא מֵחֲבֵרוֹ עָלָיו הָרְאָיָה.

- רע"ב -

וְאֵינוֹ נִלְקָח בְּכֶסֶף מַעֲשֵׂר לְאָכְלוֹ בִּירוּשָׁלַיִם. דְּשֶׁמָּא בְּהֵמָה הוּא, וְאֵין לוֹקְחִין בְּהֵמָה לִבְשַׂר תַּאֲוָה מִכֶּסֶף מַעֲשֵׂר [שֶׁלֹּא] לְהַקְרִיבָהּ

שְׁלָמִים: **וְחַיָּב בַּזְּרוֹעַ וּבַלְּחָיַיִם וּבַקֵּבָה.** דְּמַרְבִּינַן לְהוּ מִקְּרָא דִּכְתִיב (דברים יח,ג) אִם שֶׂה, לְרַבּוֹת אֶת הַכּוֹי: **שֶׁהַמּוֹצִיא מֵחֲבֵירוֹ עָלָיו הָרְאָיָה.** דְּאָמַר לֵיהּ בַּעַל הַבְּהֵמָה לַכֹּהֵן, אַיְיתִי רְאָיָה דְּמִין בְּהֵמָה הוּא וְשָׁקוֹל. וַהֲלָכָה כְּרַבִּי אֱלִיעֶזֶר:

וְאֵינוֹ נִלְקָח בְּכֶסֶף מַעֲשֵׂר לֵאָכֵל בִּירוּשָׁלַיִם — And punished with *kares* for it.[2] [a *koy*] may not be bought with *maaser sheni* money in order to be eaten in Jerusalem, just as a *beheimah* may not be bought with *maaser sheni* money in order to be eaten in Jerusalem (except as an offering).[3] וְחַיָּב בַּזְּרוֹעַ וּלְחָיַיִם וְקֵבָה — And [a *koy*] is subject to the law of giving **the foreleg, the cheeks, and the abomasum** (i.e., the fourth stomach) to a Kohen, as is the case with a *beheimah*.[4] רַבִּי אֱלִיעֶזֶר פּוֹטֵר — However, **R' Eliezer says** that one is **not obligated** to give these parts of a *koy* to a Kohen, שֶׁהַמּוֹצִיא מֵחֲבֵרוֹ עָלָיו הָרְאָיָה — because in monetary disputes the rule is that **the burden of proof rests on the person who wants to take property from another.** In this case, it is the Kohen who wants to take these parts from the owner of the animal.

─────────────── NOTES ───────────────

2. Someone who knowingly committed the sin of eating *cheilev* is punished by Heaven with *kares*. If he was seen by two witnesses and he was warned by them (or others) that eating *cheilev* is forbidden by the Torah, the court punishes him with *malkus*. If someone eats *cheilev* by mistake (i.e., he did not know that it was *cheilev* or he did not know the severity of the transgression), he must bring a *chatas* offering to atone for what he did. None of these punishments apply to someone who ate the *cheilev* of a *koy*, because a *koy* is possibly a *chayah*, whose *cheilev* is permitted (*Rav*).

3. If someone transfers sanctity from *maaser sheni* produce to money, he must use that money to buy food in Jerusalem and eat the food there. The Sages decreed, however, that one may not use *maaser sheni* money to buy an animal, unless he brings the animal as a *shelamim* offering (whose meat is eaten by the owner and his guests). The intent of this decree was to encourage people to spend their *maaser sheni* money on offerings (see *Maaser Sheni* 1:4). Therefore, the decree applies only to *beheimos* (specifically, cattle, sheep, and goats), which can be brought as offerings, and not to *chayos*, which are unfit to be offerings. One is thus forbidden to buy a *beheimah* with *maaser* (unless he will bring it as an offering) but permitted to buy a *chayah*. The Mishnah teaches that it is forbidden to buy a *koy* with *maaser*, since a *koy* might be a *beheimah* (*Rav*).

In fact, a *koy* is treated more strictly than a regular *beheimah* in this regard. As mentioned, one is allowed (and even encouraged) to buy a *beheimah* with *maaser sheni* money for the purpose of bringing it as an offering. A *koy*, however, cannot be brought as an offering, because it might be a *chayah*, and *chayos* are unfit to be offerings. It emerges that one may not buy a *koy* with *maaser sheni* money for any purpose. One may not buy a *koy* to eat as ordinary meat, because it might be a *beheimah* (which may not be purchased for the sake of ordinary consumption), nor may he buy it to bring as an offering, because a *koy* might be a *chayah* (which is unfit to be an offering) (*Rambam Commentary*).

4. The Torah obligates the owner of a slaughtered kosher *beheimah* to give its right foreleg, its cheeks with the tongue, and its abomasum (i.e., fourth stomach) to a Kohen (*Devarim* 18:3).

[41] **MISHNAH BIKKURIM** / Chapter 2: *HaTerumah*

— רע״ב —

(יא) לֹא כָּתַב לוֹ אֶת הַכּוֹי. אַף עַל פִּי שֶׁכָּתַב לוֹ שְׁנֵיהֶם, לֹא הָיָה דַעְתּוֹ אֶלָּא עַל וַדַּאי בְּהֵמָה אוֹ וַדַּאי חַיָּה. וְרַמְבַּ״ם פֵּירֵשׁ, שֶׁאִם כָּתַב לוֹ בְּהֶמְתּוֹ לְבַד, לֹא קָנָה אֶת הַכּוֹי, דְּאָמְרִינַן לֵיהּ, חַיָּה רָאֵיתִי דִבְהֵמָה הוּא, וְאִם כָּתַב לוֹ חַיָּתוֹ לְבַד, אָמְרִינַן לֵיהּ, בְּהֵמָה רָאִיתִי דְחַיָּה הוּא.

[יא] **בֵּיצַד** אֵינוֹ שָׁוֶה לֹא לְחַיָּה וְלֹא לִבְהֵמָה? אָסוּר מִשּׁוּם כִּלְאַיִם עִם הַחַיָּה וְעִם הַבְּהֵמָה. הַכּוֹתֵב חַיָּתוֹ וּבְהֶמְתּוֹ לִבְנוֹ, לֹא כָתַב לוֹ אֶת הַכּוֹי. אִם אָמַר הֲרֵינִי נָזִיר שֶׁזֶּה חַיָּה אוֹ בְהֵמָה, הֲרֵי הוּא נָזִיר. וּשְׁאָר כָּל דְּרָכָיו שָׁוִים לַחַיָּה וְלַבְּהֵמָה,

נראה מדבריו, שאם כתב לו שניהן, קנה ממה נפשך: אם אמר הריני נזיר שזה חיה או בהמה. בין שאמר הריני נזיר שזה חיה, בין שאמר הריני נזיר שזה בהמה, הרי זה נזיר, דספק איסורא לחומרא. ואפילו אמר הריני נזיר שזה חיה ובהמה, או שזה אינו לא חיה ולא בהמה, הרי זה נזיר מספק:

Therefore, in order to receive them, the Kohen must prove that a *koy* is a *beheimah*, which he cannot do.[5]

[11] **בֵּיצַד אֵינוֹ שָׁוֶה לֹא לְחַיָּה וְלֹא לִבְהֵמָה** — **How is [a** *koy*] not like a *chayah* or a *beheimah*? **אָסוּר מִשּׁוּם כִּלְאַיִם עִם הַחַיָּה וְעִם הַבְּהֵמָה** — **It is forbidden,** due to the law of *kilayim*, to mate a *koy* with a *chayah* or with a *beheimah*.[1] **הַכּוֹתֵב חַיָּתוֹ וּבְהֶמְתּוֹ לִבְנוֹ** — **If someone writes** a document giving **"his** *chayah* and his *beheimah*" to his son as a gift, and he owns a *koy*, **לֹא כָתַב לוֹ אֶת הַכּוֹי** — he did not assign the *koy* to [the son], because we assume that he meant to include only animals that are definitely *chayos* or definitely *beheimos*, as opposed to a *koy*, whose status is uncertain.[2] **שֶׁזֶּה חַיָּה אוֹ בְהֵמָה** — **If someone saw a** *koy* and said, **"I am a** *nazir*[3] **if this is a** *chayah*," or he says, "I am a *nazir* if this is **a** *beheimah*," **הֲרֵי הוּא נָזִיר** — he **becomes a** *nazir* out of doubt, because either statement might be true.[4] **וּשְׁאָר כָּל דְּרָכָיו שָׁוִים לַחַיָּה וְלַבְּהֵמָה** — **And in all other matters,** the laws of a

---

NOTES

5. The first Tanna, on the other hand, learns from a verse in the Torah that these parts must be given to a Kohen even in the case of a *koy* (see *Rav*).

[11]

1. A *koy* may not be mated with a *chayah*, because it might be a *beheimah*, which is forbidden to be crossbred with a *chayah*. It may also not be mated with a *beheimah*, because it might be a *chayah* (*Rashi, Kiddushin* 3a ד״ה שאינו שוה).

2. This law applies regardless of who gave the gift and who received it. The Mishnah specifies a father and son in order to teach that although fathers are usually generous toward their children, it is assumed that even in this case the *koy* was excluded (*Tiferes Yisrael*).

3. Someone who declares himself a *nazir* is prohibited to cut his hair, drink wine (or consume any part of a grape), or become *tamei* from a corpse (see *Bamidbar* 6:1-6).

4. Furthermore, even if he said, "I am a *nazir* on condition that this is both a *chayah* and a *beheimah*," he becomes a *nazir* out of doubt [because a *koy* is both a *chayah* and a *beheimah* in the sense that it is subject to the stringencies of both groups of animals, as we have learned in the previous Mishnah]. If someone said, "I am a *nazir* on condition that this is neither a *chayah* nor a *beheimah*," he also becomes a *nazir* out of doubt [because a *koy* could be in a category of its own] (*Rav;* see *Nazir* 5:7). [The last case mentioned by *Rav* illustrates the Mishnah's opening question, "How is (a *koy*) not like a *chayah* or a *beheimah*?" See *Tos. Yom Tov.*]

ב/יא

וְטָעוּן שְׁחִיטָה כָּזֶה וְכָזֶה, וּמְטַמֵּא מִשּׁוּם נְבֵלָה וּמִשּׁוּם אֵבֶר מִן הַחַי כָּזֶה וְכָזֶה.

koy **are similar to** those of *chayos* **and** those of *beheimos,* that is, the laws applicable to both *chayos* and *beheimos* apply to the *koy* as well; וְטָעוּן שְׁחִיטָה כָּזֶה וְכָזֶה — for example, **[a** *koy*] **requires slaughtering** before it may be eaten, **like [a** *chayah*] **and like [a** *beheimah*]; וּמְטַמֵּא מִשּׁוּם נְבֵלָה — **and it transmits** *tumah* **as a** *neveilah,* that is, if a *koy* dies without being slaughtered, it transmits the *tumah* of *neveilah;* וּמִשּׁוּם אֵבֶר מִן הַחַי — **and it transmits** *tumah* **as a limb taken from a living animal,** that is, if a limb is removed from a living *koy,* the limb transmits *tumah,* כָּזֶה וְכָזֶה — **just like [a** *chayah*] **and [a** *beheimah*] transmit *tumah* when they are dead or by means of a limb that was removed when it was alive.[5]

NOTES

5. The Mishnah does not attempt to list all the ways in which a *koy* is like both a *beheimah* and a *chayah.* There are many others. For example, one may not consume the blood of a *koy,* or the meat of a *koy* that has one of certain fatal defects (*tereifah*), or a limb that was removed from a *koy* when it was alive [all of which are forbidden by the Torah in regard to both *beheimos* and *chayos*] (*Tiferes Yisrael*).

Chapter Three

משניות ביכורים / פרק ג: כיצד

[א] כֵּיצַד מַפְרִישִׁין הַבִּכּוּרִים? יוֹרֵד אָדָם בְּתוֹךְ שָׂדֵהוּ וְרוֹאֶה תְאֵנָה שֶׁבִּכְּרָה, אֶשְׁכּוֹל שֶׁבִּכֵּר, רִמּוֹן שֶׁבִּכֵּר, קוֹשְׁרוֹ בְגֶמִי, וְאוֹמֵר: "הֲרֵי אֵלּוּ בִכּוּרִים." וְרַבִּי שִׁמְעוֹן אוֹמֵר: אַף עַל פִּי כֵן חוֹזֵר וְקוֹרֵא אוֹתָם בִּכּוּרִים מֵאַחַר שֶׁיִּתָּלְשׁוּ מִן הַקַּרְקַע.

— רע״ב —

פרק שלישי — כיצד. (א) כיצד מפרישין. שבכרה. ואפילו לא נגמר הפרי, דכתיב (דברים כו,י) הנה הבאתי את ראשית פרי, בשעת הבאה הוא פרי, אבל בשעת הפרשה אין צריך שיהיה פרי, אלא

אֲפִלּוּ בּוֹסֶר וַאֲפִלּוּ פַגִּין: הרי אלו בכורים. וְאֵין צָרִיךְ לִקְרוֹת עוֹד שֵׁם אַחַר לְקִיטָתָן: רבי שמעון אומר אף על פי כן חוזר וקורא שם. דְדָרִישׁ (שם פסוק ב) וּלְקַחְתָּ מֵרֵאשִׁית כָּל פְּרִי הָאֲדָמָה, מַה בִּשְׁעַת הַבָאָה פְּרִי אַף בִּשְׁעַת הַפְרָשָׁה פְּרִי, דְּבִשְׁעַת קְרִיאַת שֵׁם צָרִיךְ שֶׁיִּהְיוּ הַפֵּירוֹת בְּתָלוּשׁ כְּמוֹ בִּשְׁעַת הַבָאָה. וְאֵין הֲלָכָה כְּרַבִּי שִׁמְעוֹן:

---

[1] Most of this chapter describes how *bikkurim* are designated and brought to the Temple, and what is done with them there:

כֵּיצַד מַפְרִישִׁין הַבִּכּוּרִים — How does one designate *bikkurim*? יוֹרֵד אָדָם בְּתוֹךְ שָׂדֵהוּ וְרוֹאֶה תְאֵנָה שֶׁבִּכְּרָה — A person goes down into his field and sees a fig that is the first to emerge,[1] אֶשְׁכּוֹל שֶׁבִּכֵּר — or a cluster of grapes that is the first to emerge, רִמּוֹן שֶׁבִּכֵּר — or a pomegranate that is the first to emerge; קוֹשְׁרוֹ בְגֶמִי — he ties it with a reed,[2] so that he will remember which fruits they are, וְאוֹמֵר הֲרֵי אֵלּוּ בִכּוּרִים — and he says, "These are *bikkurim*." וְרַבִּי שִׁמְעוֹן אוֹמֵר — But R' Shimon says: אַף עַל פִּי כֵן — Even if he did this (i.e., he said that they are *bikkurim*), חוֹזֵר וְקוֹרֵא אוֹתָם בִּכּוּרִים מֵאַחַר שֶׁיִּתָּלְשׁוּ מִן הַקַּרְקַע — he must call them *bikkurim* again after they have been detached from the ground.[3]

[2] When bringing *bikkurim* to the Temple, many people would travel together, instead of small groups or individuals traveling on their own. By performing the mitzvah in a large group, they honored the One Whose commandment they were observing.[1] The Mishnah describes how the communal journey would begin:

NOTES
---

[1]

1. This is the stage when petals of the blossoms fall away and the budding fruits can be seen.

The Mishnah is describing the *preferred* way to perform the mitzvah. If someone failed to designate *bikkurim* when his fruits were still attached to the ground, but waited until after they were harvested, he can make the designation then (Rambam, Hilchos Bikkurim 2:19). Also, if someone failed to mark the first fruits and he does not know which ones they are, he can designate any of his fruits as *bikkurim* (*Beur HaHalachah* there ד״ה כיצד).

2. He may mark it with anything he wants. The Mishnah mentions a reed only as an example of something that was commonly used (*Tos. Yom Tov*).

3. R' Shimon and the Tanna Kamma learn their respective opinions from verses in the Torah (see *Rav*).

[2]

1. This idea is expressed in the verse (Proverbs 14:28): בְּרָב עָם הַדְרַת מֶלֶךְ, *With many people is the glory of the king* (*Rav*).

[45] **MISHNAH BIKKURIM** / Chapter 3: *Keitzad*   3/2

- רע"ב -

[ב] **כֵּיצַד** מַעֲלִין אֶת הַבִּכּוּרִים? כָּל הָעֲיָרוֹת שֶׁבַּמַּעֲמָד מִתְכַּנְּסוֹת לָעִיר שֶׁל מַעֲמָד, וְלָנִין בִּרְחוֹבָהּ שֶׁל עִיר, וְלֹא הָיוּ נִכְנָסִין לַבָּתִּים. וְלַמַּשְׁכִּים הָיָה הַמְמֻנֶּה אוֹמֵר: "קוּמוּ וְנַעֲלֶה צִיּוֹן אֶל (בֵּית) ה' אֱלֹהֵינוּ."

(ב) כל העיירות שבמעמד. עשרים וארבעה מעמדות היו בישראל, כנגד ארבעה ועשרים משמרות כהונה, ואנשי המעמד ישראלים היו שלוחים מכל ישראל, לעמוד על הקרבן עם הכהנים והלוים שבאותו משמר, כל אחד בשבת הקבוע לו, והן נקראים אנשי מעמד: **מתכנסות לעירו.** של ראש המעמד, ולא היו מביאין בכוריהם כל אחד בפני עצמו, משום דברוב עם הדרת מלך (משלי יד,כח): **ולא היו נכנסים לבתים.** מפני אהל הטומאה: **ולמשכים.** בבקר כשהם משכימים: **הממונה.** ראש המעמד: **קומו ונעלה ציון.** ובדרך היו אומרים, שמחתי באומרים לי בית ה' נלך (תהלים קכד,א). כשהגיעו לירושלים היו אומרים, עומדות היו רגלינו בשעריך ירושלים (שם פסוק ב). בהר הבית היו אומרים, הללויה הללו אל בקדשו (שם ק"נ). בעזרה היו אומרים, כל הנשמה תהלל יה (שם פסוק ו):

כֵּיצַד מַעֲלִין אֶת הַבִּכּוּרִים — **How do we bring the *bikkurim* up to the Temple?** **כָּל הָעֲיָרוֹת שֶׁבַּמַּעֲמָד מִתְכַּנְּסוֹת לָעִיר שֶׁל מַעֲמָד** — **All the people who lived in the towns of the local *maamad*[2] gather in the main town of the *maamad* (i.e., the town in which the leader of the *maamad* lived),** **וְלָנִין בִּרְחוֹבָהּ שֶׁל עִיר** — **and they sleep overnight in the town square.** **וְלֹא הָיוּ נִכְנָסִין לַבָּתִּים** — **They would not go into any houses, so that they would avoid becoming *tamei*.[3]** **וְלַמַּשְׁכִּים הָיָה הַמְמֻנֶּה אוֹמֵר** — **And in the morning, the appointed person (i.e., the leader of the *maamad*) says:** **"קוּמוּ וְנַעֲלֶה צִיּוֹן אֶל (בֵּית) ה' אֱלֹהֵינוּ"** — **Rise and let us go up to Zion, to Hashem, our God** (Jeremiah 31:5).[4]

──── NOTES ────

2. The Kohanim and the Leviim were divided into twenty-four groups that were called *mishmaros* (singular, *mishmar*), each of which served in the Temple one week at a time. The Yisraelim were divided into twenty-four groups called *maamados* (singular, *maamad*). Each *maamad* of Yisraelim was linked to a *mishmar* of Kohanim and Leviim. When the time came for a particular *mishmar* of Kohanim and Leviim to serve in the Temple, the corresponding *maamad* of Yisraelim would go to the Temple and attend the services of the public offerings. The *maamados* were established for the following reason: A person who brings an offering is obligated to attend its service in the Temple; accordingly, every Jew should have to be in the Temple every day, because offerings were brought each day on behalf of the entire Jewish people. Since this was impossible in practice, split into a different *maamad* of Yisraelim would represent the entire nation each week (*Rav*). Some members of the *maamad* actually attended the Temple services, while the others gathered in their towns, where they fasted and prayed on behalf of the nation (*Rambam Commentary;* see *Taanis* 4:2-3).

When the time came to bring their *bikkurim*, the members of each *maamad* would gather in one town. They were joined there by the corresponding *mishmar* of Kohanim (and Leviim) and they would travel from there to Jerusalem (*Meleches Shlomo*).

3. A dead body that is under a roof transmits *tumah* to any people, items of food, and utensils that are under the same roof. Accordingly, if those bringing the *bikkurim* would go into a house in which there is a corpse, they would become *tamei* and thus forbidden to enter the Temple. To avoid this problem, they would sleep outside, in the town square, where they were not covered by a roof (*Rav*).

4. The word בית, *house,* does not appear in the verse and should therefore be deleted from the Mishnah (*Meleches Shlomo*).

As they traveled, they would recite the

משניות ביכורים / פרק ג: כיצד [46]

[ג] **הַקְרוֹבִים** מְבִיאִים הַתְּאֵנִים וְהָעֲנָבִים, וְהָרְחוֹקִים מְבִיאִים גְּרוֹגְרוֹת וְצִמּוּקִים. וְהַשּׁוֹר הוֹלֵךְ לִפְנֵיהֶם, וְקַרְנָיו מְצֻפּוֹת זָהָב, וַעֲטָרָה שֶׁל זַיִת בְּרֹאשׁוֹ. הֶחָלִיל מַכֶּה לִפְנֵיהֶם, עַד שֶׁמַּגִּיעִים קָרוֹב לִירוּשָׁלַיִם. הִגִּיעוּ קָרוֹב לִירוּשָׁלַיִם, שָׁלְחוּ לִפְנֵיהֶם, וְעִטְּרוּ אֶת בִּכּוּרֵיהֶם.

- רע"ב -

(ג) תאנים וענבים. כשהם לחים: והרחוקים. מירושלים, ואין בכוריהם יכולים להתקיים כל כך: מביאין גרוגרות וצמוקים. תאנים וענבים יבשים: השור הולך לפניהם. ומקריבין אותו שלמים: ועטרה של זית בראשו. זית דאמרי, לפי שהוא

קרוב לארץ יותר מכל שאר אילנות שבשבעת המינים, דכתיב (דברים ח,ח) ארץ זית שמן. ואית דאמרי, לפי שאין בכל שאר אילנות של שבעת המינים אילן יפה ועלהו רענן כמו הזית: ועטרו את בכוריהם. וכיצד מעטרים, מי שהיו בכוריו גרוגרות, מעטרן בתאנים לחים. מי שהיו בכוריו צמוקים, מעטרן בענבים לחים. ואם מביאין ענבים, היה מראה הטובים והיפים שבכולם מלמעלה:

[3] The people bringing *bikkurim* to Jerusalem would form a festive procession, as described in this Mishnah:

הַקְרוֹבִים מְבִיאִים הַתְּאֵנִים וְהָעֲנָבִים — **Those** who live **near** Jerusalem **bring fresh figs and grapes** as *bikkurim*, because it is preferable to bring fresh fruits, rather than dry ones, וְהָרְחוֹקִים מְבִיאִים גְּרוֹגְרוֹת וְצִמּוּקִים — **but those** who live **far** from Jerusalem **bring dried figs and raisins,** because fresh fruits might spoil by the time they reach the Temple. וְהַשּׁוֹר הוֹלֵךְ לִפְנֵיהֶם — **The ox walks in front of them,**[1] וְקַרְנָיו מְצֻפּוֹת זָהָב — **and its horns are coated with gold,** וַעֲטָרָה שֶׁל זַיִת בְּרֹאשׁוֹ — **and a wreath of olive** branches **is on its head.**[2] הֶחָלִיל מַכֶּה לִפְנֵיהֶם עַד שֶׁמַּגִּיעִים קָרוֹב לִירוּשָׁלַיִם — **The flute plays in front of them**[3] **until they approach Jerusalem.** הִגִּיעוּ קָרוֹב לִירוּשָׁלַיִם — **Once they approach Jerusalem,** שָׁלְחוּ לִפְנֵיהֶם — **they send** messengers **ahead of them** to let the people of Jerusalem know that they are coming,[4] וְעִטְּרוּ אֶת בִּכּוּרֵיהֶם — **and** in the meantime **they adorn their** baskets of *bikkurim*.[5]

— NOTES —

verse: *A song of ascents: I rejoiced when they said to me, "Let us go to the house of Hashem"* (Psalms 122:1). When they reached Jerusalem, they said: *Our feet were standing in your gates, O Jerusalem* (verse 2 there). In the Temple Mount, they said: *Halleluyah! Praise God in His holy place* (150:1 there). In the Temple Courtyard, they said: *Every soul should praise God! Halleluyah!* (verse 6 there) (*Rav*, from *Yerushalmi*).

[3]

1. This ox is offered as a *shelamim* offering (*Rav*), because, as taught in Mishnah 2:4, someone who brings *bikkurim* must also bring a *shelamim* offering (*Mishnah Rishonah*). Each person owned part of the ox, so that the offering would belong

to all of them (*Meleches Shlomo*).

2. Of all the trees of the seven species from which *bikkurim* are brought, the olive tree is the most beautiful and its leaves are the freshest (*Rav*).

3. The sound of a flute can be heard from far away (*Rav* to Mishnah 4). [It announced to all within hearing range that a *bikkurim* procession is approaching.]

4. *Tos. Yom Tov.*

At this point, the flutist stops playing and they wait until the officials of the Temple come out to greet them (see below). After they are greeted, they resume their march and the flutist starts playing again, as related in the next Mishnah (*Mishnah Rishonah*).

5. Those bringing dry fruits (such as

[47] **MISHNAH BIKKURIM** / Chapter 3: *Keitzad* 3/4

- רע"ב -

הַפַּחוֹת, הַסְּגָנִים וְהַגִּזְבָּרִים יוֹצְאִים לִקְרָאתָם, לְפִי כְבוֹד הַנִּכְנָסִים הָיוּ יוֹצְאִים. וְכָל בַּעֲלֵי אֻמָּנִיּוֹת שֶׁבִּירוּשָׁלַיִם עוֹמְדִים לִפְנֵיהֶם וְשׁוֹאֲלִין בִּשְׁלוֹמָם: "אַחֵינוּ אַנְשֵׁי הַמָּקוֹם פְּלוֹנִי, בָּאתֶם לְשָׁלוֹם."

[ד] **הֶחָלִיל** מַכֶּה לִפְנֵיהֶם עַד שֶׁמַּגִּיעִין לְהַר הַבַּיִת. הִגִּיעוּ לְהַר הַבַּיִת,

הפחות. סגני כהונה: והגזברים. הממונים על הקדש: ולפי כבוד הנכנסים היו יוצאים. אם מרובים מרובים, ואם מועטים מועטים: וכל בעלי אומניות שבירושלם עומדים מפניהם. אף על גב דאין בעלי אומניות חייבין לעמוד

מפני תלמידי חכמים בשעה שעוסקים במלאכתם כדי שלא יתבטלו ממלאכתם, מכל מקום היו חייבין לעמוד מפני מביאי בכורים, דחביבה מצוה בשעתה. ומטעם זה עומדים מפני נושאי המטה שהמת בה, ומפני נושאי התינוק לברית מילה: (ד) החליל. מין כלי זמר וקולו נשמע למרחוק:

הַפַּחוֹת הַסְּגָנִים וְהַגִּזְבָּרִים יוֹצְאִים לִקְרָאתָם — The princes, i.e., the leaders, of the Kohanim, **and the treasurers** of the Temple **come out to greet them.** לְפִי כְבוֹד הַנִּכְנָסִים הָיוּ יוֹצְאִים — **According to the honor of those going in is the honor of those going out;** that is, the greater the number of people bringing *bikkurim*, the greater the number of officials going out to greet them.[6] וְכָל בַּעֲלֵי אֻמָּנִיּוֹת שֶׁבִּירוּשָׁלַיִם עוֹמְדִים לִפְנֵיהֶם — And when they enter the city, **all the craftsmen of Jerusalem stand up before them** as a show of honor for people doing a mitzvah,[7] וְשׁוֹאֲלִין בִּשְׁלוֹמָם — **and they inquire after their welfare,** saying, אַחֵינוּ אַנְשֵׁי הַמָּקוֹם פְּלוֹנִי בָּאתֶם לְשָׁלוֹם — "**Our brothers, the people of such-and-such a place, have you arrived in peace?**"[8]

[4] After those who bring the *bikkurim* are greeted by officials of the Temple, they resume their march, once again led by the flutist:[1]

הֶחָלִיל מַכֶּה לִפְנֵיהֶם עַד שֶׁמַּגִּיעִין לְהַר הַבַּיִת — **The flute plays in front of them until they reach the Temple Mount.** הִגִּיעוּ לְהַר הַבַּיִת — **When they reach**

NOTES

---

dry figs or raisins) obtain fresh ones and put them around the rim of the basket. Those bringing fresh fruits put the most attractive ones on top (*Rav*; see *Rav* to Mishnah 9).

6. Although the Mishnah's literal meaning ("the *honor* of those going in") refers to the status and prestige of the people involved, *Yerushalmi* argues that this cannot be correct, because when it comes to fulfilling mitzvos, there is no difference between people of higher and lower status; anyone doing a mitzvah is considered important and must be honored. Therefore, *Yerushalmi* explains the Mishnah as referring to the *number* of people (*Shenos Eliyahu; Derech Emunah* 4:148).

7. Someone who is busy working need not stop when a Torah scholar passes by to stand in his honor. However, he *is* obligated to stand for those who bring the *bikkurim*, because a mitzvah is especially precious at the time it is being performed. For the same reason, workers must rise in honor of people carrying a deceased person to be buried or carrying a baby to be circumcised (*Rav*, from *Yerushalmi*).

8. That is, "Have you arrived without any trouble on the way?" (*Tosefos Anshei Shem*).

[4]

1. See note 4 to the previous Mishnah.

[48] **משניות ביכורים** / פרק ג: כיצד

אֲפִלּוּ אַגְרִיפַּס הַמֶּלֶךְ נוֹטֵל הַסַּל עַל כְּתֵפוֹ וְנִכְנָס, עַד שֶׁמַּגִּיעַ לָעֲזָרָה. הִגִּיעַ לָעֲזָרָה וְדִבְּרוּ הַלְוִיִּם בְּשִׁיר: "אֲרוֹמִמְךָ ה' כִּי דִלִּיתָנִי וְלֹא שִׂמַּחְתָּ אֹיְבַי לִי".

[ה] **הַגּוֹזָלוֹת** שֶׁעַל גַּבֵּי הַסַּלִּים, הָיוּ עוֹלוֹת, וּמַה שֶּׁבְּיָדָם, נוֹתְנִים לַכֹּהֲנִים.

— רע"ב —

היה נוטל הסל על כתפו. לפי שהיה צריך ליתנו מידו ליד כהן, דכתיב (דברים כו,ד) ולקח הכהן הטנא מידך: (ה) **הגוזלות** שעל גבי הסלים. שהיו תולים מאחורי הסלים של בכורים תורים ובני יונים, ולא על גבי הסלים ממש, שלא יטנפום. והן קרבין

עולות: **ומה שבידם.** רמב"ס פירס, הגוזלות שהביאו בידס, שלא תלחום אחורי הסלים. ולי נראה, ומה שבידס, הבכורים שהביאו בידס:

---

the Temple Mount, אֲפִלּוּ אַגְרִיפַּס הַמֶּלֶךְ נוֹטֵל הַסַּל עַל כְּתֵפוֹ וְנִכְנָס — **each one of them, even King Agrippas, takes** his **basket of** *bikkurim* **on his shoulder and enters** the Temple,[2] עַד שֶׁמַּגִּיעַ לָעֲזָרָה — **carrying it until he reaches the Courtyard.** הִגִּיעַ לָעֲזָרָה וְדִבְּרוּ הַלְוִיִּם בְּשִׁיר — **Once he reaches the Courtyard, the** *Leviim* **break out in song** (*Psalms* 30:2): "אֲרוֹמִמְךָ ה' כִּי דִלִּיתָנִי וְלֹא שִׂמַּחְתָּ אֹיְבַי לִי" — *I exalt You, God, because You lifted me up and You did not let my enemies rejoice over me.*[3]

[5] It was customary to adorn the baskets of *bikkurim* by attaching small birds (pigeons or turtledoves) to them. The Mishnah teaches what is done with these birds:

הַגּוֹזָלוֹת שֶׁעַל גַּבֵּי הַסַּלִּים הָיוּ עוֹלוֹת — **The young birds that are on the basket** of *bikkurim*[1] **were brought as** *olah* **offerings,**[2] וּמַה שֶּׁבְּיָדָם נוֹתְנִים לַכֹּהֲנִים — **and what is in [the people's] hands,** i.e., the *bikkurim* themselves, **is given to the Kohanim.**[3]

NOTES

2. Those who bring *bikkurim* are not obligated to personally carry their baskets of *bikkurim* on their journey to Jerusalem; they may have them carried by relatives or servants (*Rambam, Hilchos Bikkurim* 3:12). But once they reach the Temple Mount, each owner must carry his basket of *bikkurim* himself, because the Torah states (*Devarim* 26:4): *The Kohen takes the basket from your hands,* which indicates that the Kohen takes the basket directly from the owner (*Rav*).

The Mishnah emphasizes that even if the one bringing the *bikkurim* is King Agrippas himself — an exceptionally important and powerful figure who ruled in the period of the Second Temple — he must personally carry his basket of *bikkurim* (*Rambam Commentary*).

3. This psalm was chosen because of its similarity to the *bikkurim* passage.

Just as the *bikkurim* passage begins, *An Aramean [tried to] destroy my father,* praising Hashem for saving our forefather Yaakov from his enemy Lavan, so too this psalm begins with the praise, *You lifted me up and You did not let my enemies rejoice over me* (*Mishnah Rishonah*).

[5]

1. The birds were suspended beyond the sides of the baskets, not on top of them, so that they would not soil the fruit (*Rav*).

2. Unlike the *shelamim* offering, which was obligatory (see Mishnah 2:4), these *olah* offerings were voluntary. People chose to bring them as a way of enhancing the mitzvah (*Mishnah Rishonah*).

3. *Rav's* preferred explanation.

A different approach: "What is in their hands" refers not to the *bikkurim*, but to

[49] **MISHNAH BIKKURIM** / Chapter 3: *Keitzad*

– רע״ב –

(ו) רבי יהודה אומר עד ארמי אובד אבי. ואין הלכה כרבי יהודה: ואוחזו בשפתותיו וכהן מניח ידו תחתיו מכאן משמע שהסל היה על ידו של כהן, אלא שהבעלים אוחזים הסל בשפתותיו למעלה בשעת התנופה, ושלא כדברי האומר כהן מניח ידו תחת יד הבעלים ומניף:

[ו] **עוֹדֵהוּ** הַסַּל עַל כְּתֵפוֹ, קוֹרֵא מֵ"הִגַּדְתִּי הַיּוֹם לַה' אֱלֹהֶיךָ" עַד שֶׁגּוֹמֵר כָּל הַפָּרָשָׁה. רַבִּי יְהוּדָה אוֹמֵר: עַד "אֲרַמִּי אֹבֵד אָבִי". הִגִּיעַ לַ"אֲרַמִּי אֹבֵד אָבִי", מוֹרִיד הַסַּל מֵעַל כְּתֵפוֹ וְאוֹחֲזוֹ בִשְׂפָתוֹתָיו,

[6] After entering the Temple Courtyard, the owner of *bikkurim* recites the *bikkurim* passage. The Torah describes this mitzvah as follows (*Devarim* 26:3): וְאָמַרְתָּ אֵלָיו הִגַּדְתִּי הַיּוֹם לַה' אֱלֹהֶיךָ כִּי בָאתִי אֶל הָאָרֶץ אֲשֶׁר נִשְׁבַּע ה' לַאֲבֹתֵינוּ לָתֶת לָנוּ, *... you shall say to [the Kohen]: "I declare today to Hashem, your God, that I have come to the Land that Hashem swore to our forefathers to give to us."* The next verse (4) states: וְלָקַח הַכֹּהֵן הַטֶּנֶא מִיָּדֶךָ וְהִנִּיחוֹ לִפְנֵי מִזְבַּח ה' אֱלֹהֶיךָ, *The Kohen shall take the basket from your hands and place it before the Altar of Hashem, your God.* After that, it is written (verse 5): וְעָנִיתָ וְאָמַרְתָּ לִפְנֵי ה' אֱלֹהֶיךָ, *You shall speak before Hashem, your God, and say:* אֲרַמִּי אֹבֵד אָבִי וגו', *"An Aramean [tried to] destroy my father"* etc. The recitation continues into verse 10: וְעַתָּה הִנֵּה הֵבֵאתִי אֶת רֵאשִׁית פְּרִי הָאֲדָמָה אֲשֶׁר נָתַתָּה לִּי ה' וְהִנַּחְתּוֹ לִפְנֵי ה' אֱלֹהֶיךָ וְהִשְׁתַּחֲוִיתָ לִפְנֵי ה' אֱלֹהֶיךָ, *"And now, behold, I have brought the first fruit of the ground that You have given me, Hashem." And you shall place it before Hashem, your God, and you shall prostrate yourself before Hashem, your God.*

Thus, the *bikkurim* passage begins in verse 3, is interrupted in verse 4, and then resumes in verses 5 through 10. The Mishnah cites a dispute as to whether the recitation of the passage is in fact interrupted, or whether he reads both parts together:

עוֹדֵהוּ הַסַּל עַל כְּתֵפוֹ — **While the basket is still on his shoulder,** קוֹרֵא מֵ"הִגַּדְתִּי הַיּוֹם לַה' אֱלֹהֶיךָ" — **he reads from** *I declare today to Hashem, your God,* **etc.** (verse 3), עַד שֶׁגּוֹמֵר כָּל הַפָּרָשָׁה — **and then goes straight to verse 5 and continues until he finishes the entire passage.** That is, he reads both parts one after the other, without any interruption.[1]

R' Yehudah disagrees:

רַבִּי יְהוּדָה אוֹמֵר — **R' Yehudah says:** עַד "אֲרַמִּי אֹבֵד אָבִי" — **He reads until** *An Aramean tried to destroy my father* **etc. (verse 5).** That is, he reads only the first part of the passage (*I declare today to Hashem ... to give to us*), הִגִּיעַ לַ"אֲרַמִּי אֹבֵד אָבִי" מוֹרִיד הַסַּל מֵעַל כְּתֵפוֹ וְאוֹחֲזוֹ בִשְׂפָתוֹתָיו — **and before he reaches the second part, which begins,** *An Aramean [tried To] destroy my*

— NOTES —

a second set of birds, which were not attached to the baskets but were held by hand. The birds that were attached to the basket were brought as *olah* offerings, and those that were carried by hand were given to the Kohanim as a gift (*Rav*, citing *Rambam Commentary*)

[6]
1. Although the Kohen's taking of the *bikkurim* is mentioned in the Torah between the two parts of the passage, the Kohen does not actually do this until after the second part has been read (see next note).

משניות ביכורים / פרק ג: כיצד

וְכֹהֵן מַנִּיחַ יָדוֹ תַּחְתָּיו וּמְנִיפוֹ, וְקוֹרֵא מֵאֲרַמִּי אֹבֵד אָבִי עַד שֶׁהוּא גוֹמֵר כָּל הַפָּרָשָׁה, וּמַנִּיחוֹ בְּצַד הַמִּזְבֵּחַ, וְהִשְׁתַּחֲוָה וְיָצָא.

[ז] **בָּרִאשׁוֹנָה**, כָּל מִי שֶׁיּוֹדֵעַ לִקְרוֹת קוֹרֵא, וְכָל מִי שֶׁאֵינוֹ יוֹדֵעַ לִקְרוֹת, מַקְרִין אוֹתוֹ. נִמְנְעוּ מִלְּהָבִיא.

- רע"ב -

בצד המזבח. בקרן דרומית מערבית: והשתחוה ויצא. מכאן משמע שלא היה מניף כי אם תנופה אחת בשעת הקריאה בלבד. ותנא דספרי (דברים כו,י) מצריך שתי תנופות, אחת בשעת הקריאה, דכתיב (שם פסוק ד) ולקח הכהן

הטנא מידך והניחו, וגמרינן יד יד מידיו תביאינה את אשי ה' (ויקרא ז,ל), מה להלן תנופה אף כאן תנופה, והשנית לאחר שהשלים הקריאה, דלאחר הקריאה כתיב (דברים כו,י) והנחתו, לשון לך נחה את העם (שמות לב,לד), דהיינו תנופה, שמוליך ומביא מעלה ומוריד: (ז) **נמנעו מלהביא**. מפני הבושה שאינו יודע לקרות:

---

father, he takes the basket down from his shoulder and holds it by its rim, **וְכֹהֵן מַנִּיחַ יָדוֹ תַּחְתָּיו** — and a Kohen puts his hand underneath [the basket], **וּמְנִיפוֹ** — and [the Kohen] waves it together with him.[2] **וְקוֹרֵא מֵ"אֲרַמִּי אֹבֵד אָבִי" עַד שֶׁהוּא גוֹמֵר כָּל הַפָּרָשָׁה** — [The owner] then reads the second part of the passage, from the verse, *An Aramean tried to destroy my father,* until he finishes the whole passage. **וּמַנִּיחוֹ בְּצַד הַמִּזְבֵּחַ** — He then places [the basket] at the side of the Altar, **וְהִשְׁתַּחֲוָה** — he prostrates himself on the floor of the Courtyard,[3] **וְיָצָא** — and he leaves.[4]

[7] Another law that concerns the reading of the *bikkurim* passage:

בָּרִאשׁוֹנָה כָּל מִי שֶׁיּוֹדֵעַ לִקְרוֹת קוֹרֵא — Originally, anyone who knew how to read would read the passage on his own, **וְכָל מִי שֶׁאֵינוֹ יוֹדֵעַ לִקְרוֹת מַקְרִין אוֹתוֹ** — and if anyone did not know how to read, they would dictate the passage to him, and he would repeat each word.[1] **נִמְנְעוּ מִלְּהָבִיא** — In

---

NOTES

2. That is, they move the basket in each of the four directions of the compass, and up and down (*Menachos* 62a with *Rashi*). Although verse 4 (*The Kohen shall take the basket from your hands and place it*) does not explicitly mention "waving," it is interpreted as referring to this ritual (see *Rav* ד"ה והשתחוה ויצא; *Shenos Eliyahu*).

According to the first Tanna, however, the *bikkurim* are not waved at all. This verse simply means that after the entire passage has been read, the Kohen takes the basket from the owner and places it next to the Altar (*Shenos Eliyahu*).

3. This is written in the Torah (verse 10, after the entire passage): *And he* [the owner] *shall place it before Hashem, your God, and you shall prostrate yourself before Hashem, your God.*

The owner puts the basket at the southern side of the Altar, next to the southwestern corner (*Rash*). Then he prostrates himself by lying on the ground facing the *Heichal* (main Temple building) with his arms and legs stretched out (*Tiferes Yisrael*).

The Tanna Kamma agrees that the basket is placed next to the Altar at this point, but he holds that this is done by the Kohen, not the owner. In fact, this is the very procedure described in verse 4 (see the previous note). The Torah mentions it twice in order to teach that placing the *bikkurim* next to the Altar is an essential part of the ritual; if it is not done, the *bikkurim* may not be eaten (see *Makkos* 18b with *Rashi* ד"ה והוא).

4. With his face toward the *Heichal*, he walks out backward, thus showing his respect for the *Heichal* (*Rambam, Hilchos Beis HaBechirah* 7:4).

[7]

1. The *bikkurim* passage must be read in

[51] **MISHNAH BIKKURIM** / Chapter 3: *Keitzad* 3/8

– רע״ב –

הִתְקִינוּ שֶׁיְּהוּ מַקְרִין אֶת מִי שֶׁיּוֹדֵעַ וְאֶת מִי שֶׁאֵינוֹ יוֹדֵעַ.

[ח] **הָעֲשִׁירִים** מְבִיאִים בִּכּוּרֵיהֶם בִּקְלָתוֹת שֶׁל כֶּסֶף וְשֶׁל זָהָב, וְהָעֲנִיִּים מְבִיאִין אוֹתָם בְּסַלֵּי נְצָרִים שֶׁל עֲרָבָה קְלוּפָה, וְהַסַּלִּים וְהַבִּכּוּרִים נִתָּנִין לַכֹּהֲנִים.

הִתְקִינוּ שֶׁיְּהוּ מַקְרִין. וְאַסְמַכְתָּא אַקְרָא דִּכְתִיב (דברים כו,ה) וְעָנִיתָ וְאָמַרְתָּ, וְאֵין עֲנִיָּה אֶלָּא מִפִּי אַחֵר: (ח) בִּקְלָתוֹת שֶׁל כֶּסֶף וְשֶׁל זָהָב. קוּפּוֹת מְלוּפוֹת כֶּסֶף וְזָהָב: הַסַּלִּים וְהַבִּכּוּרִים נִיתָּנִים לַכֹּהֲנִים. סַלֵּי עֲנִיִּים נִתָּנִים לַכֹּהֲנִים, וְקַלָּתוֹת שֶׁל עֲשִׁירִים מַחֲזִירִים לָהֶן, מִכָּאן אָמְרוּ (בבא קמא צב,א) בָּתַר עֲנִיָּא אָזְלָא עֲנִיּוּתָא:

---

the course of time; however, **people** who could not read **stopped bringing** *bikkurim*, because they were embarrassed to have it known that they were unable to read the passage. הִתְקִינוּ שֶׁיְּהוּ מַקְרִין אֶת מִי שֶׁיּוֹדֵעַ וְאֶת מִי שֶׁאֵינוֹ יוֹדֵעַ — To prevent this, [the Sages] decreed that the passage **would be dictated** both **to those who know** how to read **and to those who do not know** how to read. Since everyone was treated alike, there was no cause for embarrassment.

[8] *Bikkurim* must be brought to Jerusalem and given to the Kohen in a basket (or other vessel), as it is written (*Devarim* 26:2): *you shall put [them] in a basket*.[1] The Mishnah discusses the types of baskets that were used and what was done with them:

הָעֲשִׁירִים מְבִיאִים בִּכּוּרֵיהֶם בִּקְלָתוֹת שֶׁל כֶּסֶף וְשֶׁל זָהָב — **Wealthy people would bring their *bikkurim* in baskets of silver and gold,**[2] וְהָעֲנִיִּים מְבִיאִין אוֹתָם בְּסַלֵּי נְצָרִים שֶׁל עֲרָבָה קְלוּפָה — **and poor people would bring them in baskets of peeled willow branches,**[3] וְהַסַּלִּים וְהַבִּכּוּרִים נִתָּנִין לַכֹּהֲנִים — **and,** in the case of the poor, **the baskets and the *bikkurim* would be given to the Kohanim.**[4]

[9] Those bringing *bikkurim* would decorate them by hanging beautiful fruits from the rim of the basket.[1] The Mishnah cites a dispute about which types of fruit may be used for this purpose:

——————— NOTES ———————

the original Hebrew, as it is written in the Torah (*Sotah* 7:2). In the beginning of the Second Temple period, many of the Jews who had returned from the Babylonian exile could not read Hebrew (*Rambam Commentary*).

[8]

1. *Rambam, Hilchos Bikkurim* 3:7-8.
2. The baskets were coated with silver or gold (*Rav*).
3. The branches looked more beautiful without their bark (*Tiferes Yisrael*).
4. Only the wooden baskets, which were brought by poor people, were kept by the Kohanim. The baskets plated with gold and silver were returned to their owners. This is an example of the popular saying, "Poverty follows the poor" (*Rav*).

Poor people, who had only a small amount of *bikkurim*, would also give their baskets to the Kohanim, so that the gift would be substantial (*Tos. Yom Tov, Mishnah Rishonah*).

[9]

1. *Rash*. This is the decoration mentioned in Mishnah 3 (*Tos. Yom Tov* there).

ג/ט-י

— רע״ב —

(ט) מעטרים את הבכורים חוץ משבעת המינים. מקיפים את הסלים שבכורים בהם מפירות נאים ומשובחים, ואף על פי שאינם משבעת המינים, כגון פריס ואתרוג וכיוצא בהן, והוא הדין שיכולין לעטר מפירות שגדלו בחוץ לארץ: רבי עקיבא אומר אין מעטרין הבכורים אלא

משבעת המינים. ומפירות שגדלו בארץ, שחייבים בבכורים. והלכה כרבי עקיבא: (י) הבכורים. עיקר הבכורים, תאנה שבכרה או אשכול שבכר:

[ט] **רַבִּי** שִׁמְעוֹן בֶּן נַנָּס אוֹמֵר: מְעַטְּרִין אֶת הַבִּכּוּרִים חוּץ מִשִּׁבְעַת הַמִּינִים. רַבִּי עֲקִיבָא אוֹמֵר: אֵין מְעַטְּרִין אֶת הַבִּכּוּרִים אֶלָּא מִשִּׁבְעַת הַמִּינִים.

[י] **רַבִּי** שִׁמְעוֹן אוֹמֵר: שָׁלֹשׁ מִדּוֹת בַּבִּכּוּרִים: הַבִּכּוּרִים, וְתוֹסֶפֶת הַבִּכּוּרִים, וְעִטּוּר הַבִּכּוּרִים.

מְעַטְּרִין אֶת הַבִּכּוּרִים — רַבִּי שִׁמְעוֹן בֶּן נַנָּס אוֹמֵר — R' Shimon ben Nannas says: חוּץ מִשִּׁבְעַת הַמִּינִים — We may adorn the *bikkurim* even with species other than the Seven Species.[2] רַבִּי עֲקִיבָא אוֹמֵר — But R' Akiva says: אֵין מְעַטְּרִין אֶת הַבִּכּוּרִים אֶלָּא מִשִּׁבְעַת הַמִּינִים — We may adorn the *bikkurim* only with the Seven Species.[3]

[10] רַבִּי שִׁמְעוֹן אוֹמֵר — R' Shimon says: שָׁלֹשׁ מִדּוֹת בַּבִּכּוּרִים — There are three levels of *bikkurim*: הַבִּכּוּרִים — the actual *bikkurim*, i.e., the fruit that the owner designates as *bikkurim* when he first sees them on the tree (as described in Mishnah 1); וְתוֹסֶפֶת הַבִּכּוּרִים — additional *bikkurim*, which are fruit that he adds to his *bikkurim* at the time of harvesting;[1] וְעִטּוּר הַבִּכּוּרִים — and decorative *bikkurim*, which are fruit that he uses to decorate the *bikkurim* (as described in Mishnahs 3 and 9).

Additional *bikkurim* and decorative *bikkurim* must also be given to a Kohen, who has to eat them in Jerusalem.[2] The Mishnah cites other laws that apply to these two types of *bikkurim*:

NOTES

2. Although the obligation of *bikkurim* applies only to the seven species for which Eretz Yisrael is praised (see Mishnah 1:10), one may adorn his basket with beautiful, high-quality fruits of other species, such as quinces and *esrogim*. One may also use fruits that grew outside Eretz Yisrael, despite the fact that they, too, are unfit to be *bikkurim* (*Rav*).

3. In addition, it is forbidden to use fruit that grew outside Eretz Yisrael (*Rav*).

R' Akiva is concerned that someone who sees fruit around the basket might assume that they are actual *bikkurim*. Therefore, if they do not belong to the Seven Species, or if they are from outside Eretz Yisrael, he might conclude that the obligation of *bikkurim* applies even to such fruits. To prevent people from making this mistake, the Sages decreed that the basket may be decorated only with fruits that are fit to be *bikkurim* themselves (*Mishnah Rishonah*, from *Yerushalmi*).

[10]

1. That is, when the owner picks the *bikkurim* he had already designated, he adds a few more fruits of the same type (*Rav*).

2. Although additional *bikkurim* and decorative *bikkurim* do not have the Biblical sanctity of regular *bikkurim* (*Mishnah Rishonah*), they may be eaten only by Kohanim in Jerusalem (see *Derech Emunah, Hilchos Bikkurim* 2:130-131).

[53] **MISHNAH BIKKURIM** / Chapter 3: *Keitzad*   3/10

- רע"ב -

תּוֹסֶפֶת הַבִּכּוּרִים, מִין בְּמִינוֹ. וְעִטּוּר הַבִּכּוּרִים, מִין בְּשֶׁאֵינוֹ מִינוֹ. תּוֹסֶפֶת הַבִּכּוּרִים, נֶאֱכֶלֶת בְּטָהֳרָה, וּפְטוּרָה מִן הַדְּמַאי; וְעִטּוּר הַבִּכּוּרִים, חַיָּב בַּדְּמַאי.

תוספת הבכורים. בשעת לקיטת הבכורים מוסיף עליהם מאחר תאנים או מאחר ענבים: עיטור. הפירות הנאים שמקיף סביבות הסל להדור מצוה: מין בשאינו מינו. מעטר הסל של בכורי ענבים בתאנים ושל בכורי תאנים בענבים. ואפילו בפירות שאינם משבעת המינים, לדברי רבי שמעון דסבירא ליה כך לעיל: ופטורים מן הדמאי. אם לקחן הכהן מעם הארץ שהביא בכורים:

תּוֹסֶפֶת הַבִּכּוּרִים מִין בְּמִינוֹ — Additional *bikkurim* must be of **the same type** of fruit as the actual *bikkurim*, **וְעִטּוּר הַבִּכּוּרִים מִין בְּשֶׁאֵינוֹ מִינוֹ** — but decorative *bikkurim* may be of **a different type**.[3] **תּוֹסֶפֶת הַבִּכּוּרִים נֶאֱכֶלֶת בְּטָהֳרָה** — Additional *bikkurim* must be eaten in a state of **purity** (that is, when both they and the person eating them are *tahor*), and the same is true of decorative *bikkurim*.[4] **וּפְטוּרָה מִן הַדְּמַאי** — [Additional *bikkurim*] are exempt from the law of *demai*[5] (thus, if a Kohen receives additional *bikkurim* from an *am haaretz*, he does not have to separate *maasros* from them), **וְעִטּוּר הַבִּכּוּרִים חַיָּב בַּדְּמַאי** — but decorative *bikkurim* are subject to the law of *demai* (thus, a Kohen who receives decorative *bikkurim* from an *am haaretz* must separate *maasros* before eating them).[6]

— NOTES —

3. For example, if someone designated figs as his *bikkurim*, he can designate only figs as additional *bikkurim*. If he went ahead and designated a different type (such as grapes) for his additional *bikkurim*, they do not gain that status; rather, they automatically become subject to the laws of decorative *bikkurim* (*Derech Emunah* there 2:130).

According to R' Shimon ben Nannas (cited in the previous Mishnah), one may decorate his *bikkurim* even with fruit that are unfit to become *bikkurim* themselves, like quinces and *esrogim* (*Rav*).

4. *Rambam* there 2:18, as understood by *Meleches Shlomo* and *Mishnah Rishonah*.

5. *Demai* is produce obtained from an *am haaretz* (unlearned person; plural, *amei haaretz*). The Sages decreed that one must separate *maasros* from *demai*, because although most *amei haaretz* separate *maasros* from their produce, many do not. However, it is not necessary to separate *terumah* from *demai*, because even *amei haaretz* can be trusted to separate *terumah*.

6. In this respect, both additional *bikkurim* and decorative *bikkurim* are different from actual *bikkurim*. Actual *bikkurim* are completely exempt from the laws of *terumos* and *maasros*, and thus may be eaten even if these portions were *certainly* not separated from them (see *Terumos* 3:6-7). Additional *bikkurim*, on the other hand, are basically subject to the laws of *terumos* and *maasros*. Therefore, if it is *known* that additional *bikkurim* still contain *terumah* or *maasros*, Kohanim are forbidden to eat them before separating the required portions. Nevertheless, additional *bikkurim* are exempt from the Rabbinic decree of *demai*. Thus, if a Kohen received additional *bikkurim* from an *am haaretz*, the Sages did not require him to separate *maasros*, since, after all, it is likely that the *am haaretz* already did so (see previous note). Decorative *bikkurim* are a third category. They are subject not only to the Biblical laws of *terumos* and *maasros*, but also to the Rabbinic decree of *demai* (*Derech Emunah, Hilchos Maaser* 13:103).

[54] משניות ביכורים / פרק ג: כיצד ג/יא-יב

- רע"ב -

[יא] **אֵימָתַי** אָמְרוּ תּוֹסֶפֶת הַבִּכּוּרִים כְּבִכּוּרִים? בִּזְמַן שֶׁהִיא בָאָה מִן הָאָרֶץ. וְאִם אֵינָהּ בָּאָה מִן הָאָרֶץ, אֵינָהּ כְּבִכּוּרִים.

[יב] **לָמָה** אָמְרוּ הַבִּכּוּרִים כְּנִכְסֵי כֹהֵן? שֶׁהוּא קוֹנֶה מֵהֶם עֲבָדִים וְקַרְקָעוֹת וּבְהֵמָה טְמֵאָה, וּבַעַל חוֹב נוֹטְלָן בְּחוֹבוֹ,

(יא) ואם אינה באה מן הארץ. כגון שהביאו התוספת מעבר לירדן, דתנן לעיל (א,י) שמביאים משם בכורים, אף על פי שאינה ארץ זבת חלב ודבש. אי נמי מתניתין רבי שמעון היא דאמר (משנה ט) מעטרים את הבכורים חוץ משבעת המינים, והוא

הדין מפירות שגדלו בחולה לארץ. וכי היכי דאליביה מעטרים בפירות חולה לארץ, הכי נמי התוספת באה מפירות חולה לארץ, וקא משמע לן הכא שהתוספת שאינה מן הארץ אינה כבכורים:

[11] As has been mentioned, additional *bikkurim* and decorative *bikkurim* are similar to actual *bikkurim* in that they may be eaten only by a *tahor* Kohen in Jerusalem.[1] The following Mishnah cites an exception to these laws: אֵימָתַי אָמְרוּ תּוֹסֶפֶת הַבִּכּוּרִים כְּבִכּוּרִים — **When did [the Sages] say that additional** *bikkurim* **and decorative** *bikkurim*[2] **are like actual** *bikkurim*? בִּזְמַן שֶׁהִיא בָּאָה מִן הָאָרֶץ — **When they come from the Land,** i.e., the main part of Eretz Yisrael, which is west of the Jordan River (where the obligation of *bikkurim* is Biblical). וְאִם אֵינָהּ בָּאָה מִן הָאָרֶץ — **But if they do not come from the Land,** but rather from the part of Eretz Yisrael that is east of the Jordan River (where the obligation of *bikkurim* is only Rabbinic, because that region is not described as "flowing with milk and honey),[3] אֵינָהּ כְּבִכּוּרִים — **they are not like** actual *bikkurim*. Therefore, if produce that grew east of the Jordan is designated as additional or decorative *bikkurim*, it is not subject to the restrictions mentioned above, but may be eaten by anyone even outside Jerusalem.

[12] When *bikkurim* are given to a Kohen, they become his "personal property" (Mishnah 2:1). The following Mishnah teaches what this means:[1] לָמָה אָמְרוּ הַבִּכּוּרִים כְּנִכְסֵי כֹהֵן — **In what** respect **did [the Sages] say that** *bikkurim* **are the property of the Kohen?** שֶׁהוּא קוֹנֶה מֵהֶם עֲבָדִים וְקַרְקָעוֹת וּבְהֵמָה טְמֵאָה — **They are his in that he may use them** even **to buy slaves, land, or nonkosher** work animals, despite the fact that *bikkurim* are meant to be eaten by the Kohen, and these are nonfood items;[2] וּבַעַל חוֹב נוֹטְלָן בְּחוֹבוֹ — **and a creditor may take [***bikkurim*] from a Kohen as payment **for his debt,**

─── NOTES ───

[11]
1. *Meleches Shlomo;* see previous Mishnah and note 2 there.
2. *Rambam, Hilchos Bikkurim* 2:18; *Derech Emunah* there §132.
3. See Mishnah 1:10.

[12]
1. *Ri ben Malki Tzedek.*

2. The Torah (*Bamidbar* 18:13) states: *The first fruits of everything that is in their land, which they will bring to Hashem, to you [Aharon the Kohen] they will be, every tahor person in your household shall eat them.* It seems from this verse that *bikkurim* are given to the Kohen for him to eat. The Mishnah teaches that, in fact, the Kohen need not eat them; rather, he may

[55] **MISHNAH BIKKURIM** / Chapter 3: *Keitzad* 3/12

וְהָאִשָּׁה בִּכְתֻבָּתָהּ, כְּסֵפֶר תּוֹרָה. וְרַבִּי יְהוּדָה אוֹמֵר: אֵין נוֹתְנִין אוֹתָם אֶלָּא לְחָבֵר בְּטוֹבָה.

- רע"ב -

(יב) כְּסֵפֶר תּוֹרָה. כְּלוֹמַר וְסֵפֶר תּוֹרָה נַמִי הֲוֵי כְּמוֹ בִּכּוּרִים לְדִין זֶה, דְּבַעַל חוֹב נוֹטֵל בִּכְתוּבוֹ וְאִשָּׁה בִּכְתֻבָּתָהּ. פֵּירוּשׁ אַחֵר, וְסֵפֶר תּוֹרָה, וּמֻתָּר לִקְנוֹת בָּהֶם סֵפֶר תּוֹרָה. וְאַף עַל גַּב דִּתְנַן בְּהֵמָה טְמֵאָה, אַנְטְעֲרִיךְ לְמַתְנֵי סֵפֶר תּוֹרָה, דְּלֹא תֵימָא כָּל הֲנֵי נְהִי דְלֹא חֲזוּ לַאֲכִילָה, חֲזוּ לִשְׂכַר שֶׁיָּבֹא לִידֵי אֲכִילָה, אֲבָל סֵפֶר תּוֹרָה דְלֹא חֲזֵי לִשְׂכַר שֶׁיָּבֹא לִידֵי אֲכִילָה, לְפִי שֶׁאֵין מוֹכְרִין סֵפֶר תּוֹרָה, אֵימָא לֹא, קָא מַשְׁמַע לָן: **אֵין נוֹתְנִים אֶלָּא לְחָבֵר בְּטוֹבָה.** אֵין הַכֹּהֵן יָכוֹל לִיתֵּן הַבִּכּוּרִים אֶלָּא לְכֹהֵן חָבֵר שֶׁאוֹכֵל חֻלָּיו בְּטָהֳרָה, וְנוֹתֵן אוֹתָם לוֹ בְּטוֹבָתוֹ, בְּתוֹרַת חֶסֶד וּנְדָבָה, וְאֵינוֹ רַשַּׁאי לִקְנוֹת בָּהֶן דָּבָר. וְאַף לֹא לִיתְּנָן לְכֹהֵן שֶׁאֵינוֹ חָבֵר, דְּכֵיוָן שֶׁאֵין עוֹשִׂין בָּהֶן עֲבוֹדָה, חַיְישִׁינַן דִּלְמָא לֹא מִיזְדַּהַר בְּהוּ:

וְהָאִשָּׁה בִּכְתֻבָּתָהּ — **and a woman** may take *bikkurim* from a Kohen as payment **for her** *kesubah*.[3] כְּסֵפֶר תּוֹרָה — **And the same** is true of **a Torah Scroll**, that is, a Torah Scroll may also be taken by a creditor collecting his debt and by a woman collecting her *kesubah*.[4]

R' Yehudah disagrees:

וְרַבִּי יְהוּדָה אוֹמֵר — **But R' Yehudah says:** אֵין נוֹתְנִין אוֹתָם אֶלָּא לְחָבֵר בְּטוֹבָה — [A Kohen] may give [his *bikkurim*] **only to** another Kohen who is **a** *chaver* (i.e., someone who is so careful with the laws of *tumah* and *taharah* that he eats even his ordinary, non-sacred food only when he and the food are *tahor*), and he may give them to him only **as a favor**, that is, without receiving anything in exchange.[5] Thus, in contrast to the previous Tanna, who permits

───── NOTES ─────

sell them if he so chooses. Furthermore, he does not even need to sell them for money with which to buy food to eat in their place. The *bikkurim* are his "personal property," as taught in Mishnah 2:1, which he is entitled to sell or exchange for anything he wants (*Mishnah Rishonah*). [It should be noted that when *bikkurim* are sold, they retain their holiness. Thus, even after the transaction, they may not be eaten except by a *tahor* Kohen in Jerusalem (see *Meleches Shlomo*).]

Mishnah 2:1 contrasts *bikkurim* with *maaser sheni*, stating that only *bikkurim* are personal property, whereas *maaser sheni* is not. Someone who has *maaser sheni* cannot sell it, because *maaser sheni* does not truly belong to him but rather is מָמוֹן גָּבֹהַּ, *Divine property*, which is not his to sell (see *Rav* to *Maaser Sheni* 1:1). [However, it is possible to "redeem" *maaser sheni*, i.e., transfer its sanctity to money, which must then be used to buy food to eat in Jerusalem.]

3. If a man divorces his wife or dies before her, he (or his estate) must pay her a certain amount of money. This payment is called the *kesubah* (see *Kesubos* 1:2).

The Mishnah teaches that if a Kohen divorced his wife, she may take his *bikkurim* as payment. However, this law is relevant only as long as the husband is still alive. After a man's death, the general rule is that his heirs need pay the *kesubah* only with land that they inherited, and not with movable objects, such as fruit (*Tos. Yom Tov*).

The laws cited in the Mishnah here (a creditor and a divorced woman may seize *bikkurim*) apply only in the case of *bikkurim*, and not *maaser sheni*, since *maaser sheni* is not fully under the debtor's ownership (*Maaser Sheni* 1:1 and *Rav* there).

4. A Torah Scroll may not be sold other than for a pressing need, such as marriage or learning Torah (*Yerushalmi*). The Mishnah teaches that a Torah Scroll may nevertheless be seized from its owner as payment of a debt or a *kesubah* (*Rash*, second explanation).

5. R' Yehudah teaches two laws: (a) One may give his *bikkurim* only to a *chaver*, who is always careful to observe the laws

ג/יב

משניות ביכורים / פרק ג: כיצד [56]

- רע"ב -

וַחֲכָמִים אוֹמְרִים: נוֹתְנִין אוֹתָם לְאַנְשֵׁי מִשְׁמָר, נותנים אותם לאנשי
וְהֵם מְחַלְּקִין בֵּינֵיהֶם, כְּקָדְשֵׁי הַמִּקְדָּשׁ. משמר. ובין חבר ובין
שאינו חבר מחלקין אותם
ביניהס: כקדשי מקדש.

כשאר קדשי מזבח. ואף על פי שאין עושין בהם עבודה, הואיל ומכניסים אותם לעזרה, מזדהרי בהו
ולא אתו למכליניה בטומאה. והלכה כחכמים:

---

using *bikkurim* to buy whatever one wants, R' Yehudah holds that a Kohen who receives *bikkurim* may not sell or exchange them for anything.

The Sages dispute R' Yehudah's first point; namely, that *bikkurim* may be given only to a Kohen who is a *chaver*, and not to other Kohanim:

וַחֲכָמִים אוֹמְרִים — **But the Sages say:** נוֹתְנִין אוֹתָם לְאַנְשֵׁי מִשְׁמָר — **[The owner] gives [the *bikkurim*] to the members of the *mishmar* of Kohanim serving in the Temple that week,**[6] וְהֵם מְחַלְּקִין בֵּינֵיהֶם — **and they divide [the *bikkurim*] among themselves,** including those who are not *chaveirim*, כְּקָדְשֵׁי הַמִּקְדָּשׁ — **just like the offerings of the Altar in the Temple are divided among all the Kohanim of the week's *mishmar*, whether or not they are *chaveirim*.**[7]

NOTES

of *tumah* and *taharah*. Since *bikkurim* are not used in a sacrificial service (*avodah*), there is concern that an ordinary Kohen might not treat them as carefully as he should. A *chaver*, by contrast, can be fully trusted to eat them in a state of *taharah*. (b) A Kohen is forbidden to sell his *bikkurim* to anyone; he may only give them away (to a Kohen who is a *chaver*) for free, without receiving anything in return (*Rav*; see *Tiferes Yaakov* and *Meleches Shlomo*).

[The first law, which prohibits giving *bikkurim* to someone who is not a *chaver*, applies not only to the Kohen who received them in the first place, but also to their original owner. The owner, too, may give his *bikkurim* only to a Kohen who is a *chaver*.]

6. The Kohanim were divided into twenty-four groups, each of which took a turn serving in the Temple for one week at a time. Each group was known as a *mishmar* (see Mishnah 3:2 note 2).

7. The Sages are responding to the first law taught by R' Yehudah (see note 5). They hold that although *bikkurim* are not used in a sacrificial service, they resemble the sacrificial offerings in that they are brought into the Temple. Thus, giving them to ordinary Kohanim is permitted, because they can be trusted to treat them with the proper respect and avoid eating them in a state of *tumah* (*Rav*). [Here as well, there is no difference between the original owner of *bikkurim* and the Kohen who receives them. Both are free to give them to a Kohen who is not a *chaver* (*Tos. Yom Tov*).]

There is another point of disagreement between R' Yehudah and the Sages. According to R' Yehudah, the owner of *bikkurim* may give them to any Kohen he wants (as long as that Kohen is a *chaver*), while the Sages hold that he may give them only to the Kohanim of that week's *mishmar*, who divide the *bikkurim* among themselves (see *Mishnah Rishonah*).

Chapter Four

משניות ביכורים / פרק ד: תניא [58]
ד/א-ב

[א] תַּנְיָא, אַנְדְּרוֹגִינוֹס, יֵשׁ בּוֹ דְרָכִים שָׁוֶה לָאֲנָשִׁים, וְיֵשׁ בּוֹ דְרָכִים שָׁוֶה לַנָּשִׁים, וְיֵשׁ בּוֹ דְרָכִים שָׁוֶה לָאֲנָשִׁים וְלַנָּשִׁים, וְיֵשׁ בּוֹ דְרָכִים שֶׁאֵינוֹ שָׁוֶה לֹא לָאֲנָשִׁים וְלֹא לַנָּשִׁים.

[ב] שָׁוֶה לָאֲנָשִׁים כֵּיצַד? מְטַמֵּא בְלֹבֶן, כָּאֲנָשִׁים. וְנוֹשֵׂא

[1] This chapter deals with the laws of an androgyne, a person who is of unknown gender because he was born with both male and female body parts.[1] It discusses how such a person is regarded in the areas of halachah that differentiate between men and women.

Although this chapter is included in the standard editions of the Mishnah — and our commentary will therefore refer to it as Mishnah — many commentaries state that it belongs not to the Mishnah, but to the *Tosefta, Bikkurim* 2:2-6.[2] The subject of the androgyne appears there as an extension of the previous discussion regarding the *koy* (see Mishnah 2:8-11). Just as the *koy* is comparable in some ways to a *beheimah* (domestic animal), in some ways to a *chayah* (wild animal), in some ways to both, and in some ways to neither, the same four possibilities exist when comparing the androgyne to a man and a woman.[3]

תַּנְיָא — It was taught in a Baraisa: אַנְדְּרוֹגִינוֹס יֵשׁ בּוֹ דְרָכִים שָׁוֶה לָאֲנָשִׁים — An androgyne has ways in which he is like men, וְיֵשׁ בּוֹ דְרָכִים שָׁוֶה לַנָּשִׁים — and he has ways in which he is like women, וְיֵשׁ בּוֹ דְרָכִים שָׁוֶה לָאֲנָשִׁים וְלַנָּשִׁים — and he has ways in which he is like both men and women, וְיֵשׁ בּוֹ דְרָכִים שֶׁאֵינוֹ שָׁוֶה לֹא לָאֲנָשִׁים וְלֹא לַנָּשִׁים — and he has ways in which he is not like men or women. These four categories are illustrated in the next four Mishnahs.

[2] שָׁוֶה לָאֲנָשִׁים כֵּיצַד — How is [an androgyne] like men? מְטַמֵּא בְלֹבֶן כָּאֲנָשִׁים — Like men, he becomes *tamei* with a white emission; that is, if an androgyne discharges white fluid he becomes *tamei* as a *zav*, which is a law applicable only to men.[1] וְנוֹשֵׂא אֲבָל לֹא נִשָּׂא כָּאֲנָשִׁים — Like men, he

---
NOTES

[1]

1. אַנְדְּרוֹגִינוֹס, *androginos* (androgyne), is a combination of the Greek words for man, *andros,* and woman, *gyne* (see *Tos. Yom Tov* to *Yevamos* 8:6, from *Sefer HaTishbi*).

2. For this reason, *Yerushalmi* and most commentators to the Mishnah did not include this chapter in their commentaries on the tractate.

There are several different versions of this chapter. We have used the one that appears in the standard *Yachin U'Boaz* Mishnayos under the title *Nuschas Ha-Rashash*, which largely resembles the one used in the commentary of the *Rash*. (The acronym *Rashash* could refer to *Rash*, whose full name is *Rabbeinu Shimshon MiShantz*.)

3. *Rama MiPanu,* Responsa #130.

[2]

1. If a man's reproductive organ emits a *zivah* discharge, i.e., an emission that resembles the white of an egg (*Niddah* 35b), he becomes *tamei* as a *zav* (*Vayikra* 15:2). Such emissions are sources of *tumah* only when discharged by men, while similar white emissions that may be discharged by women are excluded from this law (*Rav* to *Zavim* 2:1, from *Niddah* 32b). Our Mishnah teaches that an androgyne who discharges *zivah* is *tamei,* as is the case with a man. They are,

[59] MISHNAH BIKKURIM / Chapter 4: *Tanya*   4/2

אֲבָל לֹא נִשָּׂא, כָּאֲנָשִׁים. וְאֵינוֹ מִתְיַחֵד עִם הַנָּשִׁים, כָּאֲנָשִׁים. וְאֵינוֹ נִזּוֹן עִם הַבָּנוֹת, כָּאֲנָשִׁים. וְאֵינוֹ נִקְטָף, וּמְסַפֵּר כָּאֲנָשִׁים.

---

can marry a woman **but he cannot be married** to a man;[2] that is, if a Kohen who is an androgyne marries a woman, he gives her the right to eat (Rabbinic) *terumah*, because he might be a man; however, if an androgyne is married to a male Kohen, the androgyne does not receive the right to eat any *terumah*, for since he might be a man, their marriage is forbidden.[3] וְאֵינוֹ מִתְיַחֵד עִם הַנָּשִׁים כָּאֲנָשִׁים — **Like men, he may not be alone with women.**[4] וְאֵינוֹ נִזּוֹן עִם הַבָּנוֹת כָּאֲנָשִׁים — **Like men, he is not given food with the daughters;** that is, if an androgyne's father dies and leaves behind property that is not enough to support all his sons and daughters, the daughters receive what they require for their support until adulthood, while the sons — including the androgyne — receive only what is left over.[5] וְאֵינוֹ נִקְטָף וּמְסַפֵּר כָּאֲנָשִׁים — **Like men, he does**

NOTES

however, not completely the same, for the *zivah* of an androgyne is *tamei* only out of doubt, because he might be a woman (see Mishnah 5), while that of a man is definitely *tamei* (*Rash, Rama MiPanu*).

2. The Mishnah refers to an androgyne marrying a woman in the active voice ("marry") and to an androgyne marrying a man in the passive voice ("be married to"), because the act of *kiddushin*, which effects marriage, is performed by the man (see *Kiddushin* 1:1).

3. When the Mishnah rules that an androgyne can marry a woman but not a man, it seems to mean that a marriage between an androgyne and a woman is a legally valid union (at least out of doubt), which cannot be terminated in their lifetimes except by giving a *get* (divorce document), while a marriage between an androgyne and a man has no validity at all, and they are permitted to remarry even without a *get* having been given. However, this cannot be the Mishnah's meaning, because in both cases the marriage takes effect out of doubt, which is enough for a *get* to be necessary. Rather, the Mishnah refers to a different law that pertains to marriage; namely, that if the daughter of a non-Kohen marries a Kohen, she is permitted to eat *terumah*. This permission is limited, or does not apply at all, where either of the spouses is an androgyne, because the marriage is possibly invalid. In the case where the Kohen is the androgyne and the wife is a regular woman, the wife may not eat Biblical *terumah*, since the marriage might be invalid, but she may eat produce that is *terumah* only according to Rabbinic law. [This is an application of the rule: סָפֵק דְּרַבָּנָן לְקוּלָא, *a doubt in a case of Rabbinic law is decided leniently.*] In the opposite case, though, where the "wife" is the androgyne and the husband (the Kohen) is a regular man, the Sages prohibited the androgyne to eat any kind of *terumah*. This is because marriage between a man and an androgyne is forbidden, given the possibility that the androgyne might also be a man (*Rash*). [It is permitted, however, for an androgyne to marry a woman (*Rambam, Hilchos Issurei Bi'ah* 1:15).]

4. A man is forbidden to be in a secluded place with a woman who is not a close relative (see *Kiddushin* 4:12).

Although the Mishnah mentions only an androgyne being alone with a woman, an androgyne is also prohibited to be alone with a man (Mishnah 3), since an androgyne is possibly a woman. Our Mishnah does not add that law, however, because it is listing only the ways in which an androgyne is like a man.

5. When a father dies, his sons inherit all his property, and they must give an allowance to his daughters for their support until the daughters reach adulthood. However, if someone dies and does not leave enough property to support his sons and daughters, the daughters receive the

וְאֵינוֹ מְטַמֵּא לְמֵתִים, וְחַיָּב בְּבַל תַּקִּיף וּבְבַל תַּשְׁחִית, כָּאֲנָשִׁים. וְחַיָּב בְּכָל מִצְוֹת הָאֲמוּרוֹת בַּתּוֹרָה, כָּאֲנָשִׁים.

[ג] **שָׁוֶה** לַנָּשִׁים כֵּיצַד? מְטַמֵּא בְאָדָם, כַּנָּשִׁים. וְאֵינוֹ מִתְיַחֵד עִם הָאֲנָשִׁים, כַּנָּשִׁים. וְאֵינוֹ זוֹקֵק לְיִבּוּם, כַּנָּשִׁים.

---

not wrap his **head and cut his hair;** an androgyne is forbidden to resemble women, who cover their heads (for reasons of modesty) and grow their hair long. He must carry himself with the dress and appearance of a man to ensure that he will not marry a man, which is forbidden.[6] **וְאֵינוֹ מְטַמֵּא לְמֵתִים וְחַיָּב בְּבַל תַּקִּיף וּבְבַל תַּשְׁחִית כָּאֲנָשִׁים** — **Like men, he may not become** *tamei* **from a dead body** if he is a Kohen, **and he is prohibited to round off** the corners of the head (i.e., he may not make his hairline even all around by removing the hair from the temples), **and he is prohibited to destroy** the corners of the beard (i.e., he may not shave certain parts of his beard with a razor).[7] **וְחַיָּב בְּכָל מִצְוֹת הָאֲמוּרוֹת בַּתּוֹרָה כָּאֲנָשִׁים** — **Like men, he is obligated to** do **all the** positive **mitzvos that are stated in the Torah,** including those that apply only at specific times (such as shofar, *succah,* and *lulav*).[8]

[3] **שָׁוֶה לַנָּשִׁים כֵּיצַד** — **How is** [an androgyne] **like women? מְטַמֵּא בְאָדָם כַּנָּשִׁים** — **Like women, he becomes** *tamei* **with a red** emission; that is, if an androgyne discharges red blood he becomes *tamei* as a *niddah,* like a woman who discharges red blood.[1] **וְאֵינוֹ מִתְיַחֵד עִם הָאֲנָשִׁים כַּנָּשִׁים** — **Like women, he may not be alone with men.**[2] **וְאֵינוֹ זוֹקֵק לְיִבּוּם כַּנָּשִׁים** — **Like women, he does not cause** a woman **to require** *yibum*;[3] that is, if a married man dies

---

NOTES

full amount they will need until adulthood, and the sons get only what remains (see *Kesubos* 13:3, *Bava Basra* 9:1). The Mishnah teaches that in the second case, where each daughter receives a greater amount than each son, an androgyne has no right to a daughter's portion unless he shows that he is entitled to such a portion by proving that he is a female, which is impossible. Therefore, the androgyne receives no more than one of the sons (*Rash*). [Regarding the first case, where the sons inherit the estate, see the next Mishnah.]

6. The Torah prohibits intimate relations between two men (*Vayikra* 18:22, 20:13). Since an androgyne might be a man, this prohibition applies to him out of doubt (*Rash*). To avoid the transgression of marrying a man, an androgyne must appear like a man.

Although this will not prevent the androgyne from marrying a woman, that is not a problem, because an androgyne is allowed to marry a woman, as mentioned in note 3.

7. These three prohibitions do not apply to women (see *Kiddushin* 1:7).

8. Women are generally exempt from positive commandments that are limited by time (*Kiddushin* there).

[3]

1. A women becomes *tamei* upon experiencing a flow of blood from her reproductive organ (*Vayikra* 15:19,25). This is described as a "red emission" based on the rule that only certain shades of red are *tamei,* as taught in *Niddah* 2:6 (*Rash*). The Mishnah applies this law to the androgyne as well, in view of the possibility that an androgyne is classified as a woman.

2. See note 4 on the previous Mishnah.

3. In the event that a married man dies without children, his widow must marry one of his brothers (this marriage is

[61] MISHNAH BIKKURIM / Chapter 4: *Tanya*

וְאֵינוּ חוֹלֵק עִם הַבָּנִים, וְאֵינוּ חוֹלֵק בְּקָדְשֵׁי הַמִּקְדָּשׁ, כַּנָּשִׁים.
וּפָסוּל לְכָל עֵדוּת שֶׁבַּתּוֹרָה, כַּנָּשִׁים. וְאֵינוּ נִבְעָל בַּעֲבֵרָה, כַּנָּשִׁים.
וּפָסוּל מִן הַכְּהֻנָּה, כַּנָּשִׁים.

---

leaving no children, and his only brother is an androgyne, the widow does not require *yibum* or *chalitzah* from the androgyne.[4] וְאֵינוּ חוֹלֵק עִם הַבָּנִים — Like women, **he does not receive a share** of his father's inheritance **with his father's sons**,[5] וְאֵינוּ חוֹלֵק בְּקָדְשֵׁי הַמִּקְדָּשׁ כַּנָּשִׁים — **and, like women, he does not receive a share of the holy foods of the Temple** (i.e., offerings) when they are divided among male Kohanim.[6] וּפָסוּל לְכָל עֵדוּת שֶׁבַּתּוֹרָה כַּנָּשִׁים — **Like women, he is disqualified from all testimonies of the Torah**; that is, an androgyne may not testify in all cases where the Torah requires the testimony of two men.[7] וְאֵינוּ נִבְעָל בַּעֲבֵרָה כַּנָּשִׁים — **Like women, he may not participate in cohabitation with [a man] who is forbidden** to the androgyne, such as one of an androgyne's forbidden male relatives.[8] וּפָסוּל מִן הַכְּהֻנָּה כַּנָּשִׁים — **And,**

--- NOTES ---

called *yibum*) unless one of them performs the ceremony of *chalitzah* with her, which frees her to marry anyone else (see *Devarim* 25:5-10).

4. It is learned from a verse in the Torah that the laws of *yibum* and *chalitzah* do not apply where the only surviving brother cannot father children (*Yevamos* 8:4), which is assumed to be true of an androgyne (*Rash*).

5. As mentioned above (Mishnah 2 note 3), when a man dies and leaves behind more than enough property to support his children until the daughters reach adulthood, the sons inherit all the property and give an allowance to the daughters. In this situation, an androgyne is treated like a daughter. He has no right to a son's larger portion, unless he shows that he is entitled to such a portion by proving that he is a male, which is impossible (*Rash*).

6. Some sacrificial portions (the *chatas*, *asham*, etc.) are eaten only by male Kohanim, and some sacrificial portions (the *pesach*, most of the *shelamim*, etc.) are eaten by the owner and his guests, even if they are not Kohanim. However, there is a third group of sacrificial portions (such as the breast and thigh of a *shelamim* offering), which are distributed in the Temple to male Kohanim, but once a Kohen receives his portion he may share it with his wife and daughters. Although an androgyne may certainly eat these portions (regardless of whether he is a man or a woman), the Torah requires them to be divided in the Temple only among definite males, and not androgynes (see *Rash*).

7. The Torah teaches that in areas of law where the testimony of two witnesses is required, both must be males (see *Shevuos* 30a). The testimony of an androgyne is therefore disqualified, since an androgyne is possibly a woman.

8. The Torah forbids cohabitation between close relatives, such as a brother and sister, parent and child, grandparent and grandchild. It also prohibits cohabitation between certain types of other people, for example, a man and a married woman, or a regular Jew and a *mamzer*.

The Mishnah teaches that an androgyne may not cohabit with a man if that man would be prohibited to the androgyne were the androgyne a woman. Therefore, an androgyne is forbidden to cohabit with a male relative, *mamzer*, etc.

Given the possibility that an androgyne is a man, he is also forbidden to cohabit with a *female* relative (or other forbidden woman). Moreover, he is forbidden to cohabit not only with males who are specifically forbidden (relative, *mamzer*, etc.), but also with *any* male (see *Rash*). Our Mishnah, though, does not mention these prohibitions because it refers only to ways in which an androgyne is "like women."

[ד] **שָׁוֶה** לָאֲנָשִׁים וְלַנָּשִׁים כֵּיצַד? חַיָּב עַל נִזְקוֹ, כְּאִישׁ וְאִשָּׁה. וְחַיָּב בְּכָל הַנִּזָּקִין, כְּאִישׁ וְאִשָּׁה. וְהַהוֹרְגוֹ בְמֵזִיד, נֶהֱרָג, בְּשׁוֹגֵג, גּוֹלֶה לְעָרֵי מִקְלָט, וְאִמּוֹ יוֹשֶׁבֶת עָלָיו דַּם טֹהַר, כָּאֲנָשִׁים וְכַנָּשִׁים. וְנוֹחֵל בְּקָדְשֵׁי הַגְּבוּל, כָּאֲנָשִׁים וְכַנָּשִׁים.

like women, if an androgyne who is a Kohen cohabits with a forbidden male relative, **he is disqualified from the Kehunah,** i.e., he may not eat *terumah*.[9]

[4] שָׁוֶה לָאֲנָשִׁים וְלַנָּשִׁים כֵּיצַד — **How is [an androgyne] like men and women?** חַיָּב עַל נִזְקוֹ כְּאִישׁ וְאִשָּׁה — **Like a man or woman,** if an androgyne or his property suffers damage, the person who harmed him is **liable** to pay **for his damage.** וְחַיָּב בְּכָל הַנִּזָּקִין כְּאִישׁ וְאִשָּׁה — **Like a man or woman, he is liable** to pay **for all damage** that he does. וְהַהוֹרְגוֹ בְמֵזִיד נֶהֱרָג בְּשׁוֹגֵג גּוֹלֶה לְעָרֵי מִקְלָט — **Someone who kills [an androgyne] intentionally is executed** by the court, and one who kills him **unintentionally is exiled to** one of **the cities of refuge.**[1] וְאִמּוֹ יוֹשֶׁבֶת עָלָיו דַּם טֹהַר כָּאֲנָשִׁים וְכַנָּשִׁים — **Like mothers of men and like** mothers of **women,** the mother of [an androgyne] **sits** the period of *tahor* blood upon giving birth to him,[2] וְנוֹחֵל בְּקָדְשֵׁי הַגְּבוּל כָּאֲנָשִׁים וְכַנָּשִׁים — **Like men and like**

— NOTES —

9. A Koheness (i.e., the wife or daughter of a Kohen) has the right to eat *terumah*, but she loses that right if she cohabits with a man who is forbidden to her, like a close relative or *mamzer*. This law applies only to a Koheness, and not to a male Kohen; rather, a male Kohen who engages in forbidden cohabitation remains permitted to eat *terumah*. Since an androgyne might be a woman, he must be treated with the stringencies of women. Thus, if a Kohen who is an androgyne cohabits with a forbidden male (such as a relative or *mamzer*), the Kohen becomes prohibited to eat *terumah* (*Rash*).

[However, if an androgyne-Kohen cohabited with a *forbidden female*, or with an *ordinary male* (who is not specifically forbidden, such as a relative or a *mamzer*), although he was forbidden to do so, he remains *permitted* to eat *terumah*. In this regard, it makes no difference whether an androgyne is classified as male or female: If he is a male, forbidden cohabitation does not disqualify him from eating *terumah*, and if he is a female, only cohabitation with *specifically forbidden males* effects disqualification.]

[4]

1. Someone who kills another person intentionally is put to death (see *Shemos* 21:20) and someone who kills another person unintentionally must go to live in one of the 48 towns in Eretz Yisrael that are designated as "cities of refuge" (see *Bamidbar* 35:25). These laws apply regardless of whether the victim is a man or a woman.

2. After a woman gives birth to a boy, she is *tamei* as a *niddah* for seven days. For the following 33 days, she "sits [a period of] *tahor* blood," which means that even if she has a flow of blood, she does *not* become a *niddah* [by Biblical law]. A woman who gives birth to a girl is *tamei* for 14 days and her period of *taharah* lasts 66 days (see *Vayikra* 12:4,5). Our Mishnah teaches that a woman who gives birth to an androgyne must always follow the stricter law, whether it is the law of giving birth to a girl or the law of giving birth to a boy, because the androgyne could be either a male or a female. Thus, she is *tamei* for the longer period of 14 days, like the mother of a girl, and then she is *tahor* only through the 40th day, like the mother of a boy, whose period of *taharah* ends on the 40th day. Since the mother of an androgyne resembles both the mother of a boy and the mother of a girl, she is described as being "like [mothers of] men and like [mothers of] women" (*Rash*).

[63] MISHNAH BIKKURIM / Chapter 4: *Tanya*

וְהָאוֹמֵר: "הֲרֵינִי נָזִיר שֶׁזֶּה אִישׁ וְאִשָּׁה", הֲרֵי זֶה נָזִיר.

[ה] **אֵינוֹ** שָׁוֶה לֹא לָאֲנָשִׁים וְלֹא לַנָּשִׁים כֵּיצַד? אֵין חַיָּבִין עַל טֻמְאָתוֹ, וְאֵין שׂוֹרְפִין עַל טֻמְאָתוֹ, וְאֵינוֹ נֶעֱרָךְ,

---

women, he receives a portion of the "holy things of the borders"; that is, if he is a Kohen, he may be given *terumah, terumas maaser,* and *challah*.[3] וְהָאוֹמֵר הֲרֵינִי נָזִיר שֶׁזֶּה אִישׁ וְאִשָּׁה הֲרֵי זֶה נָזִיר — And if someone sees an androgyne and says "I am a *nazir*[4] if this person is a man or a woman," he becomes a *nazir*, since one of these two options ("man" or "woman") is certainly true.

[5] אֵינוֹ שָׁוֶה לֹא לָאֲנָשִׁים וְלֹא לַנָּשִׁים כֵּיצַד — How is [an androgyne] not like men or women? אֵין חַיָּבִין עַל טֻמְאָתוֹ — One is not obligated to bring an offering on account of his *tumah*; that is, if an androgyne has both white and red discharges, in which case he is certainly *tamei*,[1] and then he (or someone else who came into contact with both discharges) entered the Temple or ate holy food (which a *tamei* person is forbidden to do), he is not obligated to bring an offering to atone for his sin. וְאֵין שׂוֹרְפִין עַל טֻמְאָתוֹ — One does not burn *terumah* on account of his *tumah*; that is, if an androgyne has either a white or a red discharge, in which case he is *tamei* out of doubt, and then touched some *terumah*, the *terumah* may not be burned (which is the usual treatment of *terumah* that is *tamei*), since it is *tamei* only out of doubt.[2] וְאֵינוֹ נֶעֱרָךְ

NOTES

3. *Terumah, terumas maaser,* and *challah* are called "holy things of the borders" because they may be eaten anywhere within the borders of Eretz Yisrael. This is in contrast to other holy foods, such as the meat of offerings and *bikkurim*, which must be eaten either inside the Temple Courtyard or inside Jerusalem (see Rashi to *Chagigah* 22b ד"ה תרומה). Our Mishnah teaches that *terumah, terumas maaser,* and *challah* may be given to an androgyne who is a Kohen. It makes no difference here whether an androgyne is a man or a woman, because these items are given to both male and female Kohanim. Likewise, *maaser rishon* may be given to an androgyne who is a Levi (*Rash*). [The meat of offerings and *bikkurim*, however, are divided only among Kohanim who are definite males, and not androgynes.]

4. Someone who declares himself a "*nazir*" is prohibited to cut his hair, drink wine (or consume any part of a grape), or become *tamei* from a corpse (see *Bamidbar* 6:1-6).

[5]

1. We have learned that an androgyne who has a white discharge becomes *tamei* out of doubt because he might be a man (Mishnah 2), and an androgyne who has a red discharge becomes *tamei* out of doubt because he might be a woman (Mishnah 3). Therefore, an androgyne who has both types of discharges is *certainly tamei*, since an androgyne is either a man or a woman. Nevertheless, if an androgyne who has both types of discharges (or a person who came into contact with both of his discharges) enters the Temple or eats holy food, he does not have to bring an offering. Although a *tamei* person who enters the Temple or eats holy food must bring an offering to atone for his sin (see *Bamidbar* 5:2-6), that law applies only to a definite male or a definite female (see verse 3 there), and not to an androgyne whose *tumah* is based on him being possibly a male or possibly a female (*Niddah* 28a-b).

2. While *terumah* that is *tamei* must be burned, one is forbidden to destroy *terumah* that is not *tamei*. Accordingly, if an androgyne has *either* a white discharge *or* a red discharge, which makes

לֹא כָאֲנָשִׁים וְלֹא כַנָּשִׁים. וְאֵינוֹ נִמְכָּר בְּעֶבֶד עִבְרִי, לֹא כָאֲנָשִׁים וְלֹא כַנָּשִׁים. וְאִם אָמַר: "הֲרֵינִי נָזִיר שֶׁאֵין זֶה אִישׁ וְאִשָּׁה", הֲרֵי זֶה נָזִיר.

לֹא כָאֲנָשִׁים וְלֹא כַנָּשִׁים — Unlike men and unlike women, [an androgyne] cannot be the subject of an *erech* vow.[3] **וְאֵינוֹ נִמְכָּר בְּעֶבֶד עִבְרִי לֹא כָאֲנָשִׁים וְלֹא כַנָּשִׁים** — Unlike men and unlike women, he cannot be sold as a Hebrew servant.[4] **וְאִם אָמַר הֲרֵינִי נָזִיר שֶׁאֵין זֶה אִישׁ וְאִשָּׁה הֲרֵי זֶה נָזִיר** — And if someone saw an androgyne and **said, "I am a *nazir* if this person is either not a man or not a woman,"** he becomes a *nazir,* since one of these two options (either "not a man" or "not a woman") is certainly true.

The rulings of this chapter until this point have been based on the premise that an androgyne is either a man or a woman, but we do not know which.

———————————— NOTES ————————————

him *tamei* only out of doubt, and then he touches some *terumah*, that *terumah* is also *tamei* only out of doubt. As such, it may not be burned, because by doing so one might be violating the prohibition against destroying *terumah* (*Niddah* 28a with *Rashi*). [In this respect, an androgyne is different from a *tamei* man (who had a white discharge) and a *tamei* woman (who had a red discharge), because they are definitely *tamei,* and *terumah* touched by one of them would have to be burned.]

The Mishnah's ruling applies only to an androgyne who had just one type of discharge, *either* red *or* white. If he had *both* a white discharge *and* a red one, which would make him definitely *tamei,* and then he touched *terumah,* it would have to be burned, because it is *tamei* without question. This is different from the Mishnah's previous ruling about an androgyne who entered the Temple or ate sacred food. In that case, he is exempt from punishment even if he had both types of discharges, because the Torah specifically excludes an androgyne from liability (*Niddah* there with *Rashi*).

3. An *erech* is a vow in which a person declares that he will give the "*erech*" (literally, *value*) of a specific person to the Temple. The Torah (*Vayikra* 27:1-8) gives a fixed *erech* for every person, based on his age and gender (for example, the *erech* of a man between 20 and 60 years old is 50 *shekalim*). Our Mishnah teaches that

someone who declares that he will give the *erech* of an androgyne does not need to give anything, because the Torah refers there only to definite males and definite females, and this excludes androgynes (see *Arachin* 4b, *Niddah* 28b).

4. A Jewish man may be sold as a "Hebrew servant" (עֶבֶד עִבְרִי) in one of two ways. If he is poor, he may sell himself in order to support himself and his family (see *Vayikra* 25:39); and if he steals and is unable to repay, the court may sell him and give the money to the victim of the theft (see *Shemos* 22:2). Each of these situations are relevant only to an adult man (at least thirteen years old). A boy cannot sell himself because he is unable to make monetary transactions (see *Gittin* 5:7), and a boy cannot be sold by the court because he is not subject to court action (see *Bava Kamma* 8:4). Regarding a woman, however, the opposite is true. An adult woman (at least twelve years old) cannot be sold to be a Hebrew servant under any circumstance (see *Sotah* 3:8; *Rambam, Hilchos Avadim* 1:2), whereas a girl under the age of twelve can be sold by her father (*Shemos* 21:7).

It emerges that a male can be sold to be a Hebrew servant only if he is an adult, while a female can be sold only if she is a minor. Therefore, an androgyne can never be sold. If he is a minor, he cannot be sold because he might be a male, and if he is an adult he cannot be sold because he might be a female (*Rash*).

[65] **MISHNAH BIKKURIM** / Chapter 4: *Tanya*

רַבִּי יוֹסֵי אוֹמֵר: אַנְדְּרוֹגִינוֹס, בְּרִיָּה בִּפְנֵי עַצְמָה, וְלֹא הִכְרִיעוּ בּוֹ חֲכָמִים אִם אִישׁ אִם אִשָּׁה. אֲבָל טוּמְטוּם, אֵינוֹ כֵן, אֶלָּא סְפֵק אִישׁ, סְפֵק אִשָּׁה.

The next Tanna, however, considers it possible that an androgyne is neither a man nor a woman, but belongs to a category of his own. This Tanna contrasts an androgyne with a *tumtum* (literally, *hidden one*), who is a person that has a thick membrane covering the reproductive organs, which makes it impossible to tell whether he is a man or a woman:

רַבִּי יוֹסֵי אוֹמֵר — **R' Yose says:** אַנְדְּרוֹגִינוֹס בְּרִיָּה בִּפְנֵי עַצְמָה וְלֹא הִכְרִיעוּ בּוֹ חֲכָמִים אִם אִישׁ אִם אִשָּׁה — **An androgyne is a creature in his own right and the Sages could not decide whether he is a man or a woman.** That is, there are three possibilities: an androgyne is either a man, or a woman, or a third type (neither male nor female).[5] אֲבָל טוּמְטוּם אֵינוֹ כֵן אֶלָּא סְפֵק אִישׁ סְפֵק אִשָּׁה — **But a *tumtum* is not like this; rather, a *tumtum* is possibly a man or possibly a woman,** but certainly not a third type. This is because a *tumtum* definitely has the organs of either a man or a woman, but we cannot tell because they are covered.

NOTES

5. In contrast to the preceding Tanna, who holds that an androgyne is either a man or a woman, R' Yose holds that an androgyne could be neither male nor female, but a distinct sort of being. One practical difference between these two opinions arises where someone said, "I am a *nazir* if this person (an androgyne) is neither a man *nor* a woman." According to the first Tanna, he is definitely not a *nazir*, because he holds that an androgyne must be one or the other, but according to R' Yose he is a *nazir* out of doubt, because it is possible than an androgyne is a third type, which is neither male nor female (*Rash*).

Hadran

הדרן

Upon the סִיּוּם, *completion*, of the study of an entire Order (*Seder*) of Mishnah, a festive meal (which has the status of a *seudas mitzvah*) should be eaten — preferably with a *minyan* in attendance. The following prayers of thanksgiving are recited by those who have completed the learning.
[The words in brackets are inserted according to some customs.]

The first paragraph is recited three times.

הַדְרָן עֲלָךְ סֵדֶר זְרָעִים וְהַדְרָךְ עֲלָן, דַּעְתָּן עֲלָךְ סֵדֶר זְרָעִים וְדַעְתָּךְ עֲלָן, לָא נִתְנְשֵׁי מִנָּךְ סֵדֶר זְרָעִים וְלָא תִתְנְשֵׁי מִנָּן, לָא בְּעָלְמָא הָדֵין וְלָא בְּעָלְמָא דְאָתֵי.

הַעֲרֶב נָא יהוה אֱלֹהֵינוּ אֶת דִּבְרֵי תוֹרָתְךָ בְּפִינוּ וּבְפִי עַמְּךָ בֵּית יִשְׂרָאֵל, וְנִהְיֶה [כֻּלָּנוּ,] אֲנַחְנוּ וְצֶאֱצָאֵינוּ [וְצֶאֱצָאֵי צֶאֱצָאֵינוּ] וְצֶאֱצָאֵי עַמְּךָ בֵּית יִשְׂרָאֵל, כֻּלָּנוּ יוֹדְעֵי שְׁמֶךָ וְלוֹמְדֵי תוֹרָתֶךָ [לִשְׁמָהּ]. מֵאֹיְבַי תְּחַכְּמֵנִי מִצְוֹתֶךָ, כִּי לְעוֹלָם הִיא לִי. יְהִי לִבִּי תָמִים בְּחֻקֶּיךָ, לְמַעַן לֹא אֵבוֹשׁ. לְעוֹלָם לֹא אֶשְׁכַּח פִּקּוּדֶיךָ, כִּי בָם חִיִּיתָנִי. בָּרוּךְ אַתָּה יהוה, לַמְּדֵנִי חֻקֶּיךָ. אָמֵן אָמֵן אָמֵן, סֶלָה וָעֶד.

מוֹדֶה אֲנִי לְפָנֶיךָ יהוה אֱלֹהַי וֵאלֹהֵי אֲבוֹתַי, שֶׁשַּׂמְתָּ חֶלְקִי מִיּוֹשְׁבֵי בֵּית הַמִּדְרָשׁ, וְלֹא שַׂמְתָּ חֶלְקִי מִיּוֹשְׁבֵי קְרָנוֹת. שֶׁאֲנִי מַשְׁכִּים וְהֵם מַשְׁכִּימִים, אֲנִי מַשְׁכִּים לְדִבְרֵי תוֹרָה, וְהֵם מַשְׁכִּימִים לִדְבָרִים בְּטֵלִים. אֲנִי עָמֵל וְהֵם עֲמֵלִים, אֲנִי עָמֵל וּמְקַבֵּל שָׂכָר, וְהֵם עֲמֵלִים וְאֵינָם מְקַבְּלִים שָׂכָר. אֲנִי רָץ וְהֵם רָצִים, אֲנִי רָץ לְחַיֵּי הָעוֹלָם הַבָּא, וְהֵם רָצִים לִבְאֵר שַׁחַת, שֶׁנֶּאֱמַר: וְאַתָּה אֱלֹהִים, תּוֹרִדֵם לִבְאֵר שַׁחַת, אַנְשֵׁי דָמִים וּמִרְמָה לֹא יֶחֱצוּ יְמֵיהֶם, וַאֲנִי אֶבְטַח בָּךְ.

יְהִי רָצוֹן מִלְּפָנֶיךָ יהוה אֱלֹהַי וֵאלֹהֵי אֲבוֹתַי, כְּשֵׁם שֶׁעֲזַרְתַּנִי לְסַיֵּם סֵדֶר זְרָעִים, כֵּן תַּעַזְרֵנִי לְהַתְחִיל סְדָרִים אֲחֵרִים וּלְסַיְּמָם, לִלְמֹד וּלְלַמֵּד מִתּוֹךְ הַרְחָבָה, לִשְׁמֹר וְלַעֲשׂוֹת וּלְקַיֵּם אֶת כָּל דִּבְרֵי תַלְמוּד תּוֹרָתֶךָ בְּאַהֲבָה. וּזְכוּת כָּל הַתַּנָּאִים

Hadran

Upon the סִיּוּם, *completion*, of the study of an entire Order (*Seder*) of Mishnah, a festive meal (which has the status of a *seudas mitzvah*) should be eaten — preferably with a *minyan* in attendance. The following prayers of thanksgiving are recited by those who have completed the learning.
[The words in brackets are inserted according to some customs.]

The first paragraph is recited three times.

הַדְרָן *We shall return to you, the Order of Zeraim, and you shall return to us. Our thoughts are on you, the Order of Zeraim, and your thoughts are on us. We will not forget you, the Order of Zeraim, and you will not forget us — neither in This World, nor in the World to Come.*

הַעֲרֶב נָא *Please, Hashem, our God, sweeten the words of Your Torah in our mouth and in the mouth of Your people, the House of Israel, and may [we all —] we, our offspring, [the offspring of our offspring,] and the offspring of Your people, the House of Israel, all of us — know Your Name and study Your Torah. Your commandment makes me wiser than my enemies, for it is forever with me. May my heart be perfect in Your statutes, so that I not be shamed. I will never forget Your precepts, for through them You have preserved me. Blessed are You, Hashem, teach me Your statutes. Amen. Amen. Amen. Selah! Forever!*

מוֹדֶה *I express gratitude before You, Hashem, my God, and the God of my forefathers, that You have established my portion with those who dwell in the study hall, and have not established my portion with idlers. For I arise early and they arise early; I arise early for the words of Torah, while they arise early for idle words. I toil and they toil; I toil and receive reward, while they toil and do not receive reward. I run and they run; I run to the life of the World to Come, while they run to the well of destruction, as it is said: But You, O God, You will lower them into the well of destruction, men of bloodshed and deceit shall not live out half their days; and I will trust in You.*

יְהִי רָצוֹן *May it be Your will, Hashem, my God, and the God of my forefathers, that just as You have helped me complete the Order of Zeraim, so may You help me to begin other Orders, and to complete them; to learn and to teach in peace, to safeguard and to perform, and to fulfill all the words of Your Torah's teachings with love. May the merit of all the Tannaim*

וְתַלְמִידֵי חֲכָמִים הַנִּזְכָּרִים בְּסֵדֶר זְרָעִים וּבְכָל הַסְּפָרִים שֶׁלָּמַדְתִּי, יַעֲמֹד לִי וּלְזַרְעִי וּלְזֶרַע זַרְעִי, שֶׁלֹּא תָּמוּשׁ הַתּוֹרָה הַקְּדוֹשָׁה מִפִּי וּמִפִּי זַרְעִי וְזֶרַע זַרְעִי מֵעַתָּה וְעַד עוֹלָם. וִיקֻיַּם בִּי מִקְרָא שֶׁכָּתוּב: בְּהִתְהַלֶּכְךָ תַּנְחֶה אֹתָךְ, בְּשָׁכְבְּךָ תִּשְׁמֹר עָלֶיךָ, וַהֲקִיצוֹתָ הִיא תְשִׂיחֶךָ. כִּי בִי יִרְבּוּ יָמֶיךָ, וְיוֹסִיפוּ לְךָ שְׁנוֹת חַיִּים. אֹרֶךְ יָמִים בִּימִינָהּ, בִּשְׂמֹאולָהּ עֹשֶׁר וְכָבוֹד. יהוה עֹז לְעַמּוֹ יִתֵּן, יהוה יְבָרֵךְ אֶת עַמּוֹ בַשָּׁלוֹם.

If a minyan *is present, the following version of the Rabbis' Kaddish is recited by one or more of those present. It may be recited even by one whose parents are still living.*

יִתְגַּדַּל וְיִתְקַדַּשׁ שְׁמֵהּ רַבָּא. (.Cong – אָמֵן) בְּעָלְמָא דִּי הוּא עָתִיד לְאִתְחַדְתָּא, וּלְאַחֲיָאָה מֵתַיָּא, וּלְאַסָּקָא יָתְהוֹן לְחַיֵּי עָלְמָא, וּלְמִבְנֵא קַרְתָּא דִירוּשְׁלֵם, וּלְשַׁכְלְלָא הֵיכְלֵהּ בְּגַוַּהּ, וּלְמֶעְקַר פָּלְחָנָא נֻכְרָאָה מִן אַרְעָא, וְלַאֲתָבָא פָּלְחָנָא דִי שְׁמַיָּא לְאַתְרֵהּ, וְיַמְלִיךְ קֻדְשָׁא בְּרִיךְ הוּא בְּמַלְכוּתֵהּ וִיקָרֵהּ, [וְיַצְמַח פֻּרְקָנֵהּ וִיקָרֵב מְשִׁיחֵהּ (.Cong – אָמֵן).] בְּחַיֵּיכוֹן וּבְיוֹמֵיכוֹן וּבְחַיֵּי דְכָל בֵּית יִשְׂרָאֵל, בַּעֲגָלָא וּבִזְמַן קָרִיב. וְאִמְרוּ: אָמֵן.

(.Cong – אָמֵן. יְהֵא שְׁמֵהּ רַבָּא מְבָרַךְ לְעָלַם וּלְעָלְמֵי עָלְמַיָּא.)
יְהֵא שְׁמֵהּ רַבָּא מְבָרַךְ לְעָלַם וּלְעָלְמֵי עָלְמַיָּא.
יִתְבָּרַךְ וְיִשְׁתַּבַּח וְיִתְפָּאַר וְיִתְרוֹמַם וְיִתְנַשֵּׂא וְיִתְהַדָּר וְיִתְעַלֶּה וְיִתְהַלָּל שְׁמֵהּ דְּקֻדְשָׁא (.Cong – בְּרִיךְ הוּא) °לְעֵלָּא מִן כָּל (°לְעֵלָּא וּלְעֵלָּא מִכָּל – *From Rosh Hashanah to Yom Kippur substitute*) בִּרְכָתָא וְשִׁירָתָא תֻּשְׁבְּחָתָא וְנֶחֱמָתָא, דַּאֲמִירָן בְּעָלְמָא. וְאִמְרוּ: אָמֵן. (.Cong – אָמֵן).

עַל יִשְׂרָאֵל וְעַל רַבָּנָן, וְעַל תַּלְמִידֵיהוֹן וְעַל כָּל תַּלְמִידֵי תַלְמִידֵיהוֹן, וְעַל כָּל מָאן דְּעָסְקִין בְּאוֹרַיְתָא, דִּי בְאַתְרָא [בארץ ישראל: קַדִּישָׁא] הָדֵין וְדִי בְכָל אֲתַר וַאֲתַר. יְהֵא לְהוֹן וּלְכוֹן שְׁלָמָא רַבָּא, חִנָּא וְחִסְדָּא וְרַחֲמִין, וְחַיִּין אֲרִיכִין, וּמְזוֹנֵי רְוִיחֵי, וּפֻרְקָנָא מִן קֳדָם אֲבוּהוֹן דִּי בִשְׁמַיָּא [וְאַרְעָא]. וְאִמְרוּ: אָמֵן. (.Cong – אָמֵן).

יְהֵא שְׁלָמָא רַבָּא מִן שְׁמַיָּא, וְחַיִּים [טוֹבִים] עָלֵינוּ וְעַל כָּל יִשְׂרָאֵל. וְאִמְרוּ: אָמֵן. (.Cong – אָמֵן).

Take three steps back. Bow left and say . . . עֹשֶׂה; *bow right and say* . . . הוּא; *bow forward and say* וְעַל כָּל . . . אָמֵן. *Remain standing in place for a few moments, then take three steps forward.*

עֹשֶׂה שָׁלוֹם בִּמְרוֹמָיו, הוּא בְּרַחֲמָיו יַעֲשֶׂה שָׁלוֹם עָלֵינוּ, וְעַל כָּל יִשְׂרָאֵל. וְאִמְרוּ: אָמֵן. (.Cong – אָמֵן).

and Torah scholars that are mentioned in the Order of Zeraim and in all the books that I have studied, stand by me and my children and my children's children, that the Holy Torah shall not depart from my mouth and from the mouth of my children and my children's children forever. May it be fulfilled for me: *When you walk, it (i.e., the Torah) will guide you; when you lie down, it will watch over you; and when you wake up, it will converse with you. For because of me (i.e., the Torah), your days will increase, and years of life will be added to you. Long days are in its right hand, and in its left hand are wealth and honor. Hashem will give might to His people, Hashem will bless His people with peace.*

If a minyan is present, the following version of the Rabbis' Kaddish is recited by one or more of those present.
It may be recited even by one whose parents are still living.

יִתְגַּדַּל May His great Name grow exalted and sanctified (Cong. — Amen) in the world that will be renewed and where He will revivify the dead and raise them up to eternal life, and rebuild the city of Jerusalem and complete His Temple within it, and uproot alien worship from the earth, and return the service of Heaven to its place, and may the Holy One, Blessed is He, reign in His sovereignty and splendor [and cause salvation to sprout and bring near His Messiah (Cong. — Amen)] in your lifetimes and in your days, and in the lifetimes of the entire House of Israel, swiftly and soon. Now respond: Amen.

(Cong. — Amen. May His great Name be blessed forever and ever.)
May His great Name be blessed forever and ever.

Blessed, praised, glorified, exalted, extolled, mighty, upraised, and lauded be the Name of the Holy One, Blessed is He (Cong. — Blessed is He), (From Rosh Hashanah to Yom Kippur add: *exceedingly*) beyond any blessing and song, praise, and consolation that are uttered in the world. Now respond: Amen. (Cong. — Amen.)

Upon Israel, upon the teachers, upon their disciples and upon all of their disciples' disciples and upon all those who engage in the study of Torah, who are in this place or anywhere else; may they and you have abundant peace, grace, kindness, and mercy, long life, ample nourishment, and salvation, from before their Father Who is in Heaven [and on earth]. Now respond: Amen. (Cong. — Amen.)

May there be abundant peace from Heaven, and [good] life upon us and upon all Israel. Now respond: Amen. (Cong. — Amen.)

Take three steps back. Bow left and say, "He Who makes peace . . ."; bow right and say, "may He . . ."; bow forward and say, "and upon all Israel . . . Amen." Remain standing in place for a few moments, then take three steps forward.

He Who makes peace in His heights, may He, in His compassion, make peace upon us, and upon all Israel. Now respond: Amen. (Cong. — Amen.)

Appendix

Appendix: Laws of Tumah

The laws of *tumah* come up throughout the Mishnah. Indeed, the last of the Six Orders of Mishnah — *Seder Tohoros* — is devoted entirely to this topic. Since these laws unfortunately do not play a significant role in daily Jewish life nowadays (as the Temple is not standing) and most people are unfamiliar with them, we present here a short introduction to this very intricate topic.

Tumah is a type of halachic impurity that attaches itself to people, utensils, and foods under certain circumstances or as a result of special conditions. The laws of *tumah* and its counterpart *taharah* (purity) are Scriptural decrees, whose roots cannot be understood through ordinary human logic and experience (*Rambam, Hil. Mikvaos* 11:12). For this reason, their terminology cannot be simply translated. Therefore, we will use a number of Hebrew terms to explain the Mishnah's discussions of these laws, with which the reader must be familiar to follow the explanations of many Mishnahs.

◆§ Sources of *Tumah*

The Torah classifies certain people and items as "sources of *tumah*." These include a human corpse, a *neveilah* (any animal carcass except for that of a kosher animal killed through *shechitah*), a *sheretz* (the carcass of one of eight species of creeping things listed in *Leviticus* 11:29-30), a *zav* (a man who experienced emissions that resemble, but are not identical to, seminal emissions), a *niddah* (menstruant woman), and others that are listed in the first chapter of *Keilim*. Each of these main sources of *tumah* is known as an *av hatumah* (literally, *father of tumah*) except for a human corpse, whose more stringent *tumah* is known as *avi avos hatumah* (*father of fathers of tumah*). An *av hatumah* [and certainly an *avi avos hatumah*] transmits *tumah* to people, utensils, and foods and beverages that touch it or come in contact with it in various other ways.

◆§ Objects That Can Become *Tamei*

As mentioned above, there are three categories of things that can become *tamei* through contact with a source of *tumah*: (a) people; (b) utensils (objects that have been fashioned to be used in some way, such as chairs, dishes, lamps, or clothing, in contrast to blocks of wood, gold, clay, or random strands of wool, etc.); and (c) beverages, or foods that have become wet through contact with one of seven liquids (dew, water, wine, olive oil, blood, milk, or honey). These different categories are subject to different levels of *tumah* (as will be explained below).

[3] **APPENDIX** / Laws of Tumah

⊷§ The Transfer of *Tumah* and Degrees of *Tumah*

Tumah is passed from an *av hatumah* to a person, utensil, food, or beverage that comes in contact with it, and these in turn can have the ability to pass the *tumah* further. The *tumah* weakens, however, each time it is passed on. Thus, when an *av hatumah* transmits *tumah* to a person or object, the person or object becomes a רִאשׁוֹן לְטוּמְאָה, *rishon* of *tumah* (first degree of received *tumah*). This level of *tumah* is too weak to transmit *tumah* to people or utensils, and it can transmit further *tumah* only to foods and beverages. These in turn can become *tamei* as a שֵׁנִי לְטוּמְאָה, *sheni* of *tumah* (second degree of received *tumah*). [These terms are generally abbreviated simply as *av*, *rishon*, and *sheni*.]

A *sheni* is too weak to transmit *tumah* to *chullin* (non-holy) food that it touches — which makes it impossible for ordinary food to possess a third degree of acquired *tumah*. Due to the greater degree of stringency associated with *terumah*, however, it can become *tamei* as a *shelishi*, or third degree of received *tumah*, if it is touched by a *sheni*. But even the *tumah* of *terumah* can go no further than this third degree. [Food that is *kodesh* (such as the parts of offerings) can receive an additional degree of *tumah*. If *kodesh* food is touched by a *shelishi*, it becomes a *revi'i* (fourth degree of received *tumah*).]

Although usually *chullin* foods touched by a *rishon* become *tamei* as a *sheni*, the Rabbis made a special decree that *beverages* touched by *tamei food* (whether the food is *tamei* as a *rishon* or as a *sheni*) always become a *rishon*. They can then render other foods a *sheni* by touching them.

⊷§ How *Tumah* Is Transmitted

All main sources of *tumah* (*avos hatumah*) can transmit their *tumah* to other objects if one touches them (מַגָּע). Most *avos* also transmit *tumah* to one who carries them even without touching them (מַשָּׂא), or even causes them to be moved without touching or carrying them (הֶיסֵּט).

Avos hatumah that are living persons (such as a *zav* or a *niddah*) also render *tamei* any bed, chair, etc. that they sit or lie upon (מִשְׁכָּב וּמוֹשָׁב), even if it is covered and they do not touch it directly or move it. Also, the bed or chair (called a מִדְרָס) is an exception to the rule discussed above, because it itself becomes an *av hatumah*, rather than a *rishon*, and has the capacity to render people and utensils *tamei* (not only foods and beverages as a *rishon* does).

A human corpse (as well as certain parts of a corpse) can also transmit *tumah* through *tumas ohel* (tent-*tumah* or roof-*tumah*). A corpse renders people or objects *tamei* through *tumas ohel* (a) if the corpse is in the same tent (under the same roof) as they are; or (b) if the corpse forms a roof over them; or (c) if they form a roof over the corpse. The details of these complex laws are discussed in Tractate *Oholos*.

⊷§ Items That Do Not Become *Tamei*

Live animals do not become *tamei*; animal food not fit for human consumption also cannot become *tamei*; nor can anything attached to the ground (such as a tree or plant) become *tamei*.

Utensils made of stone or unbaked earth do not become *tamei*. Flat wooden

utensils that have no receptacle or hollow in which something can be contained (e.g., a wooden cutting board) also cannot be rendered *tamei*.

Foods that have not been "prepared" (מֻכְשָׁר) for *tumah* by being wetted by one of the seven liquids mentioned above do not become *tamei*. [These laws are the subject of Tractate *Machshirin*.] Once they have been "prepared" they can become *tamei* even after they are dry.

Earthenware utensils (כְּלִי חֶרֶס) are unique in that they become *tamei* only if their *inside* (or even their interior airspace) is touched; even if a corpse (the most severe source of *tumah*) touches only the outside of an earthenware utensil, it remains *tahor*. Also, an earthenware utensil that is *tamei* transmits *tumah* only to objects that touch its interior.

◆§ Removing *Tumah*

Tumah is removed from people and most utensils that become *tamei* as a *rishon* through immersion in a *mikveh*. Earthenware utensils, however, cannot be purified of *tumah*; foods and beverages (other than water) also cannot be purified of *tumah*.

After immersing in a *mikveh*, the person (or utensil) is known as a טְבוּל יוֹם, *tevul yom* (one who immersed that day), and will no longer render *tamei* any food or beverage he touches. He may also eat *maaser sheni* immediately after immersion. However, he still renders *terumah* or *kodesh* that he touches *tamei* until nightfall (הַעֲרֵב שֶׁמֶשׁ) of the day of his immersion.

A person who is an *av hatumah* (such as a *zav*, or a person who touched a human corpse) requires additional procedures to remove his or her *tumah*. The procedures vary with each type of *tumah*, and sometimes include the bringing of offerings, or the passage of certain time periods.

The *tumah* of a non-living *av hatumah* (such as *neveilah*, or corpses) cannot be removed.

◆§ Consequences of *Tumah*

Tamei persons and objects may not enter the Temple (*Beis HaMikdash*). *Terumah, maaser sheni,* and *kodesh* foods that become *tamei* may not be eaten and must be burned. By contrast, *chullin* foods that become *tamei* may be eaten (although some people were careful to eat only *tahor* foods), and *tamei* utensils may be used for ordinary, non-sacred purposes.

Glossary

Glossary

Adar — the twelfth month of the Jewish calendar.

Altar — the structure in the **Temple** Courtyard upon which the blood of offerings was poured and on which part or all of their meat or flour were burned. See also **Inner Altar**.

am haaretz [plural, **amei haaretz**] — an unlearned person. This refers to someone who is not careful in his observance of the laws of **tumah** and **taharah**. *Amei haaretz* were also suspected of not separating **maaser**.

amah [plural, **amos**] — cubit; a measure of distance equaling six **tefachim**. Opinions regarding its modern equivalent range between 18.9 and 22.7 inches (48-57.7 cm.).

Antechamber — the **Ulam**; the Hall in the Sanctuary Building that led into the Sanctuary.

aravah [plural, **aravos**] — twigs of a willow tree. See **Four Species**.

arei miklat — see **ir miklat**.

Ark — the sacred chest that stood in the Holy of Holies in the **Mishkan** and the First **Temple**. It contained the Tablets of the Ten Commandments and the Torah Scroll written by Moses.

asham [plural, **ashamos**] — guilt offering; an offering brought to atone for one of several specific sins or as part of certain purification procedures. It is one of the **kodshei kodashim**.

asheirah — a tree that was designated for worship or under which an idol is placed.

asmachta — a Scriptural source that hints at a Rabbinic law.

av [plural, **avos**] **hatumah** — literally, father of **tumah**. See *tumah*.

avi avos hatumah — literally, father of fathers of **tumah**; a corpse. See *tumah*.

avodah [plural, **avodos**] — (a) a part of the sacrificial service in the **Temple**; (b) the Temple service as a whole.

Azazel — (a) the he-goat chosen by lottery to be thrown off a cliff on Yom Kippur; (b) the cliff from which it was thrown.

bagrus — the state of being a **bogeress**.

bamah — (a) major *bamah*; the **Altar** that stood next to the **Mishkan** when the Mishkan was located in Gilgal, Nov, and Givon; (b) minor *bamah*; altar built by an individual on which he offered his personal, voluntary offerings.

bechor — (a) firstborn male child; (b) a firstborn male kosher animal. Such an animal is born with sacrificial sanctity, and must be given to a **Kohen** who then offers it (if unblemished) as a *bechor* offering in the **Temple** and eats its meat.

bein hashemashos — the twilight period preceding night. The legal status of *bein hashemashos* as day or night is uncertain.

beis av — a family group within a **mishmar**.

beis din — Rabbinic court.

Beis HaMikdash — **Temple** in Jerusalem.

beis kor — 75,000 square **amos**.

beis se'ah — an area 50 **amos** by 50 *amos*.

Bircas HaMazon — the blessings recited after a meal.

bogeress — see **naarah**.

b'shogeig — inadvertently.

chadash — literally, new; the new crop of any of the five grains (wheat, barley, rye, spelt, oats). *Chadash* may not be eaten until the **omer** offering is brought on the second day of **Pesach**.

chalitzah — see **yibum**.

challah — the portion separated from a dough made of the five grains; it must be given to a **Kohen**.

chalal — the male child of a **Kohen** and a woman who is forbidden specifically to Kohanim (for example, a divorcee). Although his father is a Kohen, a *chalal* is not a Kohen. The son of a *chalal* is also a *chalal*, and his daughter is a **chalalah**.

chalalah — (a) the female child of a **Kohen** and a woman who is forbidden specifically to Kohanim; (b) the daughter of a **chalal**; (c) a woman forbidden specifically to Kohanim who cohabited with a Kohen; (d) a woman who cohabited with a *chalal*. A *chalalah* is prohibited to marry a Kohen or eat **terumah**.

chametz — grain that was mixed with water and allowed to leaven before being baked. Only five grains — wheat, barley, spelt, rye, and oats — can become *chametz*.

Chanukah — Festival of Lights; the eight-day holiday that commemorates the Maccabean victory over the Greeks.

chatas [pl. **chataos**] — sin offering; an offering usually brought in atonement for the inadvertent transgression of a prohibition punishable by **kares** when transgressed deliberately.

chatzitzah — literally, an interposition; foreign matter attached or adhering to the person or object that needs to be immersed in a **mikveh**, which prevents the water from coming in contact with the whole of its surface. This invalidates the immersion.

chaver [plural, **chaveirim**] — (a) one who observes the laws of **tumah** and **taharah** even with respect to non-consecrated foods; (b) a Torah scholar, scrupulous in his observance of mitzvos.

chavitin — a **minchah** offering that consists of flour and oil; half of it was offered with the morning **tamid** and half with the afternoon *tamid*. The **Kohen Gadol** brings a *chavitin* every day; an ordinary **Kohen** brings it on his first day of service in the **Temple**.

cherem — (a) a vow in which one uses the expression "*cherem*" to consecrate property, placing it under the ownership of the **Temple** or the **Kohanim**; (b) land or property upon which a ban has been declared, forbidding its use to anyone.

chilazon — an aquatic creature from whose blood the blue *techeiles* dye was produced.

Chol HaMoed — the intermediate days of the festivals of **Pesach** and **Succos**. These festivals begin and end with a holy day (**Yom Tov**), during which most forms of work (**melachah**) are forbidden, and they are separated by intermediate days — known as "Chol HaMoed," literally, the ordinary part of the festival — during which certain forms of *melachah* are permitted.

chullin — literally, ordinary things; any substance that is not sanctified or consecrated. See **kodesh**.

Curtain — the **Paroches**; the curtain that divided between the **Holy** and the **Holy of Holies** in the **Sanctuary**.

Cutheans — a non-Jewish tribe brought by the Assyrians to settle the part of **Eretz Yisrael** left vacant by the exile of the Ten Tribes. The Cutheans' subsequent conversion to Judaism was considered questionable and their observance of many laws was lax.

demai — produce of **Eretz Yisrael** obtained from an **am haaretz**. The Rabbis required that **maasros** be separated from *demai* because the *am haaretz* might not have done so.

eglah arufah — literally, decapitated calf; when a murder victim is found and the murderer is not known, the **beis din** measures to determine the city closest to where the corpse lies. The elders of that city decapitate a calf, in accordance with the procedures outlined in *Deuteronomy* 21:1-9.

emurin — the fats and internal organs of an animal offering that are burned on the **Altar**.

Eretz Yisrael — the Land of Israel.

Erev Pesach — the fourteenth of **Nissan**, the day before **Pesach**.

erusin — betrothal; the first act of marriage [also known as **kiddushin**]. This is effected by the man giving the

woman an object of value to betroth her. At this point, the couple is not yet permitted to have marital relations, but is legally married in most respects and the woman requires a **get** before she can marry again. The period between *erusin* (*kiddushin*) and **nisuin** is also called *erusin*.

eruv — popular contraction of **eruvei tavshilin** or **eruvei techumin**.

eruv tavshilin — food cooked before a **Yom Tov** that falls on Friday and is intended to be eaten on **Shabbos**. If one prepares such food before the Yom Tov, one is permitted on that Yom Tov to prepare food for Shabbos.

eruvei techumin — literally, merging of boundaries; a legal device that allows a person to shift his **Shabbos** residence from the place where he is to any place up to 2,000 **amos** away. One accomplishes this by placing a specific amount of food at the desired location before the start of Shabbos or by being there himself when Shabbos begins. That place is then viewed as the person's Shabbos residence, and his 2,000-*amah* **techum** limit is measured from there.

esrog — citron; one of the **Four Species**.

Four Species — it is a Biblical obligation to take the following four species on Succos: the **lulav** (branch of a palm tree), **esrog** (citron), **hadassim** (twigs of a myrtle tree), and **aravos** (twigs of a willow tree).

fourfold and fivefold payments — the fine that must be paid by a **ganav** who stole a sheep or ox and slaughtered or sold it. In addition to the value of the sheep or ox, he must pay a fine of three times as much (in the case of the sheep) or four times as much (in the case of the ox).

fund for the upkeep of the Temple — fund comprised of voluntary contributions that was used to pay for repairs to the **Temple**.

ganav — a thief who steals secretly.

gazlan — a thief who robs openly, by force or by threatening force.

ger toshav — resident foreigner; a non-Jew who agrees not to worship idols and is therefore allowed to live in **Eretz Yisrael**.

get [plural, **gittin**] — bill of divorce; the document that, when placed in the wife's possession, effects the end of the marriage.

gezeirah shavah — one of the thirteen principles of Biblical derivation. If a similar word or phrase occurs in two passages in the Torah, the principle of *gezeirah shavah* teaches that these passages are linked to each other, and the laws of one passage are applied to the other. Only those words that are designated by the Oral Sinaitic Law for this purpose may serve as a basis for a *gezeirah shavah*.

goel hadam — relative of someone who has been killed; he may avenge the death by killing the killer.

Golden Altar — see **Inner Altar**.

hadassim — twigs of a myrtle tree; one of the **Four Species**.

hagbanah — see **kinyan**.

half-pras — measure of volume that is equivalent to two eggs.

Hallel — prayer of praise to God that is recited on **Pesach, Succos, Shavuos, Chanukah,** and **Rosh Chodesh**. It consists of *Psalms* 113-118.

hazamah — a process of discrediting witnesses. After witnesses testify that a certain event took place, another set of witnesses discredits them by saying that they could not have seen the event because they were in a different place at that time.

hekdesh — (a) items consecrated to the **Temple** treasury or as offerings. *Hekdesh* can have two levels of sanctity: **monetary sanctity** and **physical sanctity**. Property owned by the Temple treasury is said to have monetary sanctity. Such property can be redeemed or sold by the Temple treasurers, with the proceeds of the redemption or sale becoming *hekdesh* in its place. Consecrated items that are fit for the Temple service (e.g., unblemished animals or

sacred vessels) are deemed to have physical sanctity; (b) the state of consecration; (c) the Temple treasury.

Holy — the chamber in the Temple that contained the **Shulchan, Menorah,** and the **Inner (Golden) Altar.**

Holy of Holies — the most sacred part of the **Temple.** During most of the First Temple era, it contained the Holy Ark; later it was empty of any utensils. Even the **Kohen Gadol** is prohibited from entering it except on **Yom Kippur.**

Inner Altar — structure inside the main chamber of the **Temple** building on which the **ketores** offerings were burned. See also **Altar.**

ir miklat (plural, **arei miklat**) — one of several towns in Eretz Yisrael to which someone who killed a person inadvertently is exiled.

Iyar — the second month of the Jewish calendar.

kares — cutting off of the soul or premature death; Divinely imposed punishment decreed by the Torah for certain classes of transgression.

kav — measure of volume equivalent to 24 eggs.

kebeitzah — an egg's volume.

keifel — the fine that a **ganav** must pay. In addition to returning the stolen item (or its value), he must pay a fine of the same value.

keilim [singular, **kli**] — utensil or vessel.

keren — literally, horn; damage that an animal does through unusual behavior, such as a tame animal goring another animal with its horns.

kesubah — (a) the marriage contract that a groom hands over to his bride when they get married, in which his commitments toward her are recorded; (b) the payment that a husband (or his estate) must make to his wife if their marriage ends in divorce or his death. If she was a virgin when she got married, the payment is at least 200 *zuz*; if she was not a virgin, the payment is at least 100 *zuz*.

Kesuvim — see **Writings.**

ketanah — an underaged girl. See **naarah.**

ketores — a mixture of aromatic spices and other substances that was burned twice every day in the **Temple,** and a third time on **Yom Kippur.**

kezayis — the volume of an olive; minimum amount of food whose consumption is considered "eating."

Kiddush — the blessing recited over wine before the evening and morning meals on the **Sabbath** and **Yom Tov.**

kiddushin — see **erusin.**

kilayim — "mixtures"; various forbidden mixtures, including: **shaatnez** (cloth made from a blend of wool and linen); cross-breeding of animals; cross-breeding (or side-by-side planting) of certain food crops; and working with different species of animals yoked together.

kinyan — an act through which a person acquires ownership of property; examples of a *kinyan* are **hagbahah** (lifting the object) and **meshichah** (drawing it away from where it is).

kiyor — large basin of water that stood in the **Temple** Courtyard to which faucets were attached. The **Kohanim** washed their hands and feet with water from the *kiyor*.

kodashim — sacrificial food.

kodashim kalim — offerings of lesser holiness (one of the two classifications of sacrificial offerings). They may be eaten anywhere in Jerusalem by any **tahor** person. They include the **todah,** regular **shelamim, bechor, nazir's** ram, **maaser,** and **pesach** offerings. This category of offerings is not subject to the stringencies applied to **kodshei kodashim.**

kodesh — (a) portions of sacrificial offerings; (b) any consecrated item.

kodshei kodashim — most-holy offerings (one of the two classifications of sacrificial offerings). They may be eaten only in the **Temple** Courtyard and only by male **Kohanim.** They include the **olah** (which may not be eaten at all), **chatas, asham,** and communal **shelamim.** These are subject to greater stringencies than **kodashim kalim.**

[11] GLOSSARY

Kohen [plural, **Kohanim**] — member of the priestly family descended in the male line from Aaron. The Kohen performs the service in the **Temple**.

Kohen Gadol — High Priest.

konam — a word that can substitute for **korban**. It is used in **nedarim**; for example, "This object is *konam* to me."

korban — a sacred offering.

lavud — rule stating that a gap of less than three **tefachim** is legally viewed as closed.

lechem hapanim — *panim* breads. The twelve loaves of bread baked in a special way that were placed on the **Shulchan** in the **Temple** each **Shabbos**. They remained until the next Shabbos, when they were eaten by the **Kohanim**.

Levi [plural, **Leviim**] — male descendant of the tribe of Levi in the male line, who performs secondary services in the **Beis HaMikdash**.

lishkah — the **lishkah** (or **terumas halishkah**) is the name of a fund in which the annual half-**shekel** contributions were collected. This fund was used to pay for the communal offerings and general expenses related to the Temple service.

log [plural, **lugin**] — liquid measure equal to the volume of six eggs.

lulav — branch of a palm tree; one of the **Four Species**.

maamar — The Sages decreed that before performing **yibum**, the **yavam** first "betroth" the **yevamah** by performing one of the acts that normally effect **erusin**. This act of pre-*yibum* betrothal is called **maamar**.

Maariv — the evening prayer service.

maasar ani — the tithe for the poor, given in the third and sixth years of the **shemittah** cycle.

maasar beheimah — the animal tithe. The newborn kosher animals born to one's herds and flocks each year are gathered into a pen and made to pass through an opening one at a time. Every tenth animal is designated as **maaser**. It is brought as an offering in the **Temple** and is eaten by the owner.

maaser [plural, **maasros**] — tithe. It is a Biblical obligation to give two tithes, each known as *maaser*, from the produce of the Land of Israel. The first tithe (**maaser rishon**) is given to a **Levi**. The second tithe (**maaser sheni**) is taken to Jerusalem and eaten there, or redeemed with coins that are then taken to Jerusalem for the purchase of food to be eaten there. In the third and sixth years of the seven-year **shemittah** cycle, the *maaser sheni* obligation is replaced with **maasar ani**, the tithe for the poor.

maaser rishon — see **maaser**.

maaser sheni — see **maaser**.

malkus — lashes; punishment given to someone who violates certain laws of the Torah.

mamzer (fem. **mamzeress**) — a child born from a forbidden union that is punishable by **kares**, or from a parent who is a *mamzer* or *mamzeress*. The Torah forbids marriage or cohabitation between a *mamzer* or *mamzeress* and a regular Jew.

maror — the bitter herb that one is obligated to eat on the first night of **Pesach**.

matzah — unleavened bread; dough that was baked before it was allowed to ferment or rise. It is a Biblical obligation to eat matzah on the first night of **Pesach**.

mazik — a person who damages the body or property of someone else, or whose property does such damage.

mechussar kapparah [plural, **mechussarei kapparah**] — literally, lacking atonement; the status accorded to a **tevul yom** in the interval between sunset of the day of his immersion and the time he brings his offerings. During that period, he retains a vestige of his earlier **tumah** and is thus forbidden to enter the **Temple** Courtyard or partake of the offerings.

mei chatas — see **parah adumah**.

me'ilah — unlawfully benefiting from **Temple** property or removing such property from the Temple ownership. One who does so inadvertently must

GLOSSARY [12]

pay the value of the item plus a quarter. He must also bring an **asham** offering.

melachah [plural, **melachos**] — labor; specifically, one of the thirty-nine labor categories whose performance is forbidden by the Torah on **Shabbos** and **Yom Tov**. These prohibited categories are known as *avos melachah*. Activities whose prohibition is derived from one of these thirty-nine categories are known as **tolados** (singular, *toladah*) — subcategories.

melikah — the unique manner in which bird offerings were slaughtered. *Melikah* differs from **shechitah** in two respects: (a) The cut is made with the **Kohen's** thumbnail rather than with a knife. (b) The neck is cut from the back rather than from the throat. Only birds for sacrificial purposes may be slaughtered by *melikah;* all others require *shechitah*.

melog — property that a bride brings into the marriage that is not recorded in the **kesubah** document. It belongs to her but the husband has the right to use it, and any profit generated from it is his.

Menorah — the seven-branched gold candelabra that stood in the main chamber of the **Temple**.

meshichah — see **kinyan**.

metzora — a person who has contracted **tzaraas** (mistakenly described as leprosy), an affliction of the skin described in *Leviticus* Chs. 13 and 14.

mezuzah [plural, **mezuzos**] — a parchment scroll that contains the passages of *Deuteronomy* 6:4-9 and 11:13-21; it is affixed to the doorpost.

midras — literally, treading; an object that acquired **tumah** when a zav, zavah, niddah, or woman after childbirth rests his or her weight on it. It is an **av hatumah**.

mikveh — a body of standing water containing at least forty *se'ah*. It is used to purify (by immersion) people and utensils of their **tumah**-contamination. A *mikveh* consists of waters naturally collected, without direct human intervention. Water drawn in a vessel is not valid for a *mikveh*.

mil — distance of 2,000 **amos**.

minchah — (a) [upper case] the afternoon prayer service; (b) [plural, **menachos**] a flour offering, generally consisting of fine wheat flour, oil, and frankincense, part of which is burned on the **Altar**.

minyan — quorum of ten adult Jewish males necessary for the communal prayer service and other rituals.

Mishkan — the portable Temple used during the forty years of national wandering in the Wilderness. After the Jews entered **Eretz Yisrael**, it was situated in different places (Gilgal, Shiloh, Nov, and Givon) until the **Beis HaMikdash** was built in Jerusalem.

mishmar [plural, **mishmaros**] — literally, watch; one of the twenty-four watches of **Kohanim** and **Leviim** who served in the **Temple** for a week at a time on a rotating basis. These watches were subdivided into family groups, each of which served on one day of the week. A family group is called a **beis av** (literally, father's house).

mi'un — By Rabbinic enactment, an underaged orphan girl may be given in marriage by her mother or brothers. She can annul the marriage anytime before reaching adulthood by declaring her unwillingness to continue in the marriage. This declaration and process are called *mi'un*.

monetary sanctity — the level of sanctity of items consecrated to the **Temple**, not to be offered on the **Altar** but to be sold for their value, with the proceeds being used for Temple purposes. See **hekdesh**.

muad — an animal that habitually does damage in a certain way.

muktzeh — literally, set aside; (a) a class of objects that the Sages prohibited moving on **Shabbos** or **Yom Tov**; (b) an animal set aside to be sacrificed for idolatry.

mussaf — (a) additional offerings brought on **Shabbos, Rosh Chodesh,**

or **Yom Tov**; (b) [upper case] the prayer service recited on the days that these offerings are brought.

naarah — There are three stages in the life of a maturing girl. She is a **ketanah** (minor) from the day of her birth until she reaches the age of twelve and grows two pubic hairs, at which point she becomes a *naarah* (partial adult). She remains a *naarah* for six months, after which she becomes a **bogeress** (full adult).

nasin (fem. **nesinah**) — a descendant of the Gibeonites, a group of Canaanites who tricked Joshua into making a peace treaty with them. An ordinary Jew is forbidden to marry a *nasin* or a *nesinah*.

nazir [plural, **nezirim**] — one who took a special vow that prohibits him, for a minimum period of thirty days, from cutting his hair, drinking wine (or eating any part of a grape), and becoming **tamei** from a corpse.

neder — a vow that renders objects, in contrast to actions, prohibited. There are two basic categories of vows: (a) prohibitive vows; (b) vows to donate to **hekdesh**. See **hekdesh**.

nesachim [singular, **nesech**] — libations; a liquid (usually wine) that is poured upon the **Altar**. It accompanies certain offerings or may be donated separately.

nesinah — see **nasin**.

neveilah — carcass of an animal that was not killed through **shechitah**.

Neviim — see **Prophets**.

nezirus — the state of being a **nazir**.

niddah — a woman who has menstruated but has not yet completed her purification process, which concludes with immersion in a **mikveh**.

Nissan — the first month of the Jewish calendar.

nisuch hamayim — the mitzvah of pouring water on the **Altar** on each day of **Succos**.

nisuin — the second act of marriage, after which the couple is allowed to live together. It is effected by a procedure called *chuppah*. The period between *nisuin* and the end of the marriage is also known as *nisuin*. See **erusin**.

nizak — a person who suffers damage to his body or his property.

nolad — literally, newborn. Objects that are **muktzeh** because they did not exist (or were not usable) before **Shabbos** or **Yom Tov** began.

nossar — part of an offering left over after the time permitted for eating it has passed.

olah [plural, **olos**] — burnt offering; an offering that is burned in its entirety on the **Altar**.

omer — a communal **minchah** offering brought on the 16th of **Nissan**. Once it was brought, the new grain crop (**chadash**) became permitted to be eaten.

ona'ah — price fraud; taking advantage of someone who does not know the true price of an item, by selling it to him for more than the market value, or buying it from him for less than the market value.

orlah — literally, sealed; fruit that grows on a tree during the first three years of the tree's existence. The Torah prohibits any benefit from such fruit.

parah adumah — literally, red cow. A completely red cow is slaughtered and burned; its ashes are mixed with spring water and then used in the purification process of people or objects who have contracted **tumah** from a human corpse.

Paroches — see **Curtain**.

Pesach — Passover; the **Yom Tov** that celebrates the Exodus of the Jewish nation from Egypt.

pesach offering — offering brought on the afternoon of the 14th day of **Nissan** and eaten after nightfall.

physical sanctity — the level of sanctity possessed by items consecrated to be used as offerings. See **hekdesh**.

Prophets (Neviim) — the second of the three sections of the Written Torah. It consists of the following books: *Joshua, Judges, Samuel, Kings, Isaiah, Jeremiah, Ezekiel, Twelve Prophets.*

prozbul — The Torah states that all loans are canceled at the end of the **shemittah** year. The Rabbis enacted a law allowing for loans to be collected after the *shemittah* year through a process whereby the lender authorizes the court in advance of *shemittah* to collect all his debts. The document that authorizes the court to assume responsibility for the collection of those debts is called a *prozbul*.

regel [plural, **regalim**] — (a) any of the three pilgrimage festivals: **Pesach, Shavuos,** and **Succos**; (b) damage that an animal does in the course of walking or other normal movement.

reshus harabim — literally, public domain; any unroofed, commonly used street, public area, or highway at least sixteen **amos** wide and open at both ends. According to some, it must be used by at least 600,000 people.

reshus hayachid — literally, private domain; any area measuring at least four **tefachim** by four *tefachim* and enclosed by partitions at least ten *tefachim* high. According to most opinions, it needs to be enclosed only on three sides to qualify as a *reshus hayachid*. Private ownership is not necessary.

revi'i of tumah — see **tumah.**

revi'is — a quarter of a **log.**

rishon of tumah — first degree of acquired **tumah**. See *tumah.*

Rosh Chodesh — (a) festival celebrating the new month; (b) the first of the month.

Rosh Hashanah — the **Yom Tov** that celebrates the new year. It falls on the first and second days of **Tishrei.**

Sadducees — heretical sect active during the Second **Temple** era, named after Tzaddok, a disciple of Antigenos of Socho. They denied the Divine origin of the Oral Law and refused to accept the Sages' interpretation of the Torah.

Sanctuary — (a) the **Holy**; (b) the main **Temple** building that included the Holy and the **Holy of Holies.**

Sanhedrin — (a) the High Court of Israel; the Supreme Court consisting of seventy-one judges whose decisions on questions of Torah law are definitive and binding on all courts; (b) [lower case] a court of twenty-three judges authorized to adjudicate capital and corporal cases.

sela — see **shekel.**

shaatnez — see **kilayim.**

Shabbos — the seventh day of the week (Saturday); a holy day when **melachah** and certain other activities are forbidden.

Shacharis — the morning prayer service.

Shavuos — the festival that celebrates the giving of the Torah to the Jewish nation at Mount Sinai.

shechitah — (a) ritual slaughter; the method prescribed by the Torah for slaughtering a kosher animal to make it fit for consumption. It consists of cutting through most of the esophagus and windpipe, from the front of the neck, with a specially sharpened knife that is free of nicks; (b) one of the four essential blood **avodos.**

shein — literally, tooth; damage that an animal does through eating or any other activity from which it benefits.

shekel (plural, **shekalim**) — Scriptural coin equivalent to the Aramaic **sela** or four *dinars*. In Mishnaic terminology, the Scriptural half-*shekel* (two *dinars*) is called a *shekel,* and the Scriptural shekel is called by its Aramaic name, *sela.*

shelamim — peace offering; generally brought by an individual on a voluntary basis; part is burned on the **Altar,** part is eaten by a **Kohen** (and the members of his household), and part is eaten by the owner.

shelishi of tumah — see **tumah.**

Shemini Atzeres — the eighth and concluding day of the **Succos** celebration. In many respects, it is a **Yom Tov** in its own right.

shemittah — the Sabbatical year, occurring every seventh year, during which the land of **Eretz Yisrael** may not be cultivated.

[15] GLOSSARY

Shemoneh Esrei — literally, eighteen; the silent standing prayer that is the main feature of the daily prayer services. It is also called *Amidah*.

sheni of tumah — see **tumah**.

sheretz — carcass of one of eight species of creeping animals (rodents and reptiles) listed in *Leviticus* 11:29-30.

shevuah — (a) a vow to perform or not to perform an action; (b) an oath stating that something is true.

shogeig — inadvertent action.

shomer — literally, guardian, watchman; a person who is responsible to watch and take care of property that belongs to someone else.

Shulchan — the sacred Table in the **Sanctuary**.

Simchas Beis HaSho'eivah — celebration held in the **Temple** on each night of **Chol HaMoed** on **Succos**.

sotah — a woman suspected of adultery. If a woman was warned by her husband not to be alone with a certain man and she disobeyed his warning, she and her husband are not allowed to live together unless she drinks the "bitter waters," which prove her guilt or innocence. These consist of water from the **Temple** mixed with dust from the Temple floor, into which the writing of certain verses that include the Name of God has been dissolved.

succah — (a) the temporary dwelling in which one must dwell during the festival of **Succos**; (b) [upper case] the Talmudic tractate that deals with the laws pertaining to the festival of Succos.

Succos — festival during which we dwell in a **succah** to commemorate the protection provided by God to the Jewish people in the Wilderness.

taharah — the absence of **tumah**.

tahor — not **tamei**.

tam — an animal that is not expected to do damage in a particular way; see **keren**.

tamei — possessing **tumah**.

tamid — a communal offering that was offered in the **Temple** twice daily — once in the morning and once after the conclusion of the Temple services (always before nightfall). It consisted of lambs in their first year.

techum [plural, **techumim**] — **Shabbos** boundary; the distance of 2,000 **amos** from a person's Sabbath residence that he is permitted to travel on Shabbos or **Yom Tov**. See **eruv techumin**.

tefach [plural, **tefachim**] — a handbreadth; the length of an average fist. Opinions regarding its modern equivalent range between 3.2 and 3.8 inches (8-9.6 cm.).

tefillin — phylacteries; they are worn on the head and the left arm.

Temple — (a) the Holy Temple in Jerusalem (**Beis HaMikdash**); (b) the **Mishkan**.

terumah [plural, **terumos**] — the first portion of the crop separated and given to a **Kohen**, usually between 1/40 and 1/60 of the total crop. It has a level of sanctity that prohibits it from being eaten by a non-Kohen, or by a Kohen in a state of **tumah**.

terumas hadeshen — the daily service of removing a portion of ash from the **Outer Altar** in the **Temple**.

terumas halishkah — (a) money withdrawn from the **lishkah** fund; (b) an alternative name of the fund itself.

tevel — produce of **Eretz Yisrael** that has become subject to the obligation of **terumah** and **maaser**. *Tevel* is forbidden for consumption until *terumah* and all the other tithes have been designated.

tevilah — immersion in a **mikveh** for the purpose of purification from **tumah**-contamination.

tevul yom — literally, one who immersed that day — a person who had been rendered ritually impure with a Biblical **tumah** from which he purified himself with immersion in a **mikveh**. A residue of the *tumah* lingers until nightfall of the day of his immersion, leaving him *tamei* in regard to offerings, **terumah**, and entering the **Temple** Courtyard. A person in this reduced state of *tumah* is known as a *tevul yom,* and he renders

terumah and **kodashim** invalid through contact.

Tishah B'Av — literally, the ninth of Av; annual fast day that commemorates the fall of the First and Second **Temples**.

Tishrei — the seventh month of the Jewish calendar.

todah — a thanksgiving offering brought when a person wants to show gratitude to God, particularly after surviving a life-threatening situation.

toladah [plural, **tolados**] — see **melachah**.

tumah [plural, **tumos**] — a type of impurity that attaches itself to people, utensils, and foods. There are different levels of *tumah*. The highest level, **avi avos hatumah** [literally, *father of fathers of tumah*], is limited to a human corpse. The next level is known as **av hatumah**, primary [literally, *father of*] *tumah*. This category includes a **neveilah**, a **sheretz**, a **niddah**, a **zavah**, a **metzora**, a woman after childbirth, and a person who received *tumah* directly from a corpse. An *av hatumah* transmits *tumah* to people, utensils, foods, and beverages that come in contact with it, for example, by touching it. These in turn have the ability to pass the *tumah* further. The *tumah* weakens, however, each time it is passed on. Thus, when an *av hatumah* transmits *tumah* to a person or object, he or it become **rishon of tumah** (first degree of acquired *tumah*). This level of *tumah* is too weak to transmit *tumah* to people or utensils; it can transmit *tumah* only to foods and beverages, which become **sheni of tumah** (second degree of acquired *tumah*). A *sheni* is too weak to transmit *tumah* to **chullin** (non-holy) food that touches it, which makes it impossible for ordinary food to possess a third degree of acquired *tumah*. However, a *sheni* can transmit *tumah* to **terumah** and **kodesh**, making either one a **shelishi of tumah** (third degree of acquired *tumah*), and a *shelishi* can transmit *tumah* to **kodesh**, making it a **revi'i of tumah** (fourth degree of acquired *tumah*).

tzaraas — see **metzora**.

tzitzis — the fringes that by Torah law must be placed on a four-cornered garment.

tzon barzel — property that a bride brings into the marriage and is recorded in the **kesubah**. The husband owns it and may use it as he wishes, but if the marriage ends in his death or divorce, he must pay her the amount the property was worth at the time of marriage.

Ulam — see **Antechamber**.

variable [chatas] offering — literally, an offering that can go up or down. This offering depends on the sinner's financial status. If he can afford an animal, he must bring a female sheep or goat; if he is poor, he need bring only two birds; and if he is so poor that he cannot afford even birds, he may bring instead a flour offering.

Writings — the third of the three sections of the Written Torah. It consists of the following Books: *Psalms, Proverbs, Job, Song of Songs, Ruth, Lamentations, Ecclesiastes, Esther, Daniel, Ezra-Nehemiah, Chronicles.*

yavam — see **yibum**.

yevamah — see **yibum**.

yibum — levirate marriage. When a man dies childless, the Torah provides for one of his brothers to marry the widow. This marriage is called *yibum*. Before this, the widow is forbidden to marry anyone else. The surviving brother, upon whom the obligation to perform the mitzvah of *yibum* falls, is called the *yavam*. The widow is called the *yevamah*. *Yibum* is effected only through cohabitation. If the brother should refuse to perform *yibum*, he must release her from her *yibum*-bond by performing the rite of *chalitzah*, in which she removes his shoe before the court and spits before him and declares: *So should be done to the man who will not build his brother's house* (*Deuteronomy* 25:5-9).

Yisrael [plural, **Yisraelim**] — a Jew who is not a **Kohen** or a **Levi**.

Yom Kippur — Day of Atonement; a day

of prayer, penitence, fasting, and abstention from **melachah**.

Yom Tov [plural, **Yamim Tovim**] — holiday; specifically, the first and last days of **Pesach, Shavuos**, the first day of **Succos, Shemini Atzeres, Yom Kippur**, and the two days of **Rosh Hashanah**. Outside of **Eretz Yisrael**, an additional day of Yom Tov is added to each of these festivals, except **Yom Kippur** and **Rosh Hashanah**. Most forms of **melachah** are forbidden on Yom Tov.

yovel — fiftieth year [Jubilee]; the year following the conclusion of a set of seven **shemittah** cycles. On **Yom Kippur** of that year, the shofar is sounded to proclaim freedom for the Jewish servants, and to signal the return to the original owner of fields that had been sold in **Eretz Yisrael** during the previous forty-nine years.

zav [plural, **zavim**] — a man who has become **tamei** because of a specific type of bodily emission. If three emissions were experienced during a three-day period, the man must bring offerings upon his purification.

zavah [plural, **zavos**] — By Biblical law, after a women concludes her seven days of **niddah**, there is an eleven-day period during which any menses-like bleeding renders her a *minor zavah*, who is **tamei** until she experiences seven consecutive days without bleeding and immerses in a **mikveh**. If the bleeding lasts for three days, she is a *major zavah* and must bring offerings upon her purification.

zomemin — witnesses who were discredited through **hazamah**.

zonah — a woman who cohabited with a non-Jew, a Canaanite slave, or one of the forbidden close relatives; a married woman who cohabited with any man who is not her husband. The Torah forbids marriage between a *zonah* and a **Kohen**. A *zonah* is forbidden to eat **terumah**.

תפילה על הנפטר אחר לימוד משניות
Prayer after the Study of Mishnah for the Deceased

[20] תפילה על הנפטר אחר לימוד משניות

It is customary to recite this prayer whenever Mishnayos are studied
in memory of a deceased.

אָנָּא יהוה מָלֵא רַחֲמִים, אֲשֶׁר בְּיָדְךָ נֶפֶשׁ כָּל חַי, וְרוּחַ כָּל בְּשַׂר אִישׁ. יְהִי נָא לְרָצוֹן לְפָנֶיךָ תּוֹרָתֵנוּ וּתְפִלָּתֵנוּ בַּעֲבוּר נִשְׁמַת (deceased's Hebrew name) בֶּן/בַּת (father's Hebrew name) וּגְמוֹל נָא עִמָּהּ בְּחַסְדְּךָ הַגָּדוֹל, לִפְתּוֹחַ לָהּ שַׁעֲרֵי רַחֲמִים וָחֶסֶד, וְשַׁעֲרֵי גַּן עֵדֶן. וּתְקַבֵּל אוֹתָהּ בְּאַהֲבָה וּבְחִבָּה, וְשָׁלַח לָהּ מַלְאָכֶיךָ הַקְּדוֹשִׁים וְהַטְּהוֹרִים, לְהוֹלִיכָהּ וּלְהוֹשִׁיבָהּ תַּחַת עֵץ הַחַיִּים, אֵצֶל נִשְׁמוֹת הַצַּדִּיקִים וְהַצִּדְקָנִיּוֹת, חֲסִידִים וַחֲסִידוֹת, לֵהָנוֹת מִזִּיו שְׁכִינָתְךָ, לְהַשְׂבִּיעָהּ מִטּוּבְךָ הַצָּפוּן לַצַּדִּיקִים. וְהַגּוּף יָנוּחַ בַּקֶּבֶר בִּמְנוּחָה נְכוֹנָה, בְּחֶדְוָה וּבְשִׂמְחָה וְשָׁלוֹם, כְּדִכְתִיב: יָבוֹא שָׁלוֹם, יָנוּחוּ עַל מִשְׁכְּבוֹתָם, הֹלֵךְ נְכֹחוֹ. וּכְתִיב: יַעְלְזוּ חֲסִידִים בְּכָבוֹד, יְרַנְּנוּ עַל מִשְׁכְּבוֹתָם. וּכְתִיב: אִם תִּשְׁכַּב לֹא תִפְחָד, וְשָׁכַבְתָּ וְעָרְבָה שְׁנָתֶךָ.

for a male:

וְתִשְׁמוֹר אוֹתוֹ מֵחִבּוּט הַקֶּבֶר, וּמֵרִמָּה וְתוֹלֵעָה. וְתִסְלַח וְתִמְחוֹל לוֹ עַל כָּל פְּשָׁעָיו, כִּי אָדָם אֵין צַדִּיק בָּאָרֶץ, אֲשֶׁר יַעֲשֶׂה טּוֹב וְלֹא יֶחֱטָא. וּזְכוֹר לוֹ זְכֻיּוֹתָיו וְצִדְקוֹתָיו אֲשֶׁר עָשָׂה. וְתַשְׁפִּיעַ לוֹ מִנִּשְׁמָתוֹ לְדַשֵּׁן עַצְמוֹתָיו בַּקֶּבֶר מֵרַב טוּב הַצָּפוּן לַצַּדִּיקִים, דִּכְתִיב: מָה רַב טוּבְךָ אֲשֶׁר צָפַנְתָּ לִּירֵאֶיךָ. וּכְתִיב: שֹׁמֵר כָּל עַצְמֹתָיו, אַחַת מֵהֵנָּה לֹא נִשְׁבָּרָה. וְיִשְׁכּוֹן בֶּטַח בָּדָד וְשַׁאֲנַן מִפַּחַד רָעָה, וְאַל יִרְאֶה פְּנֵי גֵיהִנֹּם. וְנִשְׁמָתוֹ תְּהֵא צְרוּרָה בִּצְרוֹר הַחַיִּים, וּלְהַחֲיוֹתוֹ בִּתְחִיַּת הַמֵּתִים עִם כָּל מֵתֵי עַמְּךָ יִשְׂרָאֵל בְּרַחֲמִים. אָמֵן.

for a female:

וְתִשְׁמוֹר אוֹתָהּ מֵחִבּוּט הַקֶּבֶר, וּמֵרִמָּה וְתוֹלֵעָה. וְתִסְלַח וְתִמְחוֹל לָהּ עַל כָּל פְּשָׁעֶיהָ, כִּי אָדָם אֵין צַדִּיק בָּאָרֶץ, אֲשֶׁר יַעֲשֶׂה טּוֹב וְלֹא יֶחֱטָא. וּזְכוֹר לָהּ זְכֻיּוֹתֶיהָ וְצִדְקוֹתֶיהָ אֲשֶׁר עָשָׂתָה. וְתַשְׁפִּיעַ לָהּ מִנִּשְׁמָתָהּ לְדַשֵּׁן עַצְמוֹתֶיהָ בַּקֶּבֶר מֵרַב טוּב הַצָּפוּן לַצַּדִּיקִים, דִּכְתִיב: מָה רַב טוּבְךָ אֲשֶׁר צָפַנְתָּ לִּירֵאֶיךָ, וּכְתִיב: שֹׁמֵר כָּל עַצְמֹתָיו, אַחַת מֵהֵנָּה לֹא נִשְׁבָּרָה. וְתִשְׁכּוֹן בֶּטַח בָּדָד וְשַׁאֲנַן מִפַּחַד רָעָה, וְאַל תִּרְאֶה פְּנֵי גֵיהִנֹּם. וְנִשְׁמָתָהּ תְּהֵא צְרוּרָה בִּצְרוֹר הַחַיִּים, וּלְהַחֲיוֹתָהּ בִּתְחִיַּת הַמֵּתִים עִם כָּל מֵתֵי עַמְּךָ יִשְׂרָאֵל בְּרַחֲמִים. אָמֵן.

[21] PRAYER AFTER THE STUDY OF MISHNAH FOR THE DECEASED

It is customary to recite this prayer whenever Mishnayos are studied in memory of a deceased.

אָנָּא *Please, O Hashem, full of mercy, for in Your hand is the soul of all the living and the spirit of every human being, may You find favor in our Torah study and prayer for the soul of* (deceased's Hebrew name) *son/daughter of* (father's Hebrew name) *and do with it according to Your great kindness, to open for it the gates of mercy and kindness and the gates of the Garden of Eden. Accept it with love and affection and send it Your holy and pure angels to lead it and to settle it under the Tree of Life near the souls of the righteous and devout men and women, to enjoy the radiance of Your Presence, to satiate it from Your good that is concealed for the righteous. May the body repose in the grave with proper contentment, pleasure, gladness, and peace as it is written: "Let him enter in peace, let them rest on their beds — everyone who has lived in his proper way." And it is written: "Let the devout exult in glory, let them sing joyously upon their beds." And it is written: "If you lie down, you will not fear; when you lie down, your sleep will be sweet." And protect him/her from the tribulations of the grave and from worms and maggots. Forgive and pardon him/her for all his/her sins, for there is no person so wholly righteous on earth that does good and never sins. Remember for him/her the merits and righteous deeds that he/she performed, and cause a spiritual flow from his/her soul to keep his/her bones fresh in the grave from the abundant good that is concealed for the righteous, as it is written: "How abundant is Your goodness that You have concealed for Your reverent ones," and it is written: "He guards all his bones, even one of them was not broken." May it rest secure, alone, and serene, from fear of evil and may it not see the threshold of Gehinnom. May his/her soul be bound in the Bond of Life. And may it be brought back to life with the Revivification of the Dead with all the dead of Your people Israel, with mercy. Amen.*

This volume is part of
THE **ArtScroll® SERIES**
an ongoing project of
translations, commentaries and expositions on
Scripture, Mishnah, Talmud, Midrash, Halachah,
liturgy, history, the classic Rabbinic writings,
biographies and thought.

For a brochure of current publications visit your local
Hebrew bookseller or contact the publisher:

Mesorah Publications, ltd

4401 Second Avenue / Brooklyn, New York 11232
(718) 921-9000 / www.artscroll.com

Many of these works are possible
only thanks to the support of the
MESORAH HERITAGE FOUNDATION,
which has earned the generous support of concerned people,
who want such works to be produced
and made available to generations world-wide.
Such books represent faith in the eternity of Judaism.
If you share that vision as well,
and you wish to participate in this historic effort
and learn more about support and dedication opportunities –
please contact us.

Mesorah Heritage Foundation

4401 Second Avenue / Brooklyn, N.Y. 11232
(718) 921-9000 / www.mesorahheritage.org

Mesorah Heritage Foundation is a 501(c)3 not-for-profit organization.

GW01339754